The Jewish Reformation

The Jewish Reformation

Bible Translation and Middle-Class German Judaism as Spiritual Enterprise

MICHAH GOTTLIEB

OXFORD
UNIVERSITY PRESS

OXFORD
UNIVERSITY PRESS

Oxford University Press is a department of the University of Oxford. It furthers the University's objective of excellence in research, scholarship, and education by publishing worldwide. Oxford is a registered trade mark of Oxford University Press in the UK and certain other countries.

Published in the United States of America by Oxford University Press
198 Madison Avenue, New York, NY 10016, United States of America.

Library of Congress Cataloging-in-Publication Data
Names: Gottlieb, Michah, author.
Title: The Jewish reformation : Bible translation and middle-class German
Judaism as spiritual enterprise / Michah Gottlieb.
Description: New York : Oxford University Press, [2021] |
Includes bibliographical references and index.
Identifiers: LCCN 2020037504 (print) | LCCN 2020037505 (ebook) |
ISBN 9780199336388 (hardback) | ISBN 9780199336401 (epub)
Subjects: LCSH: Bible. Old Testament. German—Versions. |
Bible. Old Testament—Versions, Jewish. | Bible. Old Testament—Translating—Germany. |
Mendelssohn, Moses, 1729–1786. |
Zunz, Leopold, 1794–1886. | Hirsch, Samson Raphael, 1808–1888. |
Jews—Germany—History—18th century. | Jews—Germany—History—19th century. |
Judaism—Germany—History—18th century. |
Judaism—Germany—History—19th century. | Germany—Ethnic relations. |
Germany—Religious life and customs.
Classification: LCC BS941 .G68 2021 (print) | LCC BS941 (ebook) |
DDC 221.5/310943—dc23
LC record available at https://lccn.loc.gov/2020037504
LC ebook record available at https://lccn.loc.gov/2020037505

DOI: 10.1093/oso/9780199336388.001.0001

1 3 5 7 9 8 6 4 2

Printed by Integrated Books International, United States of America

For Thomas 'Tommy' Gimbel Jr. ז"ל

A scholar and Mensch *who touched everyone who knew him*

A rationalized and modernized type of Judaism has emerged in Germany, however you term it, neo-orthodoxy or reform. There is indeed a sincere and genuinely-felt Jewish piety among German Jews in Germany and outside of Germany, which nobody can fail to notice, akin to the old-fashioned piety of days gone by.

—Harry Wolfson, "Escaping Judaism" (1921)

The direct encounter with God, *this* is a Christian concept.

—Emmanuel Levinas, *Ideology and Idealism* (1972)

Contents

Preface

This book is about how German Jews used Bible translation to imagine and implement a middle-class vision of Jewish selfhood. In the popular American imagination, being middle class is often conceived in narrowly economic terms as possessing a level of wealth. Scholars understand it to be a much more complex phenomenon that is as much about values and culture. Being middle class includes attitudes toward education; ways of dressing, speaking, and eating; notions of rationality and emotion; aesthetic and artistic sensibilities; conceptions of family and gender roles, etc.

The German Jewish Bible translators that I will explore sought to promote Jews' entry into the German middle class. Some recent scholars have interpreted middle-class German Judaism as primarily about attaining secular ends, namely, civil rights, economic advancement, and social respectability. I argue that for the subjects of this study, this secular interpretation of being middle class obscures what was most important about it for them. Economic prosperity, social respectability, and even civil rights were valued not as ends in themselves but as means to becoming self-actualized individuals who served God for the benefit of humanity.

I am indebted to many colleagues and friends, too numerous to mention, who helped me think through this project. I first began researching Samson Raphael Hirsch as a Tikvah fellow at Princeton University. I thank the Tikvah Fund and Leora Batnitzky for this opportunity. I am grateful to the Maimonides Centre for Advanced Studies (MCAS) at the University of Hamburg and its director Giuseppe Veltri for a summer fellowship during which time I completed final revisions on the book. My editor at Oxford University Press, Theo Calderara, showed unwavering confidence in this project, and I thank him for his patience and perseverance in shepherding it to completion. Drew Anderla, Brent Matheny, Preetham Raj, and Maria Cusano provided invaluable assistance with the final editing and publication of the manuscript.

Though I cannot list all the people who helped me conceptualize and research this book, I would be remiss not to mention a few. Marion Kaplan and David Sorkin read parts of the manuscript and offered enormously helpful suggestions and encouragement. Marion pressed me to think about gender and class, which became framing issues in the book, and David taught me much about the legal-political aspects of this project. Jonathan Green, Kylie Unell, and Sam Weiss participated in a doctoral seminar on Mendelssohn, and I learned much from their insights. I thank Jonathan Green for compiling the index and carefully proofreading the text. I am grateful to Hasia Diner, Jeffrey Rubenstein, and Daniel Fleming for their unfailing friendship and support.

I owe an enormous debt to Zev Harvey, who offered hundreds of constructive comments and edits. It is no exaggeration to say that every comment Zev made was wise, even if I did not follow every suggestion. I take full responsibility for my errors.

I could not have completed this project without the support of my wife and partner Ilana and our children, Gabriella, Jordanna, Itai, and Zachy. More than support, the life lessons that I have learned from you are at the heart of this work.

The book is dedicated to Thomas Gimbel Jr., whom we knew as "Tommy." A gentle, brilliant young scholar descended from a German Jewish family which rose to prominence in nineteenth-century America, Tommy was working with me on a doctorate before his untimely passing in 2016. The central themes of this book: Bible translation, German Jewish thought and culture, relations between Judaism, Protestantism, and Catholicism, and the possibility of bourgeois spirituality were all of keen interest to him. He would have been the book's ideal reader, and I surely would have learned much from his response to it. *Yehi Zikhro Barukh*—May his memory be a blessing.

Abbreviations

AL	Moses Mendelssohn, *Alim Literufah*
AZJ	*Allgemeine Zeitung des Judenthums*
BT	*Babylonian Talmud*
CW	Samson Raphael Hirsch, *The Collected Writings*
GS	*Gesammelte Schriften* (Mendelssohn, Zunz, or Hirsch)
IRG	*Israelitische Religionsgesellschaft*
JMW	Paul Mendes-Flohr and Jehuda Reinharz (eds.), *The Jew in the Modern World*
JT	*Jerusalem Talmud*
JubA	Moses Mendelssohn, *Gesammelte Schriften Jubiläumsausgabe*
KM	Moses Mendelssohn, *Kohelet Mussar*
NB	Samson Raphael Hirsch, *Neunzehn Briefe über Judenthum*
NL	Samson Raphael Hirsch, *Nineteen Letters on Judaism*
OL	Moses Mendelssohn, *Or Linetiva*
TTP	Benedict Spinoza, *Tractatus Theologico-Politicus*
Sermons	Leopold Zunz, *The Sermons of the Jews*
WZJT	*Wissenschaftliche Zeitschrift für jüdische Theologie*

Introduction

The Jewish Reformation

Over the past two decades the place of minorities in Western societies has become increasingly contested. The clearest example of this is the debate over Muslim immigration in Western Europe and the United States. But of late the debate has been broadened to include the question of migrants from poor European countries to affluent ones and of Latin Americans to the United States. Opponents of immigration often recur to stock complaints: immigrants bring crime and disorder; they do not speak the language of the host country; they are insular and do not integrate; they lack patriotic loyalty; they are uneducated; they steal jobs from citizens. Muslims are regularly accused of practicing an authoritarian, sexist form of religion that they surreptitiously seek to impose on Christians.

In a 2007 paper, Masahide Goto linked the contemporary debate over Muslim immigration to eighteenth-century debates over Jewish civil rights. Invoking Jiro Mizushima's expression "exclusivism in enlightenment," which describes West European opposition to Muslim immigration on the grounds that Muslims do not share enlightened, liberal values, Goto demonstrated that this argument is not new and was deployed by eighteenth-century thinkers to exclude Jews from civil rights.[1]

Scholars often date the beginning of Jewish emancipation in German lands to the publication of Christian Wilhelm Dohm's 1781 *On the Civil Improvement of the Jews (Über die bürgerliche Verbesserung der Juden)*.[2] Dohm's spirited plea for Jewish civil rights provoked a heated debate in which many Christians opposed granting Jews civil rights. In 1782, Moses Mendelssohn joined the debate.[3]

[1] See Goto, "Modern Judaism and Religious Tolerance."

[2] See Sorkin, *The Transformation of German Judaism*, 23.

[3] Mendelssohn commissioned a German translation of Menasseh Ben Israel's 1656 *Vindiciae Judaeorum*, which Menasseh had written to convince Oliver Cromwell to readmit the Jews to England from which they had been expelled in 1290. Mendelssohn included his own defense of Jewish civil rights in a preface that he added to the work. See Altmann, *Moses Mendelssohn*, 449–474.

The Jewish Reformation. Michah Gottlieb, Oxford University Press (2021). © Oxford University Press.
DOI: 10.1093/oso/9780199336388.003.0001

Mendelssohn took note of the change between medieval and Enlightenment attacks on Jews. Medieval Christians attacked Jews on religious grounds, accusing them of defiling the Eucharist, stabbing crosses, and killing Christian children to bake Passover matzot. But Mendelssohn observed that these overtly theological attacks were passé, replaced by arguments excluding Jews from civil rights on enlightened principles. He remarked that opponents of Jewish civil rights regularly claimed that Jews could not be granted civil equality because their religion imbued them with values at odds with the Enlightenment, including irrational, superstitious beliefs; antipathy toward Christian culture; arrogance and superiority; intolerance and hatred for Christians; clannishness, thievery, and fraud; disloyalty to the state; and coarse manners.[4]

Mendelssohn responded that Christian opponents of Jewish civil rights were blinded by religious stereotypes. Far from being incompatible with Enlightenment values, Judaism was *more consonant* with them than Christianity. But Mendelssohn recognized that arguments against Jewish emancipation were also driven by Christian anxiety that upheavals wrought by the Enlightenment were overturning the existing social order, causing Christians to lose their place in society.[5] Mendelssohn sought to reassure Christians by arguing that not only would granting Jews civil rights not harm Christian society, but it would also enrich it economically, morally, and religiously. At the same time, Mendelssohn made clear that abandoning Judaism could not be the price of civil rights and that if this was the offer, it must be refused.[6]

Mendelssohn did not solely defend Jews against Christian attacks. Recognizing that not all Christian complaints about German Jews were groundless, he also engaged in communal self-reflection.[7] He recognized

[4] See Mendelssohn, *JubA*, 8:6; *Moses Mendelssohn: Writings*, 43–44.

[5] In part, the problem was due to a conflict between two types of *Bürger* in German lands. The *Stadtbürger* were a group that emerged in late medieval/early modern period and constituted a corporate entity living in a city with specific legal privileges, ways of life, and social status. They saw their position threatened by Jews like Mendelssohn, who were part of a rising class of educated bourgeois (*Bildungsbürger*) and economic bourgeois (*Wirtschaftsbürger*), whose trade extended beyond the city. On these distinctions, see pp. 12–13 of this volume.

[6] These are the central claims of Mendelssohn's 1769 Open Letter to Lavater, his 1782 Preface to Menasseh ben Israel, and his 1783 *Jerusalem*.

[7] Even a staunch defender of Jewish civil rights like Dohm assumed that Jews were a corrupt people who did not view Christians as their brothers and lacked patriotic sentiments. But for Dohm Christian persecution was *solely responsible* for Jewish moral degradation. Once Jews were accepted as citizens they would naturally reform those elements of their tradition that alienated them from Christians and encouraged unjust dealings with them. As Dohm put it, "The Jew is even more man than Jew. How would it be possible for him not to love a state where he could freely acquire property and enjoy it, where his taxes would not be heavier than those of his fellow citizens, where he could

that many German Jews had a strong aversion to secular learning and German culture, harbored ill will toward Christians, engaged in unethical business practices, and felt little patriotic loyalty to the states in which they lived.[8] Mendelssohn was also keenly aware that many Jews agreed that religious authoritarianism was a foundation of Judaism.[9]

By age forty Mendelssohn was a member of the German bourgeoisie (*Bürgertum*), having become a celebrity philosopher and a prosperous manager in a silk factory. But he did not rest content with his personal success. Instead, Mendelssohn labored to promote the entry of his fellow Jews into the German middle class.[10] He recognized that this required changing not only how German Christians regarded Jews, but also how Jews related to German culture.[11] Mendelssohn considered educational reform the key to changing Jewish hearts and minds, and the centerpiece of this work was his landmark translation of the Bible into High German, the first by a Jew. Mendelssohn's efforts at reform naturally led observers to compare him to Luther.[12]

reach positions of honor and enjoy general esteem?" See Dohm, *Concerning the Amelioration*, 14. On Dohm's plea for Jewish toleration, see Liberles, "Dohm's Treatise on the Jews: A Defence of the Enlightenment." Dohm can be understood as developing arguments from Luther's 1523 essay "That Jesus Christ Was Born a Jew." See Luther, *Luther's Works*, 45:199–229.

[8] Mendelssohn famously wrote to the Christian Deist August Hennings that "my nation is, alas, so estranged [from culture] that one is almost ready to despair of the possibility of improvement." See Mendelssohn, *JubA*, 12.2:149; *Moses Mendelssohn: Writings*, 188. I will discuss this statement later. See pp. 94–101 of this volume.

[9] When the journalist August Friedrich Cranz wrote to Mendelssohn in 1782 charging that Judaism was a coercive religion, Mendelssohn responded that the "objection cuts me to the heart" since it "is taken to be correct even by many of my coreligionists." See Mendelssohn, *JubA*, 8:153; *Moses Mendelssohn: Writings*, 77.

[10] Simone Lässig notes that Jewish *embourgeoisement* involved three aspects: (1) a political-legal element; (2) a cultural-religious dimension; (3) a socio-economic element. See Lässig, *Jüdische Wege ins Bürgertum*, 17–18. While Mendelssohn could be considered middle class in terms of the second and third elements, he never achieved middle-class status in terms of the first. During his life, Prussian Jews were divided into six separate categories with only members of the highest category having the right of residence for themselves and the ability to pass this right to their children. On the six categories of Jews in Prussia, see Alexander Altmann, *Moses Mendelssohn. A Biographical Study*, Philadelphia, PA, Jewish Publication Society of America, 1973, 16–17. Despite Mendelssohn's fame, he never belonged to the highest category, and after his death his widow Fromet had to petition the new ruler Friedrich Wilhelm II for permission to remain in Prussia. See Kayserling, *Moses Mendelssohn, sein Leben und seine Werke*, 126; Zweig, "Biographical Sketches," 598. I will discuss the meanings of the terms *middle class*, *bourgeois*, and *bourgeoisie* and their German cognates shortly. See pp. 12–14 of this volume.

[11] Lässig argues that German Jews' enormous success at entering the German middle class in the nineteenth century was directly related to the protracted, uneven granting of Jewish civil rights and the demand that Jews "improve" their character in exchange for civil rights. See Lässig, *Jüdische Wege ins Bürgentum*, 15–17.

[12] In 1789 the Protestant preacher Daniel Jenisch called Mendelssohn "the Luther of the Jews," asking "what else was Mendelssohn for that nation, but the torchbearer of Enlightenment?" See Jenisch, "Skizze von dem Leben und Charakter Mendelssohn," 7, cited in Altmann, *Moses Mendelssohn*, 9. In his 1871 *Geschichte der Juden* (*History of the Jews*), Heinrich Graetz stressed the

In his 1835 *On the History of Religion and Philosophy in Germany*, Heinrich Heine described Luther's conflict with Catholicism as a conflict between coercive dogmatism and free rationality:

> In saying that his teachings could only be contradicted by the Bible itself or by means of rational argument Luther granted human reason the right to explain the Bible, and reason was thus acknowledged as the highest judge in all religious controversies. Thus arose in Germany what is called freedom of spirit (*Geistesfreiheit*), or by another name, freedom of thought (*Denkfreiheit*). Thinking became a right and the authority of reason became legitimate.[13]

For Heine, a legacy of Luther's conflict with Catholicism was the establishment of a right to freedom of thought, which reached its apotheosis with the German Enlightenment. Heine also credited Luther's Bible translation with "creating the German language" by establishing a standard German.[14]

Heine then turned to Mendelssohn. Just as Luther was a Christian reformer who overthrew the "Christian Catholicism" of the papacy, so Mendelssohn was a "reformer of the German Israelites" who overthrew the "Jewish Catholicism" of the Talmud. Heine memorably described the Talmud as "a Gothic cathedral" containing "a hierarchy of religious laws . . . so ingenuously placed above and below each other, supporting and bearing each other . . . that they make up a frighteningly defiant and colossal whole."[15] For Heine, Mendelssohn's Bible translation was the key to "destroying the reputation of Talmudism and founding a pure Mosaic religion."[16] While Heine did not explicitly link Mendelssohn with promoting freedom of thought among

significance of Mendelssohn's work on the Bible and also compared Luther and Mendelssohn. But while Graetz praised Mendelssohn, he denigrated Luther, writing: "Mendelssohn's translation of the Pentateuch together with his paraphrase of the Psalms has produced more good than Luther because instead of fossilizing the mind, it animated it. The inner freedom of the Jews, as has been said, dates from this translation." See Graetz, *History of the Jews,* 5:335. Werner Weinberg cites other writers who compared Mendelssohn to Luther, including: Franz Muncker, Simon Bernfeld, Peretz Sandler, Mendele Mokher Seforim, and Ismar Elbogen. See Weinberg, "Language Questions," 199–200. Moses Hess also makes this comparison. See Hess, *Ausgewählte Schriften,* 252.

[13] Heine, *On the History of Religion and Philosophy in Germany,* 32.
[14] Ibid., 35, 37.
[15] Ibid., 69–70.
[16] Ibid., 69.

Jews or with their acquisition of the German language, other writers ascribed these achievements to him.[17]

In portraying Mendelssohn as seeking to overthrow the Talmud, Heine exaggerated. Mendelssohn consistently upheld talmudic legal authority and had a positive view of rabbinic interpretation. Nevertheless, by pointing to his bibliocentricism, Heine was describing something important, namely, Mendelssohn's attempt to shift the center of Jewish education from the Talmud to the Bible.

In Mendelssohn's day, traditional German Jewish education for boys focused near exclusively on studying the Aramaic Talmud from a young age using a scholastic method known as *pilpul.* In Mendelssohn's view, *pilpul* aimed not at furthering understanding of the text but, rather, at showing off a student's brilliance.[18] Secular learning was largely neglected, including the study of vernacular languages, and there was no intensive instruction in the Bible or Hebrew language.[19] Mendelssohn thought that Jews' ignorance of secular subjects, vernacular languages, and the Bible and Hebrew, both prevented them from engaging the Christian world and instilled a distorted view of Judaism. By translating the Bible into elegant German based on a grammatical understanding of Hebrew, highlighting the Bible's aesthetic features, and emphasizing its rational moral teachings, Mendelssohn sought to ground a middle-class vision of Judaism.[20]

Mendelssohn's Bible translation was a watershed. From the completion of his Pentateuch translation in 1783 to the completion of the Buber-Rosenzweig translation in 1961, German Jews produced at least fifteen *different* Bible translations into High German, more than even German Protestants produced in the same period.[21] This despite the fact that by 1900

[17] See Graetz, *History of the Jews,* 5:335. The philosopher Johann Erich Biester compared Mendelssohn's contributions to the German language to Luther's. Biester's comments can be found in Mendelssohn, *JubA,* 26:24.

[18] On Mendelssohn's judgment of *pilpul,* see pp. 80–81 of this volume.

[19] This describes boys' education. I will discuss the differences between boys' and girls' education in Chapter 2. The neglect of Bible study in German lands began in the fourteenth century. See Katz, *Tradition and Crisis,* 162–167; Breuer, *Asif,* 237–259; *The Tents of Torah,* 116–128; Talmage, *Apples of Gold,* 151–171; Fishman, *The History of Jewish Education in Central Europe,* 94–109.

[20] In 1929 Rosenzweig acknowledged Mendelssohn's success in this endeavor, calling him "the first German Jew." See p. 414 note 13 of this volume.

[21] In addition to Mendelssohn's translation, there were German Jewish Bible translations by Joseph Johlson (תורה נבאים וכתובים/ *Die heiligen Schriften der Israeliten,* Frankfurt, 1831–1836); Gotthold Salomon (תורה נבאים כתובים *oder Deutsche Volks- und Schul-Bibel für Israeliten,* Altona, 1837); Leopold Zunz (תורה נבאים כתובים/*Die vier und zwangzig Bücher der heiligen Schrift,* Berlin, 1838); Salomon Herxheimer (תורה נבאים כתובים/*Die vier und zwanzig Bücher der Bibel,* Berlin, 1840–1848); Jonah Kosmann (תרגומא דבי רב /*Eine deutsche Uebersetzung vom Pentateuch,* Königsberg, 1847–1852); Ludwig Philippson (מקרא תורה נביאים וכתובים/*Die Israelitische Bibel,*

Jews constituted a mere one percent of the German population. Why so many Bible translations?

A comprehensive account of the aims of German Jewish Bible translation is beyond the scope of this book.[22] Instead, I will focus on a set of translations engaged in a common project that I call "Jewish Reformation." I distinguish "Jewish Reformation" from "Reform Judaism." While "Reform Judaism" denotes a specific religious denomination that emerged in the nineteenth century, I use "Jewish Reformation" more broadly to refer to the attempt to reshape Judaism along bourgeois, middle-class lines. Jewish Reformation writers belonged to diverse Jewish ideological groups, including Haskalah, Reform Judaism, Positive-Historical Judaism, and Neo-Orthodoxy.[23] I argue

Leipzig, 1839–1854); Samson Raphael Hirsch (חמשה חומשי תורה מתורגם ומבואר/*Der Pentateuch übersetzt und erläutert,* Frankfurt, 1867–1878); Seligmann Bamberger, Abraham Adler, Marcus Lehmann (חמישה חומשי תורה/*Uebersetzung der fünf Bücher Moses,* Frankfurt, 1873); Julius Fürst (ספרי קודש/*Illustrirte Pracht Bibel für Israeliten,* Leipzig, 1874); Joseph Wohlgemuth and Abraham Bleichrode, (חמשה חומשי תורה/*Die fünf Bücher Moses mit deutscher Übersetzung,* Rodelheim, 1899); Simon Bernfeld (תורה נביאים וכתובים/*Die heilige Schrift: Nach dem masoretischen Text neu übersetzt und erklärt,* Frankfurt, 1903); Lazarus Goldschmidt (*Die heiligen Bücher des alten Bundes,* 1921–1925); Harry Torcyner (Tur-Sinai) (מקרא ותרגומו/*Die heilige Schrift,* Frankfurt, 1935); and Martin Buber and Franz Rosenzweig (*Die Schrift,* Berlin, 1925–1961). This list includes editions comprising at least a complete translation of the Pentateuch. In addition, many translations of individual biblical books appeared. In the same period there were ten German Protestant translations: Johann David Michaelis, *Übersetzung des Alten Testaments* (Göttingen, 1769–1785); Johann Heinrich Moldenhawer, *Übersetzung und Erläuterung der heiligen Bücher des Alten Testaments* (Quedlinburg, 1774–1787); Johann Wilhelm Hezel, *Die Bibel alten und neuen Testaments, mit vollständigen erklärenden Anmerkungen* (Lemgo, 1780–1791); Johann Christian Augusti and Wilhelm Martin De Wette, *Die Schriften des Alten Testaments* (Heidelberg, 1809–1814); Christian Bunsen, *Vollständiges Bibelwerk für die Gemeinde* (Leipzig, 1858–1870); J.A. von Poseck, Carl Brockhaus, and John Darby, *Die Heilige Schrift. Erster Teil genannt Altes Testament* (Elberfeld, 1855); Eduard Reuss, *Die Bücher der Bibel* (Braunschweig, 1892–1923); Emil Kautzsch, *Die Heilige Schrift des Alten Testaments* (Freiburg: 1890–1894); Franz Schlachter, *Miniatur-Bibel* (Bonn, 1913); and Hermann Menge, *Die Heilige Schrift Alten und Neuen Testaments* (Stuttgart, 1926). In addition, German Catholics produced ten translations in this period: Franz Rosalino, *Biblia Sacra, oder die Heilige Schrift des alten und Neuen Testaments* (Vienna, 1784); Dominic Brentano, Thaddäus Dereser, and Johann Scholz, *Die heilige Schrift des alten Testaments* (1797–1837); Joseph Franz Allioli and Heinrich Braun, *Die Heilige Schrift des alten und neuen Testamentes aus der Vulgata* (1830–1837); Leander van Ess, *Die heiligen Schriften des Alten und Neuen Testamentes* (Sulzbach, 1822); Heinrich Joachim Jaeck, *Die Bibel für die Katholiken oder die ganze heilige Schrift des Alten und Neuen Testaments nach der lateinischen Vulgata* (Leipzig, 1845); Valentin Loch and Wilhelm Carl Reichel, *Die heiligen Schriften des alten und neuen Testamentes, nach der Vulgata* (Regensberg, 1851–1866); Nivard Schlögl, *Die Heiligen Schriften des Alten Bundes aus dem kritisch wiederhergestellten hebräischen* (Wien, 1922); Franz Feldmann and Heinrich Herkenne, *Die Heilige Schrift des Alten Testamente* (Bonn, 1923); Paul Riessler, *Die Heilige Schrift des Alten und des Neuen Bundes* (Mainz, 1924); and Pius Parsch and Jakob Schäfer, *Die heilige Schrift des Alten & des Neuen Bundes* (Vienna, 1934). Many of the Catholic translations were made from the Latin Vulgate Bible rather than from the Masoretic Hebrew text.

[22] Abigail Gillman has provided a more extensive (though not comprehensive) discussion of German Jewish Bible translations in her recently published book *A History of German Jewish Bible Translation.*

[23] In general, when I discuss the Reform movement or members thereof, I will use the terms *Reform* or *Reformers* with an uppercase *R.* When speaking of the reforming efforts of exponents of

that as German Jews travelled along what Werner Mosse called "the long and bumpy road of Jewish emancipation," they used Bible translation to disseminate middle-class conceptions of Judaism.[24]

German Jewish Bible translation provides insight into a crucial debate about the modernization of German Jews. Mosse argued that Jews sought acceptance within the German middle class by inscribing themselves within a universalistic concept of German culture that transcended their Judaism. To this end, they embraced the sociocultural ideal of *Bildung*, which involved "self-cultivation based on classical learning and the development of aesthetic sensibilities," and immersed themselves in classical learning and German humanistic writing.[25] David Sorkin challenged Mosse's thesis, rejecting the idea that "German-Jewry's cultural productivity was at the cost of self-denial," instead arguing that German Jews cultivated a middle-class, bourgeois sensibility by creating institutions that fostered a vibrant Jewish "sub-culture."[26]

My analysis of German Jewish Bible translation unites Mosse's and Sorkin's perspectives. Through Bible translation German Jews cultivated a bourgeois sensibility that both *transcended* and *affirmed* Judaism. Translating the Bible helped inscribe Jews as Germans, as the Bible had been a crucial part of German cultural heritage since Luther's translation.[27] German Jews saw themselves as having privileged access to the Hebrew Bible. The translators I will explore also sought to imbue German Jews with bourgeois values by stressing the Bible's aesthetic qualities, rationality, morality, positive view of work, emphasis on family and home life, and distinct gender roles.

But through translation, German Jews also sought to create a Bible that *marked them as Jews*. By translating the Bible according to its plain meaning,

"Jewish Reformation," I will use the terms *reform* and *reformers* with a lowercase *r*. The first German Jewish writer to call for a "reformation" of Judaism was Saul Ascher in his 1792 *Leviathan, oder über Religion in Rücksicht des Judenthums* (*Leviathan, or on Religion in Relation to Judaism*). See Ascher, *Leviathan*, 212–228.

[24] See Mosse, "From '*Schutzjuden*.'"

[25] Mosse, "Between Bildung and Respectability," 2–3. Sorkin offers a more expansive and accurate definition of *Bildung* as "an ideal of integral self-development by which the whole man would fully develop his inherent form by transforming all of his faculties, mind and body, into a harmonious unity." See Sorkin, "The Genesis of the Ideology of Emancipation," 19. The literature on *Bildung* is vast. For an overview of some of its anthropological and semantic meanings, see Koselleck, *The Practice of Conceptual History*, 170–207. Also see Lässig, *Jüdische Wege*, 18–20, and the sources she cites.

[26] Sorkin, *The Transformation of German Jewry*, 5–7, 122–123.

[27] On the turn to the Bible as a means of finding a common basis between Jews and Christians, see Eliav, *Jewish Education*, 164; Breuer, *The Limits of Enlightenment*, 20. I will discuss this point further in Chapter 1.

shorn of Christology and conveying both the linguistic form of the original Hebrew and the subtleties of rabbinic Midrash, German Jews sought to produce a distinctly *Jewish* German Bible.[28] Recent scholarship has emphasized German Jews' minority critique of majoritarian German Protestant culture.[29] While I will touch on this theme, my focus will be on how German Jewish translators sought to cultivate a bourgeois sensibility that *inscribed Jews within Protestant society*, while *preserving Jewish distinctiveness*.

Bible translation was not solely a means of defining Jews' relation to German culture. It was also a means of *grounding competing conceptions of Judaism*. The lives of premodern German Jews were shaped by the kehillah, a communal structure in which halakhah (Jewish law), religious custom, and theological ideas impacted all spheres of life. Leaders of the *kehillah*, primarily rabbis and wealthy laypeople, administered education, taxed members, and operated courts that adjudicated civil matters according to halakhah. Those who deviated from halakhic norms, whether civil or ritual, could be punished. Non-Jewish governmental authorities generally recognized the *kehillah*'s coercive authority over its members.[30]

By the end of the eighteenth century, the *kehillah*'s authority was waning due to internal disputes and enlightened rulers' diminishing many of its prerogatives.[31] As the authority of the *kehillah* faltered, German Jewry began to fracture. From the late-eighteenth to the mid-nineteenth centuries, new German Jewish ideologies, including Haskalah, *Wissenschaft des Judentums*, Reform, Positive-Historical Judaism, and Neo-Orthodoxy, emerged.[32] Jewish leaders sought to repair this fracture by producing new Bible translations that adumbrated a vision of middle-class Judaism that would unite German Jews. But there were many such visions, and as fissures within German Jewry deepened, Bible translation became a vehicle for religious sectarianism, culminating in the "Secession Controversy" of the 1870s.[33]

While Heine links Mendelssohn to Luther, the connection between Protestantism and German Judaism runs deeper. Living amidst Protestant

[28] See Cohen, "Urban Visibility and Biblical Visions," 762–764.

[29] See Heschel, *Abraham Geiger and the Jewish Jesus*; Wiese, *Challenging Colonial Discourse*.

[30] See Katz, *Tradition and Crisis*, 63–94; idem, *A House Divided*, 8–9. To be sure, this is a general picture. The reality was far more complex and messy. See Carlebach, "La communauté juive et ses institutions au début de l'époque moderne."

[31] See Katz, *Tradition and Crisis*, 181–236; Meyer, *Response to Modernity*, 10–13; Carlebach, "La communauté," 365–366, 387–389.

[32] These ideologies were not mutually exclusive. For example, Reform, Positive-Historical Judaism and elements of Neo-Orthodoxy all drew on aspects of Haskalah and *Wissenschaft des Judentums*.

[33] On the Secession Controversy, see pp. 402–408 of this volume.

majorities, the translators I will explore deployed Protestantism and Catholicism as *conceptual categories*, generally aligning themselves with Protestantism and tarring their opponents as Catholics. The Pauline dichotomy between the "spirit that gives life" and the "letter that kills" (II Corinthians 3:6), which Luther deployed to battle Catholicism, became a central trope for these Bible translators.[34]

Two additional themes are important in this study: gender and authenticity. Marion Kaplan has highlighted the centrality of gender in German Jews' quest to become middle class.[35] Extending Kaplan's approach, Benjamin Baader has argued that nineteenth-century German Judaism became "feminized."[36] For Baader, German Jews made elements of Judaism previously associated with female religiosity central for both males and females. While male roles had centered on Torah study and communal Hebrew prayer, Baader argues that in the nineteenth century these two elements declined in importance as Judaism became "privatized." Male and female religiosity increasingly emphasized "feminine" elements such as vernacular prayer, morality, emotional sensitivity, and the home as the center of Judaism.[37] Baader's study is important, but it does not mention a crucial element of feminization, namely, the new curricular emphasis on Bible study for *males*. Traditionally German Jewish females focused on Bible study while Jewish males focused on Talmud study. But German Jewish Bible translators sought to re-center *male* Jewish education on the Bible. I will show that this new emphasis on Bible study gradually led to greater educational equality between the sexes, though important differences persisted.

[34] I focus on how German Jewish thinkers used Protestantism and Catholicism as conceptual categories to construct their vision of bourgeois German Judaism rather than on substantive affinities between bourgeois German Judaism and Protestantism. My approach is similar to Ari Joskowicz's in his recent book. See Joskowicz, *The Modernity of Others: Jewish Anti-Catholicism in France and Germany*. Seeking substantive affinities between German Judaism and Protestantism is a fool's errand as there were multiple forms of Protestantism in the five centuries between Luther and the end of German Jewry. For example, Protestantism is often associated with the privatization of religion and Catholicism with the penetration of religion into all spheres of life including the state. But in nineteenth-century Germany, it was *Protestants* who elaborated the idea of the Germany as a Christian state. See Tal, *Christians and Jews in Germany*, 121–159.

[35] See Kaplan, *The Making of the Jewish Middle Class: Women, Family and Identity in Imperial Germany*. A large literature on this topic has emerged in the wake of Kaplan's groundbreaking work.

[36] See Baader, *Gender, Judaism and Bourgeois Culture*. Lässig makes a similar point. See Lässig, *Jüdische Wege*, 326–361.

[37] See Baader, *Gender, Judaism and Bourgeois Culture*, 4–5. While I have learned much from Baader's work, I have hesitations about several of his assertions. First, in premodern Judaism, home life, ethics, and religious sensitivity were also important dimensions of male Jewish religiosity. Second, in the nineteenth century the public synagogue service assumed *increased* importance in German Jewish religious life, which calls into question whether Judaism of this period can be described as becoming "privatized."

The German Jewish turn to Bible translation also raises the question of religious authenticity. In discussing debates between Islamists and Islamic modernists, Roxanne Euben and Muhammad Qasim Zaman note that "the claim of authenticity is an act of power," which seeks to "construct [the world] by determining who is included and excluded, who may and may not speak authoritatively, what is the proper realm of debate, and what is beyond contestation."[38] This judgment is very germane to German Jewish debates over the Bible. The question of authenticity was raised at the earliest stage of Mendelssohn's Bible translation, as some of his traditionalist opponents criticized it as a revolutionary act that undermined Jewish tradition. All the Bible translators I will explore present their middle-class Judaism not as revolutionary but as authentic Judaism grounded in ancient and medieval Jewish sources. Indeed, they charge that it is their *traditionalist critics* who created counterfeit forms of Judaism that deviate from Jewish tradition.

In this way, my study of middle-class German Judaism illustrates the dynamics of religious change. While it is tempting to assess religious authenticity on the basis of continuity and conformity with the past where adaptation of contemporary ideals represents an inauthentic break from tradition, the forms of middle-class German Judaism I will explore illustrate how engagement with contemporary ideals can lead to activating dormant elements within a religious tradition, resulting in a religious vision that is at once old and new.

The present study cannot aspire to anything approaching a comprehensive treatment of German Jewish Bible translation. Instead, I will focus on three seminal translations, each separated by about half a century: Moses Mendelssohn's 1780–1783 translation and commentary on the Pentateuch, *Sefer Netivot Hashalom* (*Book of the Paths of Peace*); Leopold Zunz's 1838 translation of the entire Hebrew Bible, *Torah Nevi'im Ketuvim/Die vier und zwangzig Bücher der heiligen Schrift* (*Torah Prophets Writings/The Twenty-Four Books of Holy Scripture*); and Samson Raphael Hirsch's 1867–1878 translation and commentary on the Pentateuch, *Hamishah Humshei Torah/Der Pentateuch* (*Five-Fifths of the Torah/The Pentateuch*). I will also devote attention to the Reformer Ludwig Philippson's *Mikra Torah Nevi'im Ketuvim/Die Israelitische Bibel* (*Bible Torah Prophets Writings/The Israelite Bible*), which I will set in relation to Hirsch's *Der Pentateuch*. While my focus will be on Mendelssohn's and Hirsch's Pentateuch translations, I will also explore their translations of the Psalms.

[38] Euben and Zaman, *Princeton Readings in Islamist Thought*, 28.

I choose these writers for several reasons. *First*, their translations were widely disseminated. Werner Weinberg has listed twenty-seven different editions of Mendelssohn's *Pentateuch* (not including reprints) through 1915 and his list is incomplete.[39] Zunz's Bible was reprinted seventeen times through 1935 and it was the most widely used synagogue Bible throughout the nineteenth and twentieth centuries.[40] Hirsch's *Pentateuch* was republished six times through 1933 and was the most important Neo-Orthodox Pentateuch translation and commentary.[41] *Second*, each of these writers was a leading representative of an influential trend in modern German Judaism. Mendelssohn, who has been called the "patron saint" of German Jewry, was the most important figure of the Haskalah.[42] Zunz founded *Wissenschaft des Judentums* and in his early life was a leading Reformer who preached in the Beer Temple in Berlin. Hirsch was the chief ideologue of nineteenth-century Neo-Orthodoxy. *Third*, each of these translators engaged in a dual polemic. They all rejected the traditional Talmud-centered German Jewish educational system for males and the mindless practice of Jewish rituals grounded in fear.[43] But they also criticized those who disregarded Jewish teachings out of greed for money, social status, and pleasure. They each presented a vision of German Judaism that would avoid both pitfalls. Finally, while all three translators criticized Talmud-centric education, they all highly valued rabbinic teachings, which they saw as key to preserving the "living spirit" of Judaism.

I will not focus on perhaps the most famous of all German Jewish Bible translations, Buber's and Rosenzweig's *Die Schrift* (*Scripture*). In addition to the enormous secondary literature on this work, I see this translation as a *reaction* to the Jewish Reformation.[44] Unlike Mendelssohn, Zunz, and Hirsch,

[39] See Mendelssohn, *JubA*, 15.1:CII–CXII.

[40] See Schorsch, *Leopold Zunz: Creativity in Adversity*, 71.

[41] Mordechai Breuer discusses why Hirsch's Bible was much more widely read than the more scholarly one penned by his Neo-Orthodox contemporary David Zvi Hoffmann. See Breuer, "Rabbi Samson Raphael Hirsch's Commentary," 349–350.

[42] See Altmann, "Moses Mendelssohn as the Archetypal German Jew," 18.

[43] On the traditional German Jewish emphasis on the study of the Talmud and neglect of Bible study, see Katz, *Tradition and Crisis*, 162–167; Breuer, *Asif*, 237–259; *The Tents of Torah*, 116–128; Talmage, *Apples of Gold*, 151–171; Fishman, *The History of Jewish Education in Central Europe*, 94–109.

[44] Important scholarship on the Buber-Rosenzweig translation includes: Benjamin, *Rosenzweig's Bible*; Fox, "Franz Rosenzweig as Translator"; Niehoff, "The Buber-Rosenzweig Translation of the Bible within German-Jewish Tradition"; Levenson, *The Making of the Modern Jewish Bible*, ch. 5; Gordon, *Rosenzweig and Heidegger*, ch. 5; Reichert, "It Is Time: The Buber-Rosenzweig Translation in Context"; Seidman, *Faithful Renderings*, ch. 4; Weintraub, *The German Translations of the Pentateuch*,

Buber and Rosenzweig were not deeply steeped in talmudic learning, were not concerned about the traditional Ashkenazic centering of male Jewish education on Talmud study, and wrote little about the Talmud's relation to the Bible. Rather, Buber's and Rosenzweig's concern was returning alienated Jews with little Jewish education to Judaism by overturning the bourgeois synthesis of the Jewish Reformation translators. I will analyze the relation of the Buber-Rosenzweig translation to the translations that form the focus of this study in the Conclusion.

Throughout this book, I will treat three clusters of questions: The first relates to *translation method*: What is the proper approach to translating the Bible? What are the obstacles to translation? What role do the critical tools of etymology, grammar, history, and literary/aesthetic considerations play in Bible translation? How does one translate the Bible when it contradicts science and philosophy? How do rabbinic Midrash and Christological considerations inform translation choices? How is language gendered in translation?

The second cluster of questions relates to *language*: What is the origin and function of language? Do Hebrew and German have a special status or defining characteristics? What is the relationship between Hebrew and Jewish nationhood? How is Yiddish regarded?

The third cluster of questions relates to *education and community*: What is each translator's vision for German Jewish education? What role do class and gender play in shaping educational models? What is the place of the Bible and Talmud in the curriculum? Who is the audience for their Bible translation? What is the purpose of Bible translation? How does Bible translation promote a middle-class sensibility? What makes a Bible translation Jewish?

A note on terminology. Like many scholars, I use the terms *middle-class* and *bourgeois* interchangeably.[45] *Bourgeois* as an adjective translates the German word *bürgerlich* and as a noun translates *Bürger*, while *bourgeoisie* translates *Bürgertum*. Jürgen Kocka notes that by the end of the eighteenth century three types of *Bürger* had emerged. The first, often rendered in English as *burghers*, referred to a group that originated in the late medieval/early modern period known as the *Stadtbürger*. This was a corporate entity living in cities that had specific "legal privileges, lifestyles, and status" within cities and included independent craftsmen organized into guilds, landlords,

37–50, 233–239; Gillman, "Between Religion and Culture: Mendelssohn, Buber, Rosenzweig and the Enterprise of Biblical Translation"; idem, *A History of German Jewish Bible Translation*, ch. 4.

45 See Kocka, "The Middle Classes in Europe," 784; Kaplan, *The Making of the Jewish Middle Class.*

doctors, lawyers, ministers, and the most successful merchants.[46] Toward the end of the eighteenth century, two new types of bourgeois developed: the *Wirtschaftsbürgertum* (economic bourgeoisie), namely, individuals with substantial economic undertakings, including entrepreneurs, manufacturers, bankers, managers, and capitalists whose business extended beyond the city; and the *Bildungsbürgertum* (educated bourgeoisie), the *intelligentsia*, which included lawyers, judges, professors, university-educated civil servants, ministers, and journalists.[47]

Unlike in England where the *Wirtschaftsbürgertum* was the largest group and clearly distinguished from the *Bildungsbürgertum*, in German lands the *Bildungsbürgertum* was dominant, and there was much overlap between this group and the *Wirtschaftsbürgertum*.[48] The *Bildungsbürgertum* was defined as much by culture as by economic and political status. Their core values included: (1) meritocracy where rewards, recognition, and influence were based on individual achievement rather than noble birth or governmental dispensation; (2) the value of regular work; (3) rationality and emotional control; (4) independence and liberty for the individual both *qua* individual and *qua* member of self-governing associations; (5) *Bildung*; (6) respect for academic/scientific pursuits (*Wissenschaft*); (7) aesthetic appreciation and creativity; (8) proper dress, speech, and manners; and (9) raising a family based on distinct gender roles, with the male sphere being public and the female being private. The primary male role was to earn income outside the home and the primary female role was to protect the home from the corrosive effects of competition and materialism to raise ethical children.[49]

While *bourgeois* translates the words *bürgerlich* and *Bürger*, this does not fully capture the meaning of these German words. *Bürgerlich* also connotes "civil" and *Bürger* "citizen." This is not incidental, for a central element of being bourgeois was seeking to secure one's civil rights against encroachment by the aristocracy and the state.[50] Given German Jews' inferior social status, it is not surprising that many embraced the bourgeois ideal, though their primary concern was not to oppose the claims of the aristocracy but, rather, to

[46] See Kocka, "The European Pattern and the German Case," 3–4; idem, "Bürgertum und Bürglichkeit," 21–23.

[47] Kocka, "Bürgertum und Bürglichkeit," 23–28; idem, "The European Pattern and the German Case," 4; idem, "The Middle Classes in Europe," 784.

[48] Kocka, "The European Pattern and the German Case,"16, 23.

[49] Kocka, "Bürger und Bürgertum," 43–44; "The Middle Classes in Europe," 787; Kaplan, *The Making of the Jewish Middle Class*.

[50] Kocka, "The European Pattern and the German Case," 8–11.

secure their rights against those who claimed that civil rights should be based on Teutonic descent and/or adherence to Christianity.

The success of German Jews in becoming middle class is astonishing. Lässig observes that nineteenth-century German Jews "enjoyed an economic and social ascent without parallel in Europe." While in 1800 nearly two-thirds of German Jews were poor, in the decades following the establishment of the German Empire in 1871, the majority of German Jews had become middle or upper class.[51] Invoking Max Weber's theories about the relation between religion and economics and Pierre Bourdieu's theory of social capital, Lässig argues that religion was a crucial factor in German Jews' social, political, and economic ascent.[52]

I do not disagree with Lässig's arguments, but I think that they are too limited. Focusing solely on the secular achievements of middle-class German Judaism conceals what was most important about it, at least for the Jewish Reformation translators who are the focus of this study. For these translators being middle class was a religious endeavor, a *spiritual enterprise.* Wealth, respectability, and even civil rights were only of value insofar as they helped Jews worship God. The purpose of middle-class Judaism was to foster the development of a community of free self-realized individuals, loyal members of both the Jewish and German nations, who served God by actualizing God's universal ethical message to benefit humanity.

[51] See Lässig, *Jüdische Wege ins Bürgertum,* 13.

[52] See Lässig, *Jüdische Wege ins Bürgertum*; idem, "The Emergence of Middle Class Religiosity." Sorkin has similarly argued that transformations in religion were central to German Jews' quest for civil rights. See Sorkin, "The Genesis of the Ideology of Emancipation."

PART I

HASKALAH

Moses Mendelssohn's Moderate Reformation

1
The Bible as Cultural Translation

From the time of its publication until today, Mendelssohn's translation of the Pentateuch into High German, formally titled *Sefer Netivot Hashalom* (*Book of the Paths of Peace*), but informally known as the *Be'ur* (*Elucidation*), has elicited outrage. Critics ranging from secular Zionists like Peretz Smolenskin to traditionalist rabbis like Ezekiel Landau condemned the work, seeing it as a way of civilizing primitive Jews by turning them into sycophantic, servile Germans.[1] Naomi Seidman has recently given voice to this worry in a postcolonialist key, writing that "Alongside the rhetoric of cultural equality and religious tolerance, German Enlightenment discourse less openly takes part in the project of internal European colonialism, the civilizing mission to the Jews of which Mendelssohn can be called a 'native agent.'"[2] For Seidman, Mendelssohn was a member of an oppressed minority who internalized the values of his oppressors, which he sought to impose on his backward brethren, thereby securing for himself the illusory feeling of being liberated whereas he was, in fact, a slave doing his tormentors' dirty work.[3]

Features of the *Be'ur* have been adduced in support of this criticism. Does not the fact that the *Be'ur* translation smooths the rough edges of the Hebrew, eliminating its strange foreign cadences in favor of a refined German style, reflect an act of violent repression on the biblical text? Is not Mendelssohn's concern with the plain meaning of the biblical text (*peshat*) the expression of an effort to efface the vibrant, polysemic meaning uncovered by the ancient rabbis by imposing a ghostly, singular identity on it?[4] By translating the Bible into proper German is not Mendelssohn opting for preserving the sense of

[1] Landau's view is cited in Altmann, *Moses Mendelssohn: A Biographical Study,* 382–383. Smolenskin's view is cited in Weinberg, "Language Questions," 201. For discussion, see Seidman, *Faithful Renderings,* 164–179. Elisheva Carlebach notes that through the end of the eighteenth century, Jewish traditionalists associated learning the German language with conversion. See Carlebach, *Divided Souls,* 160–161, 169.

[2] See Seidman, *Faithful Renderings,* 173.

[3] Yitzhak Melamed has recently presented a similar assessment of Mendelssohn. See Melamed, "Mendelssohn, Maimon, and Spinoza on Excommunication and Toleration." Olga Litvak discusses some the dynamics of this critique of Mendelssohn and responses to it. See Litvak, *Haskalah,* 71–77.

[4] See Berman, "Translation and the Trials of the Foreign," 276–278.

The Jewish Reformation. Michah Gottlieb, Oxford University Press (2021). © Oxford University Press.
DOI: 10.1093/oso/9780199336388.003.0002

the biblical text over literary form, thereby indicating his having internalized the Protestant privileging of the spirit over the letter and revealing himself as the quintessential Jewish Protestant? In his *Phaedon* Mendelssohn wrote that he had made "Socrates speak like an eighteenth-century philosopher."[5] Did he not do the same to Moses in his *Be'ur* translation, thereby revealing the "German Plato" as the archetypical Jewish Zelig?[6]

Mendelssohn's work as a translator was not limited to the Bible. His mother tongue was Yiddish, and as a youth in the rural hamlet of Dessau he was taught Hebrew and Aramaic but no European languages. When at age fourteen Mendelssohn followed his teacher, the learned Talmudist Rabbi David Fränkel, to Berlin and encountered the flowering enlightened culture there, Mendelssohn realized that to engage this culture he had to learn European languages. While Mendelssohn received some minor instruction in Latin from Abraham Kisch, and in Greek from Christian Tobias Damm, he essentially taught himself these languages as well as German, French, and English.[7] Mendelssohn practiced translation as a means of perfecting his grasp of languages. He translated Jean-Jacques Rousseau's *Discours sur l'origine et les fondements de l'inégalité parmi les hommes* (*Discourse on the Origin of Human Inequality*) from French into German in 1755, Lord Shaftesbury's *Sensus Communis: An Essay of the Freedom of the Wit* from English into German in 1762, Plato's *Republic* from Greek into German in 1763, and Alexander Baumgarten's *Ethica Philosophica* from Latin into German sometime between 1762 and 1766.[8]

The centrality of translation for Mendelssohn seems to reinforce the frequently expressed view that he was an eclectic, unoriginal thinker. Proponents of this view claim that Mendelssohn uncritically accepted Leibniz's and Wolff's enlightened rationalism, which he uncomfortably fused with English empiricism rather than develop his own original philosophy from first principles. They note that he preferred to rewrite the work of others (most famously the *Phaedon*) rather than pen original philosophical works.[9]

Critics extend this judgment regarding Mendelssohn's lack of originality to his Hebrew writings, noting that unlike later Zionist writers who wrote

[5] See Mendelssohn, *JubA*, 3.1:9; *Phaedon*, 42.

[6] See Weinberg, "Language Questions," 210.

[7] See Altmann, *Moses Mendelssohn: A Biographical Study*, 22–23, 112.

[8] These translations are found in Mendelssohn, *JubA*, 6.2:61–242.

[9] For a classical statement of Mendelssohn lack of originality, see Hegel, *Lectures on the History of Philosophy*, 3:356–357, and Cohen, *Jüdische Schriften*, 2:259–260, cited in Freudenthal, *No Religion without Idolatry*, 249, note 11.

original works in Hebrew, the genre that Mendelssohn most often used in his Hebrew writings was commentary.[10] Mendelssohn wrote a commentary on Maimonides's *Treatise on Logic*, a commentary on Ecclesiastes, and his *Be'ur* includes a Hebrew commentary. In his *Be'ur* commentary, Mendelssohn is constantly citing medieval Jewish authorities. He did not even have the intellectual independence to comment on the biblical text by itself![11]

For these reasons, the *Be'ur* can be seen as a powerful brief against Mendelssohn, the Haskalah, and the Enlightenment, tearing away their mask of compassion, tolerance, impartiality, and intellectual probity, and exposing their oppression, intolerance, treachery, and superficiality.

Scholars have rightly stressed the importance of eighteenth-century debates over Jewish civil rights for understanding Mendelssohn's Bible translation. As we have seen, opponents of Jewish civil rights routinely charged that the Jews' clannishness, immorality, and irrationality precluded them from citizenship.[12] Edward Breuer notes that Mendelssohn turned to Pentateuch translation "to highlight a common religious and cultural heritage a notion that reinforced the grounds for economic and social integration."[13] If this is true of Mendelssohn's Pentateuch translation, which was aimed at Jews, it is even more true of his Psalms translation, which was aimed at Jews and Christians alike.[14]

[10] Friedrich Niewöhner goes further, arguing that even Mendelssohn's German works are best understood as commentaries. See Niewöhner, "Mendelssohn als Philosoph-Aufklärer-Jude," 124. Niewöhner exaggerates. While he is correct in claiming that the *Phaedon* can be understood as a commentary on Plato and *Sache Gottes* as a commentary on Leibniz, Niewöhner's claim that Mendelssohn's *Morgenstunden* is a commentary on Spinoza is wrong, and he does not consider Mendelssohn's other independent philosophical works such as his *Treatise on Evidence* and his aesthetic writings, none of which can be construed as commentaries.

[11] See Barzilay, "Smolenskin's Polemic against Mendelssohn," 17. Zev Harvey has observed the irony that Mendelssohn was attacked for being both overly original and unoriginal.

[12] See p. 2 of this volume. Already in his 1543 *Von den Jüden und iren Lügen* (*On the Jews and their Lies*), Luther condemned Jews as immoral, hateful, and irrational. See Luther, *Luther's Works*, 47:137–150, 216, 226–227. On the eighteenth-century use of such arguments to deny Jews civil rights, see Katz, *From Prejudice to Destruction*, 23–73.

[13] See Breuer, *The Limits of Enlightenment*, 20. Mordechai Eliav earlier made this point in his 1960 book *Jewish Education in Germany*. See Eliav, *Jewish Education*, 164.

[14] That the intended audience of the *Be'ur* was Jews is evidenced by the German translation being in Hebrew script and the commentary being in Hebrew. Further confirmation is found in the fact that of the 515 subscribers to the original edition of the *Be'ur*, only twenty-one were Christians, many of whom subscribed for political reasons, such as the King and Crown Prince of Denmark. Mendelssohn solicited such subscriptions in order to forestall the possibility of the *Be'ur* being put under the ban by Rabbi Raphael Cohen of Altona. For discussion of the subscribers to the original edition of the *Be'ur*, see Lowenstein, "The Readership," 183, 195–209. In 1780, Josias Loeffler published the first volume of the *Be'ur* translation in Gothic script, omitting the commentary and introduction. Loeffler made clear that his edition was intended primarily for Christian scholars, not for the Christian laity. Subsequent volumes were never produced. See Altmann, *Moses Mendelssohn: A Biographical Study*, 389. In addition, a partial German translation of the prospectus for Mendelssohn's Pentateuch

Breuer's claim is surely correct, but it is incomplete. Over the next two chapters I will argue that Mendelssohn's Bible translation project has seven main goals: (1) strengthening Jewish national sentiment and religious practice; (2) invigorating German national identity; (3) promoting tolerance and love between German Jews and Christians; (4) reforming the German Jewish educational system for males; (5) restructuring the German Jewish social hierarchy; (6) fostering the moral, aesthetic and religious development of German Jews *and* Christians; and (7) advancing Jewish civil rights. Against the postcolonial critique of Enlightenment and Haskalah, I will argue that Mendelssohn's Bible project reveals the deep resources of the Enlightenment for vitalizing a premodern religious tradition by deepening its moral and spiritual teachings for the benefit both of its adherents and of society at large.

Franz Rosenzweig's nuanced view of the *Be'ur*

The best-known discussion of Mendelssohn's *Be'ur* is Franz Rosenzweig's essay "The Eternal: Mendelssohn and the Name of God" ("Der Ewige: Mendelssohn und der Gottesname"). Rosenzweig discusses Mendelssohn's rendering of the ineffable four-letter name of the God, the so-called Tetragrammaton, as a way of reflecting more generally on Mendelssohn's approach to Bible translation. Scholars typically read Rosenzweig's essay as highly critical of Mendelssohn.

On the standard interpretation, Rosenzweig rejects Mendelssohn's rendering of the Tetragrammaton as a way of expressing a fundamental difference

project titled *Alim Literufa* appeared in 1780, with the Bible translation appearing in Gothic letters. In a review published later that year, the reviewer notes that he seeks to familiarize the reader with this work since Mendelssohn's translation project "is a valuable and pleasing gift not just for the nation (*Nation*) of the its author but also for the Christian reader of the Bible (*christliche Bibelleser*)." See "Rezension *Probe einer jüdische-deutschen Uebersetzung der fünf Bucher Moses des Herrn Moses Mendelssohn*," *Allgemeine Deutsche Bibliothek* 40 (1780), 244. In contrast to the *Be'ur*, Mendelssohn's 1783 *Psalms*, which was printed in Gothic script, was aimed at both Jews and Christians, as I will explore later in the chapter. See p. 37 of this volume. Further evidence of the different audiences of these works is that while in the *Be'ur* Mendelssohn rendered Hebrew names in their Hebrew form, in his *Psalms* translation he most often translated them according to their German form. For example, in the *Be'ur* Mendelssohn preserves יצחק and מצרים in their Hebrew forms, but in his Psalms he translates the names in Germanic forms as *Isaak* and *Aegypten*. See Mendelssohn, *JubA*, 10.1:157 (Psalm 105:9), 101.1:177 (Psalm 114:1). But note that in his translation of Psalm 90 Mendelssohn translates משה as *Mosche* rather than as *Mose*. See Mendelssohn, *JubA*, 10.1:140. Also, while in the introduction to the *Be'ur* Mendelssohn emphasizes his use of the medieval Jewish commentators Rashi, Rashbam, Nahmanides, and Ibn Ezra, in the introduction to his Psalms translation he only mentions his use of Christian translators, namely Luther, G.C. Knapp, and J.D. Michaelis. See Mendelssohn, *JubA*, 14:327; 10.1:6–7; *Moses Mendelssohn: Writings*, 183.

between their approaches to Bible translation and to theology more generally. For Rosenzweig, Mendelssohn renders the Tetragrammaton as an impersonal, transcendent description of God by translating it as "the Eternal" (*Der Ewige*). By contrast, Rosenzweig translates the Tetragrammaton with a personal pronoun, thereby expressing God's living presence in the world. On the standard interpretation, Rosenzweig deems Mendelssohn's translation a monological, abstract "Hellenic" rendering of the name of God. More generally, Mendelssohn's translation evinces embarrassment at the foreign-sounding Hebrew of the Bible and so flattens it into an unthreatening German idiom. By contrast, Rosenzweig's translation is a dialogical, concrete "Jewish" translation that unabashedly imposes the form and cadences of the Hebrew original on the German. In a word, Rosenzweig sees Mendelssohn's translation as Germanizing Hebrew, whereas his own translation Hebraicizes German.[15]

In fact, Rosenzweig's interpretation of Mendelssohn is much subtler than it is often given credit for and points toward a more complex understanding of Mendelssohn's *Be'ur*. Near the beginning of the essay, Rosenzweig lavishes praise on Mendelssohn's translation, writing that "objectively considered, [it is] one of the great accomplishments of the classic decades of German translation of the era of Goethean world-literature."[16] Rosenzweig observes that in the *Be'ur* Mendelssohn pays close attention to the "oriental language and manner of speech" (*morgenländischen Sprache und Vortragsart*) of the Bible, giving the example of Mendelssohn's translation of *karat brit* in Genesis 15:18. While Luther translates the phrase into idiomatic German as *machte einen Bund* (made a covenant), Mendelssohn translates it very literally as *zerschnitt einen Bund* (cut a covenant), thereby alluding to the fact that Abraham concluded his covenant with God by cutting up animals. This manner of translating, which seeks to convey the foreign, "oriental" nature of the Hebrew Bible, is something that one would expect from Rosenzweig, not Mendelssohn.[17]

To be sure, Rosenzweig notes that Mendelssohn's translation of the Tetragrammaton as "the Eternal" reflects the fact that "the spirit of the age

[15] For this interpretation of Rosenzweig, see Gordon, *Rosenzweig and Heidegger*, 263–267; Batnitzky, *Idolatry and Representation*, 123–135; Gillman, "Between Religion and Culture," 104–114; Rosenstock, *Philosophy and the Jewish Question*, 6–7; Horwitz, "Mendelssohn's Interpretation of the Tetragrammaton as the Eternal," 200–204.

[16] Buber and Rosenzweig, *Die Schrift und ihre Verdeutschung*, 100; *Scripture and Translation*, 185.

[17] For their part, Buber and Rosenzweig follow Luther by translating *karat brit* as *schloß einen Bund* (concluded a covenant). For a recent discussion of Mendelssohn's translation of this passage, see Freudenthal, *No Religion without Idolatry*, 97–101.

made alliance with the Aristotelian spirit of Maimonides whom Mendelssohn honored all his life, against the sure instinct of Jewish tradition."[18] But Rosenzweig notes that in his *Be'ur* commentary Mendelssohn observes that the Tetragrammaton also connotes divine providence.[19] So Mendelssohn was well aware that the Tetragrammaton expressed God's relation to the world. Rosenzweig further observes that while the Tetragrammaton first appears in Genesis, Mendelssohn deferred discussing its meaning until his commentary on Exodus 3:14 where God reveals this name to Moses. For Rosenzweig, this reflects Mendelssohn's awareness that the meaning of the Tetragrammaton must be connected to revelation.[20] Rosenzweig also finds much merit in Mendelssohn's translation of the Tetragrammaton as "the Eternal", noting that this term is not an inert, dry appellation but, rather, "is animate with genuine powers of the human soul" since it expresses mortal humanity's longing for divine eternity.[21] Indeed, in his 1921 book *The Star of Redemption,* Rosenzweig generally followed Mendelssohn by translating the Tetragrammaton as "the Eternal".[22]

Rosenzweig agrees with Mendelssohn that the Tetragrammaton denotes both a transcendent, ontological aspect of God and an imminent, relational one, writing that the "Jewish uniting of the distant God with the near" constitutes "the essence of Judaism."[23] So why does Rosenzweig translate the Tetragrammaton as a personal pronoun rather than as "the Eternal"? For Rosenzweig, the difference involves the turn from rational theology to experiential religious knowledge. While Mendelssohn thinks one can logically deduce divine providence from God's eternal necessity, Rosenzweig thinks that one must derive God's eternal necessity from one's experience of God's loving providential care.[24] Clearly Rosenzweig's essay points to a more nuanced understanding of Mendelssohn's Bible translation.

[18] Buber and Rosenzweig, *Die Schrift und ihre Verdeutschung,* 105; *Scripture and Translation,* 195.

[19] See Mendelssohn's commentary on Exodus 3:14, where following a Midrash he notes that one implication of the name *Ehyeh Asher Ehyeh* (which for Mendelssohn has the same sense as the Tetragrammaton) is "I will be with them in every plight, I will be with them in this plight, and I will be with them whenever they call me." See Mendelssohn, *JubA,* 16:27; *Moses Mendelssohn: Writings,* 217.

[20] Buber and Rosenzweig, *Die Schrift und ihre Verdeutschung,* 197; *Scripture and Translation,* 106.

[21] Buber and Rosenzweig, *Die Schrift und ihre Verdeutschung,* 112; *Scripture and Translation,* 208.

[22] See Losch, "What Is Behind God's Name?," 92.

[23] Buber and Rosenzweig, *Die Schrift und ihre Verdeutschung,* 108, 190–191; *Scripture and Translation,* 194–195, 334–335.

[24] Buber and Rosenzweig, *Die Schrift und ihre Verdeutschung,* 104; *Scripture and Translation,* 192–193.

Translation as reviving Jewish national pride

In the introduction to the *Be'ur*, titled *Or Linetiva* (henceforth: *OL*), Mendelssohn describes the need for his translation. For Mendelssohn, Jewish boys receiving an immersive traditional Jewish education failed to acquire a proper understanding and appreciation for Hebrew since they did not learn the language grammatically and were not taught to appreciate its aesthetic qualities. The focus of their education was studying the Aramaic Talmud, and when they were taught the Bible they only learned to decode it by transliterating it in a hyper-literal, word-for-word fashion. The only Bible studied was the weekly pericope of the Pentateuch with the medieval commentator Rashi, who incorporated many nonliteral rabbinic comments.[25] As Rashi's commentary was quite extensive and only a small amount of time was devoted to studying the Pentateuch each week, boys generally would not complete the weekly pericope before moving on to the next week's. The result was that boys' knowledge of even the Pentateuch was piecemeal and inadequate.[26] For Mendelssohn, without a proper grammatical understanding of Hebrew and systematic instruction in the Bible, students could not properly understand the Bible's plain meaning, appreciate its aesthetic qualities, or grasp the depth of its moral and religious teachings.

Mendelssohn's desire to instill an appreciation for the Hebrew language among his fellow German Jews goes back to his earliest writings. In his 1755 Hebrew work, *Kohelet Mussar* (Preacher of Morals), Mendelssohn complains that the Jews of his day neglect Hebrew: "I have seen clearly how our Jewish brethren have abandoned Hebrew. I do not know how this evil happened (Judges 20:3) . . . Is she not the finest of languages?"[27] Mendelssohn has no patience for Jews seeking to excuse their neglect of Hebrew.[28] Appealing to

[25] See Mendelssohn, *JubA*, 14: 243; *Moses Mendelssohn: Writings*, 197. The Pentateuch is divided into weekly pericopes read over the course of a year in the synagogue.

[26] See Turniansky, "Heder Education in the Early Modern Period"; Weinberg, "Language Questions," 229. Turniansky mentions some rabbinic opponents of the traditionalist method of male Jewish education prior to Mendelssohn.

[27] Mendelssohn, *JubA*, 14:3; Breuer and Sorkin, "Moses Mendelssohn's First Hebrew Publication," 8. On the debate over whether Mendelssohn was the sole author of this work or had a collaborator, see Breuer and Sorkin, "Moses Mendelssohn's First Hebrew Publication," 3, note 1. I henceforth abbreviate *Kohelet Mussar* as *KM*.

[28] Mendelssohn notes that one of the arguments Jews use to excuse their not learning Hebrew properly is that since the Jews are exiled among the nations and suffer civil disabilities, they are like slaves who must learn their masters' language and in doing so forget their own. In response, Mendelssohn cites a midrashic teaching that when the Hebrew were *actual* slaves in Egypt, they still preserved Hebrew as their language. See Mendelssohn, *JubA*, 14:4; Breuer and Sorkin, "Moses Mendelssohn's First Hebrew Publication," 8. The midrashic tradition that Mendelssohn cites is found in *Mekhilta*, Parashat Bo, parashah 5, commentary to Exodus 12:6; *Pirkei Derabbi Eliezer* 48 (end);

Jews' sense of national pride, he writes: "Let us learn from the other nations, each with their own national language; they neither rested nor reposed until they fully developed their language."[29] More than a century before Zionism, Mendelssohn sought to renew Hebrew as a living language. In a 1756 German review written about the same time as *KM*, Mendelssohn lays down guidelines for renewing Hebrew as a living language. These include using biblical phrases and idioms for contemporary purposes by giving them new meanings far from the original intentions of the biblical writers.[30]

At the end of *KM*, Mendelssohn notes that when it comes to rendering poetry from a different language, Hebrew "has almost has no peer," and to illustrate this he translates the first sixty lines of Edward Young's poem "Night Thoughts" into Hebrew.[31] This act expresses his hope that by resurrecting Hebrew as a living language used for both holy and profane purposes, it can become a source of Jewish national cohesion.

In a striking comment on the Song of the Sea (Exodus 15) in the *Be'ur*, Mendelssohn expresses distress that young Jews assume the superiority of Gentile literature and fail to appreciate their own national poetry:

> I have seen the youths of our nation satisfying themselves with the creations of foreign peoples and taking pride in the poetic arts of foreign nations, as if the splendor and gracefulness of poetry had been granted to them. The fire of jealousy burned in my heart, to show that just as the heavens are elevated high above the earth, so too are the ways of sacred poetry elevated high above secular poetry... In terms of magnificence and beauty, sacred poetry possesses much advantage and great excellence when compared to all of the poems that are so greatly praised for these matters.[32]

Midrash Tanhuma, Balak; *Song of Songs Rabbah, Perek Gan Naul*. Mendelssohn also cites this rabbinic teaching in his 1778 prospectus to the *Be'ur, Alim Literufa*. See Mendelssohn, *JubA*, 14:323.

[29] Mendelssohn, *JubA*, 14: 4; Breuer and Sorkin, "Moses Mendelssohn's First Hebrew Publication," 10.

[30] See Mendelssohn, *JubA*, 4:186–187. Despite Mendelssohn's stressing the need to use biblical Hebrew in contemporary Hebrew writing, Eisig Silberschlag notes that in his Hebrew writings Mendelssohn also incorporates rabbinic and medieval philosophical words and phrases. See Silberschlag, *From Renaissance to Renaissance*, 82, cited in Dauber, "New Thoughts," 145, note 40.

[31] See Mendelssohn, *JubA*, 14:18–21.

[32] Mendelssohn, *JubA*, 16:134; *Moses Mendelssohn: Writings*, 215. Also see Mendelssohn's letter to J.G. Herder of June 20, 1780, where he writes that an aim of his *Be'ur* is to "educate [my children] not to feel shame" on account of their Judaism. Mendelssohn, *JubA*, 12.2:193–194.

We will discuss why Mendelssohn thinks that Hebrew poetry is superior in the next chapter.[33]

In *KM*, Mendelssohn focuses on the need for Jews to learn Hebrew, but in *AL* and *OL* he also ascribes value to *translation*. Responding to traditionalist critics who criticize Bible translation as an impious innovation, Mendelssohn notes that to prevent the forgetting of the Bible and Hebrew, Jews translated the Bible throughout history.[34] For Mendelssohn, a new translation into proper, contemporary German will help young Jews comprehend the literary subtleties of Hebrew so that they will be able to read the Bible independently and take pride in their national literature. [35]

Translating tolerance

For Mendelssohn translation was about much more than reviving Jewish national pride. As we have seen, Mendelssohn's translation efforts were not limited to translating Hebrew texts into German; he also translated French, English, Greek, and Latin writings into German. In fact, Mendelssohn was one of the few philosophers who was also a translator.[36] I This is not incidental, for translation is at the heart of his philosophy.

As a traditional Jew from a small German town whose mother tongue was Yiddish, Mendelssohn felt acute cultural anxiety when he first encountered the vibrant culture of enlightened Berlin.[37] Throughout his life, Mendelssohn was shuttling between two worlds, translating Judaism into the idiom of enlightened German culture and translating enlightened German culture into Jewish idiom.[38] Mendelssohn used translation to constitute himself as a modern German Jew.

Many of Mendelssohn's Protestant opponents could not or would not understand this, which is why he was repeatedly solicited to convert. For both the chiliastic mystic Johann Caspar Lavater and the enlightened theist August Friedrich Cranz, religious truth was *untranslatable*. Christianity was ethical,

[33] See pp. 110–113 of this volume.

[34] Mendelssohn, *JubA*, 14:232–242, 324–325. Mendelssohn located the first reference to Bible translation in the book of Nehemiah (8:8) and cited subsequent Jewish Bible translations into Greek, Aramaic, Arabic, Persian, Spanish, and Yiddish from the 2nd century BC to the 17th century AD.

[35] See Mendelssohn, *JubA*, 14:243.

[36] Modern philosophers who were translators include Schleiermacher, Buber, and Rosenzweig. But it is surprisingly rare for philosophers to be translators. I thank Zev Harvey for this point.

[37] See Feiner, *The Jewish Enlightenment*, 21–35.

[38] Mendelssohn's German writings, such as his Letter to Lavater and *Jerusalem*, are attempts to translate Judaism into Enlightenment idiom. His Hebrew commentary on Maimonides's *Logical Terms* and his Hebrew 1773 letter to Rabbi Jacob Emden are attempts to translate Enlightenment ideals into the idiom of traditionalist Judaism.

rational, and tolerant while Judaism was immoral, irrational, and coercive. If Mendelssohn was ethical, rational, and tolerant, he must be a Christian QED. Intellectual honesty demanded that Mendelssohn publicly affirm the religion to which he truly belonged.

Mendelssohn's response was that Judaism possesses a great insight missed by Christianity, namely, the translatability of moral and religious truth. For Mendelssohn these truths were universal, knowable by all people through reason or common sense. Unlike Christianity, which claimed exclusive possession of religious truths, Judaism understood that all religions were grounded in universal moral and religious truths, which they expressed using different signs.[39] For this reason, Judaism held that Gentiles need not be Jewish to be saved. In sum, Mendelssohn regarded the possibility of interreligious translation as a central teaching of Judaism and the foundation of its religious tolerance.[40]

Constituting German nationhood through translation

Mendelssohn was not only concerned with Jewish national regeneration. He was also concerned with constituting German nationhood.[41] Historians have observed that by the middle of the eighteenth century there was a crisis of national identity in the German states. This was, in part, due to the fact that in contrast to England and France, which had strong centralized governments that provided a sense of unified national identity, Germany was divided into some three hundred principalities. It was said that, at the time, German speakers would use the term *Vaterland* to refer to their particular principality while referring to everywhere else (including other German principalities) as *Ausland*.[42]

The crisis was particularly acute in Prussia where the enlightened absolutist monarch Frederick the Great disdained German language and culture and sought to spread French influence. In a review of Frederick's 1760 *Poésies Diverses*, Mendelssohn lamented "the damage to our mother tongue that has been wrought by the prince's having made French so

[39] In *Jerusalem*, Mendelssohn enumerates God's existence, divine providence and a future life as "fundamental principles on which all religions agree." See Mendelssohn, *JubA*, 8:131; *Jerusalem*, 63.

[40] I will explore this point in greater detail in the next chapter. Also see Gottlieb, "Mendelssohn's Metaphysical Defense of Religious Pluralism."

[41] See Gottlieb, *Faith and Freedom*, 26–28.

[42] See Bruford, *Germany in the Eighteenth Century*, 45.

prevalent."[43] A central aim of the *Literaturbriefe* to which Mendelssohn was a major contributor was to revitalize German language and culture. But beyond language what would constitute German nationhood? Mendelssohn was concerned that it not be Protestantism or Teutonic descent.

In his first published writing, his 1754 *Philosophical Dialogues*, Mendelssohn identified *intellectual cosmopolitanism* as a defining feature of German nationhood. Calling Germans "a people that treasures accurate thinking more than freethinking," Mendelssohn contrasted the Germans with the French, whom he described as having "made the stylishness of manners its sole concern and . . . heaping the most biting sarcasm on those who indulged in profound meditations." Obliquely alluding to Frederick's Francophilia, Mendelssohn deplored Germans who were gladly willing to "give away half their intellect if the French would only concede to them that they know how to live."[44]

For Mendelssohn, the great German philosopher Gottfried Leibniz and his follower Christian Wolff exemplified the German spirit. What Mendelssohn most admired about Leibniz was his self-described "grand manner of philosophizing" in which he sought to discover the element of truth underlying the most diverse theological and philosophical systems and integrate them into a new whole. In a 1698 letter to Pierre Bayle, Leibniz had lamented that "our greatest failure has been the sectarian spirit, which imposes limits upon itself by spurning others."[45] For Mendelssohn, seeking to develop German culture solely from within itself risked creating a narrow, stunted national vision.[46] While thinkers such as Éléazar de Mauvillon considered translation of foreign works into German evidence of the poverty of German culture, Mendelssohn regarded translation as a means of vitalizing German nationhood by actualizing Leibniz's vision of it.[47]

43 Mendelssohn, *JubA*, 5.1:188 quoted in Altmann, *Moses Mendelssohn: A Biographical Study*, 71–72.

44 Mendelssohn, *JubA*, 1:349; *Philosophical Writings*, 106. Compare Mendelssohn, *JubA*, 6.1:140–141.

45 Leibniz, *Die Philosophischen Schriften*, 4:523–524; *Philosophical Papers and Letters*, 496.

46 In an unpublished manuscript from 1756, Mendelssohn wrote, "No one misunderstands himself more than he who observes himself alone." See Mendelssohn, *JubA*, 6.1:17.

47 In his 1740 *Lettres Françoises et Germanique*, de Mauvillon had complained that instead of producing a national literature, Germans had only produced bad translations. See Altmann, "Einleitung" to Mendelssohn, *JubA*, 6.2:xxv. Herder expressed sentiments close to Mendelssohn's in his 1767 *Fragmente*, writing, "We will bring out the advantages of new citizens in the body of our language and not imitate the Spartan willfulness, which barred entry to all alien arrivals and customs, but we will also, like Academia della Crusca and Johnson in his *Dictionary*, count our natives, organize and employ them, so that foreign colonies serve only to make up for shortcomings of our state. Our language, thus, ought to be developed by *translation* and reflection" (emphasis mine). See Herder, *Selected Early Works*, 109.

Mendelssohn observed that a nation may be unable to conceive certain concepts because their language lacks the words to express them. But translation can lead to coining new terms that open up new horizons of thought.[48] For example, he noted that while historically many peoples have construed the world as subject to manipulation through magical means, the word *nature* enabled people to conceive events in the world as the result of necessary causes and effects. Translating the word *nature* according to this meaning into a language that did not possess the concept of natural, necessary causality could therefore open a new way of seeing the world.[49] For Mendelssohn, translation put Germans into conversation with great world literature, which would enrich their national identity. As he put it in an unpublished review of Herder's 1767 *Fragmente*, "The more familiar we are with the literature of other peoples, the more we learn to consider our own thoughts from different angles."[50]

For Mendelssohn, translating from a European language into German was never straightforward. In rendering Rousseau's French into German, he was translating from his third language into his second. Mendelssohn explained that in such cases Hebrew mediated his translation, writing, "I have been accustomed to translating into Hebrew every curious word I read or heard in some other language."[51] So while translating from Hebrew into German was a direct, binary process, translating from another language into German was a three-way conversation. For this reason, Mendelssohn claimed that Hebrew modes of thought enriched his ability to contribute to German culture.

For example, Mendelssohn noted that Hebrew has no word for accident or chance. The Hebrew word *mikreh*, which the medieval Jewish translators used to translate the Greek concept from Arabic, in fact, means "destiny, providence, or [unforeseen] encounter." For Mendelssohn, the reason that medieval Hebrew translators chose the word *mikreh* was because it denoted an event that was unexpected, though not pure chance. Mendelssohn thus explained that his early acquisition of Hebrew disposed him to see all

[48] See Mendelssohn's review of Johann David Michaelis' 1759 Prize Essay in Mendelssohn, *JubA*, 5.1:106–107.

[49] See Mendelssohn, *JubA*, 8:172; *Jerusalem*, 106. Mendelssohn may have in mind the introduction of the word *teva* into Hebrew in the twelfth century to render the Greek word *physis*.

[50] See Mendelssohn, *JubA*, 5.2:305.

[51] Mendelssohn, *JubA*, 3.2:89; *Morning Hours*, 65.

events as directed by divine providence.[52] Similarly, he noted that Hebrew did not have a word for "religion," which in the Christian world was associated with belief in revealed theological mysteries. The Hebrew word commonly translated as "religion," namely, *dat*, in fact, means "law," which illustrated Judaism's teaching that practice lies at the heart of religion. In this way, the Hebrew language protected Jews from Christianity's harmful view that salvation depended on confessing belief in irrational revealed doctrines.[53]

Mendelssohn contended not only that translation could enrich philosophy, but that it could also enrich aesthetics. Leibniz had regarded differences between languages as idiosyncrasies that impeded clear thinking. He dreamed of creating what his follower J.G. Sulzer called a "universal philosophical grammar" (*allgemeine philosophische Grammatik*). Mendelssohn did not share this aspiration. For Mendelssohn, were a universal philosophical language even possible, it would be unable to capture the richness of life, which includes not only philosophical concepts that appeal to the mind, but also poetic expressions that stir the heart. As he put it in a review of Sulzer, "each [language] has its own peculiarities of which the refined spirit knows how to make excellent use. One often draws beauties out of the excesses and irregularities of a language that from a strictly philosophical language one must do without."[54]

To illustrate this point, Mendelssohn noted that German distinguishes inanimate objects by gender. For example, the moon is masculine (*Der Mond*), while the sun is feminine (*Die Sonne*). From the perspective of philosophical language these gender differentiations were "superfluous." But they are very useful for the poet by putting at his disposal tools for "embellishing" his writing. Translating great literature could therefore expand the aesthetic resources of a language.[55]

For Mendelssohn, Bible translation would enhance German culture and nationhood. These benefits were bound up with the particular features of German and Hebrew.

[52] See Mendelssohn, *JubA*, 3.2:89–90; *Morning Hours*, 65–66.
[53] See Mendelssohn, *JubA*, 3.2:197; *Moses Mendelssohn: Writings*, 162.
[54] See Mendelssohn, *JubA*, 5.1:93.
[55] See Mendelssohn, *JubA*, 5.1:93. Compare Herder's discussion of Sulzer in Herder, *Selected Early Works*, 109–111.

German versus Hebrew

Mendelssohn's account of German and Hebrew connects to a distinction he makes between what he calls "root languages" (*Stammsprache*) and "derivative languages" (*abgeleitenten Sprache*). Root languages develop in agrarian and nomadic societies where people live in a more immediate relation to nature and therefore employ "mimetic signs" (*nachahmenden Zeichen*) that bear a similarity to the objects they signify. An example would be using an actual cow to signify the concept "cow." In contrast, derivative languages arise in more technologically developed, urban societies, which are more remote from nature and hence use more "arbitrary signs" (*willkürliche Zeichen*) that bear no imitative connection to the original object such as using the word "cow" to signify the concept cow. Since philosophy involves abstracting from nature by seeking the general principles that govern it, it makes considerably more use of arbitrary signs. Derivative languages are therefore better for philosophy than root languages.[56]

In a 1760 review Mendelssohn portrays German as a derivative language, writing that "the German language appears to be better suited to the purposes of philosophy than any other living language." He describes Christian Wolff as the one who raised German to this level of philosophical precision by creating a sophisticated German philosophical lexicon. The philosophical preeminence of German does not, however, mean that it lacks beauty or rich imagery. Mendelssohn notes that German "is sufficiently emphatic and rich in images to animate the most abstract doctrines through the adornment of poetic art." Nevertheless, he thinks that while German can clothe abstract metaphysical ideas in beautiful images, it is poor at presenting concrete human individuals. As he puts it, "Our poets are excellent when they present systems of philosophers . . . however, they sink to mediocrity when they descend to describe the mores of lands and individual men."[57]

Mendelssohn has an almost opposite view of Hebrew. Friedrich Nicolai reports a discussion he had with Mendelssohn about Kabbalah in which Mendelssohn told him that "the obscurity of the propositions of this oriental philosophy [Kabbalah] originated in the poverty of the Hebrew language

[56] See Mendelssohn, *JubA*, 2:108–109; 6.2:10–11. Also see Mendelssohn, *Philosophical Writings*, 269–274.

[57] See Mendelssohn, *JubA*, 5.1:265. Mendelssohn credits the scientist and poet Albrecht von Haller (1708–1777) with being the first who developed the capacities of German to express abstract ideas poetically.

in expressing philosophical concepts, combined with the use of imagery (*Bildern*) so common in the Orient, which is so characteristic of uncultivated (*unkultivierten*) languages."[58] For Mendelssohn, Hebrew is a root language with many mimetic signs, which explains why it did not naturally originate a developed philosophical lexicon.[59] But as a root language Mendelssohn regards Hebrew as very adept at representing individuals with force and vitality, which makes it especially good for composing original poems and for rendering poems originally written in other languages.[60]

Against Herder's irrationalist view of biblical poetry

In an unpublished review of Herder's 1767 *Fragmente*, Mendelssohn observes that Herder makes two points about biblical poetry. First, Herder asserts that the Bible is remote from present-day Germans because it offers an irrational picture of nature on account of the undeveloped intellect of the "coarse" (*rauhen*) biblical authors. Second, Herder praises the poetic capacities of the biblical authors because of their "wild simplicity" (*wilde Einfalt*).[61] Mendelssohn contends that Herder is wrong to portray the biblical poets as offering irrational pictures of nature. Poetry, for Mendelssohn, cannot be understood as a literal description of reality. The anthropomorphic descriptions of God in the Bible should no more be understood as literal descriptions of God than Greek poets having regarded the Muses as real, independently existing beings rather than as metaphors for attributes of the human soul.[62] There is an anti-Christological undertone to Mendelssohn's criticism of Herder. For Herder, the Hebrew Old Testament was a primitive work that was superseded by the more philosophical Greek New Testament, a point Mendelssohn emphatically rejects.

Mendelssohn accuses Herder of following Rousseau in romanticizing the primitive. But while Mendelssohn sees Rousseau as romanticizing the happiness and freedom of the primitive, he sees Herder as romanticizing the poetry of the primitive. Opposing Herder, Mendelssohn claims that poetry is not

[58] This text is cited in Meyer, *Moses Mendelssohn Bibliographie*, 113.

[59] See note 49 in this chapter on the lack of a word for "nature" in pre-medieval Hebrew.

[60] Mendelssohn stresses this point in *KM*. See Mendelssohn, *JubA*, 14:19. Also see ibid., 2:109; 6.2:11.

[61] See Mendelssohn, *JubA*, 5.2:307. Herder later developed this conception of Hebrew in his 1782–1783 work *Vom Geist der ebräischen Poesie* (*On the Spirit of Hebrew Poetry*).

[62] See Mendelssohn, *JubA*, 5.2:306.

the direct expression of "wild" nature but, rather, the result of imitation and cultivation. He notes that in nature alone there is no poetry. Mendelssohn compares what he sees as Herder's overwrought commendation of the primitive to someone who says that because fruit and flowers come from meadows and forests, the best "art garden" (*Kunstgarten*) consists of uncultivated meadows and forests. Mendelssohn agrees that "coarser" (*rauher*) people have more lively sensations, which is the basis of art. But for Mendelssohn since art involves cultivation, it is also connected with thinking.

In his 1755 essay "On Sensations," Mendelssohn describes the relationship between thought and feeling in the appreciation of beauty. Following Leibniz's and Wolff's definition of perfection as unity in multiplicity, Mendelssohn defines beauty as "an indistinct representation of a perfection" that is an indistinct representation of unity in multiplicity. For Mendelssohn, feeling senses objects as wholes, while thinking analyzes objects into parts. Beauty cannot be identified solely with feeling, which only perceives objects indistinctly as unities. Rather, appreciating beauty requires both thought and feeling. For example, we appreciate the beauty of a painting when we both feel it indistinctly as a whole and discern how the various parts contribute to the whole.[63] Given the connection between art and thought, the biblical poets who produced beautiful works of art cannot be understood as unthinking primitives.[64]

Bible translation as perfecting German and Jewish culture

For Mendelssohn, translating the Bible into German contributes to both German and Jewish culture. It benefits German culture by showing how metaphysical concepts can be powerfully portrayed through vivid, sensuous imagery. It contributes to Jewish culture since German's philosophical precision helps one better understand the concepts that are expressed poetically in the Bible. This reciprocal relationship between the poetic and the philosophical is crucial for Mendelssohn. As he puts it, "philosophy without art is bombastic chatter (*hochtrabender Schwätzer*), while art without philosophy is a

[63] See Mendelssohn, *JubA*, 5.2:307–308; *JubA*, 1:48–52; *Philosophical Writings*, 12–17. Mendelssohn's theory of beauty is part of a tradition of German aesthetic rationalism. For an excellent discussion of this tradition, see Beiser, *Diotima's Children*.

[64] This is not to say that Mendelssohn thinks that conscious thought is involved in the production of art. For Mendelssohn, there is an unconscious operation of reason, which he calls "common sense," that operates in it. On Mendelssohn's view of common sense see p. 48 note 128 of this volume.

spiritless trinket (*geistloser Tand*) that can delight children but is unworthy of men."[65]

Mendelssohn saw translation as both enabling the possibility of cross-cultural understanding and enriching individual cultures. But Mendelssohn was no naïve idealist. He was acutely aware of the perils and impediments to translation. His repeated experience with sophisticated German Christians who sought to efface his Judaism made clear to him that cultural/religious translation was no easy task. But Mendelssohn was also keenly aware of linguistic barriers to translation.

Lost in translation

In part two of *OL*, Mendelssohn makes clear that translation is no simple process, as there is a sense in which all texts are untranslatable. Specifically, Mendelssohn enumerates three impediments to translation.

First, he claims that words have unique meanings that distinguish them from every other word in their own language as well as all from cognates in other languages. In other words, there are no complete synonyms.[66] Part of the reason for this is that words have multiple meanings and nuances. There is a "primary intention" (*kavanah rishonah*, *Hauptbegriff*) or the main idea signified by a word, and there are "secondary intentions" (*kavanot sheniyot*, *Nebenbegriffe*), which signify ancillary ideas.[67] As Mendelssohn puts it, "for the most part, words will only be comparable regarding their primary and essential meaning but will differ as regards their secondary, accidental meanings even considerably."[68]

Mendelssohn gives the example of the Hebrew word *enosh*. He notes that the primary meaning of *enosh* is a "living, speaking being," which corresponds

[65] Mendelssohn, *JubA*, 5.2:308.

[66] See Mendelssohn, *JubA*, 14:230. Also see ibid., 14: 148, 229. Mendelssohn's collaborator Naphtali Wessely portrayed the lack of complete synonyms as a distinct feature of Hebrew in his 1755 *Gan Naul*. See Harris, *How Do We Know This?*, 144. For Mendelssohn, however, lack of complete synonyms was a feature of all languages.

[67] In the introduction to his 1770 commentary on Ecclesiastes, Mendelssohn introduces the distinction between the primary intention and secondary intentions of terms using the Hebrew terms *kavanah rishonah* and *kavanah sheniah*. See Mendelssohn, *JubA*, 14:149–150. For discussion of the origin of these terms, see Breuer's and Sorkin's note in Mendelssohn, *Moses Mendelssohn's Hebrew Writings*, 123–124, note 4. Mendelssohn provides the German equivalent of these terms as *Hauptbegriff* and *Nebenbegriff* in his review of Herder's 1767 *Fragmente*. See Mendelssohn, *JubA*, 5.2:304.

[68] Mendelssohn, *JubA*, 14:229.

to the German word *Mensch*. But in citing Jeremiah 17:9, "The heart is devious above all else; it is perverse (*v'anush hu*)," Mendelssohn observes that the Hebrew word *enosh* is related to the word *anush* and has the secondary meaning of "perversity." The problem is that the German word *Mensch* does not have this secondary meaning. What then is the translator to do? If she translates *enosh* as *Mensch* she will have not captured the full meaning of the original term. But if she decides to use an adjective to incorporate this secondary meaning, translating *enosh* as *geplagter Mensch* (bedeviled person), she will also not adequately convey the meaning of *enosh* since the nature of a secondary meaning is that it is subtly implied, which is not captured by adding an adjective.[69]

A second impediment to translation for Mendelssohn is that word order differs between languages.[70] To make the translated text comprehensible to the reader, the translator must follow the grammatical conventions of the target language and so change the word order. But, Mendelssohn notes, it is impossible to change the word order of the original without also "slightly changing the meaning and the effect of the statement on the soul of the listener." Mendelssohn gives the example of I Kings 20:18, which states in the original: *vayomer im leshalom yatzu tifsum hayim, v'im lemilhamah yatzu hayim tifsum.* Rendered word for word into English, the verse reads, "He said if for peace they come out take them alive (*tifsum hayim*); and if for war they come out alive take them (*hayim tifsum*)." Mendelssohn notes that the Hebrew word *tifsum* (take them) is a verb, while the word *hayim* (alive) is an adverb. In Hebrew, it is acceptable for the adverb to either precede or come after the verb. In the first clause of the verse the verb *tifsum* (take them) is placed first because it implies that in the case the enemy sues for peace while it is obvious that one should not kill them, one might think one should conclude a peace with them. So for emphasis the verse states *tifsum hayim* (take them alive) to stress that one should capture them. But in the second clause the adverb *hayim* (alive) comes first because in the case that the enemy attacks, while it is not unexpected that one should capture them, one might think that one should kill them instead. So for emphasis the verse states *hayim tifsum* (alive take them) to stress that one should leave them alive. Mendelssohn notes that in German (as in English) the adverb always comes after the verb. So if the translator translates word for word, the original statement loses its elegance

[69] Mendelssohn, *JubA*, 14:229–230; *Moses Mendelssohn's Hebrew Writings*, 272.
[70] See Mendelssohn, *JubA*, 14:327.

and becomes scarcely comprehensible. Should, however, the translator follow proper German word order but add an explanatory note, the translation would be cumbersome thereby "destroying the pleasantness of the statement and its effect on the soul [of the reader]."[71]

Finally, quoting the 16th century Hebrew grammarian Elijah Levita, Mendelssohn notes that the different rhetorical styles of languages creates impediments to translation. Sometimes the source language contains a statement in the past tense, while the conventions of the target language require rendering it in the future tense. Similarly, there are figurative expressions that are peculiar to a given language and which therefore require the translator to translate according to the meaning of the expression while abandoning the literal sense of the original expression. For example, in describing the Israelites coming out of Egypt, Exodus 14:8 states *uvnei yisra'el yotzim beyad ramah*, which would literally be translated as "The children of Israel exited with a raised hand." The problem is that in Hebrew the expression *yad ramah* connotes "openly, without fear." But this expression is not found in other languages such as Aramaic, German, or English. So if the translator translates *yad ramah* word for word he obscures the meaning of the verse, but if he translates according to the meaning of the idiom he obscures the power of the metaphor.[72]

In light of these problems, it might seem that translation is hopeless. Yet as we have seen, Mendelssohn puts great stock in translation and expends enormous effort on it. What makes translation possible for him?

Mendelssohn's universal grammatology

For Mendelssohn language is a way of structuring reality, of "thinking of the immeasurable as measurable."[73] All languages are grounded in grammar,

[71] Mendelssohn, *JubA*, 14:230; see *Moses Mendelssohn's Hebrew Writings*, 272–273. Compare Herder, *Selected Early Works*, 132.

[72] Levita observes that The first-century Aramaic translator Onkelos rendered the idiom *beyad ramah* as *bereish galei*, which literally means with "an uncovered head" but conveys the sense of "openly, without fear." See Mendelssohn, *JubA*, 14:231; *Moses Mendelssohn's Hebrew Writings*, 273–274. Mendelssohn quotes Levita's 1541 book Hameturgeman. In the *Be'ur* on Exodus 14:8 Mendelssohn chooses a middle path, translating *beyad ramah* literally as *mit aufgehobener Hand* (with a raised hand) but then adds in parentheses *das heißt öfentlich* (that means openly), a compromise that while making sense, is inadequate to the Hebrew original. See Mendelssohn, *JubA*, 9.1:244. I will discuss other examples of Mendelssohn's uses of parentheses later. For other differences between Hebrew and German syntax, see Mendelssohn, *JubA*, 14:249–267, 327. I follow Werner Weinberg's transliterations of Mendelssohn's translation of the Pentateuch found in Mendelssohn, *JubA*, 9.1 and 9.2. For Weinberg's method of transliteration, see Weinberg, "Einleitung: Die Orthographie von Mendelssohns deutscher Pentateuchübersetzung in hebräischer Schrift."

[73] Mendelssohn, *JubA*, 8:175; *Jerusalem*, 109.

and the foundation of grammar is propositional logic whose structure is innate to the human mind. Propositional logic comprises judgments consisting of a subject and a predicate connected by a copula. This structure is reflected in grammar where a subject is a noun (*shem etzem*, *Hauptwort*) while the predicate is an adjective (*shem to'ar*, *Eigenschaftswort*) that designates either the genera that the noun belongs to or an accidental feature of the subject. Subject and predicate are connected by a copula (*dibbur hametziut*, *selbstständige Zeitwort*) which is a form of "being" (*Sein*) that can be in four modalities: (1) affirmation or negation, (2) temporal designation, (3) person (first, second, or third), or (4) gender.[74]

For Mendelssohn, the fact that grammatical structure is based in universal logic makes textual translation possible. This is similar to his view that the rational basis of natural religion is what enables interreligious translation. But for Mendelssohn the fact that grammar is grounded in logic is not a sufficient basis for textual translation for two reasons.

First, he notes that while there are "essential features" (*segulot atzmiyot*) of grammatical structure "common to all language," each language has "accidental" (*mikriyot*) grammatical features, which vary. The translator therefore needs to have an excellent grasp of the specific grammatical features of the source as well as target languages. For example, Mendelssohn notes that in all the languages known to him *except Hebrew*, if the predicate describes an accidental quality then the copula and predicate are separated. In Hebrew, however, there are many cases in which the predicate describes an accidental quality yet is not separated from the copula. For example, the Hebrew proposition *yosef ya'adim* [Joseph will turn red] includes the predicate and copula in the second word but should be translated in German as *Josef wird rot*, where the copula and predicate are designated by distinct words.[75]

Mendelssohn further notes that one cannot understand a text's meaning through grammar alone since grammar cannot elucidate the meaning of specific words. Using a proper hermeneutical method can, however, help one decode linguistic meaning. So along with grammar Mendelssohn emphasizes the importance of discerning the *literary context* of a word or statement, which is its place in relation to what precedes and comes after it, and a word or statement's *linguistic usage* by comparing its meaning in different texts.[76]

[74] Mendelssohn, *JubA*, 9.1: 69; 14:251; 40–43.
[75] See Mendelssohn, *JubA*, 14:249–254.
[76] Mendelssohn, *JubA*, 14:149, 153, 198, 327.

Comparing two great projects: The Psalms and the *Be'ur*

Mendelssohn completed both of his major Bible translations in 1783.[77] As mentioned previously, the *Be'ur* was aimed at Jews alone while the Psalms translation was aimed at Christians and Jews. While scholars have recognized the different audiences of the two translations, they have not adequately explored their distinct aims and methods. I begin with the Psalms.

Anti-Christology and history in the Psalms translation

As Alexander Altmann noted, Mendelssohn first decided to translate the Psalms in the wake of the Lavater controversy.[78] For Lavater, salvation depended on confessing Christian dogma, whose truths were revealed in the New Testament but prefigured in the Old Testament, a key text being the Psalms. In a letter to Elise Reimarus, Mendelssohn made clear that an important aim of his Psalms translation was to present it shorn of messianic predictions: "As has been known to you for a long time, the Psalms do not contain what Christians and Jews have until now tried to find in them with so much critical acumen and learning. To show this was, in fact, my main purpose in translating them and in publishing the translation."[79]

Mendelssohn used *history* to produce a non-confessional Psalms translation. A striking example of this is his translation of Psalm 110. The Psalm begins with YHWH speaking to "my Lord" (*adoni*), asking him to sit at YHWH's right side (verse 1). The Psalm then describes how "the Lord" (*adonai*) will vanquish kings and wreak judgment on the nations in *eretz rabbah* (verses 5–6). The New Testament repeatedly interprets this Psalm as a messianic Davidic prophecy with "My Lord" referring to Lord Jesus,

[77] In addition to translating the Psalms and the Pentateuch, Mendelssohn translated the Song of Songs, but this was only published posthumously in 1788. He also translated the "Song of Deborah" (Judges, ch. 5), which was published as an appendix to Loeffler's transcription into Gothic characters of Mendelssohn's Genesis translation. See p. 19 note 14 of this volume. For the text of these translations, see Mendelssohn, *JubA*, 10.1:237–258. For an account of the circumstances of the composition and publication of these works, see Weinberg, "Einleitungen," lv–lxxxiii.

[78] See Altmann, *Moses Mendelssohn: A Biographical Study*, 242–245.

[79] Mendelssohn, *JubA*, 13:109, cited in Altmann, *Moses Mendelssohn: A Biographical Study*, 242 (Letter to Elise Reimarus, May 20, 1783). Also see Mendelssohn's 1770 letter to Michaelis: "I am certain and what I have read from you lately confirms me in this certainty that you treat the Psalms as poetry without seeing the prophetic and mystical in them as Christian and Jewish interpreters who have hitherto regarded the Psalms as if they were written in a cloister by penitent monks." See Mendelssohn, *JubA*, 12.1:233 (Letter to Johann David Michaelis, November 12, 1770).

whom God the Father (designated by YHWH) asks to sit at God's right side.[80] Following this line of interpretation, Luther translates Psalm 110:1 as *Ein Psalm Davids: Der HERR sprach zu meinem Herrn: Setze dich zu meiner Rechten, bis ich deine Feinde zum Schemel deiner Füße lege* (A Psalm of David: The LORD spoke to my Lord: Seat yourself at my right until I make your enemies into your footstool). Luther interprets verse 6 as alluding to Jesus's second coming when God will judge the entire world, translating the verse as *Er wird richten unter den Heiden; er wird ein große Schlacht tun; er wird zerschmeißen das Haupt über große Lande* (He will judge the pagans, he will greatly slaughter them, he will smash the head over great lands).[81]

Mendelssohn, however, interprets the Psalm as being addressed *to* King David, not as composed *by* him.[82] In a note to his translation of the Psalm, Mendelssohn writes that the context of the Psalm is "most likely" II Samuel 12:26–31, where David's general Joab captured the water city of Rabba from Ammon and then asked David to come finish the job of conquering the rest of the city. But Mendelssohn notes that we see in other places that "the nation" did not want to see David put in danger (see e.g. II Samuel 21:17). So this Psalm expresses the thoughts of a poet who imagines God warning David not to enter battle himself so as not to needlessly put himself in danger.[83] This understanding is reflected in Mendelssohn's translation of Psalm 110:1: *An David: ein Psalm. Der Ewge spricht zu meinem Herrn: Verweile hier zu meiner Rechten! Ich werde deine Feinde dir, zum Schemel deiner Füsse legen.* (To David: a Psalm: The Eternal spoke to my lord: abide here at my right! I will make your enemies into your footstool). According to Mendelssohn, God is telling David to remain in Jerusalem until Joab finishes the battle. The

[80] See Acts 2:33–36; I Hebrews 1:13; I Corinthians 15:25; Matthew 22:43–45; Mark 12:35–37.

[81] I use the 1545 version of Luther's Old Testament translation. In his 1759 *Critisches Collegium* Michaelis had followed Luther by interpreting this Psalm Christologically, adducing "proof that this Psalm speaks of the Messiah." See Michaelis, *Critisches Collegium*, 452–635. Michaelis later moved away from Christological interpretations of the Psalms. See note 79 above.

[82] Compare Friedländer, "Etwas über die Mendelssohnische Psalmenübersetzung," 546-549; Brüll, *Sefer Zemirot Israel*, 84b–85a. Michaelis recognized the anti-Christological intent of Mendelssohn's translation in his review of Mendelssohn's Psalms translation. See Michaelis's comments cited by Werner Weinberg in Mendelssohn, *JubA*, 10.2:555. Weinberg also notes that the Protestant orientalist Oluf Gerhard Tychsen recorded dissatisfaction with Mendelssohn's anti-Christological translation of the Psalm. See Weinberg, "Einleitungen," xlvii.

[83] See Mendelssohn, *JubA*, 10.1:235. Mendelssohn's notes were first printed in volume 6 of Mendelssohn's *Gesammelte Schriften*, which was published in 1845, with the editor noting that these notes were "hitherto unpublished." There are notes to ten psalms (1, 2, 4, 15, 22, 49, 68, 93, 110, and 141). See Mendelssohn, *Gesammelte Schriften*, 6:355–366. The notes were reprinted in Mendelssohn, *JubA*, 10.1:229–236. Also see David Friedländer's interpretation of the Psalm, which he reports hearing from Mendelssohn himself. See Friedländer, "Etwas über die Mendelssohnische Psalmenübersetzung," 545–549.

opponent vanquished at *eretz rabbah* is the historical king of Rabba who was forced to drink from a stream while fleeing as God destroyed his water city. Mendelssohn therefore translates verses 6–7 as: *Er wird Nationen richten Auf hochgethürmten Leichen, Der itzt das Haupt von Rabba schlug. Schon trinkt es aus dem Bach am Wege; Weil es zu stolz sein Haupt erhob.* (He will judge nations, piling corpses high, He will now smash the head from Rabbah; he will now drink from the stream on the path because he arrogantly raised his head).[84]

Empathy and enlightened ancient Hebrew poetry

In his response to Lavater, Mendelssohn had pointed to the practice of universal natural religion as the means to salvation. Mendelssohn saw the Psalms as teaching this universal natural religion. In an essay on Mendelssohn's Psalms translation published shortly after Mendelssohn's death, his leading disciple David Friedländer maintained that his teacher had sought to present the Psalms as an example of ancient Hebrew religious Enlightenment:

> He [Mendelssohn] sought to show that the Psalms present a rich treasure of concepts of God, divine attributes, the most refined service of God and the moral conduct of humanity in their purest and clearest light extracted from the dimness and darkness that cover them . . . One can designate these matters, quite genuinely as Enlightenment (*Aufklärung*) which had already been attained in the age of the Royal Singer.[85]

For Mendelssohn it was not only the *content* of the Psalms that was important but also its *literary form*. Mendelssohn originally intended to publish parts of his Psalms translation under the title "Samples of the Lyric Poetry (*lyrischen Poesie*) of the Hebrews."[86] Mendelssohn described the main features of lyric poetry in several writings. In a 1768 review of Karl Wilhelm Ramler's *Odes*, he noted that lyric poetry uses striking images to "enliven" (*Belebung*) the objects it describes. Noting that there were three main types of lyric poetry, Greco-Roman, Nordic, and Hebraic, he explained

[84] Mendelssohn's translation is found in Mendelssohn, *JubA*, 10.1:173.
[85] Friedländer, "Etwas über die Mendelssohnische Psalmenübersetzung," 525.
[86] See Mendelssohn, *JubA*, 12.1:233 (Letter to J.D. Michaelis, November 1770); Altmann, *Moses Mendelssohn: A Biographical Study*, 242–243.

that in the "oriental poetics" (*orientalische Dichtungssystem*) of the ancient Hebrews, lyric poetry was deeply tied to religion, especially to portraying how nature depends on God.[87] In a 1778 essay, Mendelssohn emphasized the importance of subjectivity and personal feelings in lyric poetry noting, that the poet is both the author of the poem as well as its subject.[88] And in his 1757 review of Robert Lowth's *On the Sacred Poetry of the Hebrews*, Mendelssohn emphasized the power of the ancient Hebrew lyric poets, especially their ability to "arouse the most sublime sensations in us by knowing the immediate path to our hearts."[89]

In the brief introduction to his Psalms translation, Mendelssohn stressed the importance of the affective element of the Psalms and how reading them personally impacted him: "I here give over to my reader the fruits of a more than decade-long labor that gave me many pleasant hours at the time and sweetened many an anguished moment."[90] For Mendelssohn, a key to accessing the meaning of the Psalms was *empathic identification* with the poet. As he put it,

> I did not translate the psalms in order, one after another, but rather chose a psalm that pleased me, agreed with my state of mind at the time, and stimulated me sometimes by its beauty and sometimes by its difficulty. I carried it around in my head throughout many different activities until I *believed myself to be as intimate with the spirit* (*Geiste*) *of my poet* as my abilities would allow. Writing it down was then a modest task. (emphasis mine)[91]

[87] Mendelssohn, *JubA*, 5.1:84–86; Weinberg, "Einleitungen," xiii.

[88] Mendelssohn, *JubA*, 3.1:337; Weinberg, "Einleitungen," xiii.

[89] Mendelssohn, *JubA*, 4:20; Weinberg, "Einleitungen," xiv.

[90] Mendelssohn, *JubA*, 10.1:6; *Moses Mendelssohn: Writings*, 183.

[91] Ibid. Mendelssohn's emphasis on empathy as a means of discerning the meaning of the Psalms recalls Herder's hermeneutical method of *Einfühlung*, which he deployed in his influential analysis and defense of biblical poetry, *On the Spirit of Hebrew Poetry* (*Vom Geist der ebraïschen Poesie*) (1782). See Herder, *The Spirit of Hebrew Poetry*, 1:27–28. Mendelssohn was familiar with Herder's approach to biblical poetry and expressed appreciation for it: "My dear sir, you have shown that you understand Hebrew very well. Perhaps you also have some knowledge of rabbinics. At least you do not seem to despise it altogether. *You also possess the gift of putting yourself, whenever you wish, in the position and mindset of your fellow man in order to judge him*" (emphasis mine). See Mendelssohn, *JubA*, 12.2:194 (To J.G. Herder, June 20, 1780). Mendelssohn had Herder's *Vom Geist der ebraïschen Poesie* in his library (see Mendelssohn, *Verzeichniß der auserlesenen Büchersammlung*, 21, #81) and seems to allude to the title of the work in his introduction to the Psalms: "Through subsequent comparisons you will find that I have greatly diverged from all of my predecessors in many places. But be assured that this never happened without critical foundation. I must have at least believed that I could better capture the *spirit* (*Geist*) of the original, come nearer to its true sense, and better express it in our language" (emphasis mine). Mendessohn, *JubA*, 10.1:6; *Moses Mendelssohn: Writings*, 183.

Mendelssohn sought to enable the reader to access the emotional power of universal religious teachings of the Psalms through direct access to the biblical text, unburdened by the weight of biblical commentary and scholarship. As he put it, "Choose a psalm that agrees exactly with your state of mind at the moment; forget for a short time all that you have read about this psalm [in the works of] translators, interpreters, and paraphrasers; read my translation and judge!"[92] For this reason, Mendelssohn presented his Psalms translation very simply with no commentary or scholarly apparatus.[93] This is not to say that Mendelssohn made no use of other works in composing his translation. In his introduction to the Psalms, he remarked that he had consulted previous translations, scholars, and commentators and drew on his deep knowledge of biblical Hebrew.[94] But in seeking to stir an emotional response by direct encounter with the text, Mendelssohn did not want to weigh the reader down with commentary and annotations.[95] To this end, Mendelssohn employed a spare design for his Psalms translation. Aside from the translation in Gothic characters, the page contained only the chapter and verse number of each Psalm. This contrasts sharply with the layout of his *Be'ur* commentary, which contains a German translation in Hebrew characters facing the original Hebrew text with an extensive Hebrew commentary and Masoretic notes.[96]

Jews as a living hermeneutical key to the Psalms

In portraying the Psalms as enlightened lyric poetry, Mendelssohn sought to show how "oriental" Jewish literature could contribute to German nationhood. But for many Protestants, there was no connection between the Hebrew Bible and contemporary Jews. In *The Spirit of Hebrew Poetry*, Herder

[92] Mendessohn, *JubA*, 10.1:6; *Moses Mendelssohn: Writings*, 183. Friedländer recalled that Mendelssohn enjoined him to forget previous translators and commentators on the Psalms and put himself in the position of being "like someone reading the original text (*Urschrift*) for the first time." See Friedländer, "Etwas über Mendelssohische Psalmen," 530.

[93] Mendessohn, *JubA*, 10.1:7; *Moses Mendelssohn: Writings*, 184.

[94] Mendessohn, *JubA*, 10.1:6; *Moses Mendelssohn: Writings*, 183. See Friedländer, "Etwas über Mendelssohnische Psalmen," 529.

[95] Mendessohn, *JubA*, 10.1:7; *Moses Mendelssohn: Writings*, 184. Mendelssohn held open the possibility that he would publish a volume in which he defended his translation choices but never did so. He did, however, compose seven annotations, which he left unpublished. See note 83 of this chapter.

[96] See Figures 2 and 4 of this volume. I will explore the reason for the design of the *Be'ur* in the next chapter. See pp. 92–93 of this volume.

wrote that Jews could contribute "nothing of value" to understanding biblical Hebrew since the languages they used incorporated a "lamentable mixture" (*trauriges Gemisch*) of Hebrew and the language of the Gentile nations they lived amidst.[97] In his 1770 book on Mosaic Law, Michaelis similarly found no value in rabbinic biblical exegesis, writing:

> Illustrations and reasons of the laws of Moses I never take from the Talmud. The oral traditions of the ignorant Rabbis which we find collected in that work, may teach us the common law of the Jews *at the period when the men lived*, but not the *sense* of the Mosaic writings. Many of the laws in the Pentateuch would make a strange figure indeed, if we were to interpret them as the Pharisees did, whose expositions, according to Christ's declaration, in many cases served to inculcate doctrines and precepts directly the reverse of what Moses had taught and commanded. (emphasis mine)[98]

As my student Jonathan Green has shown, in one of his few annotations on the Psalms, Mendelssohn sought to use the practices of contemporary Jews to illuminate the Psalms. Psalm 22 is a central text for Christians, as it begins with the words "My God, My God, why have you forsaken me?," which Jesus is said to have uttered on the cross.[99] The Psalm contains the unusual subtitle *lamenatz'eah al ayelet hashahar*, which in his note Mendelssohn translates as "On a deer that was hunted early" (*Von einer Hindinn, die früh gejagt wird*).[100] Mendelssohn explains that when a deer is continuously pursued, its tongue will cleave to its gums, and it will sink in exhaustion and cry out. When a "sensitive" (*empfindsames*) poet witnessed this, he recalled the persecution of the righteous by the godless.[101]

Mendelssohn notes several features that mark the Psalm as the work of an "oriental poet" (*orientalische Dichter*).[102] *First*, it switches seamlessly and

97 Herder, *Vom Geist*, 11; *The Spirit of Hebrew Poetry*, 32.
98 See Michaelis, *Commentaries on the Laws of Moses*, 51.
99 See Matthew 27:46; Mark 15:34.
100 Mendelssohn's translation in the note follows Luther's 1545 translation. But in his translation printed in the text, Mendelssohn translates *ayelet hashahar* as *Morgenflöte* (morning flute), following Michaelis and Knapp. See Michaelis, *Deutsche Uebersetzung des Alten Testaments*, 6:28; Knapp, *Die Psalmen*, 42. Rashi also understands *ayelet hashahar* as referring to an instrument.
101 Mendelssohn, *JubA*, 10.1:232.
102 Mendelssohn, *JubA*, 10.1:232.

without warning between the image of the deer being hunted and the image of the righteous being persecuted.[103] *Second,* it records the "oriental" practice of thanksgiving upon delivery from danger. Mendelssohn explains that when a person in the Orient escapes a danger, he will slaughter an animal and invite his friends to a celebratory meal to publicly proclaim his gratitude to God and "encourage his brethren to trust in providence and maintain hope in the midst of misery."[104] *Third,* Mendelssohn notes that the Psalm proclaims God's miracles for a universal purpose, namely, that "all earthly peoples (*Völker*) recognize the blessings of God."[105]

Mendelssohn then connects the "oriental" Psalm to contemporary Jews. He notes that the practice of offering a thanksgiving meal upon delivery from danger to encourage trust in God is "preserved by the Jews (*Juden*) in our days" and that its function is to promote universal knowledge of God's goodness.[106] Mendelssohn also describes contemporary Jews' deep attachment to the Psalms. Observing that it is a common human practice to recollect poetry when feeling deep emotion, Mendelssohn writes that Jews do so with "words of Scripture."[107] This recalls Mendelssohn's personal testimony at the end of the last letter he ever wrote: "This much is certain: the Psalms have sweetened many a bitter hour for me, and I pray and sing them as often as I feel the urge to pray and to sing."[108]

In sum, for Mendelssohn Jews are an emotionally sensitive, poetic, religious nation who express their deepest emotions through Scripture. Preserving ancient oriental practices found in the Bible, they serve as living illustrations of biblical practices and teachings that benefit humanity.

[103] For example, "Save my soul from the sword, my self from the impudent dog. Deliver me from a lion's throat; from the horns of wild *re'emim* (Psalm 22:21–22)"; "Those who see me mock me; curl their lips, shake their head: 'He complains to the Lord who helps him; Who protects him; for he is His darling'" (Psalm 22: 8–9). My translation follows Mendelssohn's. See Mendelssohn, *JubA,* 10.1:34–35.

[104] Mendelssohn, *JubA,* 10.1:232. Mendelssohn is referring to verses 26–27 of the Psalm "Therefore I loudly praise you: 'Amidst a great community of your worshippers, I pay my vow. Eat your fill those who are oppressed! Praise the Lord, you His worshippers! May your hearts always be refreshed!'"

[105] Mendelssohn, *JubA,* 10.1:232. See Mendelssohn's translation of Psalms 22:28: "So all inhabitants of the earth will be mindful of God, turn themselves towards Him: All pagan families will pray to You."

[106] Mendelssohn, *JubA,* 10.1:232.

[107] Mendelssohn, *JubA,* 10.1:232–233.

[108] See Mendelssohn, *JubA,* 13:334 (To Sophie Becker, December 27, 1785), cited in Altmann, *Moses Mendelssohn: A Biographical Study,* 719.

The two methods of the *Be'ur*: (1) *Peshat*

In his brief, German introduction to his Psalms translation, Mendelssohn writes little about his method of translation. By contrast, in his lengthy Hebrew introduction to the *Be'ur* known as *Or Linetiva* (*OL*), in *Alim Literufah* (*AL*), and in his introduction to his 1770 commentary on Ecclesiastes, he writes much about his translation method.

In *OL*, Mendelssohn writes that the translator's main task is to convey the primary or plain sense of the text, known as *peshat*.[109] To convey *peshat* the "faithful translator" will at times need to "change a statement by adding to it, subtracting from it, or altering its order." Mendelssohn denigrates hyper-literal translators who translate word for word, asserting that in doing so they obscure the meaning of the text.[110]

In making *peshat* the primary goal of his translation, Mendelssohn presents himself as a traditionalist continuing the project of the great medieval Jewish Bible commentators. He stresses this point by noting that his translation relied on "the four chief *peshat* commentators (*arba rashei hamefarshim hapashtanim*)," Rashi, Rashbam, Ibn Ezra, and Nahmanides.[111] In the *Be'ur* commentary Mendelssohn and his collaborators regularly cite and engage with these Bible commentators among others.[112] But Mendelssohn makes clear that while he holds these commentators in high esteem, he is willing to depart from them if he thinks that their interpretations do not

[109] See Mendelssohn, *JubA*, 14:244, 327.

[110] Mendelssohn adduces support for this criticism from the Talmud, which states that one "who translates a verse according to its form is a liar" (Babylonian Talmud Kiddushin 49a; Tosefta Megillah 3:41). See Mendelssohn, *JubA*, 14:231; *Moses Mendelssohn: Writings*, 192. Werner Weinberg suggests that in emphasizing the damage wrought by word-for-word Bible translation Mendelssohn is opposing the method of Bible instruction used by Polish teachers who were employed to teach German Jewish youth. See Weinberg, "Language Questions," 229. By criticizing word-for-word Bible translation, Mendelssohn repeats an attack articulated a century earlier in two Amsterdam Yiddish translations by Yekutiel Blitz and Yosel Witzenhausen, which criticized older Yiddish Bible translations, the so-called "Khumesh Taytsh." See Baumgarten, *Introduction to Old Yiddish Literature*, 103–104. Marion Aptroot has shown that these translations, which were by German Jews, aimed at changing educational practices in Central and Eastern Europe. See Aptroot, "Yiddish Bibles in Amsterdam," 42–45, 54–56; "In Galkes," 142–143. In the first half of the eighteenth century, German Pietists such as Johann Heinrich Reitz and Johann Jakob Junckherrott produced Bible translations that aroused opposition for being too literal. See Sheehan, *The Enlightenment Bible*, 64–73.

[111] See Mendelssohn, *JubA*, 14:327, 244.

[112] In *OL* and *AL* Mendelssohn writes that he also consulted David Kimhi's *Sefer Hashorashim* (*Book of Roots*). See Mendelssohn, *JubA*, 14:244, 327. In the *Be'ur* commentary Mendelssohn also cites and engages with Sa'adyah Gaon, Judah Halevi, Maimonides, Don Isaac Abravanel, Obadiah Sforno, Joseph Gikitilla and many others. He also frequently cites the Talmud, Midrashim, the Aramaic translations of Onkelos and Jonathan Ben Uziel, and even kabbalistic works such as the Book of Creation (*Sefer Yetzirah*). He will also occasionally cite Christian Bible scholars such as Herder and Robert Lowth.

accurately convey *peshat*.[113] In this way, Mendelssohn's translation should be understood neither as slavishly adhering to tradition nor as radically revolutionary but, rather, as *conservatively innovative*, where loyalty to tradition is joined with the Enlightenment value of thinking for oneself.

For Mendelssohn, determining *peshat* involves "paying careful attention to the intention, but not the words" of the text, for at the level of *peshat* one may use different words to express the same concept or idea.[114] In *AL* and *OL* Mendelssohn enumerates three elements one needs to know to determine *peshat*. We have seen that these include Hebrew and German grammar, literary context, and linguistic usage.[115] While these tools can be used to decode the meaning of any text, in the case of the Bible Mendelssohn adds a fourth element, namely, the Masoretic accents (*te'amim*), which are traditional notations indicating how the text is to be sung. For Mendelssohn, these *te'amim* act as punctuation marks that help elucidate the meaning of the biblical text.[116]

In addition to these four elements that Mendelssohn explicitly cites in determining *peshat*, he also sometimes uses historical context.[117] Mendelssohn's use of history in the *Be'ur* is, however, quite limited and conservative. He will use it to shed light on the biblical text, but never to discuss the Bible's textual or compositional history or to challenge rabbinic biblical interpretation.[118]

Peshat and rational truth

We have seen the role that rationality plays in Bible translation for Mendelssohn through his account of the logical structure of grammar. But the importance of reason also extends to the *content* of biblical teachings. As with the Psalms, Mendelssohn interprets the Pentateuch as a work

[113] See Mendelssohn, *JubA*, 14:243–244; 327.

[114] See Mendelssohn, *JubA*, 14:148.

[115] See p. 36 of this volume.

[116] See Mendelssohn, *JubA*, 14:243–244, 327. While some Jewish scholars such as Elijah Levita had claimed that the *te'amim* were post-talmudic, Mendelssohn follows Judah Halevi in asserting that they were part of the Oral Torah revealed to Moses. See Mendelssohn, *JubA*, 14:224–227; *Moses Mendelssohn's Hebrew Writings*, 263–268. I will give an example of how Mendelssohn uses *te'amim* to interpret the biblical text later. See pp. 109–110 of this volume.

[117] In a 1771 letter to Johann Zimmerman, Mendelssohn writes that "some difficult Psalms are of such a nature that you can read into them what you want probably because one is ignorant of the situation that occasioned them because the authors' time and circumstances are unknown." See Mendelssohn, *JubA*, 12.2:22; Sorkin, *Moses Mendelssohn and the Religious Enlightenment*, 79.

[118] See Breuer, *The Limits of Enlightenment*, 147-222.

of religious enlightenment. Mendelssohn's view can be best understood in relation to Maimonides's and Spinoza's views on the rationality of biblical teachings.

In his 1670 *Tractatus Theologico-Politicus* (henceforth: *TTP*), Spinoza criticized Maimonides for seeking to harmonize the Bible with philosophical truth. For Spinoza, Maimonides's rationalism conflated truth with meaning, thereby making it impossible to accurately discern the true meaning of Scripture.[119] Spinoza maintained that he did not reject any biblical passage as false ab initio but, rather, judged its truth or untruth only *after* discerning its meaning, which required among other things situating it within its historical context.[120]

For Spinoza, historical inquiry shows that the biblical prophets generally espoused primitive views about nature and God, consistent with those held by their ancient Near Eastern neighbors. As such, he regards as untenable Maimonides's contention that the prophets had scientific conceptions of nature and refined philosophical views of God.[121]

Mendelssohn's historical sense leads him to concede Spinoza's point that the prophets were not philosophers with refined intellects.[122] But as Mendelssohn affirms that the Torah was divinely revealed, he cannot agree with Spinoza that it contains errors. As he puts it in *Jerusalem*, "truth cannot conflict with truth."[123] While Spinoza and Maimonides treat the questions of whether the prophets had scientific views of nature and philosophically accurate views of God as the same question, Mendelssohn presents different approaches to each question.

[119] See Spinoza, *Opera*, 3:114; *The Collected Works*, 2:188 (*The Theological-Political Treatise*, ch. 7).

[120] See Spinoza, *Opera*, 3:9; *The Collected Works*, 2:71 (*The Theological-Political Treatise*, preface).

[121] See especially chs. 1, 2, and 7 of the *Theological-Political Treatise*.

[122] That Mendelssohn rejects Maimonides's view is clear from a rendering of Maimonides's Thirteen Principles of faith that Mendelssohn composed for David Friedländer's 1779 textbook *Reader for Jewish Children* (*Lesebuch für jüdische Kinder*). In his sixth principle of faith, Maimonides wrote that the prophets were individuals who conjoined with the active intellect. In his seventh principle he wrote that Moses "comprehended more about God than any other human being," and his "imaginative and sensuous powers" were annulled in him such that he remained "a pure intellect." See Maimonides, Commentary on the Mishnah, Introduction to Chapter 10 of Sanhedrin. But in his rendering of Maimonides's sixth and seventh principles, Mendelssohn removes any reference to the prophets' intellectual qualities. For Maimonides's sixth principle Mendelssohn simply writes that God chooses whomever God wishes to bestow prophecy upon and that prophecy does not involve special metaphysical knowledge about God but, rather, knowledge of things that can only be known through revelation—namely, God's commandments. This fits with Mendelssohn's view that Judaism is revealed legislation, not revealed religion. In his rendering of the seventh principle, Mendelsohn writes that Moses was the greatest prophet who ever has or ever will live but says nothing about Moses's intellectual gifts. For the text of Mendelssohn's rendering of Maimonides's Thirteen Principles, see Kayserling, *Moses Mendelssohn*, 565–568.

[123] See Mendelssohn, *JubA*, 8:195; *Jerusalem*, 130.

Regarding scientific truths, Mendelssohn writes that seeking such truths from the Bible betrays a basic misunderstanding of the Bible's aims. In his commentary on Genesis 1:2, Mendelssohn rejects medieval commentators such as Ibn Ezra, Maimonides, and Nahmanides, who interpret the *ru'ah elohim* in the verse as referring to the element of air. Mendelssohn writes, "Scripture here does not discuss the four elements and how they are arranged one above the other according to the nature of their coarseness and subtlety *since this does not pertain to matters of Torah or faith* (*emunah*)" (emphasis mine).[124] For Mendelssohn, the Bible does not teach scientific truth about the natural world, as such truths are not essential to religion and morality.

Mendelssohn's understanding of Genesis 1:16 further elucidates his approach to conflicts between the Torah and natural science. He translates the verse as follows: *Also machte Got die zwey große Lichter, das größere Licht zur Regirung des Tages, das kleinere Licht zur Regirung der Nacht, und die Sterne* (Then God made the two great lights, the greater light to rule the day, the lesser light to rule the night and the stars).[125] In his commentary, Mendelssohn follows Ibn Ezra, explaining that the two lights were called "great" at the beginning of the verse in comparison with the planets, which appear as stars. Ibn Ezra had noted that the problem was that astronomers had proven that all the planets with the exception of Mercury (*kokhav*) and Venus (*nogah*) were larger than the moon. Why then was the moon called a "great light"? Mendelssohn follows Ibn Ezra by answering that the moon is called a "great light" not by virtue of its mass, but on account of of its brightness as viewed on earth. For while the moon is smaller than most other planets, it is brighter than the other planets to observers on earth since it is much closer. For Mendelssohn there is no contradiction between the Bible and natural science since the biblical prophets merely describe nature as it *appears* to us. They do not seek to provide a scientific account of nature.[126]

But Mendelssohn applies a very different approach to metaphysical descriptions of God in the Bible. In *Jerusalem*, Mendelssohn makes clear that Judaism comprises three major elements: (1) rational, eternal metaphysical

[124] Mendelssohn, *JubA*, 15.2:4. See Ibn Ezra and Nahmanides, commentaries on Genesis 1:2; Maimonides, *The Guide of the Perplexed*, 2:30, 351.

[125] Mendelssohn, *JubA*, 9.1:101–102.

[126] See Mendelssohn, *JubA*, 15.2:11. Also see Mendelssohn's commentary on the first word of the Torah, *bereshit*, which he interprets as referring not to a temporal beginning but, rather, to a causal beginning since the Hebrew word *reshit* can mean wisdom. For Mendelssohn the first word of the Torah is making a theological claim namely that the universe originated in divine wisdom, rather than making a philosophical/scientific claim about its temporal origins. See ibid., 3 (Commentary on Genesis 1:1).

truths about God and the soul; (2) historical truths about the people of Israel; and (3) revealed laws.[127] Since teaching rational metaphysical truths is one of the Torah's aims, Mendelssohn cannot adopt the same approach to biblical anthropomorphism as he does toward the Bible's teachings about natural science. For while Mendelssohn agrees that the prophets were not scientists, he thinks that they had accurate, rational metaphysical views about God, which they grasped through what Mendelssohn calls "common sense."[128]

Maimonides had asserted that neither biblical *anthropomorphisms*, which ascribe physical attributes to God, nor biblical *anthropopathisms*, which ascribe emotions to God, can be taken literally. But Mendelssohn deals with these two ways of describing God very differently. He explains biblical *anthropomorphism* on the basis of the linguistic/psychological principle that "all languages are structured by likeness to the human," noting that even when describing inanimate things the Bible will sometimes use human metaphors such as speaking of the "arm of the Jordan" (Numbers 13:29) or the "heart of the sea" (Exodus 15:8). Similarly, when speaking of God the Bible will often use anthropomorphic language to metaphorically express metaphysical ideas, such as stating that "the eyes of the Eternal are on the righteous" (Psalms 34:16), to convey divine providence. Mendelssohn explains that this is because anthropomorphisms describe abstract metaphysical principles in a lively, readily comprehensible manner.[129] As we have seen, Mendelssohn regards Hebrew as particularly adept at expressing abstract ideas through vivid images.

Mendelssohn takes a very different approach to *anthropopathic* descriptions of God. He distinguishes between two types of what he calls "passions" (*Leidenschaften/hitapa'aluyot hanefesh*).[130] The first type of passion derives from what Mendelssohn calls "true powers of the soul." Originating from desire and aversion, these passions include emotions such as love, hatred, anger, joy, and sadness. Mendelssohn writes that it is a *perfection* of the soul to have these passions as long as they are in proper balance. They only become vices

[127] See Mendelssohn, *JubA*, 8:191–193; *Jerusalem*, 126–127.

[128] For a detailed discussion of Mendelssohn's concept of common sense, see Gottlieb, *Faith and Freedom*, 45–57, 87–95; Freudenthal, *No Religion without Idolatry*, 21–64.

[129] Mendelssohn cites Ibn Ezra's commentary on Exodus 19:20 verbatim. See Mendelssohn's commentary on Exodus 19:20 in *JubA*, 16:182–183. Also see his commentary on Exodus 19:18 where Mendelssohn cites the rabbinic work *Mekhilta* to show that the Bible not only uses human metaphors to describe God but even animal metaphors like stating that God "roars like a lion" (Hosea 11:10). See Mendelssohn, *JubA*, 16:182 (Commentary on Exodus 19:18).

[130] Mendelssohn uses the term *affects* (*hargashot hanefesh*) as relatively synonymous with *passions*. See Mendelssohn, *JubA*, 15.2:56 (Commentary to Genesis 6:6).

when they are experienced with such extreme intensity that they overwhelm a person, thereby driving her to commit unethical acts.[131]

By contrast, the second type of passion is grounded not in a power of the soul, but in lack. This type of passion includes emotions such as stinginess, regret, cowardice, and despondency. For example, stinginess comes from the worry that one will not have enough, regret from a sense that things are not as one had hoped they would be, cowardice from a sense of not having power, and despondency from a loss of all hope. Mendelssohn notes that while occasionally some of these affects such as regret can lead to good actions, in general they are vices. Mendelssohn concludes that the first type of passion can be rationally ascribed to God since God always has them in proper measure, so they are consistent with divine perfection. By contrast, it is irrational to ascribe the second types of passions to God since God cannot lack anything.

Mendelssohn's complex approach to biblical anthropopathism is expressed in his treatment of Genesis 6:6. He translates the verse as follows: *Da bereuete der Ewige daß er den Menschen auf Erden gemacht hatte, und hatte Ver druß in seinem Herzen* (Then the Eternal regretted that He made humanity on earth and He had vexation in his heart).[132] Since regret is the second type of passion and cannot be attributed to God, in his commentary Mendelssohn follows Ibn Ezra in describing God's regret (*vayinahem/Da bereuete*) as a metaphor for God having changed God's mind about creating humanity. According to Mendelssohn, the Bible uses this metaphor since people change their mind because they feel regret.[133]

When, however, God is described as "having vexation in his heart" (*veyitatzev el libo/hatte Ver druß in seinem Herzen*), Mendelssohn adopts a different approach. As vexation is the first type of passion, it is applicable to God. Mendelssohn therefore rejects commentators like the ancient Aramaic translator Onkelos, who seek to eliminate this anthropopathism.[134]

In Mendelssohn's willingness to attribute certain types of passions to God, we find further evidence that the claim that he presents an impersonal, "Hellenistic" concept of God in the *Be'ur* is wrong.

131 Mendelssohn, *JubA,* 15.2:56–57 (Commentary to Genesis 6:6).

132 Mendelssohn, *JubA,* 9.1:111.

133 Mendelssohn, *JubA,* 15.2:56–57 (Commentary to Genesis 6:6).

134 See Mendelssohn, *JubA,* 15.2:56–57 (Commentary to Genesis 6:6). Onkelos translates the phrase *vayitatzev el libo* as "[He] said He would destroy their strength according to His will," eliminating reference to God's vexation. Mendelssohn rejects Onkelos's translation as "deviating from peshat" and cites *Genesis Rabbah* 27:4 in support of his contention that it is perfectly legitimate to ascribe vexation to God.

The two methods of the *Be'ur*: (2) *Derash*

While Mendelssohn gives priority to *peshat* in the *Be'ur*, he recognizes that rabbinic tradition frequently employs other exegetical methods. In the introduction to his 1769 commentary on Ecclesiastes, Mendelssohn follows a kabbalistic tradition originating in the medieval Zohar by distinguishing four levels of biblical interpretation:—*peshat*, the plain sense; *derash*, the exegeted sense; *remez*, the allusive sense; and *sod*, the esoteric sense.[135] Breuer has correctly observed that while many medieval Jewish thinkers regarded these levels of meaning hierarchically, with *sod* being at the pinnacle, Mendelssohn prioritizes *peshat*, subordinating *remez* and *sod* to *derash*.[136] Mendelssohn makes clear that he eschews mystical interpretations of the Bible, instead seeing all levels of biblical interpretation as consistent with reason.[137] As he puts it, "There are four ways to elucidate our holy Torah: *peshat*, *derush*,[138] *remez*, and *sod*. They are all words of the living God[139] and are all correct. *This neither contradicts the ways of the intellect and logic, nor is strange and astonishing to human understanding*, as I will elucidate with the help of the Eternal, may He be blessed" (emphasis mine).[140]

Given the importance of *peshat* for Mendelssohn, his positive attitude toward *derash* is striking. Mendelssohn's approach to *derash* can be understood, at least in part, as a defense of rabbinic exegesis against Protestant critique.[141] Beginning with Luther, Protestants frequently claimed that the Talmud was irrational as evidenced by its absurd midrashic exegesis. Jews' reliance on rabbinic interpretation was regarded as proof of their inability to

[135] Within Judaism, the idea that Scripture has four levels of meaning was first developed in the later strata of the Zohar in the thirteenth century. See Scholem, *On the Kabbalah and Its Symbolism*, 50-62; Breuer, *The Limits of Enlightenment*, 185. On the relationship between the Zohar's doctrine of the Bible's four levels of meaning and the medieval Christian doctrine of a fourfold sense of Scripture, see Talmage, *Apples of Gold in Settings of Silver*, 114-116.

[136] Breuer, *The Limits of Enlightenment*, 184–195.

[137] Zev Harvey has shown that even when Mendelssohn cites interpretations of the Bible from kabbalistic texts, he generally omits mythical elements from them. Gideon Freudenthal has shown how Mendelssohn neutralizes ostensibly magical doctrines in Scripture. See Harvey, "Why Philosophers Quote Kabbalah," 119–121; Freudenthal, *No Religion without Idolatry*, 105–134, 165–171.

[138] Mendelssohn uses the term *derush* rather than the more common term *derash*.

[139] See *BT*, Eruvin, 13b.

[140] Mendelssohn, *JubA*, 14:148; *Moses Mendelssohn: Writings*, 176.

[141] Of course, medieval Jewish *peshat* commentators such as Rashi, Ibn Ezra, Nahmanides, and others would regularly provide *derash* interpretations in addition to *peshat* ones. So in defending *derash*, Mendelssohn was also defending a tradition of medieval Jewish biblical exegesis.

read the Bible correctly.[142] Spinoza had repeated the standard Protestant critique of midrashic interpretation, writing that the "the Rabbis are completely crazy . . . each one invents what he can according to the power of his mentality."[143] Mendelssohn's approach to biblical interpretation cuts a fascinating contrast with Spinoza's.

In Chapter 7 of the *TTP*, Spinoza famously compares the method of studying the Bible to the method of studying nature:

> To sum up briefly, I say that the method of interpreting Scripture does not differ at all from the method of interpreting nature, but agrees with it completely. For the method of interpreting nature consists above all in putting together a history of nature (*historia naturae*) from which, as from certain data, we infer the definitions of natural things. In the same way, to interpret Scripture it is necessary to prepare a straightforward history of Scripture and to infer from it the mind of Scripture's authors by legitimate inferences as from certain data and principles. For in this way everyone will always proceed without danger of error—provided he has admitted no principles or data for interpreting Scripture and discussing it other than those drawn from Scripture itself and its history. He will be able to discuss the things which surpass our grasp as safely as those we know by the natural light (*lumine naturali*).[144]

I have discussed the meaning of this passage in detail elsewhere.[145] For Spinoza, just as the essence of every finite individual is determined both by

[142] In his 1543 tract *Von den Juden und ihren Lügen* (*On the Jews and Their Lies*), Luther accused the Jews of being stubborn and irrational, as reflected by their distortion of the meaning of Scripture by relying on talmudic interpretations that "pervert and twist the [meaning of] the prophetic books." See Luther, *Luther's Works*, 47:176. In his 1711 book *Entdecktes Judentum* (*Judaism Unmasked*), Johann Andreas Eisenmenger fleshed out Luther's charge of the rabbis' irrationality by citing rabbinic passages where the talmudic rabbis claim that the Bible has multiple, even infinite meanings, and then showing the absurdity of midrashic interpretations. See Eisenmenger, *Entdecktes Judentum*, I:ch. 1; Katz, *From Prejudice to Destruction*, 17. For discussion, see Katz, *From Prejudice to Destruction*, 13–22; Manuel, *The Broken Staff*, 151–154. Even Mendelssohn's friend Lessing, who was known for his strikingly positive views of Jews, criticized the rabbis for their "petty, warped, hair-splitting" interpretations of the Bible. See Lessing, *Werke*, 10:88, #55; *Philosophical and Theological Writings*, 230, #51. For discussion of other German Enlightenment writers who regarded Midrash as irrational, see Breuer, *The Limits of Enlightenment*, 101–105.

[143] See Spinoza, *Opera*, 3:134, 147; *Collected Works*, 2:216, 235 (*Theological-Political Treatise*, chs. 9–10).

[144] Spinoza, *Opera*, 3:98; *Collected Works*, 2:171 (*Theological-Political Treatise*, ch. 7).

[145] See Gottlieb, *Faith, Reason, Politics*, 71–79.

the universal laws of nature and its place within the chain of finite natural causes,[146] so the meaning of every word in a verse is determined in relation to both the teachings found universally throughout Scripture and a text's specific narrative context.[147]

Like Spinoza, Mendelssohn compares the study of Scripture to the study of nature. But whereas Spinoza uses this analogy to *discredit* rabbinic interpretation, Mendelssohn uses it to *vindicate* rabbinic reading practices. Mendelssohn writes:

> Therefore we see clearly that the sages, may their memories be for a blessing, never rejected the *peshat* and primary intention, which leaves aside the words but preserves the sense. But they also left a place for the secondary intention, which scrutinizes every word, every letter, and even every jot on those letters. For nothing in the words of the living God appears accidentally, without intention, just as God did not create anything in God's world without a specific purpose, as is clear to every wise individual.[148]

Following Leibniz, Mendelssohn holds that God created the most perfect possible world, which involves unity with maximal diversity. This means that the world is maximally rich in the variety of beings that exist in it, but that these beings are united under a single law of divine providence. Every single detail of creation has a particular purpose in the divine plan.[149]

Taking Leibniz's idea of maximal diversity further, Mendelssohn notes that not only does each thing have its particular place in the divine order,

[146] See Spinoza, *Opera* 2:34, 69, 74; *Collected Works* 1:38-39; 432-433, 436 (*Treatise on the Emendation of the Intellect*, paragraph 92; *Ethics*, Part I, Proposition 28; Proposition 33 Scholium 1).

[147] Spinoza's attention to both the teachings found universally throughout Scripture and the specific narrative context parallels the two levels of causality in his metaphysics, which include infinite modes (universal causality) and finite modes (finite causality). For discussion of how these different levels of analysis operate in the interpretation of Scripture, see Spinoza, *Opera*, 3:102–104; *Collected Works*, 2:176–178 (*Theological-Political Treatise*, ch. 7). In addition to stressing the importance of these two factors in discerning the literal meaning of Scripture, Spinoza includes other considerations, including knowledge of: biblical Hebrew grammar, vocabulary, and phraseology; the life of the biblical author, the historical context in which he wrote, and his intended audience; and the textual history of the biblical text. See Spinoza, *Opera*, 3:100–102, 106; *Collected Works*, 2:173–175, 179–180.

[148] See Mendelssohn, *JubA*, 14:150; *Moses Mendelssohn: Writings*, 179.

[149] On Leibniz's definition of perfection, see his May 18, 1715, letter to Christian Wolff found in Leibniz, *Philosophical Essays*, 232–234. On Leibniz's account of divine providence, see Chapter 5 of the *Discourse on Metaphysics*, found in ibid., 38–39. Mendelssohn adopts Leibniz's and Wolff's accounts of God's perfection in his 1755 *On Sentiments*, while recognizing subtle differences between the two that are not relevant for our discussion. See Mendelssohn, *JubA*, 1:248–253, 294–296, 325–326; *Philosophical Writings*, 20–24, 61–63, 90–91.

but certain things also serve multiple functions. For example, Mendelssohn points out that the nose is able to breathe, smell, make us look beautiful, and expel excess moisture.[150] Divine wisdom is manifest not only when *individual things conform to a single purpose*, but also when *individual things perform multiple functions* in achieving this purpose. For individual things performing multiple functions is a further manifestation of diversity in unity, that is, of perfection.

For Mendelssohn, just as nature is a testament to divine perfection, so is the Bible. In nature everything serves a particular purpose, and in the Bible every detail exists for a reason. In nature God's wisdom is manifest in individual things performing multiple functions, and in Scripture divine wisdom is manifest when a single word or expression has multiple, indeed, infinite meanings. While Spinoza uses the analogy between the study of Scripture and the study of nature to claim that a scriptural passage only has a single meaning, Mendelssohn uses the analogy to claim that Scripture has infinite meanings.[151]

Mendelssohn's understanding of midrashic method is connected with his theory of synonyms. We have seen that Mendelssohn denies that there are any true synonyms since even words that have identical "primary intentions" possess subtle nuances that differ and hence convey different "secondary intentions." While *peshat* is concerned with the "primary intention" and does not pay attention to these subtle nuances, Mendelssohn claims that *derash* proceeds from careful attention to these nuances.[152] For Mendelssohn, there are two characteristics of *derash*. First, *derash* notices something out of place in the flow of a passage. Second, it considers the meaning of the passage in isolation from its wider context.[153] In his introduction to his commentary on Ecclesiastes, Mendelssohn provides an excellent illustration of the relationship between *peshat* and *derash*.

[150] Mendelssohn, *JubA*, 14:151; *Moses Mendelssohn: Writings*, 180–181. In the introduction to his commentary on the Pentateuch, Ibn Ezra briefly makes the same point. See his comments on the third approach to interpreting Scripture.

[151] Spinoza does occasionally allow metaphorical interpretations of the Bible, claiming that he does so only when dictated by intra-biblical considerations. But Spinoza's use of metaphorical interpretation is highly circumscribed and problematic. For discussion of Spinoza's use of metaphorical interpretation of the Bible, see Gottlieb, *Faith, Reason, Politics*, 63–97, and the relevant sources cited there.

[152] Compare Ibn Ezra's commentary with Exodus 20:1.

[153] Mendelssohn, *JubA*, 14:149; *Moses Mendelssohn: Writings*, 177.

The two methods in action

Genesis 43–44 recounts that during a famine in Canaan Joseph's brothers went to Egypt to purchase food. The brothers came before Joseph, who accused them of being spies and told them that to prove they were not spies they must return to Canaan and bring back their youngest brother Benjamin, who had stayed behind with Jacob. With Judah promising to guarantee Benjamin's security Jacob allowed the brothers to bring Benjamin down to Egypt. Joseph welcomed his brothers and gave them bags of food but secretly had his divining chalice hidden in Benjamin's bag. As the brothers were leaving, Joseph sent his men after them and accused them of stealing his chalice. Joseph's men searched the bags and found the chalice in Benjamin's bag. Judah proposed that they should all become Joseph's slaves, but Joseph insisted on only holding Benjamin. At this point we read:

> Then Judah approached him [Joseph] and said, "Please my lord, let your servant appeal to my lord and do not be angry with your servant, for you are the equal of Pharaoh." (Genesis 44:12)

Citing a Midrash, Rashi (1040–1105) comments on the phrase "for you are the equal of Pharaoh" as follows:

> You are as important in my eyes as the king, this is the *peshat*. And the midrashic explanation—you are destined to be afflicted with leprosy just as Pharaoh was afflicted by means of my ancestor Sarah on account of the single night that he detained her.[154]

On the face of it, this midrashic interpretation looks like a fanciful eisegetical comment that provides no insight into the meaning of the verse. Mendelssohn, however, considers it a keen insight into the literary nuances of the biblical text. He explains that according to the *peshat* of the phrase "for you are the equal of Pharaoh," Judah is complementing Joseph as a way of mollifying him. But the Midrash quoted by Rashi interprets the phrase "for you are the equal of Pharaoh" as a threat. Judah is comparing Joseph not to the present Pharaoh, but to the Pharaoh who was punished with leprosy in the times of Abraham. The reference is to Genesis 12, where Judah's ancestor

[154] This midrashic interpretation Rashi cites is found in *Genesis Rabbah* 93:6.

Abraham descended to Egypt to find food in a time of famine. Abraham knew that Pharaoh would find Sarah beautiful and kill him to wed her. So Abraham claimed that Sarah was his sister. As expected, Pharaoh brought Sarah to his palace intending to wed her or make her his concubine. But God then afflicted Pharaoh and his house and Pharaoh released Sarah.[155]

Mendelssohn sees Rashi's comment on Genesis 44:12 as a paradigmatic example of the different levels of meaning conveyed by the biblical text. Rashi first explains the *peshat*, which follows from the context of the verse. Judah's complementing Joseph is a natural way that a weak stranger might seek to curry favor with a powerful official in order to get his brother released. But Mendelssohn notes that Joseph's choice of words was significant. Judah could easily have told Joseph that he was a great official or that he was as great as a king in his eyes. The Midrash quoted by Rashi is pointing to a subtle message that Judah is trying to telegraph to Joseph, namely, that "even if Joseph was as great Pharaoh, he was not better than Pharaoh and could be afflicted the way that Pharaoh was afflicted."[156] Mendelssohn notes that it is the way of people speaking before those who have power to mask their anger by conveying a threat in a veiled way through what appears to be a compliment.[157] The Midrash is sensitive to this nuance of Judah's speech and shows how through a careful choice of words the divine author is able to convey many things at once. For Mendelssohn, a true understanding of Midrash therefore shows that the rabbis did not ignorantly impose their own interpretations on the Bible but, rather, discerned the Bible's literary subtext through their keen aesthetic sensitivity. As with his discussion of how Jewish practices illuminate the Psalms, Mendelssohn's interpretation of Midrash as keen literary analysis counters the Protestant claim that rabbinic Judaism is discontinuous with the Bible.

Mendelssohn's pluralist defense of the Masoretic Text

Spinoza did not limit his criticism to rabbinic exegesis. He also questioned Mosaic authorship of the Pentateuch.[158] Drawing on the fact that many

[155] See Genesis 12:10–20.

[156] See Mendelssohn, *JubA*, 14:149.

[157] It is worth considering Mendelssohn's defenses of Judaism before Christians in light of his account of Judah's actions and intentions.

[158] In questioning Mosaic authorship of the Pentateuch, Spinoza presented the rabbis as the target of his criticism despite the fact that many Christians also accepted this view, writing: "the Pharisees maintained this [Mosaic authorship of the Pentateuch] so stubbornly that they considered anyone

phrases and events in the Pentateuch seem to indicate a speaker living long after Moses, Spinoza concluded that the Pentateuch could not have been written entirely by Moses.[159] He also argued against the reliability of the Masoretic Text by pointing to maculations that reflected problems in textual transmission.[160] By the eighteenth century German Bible scholars began adducing mounting evidence for Spinoza's questioning of the Mosaic authorship and textual integrity of the Masoretic Text.[161]

Mendelssohn addresses the question of biblical authorship at the beginning of *OL* when he writes that "Moses our master, peace be on him, wrote the entire Torah from 'in the beginning' (Genesis 1:1) to 'before the eyes of all Israel' (Deuteronomy 34:12)."[162] He cites a famous talmudic dispute over whether or not Moses wrote the final eight verses of the Pentateuch, which describe his own death.[163] According to the Talmud, Rabbi Judah (others say Rabbi Nehemiah) claims that Moses wrote everything up to the last eight verses of the Torah, which were written by Joshua. R. Simeon disagrees, arguing that Moses wrote even these verses "with tears" in his eyes. In support of his view, R. Simeon cites Jeremiah 36:18, in which Jeremiah instructs the scribe Baruch to transcribe his words. While many Jewish authorities considered R. Judah's opinion on the final eight verses valid, Mendelssohn emphatically sides with R. Simeon.[164] Why is Mendelssohn so insistent on defending R. Simeon's "conservative" view when R. Judah's more "liberal" position had been deemed legitimate by many if not most post-talmudic Jewish commentators and legal decisors?[165]

Mendelssohn notes that "there have already been people" who found the fact that the Bible often speaks of Moses in the third person as indicating

who seemed to think otherwise a heretic." See Spinoza, *Opera* 3:118; *Collected Works*, 2:192–193 (*Theological Political Treatise*, ch. 8).

[159] See Spinoza, *Opera* 3:120–121; *Collected Works*, 2:195–196. Spinoza conjectures that Ezra redacted the Pentateuch as well as the books of Joshua, Judges, Ruth, Samuel, and Kings. See Spinoza, *Opera* 3:126–128; *Collected Works*, 2:202–205 (*Theological-Political Treatise*, ch. 8).

[160] For example, Spinoza claimed the marginal notes in the Masoretic Text (the so-called *keri* and *ketiv*), reflected textual variants. See Spinoza, *Opera* 3:133, 136–141; *Collected Works* 2:213–215, 217–222 (*Theological-Political Treatise*, ch. 9).

[161] For an excellent overview of this topic with an eye to its relevance for Mendelssohn, see Breuer, *The Limits of Enlightenment*, 78–101.

[162] Mendelssohn, *JubA*, 14:212; *Moses Mendelssohn: Writings*, 189.

[163] See *BT*, Baba Batra, 15a; Menahot, 30b.

[164] See Mendelssohn, *JubA*, 14:212; *Moses Mendelssohn: Writings*, 189–190.

[165] Jewish authorities who considered R. Judah's position legitimate included Rashi, Ibn Ezra, Maimonides, and R. Bahya ben Asher. See Breuer, *The Limits of Enlightenment*, 165; 288, note 81.

that Moses did not author the entire Torah. Mendelssohn is likely referring to Spinoza.[166] For example, Spinoza cites Deuteronomy 34:10, "There has never arisen in Israel a prophet like Moses whom God knew face to face," as having been written long after Moses since it declares Moses superior to all prophets who will succeed him.[167] But Mendelssohn observes that this argument depends on the assumption that Moses wrote the Bible *of his own accord.* By citing the verse from Jeremiah, Mendelssohn sees Rabbi Simeon as expressing a very different view of Mosaic authorship, portraying God as dictating the Torah to Moses, who acted as a mere copyist. The fact that Moses is described in the third person is thus no evidence against Moses having written the Torah since God is the one speaking.[168] For this reason, Mendelssohn finds it important to reject the opinion that Moses did not author the last eight verses of the Pentateuch despite the substantial rabbinic precedent for this view. For if the literary style of the Pentateuch can be used to dispute Mosaic authorship for its last eight verses, then it can also be used to dispute Mosaic authorship of other parts of the Pentateuch.[169]

The assumption that the Pentateuch is an unmediated divine revelation to Moses also helps explain Mendelssohn's previously mentioned assumption that the Pentateuch contains infinite intentions. A text composed by a human being may contain multiple intentions, but only a finite number. For a text to have infinite intentions, it must have been composed by an infinite mind.

Turning to textual criticism of the Masoretic Bible, Mendelssohn asserts that the Pentateuch possessed by contemporary Jews has been preserved

[166] See Spinoza, *Opera,* 3:119; *Collected Works,* 2:193 (*Theological-Political Treatise,* ch. 8) and Breuer's and Sorkin's note in Mendelssohn, *Moses Mendelssohn's Hebrew Writings,* 244, note 22. Spinoza himself attributed this view to Ibn Ezra, so Mendelssohn may also have had Ibn Ezra in mind. See Harvey, "Spinoza on Ibn Ezra's 'Secret of the Twelve,'" 44–47.

[167] See Spinoza, *Opera,* 3:121; *Collected Works,* 2:196 (*Theological-Political Treatise,* ch. 8).

[168] That the issue for the talmudic rabbis is not whether or not Moses wrote the Bible but whether or not God dictated it to him is clear from *BT, Sanhedrin* Sanhedrin, 99a, which states that one who admits that the entire Torah was dictated to Moses by God but that Moses composed a single verse *of his own accord* has no portion in the World to Come, a view that Maimonides codifies. See Maimonides, *Mishneh Torah: The Book of Knowledge,* 84b ("Laws of Repentance" ch. 3, law 8) and the eighth principle of faith found in Maimonides, *Commentary on the Mishnah: Tractate Sanhedrin,* 155-156 (introduction to the tenth chapter of Sanhedrin).

[169] But compare the *Be'ur* commentary on Numbers 12:3. The verse states that Moses was more *anav* than any man on earth. In a comment added by Mendelssohn himself, he explains that he translates the word *anav* as *geduldiger* (patient) rather than as *demütig* (modest) since unlike modesty, "the patient man can praise himself [for this trait]." But testifying about Moses's modesty is only an problem if Moses is saying this about himself, not if God testifies this about Moses. See Mendelssohn, *JubA,* 18:97 (Commentary on Numbers 12:3). Spinoza himself had pointed to this verse as evidence that Moses could not have composed the entire Pentateuch. See Spinoza, *Opera,* 3:121; *Collected Works,* 2:196 (*Theological-Political Treatise,* ch. 8). See pp. 400–402 of this volume.

intact and unchanged.[170] He acknowledges that "Christian translators" do not accept this view.[171] For Mendelssohn, this is a major problem since halakhic practice depends on interpretations of the precise wording of the Masoretic Text and thus presupposes the Masoretic Text's absolute textual integrity.[172] Mendelssohn criticizes Christian scholars for arbitrarily emending the biblical text, noting that they do so "according to their fancies and understanding."[173]

But Mendelssohn recognizes that this is not sufficient to defend the textual integrity of the Masoretic Bible since text criticism can be undertaken in a more modest, cautious way. Mendelssohn therefore attempts a *philosophical* response textual biblical scholarship. Addressing Christian Bible critics, he writes:

> However, I do not condemn these scholars . . . for what compels them to heed the tradition that they have not received from their ancestors, or the *Masorah* that has not been transmitted to them by individuals whom they deem trustworthy? Furthermore, they do not accept the words of the Torah in order to observe and perform all that is written there, but rather as a book of chronicles to know the events of ancient times and to understand the ways of divine providence and governance in every generation. For these purposes it does no harm if they sometimes alter details by adding or subtracting letters or words just as they do with famous, well-known secular books, which every editor changes according to his wishes. *But if this is possible for Christian scholars and their students, it is not possible for us, the house of Israel. For us, this Torah is an inheritance not only for the purposes*

170 Mendelssohn, *JubA*, 14:213; *Moses Mendelssohn: Writings*, 190–191.

171 Mendelssohn, *JubA*, 14:242; *Moses Mendelssohn: Writings*, 196. In their annotations on *OL*, Breuer and Sorkin cite, as an example of this, Michaelis's translation, noting that in the introduction to the work, he writes "I rather wish the entire work be discontinued, if I must be obliged to follow the beliefs of the Jewish Masoretes . . . which occasionally do not even yield rational sense." See Michaelis, *Deutsche Übersetzung des Alten Testaments*, 1:xxviii, cited in Mendelssohn, *Moses Mendelssohn's Hebrew Writings*, 290–291, note 83.

172 See Breuer, *The Limits of Enlightenment*, 162. Mendelssohn's assumption of textual integrity pertains to the Pentateuch alone. He had a very different view of other books of the Bible. For example, in a 1771 letter to Johann Zimmerman, Mendelssohn wrote that some of the Psalms are textually corrupt. See Mendelssohn, *JubA*, 12.1:275.

173 See Mendelssohn, *JubA*, 14:242; *Moses Mendelssohn: Writings*, 196. Mendelssohn repeats this criticism often. In a 1773 review of Benjamin Kennicott's critical notes on the Psalms, Mendelssohn criticizes the arbitrariness of his emendations, writing: "I miss in him the rare talent that being a great critic demands: penetrating acumen connected with extreme caution, and the most modest flexibility [to change one's mind]." See Mendelssohn, *JubA*, 5.1:184. Also see Mendelssohn's letters to an anonymous "Bible researcher" Mendelssohn, *JubA*, 12.2:33–34, 41–43 (Letter to a Bible researcher, February 16, 1773, February, 8, 1774), which likewise criticize Kennicott and his followers.

mentioned above, but rather to know what the Eternal our God has commanded us to study, teach, observe, and perform: it is our life and the length of our days. (emphasis mine)[174]

Mendelssohn admits that he cannot prove the integrity of the Masoretic Text. But he adopts a skeptical stance doubting that Christian scholars can prove the opposite. Since one cannot travel back in history, the question of whether the Masoretic Bible is the correct version is a matter of *faith.* According to Mendelssohn, for Jews this faith is sustained by their *trust* that their ancestors have reliably transmitted the correct text as well as by the practical needs of members of the Jewish religious community who seek to live according to the laws of the Torah as interpreted by the rabbis.[175] It is in light of this assumption that Jews seek to explain apparent maculations in the Masoretic Text through *peshat* and *derash.* For Mendelssohn, it would be foolish and irresponsible for a Jew to make her way of life dependent on the vicissitudes of biblical scholarship. By contrast, for Christian Bible critics who read the Bible primarily as a book of chronicles that reveals divine providence, there is no reason to refrain from textual emendation.[176] Mendelssohn thus responds to Bible critics by offering a *pluralist* understanding of history noting that the past can be constructed in different ways depending on one's underlying assumptions and motives. As we will see, Samson Raphael Hirsch later employs a similar response to biblical criticism.[177]

Rabbinic law and the plain meaning of the biblical text

Mendelssohn follows rabbinic tradition in affirming that along with the Pentateuch, which the rabbis refer to as the "Written Torah," God gave Moses oral explanations for how to practice the law, which were forbidden to be written down and formed part of the so-called "Oral Torah." These authoritative explanations were only written beginning in the times of the

174 Mendelssohn, *JubA,* 14:243; *Moses Mendelssohn: Writings,* 196–197.

175 Mendelssohn asserts that the Hebrew word for "faith" (*Glaube*) is *emunah,* which means "trust." See Mendelssohn, *JubA,* 8:166–167; *Moses Mendelssohn: Writings,* 89–90. Also see Mendelssohn's commentary on Chapter 8 of Maimonides's *Treatise on Logic.* See Mendelssohn, *JubA,* 14:71–72; *Moses Mendelssohn's Hebrew Writings,* 84–85.

176 In the Appendix, I use Mendelssohn's treatment of the two versions of the Decalogue (Exodus and Deuteronomy) to illustrate how he deploys the assumption that the Pentateuch was dictated to Moses and that it has multiple levels of meaning to respond to Spinoza's historical-critical approach.

177 See pp. 398–402 of this volume.

Mishnah (second century AD) when there was concern that they would be forgotten.[178]

Rabbinic legal determinations do not, however, always fit neatly with the plain meaning of the biblical text. One sees Mendelssohn trying to balance his dual commitments to *peshạt* and rabbinic legal authority when he writes in *OL* that while the primary task of his translation is to convey *peshat*, where *peshat* and *derash* do not contradict, he tries to leave open the midrashic understanding of the verse. But Mendelssohn explains that if *peshat* and *derash* contradict, he will translate according to *derash* in matters of law since translating according to *peshat* would undermine halakhah as a legal text cannot say "do x and do not do x."[179] I will explore an example of how Mendelssohn translates a legal passage where *peshat* and *derash* contradict in the next section.

The Jewish Luther and his Protestant predecessor

In his seminal 1984 article "Language Questions Related to Moses Mendelssohn's Pentateuch Translation," Werner Weinberg compares Mendelssohn's Bible translation with Luther's, writing, "[Mendelssohn] will not violate the inherent laws of good contemporary German; when sacrificing is to be done, Mendelssohn sacrifices literalness. One may say that Luther's translation was in many ways more faithful, but for Mendelssohn the aesthete, the man of letters, and celebrated German stylist, there could be no

[178] See Mendelssohn, *JubA*, 8:168–169; *Moses Mendelssohn: Writings*, 91–92. In his 1777 work *The Ritual Laws of the Jews*, Mendelssohn provides a taxonomy of halakhah as it relates to the Written and Oral Torah. He explains that the Written Law is constituted by the Pentateuch, while the Oral Law comprises five elements: (1) explanations of the Written Law, (2) determinations of the Written Law based on oral traditions from Moses, (3) determinations of the Written Law based on arguments according to hermeneutical principles transmitted through rabbinic tradition, (4) protective provisions added to the law by the prophets and later wise men of the nation whose purpose is to help safeguard Jews from transgressing the law, and (5) customs accepted by the entire Jewish nation. See Mendelssohn, *JubA*, 7:115–116. It is striking that in both *Jerusalem* and in the *Ritual Laws* Mendelssohn identifies the Written Torah only with the Pentateuch, and not with the Prophets and Writings. This seems to explain why Mendelssohn's Pentateuch translation was directed to Jews alone. For Mendelssohn saw the Pentateuch primarily as a text detailing legal obligations incumbent only on Jews. By contrast, he saw the Psalms as expressing universal religious sentiments useful for both Jews and Christians alike.

[179] In opting for such an approach to legal texts, Mendelssohn follows Rashi and Ibn Ezra and criticizes Rashbam, who interprets legal passages according to *peshat* even when such an interpretation contradicts normative halakhah. See Mendelssohn, *JubA*, 14:244–245; 16:198–199; *Moses Mendelssohn: Writings*, 199–200, 205–206. In the case of narrative sections of the Pentateuch, however, Mendelssohn allows multiple, even contradictory interpretations. Unlike law which must be practiced in a specific way, there is no need for an authoritative interpretation of biblical narratives.

compromise with the demands of the German language."[180] For Weinberg, Mendelssohn's commitment to High German exceeded Luther's to the point that Luther was more faithful to the Hebrew. Weinberg's judgment is common.and is used by those who cast Mendelssohn as a "colonial agent". In reality, Mendelssohn's translation generally *stays closer to the Hebrew than Luther* with a few notable exceptions. Consider a few examples:

1. *Preserving the repetition of Hebrew word roots.* In Genesis 3:15 God tells the serpent that Eve's "seed" (*zar'a*) will be in conflict with the serpent's, saying *hu* ***yeshufkha*** *rosh ve'atah* ***teshufenu*** *akev.* Luther ignores the linguistic similarity between *yeshufkha* and *teshufenu*, translating the phrase as *Derselbe soll dir den Kopf* ***zertreten,*** *und du wirst ihn in die Ferse* ***stechen*** (he shall **crush** your head and you will **bite** his heel). Mendelssohn, however, strives to preserve the linguistic similarity between *yeshufkha* and *teshufenu* by translating the phrase as *Diser soll dir den Kopf* ***verwunden,*** *und du ihm die Ferse* ***verwunden*** (this one shall **wound** your head and you shall **wound** his heel).[181]
2. *Preserving double phrasing of the Hebrew.* Exodus 34 describes Moses ascending Mount Sinai to receive the Decalogue and then descending to return to the people. Verse 29 reads *vayhi* ***beredet Mosheh mehar Sinai*** *ushnei luhot ha'edut beyad Mosheh* ***berideto min hahar.*** The Hebrew describes Moses's descent from Mount Sinai with the two tablets of the law and then repeats that Moses descended from the mountain. Luther ignores this redundancy, translating the verse *Da nun Mose vom Berge Sinai ging, hatte er die zwei Tafeln des Zeugnisses in seiner Hand* (When Moses went [down] from Mount Sinai, he had the two Tablets of Testimony in his hand). Mendelssohn, however, preserves the repetition of the original, translating it as ***Als Moscheh herunter ging von dem Berge Sinai,*** *die beiden Tafeln des Zeugnisses hatte Moscheh in der Hand,* ***als er von dem Berge herunter ging*** (**When Mosheh went down from Mount Sinai**, the two Tablets of Testimony had Mosheh in hand,

[180] Weinberg, "Language Questions," 210.

[181] See Mendelssohn, *JubA,* 9.1:106; 15.2:34–35. There is also a Christological divide here. Luther takes the *hu* that will crush the serpent to refer to Jesus who will crush the head of the devil. So Luther translates the word as *Der* (he). Rejecting Christology Mendelssohn translates the *hu* as *Dieser* (this), referring to Eve's seed. Luther makes his Christological interpretation of the verse clear in a 1545 marginal note where he writes, "This is the first *evangelium* and promise of Christ given to the world. That he should overcome sin, death, and hell and deliver us from the violence of the snake." See Luther's commentary to Genesis 3:15, cited in Sheehan, *The Enlightenment Bible,* 125.

as he went down from the mountain).[182] Mendelssohn's preserving the form of the Hebrew is also evident by the fact that while Luther renders the second clause in elegant German as *hatte er die zwei Tafeln des Zeugnisses in seiner Hand* (he had the two Tablets of Testimony in his hand), Mendelssohn seeks to reproduce the form of the Hebrew, translating the clause as *die beiden Tafeln des Zeugnisses hatte Moscheh in der Hand* (the two Tablets of Testimony had Mosheh in hand).

3. *Hebrew colloquialisms.* In Exodus 4 God tells Moses that he should speak to Pharaoh on behalf of the Israelites. In Exodus 4:10 Moses objects, responding *lo ish devarim anochi.* Luther translates the phrase into a comprehensible German idiom as *ich bin je und je nicht wohl beredt gewesen* (I have never been very eloquent). Mendelssohn, however, renders the verse literally as *ich bin kein Man von Worten* (I am not a man of words). Mendelssohn thinks, however, that this translation is insufficient since the meaning of *Ich bin kein Man von Worten* will not be completely clear to a German reader. So after his translation, he adds in parentheses *das heißt kein guter Redner* (that means not a good speaker).[183] By adding the parentheses Mendelssohn is signaling that this is a case where the Hebrew is untranslatable.
4. *Preserving Hebrew syntactic style.* Genesis 23:1 describes the length of Sarah's life as follows: *vayihyu hayei Sarah me'ah shanah v'esrim shanah v'sheva shanim shnei hayei Sarah.* Luther translates the verse concisely into proper German style as *Sara war hundertsiebenundzwanzig Jahre alt* (Sara was one hundred and twenty-seven years old), eliminating both the lengthy form in which the Hebrew describes Sarah's years as well as the summary at the end of the verse. By contrast, Mendelssohn preserves the distinctive syntax of the original Hebrew: *Es war das Lebensalter der Sarah, hundert Jahr, und zwangzig Jahr und siben Jahr. Dises waren die Lebens Jahre der Sarah* (The lifespan of Sarah was one hundred years, and twenty years and seven years. These were Sarah's years of life).[184]

The *Be'ur* commentary makes clear that Mendelssohn reproduces the syntax of the Hebrew original to leave open its midrashic interpretation. In his commentary Rashi cites a Midrash that states that

182 Mendelssohn, *JubA*, 9.1:293.
183 Mendelssohn, *JubA*, 9.1:221.
184 Mendelssohn, *JubA*, 9.1:141.

the verse divides Sarah's lifespan into three parts (one hundred years, twenty years, seven years) to teach that when Sarah was one hundred years old, she was as innocent as a twenty year old and when she was twenty she was as beautiful as a seven year old.[185] The Be'urist notes that Mendelssohn's translation is even more literal than Onkelos's translation,[186] explaining that this is because Onkelos's aim is to convey the "intention" (*kavanah*) of the verse, while Mendelssohn seeks to make room for the verse's midrashic interpretation.[187]

5. *Hebrew names.* In his translation, Luther Germanizes Hebrew names in the Bible, while Mendelssohn preserves their Hebrew form. So Mendelssohn's translation has *Moscheh* for משה while Luther has *Mose*, Mendelssohn has *Mizraim* for מצרים while Luther has *Ägypten*, and so on. Mendelssohn explains that he preserves the Hebrew form of biblical names rather than give them a vernacular form because biblical names generally have meanings derived from their Hebrew etymology.[188] Another factor that might have influenced Mendelssohn's decision to retain the Hebrew original is that rabbinic Midrash often engages in interpretations based on the Hebrew forms of names.
6. *Hebrew word roots.* We have seen that at times Mendelssohn translates hyperliterally even when this contravenes German literary style in order to convey the Hebrew word root. This is the case in Mendelssohn's translation of *karat brit* in Genesis 15:18 as *zerschnitt einen Bund* (cut a covenant) as opposed to Luther's more colloquial *machte einen Bund* (make a covenant). The Be'urist notes the strangeness of this translation since *zerschnitt* means cutting or separation while the German word for covenant *Bund* implies uniting.[189] The oddity of Mendelssohn's translation is also evidenced by the fact that in other places Mendelssohn translates the word *karat* in *karat brit* colloquially as *machen* (made),[190] *schließen* (conclude),[191] *verpflichten* (obligate),[192] and *festsetzen* (establish).[193] So why does Mendelssohn translate Genesis 15:18 hyperliterally? The

185 Rashi is drawing on the *Genesis Rabbah* 58:1.
186 Onkelos translates the verse as *vahavo hayei Sarah me'ah v'esrin usheva sh'nin, sh'nei hayei Sarah* (The life of Sarah was one hundred and twenty-seven years, these were the years Sarah's life).
187 Mendelssohn, *JubA*, 15.2:216.
188 See Mendelssohn's commentary to Exodus 2:10 in Mendelssohn, *JubA*, 16:16–17.
189 See *Be'ur* comment to Genesis 15:10 in Mendelssohn, *JubA*, 15.2:133.
190 Exodus 24:8, 34:10; Deuteronomy 4:23; 5:2–3; 9:9.
191 Deuteronomy 28:69; 29:24.
192 Deuteronomy 29:11.
193 Deuteronomy 29:13.

reason is that the verse is referring to the covenant that Abraham concluded with God by cutting up animals, and Mendelssohn seeks to convey this in his translation.[194] Mendelssohn uses hyperliteral translation to illuminate the meaning of the biblical text.

While Mendelssohn generally remains closer to the form of the Hebrew than does Luther, there are four areas where Luther's translation is ostensibly closer to the form of the Hebrew original, though even here matters are complicated:

1. *Midrashic law.* We have seen Mendelssohn's declaration that he will translate according to *peshat* except in legal cases where the *derash* contradicts the *peshat.* This would seem to be a case where his translation clearly must deviate from the Hebrew original. But even here matters are not simple. Consider the *lex talionis* found in Exodus 21:24–25: *ayin tahat ayin, shen tahat shen, yad tahat yad, regel tahat ragel; k'viah tahat k'viah, petzah tahat patzah, habura tahat habura.* Luther translates the verse literally: *Auge um Auge, Zahn um Zahn, Hand um Hand, Fuß um Fuß, Brand um Brand, Wunde um Wunde, Beule um Beule,* (eye for eye, tooth for tooth, hand for hand, foot for foot, burn for burn, wound for wound, bruise for bruise). The problem for Mendelssohn is that while according to *peshat* the verse refers to an actual eye for an eye, the rabbis interpret the verse to refer to monetary compensation. To follow the rabbinic interpretation of the verse while simultaneously conveying the *peshat* Mendelssohn translates the verse as follows: *(Rechtswegen sollte) Auge für Auge (seyn), Zahn für Zahn. Hand für Hand, Fuß für Fuß. Brandmal für Brandmal, Wunde für Wunde. Beule für Beule (daher muß der Tädter Geld dafür geben)* ([According to justice it should be] eye for eye, tooth for tooth, hand for hand, foot for foot, burn for burn, wound for wound, bruise for bruise [therefore the offender must give money instead]).[195]

In his commentary Mendelssohn explains that moral reason demands that one not exact a literal eye for an eye. For example, he asks if a blind person blinds another how can justice be served?[196] Given Mendelssohn's

[194] Genesis 15:10. See Freudenthal, *No Religion without Idolatry,* 97–101.
[195] Mendelssohn, *JubA,* 9.1: 260.
[196] Mendelssohn enumerates other ways in which instituting *lex talionis* could lead to injustice: If a person damages one third of the eyesight of another, how can one take exactly one third of

commitment to the Torah's moral truth, he cannot accept that it contains laws that offend moral reason. He therefore explains that his translation follows Ibn Ezra, who interprets the verse to mean that a person is liable to have the law of retribution exacted upon him until he pays the victim. Mendelssohn seeks to convey this sense by putting in parentheses at the beginning of the verse that "according to justice" the perpetrator should have the law of retribution exacted upon him, but because of the aforementioned difficulties he "must give money instead," which Mendelssohn puts in parentheses at the end of the verse. By framing the verse with parentheses that explain how the law is practiced, Mendelssohn is able to convey the *peshat* in his translation while translating according to the rabbinic legal interpretation.

In this case, Luther, who does not feel bound to rabbinic interpretation, undoubtedly translates closer to the Hebrew than Mendelssohn. But even here Mendelssohn seeks to convey the *peshat*, and his deviation from the Hebrew is certainly not due to his conviction that "there could be no compromise with the demands of the German language."

2. *The vav construction.* Luther generally translates the *vav* at the beginning of phrases as *und* (and). For example, Genesis 1:2 states: *veha'aretz haytah tohu vavohu vehoshekh al pnei tehom veru'ah elohim merahefet al pnei hamayim.* Luther translates *veha'aretz* as ***Und** die Erde* (and the earth), *vehoshekh* as ***und** es war finster* (and there was darkness), and *veru'ah* as ***und** der Geist* (and the spirit). By contrast, Mendelssohn renders *veha'aretz* as *Die Erde **aber*** (but the earth), does not translate the *vav* of *vehoshekh*, which he renders simply as *Finsternis* ("darkness"), but does translate the *vav* of *veru'ah* as ***und** der götliche* (and the divine).[197]

In his *Be'ur* commentary Mendelssohn explains that it is a grammatical error to interpret every instance of *vav* at the beginning of the word as *und* (and). Rather, he claims that the *vav* can have several meanings or be a particle that has no direct translation.[198] In the case of *veha'aretz* where

his eyesight? Or if a person burns, bruises, or wounds another in a vulnerable part of his body but the victim does not die, how can one exact retribution since doing so might kill the offender? See Mendelssohn, *JubA*, 16:206–207; *Moses Mendelssohn: Writings*, 206–208.

[197] Mendelssohn, *JubA*, 9.1:101.

[198] See Mendelssohn, *JubA*, 14:265, 327–328. Mendelssohn writes that *vav* can be a response to a conditional, in which case it is translated as *so*, or indicate an opposition, in which case it is translated

Mendelssohn renders the *vav* as *aber* (but), Mendelssohn notes in his commentary that he was led to this translation by the Masoretic accent on the word. The Masoretic accent is a *revi'i*, which indicates a pause. Mendelssohn explains that this indicates a soft opposition meaning that God created the heaven and earth, but the land was unformed at the beginning.[199] So for Mendelssohn Luther's consistent rendering of *vav* at the beginning of words as *und* does not reflect greater fidelity to the Hebrew but, rather, a lack of understanding of the subtleties of biblical Hebrew.

3. *Anthropomorphism.* We have seen that Mendelssohn affirms that the Torah cannot err in its metaphysical teachings about God.[200] For this reason, he seeks to protect the reader from the idea that the Bible ascribes anthropomorphic traits to God's essence. This leads Mendelssohn sometimes to translate literally and add a parenthetic comment that explains the anthropomorphism. At other times, Mendelssohn translates literally and only explains the metaphorical meaning of the anthropomorphic expression in his commentary.[201] But there are times when Mendelssohn deviates from the plain sense of the Hebrew in his translation to avoid an anthropomorphism. By contrast, Luther has no problem with anthropomorphic descriptions of God since he believes that God became incarnate in Jesus and so translates these phrases literally.

For example, Genesis 8:21, which reads *vayarah YHWH et re'ah haniho'ah vayomer YHWH el libo*, attributes to God the sense of smell. Luther translates the verse literally as *Und der HERR roch den lieblichen Geruch und sprach in seinem Herzen* (And the LORD smelled the sweet smell and said in His

as *aber* (but). He also notes that when listing many things Hebrew can use a *vav* in different places while in German one only puts the *und* (and) before the last word, so the *vav* would not always be translated.

199 Mendelssohn, *JubA*, 15.2:4.

200 See p. 48 of this volume.

201 An example where Mendelssohn translates an anthropomorphic expression literally, but adds a parenthesis in his translation that explains the anthropomorphism, is his translation of the Hebrew word *kapi* (my hand) in Exodus 33:22. An example where he translates an anthropomorphism literally and then explains it metaphorically only in his commentary is his rendering of *panei* (my face) in Exodus 33:23. Even when Mendelssohn adds a parenthesis that explains an anthropomorphic expression in his translation, he will often also add a further explanation in his commentary. See Mendelssohn, *JubA*, 16:347–348; *Moses Mendelssohn's Hebrew Writings*, 439–441 (Commentary on Exodus 33:22–23).

heart). Mendelssohn, however, translates the verse as *Der Ewige nam den liblichen Duft mit Wohl Gefallen an, und sprach zu sich selbst* (The Eternal accepted the sweet smell with favor and said to Himself) to soften its anthropomorphic language.[202]

4. *Christology.* The other case where Luther adheres more strictly to the Hebrew original than Mendelssohn is in certain passages that can be read Christologically. In his 1524 preface to his translation of the book of Job, Luther wrote that he aimed to translate into a "clear language, comprehensible to everyone, with an undistorted sense and meaning."[203] But as Rosenzweig points out, Luther elsewhere noted that he sometimes held rigidly to the Hebrew original in his translation as a way of "giving the Hebrew some room."[204] Luther generally did so in cases where he thought that the hyperliteral Hebrew construction alluded to Christ.

The classic example of this is Luther's rendering of Psalm 68:19. In Hebrew the verse reads *alita lamarom shavita shevi*, which Luther translates as *Du bist in die Höhe gefahren und hast das Gefängnis gefangen* (You have gone up on high and led captivity captive). Luther translates the idiom *shavita shevi* hyperliterally as *das Gefängnis gefangen* (led captivity captive) because he sees it as referring not just to the release of prisoners but, rather, to Christ's having freed human beings from captivity to sin and death by allowing them to enjoy eternal life through their faith in Him.[205] By contrast, Mendelssohn translates the verse colloquially as *Du stiegest hoch empor, Trugst Beute davon* (you have ascended up high, carried away captives).[206] While Luther's hyperliteral translation is closer to the form of the Hebrew, Mendelssohn's translation better preserves the plain sense of the text.[207]

[202] Mendelssohn, *JubA*, 9.2:115; 15.2:74. Mendelssohn's translation follows Onkelos's, but is more literal.

[203] See Luther's 1524 Preface to Job, cited in Buber and Rosenzweig, *Scripture and Translation*, 48.

[204] See Luther's commentary on Psalm 68, cited in Buber and Rosenzweig, *Scripture and Translation*, 49.

[205] See Buber and Rosenzweig, *Scripture and Translation*, 49.

[206] Mendelssohn, *JubA*, 10.1:101.

[207] The Christological motivation of Luther's translation is evident by the fact that Luther translates the expression *shavita shivyo* (Deuteronomy 21:10) in a way that does not preserve the form of the Hebrew as *Gefängenen wegführst* (led into captivity) because he does not interpret Deuteronomy 21:10 Christologically.

In sum, *Mendelssohn is often more willing than Luther to preserve the form of the Hebrew at the expense proper German style.* Sometimes this is due to purely linguistic considerations, sometimes from an aesthetic desire to make vivid the meaning of the Hebrew text, and sometimes due to his seeking to make room for the midrashic interpretation. The main instances where Mendelssohn deviates from the form of the Hebrew more than Luther is where (1) not doing so obscures the text's plain meaning (the *vav* construction, hyperliteral Christological readings); (2) the midrashic legal interpretation/moral reason contradicts *peshat*; and (3) literal translation contradicts rationalist metaphysics (anthropomorphism). But even in these cases Mendelssohn's translation does not deviate from the form of the Hebrew, because he "sacrifices literalness" for German elegance.

Luther's translation was not the only Protestant Bible translation with which Mendelssohn was familiar.[208] Comparing Mendelssohn's translation with all the Protestant Bible translations he was familiar with is beyond the scope of this book. But before concluding the chapter, I would like to compare his translation with one relatively contemporary Protestant translation, the 1735 Wertheim Bible. Comparing these two works is illuminating because they reflect two distinct enlightened religious approaches to Bible translation.

A Jewish and Protestant Enlightenment Bible

On July 2, 1756, Mendelssohn penned a letter to Georg August von Breitenbauch. At the end of letter he mentioned an intriguing Bible that he had found at a friend's house, writing "One more thing before I conclude. I saw a Bible at Herr Magister Naumann's house by the name of the 'Wertheim

[208] Mendelssohn's library contained copies of Johann David Michaelis's Old Testament translation and the first part of the 1735 Wertheim Bible. See Mendelssohn, *Verzeichniß*, 14, 16 (items # 219–231 and 254 in quarto). He also had a copy of George Christian Knapp's 1778 *Übersetzung des Psalmen* (*Translation of the Psalms*) and both parts of Herder's 1782–1783 *Vom Geist der ebräischen Poesie* (*The Spirit of Hebrew Poetry*), which contains many lengthy translations of various parts of the Bible. See Mendelssohn, *Verzeichniß*, 21–22 (items #41 and #81 in octavo). Mendelssohn's library also contained Luther's *Auserlesene erbauliche kleine Schriften* (*Select Edifying Short Writings*), which included Luther's translation and commentary on several Psalms. See ibid., 31 (item #247 in quarto). As mentioned, in his introduction to the Psalms, Mendelssohn states that he made use of the translations of Michaelis, Knapp, and Luther in preparing his own. See p. 19 note 14 of this volume. Mendelssohn was also intimately familiar with Robert Lowth's work on the Psalms, which contained many translations. Mendelssohn published a lengthy review of Lowth's 1753 *De Sacra Poesi Hebraeorum* in 1757. See Mendelssohn, *JubA*, 4:20–62.

Bible.' This is an excellent book. I hope that you have the opportunity to read it. It would please you uncommonly."[209]

The Wertheim Bible was an exceptional work with an exceptional history.[210] It was published anonymously in 1735 by Johann Lorenz Schmidt, a committed follower of the philosopher Christian Wolff. In the introduction to his Bible, Schmidt wrote that he had undertaken the translation to "promote knowledge of the divine writings" of the Old Testament, as they were not well known to the German public.[211] Guided by rationalist principles, Schmidt sought to produce a readable, comprehensible Bible to replace Luther's.

The Wertheim Bible ignited a firestorm. Pietists who a dozen years earlier had successfully lobbied for Wolff's expulsion from his professorial post in Halle on account of his rationalist theology, agitated against it. These critics led by Joachim Lange raised a litany of complaints about the Wertheim Bible, including that it adopted a historical approach that severed the connection between the Old and New Testaments, that it denied biblical miracles by interpreting them naturalistically, and that it obscured the Bible's poetic qualities.[212] The Pietist heresy hunters were successful. The Wertheim Bible was banned in Nuremburg, Saxony, Prussia, and Vienna, and Schmidt was imprisoned.[213]

Mendelssohn eventually acquired a copy of the Wertheim Bible, and Paul Spalding has argued that his *Be'ur* was influenced by it.[214] My interest is not, however, in discerning influence but, rather, in comparing Schmidt's approach to translation with Mendelssohn's. While both Mendelssohn's and Schmidt's translations were deeply informed by rationalist Wolffian principles and guided by an attempt to sever the Old Testament from the New Testament, there are instructive differences between the two works.

209 Mendelssohn, *JubA*, 11:53 (letter to G.A. von Breitenbauch, July 2, 1756).

210 There is a large literature on the Wertheim Bible. Important discussions include: Spalding, *Seize the Book*; Goldenbaum, *Appell an das Publikum*, 175–508; Sheehan, *The Enlightenment Bible*, 121–131. Paul Spalding also treats Mendelssohn's relation to the Wertheim Bible. See Spalding, "Toward a Modern Torah: Moses Mendelssohn's Use of a Banned Bible."

211 Schmidt, *Die göttlichen Schriften vor den Zeiten des Messie Jesus*, 23.

212 See Spalding, *Seize the Book*, 66–73.

213 See Spalding, *Seize the Book*, 74–150.

214 See Mendelssohn, *Verzeichniß*, 14, 16 (items # 219–231 and 254 in quarto); Spalding, "Toward a Modern Torah." Spalding greatly overestimates the Wertheim's Bible's influence on Mendelssohn. Many of Spalding's examples of Mendelssohn's use of rational theology in the *Be'ur* derive from Maimonides, not the Wertheim Bible.

Hebrew names

Like Mendelssohn's Pentateuch, the Wertheim Bible employs the Hebrew form of biblical names rather than German forms. For example, it has *Moscheh* for משה, *Mitzrai'im* for מצרים, *Jizhak* for יצחק, etc. But Mendelssohn's and Schmidt's motivations are different. Schmidt transliterates the Hebrew names because of his historical-critical sensibility while Mendelssohn is motivated by his educational desire to lead the reader back to the Hebrew original and because some Midrashim are based on the Hebrew forms of these names.[215]

Christology

Schmidt's translation is much *more* openly anti-Christological than Mendelssohn's. For example, Luther translates *ru'ah elohim* in Genesis 1:2 as *der Geist Gottes* (the spirit of God), interpreting it as referring to the third person of the Trinity. Mendelssohn opposes this Trinitarian interpretation by translating *ru'ah elohim* as *göttliche Geist* (divine spirit). Still, Mendelssohn interprets *ru'ah elohim* as referring to the divine, and his implicit rejection of the Trinitarian interpretation of this verse would have eluded many if not most of his readers. By contrast, Schmidt takes a much more combative anti-trinitarian and, indeed, naturalistic approach by translating *ru'ah elohim* as *heftige Winde* (strong wind). For Schmidt, rather than being a description of the divine, *ru'ah elohim* depicts a meteorological force on earth.[216] As he explains in a note: "Because the vapors would prefer to thin and rise into the sky at the equator rather than at the poles, thus the equilibrium of the flowing material would be destroyed. Hence the wind."[217]

215 See p. 63 of this volume.

216 Schmidt's interpretation apparently follows Spinoza, who in the first chapter of the *Theological-Political Treatise* interpreted the *ru'ah elohim* of Genesis 1:2 as "a very strong wind" (*ventus fortissimus*). See Spinoza, *Opera*, 3:24; *Collected Works*, 2:88. Schmidt was very familiar with Spinoza. In 1744, he published the first German translation of Spinoza's *Ethics*. See Spalding, *Seize the Book*, 185–186.

217 Cited in Sheehan, *The Enlightenment Bible*, 122. For other examples of Schmidt's more explicitly anti-Christological translations, compare his translations of Genesis 3:15 and 49:10 to Mendelssohn's.

Miracles

Schmidt's much more extreme rationalism can be seen by comparing his treatment of miracles with Mendelssohn's. When describing the first of the ten plagues, the plague of blood, the Bible states *vayehafkhu kol hamayim asher baye'or ledam* (Exodus 7:20). Mendelssohn's translation remains close to the Hebrew original: *Da wurden alle Wasser in dem Flusse in Blut verwandelt* (so all the water in the river changed to blood), and he does not comment on this passage, indicating that he takes this miracle literally.[218] By contrast, Schmidt's translation omits any reference to blood: *da denn das Wasser in dem Fluß sich verwandelte und roth wurde* (so the water in the river changed and became red).[219] So Schmidt does not translate the Hebrew word *dam* literally as "blood" but, rather, as "red." In his notes, Schmidt explains this miracle naturalistically: "Whoever has a concept of human and animal blood and understands the intention of this miracle will easily see that through mixture with another material the water became somewhat thick and took on a red color so it looked similar to blood."[220] For Schmidt, Moses and Aaron did not literally turn the Nile into blood; rather, they introduced a foreign substance that mixed with the Nile water, turning it thick and red so that it looked *like blood*. Schmidt's interpretation suggests that miracles performed by prophets are, in fact, clever deceptions.

Anthropomorphism

We have seen that Mendelssohn often seeks to reinterpret the Pentateuch's anthropomorphic descriptions of God. But once again Schmidt's approach is more extreme. While Mendelssohn usually strives to convey the literal meaning of the original Hebrew in his translation while offering a metaphorical interpretation either in parentheses inserted into the translation or in his

[218] See Mendelssohn, *JubA*, 9.1:60. In other writings, Mendelssohn defends the possibility of miracles philosophically and specifically rejects the idea of interpreting the miracle of blood naturalistically. See Mendelssohn, *Moses Mendelssohn: Writings*, 254. For a classic account of Mendelssohn's doctrine of miracles, see Altmann, *Die trostvolle Aufklärung*, 152–163.

[219] Schmidt, *Die göttlichen Schriften*, 288.

[220] Schmidt, *Die göttlichen Schriften*, 270, note 472; 287–288, note 507. In other places discussing the miracle of turning the Nile to blood, Schmidt translates "blood" as *roth wie Blut* (red like blood). See his translations to Exodus 4:9 and 7:17 in ibid., 269, 287.

commentary, Schmidt's rationalism leads him nearly always to radically depart from the plain sense of the Hebrew text.

For example, Mendelssohn translates Genesis 1:3, *vayomer elohim yehi or vayehi or*, quite literally as *Da sprach Got, es werde Licht: so ward Licht* (Then God said let there be light, so there was light).[221] In his commentary Mendelssohn explains that the word *amirah* (speech) in this verse refers either to will or thought, and he gives examples of other places in Scripture where *amirah* has these meanings.[222] Schmidt, however, translates the verse as *Es wurde aber bald auf derselben etwas helle, wie es die göttliche Absicht erforderte* (there was, however, immediately of itself something bright as the divine intention required). In a note, Schmidt observes that in the original Hebrew the first part of the text reads: *Gott sagte, es solte helle werden* (God said it should be bright), but he explains that when the text refers to God *saying* something should happen, this means *actualizing an intention.* So while Mendelssohn is content to translate anthropomorphism literally but explain its rational meaning in his commentary, Schmidt translates according to its rational meaning, only discussing its literal meaning in a note.[223] For Schmidt, what is important is conveying the rational meaning of the biblical text while the literary form is a dispensable shell. For Mendelssohn, however, the literary form of the Hebrew is important, as biblical aesthetics are crucial for conveying the Bible's rationalist metaphysical teachings, as we have seen.[224]

221 Mendelssohn, *JubA*, 9.1:101.

222 Mendelssohn, *JubA*, 15.2:4–5. Mendelssohn is clearly following Maimonides, who wrote that the term *amirah* "is figuratively used for the will in regard to everything that has been created in the *six days of beginning* with reference to which it is said '*He said, He said.*'" See Maimonides, *Guide of the Perplexed*, 1:67, 161.

223 Schmidt, *Die göttlichen Schriften*, 5.

224 See pp. 32–33 of this volume and the next chapter, pp. 96–113. We saw that Mendelssohn deemed smelling too vulgar a description of God and thus softened the anthropomorphism in his translation of Genesis 8:21. But he still sought to remain somewhat close to the Hebrew by including the notion of smelling in his translation: *Der Ewige nam den lieblichen Duft mit Wohl Gefallen an, und sprach zu sich selbst* (The Eternal accepted the sweet smell with favor and said to himself). Schmidt, however, feels no need to preserve the literary character of the Hebrew and removes any reference to smelling, translating the verse as *Dieses ließ sich Gott dergestalt wolgefallen, daß er bey sich beschloß* (This pleased God in such a way that that he decided). See Schmidt, *Die göttlichen Schriften*, 38–39. For an example of a case where Mendelssohn and Schmidt provide similar rationalist interpretations of an anthropomorphic description of God, with Mendelssohn providing the interpretation in a parenthetic gloss and Schmidt translating according to the rationalistic meaning, see their respective translations of Deuteronomy 4:24.

Biblical poetics

The difference between Schmidt's and Mendelssohn's approaches to biblical anthropomorphism is reflected more generally in their attitudes toward biblical poetics. Genesis 4:10 contains one of the Bible's most striking poetic images. After Cain kills Abel and attempts to flee from God, God confronts Cain, asking where Abel is. Cain responds by asking whether he is his brother's keeper. God then responds *meh asitah kol d'mei ahikha tzo'akim eilei min ha'adamah.* Mendelssohn renders the verse literally: *was hastu getahn? Die Stime von deines Bruders Blut schreyet aus der Erde zu mir* (What have you done? The voice of your brother's blood screams out to me from the earth).[225] In his commentary, Mendelssohn explains that this a "poetic expression" conveying God's confronting Cain for what he has done, through the dramatic image of Abel's blood screaming out to God from the earth.[226] Schmidt, however, worries that the imagery of the passage risks confusing the reader so translates the verse as follows: *was hast du gethan? das vergossene Blut deines Bruders ist Zeugnisses genug wider dich, und dieses erfordert eine ernstliche Strafe* (What have you done? Your brother's spilled blood is sufficient testimony against you and demands a serious punishment).[227] In case this translation did not render the meaning of the verse sufficiently obvious, in his note Schmidt observes that the Hebrew literally states *das Blut deines Bruders rufet mich an* (Your brother's blood calls to me) and provides the following explanation: "spilled blood is a sign of murder and so a testimony against Cain. For we call 'testimony' (*Zeugniß*) a statement through which a truth is confirmed. If the judge has evidence and proof that a crime has been committed, he is required to punish."[228] Schmidt's note goes on, but I will spare the reader.

In sum, while both Mendelssohn and Schmidt were religious rationalists, their approaches were not identical. Both sought to distinguish the meaning of the Old Testament from Christological interpretations and read the Bible as presenting accurate metaphysical descriptions of God. But while Mendelssohn espoused a moderate enlightened religiosity that allowed for biblical miracles, Schmidt presented a radical enlightened religiosity that followed Spinoza in denying them. Similarly, while Mendelssohn's religious

225 Mendelssohn, *JubA*, 9.1:1
226 Mendelssohn, *JubA*, 15.2:43.
227 Schmidt, *Die göttlichen Schriften*, 20.
228 Ibid., 21–22, note 43.

rationalism preserved an important place for aesthetics and literary style, for Schmidt aesthetics only confused rational religious truth and so must be excised from Bible translation.

Conclusion

Critics claim that through *Be'ur*, Mendelssohn acts as a native colonial agent who seeks to flatten Judaism to fit German Protestant sensibilities. This judgment is problematic. The *Be'ur* should be understood in the broader context of Mendelssohn's commitment to national cultural renewal through translation. For Mendelssohn, translation is *possible* because all languages are grounded in a universal grammar, and is *valuable* because language encodes distinct cultural perspectives. Mendelssohn was well aware of the obstacles to translation. But he knew that while perfect translation was impossible, translating was essential for the betterment of humanity.

Mendelssohn's work on the Bible can be understood as a project of cultural renewal. Through translation, he sought to foster Jewish national pride, which he anchored in a commitment to universal moral and religious truth, historical truths about the Jewish nation, and appreciation for the Hebrew language. Mendelssohn's Bible translation was a way of nurturing a deeper attachment to Judaism and halakhic practice by presenting a more refined understanding of the Bible's theological teachings, admiration for its aesthetic qualities, adherence to the Masoretic text, and respect for rabbinic teachings. At the same time, he sought to promote German national identity, which he interpreted as developing the German language and a cosmopolitanism that synthesized the best expressions of world thought. For Mendelssohn, translating great works of foreign literature into German including the Bible, would help renew German national culture. Of course, there were already several Christian translations of the Bible into German. But Mendelssohn thought that enlightened Christians could benefit from a Jewish Bible translation into German for several reasons: Jews' excellent knowledge of Hebrew; their understanding the Hebrew Bible independently of the New Testament; their drawing on midrashic interpretations that illuminated the Bible's literary character; and their using the lived practice of Jews to illuminate biblical teachings. By showing the organic connection between Midrash, the lived practices of contemporary Jews and the Bible, Mendelssohn countered the Protestant claim that rabbinic Judaism was utterly foreign to the Old Testament and affirmed the Jewish contribution to the German nation.

Mendelssohn's commitment to Bible translation was not, however, just about cultural translation and national pride. It was also about internal Jewish reformation to which I now turn.

2
Biblical Education and the Power of Conversation

In 1907, the artist Jacob Plessner was commissioned to create a life-sized statue of Mendelssohn. The statue was to be placed outside the Jewish Boys School in Berlin on *Große Hamburger Straße*, not far from Mendelssohn's grave. Due to a shortage of funds the commission was halted, but eventually Plessner secured sufficient funds to produce several bronze busts. One was placed in the auditorium of the school in Berlin, and another was sent to the recently opened library at Hebrew Union College in Cincinnati. The busts portrayed Mendelssohn teaching while holding a book.[1]

Mendelssohn was deeply concerned with education. He encouraged David Friedländer to establish the first modern Jewish school in Europe, the *Jüdische Freischule* (Jewish Free School), which opened in 1781.[2] Mendelssohn took an active role in his children's education, especially his son Joseph. His 1785 *Morning Hours* (*Morgenstunden*) originated in early morning lessons that Mendelssohn gave to Joseph and two other young men, and Mendelssohn included dialogues with his students in the text of the *Morning Hours*.[3] In the

[1] See Figure 1.

[2] There is a large secondary literature on the *Jüdische Freischule*. Important works include: Eliav, *Jewish Education in Germany*, 71–79; Feiner, "Educational Agendas and Social Ideals"; and the sources gathered in Lohmann (ed.), *Chevrat Chinuch Nearim: Die jüdische Freischule in Berlin*. The exact nature of Mendelssohn's involvement in the establishment of the *Freischule* is much debated. For a recent summary and contribution to the debate, see Behm, "Moses Mendelssohns Beziehungen."

[3] Along with Joseph, Mendelssohn taught his son-in-law Simon Veit (married to his eldest daughter Brendel), and Bernhard Wessely, the nephew of Mendelssohn's collaborator on the *Be'ur*, Naphtali Herz Wessely. See Altmann, *Moses Mendelssohn*, 643. Dialogues with his students appear in Chapters 4 and 16 of the *Morning Hours*. The Leo Baeck Institute in New York houses a document containing philosophical aphorisms written by Joseph with corrections in Mendelssohn's own hand. See *Aufsätze und Arbeiten von Joseph Mendelssohn*, AR10327. Since the nineteenth century, many books have appeared presenting Mendelssohn as a role model for children. These include: Schmidt, *Moses Mendelssohn: Ein Lebensbild*; Herzberg, *Moses Mendelssohn: Ein Lebensbild für die Israelitische Jugend*; Isaacs, *Step by Step: a Story of the Early Days of Moses Mendelssohn*; Pinto, *The Story of Moses Mendelssohn: A Biography for Young People*; and Behrens, *Der kleine Mausche aus Dessau*.

The Jewish Reformation. Michah Gottlieb, Oxford University Press (2021). © Oxford University Press.
DOI: 10.1093/oso/9780199336388.003.0003

introduction to the *Be'ur*, Mendelssohn wrote that he originally composed the translation to teach the Pentateuch to his young sons.[4]

Mendelssohn's traditionalist opponents immediately recognized the educational aims of the *Be'ur* and worried. Rabbi Ezekiel Landau was concerned that the *Be'ur* would lead Yiddish-speaking Jews to engage with German literature and neglect Torah study.[5] Later writers found support for Landau's concern in Mendelssohn's private correspondence. They regularly cited Mendelssohn's 1779 letter to August Hennings in which he called the *Be'ur* "the first step toward culture (*Cultur*) from which my nation, alas, is so estranged that one is almost ready to despair of the possibility of improvement."[6]

Critics saw evidence of Mendelssohn's nefarious intentions in formal features of the *Be'ur.* That Mendelssohn's true purpose was to teach German to traditionally educated Yiddish readers and eliminate the use of Yiddish seemed clear from the fact that the *Be'ur* contained an elegant, High German translation of the Pentateuch in Hebrew characters above a learned Hebrew commentary.[7] Critics regularly adduced as evidence of Mendelssohn's

[4] Mendelssohn, *JubA,* 14:243. Also see Mendelssohn, *JubA,* 19:251–252 (Letter to Avigdor Levi, May 25, 1779).

[5] See p. 17 of this volume.

[6] See Mendelssohn, *JubA,* 12.2:149; *Moses Mendelssohn: Writings,* 188. See Kayserling, *Moses Mendelssohn,* 284–285. Mendelssohn often criticized German Jews' moral, cultural, and religious shortcomings. In his response to Lavater, Mendelssohn wrote, "I shall not deny that I have observed in my religion human additions and abuses that, alas, tarnish its luster." See Mendelssohn, *JubA,* 7:9. In his preface to the German translation of Menasseh ben Israel's *Vindiciae Judaeorum* he writes of "our lack of culture (*Cultur*)" and referring to Jews' intolerance toward other Jews observes that "Revenge seeks an object, and if it can do no harm to others, then it gnaws at its own flesh." See Mendelssohn, *JubA,* 8:6, 25; *Moses Mendelssohn: Writings,* 44, 52. Addressing August Friedrich Cranz's claim that Judaism was a religion of coercion and exclusion, Mendelssohn conceded that Cranz's "objection cuts me to the heart" since its description of Judaism "is taken to be correct even by many of my coreligionists." See Mendelssohn, *JubA,* 8:153. According to his confidant Sophie Becker, towards the end of his life Mendelssohn complained to her: "True Judaism is no longer found anywhere. Fanaticism and superstition exist among us to a most abhorrent degree. Were my nation not so stupid, it would stone me on account of my *Jerusalem,* but people do not understand me." See Altmann, *Moses Mendelssohn,* 722.

[7] Zunz wrote that through the *Be'ur* Mendelssohn sought to "deal a deathblow to Yiddish." Meyer Kayserling and Franz Muncker claimed that Mendelssohn's primary aim was to teach Yiddish-speaking Jews German. Israel Zinberg ascribed both motives to Mendelssohn. Peretz Smolenskin wrote that Mendelssohn used the Holy Scriptures "as a passage to the German language" and that he "set aside the Talmud and desecrated the honor of the Torah, making her a despised handmaiden to teach by means of it the German language." See Weinberg, "Language Questions," 198–202. Wessely also claims that an aim of the *Be'ur* was to teach Jews proper German. See Wessely, *Divrei Shalom,* 23. Weinberg argues forcefully against these views, claiming that Mendelssohn neither intended the *Be'ur* to be a "textbook for German" nor to "uproot Judeo-German." He notes that German Jews began learning German well before Mendelssohn published the *Be'ur,* and that most of Mendelssohn's intended readers were Jews who had learned German as youths. Weinberg takes the fact that the German of the *Be'ur* is of a high level incomprehensible to most Yiddish readers as evidence that the work was *not* directed to Yiddish readers, and he rejects the idea that Mendelssohn

hostility to Yiddish a 1782 letter to Ernst Ferdinand Klein in which Mendelssohn wrote, "I am afraid that this jargon (*dieser Jargon*) has contributed not a little to the immorality of the common people and I expect some very good results from the use of the pure German way of speech (*reinen deutschen Mundsart*) that has been coming into vogue among my brethren for some time."[8]

In this chapter I will argue that critics are correct in claiming that Mendelssohn sought a reformation of Jewish education through the *Be'ur* that would help Jews acquire *Kultur*. But for Mendelssohn *Kultur* is not identical with German culture but, rather, is a technical term that refers to a central component of human flourishing. The educational reformation that Mendelssohn sought did not entail *abandoning* Torah study but, rather, *reimagining* it by rethinking the place of the Bible relative to the Talmud in the Jewish curriculum and stressing the value of oral instruction and dialogue so that German Jews could fully actualize themselves.

Dialogue is a thread running through Mendelssohn's life and thought from his earliest days to his death. His teacher Rabbi David Fränkel instructed students in Talmud using a "Socratic method of instruction."[9] Mendelssohn saw dialogue as a means to discover truth as epitomized by his friendship with Lessing. Mendelssohn titled his first German philosophical work, which was based on conversations with Lessing, the *Philosophical Dialogues* (*Philosophische Gespräche*), and he used dialogue as a literary device throughout his life, most famously in his 1767 *Phaedon.*[10] Dialogue is also an important theme in Mendelssohn's Hebrew writings. He interpreted the Book of Ecclesiastes as a dialogue concerning the immortality of the soul and wrote many of his Hebrew works as commentaries in which he put himself into dialogue not only with the text but also with the history of

had a negative attitude toward Yiddish since Mendelssohn continued writing letters in Yiddish even after completing the *Be'ur.* See Weinberg, "Language Questions," 203–209, 236–242. Through a careful study of the subscribers to the *Be'ur*, Lowenstein concludes that readership of *Be'ur* was not poor Jews, but wealthy ones whom he calls the "enlightened elite." See Lowenstein, "The Readership of Mendelssohn's Bible Translation," 181–186, 194; Weinberg, "A Word List," 279.

[8] See Mendelssohn, *JubA*, 7:279, cited in Altmann, *Moses Mendelssohn*, 499.

[9] Abraham Bri Bara who also studied under Fränkel recounted this. See Altmann, "Moses Mendelssohns Kindheit," 265–266.

[10] On Mendelssohn's conversations with Lessing as the basis for the *Philosophical Dialogues,* see Altmann, *Moses Mendelssohn,* 37. Dialogues also appear in Mendelssohn's 1783 *Jerusalem* and in his 1785 *Morning Hours.* Mendelssohn also used the dialogical literary device of a correspondence in his 1755 *On Sentiments.*

Jewish exegesis.[11] Mendelssohn translated texts into German and Hebrew, which, as we have seen, was a way of putting languages into dialogue with one another.[12]

Mendelssohn's critique of Jewish education

Mendelssohn's first biographer, Isaac Euchel, caustically described Mendelssohn's early childhood education: "Moses was brought to the school and learned in the way of all the youths of our nation who chirp laws of divorce and marriage, injured and injurer, and many such matters far beyond their understanding before they know how to read a single verse of the Bible properly."[13] Euchel here registers two complaints with Mendelssohn's early Jewish education. First, Talmud study centered on matters that Jewish boys had no personal experience with, such as marriage and divorce law, which inevitably created a gap between learning and life. Second, Jewish boys were taught these laws without having a proper understanding of how to read the Bible correctly, leading to a faulty understanding of the laws.

According to Euchel, Mendelssohn soon realized that the Talmud based its legal rulings on the Bible and that it was impossible to properly understand the Bible without grammatical knowledge of Hebrew. Euchel reports that the young Mendelssohn therefore "read the books of the Bible with great assiduity," learning the entire Hebrew Bible by heart. According to Euchel, Mendelssohn even accustomed himself to writing in Hebrew and by age ten was composing original Hebrew poetry.[14]

[11] In addition to the *Be'ur* commentary on the Pentateuch, Mendelssohn published a commentary on the Book of Ecclesiastes in 1770 and a commentary on Maimonides's *Treatise on Logic* in 1761.

[12] See pp. 26–29 of this volume.

[13] See Euchel, *Toldot Rabbenu*, 6. Altmann accepts Euchel's judgment, writing: "The correctness of this statement need not be doubted. The teaching method prevalent in the *Heder* or *Beth Hamidrash* aimed at familiarity with the Talmud and neglected the Bible and its classical commentaries." See Altmann, *Moses Mendelssohn,* 10. Also see Altmann's article, "Moses Mendelssohns Kindheit in Dessau," where he writes, "instruction in Bible and its classical commentaries was neglected and all emphasis was placed on subtle discussions (*pilpul*)." See Altmann, "Moses Mendelssohns Kindheit," 257. The charge that Ashkenazi Jewish boys learned to "chirp" (*metzaftzefim*) talmudic laws that they did not understand from a young age is also found in the introduction to Yekutiel Blitz's 1678 Yiddish translation of the Bible. See Baumgarten, *Introduction to Old Yiddish Literature,* 126.

[14] See Euchel, *Toldot Rabbenu,* 6. Euchel's reporting Mendelssohn's astonishing memory and facility with Hebrew from such a young age naturally invites skepticism. While Euchel's claim that Mendelssohn knew the entire Hebrew Bible by heart may be exaggerated, there is no reason to doubt his intense study of the Bible and composing original Hebrew verse. In a handwritten inscription to his copy of a book of responsa by the fourteenth-century Spanish scholar Rabbi Isaac Ben Sheshet (Ribash), the twelve-year old Mendelssohn already displayed remarkable facility not only for writing in flowery rabbinic style but also for deploying biblical idioms in creative ways. Altmann reproduces

That concern over contemporary Jewish education was one of the driving forces animating the *Be'ur* project is evident from a short essay by Naphtali Herz Wessely that Mendelssohn published as a preface to the *Be'ur.*[15] Lamenting the contemporary state of Jewish education, Wessely noted that parents would commonly send their four- or five-year-old sons to teachers in order to learn the Pentateuch. The teachers would instruct the young boys for a short time before informing the parents "your sons have already succeeded learning Mishnah and Talmud and it would not be right for them to study the Pentateuch any longer."[16] According to Wessely, while even young boys were not being taught much Pentateuch, this was all the more true of older boys whose education was devoted almost exclusively to Talmud study. An important reason for this emphasis on Talmud study was that males accrued social prestige according to their ability to master talmudic dialectics (*pilpul*) while knowledge of the Bible was not highly regarded. This had social repercussions as proficient Talmudists had better chances of marrying into the most prominent, wealthiest families and be financially supported.[17] Mendelssohn and Wessely recognized that altering educational priorities within the Jewish community would change what was valued in a husband and be a powerful catalyst for change within the German Jewish community.

Mendelssohn frequently criticized *pilpul.* In a 1769 letter to Rabbi Jacob Emden he wrote that "my soul abhors the *pilpulim* and corruption of

Mendelssohn's inscription, which reads: "Here in Berlin, the second day of the consolatory month of Av [*Ba Menahem*] [5]502. The insignificant Moses son of my lord my father, the worthy Rabbi Mendel Sofer, may his Rock and Redeemer protect him. Written in the wondrous and extraordinary house of the Torah and rabbinical scholar, the Great Gaon, Crown of our Head (Lamentations 5:16), Diadem of Beauty (Ezekiel 28:12), Holy Wreath (Exodus 29), Lover of Israel, Adornment of the Generation, Pillar of the Exile, our honored teacher, David, may his lamp burn bright, author of commentary and glosses on the Jerusalem Talmud, may God extend his days and years with all who find refuge in his shade, until [the redeemer] comes to Shiloh (Genesis 49:10) The head of the Court and head of the Academy, here in the holy community Dessau, may Zion and Jerusalem be rebuilt, in the year, 'And David was successful in all of his paths' (*v'david maSkil Bekhol deRakhav)* [I Samuel 18:14] according to the minor enumeration. This book belongs to me." See Altmann, "Moses Mendelssohns Kindheit," 267.

15 Wessely's essay is called "Mehalel Re'a" ("Praise of a Friend").

16 Wessely, "Mehalel Re'a," 9. See Katz, *Tradition and Crisis,* 162–163; Fishman, *The History of Jewish Education,* 22–24, 100–103.

17 See Katz, "Marriage and Sexual Life," 32–33. This dynamic is colorfully depicted in Salomon Maimon's 1793 autobiography. See Maimon, *The Autobiography of Salomon Maimon,* esp. pp. 24–40. According to Wessely, the reason that teachers introduced students so early to Talmud study was that the parents paid them directly. The teachers therefore sought to flatter the parents by claiming that their sons were so intelligent and their teaching methods so effective that the sons were ready to study Talmud right away. The problem was that students understood little of what they were being taught and so ended up learning little of value. See Wessely, "Mehalel Re'a," 9.

the many individuals, wise in their own eyes, who sink in great waters."[18] And in a letter to Herz Homberg, who tutored his son Joseph, Mendelssohn recalled that "a very special kind of education is required to find this exercise of the mind (*pilpul*) to one's taste. And though both of us received this education, we nevertheless agreed that we would prefer to see Joseph remain somewhat dull rather than be trained in such a sterile kind of acumen (*unfruchtbar Art des Witzes*)."[19]

Mendelssohn's opposition to *pilpul* can be understood within the context of an internal Jewish debate going back centuries. Scholars have noted that the centrality of Talmud study and relative marginalization of Bible study for males in Polish and German lands date to the fourteenth century.[20] Mordechai Breuer has noted that until the eleventh century both Ashkenazic and Sephardic communities emphasized studying Talmudic passages with a view to their practical applications. But gradually there emerged a method or, more accurately, methods of study that stressed abstract analysis over practical application.[21] *Pilpul* became widespread in Polish and German yeshivot from the sixteenth through eighteenth centuries, though it aroused opposition.[22]

The controversy over *pilpul* within the Jewish community was analogous to controversies over scholasticism within German Protestantism. In the seventeenth century there developed a form of Protestant scholasticism meant to solidify and confirm Lutheran principles.[23] This scholasticism provoked a

[18] Mendelssohn, *JubA*, 19:131 (Letter to Jacob Emden, October 27, 1769).

[19] This letter is cited in Altmann, "Moses Mendelssohns Kindheit," 257–258; *Moses Mendelssohn*, 15. But note that in his 1763 Commentary on Maimonides's *Treatise on Logic*, Mendelssohn asserted that studying logic is valuable because of it is "highly beneficial for the study of Talmud, Rashi, Tosafot, and collegial *pilpul* (*uvepilpul haverim*)." See Mendelssohn, *JubA*, 14:30; Mendelssohn, *Moses Mendelssohn's Hebrew Writings*, 73.

[20] See Katz, *Tradition and Crisis*, 162–167; Breuer, *Asif*, 237–259; idem, *The Tents of Torah*, 116–128; Talmage, *Apples of Gold*, 151–171; Fishman, *The History of Jewish Education in Central Europe*, 94–109.

[21] Breuer, *The Tents of Torah*, 84. Jacob Katz notes that in Ashkenazic Jewish communities from the sixteenth to eighteenth centuries, the yeshiva curriculum was divided into two parts, one theoretical and one practical. The theoretical part involved studying the Talmud in order to familiarize students with the talmudic form of argument, which Katz notes led to "a tendency to over intellectualize and indulge in logic games without defined purposes." Learning this theoretical method of Talmud study was thought to be an important prerequisite for the second, practical part of the curriculum, which was focused on the study of practical law through immersion in Jewish legal codes, especially the *Shulhan Arukh*. See Katz, *Tradition and Crisis*, 166–167.

[22] Many rabbis debated the propriety of *pilpul*, distinguishing between "*pilpul* of truth" (*pilpul shel emet*) and "vain *pilpul*" (*pilpul shel hevel*). Mordechai Breuer has shown that the meaning of *pilpul* was very fluid with one person's "*pilpul* of truth" often being another's "vain *pilpul*." See Breuer, *The Tents of Torah*, 168–215. For a subtle discussion of various forms of *pilpul* and debates about *pilpul*, see Reiner, "Changes in the Polish and German Yeshivot."

[23] Sorkin, *Religious Enlightenment*, 117; Beck, *Early German Philosophy*, 103–104.

reaction from two Protestant groups, the Pietists and the Neologists. While the Pietists stressed simple faith, intense religious experience, and moral action as the core of Christianity, the Neologists stressed simple rational theology and morality. Both rejected what they considered the complex, overly subtle theological arguments characteristic of Protestant scholasticism.[24] Mendelssohn's close friend Friedrich Nicolai explicitly connected *pilpul* with Protestant scholasticism in his annotations on Mendelssohn's correspondence with Lessing, writing that "He [Mendelssohn] learned in his early youth the art of scholastic talmudic disputation (*talmudisch-scholastische Art disputieren*) and he acquired facility in it. This deplorable training increases the mind's subtlety but not sustained thinking, a deficiency that may be said to attach also to many a German speculative philosopher who indicates only endless and empty arguing."[25]

Mendelssohn's critique of *pilpul* in no way implied a rejection of Talmud study, much less of talmudic authority. Mendelssohn's problem with *pilpul* was that he regarded it as a theoretical pursuit that analyzed the Talmud through overly subtle distinctions that aimed to silence criticism and separated thought from life. Rather than seeking a more accurate understanding of the Talmudic text or a law, the purpose of *pilpul* was to show off one's brilliance. For Mendelssohn, the Talmud was properly understood as a dialogue that aimed to inculcate living knowledge of the Bible and halakhic practice.[26]

A new school for a new generation

The original aim of the *Jüdische Freischule* was to supplement the traditional Talmud-based Jewish education by providing general education using modern methods that emphasized cleanliness, school rules, gradated learning, and attention to the unique capacities of individual students.[27] Its curriculum included grammatical knowledge of German, French, and Hebrew, alongside mathematics, geography, history, natural science, writing, drawing, and bookkeeping.[28] It also included subjects of universal

[24] Beck, *Early German Philosophy,* 157; Sorkin, *The Religious Enlightenment,* 158–163.

[25] This passage is cited in Altmann, "Moses Mendelssohns Kindheit," 258; *Moses Mendelssohn,* 15.

[26] This is not the place to assess whether Mendelssohn's attack on *pilpul* was justified. For a recent defense of *pilpul,* see Boyarin, "Pilpul: The Logic of Commentary."

[27] Eliav, *Jewish Education in Germany,* 72

[28] See Eliav, *Jewish Education in Germany,* 72, citing *Hame'assef,* 1784, p. 44. Wessely writes that the school met in the afternoon and the curriculum included Bible in German translation, Hebrew

religious import such as ethical teachings and principles of religion. Mendelssohn contributed selections to the school's first reader, the *Reader for Jewish Children* (*Lesebuch für jüdische Kinder*), which presented such teachings through translations from the Bible, Talmud, and other Jewish texts.[29] While the *Freischule* originally focused on general studies, it later expanded to include Jewish subjects.[30] Wessely presented an influential vision of the *Freischule*'s educational philosophy in his 1782 pamphlet *Divrei Shalom Ve'emet* (*Words of Peace and Truth*).

For Wessely, Jewish education should comprise a dual curriculum divided between what he called *torat ha'adam* (humanistic teaching) and *torat hashem* (divine teaching). *Torat ha'adam* was general knowledge accessible through reason alone. Wessely explained that through this knowledge a person actualized himself as a human being and learned to live in the world. *Torat ha'adam* included grammatical knowledge of vernacular languages, history, geography, politics, mathematics, natural science, etiquette, and rhetoric as well as ethics and rational universal principles of religion. By contrast, *torat hashem* (divine teaching) focused on knowledge binding on Jews alone, namely, biblical laws revealed to Moses (the Written Torah) and their divinely revealed interpretations (the Oral Torah). Wessely noted that the teachings of *torat hashem* were above reason and so would be unknown were it not for revelation. While laws in *torat hashem* were only binding on Jews, their purpose was to serve humanity. As such, *torat hashem* presupposed knowledge of *torat ha'adam*, which took precedence.[31] For, Wessely noted, without knowledge of *torat ha'adam* a Jew would not know how to act in the world, and "his fellowship would be burdensome to other people."[32]

grammar, German and French reading and writing, arithmetic, and geography. In the morning students studied Talmud in traditional *hadarim*. See Wessely, *Rav Tuv*, 45.

[29] See Friedländer, *Lesebuch*; Shavit, "From Friedländer's Lesebuch"; idem, "Moses Mendelssohn and David Friedländer Publish." Mendelssohn's contributions included a German rendering of Maimonides's Thirteen Principles of Judaism, the Decalogue, medieval fables by Berakhyah ben Natronai Hanakdan with morals such as "whoever persecutes others fears their own shadow," talmudic stories under the title *Moral Tales from the Talmud*, and Judah Halevi's medieval Hebrew poem "Lord, the Entirety of My Desire Lies before Thee." Mendelssohn also contributed a text called "Prayer of a Philosopher."

[30] Eliav, *Jewish Education in Germany*, 73–74.

[31] Wessely, *Divrei Shalom Ve'emet*, 1–3, 8, 16; *JMW*, 74–75.

[32] Wessely, *Divrei Shalom Ve'emet*, 3–4; *JMW*, 74–75. In claiming that *torat ha'adam* took precedence over *torat hashem*, Wessely cited two rabbinic statements. The first was the statement *derekh eretz kadmah latorah* (the way of the world preceded the Torah), found in *Leviticus Rabba* 9:3. The second statement was "a ritually unclean carcass is worthier than a scholar without knowledge" (*Leviticus Rabba* 1:15), which Wessely glossed to mean that an unclean carcass is worthier than a Jewish scholar who has knowledge of *torat hashem* without knowledge of *torat ha'adam*. Wessely also

Wessely recommended a scaffolded method of instruction in Jewish texts. Students should begin by studying Hebrew grammatically.[33] He rejected learning Talmud from a young age and the marginalization of Bible study, recommending that after studying Hebrew young boys be taught the Pentateuch using Mendelssohn's translation. He also recommended that boys be given a theoretical understanding of Judaism by being instructed in principles of Jewish faith and ethics through catechisms.[34] Wessely advised that attention be paid to individual students' different capacities, citing Proverbs 22:6, "educate a youth according to his path," which he glossed to mean "according to his qualities and capacities" as "the disposition of people and the powers of their soul are not the same," and he lamented that German Jews had abandoned this biblical teaching.[35] The Mishnah and Talmud, which were extremely complex, should only be taught to advanced students capable of understanding it while those not capable of understanding it should focus on the Bible, ethics, and professional training. As Wessely put it, "we were not all created to be talmudic masters."[36]

Wessely's attempts to reform Jewish education provoked a strong rabbinic reaction. R. David Tevele of Lissa called Wessely an "evil man" who "lacks an understanding of the profundities of the Talmud." Charging that Wessely's efforts were motivated by the Emperor Joseph II's desire to create compulsory general education for Jews in Austria, Tevele labelled Wessely a "sycophant."[37] Similar critiques of Wessely were expressed by the Chief Rabbi

claimed that *torat ha'adam* must precede *torat hashem* because knowledge of secular matters like ancient history, science, and geography elucidated important aspects of the Torah. See Wessely, *Divrei Shalom Ve'emet*, 17–18.

[33] Wessely recommended first teaching students how to read Hebrew letters and words out loud and only teaching grammar when they became capable of understanding it. See Wessely, *Rav Tuv*, 27–28.

[34] Wessely, *Divrei Shalom Ve'emet*, 23–30, 33–34; *Rav Tuv*, 28–29.

[35] See Wessely, *Divrei Shalom Ve'emet*, 1; *JMW*, 74.

[36] Wessely, *Divrei Shalom Ve'emet*, 33–34. In his treatise *Rav Tuv Leveit Israel*, which Wessely composed in response to criticisms of *Divrei Shalom Ve'emet*, he presented a model curriculum. Wessely recommended that before age five boys be taught to read Hebrew accurately. At age five, boys should be brought to school to learn the Pentateuch using a proper, elegant translation like Mendelssohn's that conveyed *peshat*. At age six, students should be taught Hebrew grammar, which would then be applied to reading the Pentateuch in Hebrew. At age seven, boys should be taught principles of Judaism and Jewish laws using catechisms in both Hebrew and the vernacular. At age seven or eight, capable students should be taught Mishnah. After several years of Mishnah study, Talmud should be introduced to capable students, with these boys becoming proficient in Talmud study by age fourteen or fifteen. Alongside the Jewish curriculum, Wessely outlined a general curriculum, which included reading and writing the vernacular, geography, and travelogues. At age seven or eight students should begin to learn principles of ethics and universal religion, and at age ten or eleven they should be taught arithmetic, geometry, and natural science. See Wessely, *Rav Tuv*, 27–36.

[37] See the excerpts from Tevele's letter in *JMW*, 78–80. Tevele himself did not oppose Joseph II's efforts to introduce German into the Jewish curriculum and even accepted teaching sciences as long

of Prague, R. Ezekiel Landau, and the Chief Rabbi of Frankfurt, R. Pinhas Horowitz. Wessely was threatened with excommunication.[38]

Mendelssohn rallied to Wessely's defense. He recommended Wessely's treatise to the leaders of the Italian Jewish community in Trieste, and in a letter to Joseph Galico, the secretary of the community, Mendelssohn called Wessely a man who "walks along a pure path" and seeks to "strengthen weak arms and rouse the sleeping from their lazy slumber."[39] Mendelssohn even enlisted seven prominent Berlin Jews to demand that Polish Jewish leaders pressure their rabbis to withdraw a threat of excommunication and publicly apologize to Wessely or else appeal would be made to the Polish authorities to intervene.[40]

Why didn't Mendelssohn teach his daughters his Bible translation?

Describing the origin of his Pentateuch translation in *OL,* Mendelssohn wrote:

> When the Eternal graced me with *male sons* (*yeladim banim zekharim*) and the time came to teach them Torah and instruct them in the words of the living God, as Scripture bids us, I began to translate the five books of the Torah into the polished, proper German that is customary in our times for the benefit of these young children. (emphasis mine).[41]

It is striking that Mendelssohn goes out of his way to write that he composed his Pentateuch translation for his "male sons." This is particularly curious when considering that from the seventeenth century, while German

as they were taught as "an adornment" to Torah knowledge. For Tevele, Wessely's mistake was that he proposed subordinating Jewish education to general education. For his part, Wessely had mentioned Joseph II's educational reforms in *Divrei Shalom Ve'emet*, writing that Joseph had "commanded that ethical treatises be composed according to philosophical views that agree with reason" for Jewish students and that Jewish students be taught German. See ibid., 19, 31; *JMW,* 77. On secular authorities' pressure to impose general education on Jews in the early 1780s, see Altmann, *Moses Mendelssohn,* 474–476; Eliav, *Jewish Education in Germany,* 39.

[38] A translation of Rabbi Landau's famous sermon denouncing Wessely can be found in Saperstein, *Jewish Preaching,* 361–373. For an excellent survey of the controversy over Wessely's treatise, see Feiner, *The Jewish Enlightenment,* 87–104.

[39] See Mendelssohn, *JubA,* 19:282; Altmann, *Moses Mendelssohn,* 477–478.

[40] See Feiner, *Moses Mendelssohn,* 158.

[41] See Mendelssohn, *JubA,* 14:243; *Moses Mendelssohn: Writings,* 197.

Jewish education for boys focused on the Talmud, a central component of girls' education was studying the Yiddish *Tsenerene* Bible.[42] The *Tsenerene* was not a translation, but a paraphrase incorporating many midrashic and aggadic stories. As we have seen, a primary goal of the *Be'ur* was to render the Pentateuch according to its *peshat*. Given the deficiencies that Mendelssohn surely found in the *Tsenerene* Bible, it would have been natural for him to have taught his Pentateuch translation to both his sons *and* daughters.

The idea of teaching females the Bible according to its plain meaning was not new. In 1678 and 1679, Yekutiel Blitz and Yosel Witzenhausen published Yiddish Bible translations in Amsterdam. Mendelssohn was aware of both these translations, which in many respects served as a model for his own.[43] Like Mendelssohn, the Amsterdam Yiddish Bible translators criticized the prevailing emphasis on Talmud study and the lack of attention to the plain meaning of the Bible, while also rejecting overly literal, word-for-word translations.[44] Both translators also expressed concern that Jewish inattention to

[42] Eliav notes that in addition to studying the Bible in Yiddish translation, German Jewish girls were taught how to read prayers and some halakhah. See Eliav, *Jewish Education*, 271. The *Tsenerene*, which was written at the end of the sixteenth century, was originally aimed at both men and women but became popular with women. See Bilik, "Tsene-rene: A Yiddish Literary Success," 99.

[43] Mendelssohn mentions both Amsterdam Yiddish translations in *OL*. He praises the "intention" of the Blitz translation though he criticizes how Blitz executed it, noting that Blitz "neither understood the nature of the holy language nor grasped the depth of its rhetoric. Moreover, whatever he did comprehend, he translated into a most corrupt and deformed language of stammering." Mendelssohn offers no assessment of Witzenhausen's translation. See Mendelssohn, *JubA*, 14:242; *Moses Mendelssohn: Writings*, 195–196. For an overview of these Bibles, see Aptroot, "Yiddish Bibles in Amsterdam." Jean Baumgarten notes that these Bibles "already seemed to anticipate the translations of the Enlightenment and the Haskalah." See Baumgarten and Frakes, *Introduction to Old Yiddish Literature*, 123. Baumgarten argues for two influences on these Yiddish Bibles, Protestant Reformation Bibles and Sephardic Bibles, both of which emphasized plain meaning rather than midrashic interpretation. See ibid., 124. Abigail Gillman has recently presented Mendelssohn's translation project as continuous with that of the Amsterdam Yiddish Bibles, even arguing that the Amsterdam Bibles were *less* traditional than Mendelssohn's *Be'ur.* See Gillman, *A History of German Jewish Bible Translation*, 15–85, esp. 29.

[44] Uri Feibush, the publisher of Blitz's translation, writes that the Blitz translation is according to the "peshat-poshut" (simple *peshat*) and that Blitz arrived at this by following the medieval Jewish *pashtanim* and taking into consideration linguistic usage (*dikduk milah*), literary context (*kishur pesukei haparashah*), Masoretic vowelization (*nikkud*), and accents (*te'amim*). See Blitz, *Torah, Nevi'im, Veketuvim*, title page. The title page of the Witzenhausen translation similarly claims that the translation follows *derekh peshutah* (the *peshat* method), relying on Rashi, Ibn Ezra, David Kimhi, Sa'adya Gaon, Gersonides, and Targum Yonatan, among others. See Witzenhausen, *Torah, Nevi'im, Veketuvim*, title page. In the preface to Witzenhausen's translation, the publisher Joseph Attias criticized the prevailing educational paradigm, which emphasized talmudic *pilpul* at the expense of plain knowledge of the Bible. As Attias put it, "the rebbe teaches a pericope or two of Pentateuch and then moves on to Mishnah and Gemara, with *harifut* and *hilukim* [two technical terms for *pilpul*—M.G.], but the main foundation, the well of living waters, the Written Torah, is neglected." See Witzenhausen, *Torah, Nevi'im, Ketuvim*, 3; http://onthemainline.blogspot.com/search?q=blitz. On Witzenhausen's and Blitz's opposition to overly literal, word-for-word translations, see Aptroot, "In Galkes," 142–143.

peshat exemplified by works like the *Tsenerene* led Gentiles to mock Jews as irrational.[45] But unlike for Mendelssohn, females were regarded as an important audience for their translations. One of the rabbinic approbations for Witzenhausen's translation praises its value for women, writing that "through this pleasant composition, the perfect law came to light, and the truth of Torah in the gates designated for the daughters of Zion, righteous women, peaceful women." An approbation for Blitz's translation praises the publisher for producing a work that "will delight the masses of Israel, the women, the youth, and the maidens."[46]

Given these precedents, two question arise. First, why did Mendelssohn not direct his translation to his daughters? Second, how did he conceive female Jewish education? Let us return to Mendelssohn's aforementioned statement regarding the origin of the *Be'ur*:

> When the Eternal graced me with male sons (*yeladim banim zekharim*) and the time came to teach them (*l'shanenam*) Torah and instruct them in the words of the living God, *as Scripture bids us*, I began to translate the five books of the Torah into the polished, proper German that is customary in our times for the benefit of these young children. (emphasis mine).

In stating that he sought to teach his sons Torah "as Scripture bids us," Mendelssohn is referring to his halakhic obligation. The Talmud states that a father has a duty to teach his sons Torah, but not his daughters, deriving this from Deuteronomy 11:19: "You shall teach your sons (*beneikhem*) to speak of them." The word *beneikhem* can mean "children," but the Talmud interprets it as referring only to sons.[47] Mendelssohn's *Be'ur* translation confirms that he accepts the Talmud's interpretation of the verse. While in other places, he translates the Hebrew word *beneikhem* as *Kinder* (children) or *Nachkommen* (descendants), in Deuteronomy 11:19 he translates it as *Söhne* (sons).[48]

[45] See Witzenhausen, *Torah, Nevi'im, Veketuvim*, 15; Blitz, *Torah, Nevi'im, Ketuvim*, title page; Baumgarten, *Introduction to Old Yiddish Literature*, 124–125.

[46] See Blitz, *Torah, Nevi'im, Ketuvim*, 3; Witzenhausen, *Torah, Nevi'im, Veketuvim*, 10.

[47] *BT*, Kiddushin, 29a–b.

[48] Compare Mendelssohn, *JubA*, 9.2:196 (translation of Deuteronomy 11:19) with Mendelssohn *JubA*, 9.2:110, 184, 394, 234 (translations of Numbers 14:33, Deuteronomy, 6:7; 11:2; 29:21). In speaking of his obligation to teach his sons Torah, it might seem that Mendelssohn is referring to Deuteronomy 6:7, which states *veshinantem l'vanekha*, since the Hebrew word he uses to refer to teaching his sons in *OL* is *l'shanenam* while the word used for teaching in Deuteronomy 11:19 is *v'limadetem*. Despite Mendelssohn's use of *l'shanenam* in *OL*, there is little doubt that in speaking of his obligation to teach his sons Torah Mendelssohn is referring to Deuteronomy 11:19, since the Talmud derives the halakhic obligation to teach one's sons Torah from Deuteronomy 11:19

What Torah should a father teach his sons? Mendelssohn's son Mendel was five when Mendelssohn began teaching him his German translation of the Pentateuch, and when Joseph turned five Mendelssohn began teaching him the Pentateuch as well.[49] In emphasizing that he was fulfilling his halakhic duty to teach his sons Torah by teaching them the Pentateuch, Mendelssohn was obliquely criticizing the prevailing Ashkenazic practice of teaching boys Talmud from a young age, which he saw as deviating from rabbinic tradition. For the Mishnah stated that one should begin teaching one's son the Bible at age five, while instruction in Mishnah should only begin at age ten and instruction in Talmud only at age fifteen.[50]

In light of his understanding that he was under no halakhic obligation to teach his daughters Torah, what Jewish education did Mendelssohn provide them?[51] Apparently very little. We have no precise information about this, but his daughters were likely taught little more than how to read and write Hebrew characters, mostly in order to recite prayers.[52] This by no means implies that Mendelssohn's daughters received no education. They received an excellent general education similar to that of the *Bildungsbürger*.[53]

and Mendelssohn's translation of this verse shows that he accepts this interpretation. By contrast, Mendelssohn translates Deuteronomy 6:7 as *Du sollst sie deinen* ***Kinder*** *einschärfen* (you must inculcate in your **children**).

[49] See Altmann, *Moses Mendelssohn*, 369. In a letter to Avigdor Levi, Mendelssohn made explicit that he had composed the *Be'ur* translation for Mendel and Joseph. See Mendelssohn, *JubA*, 19:251–252 (Letter to Avigdor Levi, May, 25, 1779).

[50] See *Pirkei Avot*, 5:24. Prominent sixteenth- and seventeenth-century Ashkenazic rabbis such R. Judah Loewe of Prague (Maharal), R. Jacob Horowitz, and R. Yair Hayim Bakhrakh had previously complained that German Jewish educational practices deviated from the Mishnah's prescriptions. See Sorkin, *The Transformation of German-Jewry*, 47–51. One also finds this criticism in the seventeenth-century Amsterdam Yiddish Bibles. See Aptroot, *Bible Translation as Cultural Reform*, 355; idem, "In Galkhes," 142–143.

[51] In his legal code the *Shulhan Arukh*, R. Joseph Karo follows Maimonides in codifying the view that not only is a father not obligated to teach his daughter Torah, but the rabbis also ruled that he should not do so, ideally not even teaching her Bible. See Karo, *Shulhan Arukh*, Yoreh De'ah, 246:6; Maimonides, *Mishneh Torah*, "Laws of Torah Study," 1:13. The authoritative Jewish legal decisor (and Mendelssohn's ancestor) R. Moses Isserles ruled that females were obligated to study the halakhic duties incumbent on them, though Isserles did not state whether a parent was obligated to teach their daughters these obligations. See Isserles's glosses on Karo, *Shulhan Arukh*, Yoreh De'ah 246:6.

[52] That Dorothea knew how to write in Hebrew characters is clear from the fact that in the 1790s she participated in the correspondence between Henriette Herz and the Humboldt brothers that was conducted in German written in Hebrew characters. But it is not clear whether or not she could understand Hebrew Her friend Henriette Herz complained that Jewish girls had to learn how to "pray in Hebrew without understanding what they were saying." See Herz, *Henriette Herz in Errinerungen, Briefen, und Zeugnissen*, 11, 207, cited in Behm, *Moses Mendelssohn und die Transformation*, 172. It is unclear whether Mendelssohn's daughters studied practical halakhah. They may have learned it mimetically from their mother.

[53] On the *Bildungsbürger*, see pp. 12–13 of this volume.

Mendelssohn hired private tutors who taught his daughters ethics, German, "foreign languages" (probably French, English, and Italian), literature, music (piano), and drawing.[54] Mendelssohn's emphasis on his daughters learning these subjects reflected the *Bildungsbürger* assumption that females had emotional, intuitive natures and a strong disposition for goodness that should be cultivated. The aim of female education was to prepare girls to be housewives capable of being intellectual companions of their husbands, conversing intelligently with guests, and educating their children.[55] Women were not, however, to be educated for careers outside the home or to be scholars.[56]

That Mendelssohn accepted these assumptions is clear from his so-called "Bridal Letters" (*Brautbriefe*) to his fiancée Fromet Gugenheim. While Mendelssohn advised Fromet to "study French assiduously" for an hour a day to "improve the heart" and sent her Rousseau's 1761 novel *Julie, ou la Nouvelle Héloïse*,[57] he cautioned her to "study with moderation (*Gemächlichkeit*)" to preserve her health.[58] In a letter dated November 10, 1761, Mendelssohn worried that Fromet was carrying her studies too far and adopted a stern, paternalist tone with her:

> I hear from R. Zalman Emmerich that you are overdoing your studiousness and nearly making it into a misuse. I cannot approve of this. What do you seek from this? To become a scholar (*Gelehrt*)? God save you from that! Reading in moderation is befitting for women but not scholarly erudition (*Gelehrsamskeit*). A young woman whose eyes are reddened from reading is worthy only of scorn. Fromet my love you must find refuge in books only when you are not in company and seek to amuse yourself, or when you need to read in order to strengthen yourself in knowledge of the good.[59]

[54] See Joseph Mendelssohn's recollection found in Mendelssohn, *Gesammelte Schriften* (henceforth: *GS*), 1:53, cited in Altmann, *Moses Mendelssohn,* 725. They also probably received some instruction in math and logic. See Behm, *Die Transformation,* 168–169.

[55] See Frevert, *Women in German History,* 35.

[56] See ibid., 18.

[57] See Mendelssohn, *Brautbriefe,* 22–23 (Letter of May, 29, 1761), and 37 (Letter of June 16, 1761). Altmann notes that Mendelssohn also paid for a French tutor for Fromet. See Altmann, *Moses Mendelssohn,* 95.

[58] Mendelssohn, *Brautbriefe,* 32 (Letter of June 5, 1761).

[59] See Mendelssohn, *Brautbriefe,* 97 (Letter of November 10, 1761), cited in Feiner, *Moses Mendelssohn,* 65. Frevert notes that the image of the learned woman was "one of the most frequent and spiteful caricatures of the late eighteenth and nineteenth centuries." See Frevert, *Women in German History,* 18.

Mendelssohn's emphasis on his girls' secular education and his neglect of their Jewish education reflected a tendency among elite German Jews that went back at least a century and a half. Beginning in the seventeenth century, wealthy German Jews gave their daughters a secular education by hiring private tutors. This was done so that the daughters could facilitate business contacts with Gentiles.[60] But this emphasis on secular education went with a neglect of Jewish education. In his 1748 *Liebes Brief*, R. Isaac Wetzler complained that while Jewish girls were taught foreign languages, they were not taught Bible, nor even sufficient Hebrew to understand the meaning of the prayers.[61]

The *Freischule* only admitted boys, and even when maskilic girls' schools were later opened, Mendelssohn's minimalist approach to his daughters' Jewish education prevailed.[62] Mordechai Eliav summarizes the maskilic attitude toward female Jewish education: ". . . girls did not need much Jewish education . . . reading and writing Hebrew, translation of prayers, and instruction in religion would suffice. *There was almost no girls' school that taught Bible, which they [the Maskilim] regarded as a non-essential subject* [for girls]" (emphasis mine).[63]

Why did Mendelssohn not teach his daughters his Bible translation? As we have seen, male Ashkenazic Jewish education centered on the legal sections of the Talmud, while female Jewish education involved studying the imaginative stories and moral lessons in the *Tsenerene* Bible. Given Mendelssohn's emphasis on Bible study with an eye to appreciating its aesthetics and moral teachings, coupled with his assumptions about the emotional, intuitive nature of females, it would have seemed natural for him to have taught his daughters his Bible translation. I Why he failed to do so is a mystery.

[60] See Eliav, *Jewish Education*, 271–272. Girls were generally taught languages, particularly French and German, as well as arithmetic and music.

[61] See Assaf, *A Source-Book*, 1:272. R. Jacob Emden also complained that girls were learning French, but not Hebrew. See ibid., 1:169; Eliav, *Jewish Education*, 278. The *Tsenerene* was generally not studied formally by females, but only read informally on the Sabbath and holidays. See Baumgarten and Frakes, *Introduction to Old Yiddish Literature*, 114; Aptroot, "Yiddish Bibles in Amsterdam," 45. The picture may be somewhat more complex as Glikl bas Leyb reports studying in a *heder* in Hamburg in the mid-seventeenth century. See Glikl, *Glikl: Memoirs*, 61. But as Turniansky notes, our knowledge about female Ashkenazic education in the early modern period remains scant. See Turniansky, "Heder Education," 36, note 117.

[62] The first maskilic girls' school opened in Hamburg in 1798. See Eliav, *Jewish Education*, 273–274.

[63] Eliav, *Jewish Education*, 278–279.

Jewish schools and class stigma

While Mendelssohn educated his girls to be bourgeois housewives, he educated his sons to be bourgeois breadwinners. Private tutors taught his sons, and by age fourteen Joseph was receiving private lessons in Latin, physics, and chemistry before being sent to a German gymnasium.[64] Mendelssohn recognized that as a Jew his son could only have a career in medicine or business, and as Joseph did not have a talent for medicine, Mendelssohn encouraged him to go into business.[65]

As regards his sons' Jewish education, I mentioned that Mendelssohn began teaching them the Pentateuch at age five. He then hired tutors to teach them. We know the most about Joseph's education. Solomon Dubno taught him Hebrew language and grammar from ages five to ten.[66] When Joseph was nine, Mendelssohn hired Herz Homberg to teach him Bible and Talmud, which Homberg did until Joseph was twelve. Mendelssohn then hired Joseph Pick to continue Joseph's Jewish education, which ended shortly after his bar mitzvah at age thirteen.[67]

Why did Mendelssohn not send his sons to the *Jüdische Freischule*? Apparently, this was due to class considerations. Being a "free school," the *Freischule* catered primarily to poor students. There were some wealthy parents who paid tuition, but most well-to-do parents preferred to hire private tutors and send their sons to a German gymnasium.[68] As we will see, class stigma continued to play a role in discouraging wealthier Jews from sending their children to Jewish schools in the nineteenth century.

[64] See Mendelssohn, *JubA,* 12:233 (Letter to Herz Homberg, November 20, 1784); Mendelssohn, *GS,* 1:54.

[65] See Mendelssohn, *JubA,* 13:185 (Letter to Herz Homberg March 15, 1784); 308 (Letter to Elise Reimarus, October 4, 1785). Joseph eventually achieved enormous financial success as the co-founder (with his brother Abraham) of the banking house Mendelssohn & Co. See Altmann, *Moses Mendelssohn,* 728.

[66] See Altmann, *Moses Mendelssohn,* 355, 726.

[67] Altmann, *Moses Mendelssohn,* 725–727.

[68] See Eliav, *Jewish Education in Germany,* 63. Eliav notes that in the early nineteenth century a number of private Jewish schools opened that were not free. Wealthy maskilic families generally preferred to send their children to these schools or to Christian public schools because the Jewish free school carried the stigma of being for the lower classes. See ibid., 76.

Bible translation and dismantling traditional Jewish hierarchy

While in *OL* Mendelssohn wrote that he composed his translation for his sons, a year later he offered a different explanation. In a 1784 Yiddish letter to a certain R. Hanokh, Mendelssohn wrote that he had composed his translation for the "masses" (*dalat ha'am*) but came to realize that "it was even more necessary for rabbis."[69] Two points are significant here. *First*, while in *OL* Mendelssohn presents the fiction that the aim of his translation was solely private, namely, to fulfill his religious duty to educate his sons, here Mendelssohn drops this mask and makes clear that his goal was to change German Jewish society. *Second*, Mendelssohn writes that not only boys and common men lack a firm grasp of the plain meaning of the Pentateuch—so do the rabbinic elite. In striving to make knowledge of the Pentateuch according to its plain meaning the foundation of Jewish education and demoting the prestige of talmudic *pilpul*, Mendelssohn understands that he is threatening the status of contemporary rabbinic leaders. In the same letter Mendelssohn observes that the more rabbis whom he calls the "*so-called* sages of the time" (*sogenannte hakhmei hador*) oppose his translation, the more it is evident to him how necessary it is.[70] Mendelssohn understands that the *Be'ur* has the revolutionary aim of restructuring the ranking of male Jewish knowledge, which will result in disrupting the existing social hierarchy of the German Jewish community.[71]

A conservative reformatory work

The layout of the *Be'ur* suggests that its aims are both conservative and reformatory. Gillman observes that the *Be'ur* bears a strong resemblance to the traditional rabbinic Bible (the so-called *Mikra'ot Gedolot*) but also differs from it in significant ways. Like the *Mikra'ot Gedolot*, the *Be'ur* is a Hebrew book that opens from right to left, includes a translation in Hebrew

[69] Mendelssohn, *JubA*, 19:296 (Letter to R. Hanokh, 1784). Altmann suggests that the recipient was R. Hanokh of Rocknitz. See Altmann, *Moses Mendelssohn*, 836, note 117. Mendelssohn's contention that he composed the Pentateuch for the "masses" contradicts Lowenstein's and Weinberg's conclusion that Mendelssohn composed it for the enlightened elite. See pp. 77–78 note 7 of this volume.

[70] Mendelssohn, *JubA*, 19:296. Also see Mendelssohn's Yiddish 1781 letter to Avigdor Levi in Mendelssohn, *JubA*, 19:279.

[71] Feiner emphasizes this impulse of the Haskalah. See Feiner, *The Jewish Enlightenment*, 87–104.

characters facing the Hebrew original, and has a Hebrew commentary below the Hebrew text and translation.[72] The commentary is similar in style to the classical medieval Jewish Bible commentators Rashi, Rashbam, Ibn Ezra, and Nahmanides, shares their aim of seeking *peshat*, and engages deeply with them often quoting or paraphrasing them. Through both its form and content, the *Be'ur* gives the impression of being a traditional Jewish work that participates in a centuries-old conversation about the meaning of the Pentateuch.[73]

But Gillman also notes that the physical layout of the *Be'ur* signals Mendelssohn's reformatory intentions. While the *Mikra'ot Gedolot* includes one or more Aramaic translations in Hebrew characters, Mendelssohn replaces all translations, including the canonical Aramaic translation of Onkelos, with his own German translation, to which he gives a Hebrew title *Targum Ashkenaz*. The *Mikra'ot Gedolot* includes several Hebrew commentaries, but Mendelssohn replaces all of them, including Rashi's with the *Be'ur* commentary.[74] Gillman's observation about the significance of these steps should be amplified. Jacob Katz notes that between the sixteenth and eighteenth centuries children in Polish and German lands nearly always studied the Pentateuch through the lens of Rashi's commentary because it effectively communicated "the fundamentals of their [Jewish] faith," including "the special status of the Jews as a chosen people, the essential and mythic distinction between Jews and the other nations, an understanding of the fate of the Jewish people in exile, and a belief in the people's ultimate redemption."[75] By replacing Rashi's commentary with his own, Mendelssohn was clearing the way for replacing Rashi's medieval understanding of Judaism with his own modern one.[76]

72 See Figures 3 and 4 of this volume.

73 Gillman, "Between Religion and Culture," 101–104. Mendelssohn also includes Masoretic notes in the *Be'ur* under the title *Tikkun Soferim*. He writes that he did so to make sure that the text of the Torah contained in the *Be'ur* is the most accurate one possible. Breuer notes that the inclusion of the highly technical *Tikkun Soferim* gives the *Be'ur* a scholarly appearance, albeit one that is firmly rooted within rabbinic tradition that does not engage with critical Christian Bible scholarship. See Breuer, *The Limits of Enlightenment*, 175.

74 See Gillman, "Between Religion and Culture," 101–104.

75 Katz, *Tradition and Crisis*, 162.

76 Gillman, "Between Religion and Culture," 100–104. Later editions of the *Be'ur* confirm that its physical layout was both conservative and reformatory. Some editions render Mendelssohn's translation in Gothic script and remove the Hebrew commentary, thereby weakening the traditional appearance of the original edition (Offenbach, 1811; Dessau and Berlin, 1815; Prague, 1815; Fürth, 1860; Pest, 1861; Sulzbach, 1839). Other editions restore Onkelos and Rashi, thereby bringing the *Be'ur* even closer to the *Mikra'ot Gedolot* (Vienna, 1795, 1817–1818, 1849; Berlin, 1831–1833; Fürth, 1801–1803 and 1824; Offenbach, 1804–1809; Sulzbach, 1829–1837; Prague, 1802, 1836; Krotoschin, 1837; Vilna and St. Petersburg, 1850–1852; Warsaw, 1837, 1887–1915). Steven Lowenstein notes that

The trouble with Yiddish

In Chapter 7 of *Divrei Shalom Ve'emet*, Wessely discusses the benefits of Mendelssohn's Pentateuch translation, writing that "When teachers teach their students the Torah with this clear German translation they will accustom youths to properly speak the language of the inhabitants of the land from their youth and through it they will properly understand the intention of Scripture (*kavanat hakatuv*)."[77] While critics saw Mendelssohn as aiming to teach Jews German so that they could engage German culture, Wessely claims that his aim was to teach Jews German to deepen their understanding and appreciation of the Torah.

Wessely explains that translation involves a teacher translating from a language that the student does not understand into a language that he understands. The teacher must therefore have a good grasp both of the source and target languages. But according to Wessely, most Jewish teachers in German lands were Polish immigrants who did not have a proper understanding of Hebrew grammar and rhetoric.[78] This made it impossible for them to faithfully convey the meaning of the biblical text.

Wessely further complains that the nature of Yiddish creates educational obstacles. This is because, like Mendelssohn, Wessely does not consider Yiddish a distinct language but, rather, a corrupt form of German that lacks

the editions of the *Be'ur* that restore Onkelos and Rashi did so for diverse reasons. In the early nineteenth century, South German editions of the *Be'ur* came to be accepted in Orthodox circles (e.g., Fürth, 1801–1803; Offenbach, 1804–1809; Sulzbach, 1829–1837). Following the Prussian decrees of 1815 that instituted compulsory secular education for Jews, knowledge of German became widespread among Jews, and a hallmark of German Orthodoxy became writing German in Hebrew script. For this reason, Mendelssohn's *Be'ur* came to appear quite traditional. By contrast, the East European editions (Krotoschin, Vilna and St. Petersburg, and Warsaw) of the *Be'ur* that included Rashi and Onkelos were printed for more revolutionary aims. In Poland, Lithuania, and Russia, Jews did not generally know German. Maskilim in these territories sought to use the *Be'ur* to teach Jews German to enable them to engage with High European culture. In the Russian Empire, Leon Mandelstamm even got the government to support the 1852 Vilna edition for use in new schools as a means of spreading maskilic ideals, and he threatened government action against the Jewish religion if traditionalist rabbis did not support the publication of the *Be'ur*. Maskilim added Rashi and Onkelos to the *Be'ur* so that it would appear less threatening to Jewish traditionalists. See Lowenstein, "The Readership," 186–194. The intended audience of Mendelssohn's German translation of the Psalms was entirely different from that of the *Be'ur*. See p. 19 of this volume.

[77] Wessely, *Divrei Shalom Ve'emet*, 23–24.

[78] The first person to express concern about Polish Jewish teachers teaching German Jewish youth was apparently Joseph Levin. In 1772 Levin wrote to Frederick II, complaining about the poor teaching methods of teachers brought in from "barbaric territories, who suffocate within us the seed of all the beautiful sciences." See Eliav, *Jewish Education in Germany*, 23.

a standard form.[79] As he puts it, "nearly every individual speaks his own language (*kimat l'khol ehad safah aheret*)."[80] This is especially problematic in German lands for while the teachers use a Polish dialect of Yiddish, their students use a German dialect, which makes conveying the proper meaning of the Bible extremely difficult.

Wessely further claims that teaching the Pentateuch by translating it into Yiddish is not educationally effective because unlike Hebrew, Yiddish does not possess beautiful rhetoric. As such, when students are taught the Bible in Yiddish it is presented in a way that "lacks taste (*sarei ta'am*)." The result is that when these students are later exposed to beautifully written heretical literature they are drawn to it because of its attractive form and so come to disdain Judaism. For these reasons, Wessely argues that Mendelssohn's beautiful German translation helps bolster Jewish religious commitment.[81]

Mendelssohn's view of German's superior ability to instill an appreciation of the Bible is quite similar to Wessely's. In *OL*, Mendelssohn stresses that an aim of his Pentateuch translation is to help his sons understand "the intended meaning of Scripture, the rhetoric of the language, and the purity of its lessons, so that they might grow up and understand it on their own."[82] Mendelssohn criticizes previous translations of the Bible into Yiddish, calling Yiddish a "corrupt and deformed language of stammering" that lacks rhetorical beauty.[83]

Careful consideration of Mendelssohn's complaint that Yiddish is "a jargon [that] has contributed not a little to the immorality of the common people" shows that like Wessely he is concerned about the lack of a standard Yiddish. Mendelssohn's complaint occurs in the context of a letter to Ernst Ferdinand Klein about Jewish oaths. Klein had been asked by the Prussian High Chancellor Count von Carmer for advice on how to revise the procedure for oath taking by Jews. Klein turned to Mendelssohn and to the Rabbi of Breslau, Joseph Jonah Fränkel, for their opinions. Fränkel apparently

[79] Eliav, *Jewish Education in Germany*, 24. On Mendelssohn's not regarding Yiddish as a distinct language, see his 1782 letter to Klein cited on p. 78 of this volume. Also see *OL* where Mendelssohn refers to Yiddish as "lashon Ashkenaz." "Ashkenaz" is the standard term used for German. The fact that Mendelssohn refers to Yiddish as "Ashkenaz" indicates that he did not see Yiddish as a distinct language. See Mendelssohn, *JubA*, 14:232; *Moses Mendelssohn's Hebrew Writings*, 275, note 17. On the emergence of the idea of Yiddish as a distinct language, see Weinreich, *History of the Yiddish Language*, 315–327.

[80] See Wessely in Mendelssohn, *JubA*, 15.1:4.

[81] Wessely, *Divrei Shalom Ve'emet*, 24–25.

[82] See p. 25 of this volume. See Mendelssohn, *JubA*, 14:243. See Weinberg, "Language Questions," 203–209, 226–234.

[83] Mendelssohn, *JubA*, 14:242: *Moses Mendelssohn: Writings*, 196.

recommended that Jews be allowed to take oaths in Yiddish. Mendelssohn's letter to Klein takes issue with Fränkel's recommendation, arguing that Jews should only be permitted to take oaths in either Hebrew or German.[84] His reasoning is that since there is no standard form of Yiddish, allowing a Jew to swear an oath in Yiddish is dangerous since she may attach a meaning to the oath that differs from that intended by the person administering the oath. This explains Mendelssohn's concern that Yiddish has "contributed [much] to [Jewish] immorality," for using it provides Jews with a means to evade their oaths.[85]

Mendelssohn's opposition to Yiddish was not absolute. Weinberg notes that he used Yiddish in private letters throughout his life, even composing Yiddish letters to men able to write Hebrew.[86] Rather, Mendelssohn's opposition to Yiddish was limited to specific contexts such as Bible translation or oaths, which demanded aesthetic sensitivity and/or linguistic precision.

In sum, like Wessely Mendelssohn thinks that appreciating the literary, poetic features of the Bible is intimately connected with one's ability to absorb its message, which requires that the Bible be translated precisely into a language with a standard form and beautiful rhetoric. To understand this point more deeply, we need to explore his concept of *Bildung* and its relation to biblical aesthetics.

Bildung and the Bible

One of the best statements of Mendelssohn's account of life's purpose is found in his commentary on the story of the Garden of Eden. Christian and Jewish theologians frequently interpreted the story as an account of the human fall from a state of perfection. Orthodox Lutherans generally read Adam and Eve's sin as a historical account of how human nature came to be tainted by humanly irreparable sinfulness that could only be overcome through faith in Christ. By contrast, Jewish philosophers such as Maimonides interpreted the Garden of Eden tale as an allegory about human realization and how to attain it through worldly effort.

[84] See Altmann, *Moses Mendelssohn*, 496–500.

[85] The association of Yiddish with immorality and criminal behavior was an important trope in medieval Christian literature. See Gilman, *Jewish Self-Hatred*, 68–87.

[86] See Weinberg, "Language Questions," 240.

For Maimonides, prior to sinning Adam was a philosopher continually engaged in contemplating truth. His sin involved turning to the imaginative faculty, which increased his desires, leading him to direct his attention to mundane, political matters. According to Maimonides, the fallen human condition is characterized by human desire being out of balance, which causes people to devote most of their energies to managing worldly affairs rather than contemplating truth. By controlling desire and realizing moral virtue, human beings can attain the emotional balance needed to focus on contemplating God in this life.[87]

Some scholars have portrayed Mendelssohn as perpetuating the Maimonidean intellectualist ideal through his commitment to the German Enlightenment (*Aufklärung*).[88] For these scholars this element of Mendelssohn's philosophy quickly made it passé, as by the end of the eighteenth century the ideal of *Bildung* came to replace the ideal of Enlightenment. Michael Meyer claims that in contrast to the Enlightenment ideal of rational perfection, *Bildung* "focused more broadly upon individual character, including the cultivation of aesthetic as well as moral sensibility." In addition to turning from philosophy to aesthetics and ethics, it is also commonly asserted that the turn to *Bildung* involved a turning away from religion, as pursuing *Bildung* became a "secular religion."[89]

A close reading of Mendelssohn's interpretation of Adam's sin makes clear that this view needs refining. Mendelssohn follows Maimonides in interpreting the story of Adam's sin as a metaphor for how to attain human excellence. But for Mendelssohn, prior to his sin Adam was not involved solely in contemplation. Rather, his faculties of cognition and desire were in a state of harmony. He contemplated truth, desired goodness, and appreciated beauty. The consequence of Adam's sin was that his faculty of desire was greatly strengthened and thus put out of balance with his other faculties. This led him to pursue pleasure above all else, thereby lessening his commitment to intellectual, moral, and aesthetic perfection. For Mendelssohn, the human task is to regain the balance of faculties originally possessed by Adam and thus attain a fully actualized, harmonious character.[90] So, unlike Maimonides, for

[87] Maimonides's interpretation of the Adam's sin is found in Maimonides, *The Guide of the Perplexed*, 1:2, 23–26.

[88] See Meyer, *German Jewish History in Modern Times*, 2:199.

[89] Meyer, *German Jewish History in Modern Times*, 2:199–201. For a classic expression of this view, see Mosse, *German Jews beyond Judaism*.

[90] See Mendelssohn, *JubA*, 15.2:22–24; *Moses Mendelssohn: Writings*, 208–211. For a trenchant comparison of Maimonides's, Nahmanides's, Mendelssohn's, and Maimon's interpretations of the Garden of Eden, see Harvey, "Mendelssohn and Maimon on the Tree of Knowledge." Harvey's

Mendelssohn refining one's intellect is not the highest expression of human excellence. Rather, human excellence involves cultivating a well-rounded personality that includes a refined aesthetic sensibility and morally good character in balance with a fully developed intellect.[91]

In his 1784 essay "On the Question: What Does 'Enlightenment' Mean?," Mendelssohn uses the term *Bildung* to describe the process of the harmonious perfection of one's faculties while noting that each faculty has its distinctive excellence. Perfecting the cognitive capacity involves knowing the true, and the process of achieving this is called "enlightenment" (*Aufklärung*).[92] Perfecting the capacity for "approval" (*Billigung*) involves feeling the good and the beautiful, while perfecting the capacity for desire involves seeking to actualize the good and create the beautiful.[93] Both are included in *Kultur.*[94] *Kultur* in its "internal" sense includes "excellence, proficiency and, beauty" in "trades and arts" (*Handwerken, Künsten*).[95] In its "external" sense *Kultur* includes "refinement" (*Politur*), which is admirable when its "splendor and elegance" is grounded in genuine moral, aesthetic, and intellectual excellence.[96]

In his "Enlightenment" essay Mendelssohn does not arrange the faculties hierarchically. But in a 1777 letter he *reverses* Maimonides's account of the relationship between moral goodness and intellectual perfection, claiming that intellectual development is the means to moral action, which is the highest

emphasis on the Platonic nature of Mendelssohn's human ideal is likely a further reason that Mendelssohn was attracted to Plato.

[91] This difference helps explain the fact that while Maimonides wrote almost nothing on aesthetics, Mendelssohn made major contributions to this field. On Mendelssohn's importance in eighteenth-century German aesthetics, see Beiser, *Diotima's Children,* 196–243. Mendelssohn's interpretation of the story of the Garden of Eden reflects philosophical commitments found in his German writings, where he distinguishes between three capacities: the "cognitive capacity" (*Erkentnissvermögen*), the "approval capacity" (*Billigungsvermögen*), and the "capacity for desire" (*Begehrungsvermögen*). See Mendelssohn, *JubA,* 3.2, 59–66, 69–71; *Morning Hours,* 41–46; 50–51. For an excellent analysis of Mendelssohn's so-called "three-faculty theory" of the soul, see Beiser, *Diotima's Children,* 240–243. Also see Altmann, "Moses Mendelssohn and Education and the Image of Man."

[92] Mendelssohn, *JubA,* 6.1:115; *Philosophical Writings,* 313–314.

[93] Mendelssohn's fullest discussion of the faculty of approval appears in his 1785 *Morning Hours.* See Mendelssohn, *JubA,* 3.2:61–69; *Morning Hours,* 42–46.

[94] Mendelssohn, *JubA,* 6.1:115; *Philosophical Writings,* 313–314.

[95] Ibid. Mendelssohn makes clear that trades and professions are included in *Kultur* in his "Preface to Menasseh ben Israel" when he writes "People continue to distance us from all the arts and sciences as well as the *other useful professions and occupations of mankind* (*nützlichen Gewerben und Beschäftigungen der Menschen*). They bar us from every path to useful improvement and make our lack of *culture* (*Cultur*) the reason for oppressing us further" (emphasis mine). See Mendelssohn, *JubA,* 8:6; *Moses Mendelssohn: Writings,* 44.

[96] Mendelssohn, *JubA,* 6.1:116; *Philosophical Writings,* 314.

aim of life. As he puts it, "The highest level of wisdom is unquestionably *doing good.* Speculation is a lower level leading to it" (emphasis in original).[97]

Mendelssohn also breaks with Maimonides in offering a wider conception of intellectual excellence. While for Maimonides intellectual excellence centers on contemplative, theoretical knowledge of God, Mendelssohn also stresses the importance of productive reason by which people rule the animal kingdom and cultivate the plant and mineral world for human use by "uprooting, shattering, digging, and quarrying."[98] For Mendelssohn productive labor is also conducive to moral goodness, as idleness breeds laziness and boredom, which nourish excessive desire. Indeed, this is how Mendelssohn interprets God's punishment for Adam's sin:

> After he [Adam] ate from the Tree of Knowledge and his desires increased, the only good for man is to toil, labor, and be preoccupied by working the cursed land. For if a man sits in peace, eats, and gets full and fat, his heart will turn from the good path and wander after his eyes, whore after them, and be far distanced from the eternal happiness which is hoped for. Therefore it is a great good for a man to enjoy the labor of his hands and eat his bread by the sweat of his face and with great toil.[99]

Adam's punishment was that he must eat his bread through great toil. This is not a retributive punishment but, rather, for the sake of Adam's improvement.[100]

Finally, Mendelssohn's embrace of *Bildung* cannot be regarded as a form of "secular religion" as he sees the Torah as promoting it. For Mendelssohn, it a basic tenet of Judaism that God desires that we perfect ourselves. He reasons that since God is perfect and cannot be improved by anything in the world, God's purpose in creating the world was *solely* to benefit humanity by

[97] Mendelssohn, *JubA,* 12.2:96 (Letter to Friedrich Wilhelm Freiherrn von Ferber, September 22, 1777). Mendelssohn thinks that intellectual perfection promotes moral goodness because, unlike Maimonides, he regards morality as a rational truth. See p. 102, note 113 of this volume. For Mendelssohn's view of how rational theology promotes moral goodness, see pp. 102–104 of this volume. Another important difference is that while for Maimonides only the elite can attain intellectual perfection, as this requires complex discursive reasoning, for Mendelssohn all people can attain intellectual perfection through common sense. On this point, see Gottlieb, *Faith and Freedom,* ch. 2.

[98] See Maimonides, *The Guide of the Perplexed,* 1:1, 21–23; Mendelssohn, *JubA,* 15.2:13. These differences signal a shift in European thought that Hannah Arendt has called "the reversal of contemplation and action." See Arendt, *The Human Condition,* 289.

[99] See Mendelssohn, *JubA,* 15.2:36–37.

[100] On Mendelssohn's claim that the sole purpose of divine punishment is human improvement, see Gottlieb, *Faith and Freedom,* 20–21, and the sources cited in notes 56–59.

providing a context in which human beings could achieve happiness and perfection, by perfecting their body and faculties, and most importantly, their moral faculty.[101] Cultivating *Bildung* is therefore a means of serving God.

Mendelssohn acknowledges that Jews do not always internalize this message. He identifies two main reasons for this. First, while Mendelssohn esteems wealth for providing security and opportunities that help a person actualize their inner capacities, he laments that many wealthier Jews deem wealth the highest goal of life, which erodes moral virtue. Responding to Michaelis' complaint that poor Jewish peddlers trade in stolen goods, Mendelssohn responds "Among my nation, at least, I have found comparatively more virtue among the poor than among the rich" (emphasis in original).[102] Second, Mendelssohn recognizes that many Jews fail to appreciate that attaining moral perfection and aesthetic refinement is a central goal of the Torah. Mendelssohn makes clear that Christian discrimination contributes to this failure. Excluded from enlightened society, many Jews adopt exclusionary, tyrannical views of Judaism and reject universal moral, aesthetic, and religious principles.[103] As he poignantly put it, "they [Christians] tie our hands and reproach us for not using them."[104] But Mendelssohn did not rest content with blaming others. He recognized that the problem began with the inadequate German Jewish educational system, and saw his *Be'ur* as helping remedy this.

In light of these considerations we can understand what Mendelssohn meant when he wrote to Hennings in 1779 that his Pentateuch translation was "the first step toward culture (*Cultur*) from which my nation, alas, is so estranged." In speaking of *Cultur*, Mendelssohn was not referring to German culture but to *Kultur* in a technical sense, claiming that the *Be'ur* helps Jews

[101] See Mendelssohn, *JubA*, 2:318–320; *Philosophical Writings*, 298–300; *JubA*, 8:125–127; *Jerusalem*, 57–59. For discussion of other Jewish thinkers before Mendelssohn who held the view that God's purpose in creating the world was to benefit humanity, see Gottlieb, *Faith and Freedom*, pp. 130–131, note 67. Of course, for Mendelssohn this is not just the view of Judaism but of all true natural religion.

[102] See Mendelssohn, *GS*, 3: 366; *JMW*, 40-41.

[103] See the sources cited on p. 77 note 6 in this volume.

[104] Mendelssohn, *JubA*, 8:6; *Moses Mendelssohn: Writings*, 44. Also see Mendelssohn's 1777 letter to Baron von Ferber in which he sought the repeal of harsh tax assessments levied specifically against Jews, noting how these discriminatory laws put pressure on Jews to be dishonest, writing, "And is the Israelite who is punished for poverty as hard as for dishonesty, still expected to be honest?" Mendelssohn's letter is cited in Altmann, *Moses Mendelssohn*, 428–429.

attain moral goodness and aesthetic refinement.[105] For Mendelssohn, biblical aesthetics are key to this end.

Biblical aesthetics and moral virtue

Aesthetics serve a crucial pedagogic function in bringing heart and mind into harmony for Mendelssohn. His account of the educational function of aesthetics grows out of a difficulty that he finds in Christian Wolff's philosophical anthropology. While Mendelssohn accepts Wolff's claim that our sole drive is to achieve perfection, from early in his literary career Mendelssohn is bothered by the problem of how a person could willingly choose imperfection.[106]

In his 1761 essay "Rhapsody," Mendelssohn distinguishes between two ways in which we can know the good. There is insight that is purely theoretical, but that has no impact on our actions, which he calls "speculative" (*speculative*) or "ineffective" (*unwirksame*) knowledge. There is also insight that stirs us to action, which Mendelssohn calls "pragmatic" (*pragmatische*) or "effective" (*wirksame*) knowledge.[107] The "effectiveness" of knowledge is a function of three factors. First is the *degree* of the perfection represented. The greater the degree of perfection represented and the more vivid our representation of it is, the stronger its effect on the will. Second is the degree of our *knowledge* of the perfection. The more clearly we know the perfection and with more cognitive certainty, the stronger the effect on our will. Finally, is the *speed* with which we perceive the perfection. The faster that we perceive it, the more powerfully it will affect our will.[108]

[105] Altmann correctly grasps this point. See Altmann, *Moses Mendelssohn,* 372. Also see Altmann, "Moses Mendelssohn on Education." Mendelssohn elaborates the understanding of *Cultur* that he presented in his essay, "What Is Enlightenment?," in a later letter to August Hennings. See Mendelssohn, *JubA,* 13:234–237 (Letter to August Hennings, November 27, 1784).

[106] See Beiser, *Diotima's Children,* 206–240. In his earliest writings, Mendelssohn accepts Plato's solution to this problem, claiming that a person chooses evil because she mistakenly perceives it as good. See Plato, *Protagoras,* 352a–357e; Mendelssohn, *JubA,* 1:257, 260, 304–305, 412; *Philosophical Writings,* 28, 30, 71, 158. But Mendelssohn soon realizes that this solution is incomplete since there are clearly cases in which people know the good intellectually yet nevertheless choose evil. Mendelssohn first discusses this problem in his 1756 essay "On Controlling Inclinations," but he addresses it most fully in his 1761 essay "Rhapsody." See Altmann, "Mendelssohn on Education," 394–401; Beiser, *Diotima's Children,* 211–217.

[107] Mendelssohn, *JubA,* 1:413; *Philosophical Writings,* 159; *JubA,* 2:326; *Philosophical Writings,* 304.

[108] Mendelssohn, *JubA,* 1:414–415; *Philosophical Writings,* 160. Compare Mendelssohn, *JubA,* 2:327–328; *Philosophical Writings,* 305–306; Altmann, *Moses Mendelssohns Frühschriften,* 383–391; Mendelssohn, *JubA,* 8:112–113; *Jerusalem,* 42–43.

On the basis of these distinctions, Mendelssohn argues that it is possible for a perfection known less clearly to have a greater power over our will than one known more clearly if we perceive it more vividly and quickly. Perfections are perceived more vividly and quickly when they are taken in sensibly than when they are known intellectually.[109] Since art is a means of representing perfections sensibly, it can therefore be a far more powerful motivator than philosophy. Mendelssohn notes that poetic images and similes are particularly effective ways of making ideas vivid.[110]

These distinctions help explain how we can know that something is evil in theory and nevertheless desire it. For while we may know that an action is vicious, if it is presented in ways that stir our senses to represent the action as leading to great perfection in the short term, we can be seduced to choose the vicious course of action. But while art can be a force that *divides* our desires from our intellect, it can also be a way of putting our intellect and desires in *harmony*. By presenting true perfection in a sensibly pleasing light, art can spur us to virtuous action. Mendelssohn notes that history and fables can makes abstract ethical principles concrete, and poetry, painting, sculpture, and rhetoric can "transform dry truths into ardent and sensuous intuitions . . . by transforming impulses into penetrating arrows and dipping them into enchanting nectar."[111]

For Mendelssohn, metaphysics are connected to ethics since belief in God's existence, divine providence, and a future life help motivate ethical action in several ways.[112] *First*, Mendelssohn thinks that conceiving God as commanding universal ethics provides an additional impetus for acting morally by locating these rules in a higher authority. While for Mendelssohn the law of universal ethics, namely, to seek one's own perfection and the perfection of others, is a rational law discernable through reason *without* reference to God, natural religion teaches that God commands this law to humanity and that it is the primary means of serving God.[113] The metaphysical conviction that a benevolent God

[109] Mendelssohn, *JubA*, 1:416; *Philosophical Writings*, 161.
[110] See Mendelssohn, *JubA*, 1:437; *Philosophical Writings*, 178.
[111] See Mendelssohn, *JubA*, 1:423; *Philosophical Writings*, 166–167. Compare Mendelssohn, *JubA*, 2:327–328; *Philosophical Writings*, 305–306; *JubA*, 14; 206 (Commentary to Ecclesiastes 12:10); *JubA*, 14:76. Also compare Mendelssohn's "Enlightenment" essay, where he writes that enlightenment is related to culture as theory is to practice. See Mendelssohn, *JubA*, 6.1:115; *Philosophical Writings*, 314. Also see Mendelssohn, *JubA*, 1:427–428; *Philosophical Writings*, 169–170.
[112] Mendelssohn, *JubA*, 8:131; *Jerusalem*, 63.
[113] For the law of universal ethics and Mendelssohn's philosophical derivation of it, see Mendelssohn, *JubA*, 2:316–321; *Philosophical Writings*, 296–300.

commands moral obedience helps motivate moral behavior by giving ethical duties "a more exalted *sanction*" (emphasis in original).[114]

Second, Mendelssohn thinks that *love of God* can motivate moral action. He notes that if we have a rational understanding of our true self-interest, we will want to obey the moral law since "*Benevolence*, in reality makes us happier than *selfishness*."[115] So Mendelssohn notes that when we *rationally* love ourselves, we will naturally love our fellow human beings. But he thinks that we can easily lose sight of this truth. When this happens, religion can provide an additional impetus for loving others. By seeing the moral law as an expression of God's will, *loving God* motivates us to *love others* and so to *love ourselves*. As Mendelssohn puts it, "We ought, from love of God, to love ourselves in a rational manner, to love his creatures."[116]

Third, divine reward and punishment provide a crucial motivation for morality. For Mendelssohn, while people generally recognize that they have a duty to seek the well-being of others, they often observe the suffering of the righteous and prospering of the wicked, which can cause them to despair of morality. For it often seems that righteousness is an impediment to prosperity while the wicked person who takes moral shortcuts gets ahead faster. Benevolence can then come to be seen as "a foppery into which we seek to lure one another so that the simpleton will toil while the clever man enjoys himself and has a good laugh at the other's expense."[117] While we have seen that the wise person will recognize that benevolence makes her happier than selfishness and thus is its own reward, Mendelssohn notes that people often forget this truth and instead consider benevolence a sacrifice (*Verlust*) that demands compensation.[118] As they do not see this compensation in this life, to act ethically they need to believe that benevolence will be rewarded in a future life.[119]

Mendelssohn recognizes, however, that the rational truths of God's existence, divine providence, and a future life only provide consolation and motivate us to act ethically if they *impact the heart*.[120] This is a central function of religion. As he puts it in *Jerusalem*,

[114] Mendelssohn, *JubA*, 8:127; *Jerusalem*, 58.
[115] Mendelssohn, *JubA*, 8:111; *Jerusalem*, 41.
[116] Mendelssohn, *JubA*, 8:127; *Jerusalem*, 58.
[117] Mendelssohn, *JubA*, 8:131; *Jerusalem*, 63. See *JubA*, 14:193 (Commentary to Ecclesiastes 9:10).
[118] See Mendelssohn, *JubA*, 3.2:236–240. On the idea of benevolence as its own reward, see Mendelssohn, *JubA*, 8:111, 116; *Jerusalem*, 41, 47; *JubA*, 6.1:38, 47; *JubA*, 1:405–408; *Philosophical Writings*, 151–154.
[119] See Mendelssohn, *JubA*, 3.2:236–240.
[120] At the end of the "Prize Essay," Mendelssohn does consider the possibility of a "fortunate genius" (*glückliche Genie*) who can be motivated by reason alone. See Mendelssohn, *JubA*, 2:329.

> the most essential purpose of religious society is *mutual edification* (*gemeinschaftliche Erbauung*). By the magic power of sympathy one wishes to transfer truth from the mind to the heart; to vivify, by participation with others, rational cognitions, which at times are lifeless, into soaring sensations. When the heart clings too strongly to sensual pleasures to listen to the voice of reason, when it is on the verge of ensnaring reason itself, then let it be seized here with a tremor of pious enthusiasm, kindled by the fire of devotion, and acquainted with joys of a higher order which outweigh even in this life the joys of the senses.[121]

Mendelssohn is here referring to power of communal worship to bring religious and ethical truths to life. But he also sees the Bible's aesthetic qualities as serving this goal.[122] In *Jerusalem*, Mendelssohn describes the Bible as a work of "divine beauty" (*göttlichen Schönheit*) that contains an "inexhaustible treasure of rational truths and religious doctrines" that it teaches in emotionally stirring ways.[123]

The sublime Bible

Among the most important concepts in Mendelssohn's aesthetics is the "sublime" (*das Erhabene*), which he calls "the height of perfection in writings."[124] Mendelssohn's conception of the sublime is dependent on his account of beauty. He defines beauty as a sensible representation of perfection, which involves unity in multiplicity. Mendelssohn distinguishes between two types of beauty, external and internal. External beauty refers to objects whose unity in multiplicity is revealed in their sensible form. But one can also perceive something as beautiful on account of its inner traits. For example, a person whose facial features harmonize forming a lovely face is beautiful in

[121] Mendelssohn, *JubA*, 8:141; *Jerusalem*, 74.

[122] Mendelssohn, *JubA*, 8:109–110; *Jerusalem*, 40–41.

[123] Mendelssohn, *JubA*, 8:166; *Jerusalem*, 99. Sorkin correctly calls attention to Mendelssohn's commitment to what he calls "practical knowledge" or "practical wisdom." See Sorkin, *Moses Mendelssohn and the Religious Enlightenment*, 55–65. For my evaluation of Sorkin's argument, see Gottlieb, *Faith, Reason, Politics*, 247–251.

[124] Mendelssohn, *JubA*, 1:455; *Philosophical Writings*, 192. On Mendelssohn's treatment of the sublime, see Beiser, *Diotima's Children*, 217–224. Also see Aaron Koller's doctoral dissertation, *The Flower of Perfection*, 228–257. Koller's subtle discussion focuses on the development of Mendelssohn's theory, especially in relation to his sustained engagement with Edmund Burke.

the external sense while a person who is able to unite her inner powers for a moral purpose is beautiful in the internal sense.[125]

External and internal beauty can come together in the appreciation of a work of art. For example, not only do we take pleasure in appreciating an actual rose, we also take pleasure in appreciating an artist's *representation* of a rose. At times we even enjoy the representation more than the object itself. For Mendelssohn, this is because in appreciating artistic representations we enjoy a double pleasure. We enjoy the unity in multiplicity of the represented rose, but also take pleasure in the genius of the artist who is able to harness the various powers of her soul to create a beautiful object according to a unified vision.

Whereas one experiences beauty when sensing complexity in a unity that one perceives all at once, Mendelssohn notes that there are also objects that cannot be perceived as a unity because of their enormity. He calls such objects "sublime." While the feeling that accompanies perceiving beauty is pleasure, Mendelssohn describes the feeling that accompanies perceiving sublime objects as "awe" (*Bewunderung*) or "astonishment" (*Erstaunen*)."[126] Awe/astonishment is a pleasant fear that we experience when we sense the immensity of the perfection of the object, which we realize is too great for us to behold.[127]

As with beauty, we can distinguish *external* and *internal* sublimity. Externally sublime objects include those that are gigantic in size such as "the unfathomable sea, a far reaching plain, or the innumerable legion of stars."[128] Internally sublime objects include those that exhibit vast "perfections of spirit" such as an "enormous intellect, enormous and uncommon sensibilities, a fortunate imagination joined with penetrating sagacity, and noble and passionate emotions that elevate themselves above the conceptions of commoner souls."[129] These two types of sublimity can come together in works of genius that represent sublime objects. In appreciating such works, we

[125] Mendelssohn, *JubA*, 1:433–434; *Philosophical Writings*, 174–174.

[126] Mendelssohn, *JubA*, 1:462; *Philosophical Writings*, 198.

[127] Mendelssohn, *JubA*, 1:458, 456, 398–399; *Philosophical Writings*, 195, 193, 144–145.

[128] Mendelssohn, *JubA*, 1:456, 398; *Philosophical Writings*, 193, 144. I choose to call both the extensively enormous and intensively enormous "sublime" even though Mendelssohn wants to reserve the term "sublime" for those that are intensively enormous while calling those that extensively large "gigantic." See Mendelssohn, *JubA*, 1:456, 459; *Philosophical Writings*, 193, 196. One reason for Mendelssohn wishing to use two different terms is that while extensively large objects arouse a pleasant shudder that ends in disgust, intensively large objects generate no feelings of disgust.

[129] Mendelssohn, *JubA*, 1:461; *Philosophical Writings*, 198.

experience awe *both* at the objects represented and at the genius of the creative artist.[130]

Mendelssohn alludes to the Bible depicting God as sublime in the *Be'ur*. He translates the beginning of Moses's Song of the Sea (Exodus 15:1), which reads in Hebrew *ashirah l'YHWH ki* ***ga'o ga'a*** as *Ich singe, dem Ewigen. Der* ***hoch erhaben*** *sich zeigt* (I sing to the Eternal who shows Himself as **highly sublime**).[131] In his commentary, Mendelssohn explains his translation of *ga'o ga'a* as "highly sublime" by noting that in Hebrew the person who is *mitga'eh b'atzmo* (haughty) "elevates himself above the proper degree and boundaries." While for human beings this is a vice, God cannot have vices. Hence, when Moses describes God as *ga'o ga'a*, he is referring to God's virtues so exceeding normal boundaries that human beings cannot properly praise God. Mendelssohn concludes that "the exaltedness of a virtue that exceeds normal bounds is called in German *Erhabenheit* (sublimity)."[132]

For Mendelssohn, there is an intimate relation between the sublime and the simple, or as he calls it, "the naïve."[133] Given the enormity of a sublime subject if the representation of it is too complex, the observer will become dumbfounded, which will disrupt her feeling of awe. This occurs, for example, when overly elaborate similes are used in writing or excessive embellishment in painting. The most effective way of representing the sublime is through simple representations in which the discrepancy between the simplicity of the representation and the enormity of the object represented calls attention to the object's perfection.[134] By not saying too much the skilled artist is able to awaken the observer to "think more than what is said to him."[135]

For example, one of the most effective tools for representing the internally sublime is to associate it with a simple image that is externally sublime,[136] for "the impressions of the inner sense . . . [are] strengthened if the outer senses are harmoniously attuned to it by a similar impression."[137] Hence, the skilled

[130] Mendelssohn, *JubA*, 1:459–460; *Philosophical Writings*, 196–197.
[131] Mendelssohn, *JubA*, 9.1:246.
[132] Mendelssohn also cites support from Rashi, who writes that the word *ge'ut* refers to doing something others are incapable of (citing Isaiah 12:5) and that the phrase *ga'o ga'a* refers to God being elevated above any praise that human beings can offer. See Mendelssohn, *JubA*, 16:135–136 (Commentary on Exodus 15:1); Gillman, *A History of German Jewish Bible Translation*, 55.
[133] Mendelssohn, *JubA*, 1:462–463; *Philosophical Writings*, 199–200.
[134] Mendelssohn, *JubA*, 1:488, 484–485; *Philosophical Writings*, 226, 222–223.
[135] Mendelssohn, *JubA*, 1:463; *Philosophical Writings*, 200.
[136] See Mendelssohn, *JubA*, 1:461; *Philosophical Writings*, 196.
[137] Ibid.

artist can induce a heightened sense of awe by associating the internally sublime object with a simple, externally sublime object.[138]

In his 1771 essay "On the Sublime and Naïve in the Fine Sciences," Mendelssohn provides the example of Psalms 36:6–7:

YHWH b'hashamayim hasdekha, emunatekha ad shehakim
tzidkatekha k'harerei el, mishpatekha tehom rabbah

Herr! deine Gnade reicht über die Himmel, und deine Wahrheit über die Wolken.
Deine Gerechtigkeit, wie die Berge Gottes, und dein Recht, eine unergründliche Tiefe!

Lord! Your grace extends above the heavens, and your truth above the clouds
Your justice, as mountains of God and your law, an unfathomable depth.[139]

For Mendelssohn, the Psalmist's associating divine justice with mountains conveys the steadfastness of God's justice, while associating God's grace

[138] Mendelssohn's translation of Psalms appeared in 1783, but he cited many examples of sublime biblical poetry from Psalms in the 1771 revised version of his 1761 essay "On the Sublime and Naïve in the Fine Sciences." See Mendelssohn, *JubA,* 1:465; *Philosophical Writings,* 202; *JubA,* 16:348 (Commentary on Exodus 33:23).

[139] Mendelssohn, *JubA,* 1:465; *Philosophical Writings,* 202. Robert Lowth also cites these verses as an example of the sublime. See Lowth, *Lectures on the Sacred Poetry,* 1:353–354. Mendelssohn's translation basically follows Luther, with the exception of his translation of *hasdekha,* which Luther renders as "goodness" (*Güte*) and Mendelssohn as "grace" (*Gnade*) and the fact that Mendelssohn translates the first verse as God's grace and truth extending **beyond** the heavens and clouds, while Luther translates it more literally as God's goodness and truth extend **"to** the heavens . . . **to** and clouds" (*so weit der Himel . . . so weit die Wolcken gehen*). Mendelssohn's rendering of *hasdekha* as "grace" apparently follows Lowth, while his rendering of God's grace and truth extending *beyond* the heavens and clouds seems prompted by his desire to make the Bible's teachings about God conform with reason as Luther's translation which describes God's grace as reaching *to* the heavens and His truth *to* the clouds can be taken to imply a limit to these attributes. In his 1783 translation of the Psalms Mendelssohn renders the verses more literally: *Herr! Deine Güte reicht bis in die Himmel! Deine Treu, so hoch die Wolken gehn! Dein Recht, wie Gottes Gebirge! Dein Rathschluß- unabsehbare Tiefe!* (Lord! Your goodness extends to the heavens! Your faithfulness as high as the clouds! Your justice, as mountains of God! Your will—a vast abyss!) See Mendelssohn, *JubA,* 10.1:57. Here Mendelssohn also follows Luther in rendering *hasdekha* as *Güte* (goodness), but he now renders *emunatekha, tzidkatekha,* and *mishpatekha* differently. I surmise that Mendelssohn understands God's "goodness extend[ing] to the heavens" as including all creation, and his "faithfulness as high as clouds" as a metaphor for God's absolute trustworthiness, thereby making the verses conform with reason. In his long 1757 review of Lowth, Mendelssohn translates these verses according to Lowth's translation: *Deine Gnade Jehova! reichet in die Himmel, Deine Wahrhaftigkeit in die Wolken. Deine Gerechtigkeit, wie die Berge Gottes, Deine Urtheile, eine unabsehliche Tiefe* (Your mercy, Jehovah extends to heaven. Your truthfulness to the clouds. Your justice as mountains of God, your judgment, a vast abyss). See Mendelssohn, *JubA,* 4:40.

with the heavens, the abode of the eternally happy angels conveys the grandeur of divine love. By employing simple, naïve images obviously inadequate to the concept represented, the Psalmist is able to awaken in his audience a heightened feeling of awe for God, who exceeds human comprehension. Furthermore, the poetic skill of the divinely inspired prophet inspires awe at the power of God to move a person to produce such work of genius. For Mendelssohn, the Psalms are a remarkably effective means of instilling an emotionally moving sense of God's power, wisdom, and goodness, which can then spur a person to moral action.

We have remarked that for Mendelssohn we can experience awe/astonishment not just in viewing the objects depicted by an artist but also in appreciating the genius of the artist themselves. Mendelssohn sees this happening when one reads the Bible with proper understanding. We have discussed Mendelssohn's introduction to Ecclesiastes where he notes that the Bible contains infinite meanings intended by God and *Jerusalem,* where he writes that the Bible contains an "inexhaustible (*unergründlichen*) treasure of rational truths and religious doctrines."[140] But Mendelssohn also stresses that what makes these features of the Bible so moving is that the they appear in a book that at the surface seems very simple. As he puts it:

> The more you search in it, the more you will be astonished (*erstaunt*) at the depths of insight that lie concealed in it. At first glance, to be sure, the truth presents itself therein in its simplest attire and, as it were, free of any pretensions. Yet the more closely you approach it, and the purer, the more innocent, the more loving and longing is the glance with which you look on it, the more it will unfold before you its divine beauty (*göttlichen Schönheit*), veiled lightly, in order not to be profaned by vulgar and unholy eyes.[141]

In other words, the dynamic of the naïve accenting the enormity of the sublime is at play in the Bible as its apparent simplicity accents the infinite wisdom concealed within it. That Mendelssohn is referring to the sublime is clear from his describing the emotion accompanying this appreciation of the Bible as feeling "astonished" (*erstaunt*) the very emotion that he characterizes as present when one perceives the sublime.[142]

140 See pp. 53 and 104 of this volume.
141 Mendelssohn, *JubA,* 8:166; *Jerusalem,* 99.
142 See p. 104 of this volume.

Orality and biblical aesthetics

The sublime is just one element of Mendelssohn's account of biblical aesthetics. In Chapter 1, we saw that Mendelssohn regards Hebrew as having exceptional poetic capacities on account of it being an imaginatively rich language. In the *Be'ur* he expands on this idea by following Judah Halevi in claiming that biblical Hebrew is an oral language *par excellence* that is able to preserve many of the features of oral communication in writing.[143] Oral communication is superior to written communication because it can convey meaning and arouse emotions through intonation, stresses, and gestures. The Bible is able to convey these emotions through its special accents known as *te'amim*.[144] In *AL* and *OL*, Mendelssohn writes that these accents help guide his translation choices as they serve as punctuation marks that indicate questions, emphases, where a statement ends, etc.[145] But they are *superior* to conventional punctuation marks, as they also help the listener distinguish the different grammatical parts of the verse. Consider Genesis 4:10, when God confronts Cain after his having slain Abel:

vayomer meḥ asita	*kol d'mai ahikha*
Then [God] said: "What have you done?	The blood of your brother
tzo'akim eilei	*min ha'adamah*
cries out to me	from the ground!"

Mendelssohn notes that there is a major pause indicated by the accent *etnahta* under *asita* (have you done). This indicates that the voice should be raised as a question. But there are also minor pauses indicated by the accent *zakef katon* under *ahikha* (of your brother) and *tifha* under *eilei* (to me) before the verse closes with *min ha'adamah* (from the ground). According to Mendelssohn, these minor pauses indicate different grammatical parts of the verse. *Kol d'mai ahikha* (the blood of your brother) refers to the actor in the

143 See Halevi, *Kuzari*, 2:72, 126–127. For discussion of Mendelssohn's relation to Halevi on this point, see Jospe, "The Superiority of Oral over Written Communication," 127–136. Mendelssohn alludes to the oral quality of Hebrew in the introduction to his commentary on Ecclesiastes, where he compares the style of the Bible to the way the "natural *speaker*" (*hamedaber hativ'i*) communicates. See Mendelssohn, *JubA*, 14:148–151.

144 On Mendelssohn's use of the *te'amim* in his biblical interpretation, see Levenson, *Moses Mendelssohn's Understanding*, 1–64.

145 See Mendelssohn, *JubA*, 14:244, 327.

verse, *tzo'akim eilei* (cries out to me) refers to the action, while *min ha'adamah* (from the ground) refers to the place where the action occurs.[146] By distinguishing these different logical parts of the verse, the accents help "external speech [the verse] be aligned to internal speech [thought] with great perfection."[147]

The intelligibility of biblical poetry

Mendelssohn's emphasis on the superior comprehensibility of the Bible is especially evident in his approach to biblical poetry, which he contrasts with Greek and Latin poetry. He asserts that while Greek and Latin poetry focus primarily on the enjoyment of sounds, the Bible stresses imprinting understanding on the heart. This explains why Greek and Latin poetry depend on metrical rules based on the number of long or short syllables or on rhyming, but biblical poetry does not. While meter and rhyming are pleasant to the ear, they are rigid structures that make conveying meaning more difficult. Mendelssohn also claims that biblical poetry's focus on understanding rather than pleasant sounds makes it more translatable than "foreign poems," since it is very difficult to convey rhyme and meter in translation without spoiling the poem's "poetic majesty."[148]

Mendelssohn seeks to incorporate this understanding of biblical poetry into his translations. In a 1770 letter to Johann David Michaelis, Mendelssohn complained that he was "little satisfied with all translations of the Psalms that I have seen, even less with the poetic translations as with the prose. When they accidentally get the sense [right] they spoil the Hebraic art of poetry through *occidental versification* (*occidentalische Versgebäude*)" (emphasis mine).[149] For Mendelssohn, many German Christian translators ruined the poetic qualities of the Bible by rendering it according to Western conceptions of poetry, which depend on rhyme and meter. Instead, Mendelssohn sought

[146] See Figure 14.
[147] See Mendelssohn, *JubA*, 14:217.
[148] See Mendelssohn, *JubA*, 16:125–128; *Moses Mendelssohn's Hebrew Writings*, 344–347; *JubA*, 1:445–447; *Philosophical Writings*, 185–187. See Halevi, *Kuzari*, 2:70–74, 125–127.
[149] See Mendelssohn, *JubA*, 12.1:233 (Letter to J.D. Michaelis, November 12, 1770). In a draft of the letter that he did not send, Mendelssohn complained that existing Psalms translations were inadequate due to their adherence to "occidental rhyme construction" (*occidentalische Reimgebäude*)." See ibid., 328.

to remain true to the Hebraic character of the Psalms by translating them according to "free meter" (*freyen Sylbenmaße*).[150]

Biblical poetry as unifying heart and mind

Mendelssohn also claims that biblical poetry has a special structure through which it conveys meaning and connects heart and mind.[151] Citing Azariah de Rossi and Robert Lowth, Mendelssohn writes that biblical poetry consists of short units of words (which modern scholars call *versets*) that are parallel to one another. The parallels usually consist of versets that are of similar meaning but use different terms, or of versets that are opposed in meaning but use similar terms, though sometimes the parallel between the versets is only partial.[152] Employing short units is effective in transmitting concepts, for it allows frequent rest periods, which gives the audience time to absorb the idea, reflect on its meaning, and remember it.[153] Furthermore, by repeating concepts in different ways the concept can penetrate the heart more easily, for it allows one "to consider the matter on all sides until nothing is unclear or hidden."[154]

An example of parallelism brought by Mendelssohn is Deuteronomy 32. The parallelism of the first verse is as follows:

ha'azinu	*hashamayim*	*va'adaberah*
v'tishma	*ha'aretz*	*imrei-fi*

[150] See Mendelssohn, *JubA*, 12.1:233 (Letter to J.D. Michaelis, November 12, 1770).

[151] Mendelssohn, *JubA*, 16:126.

[152] See Mendelssohn, *JubA*, 15.2:46–49 (Commentary on Genesis 4:23). This three-fold classification of parallelism reflects Lowth's distinction between "synonymous," "antithetical," and "synthetic" parallelism. See Lowth, *Lectures on the Sacred Poetry of the Hebrews*, 2:24–59. As mentioned above, Mendelssohn published a lengthy, glowing review of Lowth's work in 1757. See p. 68 note 208 of this volume. In a Hebrew letter from Mendelssohn to Lowth dated April 26, 1781 that Mendelssohn enclosed with a copy of his *Be'ur* to Genesis and Exodus, Mendelssohn addressed Lowth as a "prince of Torah and wisdom (*sar hatorah v'hahokhmah*)" and thanked Lowth for his writings on biblical poetry, which were like "good wine to my palate." See Mendelssohn, *JubA*, 19:274. Recent scholars have challenged Lowth's classification of Hebrew poetry. J.P. Fokkelman notes that "synthetic" parallelism is "a basket term that covers everything that cannot be called synonymous or contrasting" and as such is "a counsel of despair . . . which strikes at the root of the entire triadic structure." See Fokkelman, *Reading Biblical Poetry*, 26.

[153] Mendelssohn notes that typically versets have two to four components. At times versets with the same number of components follow one another, while at other times versets of differing length alternate with one another. See Mendelssohn, *JubA*, 16:126.

[154] Mendelssohn, *JubA*, 16:126. In his German writings on aesthetics Mendelssohn notes that an effect similar to parallelism can be achieved by using "unfinished sentences, interrupted references, or monosyllabic words." See Mendelssohn, *JubA*, 1:465–466; *Philosophical Writings*, 202–204.

Listen	O Heavens	And I will speak
Hear	O Earth	The words of my mouth

While recent scholars have questioned the provenance of parallelism in Hebrew poetry and demonstrated the greater complexity in it than was recognized by Mendelssohn, parallelism remains a central concept in the modern study of biblical poetry. In a study of biblical poetry, James Kugel, one of the strongest recent critics of the emphasis on parallelism, nevertheless concludes that parallelism "is the most striking characteristic of this style."[155]

The musical Bible

We have seen that for Mendelssohn, the biblical accents aid comprehension due to their grammatical nature. But he notes that the accents' value for absorbing the Bible's teachings goes further, as they also serve as musical tropes. Mendelssohn writes that these tropes convey emotions such as "love, hatred, anger, pleasure, warning, vengeance, joy, and sadness." While one may state a concept with great precision, if one does so without voice modulation it will remain "as a dish without salt that will not enter the heart of the listener." Music, however, is able to "sweeten an idea like honey, such that its intentions enter the heart like stakes and pegs that are implanted in the hearts of the listeners." By indicating how the verse is to be sung, the accents help the written word preserve the features of oral communication and penetrate the heart.[156] In a striking passage, Mendelssohn writes that the prophets were highly skilled musicians and delivered most of their parables, rebukes, praises of God, and prophecies in song.[157]

Mendelssohn notes that biblical poetry's lack of rhyme and meter make it eminently adapted to being set to music. For while it is very difficult to adapt metered and rhyming poetry to music without rearranging words, which frequently distorts the poem's meaning, there is no such problem with biblical poetry.

[155] See Kugel, *The Idea of Biblical Poetry,* 51. On parallelism, see Alter, *The Art of Biblical Poetry,* 3–27; Fokkelman, *Reading Biblical Poetry,* 15–36, 61–87.
[156] Mendelssohn, *JubA*, 16: 126; *Moses Mendelssohn's Hebrew Writings*, 345–346.
[157] See Mendelssohn, *JubA*, 16:126; *Moses Mendelssohn's Hebrew Writings*, 346.

Mendelssohn acknowledges that "due to the length of the exile and the many afflictions and dislocations" Jews have suffered, much of the musical art of the Bible has been lost, including the melodies, the instruments used to play them, and even "the correct way of enunciating and pronouncing the syllables." But in emphasizing the centrality of a distinct Hebrew art of poetry and music that "was once widely disseminated in the nation," Mendelssohn is stressing that aesthetics is not solely the province of Gentiles, but *native to Judaism*. Despite important elements of biblical music and poetry having been forgotten, Mendelssohn writes that "there remains great appeal in *sacred poetry* (*beshirei hakodesh*), which is felt by any intelligent reader even if he does not comprehend its source" (emphasis mine). Mendelssohn is likely here referring to the great interest in biblical poetry among contemporary Christians such as Lowth, perhaps even alluding to the title of his book *On the Sacred Poetry of the Hebrews*.[158]

By highlighting a distinct biblical aesthetics that includes poetry, prose, and music, Mendelssohn seeks to stimulate German Jews' national pride. But he also seeks to motivate German Jews to cultivate *Kultur* and contribute to German Christians' acquisition of *Kultur*.

Biblical letter and rabbinic spirit

While Mendelssohn conceived the Pentateuch as the central text in male Jewish education, this does not mean that he envisioned no place for the Talmud. We have seen that Mendelssohn had Joseph taught Talmud once he was older and that Wessely recommended that Talmud be taught to elite, mature students.[159]

Mendelssohn's conception of Judaism helps explain why he gives the Bible educational priority. As we have seen, in *Jerusalem* Mendelssohn asserts that Judaism comprises three elements: (1) eternal truths about God, divine providence, and a future life; (2) historical truths about the people of Israel; and (3) revealed laws.[160] Given that the Pentateuch (the Written Torah) presents a coherent narrative of God's providential guidance of the history of Israel and the foundations of the Mosaic laws while the Talmud and other rabbinic

[158] Mendelssohn, *JubA*, 16: 126; *Moses Mendelssohn's Hebrew Writings*, 346–347. On Mendelssohn's emphasis on music in his treatment of the Bible, especially the Psalms, see Sela, "The Voice of the Psalmist."
[159] See pp. 84, 91 of this volume.
[160] See Mendelssohn, *JubA*, 8:191–193; *Jerusalem*, 126–127. See pp. 47–48 of this volume.

writings (the Oral Torah) consist mostly of legal and narrative exegeses of the Bible, subtle legal discussions, and disconnected stories (*aggadot*), it makes sense that for Mendelssohn the Pentateuch would serve as the foundation of Jewish education, with students only later being introduced to rabbinic materials as a means of clarifying the nuances and details of Mosaic law.[161] But Mendelssohn's view of the educational value of the Talmud goes beyond this.

Many Protestants beginning with Luther charged that Jews were obsessed with the biblical letter as reflected in their overly literal interpretation of the Bible, absurd midrashic exegesis, and continued practice of the ritual laws. For these Protestants, the rabbis had calcified Judaism by rejecting the spiritual message of Jesus, which caused Judaism to cease being a vibrant, living force.[162]

Mendelssohn accepts the Pauline-Protestant dichotomy between *dead letter* and *living spirit*. But he appeals to *orality* to show how Judaism preserves the Bible's living spirit. Mendelssohn locates this orality in rabbinic teaching, known as the "Oral Torah." For Mendelssohn, the biblical accents (*te'amim*) were revealed to Moses on Mount Sinai and transmitted orally, and as we have seen, he regards them as helping keep the Bible alive by conveying its oral qualities.[163] But Mendelssohn's most extensive discussion of Judaism's orality occurs in his treatment of the Talmud and rabbinic literature. While he asserts that Judaism is distinguished from natural religion primarily by its emphasis on revealed law (*halakhah*), in a striking reversal of the Christian charge that halakhic observance reflects attachment to the dead letter, Mendelssohn calls halakhah a "living script (*lebendige Schrift*)."[164] His philosophy of halakhah is bound up with his emphasis on the centrality of inner conviction in religion that Luther stressed in his critique of Catholicism.[165]

In *Jerusalem*, Mendelssohn writes that "divine religion . . . commands actions only as tokens (*Zeichen*) of convictions (*Gesinnung*)"[166] and that religious acts practiced without proper convictions *have no religious*

[161] On Mendelssohn's account of the components of the Oral Law see p. 60 note 178 of this volume.
[162] Condemnation of the Talmud was not unique to Protestantism and was prevalent among medieval and modern Catholics. On medieval Catholic attacks on the Talmud, see Cohen, *Living Letters of the Law*, 210–211, 263–265, 317–363.
[163] On Mendelssohn's account of the origin of the *te'amim*, see p. 45 note 116 of this volume.
[164] Mendelssohn, *JubA*, 8;169; *Jerusalem*, 102.
[165] See pp. 8–9 of this volume.
[166] Mendelssohn, *JubA*, 8:140; *Jerusalem*, 73.

value.[167] If, what counts in religion is only inner conviction, why is halakhic *practice* the distinguishing feature of Judaism?

Mendelssohn's answer is that halakhah plays a crucial role in *promoting proper religious conviction*. The ritual laws are a script that direct the practitioner to contemplate the historical and eternal truths upon which Judaism is grounded. For example, by eating unleavened bread (*matzah*) on Passover, a Jew is reminded of the historical truth of the exodus from Egypt and by implication of the eternal truth of the existence of a providential God, since *matzah* symbolizes the bread that the Israelites ate hastily after God miraculously freed them from Egyptian slavery.[168]

In one respect the value of attaching ideas to practices is very simple. Enacting metaphysical moral truths is a way of changing them from inert propositions into living truths, thereby fusing "doctrine and life (*Lehr und Leben*)."[169] In this way, halakhah plays a similar role to biblical poetry. But halakhah's ability to promote religious conviction is also connected to the pedagogic role played by the Oral Law.

Elias Sacks notes that for Mendelssohn a feature of language is that the meaning of words changes over time, while the form of written words remains rigid.[170] For example, the word, "God," means something quite different to an Aristotelian than to a Cartesian. This presents a serious problem for understanding the Bible, which was composed in a time far removed from the present day and thus risks becoming a dead letter. For Mendelssohn, the Oral Law helps alleviate this problem as it is a lived conversation between a teacher and student, which gives the teacher the opportunity to convey the purpose of halakhah and the meaning of biblical doctrines in terms that the student can understand.[171] For Mendelssohn,

[167] As Mendelssohn puts it, "religious actions . . . either flow from the free impulse of the soul or they are an empty show and contrary to the true spirit of religion." See Mendelssohn, *JubA*, 8:128; *Jerusalem*, 60; *JubA*, 14:25.

[168] See Mendelssohn, *JubA*, 16:95–96 (Commentary to Exodus 12:15), and especially Mendelssohn, *JubA*, 16:111 (Commentary to Exodus 13:16), which emphasizes the connection between historical truth and metaphysical truth. Michael Morgan and Arnold Eisen debate the precise mechanism by which halakhah links the mind to religious doctrines. See Morgan, "History and Modern Jewish Thought," 476; Eisen, "Divine Legislation," 253–255. For a nice discussion of the debate, see Arkush, *Moses Mendelssohn and the Enlightenment*, 212–218. For a more elaborate discussion of the semiotics of halakhah, see Freudenthal, *No Religion without Idolatry*, 89–104.

[169] See Mendelssohn, *JubA*, 8:184; *Jerusalem*, 118.

[170] See Mendelssohn, *JubA*, 8:168–169; *Jerusalem*, 102; *JubA*, 2:290; *Philosophical Writings*, 272.

[171] Mendelssohn, *JubA*, 8:193; *Jerusalem*, 127–128. As Mendelssohn puts it when discussing the revelation of Sinaitic law: "Yet only the most essential part of them [the laws revealed on Sinai] was entrusted to letters, and without the unwritten explanations, delimitations, and more precise determinations [that were] transmitted orally and propagated through *oral, living instruction*, even these written laws are mostly incomprehensible, or inevitably became so over the course of time. For

ritual law is extremely well suited to provoking conversation since the nature of ritual is that its purpose is often opaque, which naturally leads the student to inquire about its meaning. In this way, ritual law and oral instruction help keep biblical teachings alive.[172]

Mendelssohn contrasts the Jewish concern with oral conversation stemming from the semiotic function of ritual with the contemporary European emphasis on book learning by invoking the distinction between dead letter and living spirit. He laments that "we teach and instruct one another only through writings. We learn to know nature and man only from writings. . . . Everything is dead letter (*todter Buchstabe*). The spirit of living conversation (*lebendigen Unterhaltung*) has vanished."[173] For Mendelssohn, European book culture has led to social alienation and lack of respect for lived tradition. He sees Judaism's emphasis on orality and lived instruction as providing a model for a cultural corrective that transcends religious concerns.[174]

Mendelssohn also suggests that the Oral Law keeps halakhic practice from becoming dead letter by providing a mechanism for adapting it to new circumstances. Were the entire law spelled out in detail in the Bible, it would be difficult for it to accommodate new realities. But biblical law is often ambiguous, leaving it open to being adapted. The mechanism by which the Torah is applied to new circumstances is the rabbinic Oral Law, which has a fluidity not possessed by the Bible. Talmudic orality is thus key to keeping Judaism living.[175]

Bible translation and civil rights

Mendelssohn's *Be'ur* is connected with his plea for Jewish civil rights.[176] Enlightenment writers regularly argued that Jews could not be granted civil

no words or written signs preserve their meaning unchanged throughout a generation (emphasis mine)." Also see Mendelssohn, *JubA*, 8:168–169; *Jerusalem*, 102.

[172] Mendelssohn, *JubA*, 8:184–185; *Jerusalem*, 118–119. See Sacks, *Moses Mendelssohn's Living Script*, 61–92.

[173] Mendelssohn, *JubA*, 8:169–170; *Jerusalem*, 103–104.

[174] See Hilfrich, *Lebendige Schrift*.

[175] Mendelssohn, *JubA*, 8:185; *Jerusalem*, 119–120. As Mendelssohn puts it, "the unwritten laws, the oral tradition, the living instruction from man to man, from mouth to heart, were to explain, enlarge, limit, and define more precisely what, for wise intentions and with wise moderation, remained undetermined in the written law."

[176] I treat other elements of his argument for Jewish civil rights elsewhere. See my article Gottlieb, "From Tolerance to Acceptance: Moses Mendelssohn's Solution to the Jewish Problem."

rights because of their immorality and hatred for Christians. In his 1750 *General-Privilegium* Frederick the Great had noted the "various faults and abuses among the licensed and tolerated Jews" and expressed concern that the "rampant increase of these abuses has caused enormous damage and hardship not only to the public but particularly to *the Christian inhabitants and merchants*" (emphasis mine).[177] Thirty-two years later, Michaelis pointed to the "deceitfulness of the Jew" to argue against granting Jews civil rights, claiming that a Jew was twenty-five times more likely to be a member of a "gang of thieves" than a German Christian.[178]

Michaelis further argued that it was illogical to grant Jews the right to be Prussian citizens since Jews self-segregated through their strict religious laws and did not regard Christians as their kinsmen. As Michaelis put it, "As long as Jews . . . refuse, for example, to eat together with us and to form sincere friendship at the table, they will never become fully integrated in the way that Catholics, Lutherans, Germans, Wends, and French live in one state."[179] Michaelis further contended that Jews did not regard fellow Christians as brothers due to their "national pride" (*Nationalstoltz*) deriving from "their conception of themselves as God's chosen people."[180]

Mendelssohn responded to these arguments by adapting an influential Augustinian argument. Augustine had claimed that God preserved the Jews as a separate group to bear witness to the truth of Christianity. God allowed the Jews to survive in a subjugated, lowly state to show that God had rejected them for not accepting Christ.[181] Mendelssohn drew on this concept of the Jews as divine witnesses but gave it a new interpretation. For Mendelssohn, the reason that Jews must maintain themselves as a separate group is because through their symbolic ritual practices, which are binding on themselves alone, they bear witness to the eternal truths of natural religion that promote universal morality for the benefit of humanity.[182] The meaning of

[177] Frederick the Great also worried that Jewish "foreigners" (*Fremden*) were surreptitiously entering Prussia and harming Christians through their fraudulent activities. He therefore banned all foreign Jews from emigrating to Prussia unless they brought a fortune of 10,000 Reichsthaler with them and paid a hefty entry tax. See Frederick the Great's "Charter Decreed for the Jews of Prussia" in *JMW*, 21–26.

[178] See Michaelis's 1782 response to Dohm in ibid., 34–35.

[179] Ibid., 36.

[180] See Michaelis' response to Dohm in *JMW*, 35.

[181] For discussion of Augustine's doctrine of witness, see Cohen, *Living Letters of the Law*, 23–65; Fredrikson, *Augustine and the Jews: A Christian Defense of Jews and Judaism*.

[182] Mendelssohn emphasizes the non-proselytizing nature of Judaism in several writings beginning with his 1769 Open Letter to Lavater. See Mendelssohn, *JubA*, 7:10–12; 8:191–193; *Moses Mendelssohn: Writings*, 9–10, 112–113.

Jewish election is not *Jewish superiority* but, rather, *superogatory Jewish responsibility* to humanity.

Following the publication of *Jerusalem*, Mendelssohn's close friend Herz Homberg asked him whether Jewish difference was still necessary. Mendelssohn responded that given that "polytheism, anthropomorphism, and religious usurpation (*religiös Usurpation*) [still] dominated the world," Jews were vitally needed to preserve "genuine" (read: rational) "theism."[183]

For this reason, Mendelssohn argued that granting Jews civil rights would *strengthen* Prussian society. Greater civil rights would increase sociability between Prussian Christians and Jews, which would bolster rational theism and morality. Given the importance Mendelssohn placed on the *Be'ur* for German Jews' moral and spiritual development, it is clear that he saw the *Be'ur* as not just benefitting Jews, but also Christians and all humanity.

While Mendelssohn's *Be'ur* is intimately connected to his endeavor to promote German Jews' entry into the middle-class, he declared adherence to Judaism nonnegotiable. We have seen that Michaelis claimed that halakhah separated Jews from Christians, thereby rendering them ineligible for civil rights. But Michaelis put Jews in a double bind by claiming that Jews who abandoned halakhah could not be granted civil rights since they evinced a lack of moral backbone. As Michaelis put it, "when I see a Jew eating pork in order no doubt to offend his religion, then I find it impossible to trust his word since I cannot see into his heart."[184]

Mendelssohn emphatically asserted the inviolability of halakhah given its origin in divine revelation and its role in promoting the Jews' mission to humanity. As such, he deemed any demand that Jews barter commitment to halakhah for civil rights a nonstarter. As he put it in *Jerusalem*, "if civil union cannot be obtained under any other condition than our departing from the laws that we still consider binding on us, then we are sincerely sorry to find it necessary to declare that we must rather do without civil union."[185]

[183] Mendelssohn, *JubA*, 13:134 (Letter to Homberg September 22, 1783); *Moses Mendelssohn: Writings*, 124. For Mendelssohn, Christian ideas such as the Incarnation and the Trinity undermined rationality, Original Sin and Vicarious Atonement threatened moral improvement, and the idea that salvation required confessing faith in Jesus led Christians to persecute non-Christians (or even Christians of different denominations). Jews were called to bear witness against these dangerous Christian falsehoods. Mendelssohn never, however, publicly stated his criticisms of Christianity for fear of alienating the Christian majority. For detailed discussion of this point, see Gottlieb, *Faith and Freedom*, chs. 2 and 4.

[184] See *JMW*, 35.

[185] Mendelssohn, *JubA*, 8:200; *Jerusalem*, 135.

Mendelssohn further claimed that it violated the Enlightenment principle of *liberty of conscience* to insist that Jews abandon religious difference for the sake of civil rights. Cranz had proposed that the best way to promote tolerance and love among Jews and Christians would be to unite them under a single, enlightened religious faith. Mendelssohn rejected this proposal, contending that if a single set of religious symbols came to be regarded as the foundation of tolerance and social harmony, anyone who questioned them would come to be demonized as a threat to society. As he put it, "Establish, once and for all, the articles [of a unique religious faith] . . . then woe to the unfortunate, who comes a day later and finds something to criticize even in these modest, purified words! He is a disturber of the peace. To the stake with him!"[186] For Mendelssohn, true toleration required preserving rights for Jews not only as individuals, but also as members of a separate national and religious group.[187]

The Bible and Prussian patriotism

Michaelis argued that since Jews regarded the German states in which they resided as "temporary homes" as they awaited their messianic restoration to Palestine, they could not be granted civil rights since they would never be patriotic, loyal citizens.[188] In a response to Michaelis, Mendelssohn appealed to the Talmud, noting that it prohibited Jews "*even to think* of a return to Palestine by force" and that absent the miracles depicted in the Bible as preceding the final redemption, Jews were commanded to "not take the smallest step in the direction of forcing a return and a restoration of our nation."[189]

But Mendelssohn recognized that there were Jews who felt little patriotic loyalty to the state, and *he used the Bible* to promote patriotism among Jews. During the Seven Years War (1756–1763), Mendelssohn composed and/or translated several patriotic hymns, sermons, and odes, many of which were

186 Mendelssohn, *JubA*, 8:198, 203; *Jerusalem*, 137–138. For further discussion of this argument see Gottlieb, "Mendelssohn's Metaphysical Defense of Religious Pluralism."

187 Leo Baeck made this point about Mendelssohn in a speech at a Mendelssohn celebration in 1929. See Baeck, *Mendelssohn Gedenkfeier*, 17–18.

188 See Michaelis' response to Dohm in *JMW*, 35.

189 See Michaelis's response to Dohm and Mendelssohn's reply to Michaelis in *JMW*, 35–36, 41. Mendelssohn cites the three oaths from *BT*, Ketubot, 110a–111b, which interpret Song of Songs 2:7, 3:5, and 8:4.

recited in the synagogue.[190] His 1763 *Sermon on Peace (Friedenspredigt)*, written to celebrate the end of the Seven Years War, was read at a special thanksgiving service in the central synagogue in Berlin. In the sermon, Mendelssohn adduced biblical sanction for Jewish patriotism by comparing Frederick the Great to Moses:

> What did *Frederick* do as the bolts of projectiles rained around him on all sides seemingly having him as their target? He did his duty [. . .] unstoppable like a divine wind-storm, he brought his protection from province to province and defended the innocent. He did what God and justice demand from the wise, and brought success to those of us who entrusted our fate to his wisdom and leadership. As the children of Israel left Egypt and saw before them the open sea and behind them the powerful armies of their pursuers, Moses cried out to the Lord. But the Lord answered him: 'Why do you cry to me? *Tell the Children of Israel to move forward.*'[191] The Talmud adds: 'They [the Israelites] have no other duty than to give themselves over and entrust themselves to My promise. Let them do their duty; Moses do your duty and lead them and I will direct the escape according to My wise council.'[192] In the same way the Lord teaches through His law (*Gesetz*) that when danger arises, calmly observe your duties, steadfastly hold firm at the post to which God and the Fatherland have placed you, and with unwavering feet follow the voice of virtue through all violent storms (*Ungewitter*) to the very edge of the precipice and then 'you will not fear when the earth reels and the mountains topple into the sea' (Psalms 46:3).[193]

Mendelssohn compares Frederick's devotion to protecting his nation to Moses's. Just as the Bible depicts ancient Jews expressing faithfulness to God

[190] The *Jubiläumsausgabe* includes two patriotic hymns (*Danklied über den Sieg bie Roßbach, Danklied über den Sieg bei Leuthen*), two sermons (*Dankpredigt über den Sieg bei Leuthen, Friedenspredigt*), and several odes. See Mendelssohn, *JubA*, 10.1:271–304. Mendelssohn translated into German the two Hebrew hymns which were originally written by Leo Hartog and composed the *Friedenspredigt* himself. There is a scholarly disagreement over whether Mendelssohn composed the *Dankpredigt über den Sieg bei Leuthen* or whether it was written by the Chief Rabbi of Berlin, David Fränkel, and translated by Mendelssohn. For an argument that Fränkel was the author, see Gad Freudenthal, "Rabbi David Fränckel, Moses Mendelssohn, and the Beginning of the Berlin Haskalah: Reattributing a Patriotic Sermon."

[191] See Exodus 14:15.

[192] Mendelssohn seems to be drawing on Rashi's commentary on Exodus 14:15, which is based on the rabbinic midrashic collection *Mekhilta D'rabbi Yishmael* Beshalah, parashah 14, commentary to Exodus 15:1–2.

[193] Mendelssohn, *JubA*, 10.1:294.

by trusting Moses's leadership, contemporary Jews can express faithfulness to God by being loyal to Frederick the Great and the Prussian state.

Judaism as Protestant religion for Mendelssohn

Protestants saw themselves as preserving the living spirit of Christianity and charged Catholics and Jews with being slaves to the dead letter. We have seen that Mendelssohn accepts the Pauline-Protestant dichotomy between living spirit and dead letter, but asserts that rabbinic tradition preserves Judaism as living spirit and he criticizes contemporary Christian culture as being beholden to the dead letter. Before leaving Mendelssohn, it is worth exploring how he deploys Catholicism and Protestantism as exemplary categories, connecting Judaism with Protestantism and tarring his opponents with acting like Catholics.

Mendelssohn identified Catholicism with *religious despotism* whose goal was to regulate all spheres of life, including the political. As he put it at the beginning of *Jerusalem*: "Despotism has a definite answer to every question. You need not trouble yourself any more about limits; for he who has everything no longer asks how much? The same holds true for *ecclesiastical government according to Roman Catholic principles*. It deals fully with every circumstance and is, as it were, all of one piece" (emphasis mine).[194]

Mendelssohn also presented Catholicism as *stifling independent inquiry and freedom of conscience*. In the introduction to his 1763 "Prize Essay," he wrote that "it is better for an individual to judge in accordance with his meager insights than to recognize and blindly follow some *philosophical pope* (*philosophischen Papst*) wherever the latter wants to lead him" (emphasis mine).[195] In speaking of a "philosophical pope" Mendelssohn was not referring to a Catholic philosopher, but to a despotic attitude toward philosophical truth.

Mendelssohn also linked Catholicism with *intolerance and anti-Judaism*. In his preface to Menasseh ben Israel, he wrote that, "I have often conversed with many insightful and otherwise not unreasonable, thinking Christians from Poland *and other Catholic countries* who could not entirely divest themselves of prejudices (*Vorurtheile*) against our nation" (emphasis mine).[196]

194 Mendelssohn, *JubA*, 8:103–104; *Jerusalem*, 34. See Joskowicz, *The Modernity of Others*, 63–64.
195 Mendelssohn, *JubA*, 2; Mendelssohn, *Philosophical Writings*, 278.
196 Mendelssohn, *JubA*, 8:9; Joskowicz, *The Modernity of Others*, 69.

For Mendelssohn, Catholicism's tendency to foster prejudice and superstition naturally caused those under its orbit to espouse hateful attitudes toward Jews. In this respect Mendelssohn would likely have classified the Protestant anti-Judaism of a Luther or Eisenmenger as reflecting a "Catholic" frame of mind.

By contrast, Mendelssohn associated Protestantism with *intellectual freedom* and the *liberation of politics from religious power*. After describing Catholic despotism at the beginning of *Jerusalem*, he wrote, ". . . the extraordinary confusion, the civil as well as ecclesiastical disturbances during *the early years of the Reformation* . . . the despotism of the Roman church was abolished, but what other form was to be introduced in its place? (emphasis mine)"[197] Mendelssohn interpreted the Protestant Reformation as a rebellion against Catholic despotism.[198]

Mendelssohn also used *Jesuitism* as a synonym for *hypocrisy and deception.*[199] For example, he wrote that he would not accuse a religious teacher of "hypocrisy or Jesuitry" just because he mixes "some untruth" into his "otherwise salutary exposition of truths beneficial to the public."[200] Similarly, Mendelssohn labelled the Christian attempt to convince Jews that a union of religions is the best path to peace as a "Jesuitical trickery" that masked a secret agenda of seeking to convert Jews to Christianity.[201]

In sum, for Mendelssohn Protestantism represented freedom of conscience and the liberation of politics from religious control while Catholicism represented despotism that sought to stifle freedom inquiry and control all spheres of life, including politics, through hypocrisy and deception.[202] That

[197] Mendelssohn, *JubA*, 8:104; *Jerusalem*, 34.

[198] Mendelssohn understood that eighteenth-century Protestant Enlightenment operated on a different basis than Luther's sixteenth-century Protestantism, as reason came to replace faith as the touchstone of individual conscience. As he put it in his unpublished outline for *Jerusalem*, "The modern Reformation of the eighteenth century, is no longer founded on revelation, leaves everything to reason." But conceptually he identified Protestantism with liberty of conscience. See Mendelssohn, *JubA*, 8:96; *Jerusalem*, 248.

[199] In the eighteenth century some Enlightenment figures feared that Jesuits were appealing to Enlightenment ideals like freedom and tolerance to promote despotism and intolerance. See Gottlieb, *Faith and Freedom*, 78–79; Blum, *J.A. Starck et la Querelle du Crypto-Catholicisme en Allemagne;* Di Giovanni, "Hegel, Jacobi, and Crypto-Catholicism," 53–72. As one opponent of Jesuitism put it in 1786, "In the nations which are still subject to Rome the Jesuits continue to foster superstition and seek desperately to prevent the introduction of Enlightenment, while in 'enlightened' nations they vigorously promote Enlightenment with the deliberate purpose of blinding the people through an excess of light." August Anton Göchhausen, *Enthüllung des Systems der Weltbürger-Republik* (*Exposure of the Cosmopolitan System*), quoted in Epstein, *The Genesis of German Conservatism*, 99.

[200] Mendelssohn, *JubA*, 8:139; *Jerusalem*, 72.

[201] Mendelssohn, *JubA*, 13:134; *Moses Mendelssohn: Writings*, 124 (Letter to Herz Homberg, September 22, 1783).

[202] Mendelssohn's description of Catholicism as defined by seeking to put all spheres of life under the dominion of religion was later repeated by Ernst Simon in his 1951 Hebrew essay *Are We Still*

Mendelssohn used "Protestantism" and "Catholicism" as ideal categories can be seen in his applying the Catholic label "Jesuistical" to Protestants like F.H. Jacobi whom he saw as hypocritical and deceptive.[203] In Mendelssohn's view, by denying power to religious institutions, giving priority to individual rational conscience in religious matters, and espousing religious tolerance and pluralism Judaism expressed a "Protestant" concept of religion.

Conclusion

When the issue of Jewish civil rights began to be publicly debated in Prussia, critics routinely argued that the Jews' moral defects precluded them from citizenship. Mendelssohn defended Jewish civil rights, offering an ethical-religious argument. He adamantly rejected the idea that Jews trade halakhic commitment for civil rights, seeing this as contradicting the Jewish mission to humanity and as violating liberty of conscience.

But Mendelssohn recognized that critics were not entirely wrong in discerning cultural, moral, and intellectual deficiencies among German Jews. While he regarded Christian persecution as largely to blame for these problems, he did not think Jews could wait for Christians to fix their problems. Jews must take responsibility for their own self-development.[204]

For Mendelssohn, the problem was not Judaism but, the prevailing Jewish educational system, which distorted Jewish teachings by focusing almost exclusively on talmudic *pilpul* while largely neglecting secular education, the Bible, Hebrew, ethics, and rational principles of religion.[205] Mendelssohn reformatory efforts comprised two main elements. The first involved showing that classical Jewish religious texts promoted middle-class values of *Kultur* and *Bildung*. He did this primarily through the *Be'ur* by emphasizing the Bible's aesthetic qualities and moral teachings, but also by showing how the Talmud and rabbinic literature inculcated *Kultur* and *Bildung* by preserving the "living spirit" of biblical teachings. The theological foundation

Jews? This essay was republished in Simon, *Are We Still Jews?: Essays*, 9–46. A partial English translation appeared in *Commentary Magazine* under the title "Are We Israelis Still Jews?: The Search for Judaism in the New Society" in April 1953.

[203] See Gottlieb, *Faith and Freedom*, 78–81.

[204] See Mendelssohn, *JubA*, 8:6, 7:9; *Moses Mendelssohn: Writings*, 43, 8.

[205] Mendelssohn's emphasis on ethics and rational principles of religion can be seen in his contributions to Friedländer's *Reader*. See p. 83 note 29 of this volume.

of Mendelssohn's view was his conviction that God's purpose in creating the world was to enable human beings to perfect themselves. In emphasizing that the divinely revealed Torah aimed to inculcate *Kultur* and *Bildung* through obedience to God's commandments, we can see that for Mendelssohn being middle-class was a way of serving God.

The second element of Mendelssohn's reformatory project involved establishing modern Jewish schools. He supported the *Jüdische Freischule*, which was founded by David Friedländer, Isaak Daniel Itzig, and Naphtali Herz Wessely. In *Divrei Shalom Ve'emet,* Wessely presented an influential critique of German Jewish education and offered a new vision of it. The *Be'ur* was Mendelssohn's main contribution to this project, and he hoped it would become the centerpiece of the new German Jewish curriculum.

The education that Mendelssohn gave to his son Joseph is close to Wessely's vision and dovetails with the curriculum of the *Freischule*. But Mendelssohn did not send his sons to the *Freischule*, instead employing private tutors to educate them. This reflected class stigma as many maskilic schools were regarded as schools for the poor. While Mendelssohn actively sought to reform Jewish education for *males*, he remained quite traditional in his approach to *female education*, providing no real Jewish education to them and only a general education that aimed to prepare them to become cultured middle-class Jewish housewives.

Heine was wrong in claiming that Mendelssohn's reformation involved returning to the Bible and rejecting the Talmud. Rather, Mendelssohn's reformation involved *rethinking* the educational functions of the Written Torah and Oral Torah to formulate a new ethical-religious vision of German Judaism deeply steeped in tradition. But Heine's intuition that Mendelssohn sought to displace the Talmud as the center of Jewish education and replace it with the Bible is correct. The centerpiece of Mendelssohn's educational efforts was the *Be'ur*, which he envisioned would further the moral and religious education of German Jews, Christians, and all humanity.

Mendelssohn internalized Protestant dichotomies, most notably the distinction between living spirit and dead letter. His defense of Judaism included portraying the rabbinic Oral Torah as what preserves the Bible's living spirit. More generally, Mendelssohn used Protestantism as a shorthand for free religion based on conviction, and Catholicism for despotic religion grounded in coercion. He aligned Judaism with Protestantism while critiquing "Catholic" forms of religion.

PART II

WISSENSCHAFT AND REFORM

Leopold Zunz between Scholarship and Synagogue

3
Translation versus Midrash

Leopold Zunz (1794–1886) is generally deemed the founder of *Wissenschaft des Judentums* (the academic study of Judaism).[1] In 1819, he helped establish the first organization devoted to *Wissenschaft*, the *Verein für Kultur und Wissenschaft des Judenthums* (Society for the Culture and Science of Judaism), and in 1823 he launched the first Jewish studies journal, the short-lived *Zeitschrift für die Wissenschaft des Judenthums* (*Journal for the Academic Study of Judaism*). Zunz was a prolific writer whose works include the 1818 essay *On Rabbinic Literature* (*Etwas über die rabbinische Literatur*), which Giuseppe Veltri calls the "*Magna Charta* of modern research on Jewish history and literature,"[2] and his 1832 *The Sermons of the Jews* (*Die gottesdienstlichen Vorträge der Juden*), which the 1906 *Jewish Encyclopedia* called "the most important Jewish work published in the nineteenth century."[3]

Zunz served as an elector to the Prussian parliament, giving fiery speeches in support of democracy and liberty, and he was a passionate and eloquent advocate of Jewish emancipation. He served as preacher in the Reform Beer Temple in Berlin from 1821 to 1822 and was intimately involved in Jewish education, serving as the director of a Jewish community school from 1825 to 1829 and as founding director of a school for Jewish teacher training from 1840 to 1850.

[1] I will use the German word *Wissenschaft* untranslated to refer to the scholarly study of Judaism because the German word implies science, which is missing from the English word "academic", while the English word "science" is generally limited to the natural sciences. When I use the word *Wissenschaft* by itself, I am referring to *Wissenschaft des Judentums*.

[2] See Veltri, "A Jewish Luther," 339. More recently, see Veltri, *Alienated Wisdom*, 121–126.

[3] See Hirsch, "Zunz, Leopold," 701. The prominent Reform Rabbi Emil Hirsch authored this entry. Abraham Geiger called the *Sermons* "a historical event, a turning point in the movement of spirit. It inaugurated new activity in all spheres; and there is not a scholar who would not acknowledge the impulse and the instruction that he received from this work." See Geiger, *Abraham Geiger's nachgelassene Schriften*, 1:307. David Kaufmann characterized the *Sermons* as "no book, but an event; not a literary work, but a school has been founded" (*Jewish Chronicle,* August 15, 1884, p. 7). These and other sources praising the *Sermons* are cited in Cohon, "Zunz and Reform Judaism," 262–263. Also see the praise from the historian of rabbinic Judaism, Isaac Hirsch Weiss, cited in Schorsch, *Leopold Zunz*, 84.

The Jewish Reformation. Michah Gottlieb, Oxford University Press (2021). © Oxford University Press.
DOI: 10.1093/oso/9780199336388.003.0004

We have seen that Mendelssohn placed much more emphasis on the Bible than on the Talmud both in his vision of Judaism and in his work on Jewish texts. While Heine is wrong to claim that Mendelssohn rejected the Talmud, his intuition that Mendelssohn and the Maskilim sought to center Judaism on the Bible is correct. But in the introduction to his 1895 collection of essays *On the Parting of the Ways* (*Al Parashat Derakhim*), the Zionist thinker Asher Ginsburg, better known by his pen name Ahad Ha'am, criticized *Wissenschaft* not for *overemphasizing* the Bible, but for *neglecting* it in favor of post-biblical writings. For Ginsburg this reflected *Wissenschaft* scholars' attachment to exilic Judaism and indifference to what he called the "distinctive spirit of our nation."[4]

Ismar Schorsch has recently shown that Ahad Ha'am's critique of *Wissenschaft* is "only partially correct" in the case of Zunz. While it is true that in *On Rabbinic Literature* Zunz defined the field of *Wissenschaft* as post-biblical, "rabbinic" Jewish literature and that the vast majority of Zunz's scholarship focused on these writings, near the end of his career Zunz published a series of essays on biblical criticism titled *Critical Studies of the Bible* (*Bibelkritisches*).[5] Zunz's early scholarly work did not focus on the Bible taken on its own, but the first chapter of *The Sermons of the Jews* (henceforth: *Sermons*) was devoted to a critical exposition of the Book of Chronicles, and a central concern of the work was to explore the relationship between rabbinic teachings and the Bible.[6] In 1838 Zunz edited the first German Jewish translation of the entire Hebrew Bible, titled *The Twenty Four Books of Holy Scripture* (*Die vier und zwanzig Bücher der Heiligen Schrift*).[7]

I will not focus on Zunz's 1873 essays on biblical criticism, which have been well treated by Schorsch.[8] Instead, over the next two chapters I will focus on Zunz's early scholarly work through the 1838 Bible translation. Four questions will be considered: *First*, how does Zunz conceive the relationship between the Bible and rabbinic literature? *Second*, what is the role of each for contemporary Judaism? *Third*, how does Zunz's early scholarly work on rabbinic literature relate to his Bible translation? And *fourth*, what are the aims and distinctive features of his Bible translation?

4 Ahad Ha'am, *Al Parashat Derakhim*, 4 vols. 1:xi, cited in Schorsch, "Leopold Zunz on the Hebrew Bible," 433.

5 Zunz published these essays from 1873 to 1874. They were reprinted in Zunz, *GS* 1:217–270.

6 I would add that Zunz's subtitle to *The Sermons of the Jews* is "a contribution to the study of antiquity, *biblical criticism* (*biblischen Kritik*), and religious literature and history" (emphasis mine).

7 See Schorsch, "Leopold Zunz on the Hebrew Bible," esp. 431–441.

8 Schorsch, ibid., 445–447; *Leopold Zunz*, 215–219.

Hermann Cohen famously quipped to Franz Rosenzweig that Zunz "could have been a great historian, but was actually nothing but an antiquarian."[9] In distinguishing the "antiquarian" from the "great historian," Cohen was claiming that Zunz was a scholar obsessed with minutiae who sought knowledge for its own sake, unconcerned with the practical implications of his work. Cohen was no doubt familiar with Zunz's political activities and involvement in Jewish education. So he was claiming that Zunz's scholarly work was *isolated* from his moral, political, and religious concerns. I will show how Zunz's scholarly work is, in fact, intimately tied to practical concerns.[10]

In this chapter I will focus on how Zunz conceives the Bible's relation to rabbinic literature and the function of Bible translation in the *Sermons*. In the next chapter, I will explore the aims and methods of Zunz's own Bible translation.

The politics of scholarship: Zunz's vision of *Wissenschaft*

To understand Zunz's project in the *Sermons*, it is important to appreciate his vision of academic Jewish studies and the political context that spawned it. In 1818 Zunz, then a twenty-three-year old student at the University of Berlin, published *On Rabbinic Literature*, which called for creating a new academic field focused on what he called "rabbinic" or "neo-Hebraic" literature.[11] For Zunz, "rabbinic" literature included not only the Mishnah, Midrash, and Talmud but all post-biblical Jewish writing.[12] Near the beginning of the essay, Zunz notes that this literature is largely neglected because Christian scholars adopt a derogatory attitude toward it, seeing it as containing perverse, warped interpretations of Scripture that occlude Scripture's meaning.[13] For Christians, the Bible alone is the true word of God and so worthy of study.

[9] See Cohen, *Jüdische Schriften*, 1:332. Schorsch notes that the first person to call Zunz an antiquarian was the historian Isaak Markus Jost in 1846 when he wrote, "In antiquarian research, especially in biblical criticism, and the field of Jewish literature, Dr. Zunz stands nearly alone." See Schorsch, *Leopold Zunz*, 4.

[10] This approach is also taken by Schorsch in his recent biography of Zunz.

[11] See Zunz, *GS*, 1:3, note 1; "On Rabbinic Literature" in *JMW*, 246.

[12] In his later 1845 work, *On History and Literature* (*Zur Geschichte und Literatur*), Zunz observes that Christian theologians gave post-biblical Jewish literature the name "rabbinic" because Jewish books were only seen from the standpoint of theology and Jews were only of interest as "church material" (*Kirchenmaterial*), that is, as witnesses or adversaries of triumphant Christianity. See Zunz, *Zur Geschichte*, 20.

[13] See Zunz, *GS*, 1:3; "On Rabbinic Literature" in *JMW*, 246. See Luther, *Luther's Works*, 47:176. See Manuel, *The Broken Staff*, 249–324; Katz, *From Prejudice to Destruction*, 13–33, 51–106, 147–222.

Zunz observes that this prejudice towards rabbinic literature continued even when Protestant Bible scholars discarded an explicitly theological agenda.[14]

Zunz's essay must be understood in the context of political upheaval in Prussia. In 1807, Napoleon created the Kingdom of Westphalia, merging the Prussian territories west of the Elbe—Hanover, Brunswick, and Hesse. He installed his brother Jerome as King of Westphalia, and Jerome created an egalitarian legal system, which emancipated the Jews. Under French influence Prussia began to liberalize, and in 1812 Jews were granted civil equality on condition they use fixed family names signed in German or Latin and German or another "living language" for their commercial dealings.[15] But in 1813 Napoleon was defeated, and two years later Prussia, Austria, and Russia created the Holy Alliance, which sought to turn back democracy, revolution, and secularism by uniting Europe through Christian values. This led to increasing anti-Jewish rhetoric, and Prussian Jews saw their recently won rights contested.

Protestant writers such as the philosopher Jakob Friedrich Fries argued that Jews' adherence to the Talmud led to their inferior morals, lack of patriotism, and general misanthropy. For this reason, Fries argued, they should only be granted citizenship if they publicly proclaimed their willingness to abandon the Talmud.[16] In 1815 Christian Friedrich Rühs, a nationalist professor of history at the University of Berlin, published a pamphlet titled *On the Claims of the Jews to Civil Rights in Germany*, in which he argued that Jews were ineligible for citizenship because they were concerned solely with the well-being of their own nation, whose mentality was fundamentally alien to Germans. Rühs reasoned that since "no man can serve two masters," it was a "strange contradiction that a citizen of the Jewish kingdom should seek to be at the same time a citizen of the Christian state."[17] Zunz was very familiar with Rühs, having taken a history course with him, though he apparently left the course after Rühs published his pamphlet.[18]

[14] See Zunz, *GS*, 1:4; "On Rabbinic Literature" in *JMW*, 246.

[15] See "Emancipation in Prussia" in *JMW*, 163.

[16] Fries wrote this in his 1816 tract *Über die Gefährdung des Wohlstandes und Charakters der Deutschen durch die Juden* (*On the Danger Presented by the Jews to the Well-Being and Character of the Germans*). See Katz, *From Prejudice to Destruction*, 82.

[17] See Rühs, *Ueber die Ansprüche der Juden an das deutsche Bürgerrecht* (*On the Claims of the Jews to Civil Rights in Germany*), 5–6, cited in Katz, *From Prejudice*, 79–80.

[18] See Zunz, *Das Buch Zunz*, 19. Zunz wrote a treatise against Rühs in March 1816 that was never published. See Trautmann-Waller, *Philologie Allemand*, 26, 68–69. Zunz only mentions Rühs once in *On Rabbinic Literature*, but Schorsch has analyzed a preliminary draft of the work that contains a bitter, sarcastic response to Rühs. See Schorsch, *Leopold Zunz*, 12–18.

In *On Rabbinic Literature*, Zunz notes that it is not only Christian scholars who neglect studying "rabbinic literature," but also Jewish scholars. He enumerates several reasons for this, including: (1) poor job prospects for Jewish scholars of rabbinic texts, (2) the "superficiality" (*ungründlichkeit*) and coldness toward religion among contemporary Jews, and (3) the prevailing emphasis on practicality as the measure of knowledge's value.[19] Zunz observes that the only Jews who study rabbinic texts are those committed to what he calls "vulgar rabbinism" (*vulgo-Rabbinismus*). Their study is not "scientific" and objective, but instead grounded in the tortured, pilpulistic method that Zunz calls *Talmudquäler* (tortured talmudism) or *Klopffechterei* (exhibitionist jousting).[20]

In calling for creating a new academic field to study post-biblical Jewish literature, Zunz invokes an emergent conception of scholarship that has been called *Wissenschaftsideologie*. This ideology guided Wilhelm von Humboldt's vision for the University of Berlin, which Zunz entered in 1815, five years after its opening. Roy Turner credits six theorists with developing *Wissenschaftsideologie*: J.G. Fichte, F.W.J. Schelling, Heinrich Steffens, Friedrich Schleiermacher, Humboldt, and F.A. Wolf.[21] Zunz was a devoted student of Wolf's and took five courses with him.[22]

Four components of *Wissenschaftsideologie* are relevant for understanding *On Rabbinic Literature*. *First*, *Wissenschaftsideologie* stressed original, creative research rather than the rote transmission of existing knowledge.[23] *Second*, it rejected the prevailing emphasis on professional studies, which it derisively called *Brot-studien* (bread studies), instead valuing scholarly research for its own sake.[24] *Third*, research was given an Idealist philosophical

[19] Zunz, *GS*, 1:23–27; "On Rabbinic Literature" in *JMW*, 250–251. Roy Turner notes that the widespread emphasis on practicality as the measure of knowledge's value was reflected in the Prussian university system of the late eighteenth century, which was highly focused on professional training. See Turner, *The Prussian Universities*, 29–32.

[20] See Zunz, *GS*, 1:29, note 1. This note is not translated in the *JMW*.

[21] Turner, *The Prussian Universities*, 248–250.

[22] The courses were: Greek Antiquities, Greek Literature, Roman Antiquity, Encyclopedia of Ancient Science, and Introduction to Herodotus. See Zunz, *Das Buch Zunz*, 19–20. For further discussion of Zunz's relation to Wolf, see Veltri, "Altertumswissenschaft und Wissenschaft des Judentums"; Wallach, *Liberty and Letters*, 12–16; Trautmann-Waller, *Philologie Allemand*, 177–180; Bitzan, "Leopold Zunz and the Meanings of *Wissenschaft*."

[23] Turner, *The Prussian Universities*, 254–257.

[24] Wolf wrote: "now when the theology student attends only the most necessary bread-courses . . . when the law student who usually pursues not a word of philosophy, of Roman history, of classics, sinks to a true mechanic—then it is simply impossible that superficial studies should not engender laziness, debauchery and all kinds of crudeness." See Wolf, *Ueber Erziehung, Schule, Universität*, 296–297, cited in Turner, *The Prussian Universities*, 257.

underpinning stressing the absolute unity of all reality and truth and the identity of the ideal, which is unconditioned and free with the real, which is conditioned and limited.[25] Finally, *Wissenschaftsideologie* stressed that scholars should have a high moral character and that their scholarship should serve a moral purpose.[26]

In *On Rabbinic Literature,* Zunz asserts that the unity of scientific knowledge, studied for its own sake, is a critical underpinning of *Wissenschaft des Judentums.* Zunz writes, "Let not philosophical inferiors (*Subaltern-Philosoph*) hinder this flight to the Kingdom of Hope *by their questions of utility.* We have nothing to say to whomever fails to grasp the highest relations of science, its most estimable greatness, and every detail as an integral part of spiritual creation" (emphasis mine).[27]

For Zunz, the scholarly neglect of rabbinic literature manifests a lack of appreciation of the scientific ideal. He elaborates this point twenty-seven years later in his 1845 *On History and Literature* (*Zur Geschichte und Literatur*), where he writes that the "single primordial spirit" (*einzigen Urgeist*) can be known by studying world literature.[28] For Zunz, this "speculative spirit" (*speculativen Geist*) can never be grasped in its totality, but only by studying it in its specific literary manifestations. The more diverse the literatures studied, the better the "spirit" is known, and for this reason, there is value in studying every nation's literature.[29]

In *On Rabbinic Literature,* Zunz maintains that rabbinic literature should be studied not to better understand Christianity or to describe a specific aspect of Judaism or Jewish life but, rather, to penetrate the "spirit" (*Geist*) of Judaism, which he glosses as the Jewish people's "inherited ideas . . . mores and will."[30] In emphasizing philology as the key to understanding the Jewish spirit, Zunz adopts the Herderian idea that a nation is best understood through its literature, which allows one to penetrate the essence of its cultural achievements and so discern its specific philosophy.[31] For Zunz,

[25] Turner, *The Prussian Universities,* 260–262, 331–332.
[26] Ibid., 263–266.
[27] Zunz, *GS,* 1:28; "On Rabbinic Literature," in *JMW,* 251.
[28] Zunz, *Zur Geschichte,* 1.
[29] See ibid., 1–2.
[30] Zunz, *GS,* 1:4–5; "On Rabbinic Literature," in *JMW,* 247. I have altered the English translation.
[31] See Zunz, *GS,* 1:6–7; "On Rabbinic Literature," in *JMW,* 247–248. Zunz's affinity with Herder is reflected in his statement that "Herder is greater than Goethe the poet or Humboldt the thinker. The last probes, the second pleases, the first loves." See Wallach, *Liberty and Letters,* 204. In his 1859 work *Die Ritus des synagogalen Gottesdienst* (*Rites of the Synagogue Service*), Zunz praises Herder's great appreciation of Midrash and Jewish poetry. See Zunz, *Die Ritus,* 178, cited in Schorsch, *Leopold Zunz,* 207.

the ultimate aim of *Wissenschaft des Judentums* is to uncover the philosophy of Judaism that constitutes Jews' unique contribution to world civilization.[32]

For Zunz, *Wissenschaft des Judentums* must replace talmudism.[33] *Wissenschaft* begins with the accumulation of texts producing "critical editions of manuscripts and good translations" and then "accurate reference works and biographies" to help illuminate the texts.[34] The texts must be analyzed in three ways: "doctrinally" (*doctrinale*), which includes extracting and analyzing the main ideas found in the texts; "linguistically" (*grammatische*), which includes having a good knowledge of the language of the original; and "historically" (*historische*), which involves tracing the history of ideas from their origins through the present.[35]

Zunz emphasizes two features of historical understanding that highlight Judaism's connection to the larger world. First, Jewish ideas must be understood in relation to the non-Jewish intellectual context in which they were formed. For example, Zunz recommends comparing talmudic law with Roman law.[36] Second, Jewish ideas should be studied not only as they were transmitted within Jewish circles but also insofar as they impacted the broader world. For example, Zunz suggests that by examining medieval Jewish philosophical works one can appreciate Jewish contributions to the sciences.[37]

In keeping with his view of scientific truth, Zunz writes that it is crucial that *Wissenschaft des Judentums* be undertaken in an objective, disinterested manner. At the same time, he thinks that studying Judaism academically will inevitably have salutary political consequences, ameliorating Jews' civil standing by refuting the idea that they are a clannish, ignorant, uncreative

32 Zunz, *GS*, 1:27–28; "On Rabbinic Literature," in *JMW*, 251. Zunz strongly advocated establishing a chair in Jewish history and literature at a German university and did not support situating Jewish studies within rabbinical seminaries. On Zunz's failed efforts to establish a chair in Jewish history and literature at the University of Berlin, see Trautmann-Waller, *Philologie Allemand*, 112–125.

33 In important respects Zunz modeled *Wissenschaft des Judentums* on Wolf's *Altertumswissenschaft* (scholarly study of antiquity). Wolf wrote that *Altertumswissenschaft* comprised "the sum-total of that knowledge and information which acquaints us with the deeds and the fates of the Greeks and the Romans, their political, intellectual and domestic circumstances; with their languages, arts, sciences, morals, religions, national characters, and patterns of thought . . ." See Wolf, "Darstellung der Alterthumswissenschaft" in Wolf, *Kleine Schriften*, 2:826, cited in Turner, *The Prussian Universities*, 282.

34 Zunz, *GS*, 1:7; "On Rabbinic Literature," in *JMW*, 248. I have altered the translation.

35 Ibid.

36 Zunz, *GS*, 1:9; "On Rabbinic Literature," in *JMW*, 248. Zunz notes that Michaelis put biblical law in a broader context in *Mosaische Recht*, but no one has yet done this with rabbinic law. See note 4, ad loc.

37 Zunz, *GS*, 1:14–15; "On Rabbinic Literature," in *JMW*, 249.

people who have always isolated themselves from Gentiles.[38] As he puts it in *On History and Literature*, "The equality of Jews in mores and life will be produced from the equality of *Wissenschaft des Judenthums*."[39]

Contextualizing *The Sermons*

If *On Rabbinic Literature* established a vision for *Wissenschaft*, Zunz's 1832 the *Sermons* was a response was his first major contribution to actualizing this vision. While we have seen that rising anti-Judaism and attacks on Jewish civil rights formed the context of *On Rabbinic Literature,* the *Sermons* was a response to three subsequent developments: (1) reactionary Protestant attacks on Jewish religious reform, (2) the use of Protestant Bible criticism to oppose Jewish civil rights, and (3) a Catholic attempt to reform Judaism by returning it to the Bible.

First context: Protestant relgious reaction

Following the fall of Napoleon, the Holy Alliance declared itself opposed to the rationalist Napoleonic social, political, and religious reforms and adopted a conservative agenda that emphasized the role of tradition and faith in ensuring national stability along with the need to maintain clear distinctions between Jews and Christians. Worried that Reform Jewish religious services were too similar to Protestant religious services, in September 1823 the Prussian authorities closed the Reform Beer Temple in Berlin, and on December 9, 1823 Friedrich Wilhelm III issued an order that Jewish services could be held "only according to the traditional rite without the slightest innovation in language, ceremonies, prayers, and hymns wholly according to the old tradition."[40] This included restricting efforts to reform Jewish synagogue services in three crucial areas, namely: (1) instituting vernacular prayers; (2) playing an organ during services; and most importantly for our

[38] See Zunz, *GS*, 1:30–31; "On Rabbinic Literature" in *JMW*, 252.

[39] Zunz, *Zur Geschichte,* 21. Schorsch points out that this passage was written in response to the erosion of Jewish civil rights under Friedrich Wilhelm IV, who ascended the Prussian throne in 1840. See Schorsch, *From Text to Context,* 152–153. But a similar sentiment is already found in *On Rabbinic Literature,* which was written twenty-two years earlier. See the previous note.

[40] See Meyer, "The Religious Reform Controversy," 148–150; Lowenstein, *The Berlin Jewish Community,* 138–139.

purposes, (3) preaching vernacular sermons. In the *Sermons* Zunz sought to legitimate introducing reforms in Jewish services by showing that these reforms did not deviate from Jewish tradition.[41]

Second context: Protestant Bible criticism and the rollback of Jewish civil rights

A second impetus for Zunz writing the *Sermons* was the worsening of the political situation of German Jews. In 1819, anti-Jewish "Hep Hep riots" spread throughout German states. Arguments against granting Jews civil rights were again raised, and Zunz came to realize that these arguments were being based not merely on political or theological considerations, but also on hard-nosed biblical scholarship.

Zunz's most beloved professor at the University of Berlin was the Protestant Bible critic Wilhelm De Wette. De Wette was an enormously important scholar whom some consider the founder of modern biblical criticism.[42] Zunz took two courses with De Wette and visited him multiple times in his home.[43] Zunz testified that of all his university teachers, he felt closest to De Wette. In an 1838 letter to De Wette, Zunz wrote "I owe you my understanding of biblical criticism and indeed to you and Friedrich August Wolf whatever I acquired of a scholarly perspective." And in his 1872 *The Monthly Days of the Calendar Year* (*Die Monatstage des Kalendarjahre*), Zunz called De Wette a scholar in whose writings one finds "an unprejudiced critic fighting spiritless fundamentalism (*geistlos Buchstabenglauben*)."[44]

Yet Zunz could not have been unaware that De Wette opposed Jewish civil rights and that this was intimately tied to his scholarship. Among De Wette's most important scholarly contributions was his sharp distinction between pre-exilic and post-exilic Israelite religion, which he regarded as two different faiths, which he called "Hebraism" and "Judaism."[45] In his 1815 *On Religion and Theology* (*Über Religion und Theologie*), De Wette argued that Mosaic Hebraism was a form of ethical monotheism though

41 See Trautmann-Waller, *Philologie Allemand*, 83–84.

42 See Rogerson, *Old Testament Criticism in the Nineteenth Century*, 34.

43 The two courses were The Book of Daniel and Introduction to the Old Testament. See Zunz, *Das Buch Zunz*, 20, and Kaufmann, *Gesammelte Schriften*, 3:336, cited in Schorsch, "Leopold Zunz on the Hebrew Bible," 439.

44 See Schorsch, "Leopold Zunz on the Hebrew Bible," 439–440.

45 Pasto, "W.M.L. De Wette and the Invention of Post-Exilic Judaism," 42.

an "incomplete and raw" form. Over the centuries Hebraism went through periods of decline and renewal, with a high point being the teachings of the prophets who refined the ethical teachings of Moses. But Hebraism collapsed with the fall of the Judean kingdom and the exile of the Judeans to Babylonia. In exile the Judeans created a new religion called "Judaism" and became a new people, the Jews. Seeking to account for their traumatic political disaster, the Jews developed the idea that they were God's chosen people and that their exile was punishment for having been insufficiently punctilious in observing their religious ceremonies. Seeking to counter the influence of Persian mythology, the Jews stressed conceptual religious knowledge and regarded their sacred texts as literally true.[46] Since Jews came to focus on "concepts and devotion to the letter," De Wette characterizes Judaism as "degenerate, petrified Hebraism."[47]

According to De Wette, Christ restored the "free, living spirit" of Hebraism by centering its worship on "spirit and truth." Christ restored the Mosaic teaching that God was "the creator and father of all" and stressed the universal ethical content of Hebraism over the zealous practice of religious rites. De Wette noted, however, that Christ's teachings were soon corrupted. Christianity became institutionalized as Catholicism, which emphasized hierarchy, dogma, and obedience to religious rituals, thereby becoming what De Wette calls "Christianity sunken in Judaism." It took Luther and the Protestant Reformation to again restore Jesus's "love of truth and independence" and reject the Catholic emphasis on empty works and obedience. But for De Wette, later Protestantism again sunk to worshipping the biblical letter, and so it falls to Bible scholars to restore the true Hebraic religion of freedom, morality, and truth by using historical scholarship to show how Israelite religion gradually declined.[48]

James Pasto has shown that De Wette's biblical scholarship found expression in his politics. Following Napoleon's demise, De Wette favored the formation of a unified German state under Prussian leadership, arguing that the new German state should be a Hebraic Protestant state grounded in the Old and New Testaments as understood through biblical criticism and reason. Protestantism and the German state would work in tandem, with the

[46] Pasto, "W.M.L. De Wette and the Invention of Post-Exilic Judaism," 40–41; Rogerson, *W.M.L. De Wette*, 109–110.

[47] See De Wette, *Biblische Dogmatik*, 114, cited in Pasto, "W.M.L. De Wette and the Invention of Post-Exilic Judaism," 43.

[48] See Pasto, "W.M.L. De Wette and the Invention of Post-Exilic Judaism," 41–42; Rogerson, *W.M.L. De Wette*, 110.

German state recognizing Protestantism as its official religion and protecting freedom of worship, and Protestantism promoting patriotic loyalty. De Wette rejected a proposal that the new German state include Catholic Austria as he worried that this would lead to an influx of mythology and mysticism that would strengthen retrograde Protestants who favored religious dogma and hierarchy.[49]

In this context, De Wette argued *against* Jewish civil rights. In his 1822 semiautobiographical book *Theodor*, De Wette wrote that since Judaism is a national religion, granting Jews civil rights would lead them to form a "state within a state."[50] While the German state should tolerate Jews, it should seek to "restrain their growth," encourage them to learn Christian customs, and support every Jewish movement that seeks to free Jews from "service to the letter and rabbinical hierarchy."[51] For De Wette, Judaism's opposition to Hebraism made Jews ineligible for citizenship in a Hebraic Protestant German polity.

Zunz makes clear that one task of the *Sermons* is to counter Christian misconceptions about Judaism and to further Jews' civil rights. As he puts it in the introduction, "The neglect of Jewish scholarship goes hand in hand with civil discrimination against the Jews."[52] We will see how Zunz's discussion of Midrash and the Bible in the *Sermons* seeks to undo De Wette's sharp distinction between pre-exilic Hebraism and post-exilic Judaism.

Third context: a Catholic reformation of Judaism

In addition to legitimating religious reforms and promoting Jewish civil rights, the *Sermons* must be understood within a third context, namely, a Catholic attempt to reform Judaism. To the best of my knowledge scholars have not set the *Sermons* in this context, so I will spend some time sketching it.

In 1825, the Polish Dutchy of Warsaw, then a puppet state of Czar Nicholas I, sought to reform Jewish education. Through a decree of the czar an "Israelite

[49] Pasto, "W.M.L. De Wette and the Invention of Post-Exilic Judaism," 44–46; Rogerson, *W.M.L. De Wette*, 120–124.

[50] On this epithet see Katz, *Emancipation and Assimilation*, 48–76.

[51] See De Wette, *Theodore*, 2:368; Pasto, "W.M.L. De Wette and the Invention of Post-Exilic Judaism," 47–49.

[52] See Zunz, *Vorträge*, vii; "Scholarship and Emancipation" in *JMW*, 254. I cite from the 1892 second edition of the *Vorträge*, which includes corrections based on Zunz's manuscript.

Committee" (*Israeliten-Committee*) consisting entirely of Christians was formed to open an enlightened rabbinical school. The committee designed a five-year course of study that included classes in Bible, Talmud, and Hebrew grammar, alongside courses in secular subjects including history, geography, mathematics, Polish, German, and French. Only those graduating from the rabbinical school would be permitted to be rabbis or allowed to teach Jewish children.[53]

Three years later, the "Israelite Committee" established a new program for Christians that would teach them "Hebraic, talmudic and rabbinic languages, Jewish history, and the dialect of Polish Jews." The course had a very specific agenda, namely, to teach participants to compare the "spirit (*Geist*) of the written law with the oral [law]" so that Christians would be able to understand how the Talmud distorted biblical teachings.[54]

The course, however, required translations of rabbinic texts. To this end, the committee granted an Italian professor at the University of Warsaw named Luigi Chiarini 72,000 zlotys to translate the entire Talmud.[55] While Luther had translated the *Bible* to reveal how the Catholic Church corrupted biblical teachings, the committee saw translating the *Talmud* as a way of revealing how the rabbis did the same. In 1830, Chiarini published *Theory of Judaism Applied to the Reform of Israelites in all European Countries* (*Théorie du judaïsme appliquée à la Réforme des Israélites de tous les Pays de l'Europe*), which was to serve as an introduction to his Talmud translation.[56]

Chiarini described the aims of his book in an article in *Dziennik Warszawski* (*Warsaw Daily*) in August 1829:

> We are using our theory for a certain type of reform which should not terrify the disastrous relics of Israel, since the word "reform" in our meaning does not stand—like somewhere else—for the tainting of religious principles, corruption of habits, or persecution. By the reform of scattered Jews *we mean their voluntary and gradual conversion from Judaism to Mosaism, that is from the Talmud to the Bible* by way of a better plan of education which might be supervised by the public authorities and by this plan of education

53 Zunz, *GS*, 1:272.

54 Ibid., 1:272–273; Marcinkowski, "Luigi Chiarini," 241.

55 According to an administrative decree of June 22, 1829, Chiarini would be given 12,000 zlotys per volume of his translation of the Talmud, which would be divided into six volumes. See Marcinkowski, "Luigi Chiarini," 243.

56 Chiarini, who died in 1832, only published two volumes of his translation. See Marcinkowski, "Luigi Chiarini," 240–241.

> we simply mean the learning from the Hebrew rules and the translation of the Bible in accordance with the principles of sound criticism. (emphasis mine)[57]

In other words, Chiarini conceived his work as aimed not primarily at informing Christians about Judaism but, rather, at convincing Jews to reform Judaism. By showing how the Talmud deviated from the Bible, Chiarini hoped Jews would gradually throw off its yoke and return to pristine biblical religion.

Chiarini's *Theory of Judaism* consists of three parts. In the first part, he discusses the impediments to understanding Judaism and surveys several works on Judaism. In the second part, he presents his theory of Judaism, while in the third part he presents his proposal for reforming Judaism by transforming it into pure Mosaism.

Shortly after the appearance of Chiarini's book, Zunz penned a long, devastating review of it.[58] The first half of the review summarizes key elements of Chiarini's book, while the second half criticizes Chiarini. Given that my focus is on Zunz, I will follow his summary of the key elements of Chiarini's argument.

Chiarini's assault on the Talmud

Chiarini begins the first part of his book by lamenting that the Talmud, which he calls "this unformed chaos, this collection of error and prejudice, full of reveries and mad fanaticism," has never been translated.[59] Chiarini gives several reasons for this, including Jews' opposition to translating the Talmud, the intrinsic difficulty of the work, and Christians' mistaken belief that the Old Testament forms the foundation of contemporary Judaism.[60] Since, however, it is the Talmud, not the Bible, that governs contemporary

[57] This text is cited in Marcinkowski, "Luigi Chiarini," 245.

[58] Zunz's review appeared as a separate pamphlet. See Zunz, *Beleuchtung*. Zunz later republished it in *GS*, 1:271–298.

[59] See Chiarini, *Théorie*, 1:6, cited by Zunz, *GS*, 1:274. On the lack of a complete Talmud translation prior to the twentieth century, see Mintz, "Translating the Talmud," 121–124; Schorsch, "Missing in Translation."

[60] Chiarini, *Théorie*, 1:11, cited by Zunz, *GS*, 1:274–275.

Jewish life, Christians' lack of familiarity with it makes Judaism as unknown to Christians as a "horde of nomads" in a distant land.[61]

Chiarini recognizes that the Talmud is no easy work, and he enumerates five impediments to understanding it. The *first* problem is its language. Without scientific knowledge of Hebrew and Aramaic grammar, vocabulary, phraseology, and abbreviations, comprehending the Talmud is more difficult than understanding Chinese. The *second* problem is the different literary genres and techniques found in the Talmud. Specifically, one must understand the difference between halakhah and aggadah and the hermeneutical principles employed by the rabbis. A *third* problem is that one must appreciate that the Talmud consists of different layers, most importantly, the Mishnah and Gemara, and the relationship of these layers to one another. While Chiarini describes the Mishnah as a classical ancient work with a strong connection to the Bible, he describes the Gemara as a work filled with strange fables and imagery similar to those found "among all other oriental peoples" (*tous les peuples d'Orient*). The *fourth* problem is that one must understand which elements of rabbinic literature Jews consider obligatory and which they deem non-obligatory. The *final* problem is that the Talmud was composed amidst of competing ancient sects that held conflicting views of biblical authority and employed different methods of interpreting it. So to understand the Talmud, one must understand these different sects and their viewpoints.[62]

Surveying Christian writers on the Talmud, Chiarini spends most of his time on Eisenmenger. While he praises Eisenmenger for his erudition, Chiarini also criticizes his work. Chiarini's criticisms include Eisenmenger's frequent use of bitter and biting comments to attack the Talmud; his blind zeal for converting Jews; his cherry-picking the Talmud for hateful, anti-Christian passages; his taking talmudic passages out of context; his mistaking figurative expressions for literal ones; his considering all talmudic statements of equal authority; and his paying no attention to actual halakhah.[63] For Chiarini, a proper understanding of Judaism requires a scholarly translation of the *entire* Talmud. Rather than seeking to one-sidedly indict the Talmud, one must show the good with bad. Chiarini claims that he has found over five hundred excellent talmudic teachings.[64]

[61] See Zunz, *GS*, 1:275. Chiarini's comparing Judaism to a "horde of nomads" is not coincidental given the Christian stereotype of the alien, wandering Jew.
[62] See Chiarini, *Théorie*, 1:49–86; Zunz, *GS*, 1:275–276.
[63] Chiarini, *Théorie*, 1:117–123; Zunz, *GS*, 1:277.
[64] Chiarini, *Théorie*, 1:147–159; Zunz, *GS*, 1:278.

Chiarini then identifies *eight* features of contemporary Judaism: (1) certain books and rabbis possess unlimited authority; (2) Judaism contains a great variety of articles of faith, holy customs, and traditions; (3) Jewish males are taught almost exclusively the oral law, while the education of Jewish females is largely neglected; (4) Judaism inculcates suspicion of Gentiles and teaches Jews to be cunning and deceitful; (5) Judaism promotes hairsplitting, sophistical methods to study halakhah, and it regards prejudices, allegories, and fables as principles of morality and religion; (6) Judaism promotes arrogance, hatred, and intolerance toward non-Jews but hides its antisocial teachings out of fear of reprisals; (7) Judaism teaches Jews to discreetly harm the state as vengeance for their persecution; (8) because of their unsteady, wandering existence Jews embrace occupations that prize petty profits, but which are unfruitful and damaging to the state.[65]

Chiarini criticizes Jewish education in Poland, which teaches Jews to write their Yiddish "jargon" from right to left, promotes marrying daughters off at a very young age (sometimes even before puberty), and neglects female education. After complaining about how Jews treat their women, Chiarini launches into his own misogynistic attack on them. Likening Jewish females to beautiful wild fruit that has a tart, unpleasant taste, Chiarini writes that while Jewish women are often more beautiful than their Polish counterparts, their manners and behavior are unbecoming. Jewish women are lazy about cleaning, nonchalant in performing their maternal duties, not very attached to their husbands, full of prejudices, and unsightly except on holidays when they bathe and make themselves up.[66]

Chiarini then turns to the issue of reformation, claiming that a reformation of Judaism is needed in order for Jews to be granted equal civil rights. He notes that Jews are commonly understood to have *six* characteristics deriving from their religion that preclude their being granted civil equality: (1) hatred and mockery of non-Jews; (2) disobedience of public authorities; (3) failure to promote the welfare of the states they live in, as they do not regard these states as their "homeland" (*patrie*); (4) cheating non-Jews in business; (5) not engaging in the arts, sciences, or useful professions; and (6) not engaging in agriculture or military service.[67]

65 Chiarini, *Théorie*, 1:178–179; Zunz, *GS*, 1:278–279.
66 Chiarini, *Théorie*, 1:249–259; Zunz, *GS*, 1:279–280.
67 Chiarini, *Théorie*, 2:154.

Chiarini claims that it is the *Talmud* rather than the Bible that promotes these traits. Were Jews to cast off the Talmud and return to the Bible, they would eliminate the pernicious traits that stand in the way of civil emancipation. Chiarini notes that the Talmud is so dominant among Polish Jews that not only does it form the center of the curriculum, but even when the Bible is studied, it is nearly always studied with Rashi's commentary, which refracts the Bible through a rabbinic lens.[68]

Chiarini acknowledges that Christians cannot reform Judaism—it is up to Jews to abandon the Talmud and return to the Bible. The key to Jews doing this is *education*. Chiarini predicts that by teaching Jews grammatical knowledge of Hebrew and making available to them good translations of the Talmud, Jews will understand how the Talmud corrupts the Bible and cast off its yoke.[69]

Chiarini does not, however, content himself with rhetoric but, rather, seeks to illustrate in *detail* how the Talmud corrupts the Bible's teachings. For Chiarini, the foundation of biblical teaching is to love one's neighbor as oneself, which applies to Jews and Gentiles alike.[70] Chiarini also notes that the Bible teaches one to love the foreigner[71] to love one's enemy,[72] and prohibits defrauding another whether Jew or non-Jew.[73] He further observes that in the Bible interactions with Gentiles are not generally condemned. The patriarchs lived among foreign nations, adopted their customs, and intermarried with them. Jews were permitted to make treaties with Gentile nations as evidenced by the actions of David, Solomon, and the Maccabees.[74] Moses feared the arrogance of the Jews and, therefore, enjoined them to remember that they were not superior to any other nation

[68] Chiarini, *Théorie,* 2:127–149; Zunz, *GS,* 1:282. See p. 93 of this volume.

[69] Chiarini, *Théorie,* 2:185–194; Zunz *GS,* 1:282. Chiarini's claim recalls Luther's assertion that were Jews to free themselves from rabbinic influence and read the Bible with a clear mind, "they would stone all their rabbis and hate them more violently than they do us Christians." See Luther, *Luther's Works,* 47:176–177.

[70] See Leviticus 19:18. Chiarini cites Exodus 2:13 and 11:2 as evidence that the Hebrew root *re'a* can refer both to a fellow Jew and a Gentile. See Chiarini *Théorie,* 2:154.

[71] Chiarini cites Leviticus 19:34: "The foreigner (*hager*) who resides with you shall be to you as one of your citizens; you shall love him as yourself, for you were foreigners (*gerim*) in the land of Egypt. I am the Lord your God." Chiarini observes that the term *ger* in the verse cannot refer to a convert because the Jews are referred to as *gerim* in Egypt. See Chiarini, *Théorie,* 2:155.

[72] Chiarini cites Exodus 23:4–5, which states that if one sees one's enemy's donkey collapsing under a heavy load, one must help one's enemy raise it. See Chiarini, *Théorie,* 2:155.

[73] Chiarini cites Leviticus 19:36; 37:21; Deuteronomy 25:12–16. See Chiarini, *Théorie,* 2:166.

[74] Chiarini cites Genesis 19:14; 21:8 and 33; Genesis ch. 22; 41:14; 42:15–16; ch. 50. See Chiarini, *Théorie,* 2:156–157.

because of any intrinsic merit. God distinguished them solely from God's free choice.[75]

Chiarini claims that it was the *Pharisees* who distorted the Bible's teachings by limiting the commandment to love one's neighbor as oneself to a fellow Jew,[76] interpreting the commandment to love the foreigner as referring to a convert to Judaism,[77] and limiting the laws against defrauding others to Jews.[78] When the rabbis discussed the commandment to love one's neighbor as oneself, they changed it from the positive to the negative, with Hillel restating it as "that which is hateful to you, do not do to your fellow. That is the whole Torah."[79] This contrasts with the New Testament where Jesus formulates the idea positively, stating, "So in everything do unto to others what you would have them do to you, for this sums up the Law and the prophets."[80] For Chiarini, this difference illustrates the rabbis' inferior moral sense since not acting hatefully toward another is easier than loving another.[81]

Chiarini recognizes, however, that there are several passages in the Bible that seem to imply a more hostile relationship to Gentiles. Moses commanded Jews not to overly mingle with Canaanites, Moabites, Ammonites, Philistines, and Egyptians or follow their practices,[82] and he commanded Jews to expel and/or exterminate the Canaanites and the Amalekites.[83] How does this fit with the biblical commandment to love the other? Chiarini responds that Moses enjoined not mingling with other nations not because of any hatred for Gentiles but, rather, out of concern that Jews might come to practice idolatry. It was the Pharisees who transformed the commandment to keep away from the rites and mores of idolaters into a more general commandment to keep away from all non-Jews.[84]

Chiarini explains that the commandment to exterminate the Canaanites and Amalekites was a reprisal for the actions taken by those specific nations

[75] Chiarini cites Deuteronomy 7:6; 9:4–24. See Chiarini, *Théorie*, 2:156–157.

[76] See Chiarini, *Théorie*, 2:162. Chiarini does not provide a talmudic passage in support of this claim.

[77] Chiarini, *Théorie*, 2:155, note 1. Chiarini does not provide a talmudic passage in support of this claim.

[78] Chiarini cites *BT*, Baba Batra, 54b; and *BT*, Baba Kamma, 113b. See Chiarini, *Théorie*, 2:58–59. Chiarini seems to identify the Pharisees and the rabbis.

[79] Chiarini cites *BT*, Shabbat, 31a.

[80] Matthew 7:12.

[81] See Chiarini, *Théorie*, 2:59–60.

[82] Chiarini cites Genesis 9:18–27; 12:11–20; 19:30–38; 20:1–2; Leviticus 18:3. See Chiarini, *Théorie*, 2:158.

[83] Chiarini cites Exodus 23:33; 17:14; Deuteronomy 7:1; 20:16. See Chiarini, *Théorie*, 2:160.

[84] Chiarini, *Théorie*, 2:161–162.

against Israel in accordance with the ancient right of war. In other words, it was an exceptional command.[85] It was the Pharisees who extended the notion of a perpetual war between the Jews and Amalekites to a perpetual hatred between Jews and non-Jews in all times and places. In doing so, they neglected the biblical commandment "do not abhor the Edomite for he is your brother" (Deuteronomy 23:8), which should apply to Christians who are, after all, Jews' brothers in worshipping the same God![86]

Chiarini contrasts contemporary Jews' lack of involvement in the arts and sciences with biblical heroes including Moses, Job, Ezekiel, and Daniel, all of whom were raised outside of Palestine and learned the arts and sciences from the foreign nations amidst whom they lived. According to Chiarini, all biblical writers who lived after the return from the Babylonian exile show evidence of Chaldean and Babylonian learning.[87] By contrast, the talmudic rabbis prohibited reading "foreign books."[88] While the biblical figures Bezalel and Oholiab were expert artisans schooled by Egyptians whom Moses praised for their artistic expertise,[89] the Talmud recommended that one exclusively study Torah and practice petty commerce.[90]

Chiarini claims that the Jews were not always averse to agriculture. The Bible records that Jews raised sheep in Egypt[91] and Moses gave numerous laws governing agriculture.[92] In line with his favorable attitude toward the Mishnah, Chiarini notes that the first of the six tractates of the Mishnah is devoted to agricultural laws. While the Jerusalem Talmud comments on these laws, the Babylonian Talmud, which is the foundation of contemporary Judaism, does not. One might think that the Babylonian Talmud neglects these laws because they do not apply outside of Palestine. But the Babylonian Talmud contains a tractate on laws pertaining to sacrifices even though they were only practiced in the Temple, which was destroyed centuries before the Talmud was completed. For Chiarini the Babylonian rabbis did not

[85] Ibid.

[86] Chiarini, *Théorie,* 2:162–163. The Talmud itself identifies Edom with Rome/Christianity. For sources, see Boyarin, *Dying for God,* 3.

[87] Chiarini, *Théorie,* 2:168.

[88] Chiarini cites *BT*, Sanhedrin, 90a. See Chiarini, *Théorie,* 2:169.

[89] Chiarini cites Exodus 35:30–35. Chiarini also mentions Joab from the tribe of Judah, who is called an "artisan" (*harash*) in I Chronicles 4:14. He also notes that according to the Bible many Jews learned to be artisans from the Tyreans in the times of David and Solomon (see I Chronicles 14:1, 22:15). See Chiarini, *Théorie,* 2:170.

[90] See Chiarini, *Théorie,* 2:170. Chiarini does not cite a talmudic source.

[91] Chiarini cites Genesis 46:32, 47:6; Exodus 9:4, 7, and 26. Of course all the biblical patriarchs were shepherds.

[92] See Chiarini, *Théorie,* 2:171.

comment on agricultural laws because they did not esteem agriculture[93] and because they considered the land in which they dwelled impure.[94]

On the question of the Jews' relationship to non-Jewish political authority, Chiarini notes that Jeremiah and Ezra both instructed Jews to submit to the political powers amidst which they lived and to integrate into Gentile society.[95] By contrast, the Talmud teaches Jews to regard non-Jewish kings as donkeys and only deems Jews human beings.[96] When the Talmud recommends praying for the welfare of the states in which Jews live, it is solely from prudential considerations, namely, because of the necessity of social order, not because of any positive feelings toward non-Jewish authorities.[97]

Finally, Chiarini turns to the question of Jewish military service. He notes that Jews commonly give three reasons for not serving in the military: *first*, because Jews take oaths very seriously and are loathe to swear them; *second*, because they are prohibited from bearing arms on the Sabbath; and *third*, because of the strict Jewish dietary laws that would be difficult to observe in the army.[98]

On the question of oaths, Chiarini writes that the Bible only prohibits taking God's name in vain. It was the rabbis who made oath taking in general problematic. Chiarini offers several observations regarding bearing arms on the Sabbath. First, he claims that there is no evidence that Jews held scrupulously to this prohibition during the biblical period, as the Bible describes many Jewish wars without mentioning the problem of bearing arms on the Sabbath. It was only after the Babylonian exile when some Jews became fanatical and believed that their suffering was due to violating halakhah that this became an issue, especially during the Maccabean era. But Jews could never have universally accepted the prohibition against bearing arms on the Sabbath, for otherwise, they could never have become respected Greek or Roman citizens as many did. Chiarini also notes that the Talmud itself claims

[93] Chiarini cites *BT*, Yebamot, 63a.

[94] Chiarini, *Théorie*, 2:170–174.

[95] Chiarini cites Jeremiah 27:12; 29:5–9; Ezra 7:26–27. See Chiarini, *Théorie*, 2:163–164.

[96] Chiarini, *Théorie*, 2:164–165, 190. Chiarini cites *BT*, Berakhot, 58a.

[97] Chiarini cites *Pirkei Avot* 3:2; see Chiarini, *Théorie*, 2:61–62. Chiarini considers talmudic statements that seem to oppose his argument, namely, the injunction to greet non-Jewish as well as Jewish kings (*BT*, Berakhot, 19b) and the principle "the law of the regime is the law" (*BT*, Baba Kamma, 113b). Regarding the first, he explains that the Talmud itself explains that the reason Jews are to greet non-Jewish kings is to recognize the difference between them and Jewish kings. As to the second, he notes that respecting the law of regime only applies where it does not contradict Jewish law, thereby showing that Jews' primary loyalty is to their own religion. See Chiarini, *Théorie*, 2:82–83.

[98] Chiarini, *Théorie*, 2:174–175.

that it is permissible to violate the Sabbath if this involves saving a single life, which should have made bearing arms on the Sabbath permissible.[99]

On the problem of Jewish dietary laws, Chiarini notes that Moses frequently changed laws or presented them in ways that made clear that they were time-limited.[100] For this reason, contemporary Jews do not follow all the ritual laws such as those pertaining to the Temple. Given that the main function of the dietary laws was to separate Jews from idolaters and that Christians are not idolaters, these laws should be abandoned.[101]

Chiarini concludes that by promulgating a reformation that returns Judaism to biblical Mosaism, Jews can become useful members of the nations in which they live, thereby meriting full civil rights.

Zunz's skillful defense

After carefully sketching Chiarini's arguments, Zunz uses an historical-critical scholarly approach to rabbinic literature to deliver a devastating rebuttal. Zunz begins by challenging Chiarini's distinction between the Mishnah, which Chiarini excludes from opprobrium since he regards it as containing legitimate traditions from the Bible, and the later Talmud, which Chiarini thinks contains hateful points of view that distort biblical teachings. Zunz notes that many of the passages that Chiarini points to as expressing the Talmud's problematic teachings are actually from Midrashim that are *older* than the Mishnah, such as the Mekhilta, Sifra, Sifre, and Tosefta. He also observes that many of the aggadot found in the Talmud are actually from Mishnaic times. In this way, Zunz undercuts Chiarini's sharp division between the Mishnah and Talmud, concluding that the two works must be "judged guilty or not guilty" (*Schuld oder Unschuld*) together.[102]

Zunz further argues that Chiarini errs by treating the Talmud as a unified work with a singular message or perspective. Rather, the Talmud is a literary representation of the laws, mores, and concepts of Jews who lived over several centuries. Zunz notes that the Talmud does not strive for uniformity and

[99] Chiarini cites *BT,* Eruvin, 45a.
[100] As evidence of laws that Moses changed or presented in a time-limited fashion, Chiarini cites Exodus 12:3, 11, 24; Leviticus 25:35; Deuteronomy 15:12.
[101] See Chiarini, *Théorie,* 2:181–182.
[102] Zunz, *GS,* 1:284–285.

is remarkable in the diversity of opinions contained in it. It contains sublime statements next to incomprehensible ones and virtuous pronouncements alongside those that "according to our concepts" are morally reprehensible. For Zunz, the Talmud is an honest book that avoids self-censorship and does not shy away from portraying the sufferings, hatreds, comforts, and even failings of rabbis "openly and unadorned." In this way, he sees it as similar to the Bible, which is not afraid to portray the failings of its heroes and contains excellent moral teachings alongside teachings that contemporary people would judge to be immoral.[103]

For Zunz, Chiarini's ignorance expresses itself clearly in his claim that when contemporary Jewish practice deviates from a talmudic statement, this is an example of "Jewish hypocrisy (*Heuchelei*), ignorance (*Unwissenheit*), or non-Judaism (*Unjudenthum*)." Zunz responds that Chiarini lacks the historical sense to appreciate that while the foundation of religions is contained in books, religious life is a "multifaceted fruit" (*vielgestaltige Frucht*) that often modifies or diverges from what is found in the written text.[104]

For Zunz, a serious problem is Chiarini's failure to appreciate the *orality* of the Talmud. The reason that Jews place the Talmud above the Bible is that they understand the Talmud to be an "oral teaching" (*mündliche Belehrung*) that develops halakhah in accordance with new circumstances through the legal decisions of "living authorities" (*lebendige Autorität*). Jews do not regard the Talmud as the *sole* source of Judaism but, rather, as containing many old and venerable traditions. While much of Jewish law is based on the Talmud, rabbis in different communities decide which customs, ideas, and laws are binding at present. By surveying the diversity of Jewish practices among Jewish communities in different lands over time, it becomes clear that Judaism developed in diverse ways in response to changing local circumstances.[105]

Zunz also notes that Chiarini mistakenly assumes that everything in the Talmud is of unlimited, binding authority. Chiarini's assumption is belied by the fact that the Talmud contains many contradictory legal opinions, whereas only one opinion can be legally binding. Similarly, the Talmud often explicitly rejects statements by certain rabbis, which shows that not everything in the Talmud is binding.

[103] Ibid., 1:285.
[104] Ibid., 1:287.
[105] Ibid.

Zunz accuses Chiarini of committing the same errors that he had chastised Eisenmenger for, namely, selectively citing inflammatory passages from the Talmud. Zunz considers the possibility that this is because Chiarini thinks that Jews regard only the morally reprehensible statements in the Talmud as authoritative. If this is the case, then *Jews, not the Talmud*, are the true enemies of reform. In fact, given that Judaism is a historical, developing tradition, one can only determine that a talmudic statement reflects negatively on Jews if later Jewish "legal authorities" (*Gesetzeslehren, Poskim*) confirm the statement, Jewish moral treatises espouse it, and it is reflected in the actions of Jews.[106] In fact, later Jewish moral and legal authorities rarely affirm offensive talmudic rulings. Zunz takes as an example the talmudic idea that a Jew may steal from a non-Jew.[107] He notes that not only is this idea rejected in other places in the Talmud,[108] but it is also rejected in later legal works such as *Sefer Mitzvot Gadol*,[109] in talmudic commentaries such Menahem Meiri's *Bet Habehirah*,[110] in ethical treatises such as Jonah Gerondi's *Sefer Hayirah*,[111] and in biblical commentaries such as Rabbi Bahya's.[112] Lest one think that these works reflect opinions written when Jews lived in relative peace with Gentiles, Zunz notes that all these works were written in the thirteenth century, which was "not lacking in persecution [of Jews]."[113] Zunz further notes that Jewish courts have never confirmed the right of Jews to deceive Gentiles or steal from them.[114]

Like Eisenmenger, Chiarini sees in the Talmud and later Jewish writings evidence of Jewish hatred non-Jews. But Zunz notes that Chiarini does not set such statements within the context of Roman and Christian persecution of Jews. In this way, both Eisenmenger and Chiarini fail to understand religion *historically*, as they do not consider how social conditions shape religious tenets. A basic feature of human psychology is that those who lack power turn their grievances into "God's cause" (*Sache Gottes*). In this way, Zunz uses history to humanize Jewish expressions of hatred toward Christians. He further observes that using religion to express hatred is not

106 Ibid., 1:286.
107 *BT*, Baba Batra, 54b. See Chiarini, *Théorie*, 2:58.
108 *BT*, Baba Kamma, 113b.
109 See Moses of Coucy, *Sefer Mitzvot Gadol*, 61.
110 Zunz quotes Menahem Meiri as found in *Shitah Mekubetzet*, Baba Kamma 178.
111 Gerondi, *Sefer Hayirah*, 42.
112 See Bahya's commentary on Leviticus 25:50.
113 Zunz, *GS*, 1:287.
114 Ibid.

limited to the weak and persecuted. Christians expressed hatred for non-Christians theologically by denying salvation to all who were not members of their religion. This hatred expressed itself not only in doctrine, but also in actions such as the Inquisition, where heretics were burned at the stake, and in the Jesuit injunction to treat Jews disgracefully as a way of expressing divine love.[115]

Turning to Chiarini's effort to stimulate a reformation of Judaism, Zunz observes that this effort is stillborn. Jews are not going to reform their religion because a Christian denounces one of their most sacred texts. The best way Christians can promote the reformation of Judaism is to improve Jewish civil rights, which will lead Jews to adopt a more positive approach to Gentiles and a more flexible approach to halakhah, as they seek greater interactions with Christians.[116]

Zunz calls Chiarini's specific proposal of grounding Judaism in pure Mosaism of the Bible a form of Karaism (*Karäerthum*). The Karaites, whose roots go back to talmudic times, rejected talmudic tradition and sought to base Judaism on the Bible alone. But Zunz notes that the Karaites have almost ceased to exist because *adaptation* is the key to reform, not return to a pristine text. As Zunz puts it, a living people cannot allow itself to become a "serf to the rigid letter (*starren Buchstaben*)." History shows that pure Mosaism never existed and that the authorities of every age, whether prophets, priests, kings, or rabbis, always adapted Judaism to the "spirit" (*Geist*) of existing institutions.[117] For Zunz, rabbinic literature is crucial for the reformation of Judaism, both because it provides examples of how the rabbis adapted biblical teachings to contemporary circumstances and because the many opinions found in these writings provide resources that contemporary rabbis can draw upon to legitimate halakhic changes.

Two years after publishing his review of Chiarini, Zunz published the *Sermons*, in which he and developed many of the themes he had discussed concerning the Talmud and its relation to the Bible.

[115] Ibid., 1:288.

[116] Ibid., 1:296.

[117] Ibid., 1:296–297. Zunz's criticism of Chiarini's call for a Protestant-like reformation of Judaism recalls Lessing's criticism of orthodox Lutheran bibliocentrism, which he saw as reflecting attachment to the dead letter. As Lessing memorably put it, "The letter is not the spirit and the Bible is not religion." See Lessing, *Philosophical and Theological Writings*, 63 (commentary on the *Fragments* of Reimarus).

Entangling the Bible and rabbinic literature

Zunz begins the *Sermons* by noting that German Jews have until now been given civil rights piecemeal as "concessions born of pity" and that it is high time that Jews in Europe and especially in Germany demand "complete, uplifting civil rights."[118] He observes that much of the debate over Jewish civil rights revolves around outdated Christian notions of Judaism that "have not progressed beyond the point where Eisenmenger left it 135 years ago."[119] This leads Christians to make offensive suggestions regarding the civil status of Jews, which are often grounded in theological prejudices. Zunz singles out Rühs, who argues that Jewish civil equality depends on converting to Christianity, and Chiarini, who makes Jewish civil equality dependent on their overthrowing the Talmud and re-establishing biblical Judaism.[120]

For Zunz, gaining an accurate picture of Judaism requires a *scholarly* study of rabbinic literature. He notes that "humankind has acquired all its possessions through oral instruction (*mündliche Belehrung*)." This is also true of Judaism, as "the words of teaching have passed from mouth to mouth (*von Mund zu Mund*) in all ages." Oral instruction has kept Judaism vital by keeping it up-to-date with the times. The root of living instruction within Judaism is the sermon or *derashah*.[121]

Zunz notes that the synagogue was the locale for the sermon, and he stresses that it was never merely a place of prayer but, rather, a place of communal gathering. In Hebrew, the synagogue is called a "house of assembly" (*Beit Hakenesset*) rather than a "house of prayer" (*Beit Tefillah*). Zunz observes that the center of the synagogue service is the reading of the Torah, which historically involved not only reading the text of the Pentateuch, but also translating and interpreting it orally. Jews' sense of "national identity" (*Nationalität*) was reinforced through this practice, which allowed the prescriptions of Jewish faith and morality to be transmitted in their purity.[122] Zunz's stressing the national dimensions of Judaism is important because, like Mendelssohn, he thinks that Jewish civil equality requires instilling respect for Jews not only as individuals, but also as a nation.

[118] Zunz, *Vorträge*, iii.
[119] Ibid., vii–viii.
[120] Ibid., xi.
[121] Ibid., x.
[122] Ibid., 5–6.

Zunz's makes *three* basic arguments in the *Sermons*. First, against Friedrich Wilhelm III Zunz argues that reforming Judaism does *not* deviate from traditional Judaism, as history reveals precedents for contemporary synagogue reforms, especially for the vernacular sermon. Second, against De Wette Zunz argues that rabbinic writings constitute no break from pre-exilic biblical religion but are a natural continuation of it. Third, against Chiarini Zunz argues that there is no sharp dichotomy between the Bible and rabbinic writings, as midrashic methods are already found in the later books of the Bible.

Translation versus Midrash

Near the beginning of the *Sermons*, Zunz notes that there are *two* basic ways that Jews sought to make the Bible intelligible: *translation* and *interpretation*. He observes that the project of Bible translation is very old, preceding the Hasmonean era (second century BCE). From the time of the Babylonian exile in the sixth century BCE, Aramaic was the vernacular of most Jews. Recognizing that the mass of Jews could not understand the Bible in the synagogue, Jewish leaders prescribed reading the Bible with a simultaneous Aramaic translation known as *Targum*. Originally the *Targum* was extemporaneous and oral, but by the third century BCE, the first written Aramaic *Targumim* began to appear. Eventually, written translations supplanted the extemporaneous oral ones.[123] Zunz observes that throughout the ages Jews used Bible translations. As the Jews' use of Aramaic declined, translations were composed first in Greek, then in Persian and Arabic. In the ninth and tenth centuries, the Gaonic rabbis stressed the need for translation into a language that the people could understand.[124]

But according to Zunz, Jews always recognized that translation was never sufficient. The Bible contains many passages that are contradictory or obscure, and a nation's concepts change over time, which means that it always requires new ways of understanding the Bible. So in addition to translation, the Bible requires interpretation.[125] For Zunz, the function of Midrash is to interpret the Bible. But while Midrash is generally considered a rabbinic

123 Ibid., 8–9.

124 Ibid., 9–10. In *OL*, Mendelssohn had also stressed the long history of Jewish Bible translation. See p. 25 note 34 of this volume.

125 Zunz, *Vorträge*, 11. This recalls Mendelssohn's argument in *Jerusalem*. See pp. 113–116 of this volume.

concept, Zunz contends that its roots are in the Bible itself, as later books of the Bible interpret earlier books. For example, the Book of Daniel interprets the prophecies of Jeremiah, the Book of Ezekiel interprets laws found in the Pentateuch, and the Book of Chronicles is filled with biblical exegesis. For Zunz, this intra-biblical exegesis is a form of proto-Midrash since the later books of the Bible interpret the earlier books "according to present day concerns and so in a certain sense alter [them]."[126] Midrash is, therefore, not a rabbinic creation but, rather, the natural successor of methods found in the Bible. By using an historical approach to show continuity between the Bible and rabbinic literature, Zunz undermines Chiarini's attempt to draw a bright line separating the Bible from rabbinic literature. Obliquely referring to Chiarini, Zunz concludes that "there is no basis for distinguishing between the Written and Oral [Torah] in terms of authority (*Autorität*) and inner necessity (*innere Nothwendigkeit*)."[127]

Zunz locates the emergence of Midrash in the three centuries between the Hasmoneans (140 BCE) and the Roman Emperor Hadrian (d. 138 AD), claiming that in this period the divisions between the Sadducees and Pharisees emerged. For Zunz, the Sadducees were sectarians who absorbed foreign influence and "worshipped the letter (*Buchstabe*)," rejecting the Oral Torah. By contrast, the Pharisees were patriotic nationalists who embraced the Oral Torah. While the Pharisees were well aware of Greco-Roman culture, they did not blindly embrace it like the Sadducees and were willing to both criticize it and adapt it to Judaism. They also sought to preserve the "spirit" of the Bible by adjusting it to the needs of the present.[128]

For Zunz, translation and Midrash developed in opposite directions. While translation was originally oral and came to be written, Midrash was originally written (in the form of intra-biblical exegesis), then became oral, and only later was again written in early rabbinic literature. Zunz identifies three characteristics of midrash: (1) "exegesis" (*Auslegung*) of biblical texts, (2) "subordination" (*Unterordnung*) to the authority of the Bible, and (3) "amplification" (*Amplification*) of the Bible.[129] For Zunz, there are two basic divisions of Midrash, namely, *midrash halakhah* and *midrash haggadah*.[130]

[126] Zunz, *Vorträge*, 37. Recent scholars have paid attention to this phenomenon, which has been dubbed "inner-biblical exegesis." See Fishbane, *Biblical Interpretation in Ancient Israel*.
[127] Zunz, *Vorträge*, 47.
[128] Ibid., 40–41.
[129] Ibid., 42.
[130] Ibid., 44.

Halakhah is law. It is communal, involving practices that link generations to one another and unite the Jewish nation. The authority of halakhah derives from the *Beit Midrash* (house of study), the central institution of rabbinic learning. Zunz notes that another word for halakhah is *shmateta* (literally "heard") because to be authoritative halakhah had to be *heard/received* from a teacher. The function of midrash halakhah is to show the scriptural basis for a received halakhah. Hence, it involves coordinating the oral law with the written text. Zunz links halakhah with *obedience.*[131]

Haggadah refers to ideas. Zunz describes it as an individual process involving the "free application of the content of Scripture according to the opinions and needs of the times."[132] Haggadah need not be heard from another and is not binding. The product of *individual free insight*, it is spoken and flexible, addressing present-day concerns using contemporary concepts. Its authority derives from people trusting the preacher on the basis of his personal piety, moral rectitude, sound judgment, and love for the Jewish people.[133]

For Zunz, midrash halakhah is a successor to the biblical priests, while midrash haggadah is a successor to the biblical prophets. In the Bible, the priests were the guardians of the law and the Holy Ark, while the prophets propagated the fundamental ideas of the Bible through oral exhortation, applying them to the present generation through what Zunz calls "the fire of freedom" (*Feuer der Freiheit*).[134] In stressing the continuity between midrash haggadah and biblical prophecy, Zunz is responding to De Wette by showing that midrash Haggadah reflects a "Hebraic" emphasis on freedom and seeking the spirit of the law that is characteristic of the biblical prophets. For Zunz, through midrash haggadah, Jews preserve a Hebraic form of religion that De Wette associates with Protestantism.

Zunz notes that there is overlap between Targum (translation) and midrash haggadah, as both aim to make Bible comprehensible. The major difference between the two is in their *degrees* of freedom. For Zunz, the biblical "letter" (*Buchstabe*) binds translator. As such, he is constrained in his ability to make the text relevant to the contemporary reader who is operating with different concepts than those found in the Bible. Zunz links translation with seeking the plain meaning of the text (*peshat*) and

[131] Ibid., 44–45.
[132] Ibid., 338.
[133] Ibid., 61–62.
[134] Ibid., 334.

sees it as oriented toward the *past*, that is, recovering the original meaning of the text.[135] By contrast, midrash haggadah is much freer in its interpretation and through playful exegesis the preacher makes the Bible relevant for the listener by putting it in terms that are familiar. It addresses the *present*, seeking to penetrate the "spirit" (*Geist*) of the Bible and give the biblical words a new appearance, attaching new lessons to it, and drawing comfort from it.[136] Zunz notes that *darshanim* (preachers) employed a range of techniques. They could build their sermon around the "plain meaning" (*natürlische Sinn*) of the Bible; the orthographic features of the text regardless of whether these features reflected how the text was read;[137] the similarity of words in the Bible or with other languages, including Greek, Aramaic, and Arabic; the literary context of a verse; the shapes of letters; acronyms (*Notrikon*) and mathematical calculations of the value of letters (*Gematria*); the Masorah, including special marks such as dots above letters, and the Targum.[138] In addition to Targum and Midrash, Zunz adds a third level of traditional Jewish exegesis, which interprets the Bible allegorically in terms of philosophical or mystical ideas or eschatologically about the end of days. For Zunz, this is *sod* or the esoteric meaning, which is oriented toward the *future* or *eternity*.[139]

For Zunz, the rabbinic description of Talmud and Midrash as the Oral Torah embodies a crucial truth. To be sure, he does not accept the traditional rabbinic notion that the entire Oral Torah was given to Moses on Sinai and then passed down orally until the second century, when Rabbi Judah the Prince wrote the Mishnah to prevent it from being forgotten. Zunz's critical historical sense prevents him from accepting such a supernaturalist, ahistorical view.[140] Nevertheless, Zunz thinks that by calling their writings "Oral Torah," the rabbis were alluding to a crucial feature of rabbinic literature,

[135] Zunz is thinking of Targumim like Onkelos that adhere quite closely to the biblical text. Others like Targum Yerushalmi incorporate many midrashic elements. See ibid., 62, 66.

[136] Ibid., 62, 64.

[137] Ibid., 338. For example, the rabbis will sometimes derive meaning based on whether a Hebrew word is written *plene* or not. Two talmudic dictums relevant to this that Zunz mentions are *yesh em lemikra* and *yesh em lamasoret*, that is, whether the enunciated or orthographic text has priority. See *BT*, Pesachim, 86b; *BT*, Sukkah, 6b; *BT*, Kiddushin, 18b; *BT*, Sanhedrin, 4a; *BT*, Keritot, 17b; *BT*, Zevahim, 38a; *BT*, Bekhorot, 34a.

[138] Zunz, *Vorträge*, 338–340.

[139] Ibid., 62. It is not clear how Zunz understands the third level of scriptural interpretation, *remez*, as he seems to include it in *sod*. On the four levels of interpretation, see p. 50 of this volume. Zunz translates *remez* as "*inspirirten Deutung*" (imbued meaning). See ibid., 423.

[140] While Zunz is circumspect about how the Oral Law developed, he acknowledges that many laws found in it are ancient, predating the rabbis. See ibid., 12.

namely, that it developed in oral contexts. Midrash halakhah was heard in the Beit Midrash (house of study), while midrash haggadah was spoken in the synagogue.[141]

The need for a Jewish reformation

Like Mendelssohn, Zunz accepts that much of contemporary German Judaism is corrupt and in need of reformation. But while many Christians, both Catholic and Protestant, considered this corruption endemic to rabbinic (or post-exilic) Judaism, Zunz saw it as *limited to Polish and German Judaism of the sixteenth to eighteenth centuries.*

Toward the end of the *Sermons,* Zunz notes that the Renaissance and Protestant Reformation brought Europeans a number of salutary developments: a revival of classical learning spread through printing, Luther's defense of the individual's right to think more freely about religion, and the discovery of America, which led to new ways of thinking about "customs, laws, institutions, power, and civilization."[142] At the same time, the Jews who were exiled from Spain in 1492 brought their traditions of grammatical investigation of Scripture, talmudic scholarship, and philosophical and kabbalistic studies to the communities they entered. Among these Spanish exiles, consciousness of their catastrophe ignited a "warm religiosity," which awakened a "passion for learning" (*Lerneifer*). These developments benefitted certain Jewish communities. In Italy and Amsterdam, where Jews enjoyed relative tolerance, Jews learned the vernacular and embraced a diverse curriculum that included multiple areas of general and Jewish learning, and the classical sermon in which older religious texts were used to support new ideas was revived.[143] One would have expected that these beneficial developments to have spread to Ashkenazic Jewish communities, but Zunz notes that by and large this did not happen.

Zunz observes that with the rise of Protestantism in the sixteenth century some of the medieval persecutions of Ashkenazi Jews ceased, but hate and discrimination persisted. Ashkenazi Jews continued to be excluded from professions, positions of civil authority, and scientific learning. While

[141] Ibid., 61.
[142] Ibid., 441.
[143] Ibid., 441–442.

in the Middle Ages Jews' level of culture and learning was generally higher than that of Christians, the Reformation changed this. As Protestantism was linked with Renaissance humanism, many Ashkenazic communities came to equate secular learning with Christianity and so came to reject it because of the Protestant persecution they endured. Zunz presents language as a crucial marker of Ashkenazic insularity. Before the sixteenth century, German Jews spoke German at a level comparable to Christians, but by the sixteenth century they turned away from it. Yiddish, a language that mixed German, often in archaic usage, with Hebrew (and in other countries with Polish, French, or Dutch), became Ashkenazi Jews' exclusive tongue. Since German and Polish rabbis who read Hebrew did not study the language grammatically, by the seventeenth and eighteenth centuries they essentially knew "no language at all." According to Zunz, German and Polish Jews also neglected Bible study because with Luther's emphasis on *Sola Scriptura*, it came to be seen as a defining feature of Christian piety.[144]

For Zunz, the near exclusive emphasis on pilpulistic Talmud study and kabbalistic exegesis exemplifies the decay of Ashkenazi Jewish education. Zunz portrays this decay as reflecting a decline in midrash haggadah.[145] He notes that in the seventeenth and eighteenth centuries Ashkenazi Jews did not lack preachers. But these itinerant Yiddish preachers tended either to scold their listeners or engage in pedantic talmudic exegesis, meaningless wordplays, or kabbalistic superstitions disconnected from the spirit of the Bible.[146] True midrash haggadah, which involved free application of the biblical spirit to contemporary concerns, was lost.

For Zunz, it was only at the beginning of the eighteenth century that early Maskilim familiarized themselves with Sephardic, Italian, and Dutch Jewish learning and opened themselves to secular subjects, paving the way for Mendelssohn.[147] As we will see in the next chapter, Zunz regards Mendelssohn's *Be'ur* as a major impetus for the cultural regeneration of Ashkenazic Jewry.[148]

[144] Ibid., 452–458.
[145] Ibid., 442.
[146] As Zunz put it, "The printed word sighed under contrived explanations and kabbalistic fantasies." See ibid., 458–463.
[147] Ibid., 460.
[148] Ibid., 463–469.

Reviving Midrash and synagogue reform

As we have seen, in the *Sermons* Zunz places the synagogue at the center of Judaism, writing that following the fall of the Temple, the synagogue became the "sole bearer of their [the Jews'] nationality" (*einziger Träger ihrer Nationalität*) and the "guarantor of their religious existence."[149] It is, therefore, not surprising that Zunz regards the synagogue as central to Jewish reformation.[150] For Zunz, a *deutsche Synagoge* to serve middle-class German Jews was urgently needed.[151] Zunz discusses four elements of the *deutsche Synagoge* service that were at the heart of controversies between reformers and their traditionalist opponents, namely: a regular vernacular sermon, prayers in the vernacular, changes in the traditional liturgy, and having a choir and organ accompany the service. Zunz emphasizes the role of gender in the drive for synagogue reform.[152]

We saw that in the *Sermons* Zunz identifies halakhah with the authority of the Beit Midrash (house of study). For Zunz, halakhic observance is not something that individuals can freely discard or change based on personal preference. Rather, legal reforms within Judaism must be grounded in *precedent*. Zunz distinguishes between three types of legal reform: (1) introducing new customs; (2) altering existing customs; and (3) returning to ancient, neglected customs. He appeals to precedent to justify all three.[153]

As an example of introducing a new custom, Zunz discusses using an organ and choir in the prayer service. While this is a new custom among German communities, Zunz notes that it is not without antecedent. Musical instruments were a central component of the service in the ancient Temple in Jerusalem, and an organ was used on Friday nights in the synagogue in Prague during the seventeenth and early eighteenth centuries.[154] Regarding synagogue choirs, Zunz notes that there is an old custom of having three

149 Ibid., 1, 469.

150 The centrality of the synagogue is evident in Zunz's later scholarly work. From 1855 to 1865 he published a trilogy on the synagogue liturgy *Die synagogale Poesie des Mittelalters* (Medieval Synagogue Poetry) (1855), *Die Ritus des synagogalen Gottesdienstes* (Rites of the Synagogue Service) (1859), and *Literaturgeschichte der synagogalen Poesie* (Literary History of Synagogue Poetry) (1865). This trilogy constituted the most important scholarly contributions of Zunz's later career.

151 On Zunz's concern with creating a *deutsche Synagoge*, see Schorsch, *Leopold Zunz*, 47–48.

152 Zunz, *Vorträge*, 474.

153 Ibid., 490.

154 For discussion of the use of an organ in the Prague synagogue, see Ellenson, *After Emancipation*, 121–138.

hazanim (cantors) sing during the service, which is a mini choir. For these reasons, there is ample justification for introducing an organ and choir into the synagogue service.[155]

As an example of altering an existing custom, Zunz discusses changing the content and language of the prayer book. He notes that the only ancient parts of the prayer book are the *Shema*, the silent prayer (*Amidah*), some blessings, and the thanksgiving prayer (*Hallel*). Many elements such as the lamentations (*kinot*), penitential prayers (*selihot*), and liturgical poems (*piyutim*) were added in the Gaonic period (tenth–eleventh centuries). Zunz also notes the great variety in the prayer books of different Jewish communities, which reflect local social and political realities. He therefore contends that communities have the right to add or remove prayers as long as the ancient prayers are preserved. Regarding introducing German prayers, Zunz notes that all legal authorities permit praying in the vernacular, and many even *require* it if one does not understand what one is saying. Nevertheless, Zunz recommends retaining Hebrew for the oldest and most important prayers as a way of maintaining Jewish national unity.[156]

Zunz calls returning to ancient customs the "most important means" of improving the prayer service. He cites many halakhic authorities who complain about corruptions that have entered the Polish-German prayer service, including: (1) disorder; (2) screaming and excessive body movements; (3) lack of concentration and intention; (4) appointment of morally unworthy cantors; (5) use of inappropriate melodies; (6) chanting the Torah reading using *trop* (Masoretic accents and notations);[157] (7) selling the honors associated with the Torah service; (8) impudent behavior of the rich in the synagogue; and "above all," (9) lack of regular sermons.[158]

Zunz dwells on this final point. He notes that in 1785 eight Italian rabbis supported Wessely when he attacked the useless, "pilpulistic discourse"

155 Zunz, *Vorträge*, 491.

156 Ibid., 491–493.

157 Zunz notes that the Masoretic accents and melodies are a late, post-Mishnaic development. He worries that chanting the Torah with accents and melodies has led to the person being called to the Torah not being able to read from the Torah himself since it is too difficult to memorize the complicated accents and melodies. Instead, the person called to the Torah must follow a professional reader. This results in contravening the original intention of the public Torah reading, which was that each individual read the section he was called up for by himself. See ibid., 424–426. Zunz also notes that the "Mozarabic Jews," that is, the Jews from southern Spain, did not chant the Torah according to Masoretic notations. See ibid., 495.

158 Ibid., 494–496.

(Disputir-Derascha) that German and Polish rabbis would deliver in synagogue. For Wessely, these discourses, which were given irregularly on obscure talmudic subjects in Yiddish, aimed to confuse rather than enlighten the listeners, as the public's inability to understand the discourse was taken as evidence of the speaker's great profundity and learning. The result was that these speeches held absolutely no value for women and the "masses" (*Menge*) of men.[159] Zunz notes that it took a generation after Wessely's attack before the "Polish-German style rabbinic *derashah*" (*Derascha's der polnisch-deutschen Rabbiner*) was replaced by a regular vernacular sermon that was rhetorically effective, eloquent, and edifying. It first appeared in the Jacobson Temple founded in Seesen in 1808.[160]

For Zunz, the vernacular sermon is a legitimate heir to midrash haggadah that aims to instruct the public by conveying the spirit of the Bible in contemporary language. By contrast, the German-Polish talmudic discourse does not address the mass of the Jewish community, thereby deviating from the tradition of midrash haggadah. So, while Friedrich Wilhelm prohibited innovations in Jewish services, Zunz argues that it is the Yiddish *derashah* that is the inauthentic innovation, not the vernacular sermon.

The guiding principle of Zunz's approach to synagogue reform is promoting true inner religiosity. The external forms of the synagogue service are subordinate to internal piety. As he puts it, "Reform does not consist in externals (*Aeusserlichkeiten*) but in the divine spirit (*göttlichen Geiste*) of piety and knowledge . . . When the inner is prepared for reform, the outer form easily adjusts."[161] Zunz's emphasis on interiority as the mark of true religiosity explains why he puts such emphasis on vernacular prayers and sermons. But Zunz recognizes that changing certain rites may be so contentious that they do not ultimately promote inner edification. Given the importance of Jewish national unity for edification, Zunz concludes that if instituting an organ or choir will split the community, it is best not to introduce it.[162]

[159] Ibid., 463–464, 466–467, 474–475. Zunz is referring to Wessely's 1785 letter *Rehovot*, which was his so-called "fourth letter" of *Divrei Shalom Ve'emet*. See the reference cited by Zunz, *Vorträge*, 474, note b.

[160] Ibid., 475.

[161] Ibid., 490. Also see Zunz's letter of March 4, 1845, to Geiger found in Geiger, *Abraham Geiger and Liberal Judaism*, 115–116.

[162] Zunz, *Vorträge*, 491.

Conclusion

Zunz's vision of *Wissenschaft des Judentums* is intimately tied to his promoting Jewish emancipation and reform. For Zunz, a scholarly treatment of rabbinic literature shows that Christian opponents of Jewish emancipation are incorrect in claiming that Jews have always isolated themselves or that Judaism reflects a degenerate form of religion alien to the noble, "Hebraic" teachings of the Bible exemplified by Protestantism. Through his pioneering scholarship, Zunz demonstrates that rabbinic literature is bound to world literature, and that rabbinic literature is organically connected to biblical teachings.

Zunz agrees with Christian critics such as Chiarini that Jews need reformation. But he rejects Chiarini's claim that reform depends on Jews rejecting the Talmud and returning to the Bible. Instead, Zunz argues that Bible translation and midrash haggadah are complementary means Jews have historically used to keep biblical teachings alive. Translation makes the meaning of the biblical text comprehensible and midrash haggadah adapts the biblical message to contemporary needs. For Zunz, both methods are needed for Judaism to remain a living religion of spirit. Reformation comes not by rejecting rabbinic literature and returning to the Bible but by employing the methods of midrash haggadah. Zunz advocates introducing reforms into Jewish ritual especially in the synagogue service and uses scholarship to ground these reforms by showing the variety of halakhic practices over space and time.

Zunz also uses scholarship to argue that the traditionalist German Jewish curriculum, which largely neglects the Bible, secular studies, and knowledge of the vernacular, deviates from Jewish tradition. In the next chapter, I will explore Zunz's practical efforts to implement a Jewish reformation, paying particular attention to his 1838 Bible translation.

4
Bible translation and the centrality of the synagogue

In the previous chapter we saw that in his 1832 *The Sermons of the Jews* Zunz argued that translation was the basic means Jews used to make the Bible intelligible and that Bible translation was first employed in the synagogue service. Long before publishing the *Sermons*, Zunz was thinking about producing his own Bible translation. At an 1823 plenary session of the *Verein für Kultur und Wissenschaft des Judenthums* (Society for the Culture and Science of Judaism), Zunz advocated for a new Bible translation to replace Mendelssohn's.[1] The *Verein* adopted Zunz's proposal, but its collapse a few months later left the project stillborn.[2]

Thirteen years after Zunz's original proposal, the publisher Moritz Veit approached Zunz about editing a new Bible translation.[3] Zunz accepted, dividing the translations between three scholars: Heymann Arnheim, Michael Sachs, and Julius Fürst.[4] Zunz himself translated Chronicles and edited all the translations.[5] In 1838 Zunz's translation appeared under the title

[1] The meeting took place on in Berlin on August 31, 1823. See next note.

[2] Gotthold Salomon was actually the first to suggest a new Bible translation, and he published his own translation a year before Zunz did. See Schorsch, *Leopold Zunz,* 45–46.

[3] See Schorsch, *Leopold Zunz,* 62. Gillman notes that originally the publisher H. Prausnitz revived the idea of producing a new Bible translation, enlisting Michael Sachs and Heymann Arnheim to work on it. Prausnitz then presented the idea to Veit, who offered Zunz editorship of the project. See Gillman, *A History of German Jewish Bible Translation,* 115.

[4] Arnheim was a preacher in Glogau who published a translation of Job in 1836. Sachs was a preacher and scholar who in 1835 published a translation of the Psalms, which Zunz reviewed positively. Fürst was a Polish-born Jew living in Leipzig who was a pupil of the great German orientalist H.F.W. Gesenius and an expert in ancient languages. See Rosin, "Die Zunz'sche Bibel," 507–508. Zunz's review of Sachs is found in Zunz, *GS,* 3:116–121. For the Zunz Bible, Arnheim translated Genesis, Exodus, Leviticus, Numbers, Kings, Ezekiel, Hosea, Obadiah, Jonah, Micah, Zachariah, Proverbs, Job, Ruth, Ecclesiastes, Esther, and Nehemiah. Sachs translated Deuteronomy, Joshua, Judges, Samuel, Isaiah, Joel, Amos, Habakuk, Zaphaniah, Nahum, Haggai, Malachi, Psalms, Song of Songs, and Lamentations. Arnheim and Sachs translated Jeremiah together. Fürst translated Daniel and Ezra, and Zunz translated Chronicles himself. In the introduction to his Bible translation, Zunz attributes the translation of Nahum to Arnheim, but David Rosin reports that Sachs told him personally that he had done it. See Rosin, "Die Zunz'sche Bibel," 508, note 1.

[5] It was natural that Zunz would translate Chronicles as he had devoted a chapter to that biblical book in the *Sermons.* In his introduction, Zunz describes the editing process in more detail. The translators drafted translations, which they circulated among themselves. Zunz then edited the entire

The Jewish Reformation. Michah Gottlieb, Oxford University Press (2021). © Oxford University Press.
DOI: 10.1093/oso/9780199336388.003.0005

Die vier und zwanzig Bücher der Heiligen Schrift (The Twenty-Four Books of Holy Scripture).

Zunz's Bible was not a purely scholarly enterprise. Veit noted Zunz's desire to produce a Bible for popular use writing that Zunz aimed to produce a "Bible for Israelites" (*Bibel für Israeliten*).[6] At the same time, Veit made clear that Zunz did not leave scholarship aside completely, writing that Zunz wished his translation to be "both popular and scholarly" (*zugleich popular und wissenschaftlich*).[7]

Zunz's Bible was an enormous success. It quickly displaced the *Be'ur* as the standard German Jewish Bible and ran into seventeen editions through 1935.[8] To understand the reasons for this success, we must situate Zunz's translation in relation to his efforts to promote Jewish educational reform. Like Mendelssohn, Zunz's reformatory efforts were rooted in early childhood experiences.

The miseducation of Leopold Zunz

Zunz was born Yom Tov Lippmann on October 10, 1794, in Detmold, in the German province of Lippe. Shortly after his birth, his family moved to Hamburg because of his father's poor health.[9] In his notebooks, Zunz described his earliest education: "My first memories date from my fourth year. When I was five years old, I chanted *Dror Yikra*[10] by heart and began learning Talmud. My father taught me Hebrew grammar, the Pentateuch, and Yiddish writing."[11] In 1802, Zunz's father died, and the next summer eight-year old Yom Tov was sent to the *Philipp Samson Beit Midrash* in Wolfenbüttel. Philipp Samson, a wealthy banker from Braunschweig, had established the school for poor children in 1786 and was its director. In

handwritten manuscript, making changes where he deemed necessary with an eye to giving the entire translation an even and uniform tone. After the manuscript went into proofs, Zunz revised it once more. See Zunz, *Die vier und zwanzig Bücher*, iii–iv; Rosin, "Die Zunz'sche Bibel," 511.

6 See Veit to Sachs August 6, 1835, in Sachs and Veit, *Michael Sachs und Moritz Veit: Briefwechsel*, 2.

7 See ibid.

8 When in the 1990s the Basel Jewish book publisher Victor Goldschmidt Verlag sought to issue a German Bible translation for contemporary German-speaking Jews, it chose to reissue the Zunz bible. See Zunz, *Die Heilige Schrift: Hebräische-Deutsch*.

9 See Schorsch, *Leopold Zunz*, 8. Zunz first adopted the name "Leopold" when J.H. Samson hired him as a teacher. See Trautmann-Waller, *Philologie Allemand*, 60.

10 A medieval Hebrew poem traditionally recited at Sabbath meals.

11 See Zunz, *Das Buch Zunz*, 12.

1796, the widow of Philipp's brother Herz Samson established a sister school. The two schools followed the traditional Ashkenazic curriculum for boys, focusing nearly exclusively on Talmud study using pilpulistic methods. Minimal general education was provided.[12]

In an autobiographical essay, Zunz describes being brought to the house of the school director Philipp Samson on June 5, 1803. After feeding the nine-year-old boy some brown cabbage, Samson tested Zunz's Torah knowledge and then led him to the classroom. The school was small, with eight to ten students ages ten to fifteen. Most teachers were either Polish Jews or German Jews who had been educated by Polish teachers.[13] Students were divided into two classes, with Zunz placed in the higher class. From eight or nine in the morning until five in the afternoon, Rabbi Kalman Jacob from Ellrich taught Zunz Talmud.[14] The only Bible Zunz was taught was the Pentateuch, which he learned on Friday mornings.[15] Curious students were left to study the other books of the Bible on their own. Aside from Talmud and a little Pentateuch, the only other subjects taught in the school were Yiddish writing for two hours a week and German language and arithmetic for a combined four hours weekly.[16] German books were banned, and those found reading them were punished. Zunz first read a German book when he was eleven.[17] Zunz recounts that when he asked his Christian math teacher Mr. Bertrand what algebra was, Bertrand responded: "something I will never understand."[18]

Zunz describes conditions at the school in Dickensian terms. There were no school rules or protocol, and no thought was given to pedagogy. During recess the students were left alone and would often fight. The older boys bullied the younger boys, and the teacher would use a strap to administer corporal punishment.[19] Apart from school fights, the only exercise the students received was on holidays and Friday afternoons when they could take

[12] Eliav, *Jewish Education in Germany,* 102–103.

[13] See ibid.; Ehrenberg, "Die Samson'sche Freischule zu Wolfenbüttel," 69.

[14] The day began at 8 a.m. in the summer and at 9 a.m. in the winter, presumably because for much of the winter the sun did not rise until after 8 in Wolfenbüttel, so the morning prayers could not be completed until well after 8. See Ehrenberg, "Die Samson'sche Freischule zu Wolfenbüttel," 71.

[15] Zunz recounts that Rabbi Kalman used Mendelssohn's translation to teach the Pentateuch. See Zunz, "Mein erster Unterricht," 131–132. This suggests the widespread acceptance of the *Be'ur*, even in traditionalist German Jewish circles at the time.

[16] See Ehrenberg, "Die Samson'sche Freischule zu Wolfenbüttel," 69–71; Zunz, "Mein erster Unterricht," 131–132. Christian teachers taught German language and arithmetic.

[17] See Eliav, *Jewish Education,* 103.

[18] See Zunz, *Das Buch Zunz,* 14.

[19] Zunz, "Mein erster," 132–133; Ehrenberg, "Die Samson'sche Freischule zu Wolfenbüttel," 71.

walks within the school gates.[20] Vacation consisted of 24–25 half-days over the entire year.[21]

Living conditions were harsh. The building was not heated, and the rooms where the children slept was cold as an icebox in winter. The food was awful and not plentiful. Breakfast consisted of tea or milk, and lunch was a piece of dry bread with either bug-infested cheese or a plate of lettuce. Zunz recalls that on the Sabbath, kugel (a traditional Ashkenazic pudding) was served, but it was so badly burnt that despite his gnawing hunger, Zunz would hide it under the table before surreptitiously throwing it away.[22]

Little attention was given to hygiene. Students never took baths and only washed the bare minimum demanded by the authoritative Jewish legal code, the *Shulhan Arukh*. One hand towel served many students, and a student would not normally see a toothbrush until his third year at school. The clothes worn by the students were ragged and filthy, and they only changed their shirts prior to the Sabbath.[23] Not surprisingly, people at the school frequently fell ill. Zunz recounts having a terrible fever over many weeks during the summer of 1804. That same year Zunz's teacher Rabbi Kalman and the teacher of the other class, Rabbi Lik, died.[24] The following year the school director Philipp Samson passed away.

Following the death of Philipp Samson, his nephew Isaak Herz Samson took over the two Samson schools and united them, appointing a former pupil, Samuel Meyer Ehrenberg, as the school inspector and director.[25] Ehrenberg transformed the school from a traditional Talmud school into a modern maskilic school, renaming it *Die Samson'sche Freischule* (The Samson Free School). He improved living conditions, introduced physical exercise, allowed the students free play, organized school excursions, and introduced rules and discipline.[26] But his most dramatic reforms were

[20] Ehrenberg, "Die Samson'sche Freischule zu Wolfenbüttel," 71–72.

[21] See Eliav, *Jewish Education,* 103.

[22] Zunz, "Mein erster," 134. See Ehrenberg, "Die Samson'sche Freischule zu Wolfenbüttel," 71. In 1806, Zunz wrote a satire lampooning the school in Hebrew. His friends at school read the work with gusto, but when the school administrators discovered it, they destroyed it. See Zunz, *Das Buch Zunz,* 14. Zunz's satirizing traditional Jewish education in Hebrew shows the ways in which even at the age of twelve he was following the path of late eighteenth-century Maskilim. For an analysis and selection of such works see Friedlander, *Studies in Hebrew Satire.*

[23] Ehrenberg, "Die Samson'sche Freischule zu Wolfenbüttel," 70–71.

[24] Zunz, "Mein erster," 134–135. Ehrenberg writes that the teacher's name was R. Löb from Burgeberach. See Ehrenberg, "Die Samson'sche Freischule zu Wolfenbüttel," 69, 72.

[25] Ehrenberg, "Die Samson'sche Freischule zu Wolfenbüttel," 73.

[26] Eliav, *Jewish Education,* 105. Chanan Gafni has recently published a list of school rules written in Hebrew that Ehrenberg instituted in 1807. See Gafni, "Rulebook for Students in the Wolfenbüttel Study House," 38–44.

curricular. Ehrenberg hired three new teachers, including two Christians, and greatly expanded the general curriculum, introducing German, French, Hebrew, arithmetic, geography, history, and calligraphy. Within a short time Ehrenberg added mathematics, Latin, Greek, music, and drawing to the curriculum.[27] Talmud study was reduced to ten hours a week and study of the Bible was emphasized. Students were taught Hebrew grammar and how to translate the Pentateuch into German. The books of the Prophets and Writings were taught and read grammatically. The Bible also served as a starting point for systematic instruction in religion which was studied for three hours weekly, with special emphasis given to the Bible's moral teachings of religion. Ehrenberg made the *Samson'sche Freischule* the first Jewish school in Europe to teach catechisms of Jewish faith, and in 1807 the school introduced the confirmation ceremony, with Zunz being the first student confirmed.[28] Zunz, who was thirteen when Ehrenberg took over the school, described Ehrenberg's impact in near-messianic terms: "We literally passed from a medieval age to a new age in one day, emerging from Jewish serfdom (*Helotie*) to civil freedom (*bürgerliche Freiheit*)."[29]

Celebrating a hero: Zunz on Mendelssohn

Given Zunz's childhood redemption through maskilic intervention, it is not surprising that he revered Mendelssohn. On the centenary of Mendelssohn's birth in September 1829, German Jews held the first of what were to become regular Mendelssohn celebrations. Events were held in several German cities, but the largest event was in Berlin, where Zunz delivered the final address of the evening. He spoke about Mendelssohn's accomplishments for his contemporaries and for posterity.[30]

Zunz began by observing that "through his example, actions, and writings, Moses Mendelssohn still lives." Zunz called those gathered at the celebration Mendelssohn's "spiritual possessions" (*geistige Habe*) who belong to him as

[27] Eliav, *Jewish Education*, 105. After graduating from the school, Zunz taught there for several years. The subjects he taught included German, French, Latin, Greek, arithmetic, and mathematics. It is noteworthy that Zunz did not teach any Jewish subjects. See Rosenstock, *Festschrift zur hundertjährigen Jubelfeier*, 17.

[28] See Ehrenberg, "Die Samson'sche Freischule zu Wolfenbüttel," 74–76; Eliav, *Jewish Education*, 104–105.

[29] Zunz, "Mein erster," 136–137.

[30] The other speeches were given by Moses Moser, a founder of the *Verein für Cultur und Wissenschaft der Juden*, and the historian Isaak Marcus Jost. See Zunz, *GS*, 2:112–113.

students to a revered teacher. For Zunz, Mendelssohn's influence would not be limited to the present generation since "the actions of the noble are infinite, immortally extending over lands and generations."[31]

Zunz noted that Mendelssohn's great virtue "enraptures" people. Mendelssohn was always humble, never seeking titles or official positions for himself.[32] He never set himself above others and always showed compassion for others' suffering. Throughout his life, Mendelssohn had great love for the Jewish people. He was an eloquent, passionate fighter for Jewish civil rights and opposed religious persecution and political oppression.[33] Despite enormous personal challenges, Mendelssohn lost neither his religious piety, nor his love for humanity.[34]

Zunz then observed that Mendelssohn was always occupied with the highest human interests.[35] He was passionately devoted to searching for truth and was a tireless defender of freedom of conscience. As it was more important for Mendelssohn to know truth than to be right, he was very tolerant of those who disagreed with him. While it was said that Socrates brought truth from heaven and that Plato showed truth's way into the heart, Mendelssohn did both. Not only did he think deeply, he also advanced morality and religious piety. Mendelssohn's clarity of thought and love of truth stimulated a scientific spirit among his fellow Jews, who devoted themselves to "excavating" old and new wisdom.[36]

Zunz then turned to Mendelssohn's writings. Mendelssohn's beautiful, accurate Bible translation promoted a correct understanding of the Bible and of Hebrew among German Jews. His Hebrew writings sparked the revival of Hebrew as a living language. Mendelssohn's German writings helped establish modern German literary style and spurred German *Christians* to seek *Bildung*.[37]

Zunz noted that the *Be'ur* played a crucial role in changing the language of German Jews. While half a century earlier rabbis had opposed Mendelssohn's translation for promoting German at the expense of Yiddish, Zunz observed that German Jews scarcely used Yiddish any more. Every Jewish

[31] Ibid., 102.
[32] Ibid., 103.
[33] Ibid., 108.
[34] Ibid., 103.
[35] Ibid., 105.
[36] Ibid., 105–106.
[37] Ibid., 109–110.

school in German lands now taught the Bible in High German and all rabbis delivered sermons in German.[38]

Preaching *Bildung*

Zunz's assessment of Mendelssohn's achievement in reforming Jewish education reflects his identification with Mendelssohn's concept of *Bildung*. In the first chapter, we saw that for Mendelssohn, *Bildung* constitutes life's purpose and is the way to serve God. It involves perfecting one's intellect, cultivating one's aesthetic taste and artistic abilities, and above all, acquiring moral virtue. We saw that for Mendelssohn the Bible was the primary means of promoting *Bildung* among Jews.

Serving as preacher in the Reform Berlin Beer Temple from 1821 to 1822, Zunz advocated the Mendelssohnian ideal of *Bildung*.[39] It is no accident that his sermons relied heavily on biblical rather than rabbinic texts.[40]

In a sermon delivered in September 1817 before a circle of friends, Zunz uses a striking image to express his commitment to *Bildung*. Commenting on Ecclesiastes 12:1, "Remember your Creator in your youth, before the evil days comes, before the year's approach in which you say, I love them not," Zunz describes youth as both an earthly and heavenly "garden." The earth endows the youth with physical strength and beauty, while heaven plants the seeds of "moral virtue" (*Tugend*), "knowledge" (*Wissenschaft*), and "art" (*Kunst*), which must be cultivated.[41] In a later 1862 essay titled

[38] Zunz, *GS*, 2:110. Zunz doubtlessly exaggerated the importance of the *Be'ur* in effecting this linguistic change. Government regulations mandating that Jews use German also played an important role. Lowenstein notes that "compulsory secular education for Jews was introduced in virtually all parts of Germany by 1815, and Jews were also required to keep their business records in German." See Lowenstein, "The Readership," 189. Zunz was lifelong devotee to the German language. In 1872, he published *Deutsche Briefe* (German Letters), in which he argued for using a pure form of German.

[39] Zunz expressed his commitment to *Bildung* in calling for "self-perfection" (*Selbstvervollkommnung*), "ennoblement" (*Veredelung*), or simply "improvement" (*Verbesserung*). See Altmann, "Zur frühgeschichte," 29–30. Two of Zunz's sermons delivered before he was appointed preacher at the Beer Temple, one in 1817 ("On Religiosity") and another in 1820 ("Arousal to Progress"), are found in his *Gesammelte Schriften*. See Zunz, *GS*, 2:83–101. A third sermon based on a sermon Zunz preached in 1822 but only published in 1844 on Tefillin (phylacteries) is found on pp. 172–176. See p. 168 note 44 from this volume. Zunz gave a total of sixty-six sermons during his career as a preacher. In addition to the three published in *GS*, he published sixteen more in 1823. See Zunz, *Predigten*. Most of the other sermons are in manuscript, though some have been lost. Alexander Altmann analyzed the sermons in a long, important article. See Altmann, "Zur frühgeschichte." More recently, see Niehoff, "Zunz's Concept of Haggadah."

[40] See Schorsch, *Leopold Zunz*, 53.

[41] See Zunz, *GS*, 2:84.

"Political and Nonpolitical", Zunz writes that *Bildung* constitutes the perfection of the human being qua human. To this Zunz adds two further perfections: "labor" (*Arbeit*), which is a perfection of the human being qua worker, and political participation, which is a perfection of the human being qua citizen.[42] Zunz casts the perfection of human being qua human as the province of religion and the perfection of human being qua citizen as the province of politics. Zunz espoused the bourgeois ideal of *Bildung* throughout his life.[43]

On January 26, 1822, Zunz delivered a sermon at the Beer Temple titled "The Ceremonial Law" in which he defended the ritual of putting on phylacteries in quasi-Mendelssohnian terms.[44] While some Reformers had sought to discard this ritual, Zunz defended it for its symbolic value, writing that the wrapping of the phylacteries is a "sensible" (*sinnbildlich*) symbol of being bound to God, which helps inculcate a sense of humility, curb one from acting viciously, and inspire one to act nobly.[45] For Zunz, putting on phylacteries also bound Jews together, moving them to show care and compassion for one another.[46] Some two decades later, Zunz presented a similar style defense of circumcision against Reformers who wished to eliminate the ritual arguing that the ritual promoted *Bildung* and Jewish unity.[47] In this essay, Zunz explicitly appealed to Mendelssohn's defense of the ceremonial law noting that Mendelssohn could have never imagined abandoning the rite of circumcision.[48]

[42] See Zunz, *GS*, 1:326–327. We have seen that for Mendelssohn labor contributes to man's perfection, but he does not speak of political participation as a perfection as far as I know. This is likely due to the lack of Jewish civil rights in Prussia in his time as well as the fact that Prussia was a monarchy.

[43] See Zunz, *GS*, 1:326–327.

[44] "Ceremonial law" (*Zeremonialgesetz*) is the term that Mendelssohn used for the ritual laws in *Jerusalem*. Zunz first published the 1822 sermon in a shortened form under the title "Thefillin, eine Betrachtungen" (Tefillin, some Observations) in 1844 in the *Jahrbuch für Israeliten*. See Zunz, "Thefillin". Zunz's *Gesammelte Schriften* includes the shortened version. See Zunz, *GS*, 2:172–176. For a detailed discussion of the sermon, see Altmann, "Zur Frühgeschichte," 43–49.

[45] Zunz, *GS*, 2:173.

[46] Ibid. While the emphasis on the symbolic significance of the ritual connecting heart and mind is Mendelssohnian, Zunz gave it his own direction. Mendelssohn stressed the value of rituals for inculcating *theological or historical truths* such as divine providence or the Exodus from Egypt. By contrast, Zunz stresses rituals' value in inculcating *moral virtue*.

[47] Zunz's essay defending circumcision is reprinted in Zunz, *GS*, 2:191–203. For discussion, see Schorsch, *Leopold Zunz*, 116–123.

[48] See Zunz, *GS*, 2:195, 198.

Zunz's targeted attack on Ashkenazic education

Like Mendelssohn, Zunz sees reforming education as the key to promoting *Bildung* among Jews. In the *Sermons*, Zunz takes stock of the German Jewish educational system that prevailed through the end of the eighteenth century, repeating many of the criticisms Mendelssohn and Wessely had leveled half a century earlier. He deplores the fact that German Jews commonly employed Polish teachers who taught using Yiddish, which he calls a "corrupt dialect" (*verdorbene Dialekt*) that led German Jews to "linguistic confusion" (*Sprachverwirrung*).[49]

Zunz laments the near-exclusive emphasis on Talmud study and the neglect of the Bible, writing "even worse is the situation of the schools for Jewish youth which teach the students only Talmud from early age while Holy Scripture is almost never taught."[50] Zunz complains about the pilpulistic method of Talmud study, which he groups with "superstitious confusions of the Kabbalah," as both draw one's attention away from the real world—*pilpul* by losing one in "hairsplitting" analyses of law, and kabbalah by teaching that one can magically change the world by performing religious rites. Zunz also links study of the Aramaic Talmud and Kabbalah with a neglect of Hebrew concluding that seventeenth- and eighteenth-century rabbis "essentially knew no language and so had no power to communicate true understanding in any area."[51] In these ways, Zunz makes clear how traditional Ashkenazic education impeded the acquisition of *Bildung*.

Zunz notes that the Maskilim were not the first to criticize Ashkenazic Jewish education. Earlier critics included Judah Loewe of Prague (Maharal), Leone de Modena, Ephraim Luntschitz, Elijah Delmedigo, and Judah Abas.[52] He contrasts the Polish-German educational system with the one employed by Arab, Spanish, and Italian Jewish communities, whose members were always fluent in their vernaculars, in part because they would regularly use vernacular translations of the Bible and of the prayer book. Zunz also writes approvingly of the Spanish-Portuguese Jews who used "bildende Lehrbücher" (educational textbooks) penned in the vernacular, while through

[49] Zunz, *Vorträge*, 458. Also see Zunz's 1825 plan for a new Jewish community school where he decries the damage done by Polish rabbis. See Zunz, "Leopold Zunz' Plan," 1065.

[50] Zunz, *Vorträge*, 458.

[51] Ibid.

[52] See ibid., 462, note a.

the end of the eighteenth century their Polish and German counterparts used Yiddish textbooks.[53]

Zunz opines that since Mendelssohn, German Jewish education has been improving. As new social opportunities opened and German Jews came to appreciate general culture and learning, "the Yiddish dialect fled with the Polish teachers. The corner schools (*Winckelschulen*)[54] were closed and the indignity of ignorance was removed." For Zunz, the maskilic resurrection of Hebrew was part of the revival of the great medieval Sephardic tradition of biblical, literary, and philosophical works which opened Jews to *Bildung*.[55] Zunz presents Mendelssohn's *Be'ur* as a key part of this process. The *Be'ur* delivered a "death blow" (*Todesstreich*) to Yiddish and prompted translations into German of the prayer book, women's prayers (*tehines*), the Passover Haggadah, lamentations (*kinot*), and eventually even the Mishnah and selections from the Talmud. Mendelssohn's emphasis on Hebrew grammar and poetry sparked a renaissance of Hebrew literature and poetry. The Maskilim spread knowledge of philosophy, ethics, and science to fellow Jews through Hebrew writings, especially through the journals *Hame'asef* and *Bikkurei Ha'itim*.[56]

For Zunz, there have been *three stages* in the reformation of German Jews. In the first stage, which he calls "Haskalah," Jews cultivated "language and knowledge" (*Sprache und Kenntnissen*). He dates this stage to the life of Mendelssohn. The second stage, which he calls "Bildung," dates from 1783 to 1800 and involves changes in pedagogy and manners.[57] The third stage, which Zunz calls "Reform," is ongoing and uses *Wissenschaft* as a basis for reforming Jewish institutions, namely, the rabbinate, the school, and the synagogue.[58]

Zunz's critique of Ashkenazic culture and education is nuanced. While the Maskilim rarely found Ashkenazic models for themselves before Mendelssohn, in 1822 Zunz penned a glowing biography of the eleventh-century Franco-German commentator Rashi.[59] To be sure, Zunz did not see

[53] Ibid., 457.

[54] This is a reference to the traditional *hadarim*.

[55] As he put it, a "glittering series of authors . . . remind us of the flowering of Arab-Spanish culture that adorned this epoch, which has not yet ended." See ibid., 465. On the German Jewish embrace of the medieval Sephardic tradition, see Schorsch, *From Text to Context*, 71–92; Marcus, "Beyond the Sephardic Mystique"; and most recently, Efron, *German Jewry and the Allure of the Sephardic*.

[56] Zunz, *Vorträge*, 463–469.

[57] Zunz puts the beginning of the *Bildung* stage at 1783 because that was the year in which Mendelssohn completed the *Be'ur* and published his Psalms translation.

[58] See Zunz, *Vorträge*, 465.

[59] See Zunz, "Solomon ben Isaac genannt Rashi." Schorsch notes that Zunz's Rashi essay "marks the first time since the *Haskalah* began to cultivate the genre of didactic biography that an Ashkenazic Jew other than Mendelssohn was deemed fit for biographical treatment." See Schorsch, *From Text to*

Rashi as a model in every respect. He acknowledged Rashi's limited knowledge of vernacular languages and that he did not know Persian, Arabic, Latin, or Greek. Zunz noted that even Rashi's knowledge of German was fairly weak and that he lacked a thorough grammatical understanding of Hebrew. Rashi was not very learned in sciences such as astronomy, geography, and medicine and harbored superstitious beliefs. He was also not very tolerant, in part because of having witnessed the First Crusade.[60] But Zunz argued that several other features of Rashi's work made him a model worthy of emulation. First, in his Talmud commentary Rashi sought to explicate the plain meaning of the text and eschewed the pilpulistic methods ("Deutelei und Sophisterei"—hairsplitting and sophistry) that characterized later talmudic commentators. Second, although his understanding of "academic grammar" (*wissenschaftlicher Grammatik*) lagged, Rashi had an outstanding, "intuitive" command of Hebrew and Aramaic.[61] Third, Rashi had a critical philological sense as evidenced by his introducing Talmudic variants based on different manuscripts.[62] Fourth, in his Bible commentary Rashi sought the plain meaning of the text.[63] Fifth, Rashi had an excellent literary style that was "concise, but clear." Finally, Zunz praised Rashi's fiercely independent mind and critical sense. Rashi was willing to disagree with his teachers and even reject talmudic opinions. He was also humble enough to admit when he did not know something.[64]

For Zunz, the problems in German Jewish education are therefore not endemic to Ashkenazic society as a whole but reflect a decline that he dates to the Protestant Reformation as we saw in the last chapter.[65] Put differently, for Zunz the Ashkenazic Dark Ages are not the medieval period but, rather, the early modern period.[66] While Zunz's praising his Ashkenazic forbearers

Context, 225. Schorsch has recently shown that a central aim of Zunz's 1845 *On History and Literature* was to counter the idealization of medieval Sepharad and denigration of medieval Ashkenaz by German Jewish Reformers by showing that Ashkenazic literature from 1000 to 1500 contained teachings of universal significance. For Zunz's argument and Geiger's heated response, see Schorsch, *Leopold Zunz*, 131–155.

60 See Zunz, "Solomon ben Isaac," 285–290.
61 Ibid., 325–326.
62 Ibid., 331.
63 Ibid., 325.
64 Ibid., 326.
65 See pp. 155–156 of this volume.
66 See Zunz's anonymous piece "Geist der Rabbiner" ("Spirit of the Rabbis"), which he originally published in 1819 in the *Spenescher Zeitung* and was reprinted posthumously in 1916. Zunz complained that "contemporary rabbinism has become a degenerate institution of ignorance, arrogance, and fanaticism that directly contradicts the better strivings of Jews and the humanitarian demands of the government." Picking up a stock Christian critique of Judaism, he called contemporary

deviated from the standard maskilic approach, it followed Mendelssohn, who, as we have seen, drew heavily on medieval Ashkenazic commentators like Rashi and Rashbam alongside Sephardic commentators like Ibn Ezra, Nahmanides, and David Kimhi.

An educational vision to unite German Jews

Zunz's discussion of Jewish reformation in the *Sermons* was not purely theoretical. In 1825, three years after departing from his post as preacher in the Beer Temple, the Berlin Jewish community asked Zunz to submit a plan for a new community school. As we have seen, the *Jüdische Freischule*, which had opened in Berlin in 1781, primarily catered to poor Jewish boys.[67] The school had initial success, but gradually the number of students declined and it encountered financial problems. In 1806, the radical Maskil Lazarus Bendavid was appointed to lead the school.[68] He drastically reduced the school's Jewish content and sought to attract Christian students. But in 1819 the Prussian government banned Christians from attending Jewish schools, and by 1822 it was clear that the school was in serious danger of closing.[69] The Jewish community therefore sought plans for a new school from Bendavid and J.L. Auerbach but, dissatisfied with their proposals, turned to Zunz.[70]

Zunz opened his plan by depicting a great divide between two extremes within the Berlin Jewish community, both of which threatened *Bildung*. He noted that these two groups of Jews were so opposed that it was as if they belonged to "two different centuries and [two] different parts of world."[71]

Ashkenazic Judaism "pharisaic barbarism (*pharisäische Barbarei*)." But Zunz distinguished between what he called the "earlier, learned period of rabbinic Judaism," which he dated from the close of the Bible through the Protestant Reformation, and the later "barbaric period" of Jewish history, which afflicted Polish and German Jews from the sixteenth century through the eighteenth centuries. See Zunz, "Geist der Rabbiner," 413–414. Similarly, when Zunz defended Ashkenazic culture in *On History and Literature*, he limited his discussion to pre-Reformation Ashkenazic culture. See pp. 170–171 note 59 of this volume.

[67] The *Freischule* was supposed to include both rich and poor students, with the rich paying a fee and the poor attending for free, but it never succeeded in attracting many wealthy families. See Eliav, *Jewish Education*, 74–75. See p. 91 of this volume.

[68] Eliav, *Jewish Education*, 77–78.

[69] Ibid., 78–79.

[70] Zunz submitted his plan on February 10, 1825. See ibid., 213–214.

[71] Zunz, "Leopold Zunz' Plan," 1062.

On one extreme stood traditionalist Jews whom Zunz called "rusted" (*verrostet*), both because of their linguistic and cultural deficiencies and because of their "blind reverence for the inessential" in Judaism, which led them to emphasize mindless ritual practice over ethical rectitude and to persecute Jews who thought differently than themselves.[72] At the other extreme stood a generation of young, "enlightened" (der *Aufgeklärte*) Jews who, according to Zunz, "throw off religion like a yoke." Repelled by the old ways that seemed "completely foolish and vain, mendacious and hideous," these younger Jews came to "replace blind faith (*blinden Glaube*) with an irreligiosity that they falsely called 'Enlightenment' (*Aufklärung*)," trading austerity and self-sacrifice for indulgence and selfishness. In this way, these "enlightened" young Jews espoused values as "barbaric" as those of the traditionalist "rusted" Jews. Zunz noted that many "enlightened" Jews did not stop at casting off their religious obligations, but even sought to discard all marks of their Jewishness. As Zunz put it, "ashamed of his origins . . . one does not recognize the Jew in him."[73]

For Zunz, the young generation was led astray by misunderstanding the Enlightenment's emphasis on individual happiness and perfection as the goals of life. While *Bildung* involved cultivating ethical perfection alongside intellectual and aesthetic perfection, many young Jews interpreted happiness as pleasure, which they equated with egoistic forms of gratification such as

[72] Ibid. Zunz's criticisms of traditionalist Jews continued a theme he had begun while preaching in Berlin. In his 1820 sermon "Arousal to Progress," Zunz denounced the hypocrisy of Jews who piously adhered to halakhah but were dishonest in business, writing, "Look at yourselves who cheat your neighbors" while "going to the Temple three times a day to lie to God in repentance." Zunz also criticized the hypocritical intolerance of traditionalist Jews who "persecute those who think differently than you with hatred, bans, and murder (*Hass und Bann und Mord*) while calling out a hundred times 'All-gracious, all-merciful is the Lord, forbearing and of great goodness' (Exodus 34:6)" in synagogue. See Zunz, *GS*, 2:96. These biblical phrases are recited in the prayers. For Zunz, not only was religious coercion morally wrong, it contradicted the spirit of Judaism as expressed in the Bible. Zunz also denounced religious coercion in the *Sermons*. See, for example, Zunz, *Vorträge*, 475, 481.

[73] Zunz, "Leopold Zunz' Plan," 1061–1062. Zunz had been concerned about bourgeois selfishness while preaching in Berlin. In one sermon, he criticized Jews who appear only rarely at Temple, for whom nothing is more important than to "breathe, earn, and eat (*zu athmen, und zu verdienen, und zu essen*)" and whose prayers are "empty, thoughtless, mechanical service" offered like an "imposed tax." See Zunz's 1820 sermon "Arousal to Progress" found in Zunz, *GS*, 2:95. Zunz's attacks on wealthy congregants ultimately led to his dismissal. The immediate impetus was a sermon titled "Ünglückseligkeit" ("Misery"), which he delivered on the fast on the Ninth of Av, which mourns the destruction of the ancient Temples in Jerusalem. In a letter to Isaak Noa Mannheimer, Zunz wrote that in his sermon he had linked the corruption of the leaders of the Beer Temple with the corruption that led to the destruction of the ancient Jewish Temples: "[I] did not spare the [Temple] Commission and listed lack of religiosity, vanity, and pride in worldly possessions as causes of the downfall." This letter is found in M. Brann and M. Rosenmann, "Der Briefwechsel zwischen Isak Noa Mannheimer und Leopold Zunz," 97, cited by Meyer, *The Origins of the Modern Jew*, 156.

amassing wealth, maximizing sensual enjoyment, and impressing others. The result was what Zunz called "sham enlightenment" (*falscher Aufklärung*).[74]

But, Zunz claimed, most Jewish Berliners identified with neither extreme, valuing Enlightenment and *Bildung* alongside the "religion and the wisdom of their fathers and the well-being . . . of their co-religionists."[75] For Zunz, what was needed was a middle path that could unite German Jews through a reformation that promoted rather than inhibited *Bildung*.

Unlike the *Jüdische Freischule*, which primarily served poor students, Zunz proposed that a new school be a true community school that would cater to both rich and poor.[76] Clearly influenced by his experience at the *Samson'sche Freischule*, Zunz recommended that the new school be professionally run, having strict rules that would be enforced.[77] Teachers must be properly trained, and all students must undergo thorough examinations.[78] The aim was to raise a new generation of middle-class German Jews loyal to both Prussia and Judaism, capable of "assuming unlimited civil rights."[79] To this end, the school should seek to instill "true piety" that did not involve mere show or "mindless parroting" of moral and religious doctrines but, rather, evinced "a spirit of sincere love, fundamental knowledge, (and) true humility."[80]

Gender and Jewish education

Zunz's plan comprised three elements: (1) reorganization of the *boys' school*, (2) creating a *seminary* to educate future rabbis and teachers, and (3) creating a *girls' school*. Zunz lamented the widespread neglect of female Jewish education: "For girls nearly nothing is done and a religious education is indispensable for them. The degeneration (*Ausartung*) of this sex at the earliest age is perceptible and pernicious."[81]

As we have seen, Mendelssohn and the Maskilim generally put little emphasis on female Jewish education, and by the first quarter of the nineteenth century there was rising concern about this.[82] Mendelssohn's daughter

[74] See Zunz's 1823 letter to the Berlin Jewish community on behalf of the *Verein für Cultur und Wissenschaft der Juden*. Zunz, *GS*, 2:221.
[75] Zunz, "Leopold Zunz' Plan," 1062.
[76] Ibid., 1063.
[77] Ibid., 1076–1079.
[78] Ibid., 1070–1071, 1078.
[79] See Zunz, "Leopold Zunz' Plan," 1063.
[80] Ibid., 1064.
[81] Ibid., 1062.
[82] See pp. 85–90 of this volume.

Brendel had become Dorothea and left her Jewish husband Simon Veit for the German philosopher Friedrich Schlegel, converting first to Protestantism in 1804 and then to Catholicism in 1810. Two years later, her sister Henriette also converted to Catholicism. The Jewish salonière Rachel Levin converted to Protestantism in 1814, marrying Karl August Varnhagen, and her friend Henriette Herz converted to Protestantism in 1817.[83]

Deborah Hertz notes that the percentage of Berlin Jews converting to Christianity peaked in 1815 and then declined, only to tick upward again in 1823. She notes that the rate of female and male Jewish conversion was about even through 1820, and subsequently, a higher percentage of Jewish males converted. But Hertz notes that a higher proportion of converted Jewish females intermarried. This suggests that anxiety over female conversion was driven by the bourgeois/traditionalist Jewish view of the female as the guardian of the home and concern that the wave of conversion would undermine Jewish family life.[84]

We have seen that Mendelssohn's neglecting to provide his daughters a Jewish education reflected, at least in part, his commitment to the prevailing Ashkenazic view that a father had no obligation to teach his daughters Torah. Mendelssohn followed the Talmud's interpretation of Deuteronomy 11:19, which he translated as *Lehret sie eure* ***Söhne*** (beneikhem) (teach your **sons**).[85] Zunz's deviation from this tradition and from Mendelssohn can be seen in his Bible translation of the same verse, which he renders as *Und lehret sie eure* ***Kinder*** (beneikhem) (and teach your **children**) (emphasis mine).[86]

While Zunz stressed the need for a girls' school, he thought that it should be separate from the boys' school and have different aims that aligned with the different vocations of boys and girls. For Zunz, the aim of boys' education should be to prepare Jewish males to become useful citizens who acted honorably in the public sphere and developed their minds and hearts. While preparing boys for a respectable profession was an important goal, Zunz did not think that the *Freischule* should be a vocational school. Rather it should provide boys with a base of knowledge so that they could become "teachers, rabbis, merchants, artisans, managers, artists, and university professors."[87] By contrast, Zunz thought that a girls' school should aim at forming women who would succeed in their "vocation" (*Beruf*) of tending the home and

[83] See Meyer, *Origins of Modern Jew*, 90–114; Hertz, *How Jews Became Germans*, 43–77, 165–216; Arendt, *Rahel Varnhagen*. Nahum Glatzer cites an 1822 letter from Zunz to Jost that indicates that Zunz himself contemplated converting. See Glatzer, *Leopold and Adelheid Zunz*, 16.

[84] See Hertz, *How Jews Became Germans*, 192–193, 224–225.

[85] See p. 87 of this volume.

[86] See Zunz, *Die vier und zwanzig*, 178.

[87] Zunz, "Leopold Zunz' plan," 1063.

raising children with good morals, *Bildung*, and religious piety.[88] For Zunz, the most important quality to be inculcated in girls was proper moral and religious "sentiment" (*Gefühl*), which must not be "deadened" by excessive intellectual exertion or "overeducation" (*Ueberbildung*), which distort the female "disposition" (*Gemüth*).[89] Zunz's conception of the different aims of male and female education was reflected in his curricular recommendations for each school.

For Zunz, the boys' school was to consist of four classes, and students aged 5–15 would be accepted.[90] There would be thirty-four hours of weekly instruction, and the curriculum would comprise twenty-five subjects studied over the four classes, namely, Jewish law, biblical history, Bible, Talmud, post-biblical Jewish history, Yiddish calligraphy, Hebrew reading, Hebrew language, German calligraphy, German reading, German language, Latin, Greek, French, mental arithmetic, arithmetic, geometry, world history, history of the fatherland, geography, natural science, natural history, public speaking, drawing, and singing.[91]

In the first class, boys would learn to read Hebrew and study biblical history. Biblical history involved reading passages from the Bible in German and memorizing them, as well as learning the Ten Commandments, doctrines about God, religious ceremonies, Jewish holidays and the names of the Jewish months.[92] In the second and third classes boys would study the Bible in Hebrew beginning with the Pentateuch, while in the fourth class, Bible study would give way to Talmud study, which would occupy nine teaching hours weekly, more than double any other subject, Jewish or general. Of the 34 weekly teaching hours, 5–14 would be devoted to Jewish subjects, depending on the class.[93]

Zunz's proposed girls' school also included thirty-four hours of weekly instruction but only covered twelve subjects taught over two classes. The subjects were: biblical history, Hebrew reading, Yiddish calligraphy, German calligraphy, German reading, German language, French, arithmetic, world history, geography, drawing, and needlework.[94] The study of biblical history would mirror the boys' study of this subject, including reading biblical

[88] Ibid., 1079–1080.
[89] Ibid.
[90] Ibid., 1073, 1076.
[91] Ibid., 1072–1075.
[92] Ibid., 1073.
[93] Ibid., 1074–1075.
[94] Ibid., 1080.

passages in German, learning the Ten Commandments, doctrines about God, the holidays, etc. But in the first class there would also be an emphasis on the "duties of the female sex." Of the 34 hours of weekly instruction, about one third (10–12) would be devoted to needlework, while only 2–4 hours would be devoted to Jewish subjects, depending on the class.[95]

Zunz's plan for the boys' school was immediately accepted with some significant changes, and a Jewish community school for boys was opened in January 1826 with Zunz appointed as its director. But his proposal for the girls' school was not immediately accepted, and the Berlin Jewish Community only opened a girls' school in 1835, six years after Zunz had left his post as school director.[96] While Zunz clearly went beyond Mendelssohn and most Maskilim in stressing the importance of female Jewish education, his approach was still informed by his middle-class conception of women's vocation as centered on cultivating proper moral and religious sentiments, tending the home, and raising children. As such, female Jewish education fell well short of male Jewish education and did not even involve studying the Bible in Hebrew, though the Bible was to be studied in German translation.

In sum, Zunz saw a reformed Jewish education as a basis for uniting the vast majority of Berlin Jewry. The new generation would be cultured, well-rounded German Jews who combined loyalty to the Jewish people with Prussian patriotism by being fluent in Hebrew and German, knowledgeable in both Jewish and secular subjects, and imbued with understanding and love for moral and religious principles.[97] Males would be prepared to be gainfully employed and females to care for the home and raise a family. By educating rich and poor Jews together, while steering clear of the extremes of persecutory Talmudism and unjewish pseudo-enlightenment, a sense of equality and communal solidarity would be fostered among all segments of Berlin Jewry. In this way, Zunz sought to raise a new generation of middle-class German Jews.

95 Ibid.

96 Eliav, *Jewish Education*, 277.

97 Zunz's Prussian patriotism is reflected in a speech he gave at the Berlin community synagogue in "homage" (*Huldigung*) to Friedrich Wilhelm IV's ascension to the throne in 1840. The speech is full of passages stressing that Judaism requires loyalty to the non-Jewish ruler. It is found in Zunz, *GS*, 2:116–125.

A new Bible for German Jews

We have seen that Zunz sought to produce a Bible translation to replace Mendelssohn's. To better understand why Zunz thought that Mendelssohn's *Be'ur* needed replacing, it is worth comparing differences in the content and layout of the two works. Mendelssohn's *Be'ur* contains the Pentateuch in five volumes, while Zunz's contains all twenty-four books of the Hebrew Bible in one volume. Mendelssohn's *Be'ur* is arranged like a classical rabbinic Bible, with the Hebrew original facing a German translation in Hebrew characters above a Hebrew commentary in Rashi script with Masoretic notes. The *Be'ur* opens from right to left and reads like a Hebrew book. Zunz's Bible only contains the German translation in Gothic characters and opens from left to right like a German book. The only Hebrew found in the Zunz Bible is the name of the biblical book on the top of the page (e.g., בראשית) and the name of the weekly portion (e.g., תולדות). Mendelssohn's Bible has only a Hebrew title *Sefer Netivot Hashalom*, which is adapted from a biblical verse (Proverbs 3:17), while Zunz's includes generic Hebrew and German titles: תורה נביאים כתובים (*Torah, Prophets, Writings*)/*Die vier und zwangzig Bücher der heiligen Schrift* (*The Twenty-Four Books of Holy Scripture*).[98]

Despite these differences, in important respects Zunz's aims are continuous with Mendelssohn's. Like Mendelssohn, Zunz seeks to produce a Bible for the broad swath of German Jews that addresses both enlightened and traditionalist Jews. Zunz also follows Mendelssohn in striving to balance intelligibility with faithfulness to the original. Nevertheless, the differences between Zunz's Bible and Mendelssohn's *Be'ur* are significant and stem from four main factors: (1) linguistic and social changes in the Berlin Jewish community, (2) a historical rather than theological/philosophical sensibility, (3) seeking to create a Bible for German Jews of *all* economic classes, and (4) an emphasis on the centrality of the synagogue.

A Bible for all Israelites: religious ideology

We have mentioned Moritz Veit's claim that Zunz aimed to produce a "Bible for Israelites" (*Bibel für Israeliten*).[99] That Zunz intended his Bible for both

[98] We will discuss why Zunz selected this German title later. See pp. 92–93 of this volume, and Figures 4 and 5.

[99] See p. 162 note 6 of this volume.

"enlightened" and traditionalist German Jews is evident from the fourteen-page *Zeittafel* (chronological table) that he included near the beginning of the translation. The *Zeittafel* provides the dates of the major events in the biblical period from Adam and Eve through the rise of Alexander the Great.[100] Zunz's inclusion of a chronological table brings to mind another Jewish work of chronology, David Gans's 1592 *Zemah David.* Zunz recalled that his first "awakening" to *Wissenschaft* came from reading this work as a youth.[101]

There are striking differences between Zunz's and Gans's approaches to chronology. Gans divides *Zemah David* into two parts, the first part treating Jewish history from creation to the present, while the second part treats non-Jewish history up to the present.[102] By contrast, Zunz presents a *single* chronology focused on biblical Jewish history that also includes dates of relevant events in the Ancient Near East. While Gans only gives dates for events in Jewish history according the Jewish calendar, Zunz includes dates according to both the Jewish and Gregorian calendars, setting them side by side.

Close inspection of these dates reveals Zunz's multiple audiences. When giving the date from the Gregorian calendar, Zunz follows the scholarly view even if this contradicts rabbinic tradition. For example, the rabbinic work *Seder Olam* dates the destruction of the First Temple to 3338, which corresponds to 423 BCE and Gans provides this date. Zunz, however, follows the scholarly consensus, dating the destruction of the First Temple to 586 BCE.[103] But next to the Gregorian date, Zunz provides the Hebrew date of 3402, which is 64 years *later* than Gans's date and corresponds to 359 BCE.[104] Zunz had an excellent mathematical mind and was well aware that the Gregorian and Hebrew dates he gave contradicted.[105] The fact that he included contradictory dates side by side is evidence that he sought to produce a Bible rooted in history that would neither offend the sensibilities of

[100] See Figure 15.

[101] See Zunz's letter to David Kaufmann, March 26, 1877, in Brann, "Mittheilungen," 183, cited in Schorsch, *From Text to Context,* 161. Gillman points out that Joseph Johlson's Pentateuch translation, which appeared seven years before Zunz's Bible, also included a biblical chronology, though it was not nearly as detailed as Zunz's and did not include dates according to both the Jewish and Gregorian calendars. See Gillman, *A History of German Jewish Bible Translation,* 117–118.

[102] Mordechai Breuer shows that despite this organizational structure, in practice Gans will occasionally introduce events from non-Jewish history into the section on Jewish history and vice versa. See Breuer, "Modernism and Traditionalism," 77–78.

[103] See Gans, *Zemah David,* 21; Zunz, *Die vier und zwanzig Bücher,* 12.

[104] Zunz's reason for deviating from *Seder Olam* when providing dates according to the Jewish calendar requires further exploration. Schorsch notes that Zunz follows *Seder Olam*'s chronology from creation through the death of Joseph but thereafter begins to deviate from *Seder Olam.* See Schorsch, *Leopold Zunz,* 73.

[105] On Zunz's affinity for mathematics and numbers, see Schorsch, *Leopold Zunz,* 8.

the "enlightened" younger Jews nor of the traditionalist older Jews, even if this resulted in inconsistencies.

That Zunz aimed his Bible for the broad spectrum of German Jews is also suggested by the fact that his translation follows the Masoretic text. In his 1836 review of Sachs's Psalms translation, Zunz criticized the translation as insufficiently scholarly since Sachs worked exclusively off the Masoretic text, ignoring biblical text criticism.[106] But when Zunz published his Bible translation two years later, he made clear that his translation "strictly followed the Masorah and the accents."[107] Zunz evidently worried that introducing text-critical considerations would alienate traditionalist Jews.[108]

The differences in layout and content of Mendelssohn's and Zunz's Bible are therefore not the result of their being addressed to different segments of the Jewish community, as both sought to appeal to both traditionalist and enlightened Jews. Rather, the differences between their Bibles reflect cultural changes that Berlin Jewry had undergone over the previous half century. While in the 1780s even enlightened Berlin Jews knew Yiddish and some Hebrew while many Jews had an imperfect grasp of German, by the 1830s all Berlin Jews knew German, and even among traditionalists knowledge of Yiddish and Hebrew was greatly declining.[109] For Zunz, a new Bible translation for German Jews must have a German title, be in Gothic script alone, and eschew the model of the rabbinic Bible.

Faithfulness, elegance, intelligibility

We have seen that in his translation Mendelssohn strives to balance three things: (1) communicating the plain, grammatical sense of the original; (2) conveying the form of the Hebrew; and (3) producing an intelligible, elegant German text.[110] Zunz seeks a similar balance. In the introduction to his

[106] Zunz, *GS*, 3:117.

[107] Zunz, *Die vier und zwanzig Bücher*, iii. But Zev Weintraub notes at least one instance where the Zunz translation follows the Septuagint rather than the Masoretic Bible (Genesis 49:21). See Weintraub, *The German Translations*, 228–229.

[108] There are other reasons that Zunz followed the Masoretic text. Lacking a critical apparatus, Zunz's deviations from the Masoretic text would have seemed arbitrary. Rosin notes that while Zunz adhered to the Masoretic text, he also sought to incorporate advances in biblical philology, Hebrew grammar, and Hebrew lexicography into his translation. See Rosin, "Die Zunz'sche Bibel," 513. I will mention a third reason that Zunz followed the Masoretic text later. See pp. 188–189 of this volume.

[109] See Lowenstein, "The Pace of Modernization," 44; Rosin, "Die Zunz'sche Bibel," 506.

[110] See pp. 60–74 of this volume.

translation, Zunz writes that the translators sought to be "faithful" (*treu*) to the "correct sense" (*richtige Sinn*) of the Hebrew original, while conveying it "in a clear and appropriate manner" to the reader.[111]

Zunz's desire that his translation be "clear and appropriate" included his wish that it not seem overly unfamiliar to the reader even if this meant sacrificing strict accuracy. An anecdote recounted by Sachs vividly illustrates this. Sachs recalls that when Arnheim gave him his translation of Genesis for review, Sachs suggested that Arnheim translate Genesis 1:1 as ***Früher** schuf Gott den Himmel und die Erde* (**previously** God created the heaven and the earth). Sachs's reasoning was that the Hebrew word *Bereshit* is notoriously ambiguous and, as Rashi had pointed out, does not mean "In the beginning" as it was commonly translated, most famously by Mendelssohn and Luther.[112] Sachs reports that Zunz agreed with his suggestion in *principle* but ultimately decided not to follow it. Zunz did not want to give the reader a translation so different than the common one that she would reject it out of hand.[113]

At the same time, Zunz strove to reproduce elements of the Hebrew even if this resulted in the translation sounding somewhat awkward in German. For example, Genesis 34:1 reads in Hebrew: ***vateitze dinah** bat le'ah asher yaldah **l'ya'akov lirot** bivnot ha'aretz.* Compare Luther's, Mendelssohn's, and Zunz's translations:

> **Luther:** *Dina **aber**, Leas Tochter, die sie **Jakob** geboren hatte, **ging heraus**, die Töchter des Landes **zu sehen*** [**But** Dina, Leah's daughter who was born to **Jacob went out to see** the daughters of the land]
>
> **Mendelssohn:** *Dinah Leahs Tochter, die sie dem **Jaakow** gebohren, **ging aus**, Sich **umzusehen** unter den Töchtern des Landes* [Dinah, Leah's daughter, who bore her to **Ya'akov went out, to look** among the daughters of the land]

[111] Zunz, *Die vier und zwanzig Bücher*, iii–iv. The idea of producing a very literal translation seems to have originated with Veit, who in a correspondence with Sachs wrote that in the Bible translation there should be "no place for imprecision, randomness, modernization or the aesthetic embellishment of the original." See Gillman, "The Jewish Quest for a German Bible," Section 3. Zunz expressed the need to balance accuracy and intelligibility in his 1836 review of Michael Sachs's translation of the Psalms where he praised Sachs for producing a faithful translation but worried that it was sometimes so literal that it suffered from "stiffness and clumsiness" (*Steifheit und Ungelenkigkeit*). See Zunz, *GS*, 3:117.

[112] Mendelssohn used *Im Anfang*; Luther used *An Anfang*. See Rashi's commentary on Genesis 1:1.

[113] Rosin recounts that Sachs personally told him this story. See Rosin, "Die Zunz'sche Bibel," 511.

> **Zunz:** ***Und ausging*** *Dinah, die Tochter Leah's, die sie geboren hatte dem* ***Jaakob****, um sich* ***umzusehen*** *unter den Töchtern des Landes* [**And out** went Dinah, the daughter of Leah that she bore to **Ya'akob** in order **to look** among the daughters of the land]

Unlike Luther, who Germanizes the names of the Bible (e.g., *Jakob*), both Mendelssohn and Zunz transliterate the names (*Jaakow, Jaakob*). And unlike Luther who follows proper German usage by placing the verb *sehen* at the end of the verse, Mendelssohn and Zunz replicate the Hebrew by placing it before the object. However, while Mendelssohn and Luther both follow proper German usage by putting the verb *vateitze*, which begins the Hebrew verse, at the end of the first clause (Luther: *ging heraus*/Mendelssohn *ging aus*), Zunz seeks to convey the form of the Hebrew by putting the verb at the beginning of the sentence, before the subject (*Und ausging Dinah*). Finally, both Luther and Zunz translate the *vav* (Luther as *aber* and Zunz as *und*), while Mendelssohn leaves it untranslated. While both Zunz and Mendelssohn seek to convey the form of the Hebrew original, Zunz does so even more than Mendelssohn.

Similarly, consider Exodus 4:10, where Moses asks God not to send him to Pharaoh because *lo ish devarim anochi*. Luther translates the phrase colloquially as *ich bin je und je nicht wohl beredt gewesen* (I have never been very eloquent). Mendelssohn seeks to convey the original Hebrew expression by translating the phrase literally as *Ich bin kein Man von Worten* (I am not a man of words), and Zunz follows him, translating as *Ich bin kein Mann von Reden* (I am not a man of speaking). But while Zunz leaves it to the reader to figure out what the phrase means, Mendelssohn adds in parentheses *das heißt kein guter Redner* ("that means not a good speaker"). Again, both Mendelssohn and Zunz seek to convey the original Hebrew more than Luther, but Zunz is less concerned with intelligibility than Mendelssohn when doing so disrupts the flow of the translation.

But while Zunz is concerned with preserving the form of the Hebrew, it would be incorrect to conclude that he *always* produces a more Hebraic translation than Mendelssohn. Consider Luther's, Mendelssohn's, and Zunz's translations of the expression *karat brit* in Genesis 15:18:

> **Luther:** ***schloß*** *einen Bund* [concluded a covenant]
>
> **Mendelssohn:** ***zerschnitt*** *einen Bund* [cut a covenant]
>
> **Zunz:** ***machte*** *einen Bund* [made a covenant]

Zunz is much closer to Luther's approach, which seeks to communicate the *sense* of the original. Only Mendelssohn seeks to convey the imagery of cutting through a hyper-literal translation. This is not an isolated example. Both Mendelssohn and Zunz seek to convey the Hebrew in intelligible German, but they do so in different ways. Zunz generally (though not always) hews closer to the *syntax* of the Hebrew original than Mendelssohn, while Mendelssohn generally (though not always) preserves Hebrew *word roots* more faithfully than Zunz. We will explore further examples of this shortly.[114]

Zunz the historian versus Mendelssohn the philosopher

Despite the fact that Zunz's *aims* are generally continuous with Mendelssohn's, there are important differences between their *approaches* to translation. Some of these differences are informed by the fact that while Mendelssohn's translation is animated by a *philosophical sensibility*, Zunz's is guided by an *historical* one. These differences can be seen in their approaches to three issues: (1) biblical anthropomorphism, (2) Christology, and (3) Midrash.

Biblical anthropomorphism

Genesis 8:21: ***vayarah YHWH et re'ah haniho'ah** vayomer YHWH el libo*

Luther: *Und der **HERR** roch den lieblichen Geruch und sprach in seinem Herzen* [And the LORD **smelled the sweet smell** and said in His heart]

Mendelssohn: ***Der Ewige nam den liblichen Duft mit Wohl Gefallen an,** und sprach zu sich selbst* [The Eternal **accepted the sweet smell with favor,** and said to Himself]

Zunz: ***Und der Ewige roch den lieblichen Geruch,** und der Ewige sprach zu seinem Herzen* [**And the Eternal smelled the sweet smell** and the Eternal spoke to His heart]

[114] While Mendelssohn more often preserves Hebrew word roots than Zunz, Weintraub notes instances where Zunz preserves Hebrew word roots, such as his translation of Genesis 1:20, and he shows that Mendelssohn is not always consistent in preserving Hebrew word roots in his translation. See Weintraub, *The German Translations,* 128–130.

Mendelssohn seeks to eliminate crude anthropomorphism by translating *vayarah YHWH et re'ah haniho'ah* as "the Eternal accepted the sweet smell" (*Der Ewige nam den liblichen Duft*). Zunz's translation "And the Eternal smelled the sweet smell" (*Und der Ewige roch den lieblichen Geruch*) is nearly identical to Luther's, except that Zunz follows Mendelssohn in translating the Tetragrammaton as *Der Ewige* rather than as *Der HERR* and unlike both Luther and Mendelssohn, Zunz reproduces the repetition of the Tetragrammaton in his translation.

The differences between the three translators reflect their respective ideological stances. For Luther who believes that God became incarnate, anthropomorphism poses no theological problem. For Mendelssohn, however, the Bible must conform to rational theology, so he does not translate God's smelling literally. Zunz reads the Bible like a historian understanding it as a human document written by an ancient people. As surrounding peoples of the time generally believed that gods have senses, it stands to reason that so did the ancient Israelites and one should therefore translate the passage literally. While later philosophers sought to make the Bible conform to philosophy, Zunz regards this as part of the *development of Judaism*, which should not be conflated with the original meaning of Scripture.

Christology

Genesis 3:15: ***hu yeshufkha rosh ve'atah teshufenu akev***

> **Luther:** ***Der** selbe soll dir den Kopf **zertreten**, und du wirst ihn in die Ferse **stechen*** [**he** will **crush** your head and you will **bite** his heel]
> **Mendelssohn:** ***Diser** soll dir den Kopf **verwunden**, und du ihm die Ferse **verwunden*** [**this one** will **wound** your head and you will **wound** his heel]
> **Zunz:** *er wird dir **zermalmen** den Kopf und du wirst ihn **stechen** in die Ferse* [**he** will **crush** your head and you will **bite** his heel]

We saw that Luther interprets the curse of the serpent as referring to Jesus's battle with the devil. For Luther, *hu* refers to a specific person, namely, Jesus, and Luther therefore translates it by the definite pronoun *der* (he). Mendelssohn seeks to undercut this Christological interpretation and therefore interprets *hu* as referring to the seed of Eve mentioned in the beginning of the verse who will crush the head of the serpent. As such, he translates *hu* as *Diser* (this). Zunz chooses to leave the term ambiguous and thus translates it as *er* (he), which he thinks is closest to the plain sense of the Bible. Unlike Mendelssohn the philosopher, Zunz the historian does not feel the need to exclude the Christological interpretation of the verse.

One other point is worthy of note. As we saw, while Luther uses two different words to translate *yeshufkha* and *teshufenu* (*zerstreten* and *stechen*), Mendelssohn strives to convey the repetition of the word root *y-sh-f* in the verse by translating both *yeshufkha* and *teshufenu* as *verwunden* (wound). Zunz's approach is closer to Luther's translating *yeshufkha* as *zermalmen* (crush) and *teshufenu* as *stechen* (bite). Again, we find Mendelssohn preserving a Hebrew word root, while Zunz does not.

Genesis 1:2: *vehaʼaretz haytah tohu vavohu vehoshekh al pnei tehom* ***veruʼah elohim*** *merahefet al pnei hamayim*

> **Luther**: *Und die Erde war wüst und leer, und es war finster auf der Tiefe;* ***und der Geist Gottes*** *schwebete auf dem Wasser* [And the earth was formless and void and there was darkness over the deep; **and the spirit of God** hovered over the water]
>
> **Mendelssohn**: *Die Erde aber war unförmlich und vermischt. Finsternis auf der Fläche des Abgrundes,* ***und der götliche Geist*** *webend auf den Wassern* [The earth, however, was unformed and mixed up; darkness over the surface of the abyss, **and the divine spirit** hovered over the waters]
>
> **Zunz**: *Und die Erde war öd und wüst, und Finsterniß auf der Fläche des Abgrundes,* ***und der Geist Gottes*** *schwebend über der Fläche der Wasser* [And the earth was barren and void, and darkness over the surface of the abyss, **and the spirit of God** hovered over the surface of the water]

Zunz follows Luther in translating every *vav* at the beginning of a word in this verse as *und*, unlike Mendelssohn who thinks that the *vav* can have different meanings, and therefore translates them differently in different places. Mendelssohn and Zunz are more literal than Luther, as they both translate *al pnei tehom* as "over the surface of the abyss" (*auf der Fläche des Abgrundes*) while Luther omits the word *pnei*, translating the phrase as "over the deep" (*auf der Tiefe*). Zunz is more literal than either Mendelssohn or Luther, as he translates *al pnei hamayim* as "over the surface of the water" (*über der Fläche der Wasser*) while both Mendelssohn and Luther omit the word *pnei* and translate the phrase as "over the water(s)" (*auf dem Wasser[n]*).

I would, however, like to focus on the translation of *ru'ah elohim.* We saw that Luther translates this as *Geist Gottes* (spirit of God), where *ru'ah* is a noun. He does so because he interprets this phrase as a reference to the Holy Spirit, the third person of the Trinity. Mendelssohn, however, is worried about this Christological interpretation and thus translates *ru'ah elohim* as *götliche Geist* (divine spirit), where *ru'ah* is an adjective. Zunz translates the phrase exactly like Luther because he thinks that this is the most literal, historical sense of the verse and is unconcerned by its possible Christological interpretation.

The differences between Zunz's and Mendelssohn's approaches to Christology reflect not only their different intellectual orientations, but also the different eras in which they lived. In Mendelssohn's time even critical Bible scholars defended Christological interpretations of the Hebrew Bible, and Mendelssohn endured several attempts to convert him to Christianity.[115] By contrast, in Zunz's time the historical study of the Bible had progressed to the point where most serious scholars did not feel bound to accept Christological interpretations.[116]

Midrash

Genesis 23:1: *vayihyu hayei Sarah* ***me'ah shanah v'esrim shanah v'sheva shanim*** *shnei hayei Sarah*. Luther, Mendelssohn, and Zunz translate the verse as follows:

> **Luther:** *Sara ward* ***hundertsiebenundzwanzig Jahre alt*** [Sara was **one hundred and twenty-seven years old**]
>
> **Mendelssohn:** *Es war das Lebensalter der Sarah,* ***hundert Jahr, und zwangzig Jahr, und siben Jahr.*** *Dises waren die Lebens Jahre der Sarah* [The lifespan of Sarah was **one hundred years, and twenty years, and seven years.** These were Sarah's years of life]
>
> **Zunz:** *Und es war die Lebenszeit Sarah's* ***hundert und sieben und zwanzig Jahre;*** *dies die Jahre der Lebenszeit Sarah's* [And the lifespan of Sarah was **one hundred and seven and twenty years;** These were the years of Sarah's lifetime]

[115] See p. 38 note 81 of this volume.
[116] See pp. 197–199 of this volume.

Luther gives the proper German rendering of one hundred and twenty-seven years old as *hundertsiebenundzwanzig Jahre alt*, while Mendelssohn translates hyper-literally as *hundert Jahr, und zwangzig Jahr, und siben Jahr* (hundred year, and twenty year, and seven year), putting the twenty before the seven, which violates German linguistic form and he translates *shanah* in the singular as *Jahr* like the Hebrew. Zunz adopts a middle position that is closer to the Hebrew than Luther's translation, but not as close as Mendelssohn's, translating Sarah's age as *hundert und sieben und zwanzig Jahre* (one hundred and twenty and seven years). Zunz preserves proper German form by putting the seven before the twenty, but he alludes to the Hebrew by putting *und* between the hundred and the seven. He does not, however, repeat *Jahr* like Mendelssohn, nor use the singular form.

In the first chapter, we saw that Mendelssohn translates this verse hyper-literally to leave open the midrashic interpretation that Sarah was as sinless when she was one hundred as when she was twenty and as beautiful when she was twenty as when she was seven. Zunz is not concerned with leaving open the midrashic interpretation and thus sees no need to translate the verse in a way that sounds so odd in German.

Zunz's lack of concern with justifying rabbinic interpretation is similarly clear by comparing his method of translating *lex talionis* in Exodus 21:24–25 with Mendelssohn's:

Exodus 21:24–25: *ayin tahat ayin shein tahat shein yad tahat yad, regel tahat ragel k'viah tahat k'viah petzah tahat patzah haburah tahat haburah*

Luther: *Auge um Auge, Zahn um Zahn, Hand um Hand, Fuß um Fuß, Brand um Brand, Wunde um Wunde, Beule um Beule* [eye for eye, tooth for tooth, hand for hand, foot for foot, burn for burn, wound for wound, bruise for bruise]

Mendelssohn: *(Rechtswegen sollte) Auge für Auge (seyn), Zahn für Zahn, Hand für Hand, Fuß für Fuß, Brandmal für Brandmal, Wunde für Wunde. Beule für Beule (daher muß der Tädter Geld dafür geben)* [(According to justice it should) eye for eye (be), tooth for tooth, hand for hand, foot for foot, burn for burn, wound for wound, bruise for bruise (therefore the offender must give money instead)]

Zunz: *Auge um Auge, Zahn um Zahn, Hand um Hand, Fuß um Fuß, Brandmal um Brandmal, Wunde um Wunde, Strieme um Strieme* [eye for eye, tooth for tooth, hand for hand, foot for foot, burn for burn, wound for wound, bruise for bruise]

Luther translates the verse literally. Mendelssohn seeks to convey both the literal sense of the original and its rabbinic interpretation by using parentheses. Zunz translates almost exactly like Luther. Both Luther's and Mendelssohn's translations are informed by theological commitments. Luther translates the passages literally because this confirms the Christian idea that the Old Testament teaches harsh, retributive justice, while the New Testament teaches love and mercy. Mendelssohn, however, regards talmudic law as authoritative. Since the talmudic law contradicts the *peshat* of biblical law, Mendelssohn translates in a way that plain conveys the midrashic interpretation, while seeking to preserving the sense of the original Hebrew. For Mendelssohn, the rabbinic legal interpretation is the true meaning of the Bible and reflects the fact that the Bible, which is an unmediated expression of the divine will, conforms with moral reason. Zunz, however, reads the Bible with a historian's sensibility and so does not believe that the rabbis necessarily read the Bible correctly or that the Bible must conform to moral reason. He therefore translates the *lex talionis* literally.[117]

Zunz's synagogue Bible versus Mendelssohn's study Bible

Mendelssohn's *Be'ur* is a study Bible, which is why it contains an extensive commentary and Masoretic notes. That Mendelssohn did not intend his Bible for liturgical use in the synagogue is clear from the fact that the *Be'ur* does not identify the festival readings or contain the selections from the prophetic writings (*Haftarot*) that are read after the weekly portion from the Pentateuch in the synagogue service.

In the introduction to his translation, Zunz indicates his hope that it will be used in "school and home" (*Schule und Haus*).[118] But unlike Mendelssohn's *Be'ur*, Zunz's Bible contains a chart listing the festival readings from the Bible and Prophets and it indicates the prophetic passage from which the *Haftarah*

[117] This is not to say that Zunz is always indifferent to midrashic interpretations. Weintraub cites several examples where Zunz incorporates midrashic interpretations into his translation. But this is because he thinks they make good sense of the *peshat* of the text, not because he deems them authoritative. See Weintraub, *The German Translations*, 26.

[118] Zunz, *Die vier und zwanzig Bücher*, iv.

is to be read at the end of each weekly portion.[119] Containing all twenty-four books of the Bible, Zunz's translation thus also includes the *Haftarot*. That Zunz wished his Bible to be used not only for study but also for liturgical purposes is clear from his original 1823 proposal. Zunz wrote that "what is lacking at this moment when German sermons and German religious education ought to be reintroduced into our *synagogues* is a completely new Bible translation" (emphasis mine).[120]

We have seen that in the *Sermons* Zunz defended synagogue reforms that would create a *deutsche Synagoge* appropriate for middle-class German Jews. Zunz saw his Bible as an important contribution to such a synagogue, as it would serve as the contemporary written equivalent of the oral vernacular translations that were used in the ancient synagogue.[121] Zunz's desire that his Bible be used for liturgical purposes may be another reason why his translation followed the Masoretic Text. The liturgical reading of the Bible in the synagogue had to follow a standard text and deviating from the Masoretic Text would have created confusion. Finally, given Zunz's conviction that the synagogue was the central institution in national Jewish life, it is not surprising that he wished to contribute to renewing its vitality.[122]

A Bible for all Israelites: class and gender

While Zunz follows Mendelssohn in striving to produce a Bible that appeals to German Jews from *different ideological stripes*, Zunz alone seeks to create a truly inclusive Bible that is also addressed to Jews from *different economic classes*, and to both *males and females*. Mendelssohn's Bible was in five volumes and expensive. Only wealthier Jews could afford it.[123] By contrast, in his original 1823 proposal Zunz expressed the desire that his Bible be "inexpensive, compact, and readily accessible."[124] When Veit published Zunz's Bible, he made sure that it was reasonably priced.[125]

[119] Zunz's Bible does not contain the seven traditional divisions according to which each weekly portion is read (*aliyot*). This is probably because many Reform congregations at the time did not follow the traditional divisions. See Philipson, *The Reform Movement in Judaism*, 256–257.

[120] See Schorsch, *Leopold Zunz*, 45.

[121] See p. 151 of this volume.

[122] See p. 157 of this volume.

[123] Lowenstein confirms that the readership of the *Be'ur* consisted primarily of wealthier Jews. See Lowenstein, "The Readership of Mendelssohn's," 181–186, 194.

[124] See Schorsch, *Leopold Zunz*, 45.

[125] See Rosin, "Die Zunz'sche Bibel," 506, 509.

We have seen Mendelssohn's assertion that he composed his Pentateuch translation for his sons and that he provided his daughters with minimal Jewish education.[126] By contrast, Zunz clearly included Jewish females in the intended audience of his Bible translation given his commitment to female Jewish education and his desire that his Bible be used in a reformed *deutsche Synagogue* that would cater to both Jewish males *and* females. Indeed when Zunz discusses the need for synagogue reforms in the *Sermons* he stresses that women in particular are agitating for it.[127] For Zunz a "Bible for Israelites" must be for *all German Jews* regardless of religious ideology, economic status, or gender.

A Jewish revision of a Protestant model: Zunz and De Wette

We have discussed Zunz's relation to De Wette and his reply to his teacher in the *Sermons*. But De Wette is important not only for understanding the *Sermons*, but also for understanding Zunz's Bible translation. From 1809 to 1810 De Wette and the orientalist J.C. Augusti published a new translation of the Old Testament, under the title *The Old Testament Scriptures* (*Die Schriften des Alten Testaments*).[128] In 1831, De Wette replaced Augusti's translations with his own and published a second edition under his sole authorship under the title *The Holy Scripture of the Old and New Testaments* (*Die Heilige Schrift des Alten und Neues Testaments*).[129] Zunz's Bible can be seen not only as a nineteenth-century update of Mendelssohn's Bible, but also as a Jewish revision of De Wette's. Comparing Zunz's and De Wette's Bible translations is a good way of understanding the similarities and differences between a liberal Jewish historian and a liberal Protestant historian in the first half of the nineteenth century.

[126] See pp. 85–90 of this volume.

[127] See Zunz, *Vorträge*, 474.

[128] De Wette translated the Pentateuch, Samuel, Kings, Chronicles, Psalms, Job, Jeremiah, Lamentations, Daniel, and the twelve minor prophets with the exception of Jonah. Augusti translated Joshua, Judges, Ruth, Nehemiah, Ezra, Esther, Ecclesiastes, Proverbs, Song of Songs, Isaiah, Ezekiel, and Jonah. See Augusti, "Vorrede," v.

[129] The only book that De Wette did not translate himself in the new edition was the book of Isaiah, for which he used a translation supplied by H.F. Gesenius. See De Wette, "Vorrede," v.

De Wette's Bible

In the preface to his 1831 edition, De Wette writes that his Bible translation has two main audiences. The first and primary audience is students of theology who wish to become acquainted with the original text of the Bible. For these individuals, De Wette seeks to stay as close as possible to the original Hebrew by producing a lexicographically and grammatically accurate translation.[130] The secondary audience of his translation is "unlearned Christians," including women who seek to understand the Old Testament. For this group, a clear translation is most important. De Wette writes that he would have liked to include short notes clarifying the meaning of certain verses for this group, but given his desire that the Bible be inexpensive, he could not do so.[131] He acknowledges that his two aims, namely, accuracy and faithfulness on the one hand, and intelligibility on the other hand, sometimes came into conflict. Given that his primary audience was students of theology, he erred on the side of accuracy.[132]

In his preface to the 1809 edition, Augusti notes the paucity of contemporary German translations of the entire Old Testament, identifying only three recent Protestant translations.[133] For Augusti, these translations do not meet even the "most moderate demands of good translation." He singles out Michaelis's translation for failing to convey the "dignity and nobility of the German language."[134] Augusti further notes that all the translations are out of date.[135] He expresses more regard for a Catholic translation begun by Dominic Brentano and continued by Thaddäus Dereser but does not think that a Catholic translation can meet the needs of Protestant readers.[136]

While criticizing Luther's translation, both De Wette and Augusti make clear that it forms the foundation of their own.[137] De Wette writes that he follows Luther's translation in style and tone since it is not only of ecclesiastical

130 De Wette, "Vorrede," v. De Wette also notes that preachers with little or no knowledge of Hebrew will benefit from his translation. For they often give sermons based on ideas not found in the original text by relying on Luther's "error-laden translation." De Wette recalls that one reader expressed great consternation that he could not find a text in De Wette's translation about which he had heard a particularly edifying sermon. See ibid.

131 Ibid., vi.

132 Ibid., iv.

133 The translations Augusti mentions are: Hezel, *Die Bibel Alten und Neuen Testaments, mit vollständig-erklärenden Anmerkungen* (Lemgo, 1780–1791); Michaelis, *Übersetzung des Alten Testaments* (Göttingen, 1769–1785); Moldenhawer, *Übersetzung und Erläuterung der heiligen Bücher des Alten Testaments* (Quedlinburg, 1774–1787). See Augusti, "Vorrede," ii.

134 Ibid.

135 Ibid., iii.

136 See Brentano and Dereser, *Die heilige Schrift des alten Testaments* (1797–1803); Augusti, "Vorrede," iii.

137 Ibid., vii; De Wette, "Vorrede," iii–iv.

importance but also of "national" (*volksmäßig*) significance.[138] De Wette notes that Luther did much to encourage Germans to "befriend Hebraism," introducing many Hebraic expressions into the German language through his translation.[139] De Wette acknowledges that Luther's approach is no longer fashionable, and Augusti recalls that the most recent call has been to produce a "flowing German" translation "free of Hebraisms" (*hebraismenfrey*).[140] But De Wette's scholarly sensibility shines through when he writes that content and form "belong together organically," so he seeks to preserve the Hebraic form of the original as long as it does not render the German unclear or damage "good taste" (*guten Geschmack*).[141] De Wette's desire to convey the form of the Hebrew is also informed by his valuing of Hebraic culture. Consistent with his view of Hebraism that we have explored, in the introduction to his Bible translation De Wette notes that Hebraism espouses ideas of universal significance, though it expresses them in a "childlike, naïve form of thinking and speaking." For this reason, De Wette considers it important to go further than Luther in conveying the form of the Hebrew.[142]

De Wette and Augusti recognize that some might object to updating Luther's translation. But they argue that doing so is completely in Luther's spirit. Luther himself revised his translation multiple times, and they are open to having their own translation corrected.[143] As Augusti puts it, the aim is to "perfect the excellent work of the great man [Luther]" not to discard it.[144] For De Wette and Augusti, revising Luther's translation embodies the Protestant spirit of free inquiry and devotion to truth. At the end of his preface, De Wette expresses his hope that his translation will promote "acquaintance with the undistorted (*unverfälschten*) sense of our Holy Scriptures" and thus contribute to promoting "purified Christianity" (*geläuterten Christenthums*), expressed in the basic credo: "Every truth is better than error and is most pious."[145]

Comparing the two Bibles

The layout of Zunz's Bible is strikingly similar to De Wette's, containing just the German in two columns, and Zunz likely modelled the layout of his Bible

138 Ibid., iii.
139 Ibid., iv.
140 Ibid.; Augusti, "Vorrede," ix.
141 De Wette, "Vorrede," iv.
142 Ibid. See pp. 135–137 of this volume.
143 See De Wette, "Vorrede," vii; Augusti, "Vorrede," ix.
144 Ibid., ix–x.
145 De Wette, "Vorrede," vii.

on De Wette's.[146] Zunz seems to have adapted his title from De Wette's Bible, giving it a Jewish twist. De Wette's Bible is called *Die Heilige Schrift des Alten und Neuen Testaments* (*The Holy Scripture of the Old and New Testaments*). Zunz's has a dual title, תורה נביאים כתובים (*Torah, Prophets, Writings*) and *Die vier und zwanzig Bücher der heiligen Schrift* (*The Twenty-Four Books of Holy Scripture*). Like De Wette, Zunz calls the Bible "Holy Scripture," but Zunz drops the reference to the Christian designation of the Hebrew Bible as "Old Testament" and instead refers to "twenty-four books," which is the traditional Jewish enumeration of the number of books of the Hebrew Bible and differs from the Protestant enumeration.

There are other important differences in the layout of De Wette's and Zunz's Bibles. De Wette's Bible is divided thematically, while Zunz's is divided according to weekly pericopes read in the synagogue. For example, De Wette's translation begins with "Creation of the World" (Genesis I–II.3) and then moves to "Creation of man, woman, paradise, fall into sin, expulsion of human beings" (Genesis II.4–III), etc.[147] Although chapters and verses are given, De Wette occasionally alters the traditional verse number, if he thinks it makes better sense.[148] Unlike Zunz's Bible, which gives chapter and verse at the top of the page in Hebrew and German and prints the weekly pericope in Hebrew at the top on each column, there is no Hebrew script in De Wette's translation. And unlike Zunz's Bible, De Wette's contains brief notes that I will discuss.[149]

Examples from their translations provide greater insight into the relation between Zunz's and De Wette's Bibles:

1. Genesis 4:8: *Vayomer kayin el hevel ahiv vayehi biyotam basadeh vayakom kayin el hevel ahiv vayahargeihu*

Luther: *Da redete Kain mit seinem Bruder Habel. Und es begab sich, da sie auf dem Felde waren, erhub sich Kain wider seinen Bruder Habel und schlug ihn tot* [Then Cain spoke with his brother Abel. And it happened that they were in the field, Cain raised himself against his brother Abel and struck him dead]

[146] The first edition of the translation by De Wette and Augusti published in 1809 did not split the text into two columns. De Wette first adopted this model for his 1831 edition. It is also possible that Zunz modelled his Bible on Gotthold Salomon's translation. But Salomon's translation appeared in 1837, and while Zunz's full translation has a date of 1838, his translation of the Pentateuch, which already employed the two column format, has a date of 1837. See Figures 5, 6, and 8.

[147] See De Wette, *Die Heilige Schrift*, 1–4.

[148] See, for example, De Wette's rendering of Exodus 21:36–22:1 and his note there. De Wette, *Die Heilige Schrift*, 83.

[149] In the first edition of 1809 and the second edition of 1831, the notes are placed below the text and contain no Hebrew script. In the third edition of 1839, De Wette moves the notes to the end of the book and occasionally inserts words in Hebrew script.

Mendelssohn: *Kajin sprach zu seinem Bruder Hewel. Als sie nun einst auf dem Felde waren, erhub sich Kajin über seinen Bruder Hewel und erschlug ihn.* [Kayin spoke to his brother Hevel. As they were now in the field, Kayin raised himself over his brother Hevel and smote him.]

Zunz: *Und es sprach Kajin zu Hebel seinem Bruder. Und es geschah wie sie waren auf dem Felde, da machte sich Kajin an seinem Bruder Hebel und erschlug ihn.* [And Kayin spoke to Hebel his brother. And it happened as they were in the field, Kayin turned on his brother Hebel and smote him.]

De Wette: *Und Kain sprach zu Habel seinem Bruder* und es geschah, als sie auf dem Felde waren, da erhob sich Kain gegen Habel seinen Bruder, und ermorderte ihn.* [And Cain spoke to Abel his brother* and it happened as they were out in the field, there Cain raised himself against Abel his brother and murdered him]

* Septuagint, Syriac, Vulgate, etc. add *laß uns auf's Feld gehen* [let us go to the field]

Several features of De Wette's and Zunz's translation methods can be seen from this passage. *First,* while Zunz follows Mendelssohn in rendering names in their Hebrew transliteration (*Kajin, Hebel*), De Wette follows Luther in rendering names in their Germanic form (*Kain, Habel*). *Second,* there are four *vav* prefixes in the verse (***vayomer, vayehi, vayakom, vayahargeihu***). Luther translates one as *da,* two as *und,* and leaves one untranslated. Mendelssohn translates one as *als,* one as *und,* and leaves two untranslated. Zunz translates three as *und* and one as *da,* leaving none untranslated. De Wette does the same. Indeed, both Zunz and De Wette consistently translate *vav* prefixes, usually as *und.* De Wette explains this decision by noting that the Bible's common use of the *vav* prefix is characteristic of "childlike" (*kindliche*) languages. He compares this to how children and common people often pepper their speech with superfluous connecting words (a contemporary analogy might be the way many American children frequently add "like" to their sentences). De Wette seeks to convey this flavor of the Hebrew original in his translation.[150]

Third, both Luther and Mendelssohn follow German word order in rendering *el hevel ahiv,* which appears twice in the verse as *mit/zu/wider/über*

[150] De Wette, "Vorrede," iv.

seinem Bruder Hewel (with/to/against/over his brother Abel). By contrast, both Zunz and De Wette seek to preserve the form of the Hebrew by translating it in the first clause as *zu Hebel/Habel seinem Bruder* (to Hebel/Abel his brother), though only De Wette preserves this form in the second clause while Zunz reverts to proper German translating it as *an seinem Bruder Hebel*. Augusti points to the importance of preserving Hebrew word order in their translation, writing that Luther sometimes violated the "oriental style of word order" (*orientalisch Manier der Wort-Folge*) in the Bible and that he and De Wette sought to preserve it wherever possible.[151]

Finally, De Wette is the only one who provides a textual variant to the Masoretic Text. In the second and third editions, he places this variant in a note but in the first edition he inserts the addition into the text itself.[152]

Despite the similarities between Zunz's translation and Mendelssohn's, one is struck by the fact that, in general, Zunz's translation is much closer to De Wette's than to Mendelssohn's.

2. Exodus 34:29: *vayehi beredet Mosheh meihar Sinai* ***ushnei luhot ha'edut beyad Mosheh berideto min hahar***

Luther: *Da nun Mose vom Berge Sinai ging,* ***hatte er die zwo Tafeln des Zeugnisses in seiner Hand*** [When Moses went [down] from Mount Sinai, **he had the two Tablets of Testimony in his hand**]

Mendelssohn: *Als Mosche herunter ging von dem Berge Sinai,* ***die beiden Tafeln des Zeugnisses hatte Mosche in der Hand, als er von dem Berge herunter ging*** [When Moshe went down from Mount Sinai, **the two Tablets of Testimony Moshe had in hand, as from the mountain he went down**]

Zunz: *Und es geschah, als Moscheh herabkam vom Berge Sinai*—***und die zwei Tafeln des Zeugnisses (waren) in der Hand Moscheh's, indem er herabkam vom Berge*** [And it happened, when Mosheh descended from Mount Sinai—**and the two Tablets of Testimony (were) in the hand of Mosheh as he descended from the mountain**]

De Wette: *Und es geschah, als Mose herabstieg vom Berge Sinai,* ***die zwo Tafeln den Gesetzes in Moses hand, als er herabstieg vom Berge*** [And it happened, as Moses descended from Mount Sinai, **the two Tablets of Law in Moses's hand, as he descended from the mountain**]

151 Augusti, "Vorrede," ix.
152 See Augusti and De Wette, *Die Schriften des Alten Testaments,* 1:9.

Several points are worthy of note. First, De Wette alone translates *luhot ha'edut* as "Tablets of Law" (*Tafeln den Gesetzes*) rather than as "Tablets of Testimony" (*Tafeln des Zeugnisses*), presumably because he reads the Hebrew not as *edut* (testimony) but, rather, as *edot* (laws). This reflects De Wette's willingness to depart from the Masoretic Text, unlike Luther, Mendelssohn, or Zunz. Second, Zunz alone follows the form of the Hebrew in translating the tablets as being "in the hand of Mosheh" (*beyad Moshe/ in der Hand Moscheh's*) rather than following proper German form as "in Mosheh's hand" (*hatte Moshe in der Hand/in Moses Hand*). Third, De Wette departs from Luther and, like Mendelssohn, translates the repetition of Moses descending the mountain despite its superfluity to the meaning of the text. Zunz follows suit. Fourth, both De Wette and Zunz alone translate *vayehi* in the beginning of the verse as *Und es geschah.* Fifth, only De Wette and Zunz follow the Hebrew word order in translating *berideto min hahar* as *indem er herabkam vom Berge/als er herabstieg vom Berge* (as he went down from the mountain). Sixth, De Wette alone seeks to reproduce the Hebrew form *ushnei luhot ha'edut beyad Mosheh*, which lacks an existential verb in German, translating the phrase as *die zwo Tafeln den Gesetzes in Moses hand.* By contrast, Luther and Mendelssohn include *hatte* to make the clause conform the German style while Zunz seeks a compromise by including *waren*, but only in parentheses to indicate that the word is lacking in the original Hebrew.

Again, Zunz's translation is generally closer to De Wette's than to Mendelssohn's, and both are more faithful to the syntax of the Hebrew than Mendelssohn's.

3. Psalm 110:1, 6–7: ***l'David mizmor: ne'um YHWH ladoni*** *sheiv limini ad ashit oyvekha hadom leraglekha . . . yadin bagoyim malei geviyot mahatz rosh al eretz rabbah minahal baderekh yishteh al kein yarim rosh*

Luther: ***Ein Psalm Davids: Der HERR sprach zu meinem Herrn:*** *Setze dich zu meiner Rechten, bis ich deine Feinde zum Schemel deiner Füße lege . . . er wird richten unter den Heiden, er wird ein großes Schlagen unter ihnen tun, er wird zerschmettern das Haupt über große Lande. Er wird trinken vom Bach auf dem Wege; darum wird er das Haupt emporheben.*

[**A Psalm of David: The LORD spoke to my Lord:** Sit yourself at my right until I make your enemies into your footstool . . . He will judge among the pagans, he will strike them a great blow, he will smash the head over great lands. He will drink from the stream on the way, therefore he will lift his head].

Mendelssohn: ***An David: ein Psalm. Der Ewge spricht zu meinem Herrn:*** *Verweile hier zu meiner Rechten! Ich werde deine Feinde dir, zum Schemel deiner Füsse legen . . . Er wird Nationen richten Auf hochgethürmten Leichen, Der itzt das Haupt von Rabba schlug. Schon trinkt es aus dem Bach am Wege; Weil es zu stolz sein Haupt erhob.* [**To David, a Psalm: The Eternal spoke to my lord:** abide here at my right! Until I make your enemies into your footstool . . . He will judge nations, piling corpses high, he will now smash the head from Rabbah. He will now drink from the stream on the path because he arrogantly raised his head.]

Zunz: ***Von Dawid. Ein Psalm. Spruch des Ewigen an meinen Herrn*** *Setzt dich mir zur Rechten, bis ich hinlege deine Feinde, einen Schemel deinen Füßen . . . Gericht hält er unter den Völkern—eine Fülle von Leichen; er zerschmettert Häupter auf Weitem Lande. Aus dem Bache trinkt er am Wege; darum erhebt er das Haupt* [**Of David, a Psalm. A saying of the Eternal to my lord:** Sit yourself at my right until I put your enemies down as a footstool to your feet . . . He will judge among the nations—an abundance of corpses, he will shatter heads over great lands. From the stream on the way he will drink, therefore he will lift up the head]

De Wette: ***Von David ein Gesang. Das ist Jehova's Spruch zu meinem Herrn:*** *"Sitze zu meiner Rechten, bis ich deine Feinde mache zum Schemel deiner Füße." . . . Er hält Gericht unter den Völkern, erfüllt von Leichen; zerschmettert Häupter auf weitem Land. Aus dem Bache trinkt er auf dem Zuge, darum erhebet er das Haupt.* [**Of David, a song. This is Jehova's saying to my lord.** "Sit at my right until I make your enemies a footstool to your feet." . . . He will judge among the nations, full of corpses; shatter heads over great lands. From the stream he will drink on the way, therefore he will lift up the head.]

Once again, De Wette's and Zunz's translations are closest. Both render *L'david mizmor* as the ambiguous *Von David* (of David), which could either mean "by David" or "about David." Both also render *ne'um* as a noun (*Spruch*) rather than change it into a verb like Luther and Mendelssohn. De Wette is more precise than any other translator in rendering *Mizmor* as *Gesang* (song), presumably to distinguish it from the term *Tehillah*, which would be rendered as *Psalm.* De Wette's and Zunz's rendering of verses 6–7 are very similar, neither pointing to nor excluding a Christological interpretation. De Wette's noncommittal view of what the Psalm refers to is reflected in his subtitling the

Psalm *Der Statthalter Gottes* (The Viceroy of God). Both also follow the form of the Hebrew at the beginning of verse 7 by placing the object before the subject and translating the phrase identically (*minahal baderekh yishteh/Aus dem Bache trinkt er*).

The one major difference between them concerns the rendering of the Tetragrammaton. De Wette renders it with the proper name *Jehova* rather than as Luther's *Der HERR* or Mendelssohn's *Der Ewige*, presumably because of his scholarly sense that this is the proper name of a particular ancient Near Eastern god. Such an approach is, however, impossible for Zunz, who seeks to address a broad Jewish audience, many of whom would be uncomfortable with such a translation given the traditional Jewish strictures on pronouncing God's name.[153] To appeal to Jewish sensibility, Zunz follows Mendelssohn's famous translation.

4. I Samuel 13: 1–2: *Ben shanah Shaul bemolokho ushtei shanim malakh al yisrael vayivkhar lo shaul shloshet alafim miyisrael*

Zunz: *Als Schaül ein Jahr König war—er regierte aber zwei Jahre über Jisraël—Da wählte Schaül sich drei Tausend aus Jisraël* [When Shaul was king for a year over Yisrael—he ruled however two years over Yisrael—then Shaul chose for himself three thousand from Yisrael]

De Wette: . . .[1] *Jahr alt war Saul, als er König ward, und zwei Jahr regierte er*[2] *über Israel: da wählete sich Saul dreitausend Mann aus Israel* [. . . years old was Saul when he became king and he ruled two years over Israel: then Saul chose for himself three thousand men from Israel]

[1]Hier *fehlt die Zahl des Alters.* [The year of his age is missing here.]

[2]*Andere: Ein Jahr war Saul König gewesen, und regierte das zweite Jahr.* [Others: in one year Saul became king and he ruled in the second year.]

This verse presents a classic difficulty. Its literal meaning is that Saul was one year old when he became king and that he ruled for two years over Israel. To avoid this problem, Zunz follows the classic medieval Jewish commentator David Kimhi, who reads the two verses together, with the description of Saul's being king for two years as a parenthetical comment. Zunz therefore translates the verse to mean that when Saul had been king for a year (having

[153] See, for example, Mishnah Sanhedrin 10:1.

ruled for two years) he selected three thousand men. By contrast, De Wette is open to the text being corrupt, which he indicates by inserting an ellipsis. De Wette's assumption is that there is a number such as twenty or thirty missing, namely, that Saul was twenty-one or thirty-one years old when he became king, and he ruled for two years. De Wette also presents an alternate version of the text, which reads that Saul first became king and only ruled the subsequent year.

In sum, Zunz's and De Wette's Bibles share much in common. Both translate the entire Hebrew Bible into German in two parallel columns, leaving out the Hebrew original. Zunz's title for his translation seems to be a Jewish adaptation of De Wette's. Many of their translations are extremely similar, with both seeking to provide an accurate translation that preserves both the sense *and* form of the Hebrew even if this renders passages less elegantly in German. Both see their work as of value for religious edification and not for scholars alone.

The differences between Zunz's liberal Judaism and De Wette's liberal Protestantism do, however, have important repercussions for their translations. For Protestants, the Old Testament may have value as a work of religious edification, but it is not indispensable. As such, De Wette's primary audience is students of theology. Reading the Old Testament in Hebrew does not have a central liturgical role in Protestantism, so De Wette is willing to take liberties with the Masoretic Text, introduce textual variants, alternative vocalizations, and change the way the verses are numbered. As a liberal historian, De Wette does not feel bound to accommodate Christological interpretations.

By contrast, for Zunz the Masoretic Bible has a central educational and liturgical role in Judaism and unifies German Jews. As such, he divides the biblical text according to the way it is read in the synagogue and does not deviate from the Masoretic Text or vowels, though he is cognizant that they are not always reliable.[154] Zunz considers reading knowledge of Hebrew script of value for the general Jewish public, especially in the context of the synagogue and thus prints the names of the books and weekly pericopes in Hebrew. He follows Mendelssohn in transliterating biblical names from the Hebrew and seeks to make his translation familiar to Jewish readers by following Mendelssohn's translation of the Tetragrammaton as

[154] See p. 180 of this volume.

Der Ewige.[155] Finally, while Zunz and De Wette are both independent scholars willing to deviate from their predecessors, De Wette sees his work as a revision of Luther's, while Zunz's relation to his Jewish predecessors is more ambiguous. Zunz's Bible can be seen as both a historically informed revision of Mendelssohn's translation and as a Jewish revision of De Wette's.

Protestantism and Catholicism as ideological categories for Zunz

Like Mendelssohn, Zunz associates freedom and intellectual honesty with Protestantism and coercion and manipulation with Catholicism. In a notebook entry Zunz presents Luther as a defender of liberty of thought, writing: "Lawbooks (*Gesetzbücher*) must be studied according to rules of reason, not rules of reason subject to lawbooks (Luther)."[156] In a political speech from 1865 titled "Revolution," Zunz asserts that the "Roman clergy" (*römische Geistlichkeit*) sought a "monopoly over thinking," deeming "every opinion that deviated from their own not merely false, but a crime to be punished with dungeons, torture, and fire."[157] Zunz also follows Mendelssohn in seeing Catholicism as subjugating the state to clerical rule.[158] And like Mendelssohn, Zunz deploys "Jesuitism" as a metaphor for duplicity, writing that, "it is no longer possible to be a theologian without Jesuitism, without unworthy distortion and corruption of truth."[159]

But Zunz also uses Protestantism and Catholicism differently than Mendelssohn on account of his different politics. While Mendelssohn may have harbored democratic sympathies, he publicly supported Frederick the Great's enlightened despotism and rejected the idea that democracy was the best form of government in all circumstances.[160] By contrast, Zunz was an

[155] Prior to Zunz's translation, the only other German Jewish translations of the Pentateuch were by Mendelssohn and Johlson, both who rendered the Tetragrammaton as "the Eternal." That Zunz's wish not to alienate his readers guided his use of "the Eternal" seems likely given that Mendelssohn's decision to use this term was guided by philosophical considerations, which were not Zunz's concern.

[156] Zunz, *Das Buch Zunz*, 28.

[157] Zunz, *GS*, 1:350.

[158] See Zunz's 1861 speech in Zunz, *GS*, 1:324.

[159] Zunz, *Das Buch Zunz*, 27.

[160] On Mendelssohn's democratic leanings, see Harvey, "Mendelssohn's Heavenly Politics." On Mendelssohn's praise for Frederick the Great, see Mendelssohn, *JubA*, 8:4, 146–147; *Moses*

outspoken democrat who actively supported the 1848 revolutions and was later a member of the "Progressive Party" (*Fortschrittspartei*).[161] In a political speech from 1861, he presents Luther's emphasis on individual conscience as paving the way for democracy, calling Luther and the reformer Ulrich von Hutten "dangerous agitators and democrats."[162] Zunz links Catholicism with tyranny, militarism, and mob rule, seeing them as mutually reinforcing: "Princes, popes, police, the mob, stand and fall with one another; churches, cloisters, barracks, dungeons are their monuments."[163] For Zunz, popes and tyrants seek to consolidate power by joining forces with villains and the wealthy and using superstition to manipulate the poor masses: "Tyrants and Popes have three supporting armies: scoundrels, the disgraced, and jackasses; three supporting sciences: sophistry, charlatanism, superstition; and three allies: poverty, wealth and ignorance."[164]

That Zunz conceived Protestantism and Catholicism as ideal categories is evident from the fact that he sometimes charged *Protestants* with acting like *Catholics*. The *Kreuzzeitung* (*Newspaper of the Cross*) was the chief organ for ultraconservative Protestants who advocated that Germany be a Christian state.[165] In his 1872 *Deutsche Briefe*, Zunz approvingly cites a liberal named Gerstner, who wrote: "To me, a Jesuit sermon is not as disgusting as a lead article in the *Kreuzzeitung*."[166] Zunz also compared the hatred of Jews among some liberal Protestants to Catholicism, writing that "in its despising of Jews, so-called 'free Protestantism' (*freiere protestantische Richtung*) is no better than Ultramontanism."[167]

Zunz also uses Protestantism and Catholicism to describe *different groups of German Jews*. For Zunz, traditionalist German Jews who

Mendelssohn: Writings, 41; *Jerusalem*, 78–79. Mendelssohn made clear that democracy was not the best form of government for a populace not ready for it, writing that "Certainly despotically ruled nations would be extremely miserable if they were left to govern themselves." See Mendelssohn, *JubA*, 8:111; *Jerusalem*, 42.

161 See Wallach, *Liberty and Letters*, 128. On Zunz's involvement in politics, see Schorsch, *Leopold Zunz*, 156–181.
162 Zunz, *GS*, 1:317
163 Zunz, *Das Buch Zunz*, 28.
164 Zunz, *Das Buch Zunz*, 28.
165 For a good discussion of the drive to define Germany as a Christian state following unification and its implications for German Jews, see Tal, *Christians and Jews in Germany*, 121–159, especially his remarks on p. 124.
166 Zunz, *Deutsche Briefe*, 48.
167 Ibid., 46. See Joskowicz, *The Modernity of Others*, 234. Ultramontanism is the Catholic doctrine that emphasizes supreme papal authority.

emphasize pilpulistic Talmud study and reject general education are advocating a "Catholic" form of Judaism. Using language that recalls Luther's struggle with the Church, Zunz writes, "Until the Talmud is overthrown (*gestürtz*), nothing can be done."[168] Similarly, in an 1843 response to a Prussian government query concerning the proper role and authority of rabbis, Zunz wrote that rabbis' authority stemmed from the consent of their community and was granted solely the basis on the rabbi's "morality, piety and scholarship." Zunz contrasted the role of the rabbi with that of the Catholic priest, noting that the rabbi is an "articulate teacher of the law and chosen leader *neither a priest nor a cleric.* He does not constitute a separate estate, nor receive an investiture."[169]

To the question whether the Jewish community could impose penalties on individual members, Zunz wrote that it could only do so as long as its judicial authority was confirmed by the government and accepted by the members of the Jews community. Even then it could only impose penalties in civil disputes or on matters that threatened public order. Imposing halakhah in private life was a misuse of authority. For Zunz, Judaism had a "Protestant" view of rabbinic authority, which he saw as dependent on the democratic principle of communal consent and which did not extend to individual conscience. Jewish traditionalists who sought to impose halakhic norms against people's will were imitating "medieval priestly despots and inquisitors."[170]

Conclusion

Like his hero Mendelssohn, Zunz embraces a middle-class vision of German Judaism that presents *Bildung* as a religious goal, and sees the Torah as a means of helping Jews acquire it. And, like Mendelssohn, Zunz seeks to actualize a vision of middle-class German Judaism that will unite enlightened

[168] See Zunz's Letter to Ehrenberg, October 13, 1818, as found in Geiger, "Zunz' Tätigkeit für die Reform," 114. The translation follows Meyer, *The Origins of the Modern Jew,* 152. I take Zunz not to be rejecting the Talmud completely given the positive view of rabbinic literature he expressed in *On Rabbinic Literature.* He is rejecting talmudism. Zunz's language is reminiscent of that used seventeen years *later* by Heine when he compared Mendelssohn to Luther, writing, "Just as Luther overthrew (*stürtze*) the papacy, so Mendelssohn overthrew the Talmud and in exactly the same way." See p. 4 of this volume.

[169] See Zunz, *GS,* 2:208; Schorsch, *Leopold Zunz,* 112.

[170] See Zunz, *GS,* 2:212–213.

and traditionalist Jews by reforming Jewish education and producing a new Bible translation. In their Bible translations both Mendelssohn and Zunz seek to balance communicating the plain meaning and form of the Hebrew original with producing a readable, elegant German translation. The differences between their Bibles reflect changes in the Jewish community and their distinct intellectual orientations. Mendelssohn knew that many of his readers were deeply steeped in Jewish texts, so he sought to produce a Bible that felt like the traditional rabbinic study Bible. While seeking to acquaint his readers with the form of the Hebrew, he also knew that many of his readers had an imperfect grasp of German. As such, his translation was in elegant High German, and he often changed the Hebrew syntax to conform with proper German style. This would both improve his readers' understanding of German and convey biblical ideas in aesthetically pleasing ways that moved the heart.

In Zunz's time, knowledge of Yiddish, Hebrew, and Jewish texts had greatly declined among both enlightened and traditionalist Jews while knowledge of German was taken for granted. As such, Zunz produced a German translation without the Hebrew original. While Zunz wished that his translation be comprehensible, he was concerned that his readers appreciate the form of the Hebrew and thus was often more willing than Mendelssohn to sacrifice proper German style to convey Hebrew syntax. Mendelssohn, however, more often preserved Hebrew word roots in his translation than did Zunz.

Mendelssohn's Bible was informed by a philosophical/theological sensibility and sought to synthesize the Bible with rational theology, exclude Christology, and make room for rabbinic interpretation. By contrast, Zunz was guided by a historical sensibility and so did not feel the need to accommodate rational theology, exclude Christology, or accommodate rabbinic interpretations. The historical sense informing Zunz's Bible can be seen from its proximity to De Wette's Bible. But while De Wette's translation was aimed primarily for scholars of theology, Zunz's intended audience was the mass of German Jews. Not wishing to alienate readers, unlike De Wette, Zunz did not depart from the Masoretic Text and was sometimes willing to sacrifice accuracy to appeal to popular Jewish taste. Zunz's Bible is best understood as both a *wissenschaftlichen* revision of Mendelssohn's and as a Jewish revision of De Wette's.

Zunz's Bible reflects a shifting view of the center of Judaism. While Mendelssohn considers the home the center of Jewish life and thus produces a study Bible, Zunz regards the synagogue as central and produces a Bible appropriate for liturgical use.

Both Mendelssohn and Zunz produced Bibles addressed to diverse audiences, but Zunz's intended audience was broader. Mendelssohn hoped that his Bible would be used by Jews from different *ideological* viewpoints, but his Bible was directed to *wealthy males*. By contrast, Zunz hoped that his Bible would be used not only by Jews from different *ideological* viewpoints, but also by *rich and poor, males and females*.

Finally, Zunz follows Mendelssohn by aligning Judaism with Protestantism and criticizing his opponents for acting like Catholics. But there are two important differences. First, Zunz's commitment to democracy means that, unlike Mendelssohn, he identifies Protestantism not only with intellectual and religious liberty but also with democratic politics. Second, while Mendelssohn only deploys the concepts of Protestantism and Catholicism *inter-religiously*, contrasting "Catholic" forms of Christianity with "Protestant" Judaism, Zunz also deploys these concepts *intra-religiously*, contrasting "Catholic" forms Judaism with his own "Protestant" Judaism.

Figure 1. *Bust of Moses Mendelssohn* teaching while holding a book (Jakob Plessner, 1929), Courtesy of Leo Baeck Institute, New York.

43

XXII.

1. Dem Sangmeister auf der Morgenflöte, ein Psalm Davids.

---

2. Mein Gott! mein Gott! warum verlässest du mich?
Warum sind meine Klagen so fern von Hülfe?
3. Mein Gott! des Tages ruf ich, nichts erwiedert;
Des Nachts — nichts stillet meinen Jammer.
4. Aber du, Allerheiligster!
Thronest unter Lobgesängen Israels!
5. Dir vertrauten unsre Väter;
Vertrauten dir, und du halfest aus.
6. Zu dir schrien sie, und fanden Rettung;
Dir vertrauten sie, und wurden nicht zu schanden.
7. Ich bin ein Wurm, kein Mann;
Der Leute Spott, des Volks Verachtung;
8. Die mich sehen, höhnen mich;
Verziehen Lippen, schütteln mit dem Haupte:
9. „Er klag's dem Herrn; der hilft ihm aus;
„Der rettet ihn; er ist sein Liebling."

Figure 2. Psalm 22 from the second edition of Moses Mendelssohn, *Die Psalmen* (Berlin: Friedrich Maurer, 1788), 43.

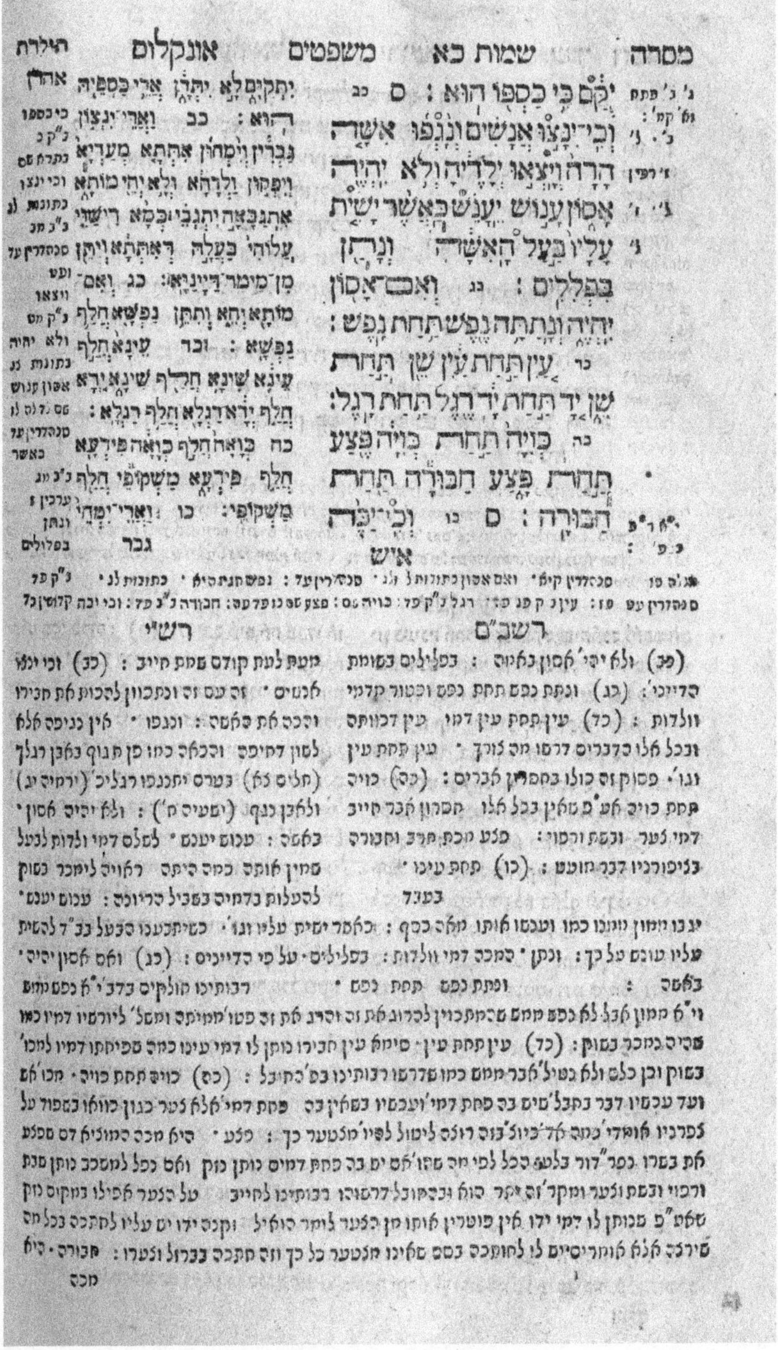

מסרה שמות כא משפטים אונקלוס תולדת

יקם כי כספו הוא: ס כב
וכי ינצו אנשים ונגפו אשה
הרה ויצאו ילדיה ולא יהיה
אסון ענוש יענש כאשר ישית
עליו בעל האשה ונתן
בפללים: כג ואם אסון
יהיה ונתתה נפש תחת נפש:
כד עין תחת עין שן תחת
שן יד תחת יד רגל תחת רגל:
כה כויה תחת כויה פצע
תחת פצע חבורה תחת
חבורה: ס כו וכי יכה
איש

יתקים לא יתדן ארי כספיה
הוא: כב וארי ינצון
גברין וימחון אתתא מעדיא
ויפקון ולדהא ולא יהי מותא
אתגבאה יתגבי כמא דישוי
עלוהי בעלה דאתתא ויתן
מן מימר דיינא: כג ואם
מותא יהא ותתן נפשא חלף
נפשא: כד עינא חלף
עינא שנא חלף שנא ידא
חלף ידא רגלא חלף רגלא:
כה כואה חלף כואה פידעא
חלף פידעא משקופי חלף
משקופי: כו וארי ימחי
גבר

רשב"ם

רש"י

Figure 3. Exodus 21:22–26 from *Mikra'ot Gedolot: Hamishah Humshei Torah: Shemot* (Berlin: Yablonski Hof Fridiger, 1705), 214b.

(כה) כְּוִיָּה תַּחַת כְּוִיָּה פֶּצַע
תַּחַת פָּצַע חַבּוּרָה תַּחַת
חַבּוּרָה׃ ס (כו) וְכִי־
יַכֶּה אִישׁ אֶת־עֵין עַבְדּוֹ אוֹ־
אֶת־עֵין אֲמָתוֹ וְשִׁחֲתָהּ
לַחָפְשִׁי יְשַׁלְּחֶנּוּ תַּחַת עֵינוֹ׃
(כז) וְאִם־שֵׁן עַבְדּוֹ אוֹ־שֵׁן
אֲמָתוֹ יַפִּיל לַחָפְשִׁי יְשַׁלְּחֶנּוּ
תַּחַת שִׁנּוֹ׃ פ
(כח) וְכִי־יִגַּח שׁוֹר אֶת־
אִישׁ אוֹ אֶת־אִשָּׁה וָמֵת
סקול

(כה) בראנדמאל פיר בראנדמאל, וואונד פיר וואונדי: ביילי פיר ביילי (דאהער מוז דער טעדטר געלד דאפיר געבן): (כו) ווען יעמאנד דש אויגי זיינש קנעכטש אדר דש אויגי זיינר מאגד שלעגט, אונד עש פערדערבט: מוז ער איהן צור פרייאהייט אוישגעהן לאסן פיר זיין אויגי:
(כז) שלעגט ער זיינם קנעכט אדר זיינר מאגד איינן צאהן אויש: מוז ער איהן צור פרייאהייט אוישגעהן לאסן פיר זיינן צאהן:
(כח) ווען איין אכס איינן מאן אדר איינע פרויא שטעסט, דש ער שטירבט:

תקון סופרים

(כח) וכי יגח שור, כתוב (א"ת) סקול:

באור

כבר לקחנו נקמתו ממנו, כי עשינו לו כאשר עשה בשוה עכ"ל, וכוונת הכתוב כמו שכת' הראב"ע שמדין הגמול הוא חייב בכך, אם לא יתן כפרו, והכתוב אומר שלא נקח כופר לנפש רוצח אשר הוא רשע למות, אבל נקח כופר במי שהוא רשע לכרות אחד מאיבריו, לכן לא נכריתנו לעולם, אבל ישלם כפרו, ואם אין לו, יהי' עליו החוב עד שתשיג ידו, וכן מתורגם בל"א: והנה התחיל בחסרון איברים, ודבר בהוה על הרוב, שכן דרך המכה את חבירו להזיקו בעין או בשן או ביד או ברגל, ומהם תקיש על יתר האיברים: (כה) כויה וגו', בכל אלו אין בהם חסרון אבר, ומשלם דמי צער ובושת ורפוי: כויה, מכות אש: פצע, היא מכה המוציא' דם שפוצע את בשרו נצר"דור בלע"ז (בל"א אפני וואונדי, עיין בפ' בראשית ד' כ"ג), הכל לפי מה שהוא, אם יש בה פחת דמים נותן נזק, ואם נפל למשכב נותן שבת ורפוי ובשת וצער (רש"י): חבורה, היא מכה שהדם נצרר בה, ואינו יוצא אלא שמאדים הבשר כנגדו, ולשון חבורה טק"א בלע"ז (וברש"י כ"יטיי"א בלע"ז, והוא טאשי, ובל"א פלעק, מאהל), כמו ונמר חברברתיו (ירמי' י"ג כ"ג), ותרגומו משקופי לשון חבטה בט"דורא בלע"ז (ובל"א שלאג), וכן שדפות קדים (בראשי' מ"א כ"ג), שקיפן קדום, חבוטות ברוח, וכן על המשקוף (לעיל י"ב כ"ג), על שם שהדלת נוקש עליו (רש"י): והרד"ק בשרשי' שרש חבר כתב שהמכה שנצרר בה הדם נקראת חבורה, על שם הדם שנחבר שם, ומשם הושאל לכתמי הנמר הדומין לכתמי החבורה: (כו) עבדו, הכנעני, אבל עברי אינו יוצא בשן ועין, כמבואר למעלה: (כז) ואם שן, דבר הכתוב על ההוה ברוב כאשר הזכרנו, והוא הדין לשאר האיברים, וחז"ל אמרו בכ"ד ראשי איברים העבד יוצא לחירות: תחת שנו, נוה השם שיצא העבד חפשי תחת עינו או תחת שנו, שלא יהי' אדוניו אכזרי, שיכנו מכה נמרצה, כי אם ישחית עינו או אפי' שנו, יצא מרשותו ויאבד ממונו: (כח) שור, אחד שור, אחד כל בהמה וחי' ועוף, אלא שדבר הכתוב בהווה: אשה, הזכיר פה את האשה בפירוש, וכן פרט או בן יגח או בת יגח, שהם קטנים, לומר לך שאין בעל השור יכול לערער, שלא הי' לאשה לצאת אל מקום השוורים, ושהי' לאבות לשמור את ילדיהם שלא יוזקו (מדברי הראב"ע):
ולא

Figure 4. Exodus 21:25–28 from the first edition of Moses Mendelssohn, *Sefer Netivot Ha-shalom: Shemot* (Berlin: G.F. Starcke, 1781), 130a.

72 Exodus, 21, 22. ואלה שמות כא כב

ואלה השפטים

6. So bringe ihn sein Herr vor die Richter, und bringe ihn an die Thüre, oder an den Thürpfosten, und sein Herr durchsteche ihm das Ohr mit einer Pfrieme, und er sei bei ihm Knecht für immer.

7. Und wenn jemand seine Tochter verkauft als Magd, so soll sie nicht ausgehen, wie die Knechte ausgehen.

8. Mißfällt sie den Augen ihres Herrn, der sie sich bestimmt hatte, so muß er ihr zum Loskaufe verhelfen; an fremde Leute hat er nicht Gewalt sie zu verkaufen, da er treulos an ihr handelt.

9. Und wenn er sie seinem Sohne bestimmt, soll er nach dem Rechte der Töchter ihr thun.

10. Wenn er sich eine andere dazu nimmt: soll er ihre Kost, ihre Kleidung und ihre Wohnung nicht verringern.

11. Und wenn er diese drei Dinge ihr nicht thut, so geht sie umsonst aus, ohne Geld.

12. Wer einen Menschen schlägt und er stirbt, soll des Todes sterben.

13. Wer aber nicht aufgelauert hat, sondern Gott hat es ihm unter die Hand geschickt, so werde ich dir einen Ort einrichten, wohin er fliehen soll.

14. So aber jemand an seinem Nächsten frevelt und ihn umbringt mit List, von meinem Altar weg sollst du ihn führen zum Tode.

15. Und wer seinen Vater oder seine Mutter schlägt, soll des Todes sterben.

16. Und wer einen Menschen stiehlt und ihn verkauft, und er wurde in seiner Hand gefunden, soll des Todes sterben.

17. Und wer seinem Vater oder seiner Mutter flucht, soll des Todes sterben.

18. Und so Männer Streit haben und einer schlägt den andern mit einem Stein oder mit der Faust, und er stirbt nicht, sondern fällt aufs Lager;

19. Wenn er aufsteht und wandelt auf der Straße an seiner Krücke, so ist der Schläger frei; nur soll er erlegen Versäumniß und lasse ihn heilen.

20. Und so jemand seinen Knecht, oder seine Magd schlägt mit dem Stocke und er stirbt unter seiner Hand, so werde es gerächt.

21. Doch wenn er einen Tag oder zwei Tage am Leben bleibt, so soll es nicht gerächt werden; denn es ist sein Geld.

22. Und wenn Männer mit einander zanken und stoßen ein schwangeres Weib, daß ihr die Kinder abgehen, aber es ist keine Lebensgefahr: so werde er am Gelde gebüßt, so viel ihm der Gatte des Weibes auflegt und er zahle durch die Richter.

ואלה השפטים

23. Wenn aber Lebensgefahr ist, so gieb Leben um Leben,

24. Auge um Auge, Zahn um Zahn, Hand um Hand, Fuß um Fuß,

25. Brandmal um Brandmal, Wunde um Wunde, Strieme um Strieme.

26. Und so jemand schlägt in das Auge seines Knechtes, oder in das Auge seiner Magd und zerstört es, so soll er ihn frei lassen für sein Auge.

27. Und wenn er den Zahn seines Knechtes, oder den Zahn seiner Magd ausschlägt, soll er ihn frei lassen für seinen Zahn.

28. Und so ein Ochse stößt einen Mann, oder ein Weib, daß er stirbt: so soll der Ochse gesteiniget werden und sein Fleisch darf nicht gegessen werden; aber der Herr des Ochsen ist frei.

29. Und wenn es ein stößiger Ochse ist von gestern, ehegestern, und sein Herr ist verwarnet worden und hat ihn nicht verwahrt, und er tödtet einen Mann oder ein Weib, so soll gesteinigt werden der Ochse und auch sein Herr hat den Tod verwirkt.

30. Wenn eine Sühne ihm aufgelegt wird, so giebt er die Lösung seiner Person, alles, wie es ihm aufgelegt worden.

31. Mag er einen Sohn stoßen oder eine Tochter stoßen, nach diesem Rechte geschehe ihm.

32. Wenn der Ochse einen Knecht stößt, oder eine Magd, dreißig Schekel-Silber erlege er seinem Herrn, und der Ochse werde gesteinigt.

33. Und so jemand öffnet eine Grube, oder wenn jemand eine Grube höhlet und sie nicht zudeckt, und es fällt darein ein Ochse oder ein Esel,

34. So soll der Eigner der Grube bezahlen, Geld erstatte er an dessen Eigner, und das todte Vieh bleibe sein.

35. Und so jemandes Ochse stößt den Ochsen eines andern und er stirbt; so verkaufen sie den lebenden Ochsen und theilen das Geld, und auch den todten theilen sie.

36. Wenn es aber bekannt geworden, daß der Ochse stößig ist von gestern, ehegestern und sein Herr hat ihn nicht verwahrt, so soll er erstatten Ochsen um Ochsen, und der todte bleibe sein.

37. So jemand stiehlt einen Ochsen oder ein Lamm und schlachtet es oder verkauft es, soll er fünf Rinder erstatten um den Ochsen und vier Schafe um das Lamm.

Das 22. Kapitel.

1. Wenn der Dieb beim Einbruch betroffen

Figure 5. Exodus 21:6–22:1 from Leopold Zunz, *Torah Nevi'im Ketuvim: Die vier und zwanzig Bücher der Heiligen Schrift* (Berlin: Veit & Comp., 1838), 72.

Das zweite Buch Mose. XXI, 22 — XXII, 10. 83

es nicht gerochen werden; denn es ist sein Geld. 22. Und so Leute sich mit einander zanken, und schlagen eine schwangere Frau, daß ihre Frucht abgehet, und ihr ist kein Schade geschehen: so soll er um Geld gestraft werden, wie viel ihm der Mann des Weibes auflegt, und soll es geben vor [1]) Schiedsrichtern. 23. Wenn aber Schade geschehen, so sollst du Leben geben um Leben, 24. Auge um Auge, Zahn um Zahn, Hand um Hand, Fuß um Fuß, 25. Brandmaal um Brandmaal, Wunde um Wunde, Beule um Beule. 26. Und so jemand das Auge seines Knechtes oder das Auge seiner Magd schlägt, und es verderbet: so soll er sie als frei entlassen für ihr Auge. 27. Und wenn er den Zahn seines Knechtes oder den Zahn seiner Magd ausschlägt, so soll er sie als frei entlassen für ihren Zahn. 28. Und so ein Ochse einen Mann stößet oder eine Frau, daß sie sterben, so soll der Ochse gesteiniget, und sein Fleisch nicht gegessen werden, aber der Herr des Ochsen soll ungestraft seyn. 29. Wenn aber der Ochse stößig gewesen seit gestern und ehegestern, und man hat seinen Herrn gewarnet, und er hat ihn nicht verwahret, und er hat einen Mann oder ein Weib getödtet: so soll der Ochse gesteiniget, und auch sein Herr soll getödtet werden. 30. Wenn eine Sühne ihm auferlegt wird, so zahle er die Lösung seines Lebens, wie viel ihm auferlegt ist. 31. Mag er einen Sohn oder eine Tochter stoßen, so soll ihm nach diesem Rechte geschehen. 32. Wenn der Ochse einen Knecht oder eine Magd stößet, so soll er dreißig Seckel Silber seinem Herrn zahlen, und der Ochse soll gesteiniget werden. 33. Und so jemand eine Grube aufthut, oder so jemand eine Grube gräbt, und sie nicht bedecket, und es fällt ein Ochse oder Esel hinein: 34. so soll der Herr der Grube erstatten, Geld soll er dem Herrn bezahlen, und das Todte soll sein seyn. 35. Und so jemandes Ochse den Ochsen des andern stößet, daß er stirbt, so sollen sie den lebendigen Ochsen verkaufen, und seinen Preis theilen, und auch den todten theilen. 36. Ist es aber bekannt, daß der Ochse stößig gewesen seit gestern und ehegestern, und sein Herr hat ihn nicht verwahret, so soll er Ochsen für Ochsen erstatten, und der todte soll sein seyn.

XXII. 1. [1]) So jemand einen Ochsen stiehlt oder ein Schaf, und schlachtet es, oder verkauft es: so soll er fünf Ochsen erstatten für den Ochsen, und vier Schafe für das Schaf. 2. [2]) Wenn beim Einbruche der Dieb betroffen wird, und geschlagen, daß er stirbt, so hat man keine Blutschuld. 3. Wenn aber die Sonne aufgegangen über ihm, so hat man Blutschuld. Er soll wieder erstatten; wenn er nichts hat, so soll er verkauft werden für seinen Diebstahl. 4. Wenn sich das Gestohlene in seiner Hand findet, es sei Ochse oder Esel oder Schaf, lebendig: so soll er das Doppelte erstatten. 5. So jemand ein Feld oder einen Weinberg abweidet, und sein Vieh hintreibt, und es weiden lässet auf dem Felde eines andern: so soll er das Beste von seinem Felde und das Beste von seinem Weinberge erstatten. 6. So Feuer auskommt, und ergreift die Dornen, und es wird ein Garbenhaufe oder die Saat oder das Feld verzehrt: so soll erstatten, wer den Brand angesteckt. 7. So jemand dem andern Geld oder Geräthe gegeben zur Verwahrung, und es wird gestohlen aus dem Hause des Mannes: wenn der Dieb gefunden wird, so soll er das Doppelte erstatten. 8. Wenn der Dieb nicht gefunden wird, so soll der Herr des Hauses vor Gott [3]) treten, ob er nicht seine Hand gelegt an die Sache des andern. 9. Ueber jeden Handel wegen Vergehen, über Ochs, über Esel, über Schaf, über Kleidung, über alles Verlorne, wovon man sagt, das ist es: vor Gott soll beider Handel kommen; wen Gott verdammet, der soll das Doppelte dem andern erstatten. 10. So jemand dem andern einen Esel oder

1) Oder: bei, unter, mit Zuziehung; oder: durch, nach Entscheidung.

1) Hebr. Text: XXI, 37.
2) Hebr. Text: XXII, 1.
3) D. h. vor Gericht.

6 *

Figure 6. Exodus 21:22–22:10 from Wilhelm De Wette, *Die Heilige Schrift des Alten und Neuen Testaments* (Heidelberg: J.C.B. Mohr, 1831), 83.

160 משפטים · שמות כא Exodus 21. Civilgesetze.

9 Wenn er sie aber seinem Sohne bestimmt: so soll er nach dem
10 Rechte der Töchter an ihr thun. || Wenn er ihm eine Andere
nimmt: so soll er doch ihre Kost, Kleidung und Wohnung nicht
11 verringern. || Und wenn er diese drei Dinge ihr nicht schaffet:
so soll sie umsonst ausgehen, unentgeldlich.

12 Wer einen Menschen schlägt, daß er stirbt, der soll getödtet
13 werden. || Und welcher es nicht geflissentlich gethan *) sondern
Gott fügte es in seine Hand: so setze ich dir einen Ort, wohin
14 er fliehen soll. || Frevelt aber Jemand an seinem Nächsten, daß
er ihn umbringet mit Hinterlist: so sollst du ihn von meinem
Altare wegnehmen, daß er sterbe.

15 Wer seinen Vater oder seine Mutter schlägt, soll getödtet
16 werden. — Wer einen Menschen stiehlt und verkauft ihn,
und er ward gefunden in seiner Hand, der soll getödtet werden.—
17 Wer seinem Vater oder seiner Mutter flucht, soll getödtet werden.

18 Wenn Leute hadern, und einer schlägt den Andern mit einem
Steine oder mit der Faust, und er stirbt nicht, aber er fällt aufs
19 Lager; || wenn er aufstehet und wandelt auf der Straße an
seinem Stabe: so wird der Schläger frei; nur seine Versäumniß
soll er erstatten, und ihn heilen lassen.

20 Schlägt Jemand seinen Knecht oder seine Magd mit dem
Zuchtstocke, und er stirbt unter seiner Hand: so soll es gerächet
21 werden. || Aber wenn er einen Tag oder zwei Tage sich erhält,
soll es nicht gerächet werden; denn es ist sein Geld.

22 Wenn Leute sich mit einander schlagen, und verletzen ein
schwangeres Weib, daß ihr die Kinder abgehen, und ihr kein
Schaden geschieht: so soll er an Geld gestraft werden, wie der
Ehemann des Weibes ihm auflegt, und er gebe es nach richter-
23 lichem Ausspruche. || Wenn ihr aber Schade geschehen: so gieb
24 Leben um Leben, || Aug' um Auge, Zahn um Zahn, Hand
25 um Hand, Fuß um Fuß, || Brandmahl um Brandmahl,
Wunde um Wunde, Beule um Beule. **)

---

*) oder: Hat er ihm nicht nachgestellt . . .

**) Es wird ihm aber eine Geldbuße dafür auferlegt; wie aus V. 30 erhellet.

Figure 7. Exodus 21:9–25 from Joseph Johlson, *Torah Nevi'im Veketuvim*: *Die heiligen Schriften der Israeliten* (Frankfurt am Main: Ändreäischen Buchhandlung, 1831), 160.

94 משפטים

Das zweite Buch Mose. Cap. 21.

7. Wenn aber Jemand seine Tochter verkauft zur Magd: so soll sie nicht ausgehen, wie die Knechte ausgehen. 8. So sie jedoch misfällig ist in den Augen ihres Herrn, daß er sie nicht für sich bestimmt: so soll er sie losgeben; aber an ein fremdes Volk ist er nicht ermächtigt, sie zu verkaufen, da er treulos gegen sie ist. 9. Und so er sie für seinen Sohn bestimmt: so soll er nach dem Rechte der Töchter an ihr thun. 10. So er sich eine andere nehmen wird: so soll er ihren Unterhalt, ihre Kleidung und ihre Wohnung nicht vermindern. 11. So er aber jene drei nicht für sie thut: so soll sie umsonst ausgehen, ohne Entgeld.

12. Wer einen Menschen schlägt, daß er stirbt, soll getödtet werden. 13. So er ihm aber nicht nachgestellt, und der Herr hat ihn in seine Hand fallen lassen: so werde ich dir einen Ort setzen, wohin er fliehen soll.

14. Wenn aber Jemand frevelt an seinem Nächsten, daß er ihn erschlage mit Hinterlist: von meinem Altare hinweg sollst du ihn nehmen, daß er sterbe.

15. Und wer da schlägt seinen Vater oder seine Mutter, soll getödtet werden.

16. Wer einen Menschen stiehlt, mag er ihn verkaufen, oder werde er in seiner Gewalt gefunden, er soll getödtet werden.

17. Wer da flucht seinem Vater, oder seiner Mutter, soll getödtet werden.

18. Wenn Männer streiten und es schlägt einer den andern mit dem Stein, oder mit der Faust, daß er nicht stirbt, aber bettlägrig wird: 19. So er aufkommt und ausgehet an seinem Stabe: so soll der Schläger frei sein; nur seine Versäumniß soll er geben und heilen soll er ihn lassen.

ש׳ 20. Wenn Jemand schlägt seinen Knecht, oder seine Magd, mit dem Stabe, daß er stirbt unter seiner Hand: so soll es gerochen werden. 21. Jedoch wenn er einen, oder zwei Tage aufrecht bleibt: so soll es nicht gerochen werden, denn sein Geld ist es.

22. Und wenn sich Männer hadern nnd stoßen ein schwangeres Weib, daß ihr die Kinder abgehen, aber kein Schaden geschieht: so soll er an Gelde gestraft werden, so viel ihm auflegen wird der Ehemann des Weibes, und er giebt es durch Schiedsrichter. 23. Wenn aber Schaden geschieht; so sollst du Seele um Seele geben, 24. Auge um Auge, Zahn um Zahn, Hand um Hand, Fuß um Fuß, 25. Brandmaal um Brandmaal, Wunde um Wunde, Beule um Beule.

26. Wenn Jemand schlägt das Auge seines Knechtes, oder das Auge seiner Magd, und verderbt es: so soll er ihn als frei entlassen für sein Auge. 27. Und wenn er den Zahn seines Knechtes, oder den Zahn seiner Magd, ausschlägt: so soll er ihn als frei entlassen für seinen Zahn.

28. Wenn ein Ochse stößt einen Mann oder ein Weib, daß sie sterben: so soll der Ochse gesteinigt werden, und sein Fleisch darf nicht gegessen werden; jedoch der Herr des Ochsen ist schuldlos. 29. Wenn aber der Ochse stößig gewesen seit gestern und vorgestern, und sein Herr ist gewarnt worden, er hat ihn aber nicht gehütet, und nun tödtete er einen Mann, oder ein Weib: so soll der Ochse gesteinigt werden und auch sein Herr soll getödtet werden. 30. So ihm aber ein Lösegeld aufgelegt wird: so soll er geben die Lösung seiner Person, so viel, wie ihm aufgelegt wurde. 31. Ob er einen Sohn stößt, oder eine Tochter stößt, nach diesem Rechte soll ihm geschehen. 32. Wenn einen Knecht der Ochse stößt, oder eine Magd, so soll man dreißig Schekel Silber seinem

Figure 8. Exodus 21:7–32 from Gotthold Salomon, *Torah Nevi'im Ketuvim oder Deutsche Volks-und Schul-Bibel für Israeliten* (Altona: Johann Friedrich Hammerich, 1837), 94.

428 2 Mos. 12, 15—25. שמות משפטים כא׳ טו־כה תכח

aber Einer frevelt an seinem Nächsten, indem er ihn mordet mit Hinterlist, von meinem Altare sollst du ihn wegnehmen zu sterben. 15. Und wer seinen Vater oder seine Mutter schlägt, soll getödtet werden. 16. Und wer einen Menschen stiehlt, und ihn verkauft, oder er wird gefunden in seiner Hand, der soll getödtet werden. 17. Und wer seinem Vater oder seiner Mutter flucht, soll getödtet werden. 18. Und so Männer sich streiten, und einer schlägt den Andern mit einem Steine oder mit der Faust, und er stirbt nicht, fällt aber auf's Lager: 19. steht er wieder auf und wandelt auf der Straße an seinem Stabe, so ist der Schläger frei, nur Versäumniß soll er erstatten und ihn heilen lassen. 20. Und so Jemand seinen Knecht oder seine Magd schlägt mit dem Stocke, und er stirbt unter seiner Hand: so soll es gerochen werden. 21. Doch wenn er einen oder zwei Tage leben bleibt, soll es nicht gerochen werden, denn es ist sein Geld. 22. Und so Männer sich zanken, und stoßen ein schwangeres Weib, daß ihr die Kinder abgehen, es ist aber kein Schaden geschehen: so soll er an Geld gebüßt werden, so viel ihm der Mann des Weibes auflegt, und gebe es vor Schiedsrichtern. 23. Ist aber Schaden geschehen, so gieb Leben um Leben, 24. Auge um Auge, Zahn um Zahn, Hand um Hand, Fuß um Fuß, 25. Brandmal um Brandmal, Wunde

אִישׁ עַל־רֵעֵהוּ לְהָרְגוֹ בְעָרְמָה מֵעִם
מִזְבְּחִי תִּקָּחֶנּוּ לָמוּת׃ ס (טו) וּמַכֵּה
אָבִיו וְאִמּוֹ מוֹת יוּמָת׃ ס (טז) וְגֹנֵב
אִישׁ וּמְכָרוֹ וְנִמְצָא בְיָדוֹ מוֹת יוּמָת׃
ס (יז) וּמְקַלֵּל אָבִיו וְאִמּוֹ מוֹת
יוּמָת׃ ס (יח) וְכִי־יְרִיבֻן אֲנָשִׁים
וְהִכָּה־אִישׁ אֶת־רֵעֵהוּ בְּאֶבֶן אוֹ בְאֶגְרֹף
וְלֹא יָמוּת וְנָפַל לְמִשְׁכָּב׃ (יט) אִם־יָקוּם
וְהִתְהַלֵּךְ בַּחוּץ עַל־מִשְׁעַנְתּוֹ וְנִקָּה הַמַּכֶּה
רַק שִׁבְתּוֹ יִתֵּן וְרַפֹּא יְרַפֵּא׃ ס [שני]
(כ) וְכִי־יַכֶּה אִישׁ אֶת־עַבְדּוֹ אוֹ אֶת־
אֲמָתוֹ בַּשֵּׁבֶט וּמֵת תַּחַת יָדוֹ נָקֹם יִנָּקֵם׃
(כא) אַךְ אִם־יוֹם אוֹ יוֹמַיִם יַעֲמֹד לֹא
יֻקַּם כִּי כַסְפּוֹ הוּא׃ ס (כב) וְכִי־
יִנָּצוּ אֲנָשִׁים וְנָגְפוּ אִשָּׁה הָרָה וְיָצְאוּ
יְלָדֶיהָ וְלֹא יִהְיֶה אָסוֹן עָנוֹשׁ יֵעָנֵשׁ
כַּאֲשֶׁר יָשִׁית עָלָיו בַּעַל הָאִשָּׁה וְנָתַן
בִּפְלִלִים׃ (כג) וְאִם־אָסוֹן יִהְיֶה וְנָתַתָּה
נֶפֶשׁ תַּחַת נָפֶשׁ׃ (כד) עַיִן תַּחַת עַיִן
שֵׁן תַּחַת שֵׁן יָד תַּחַת יָד רֶגֶל תַּחַת
רָגֶל׃ (כה) כְּוִיָּה תַּחַת כְּוִיָּה פֶּצַע תַּחַת

Dienst verrichtet. Es bezieht sich aber darauf, daß der Altar im Alterthum (s. z.B. die Erzählung von Lysimachus' Flucht in den Tempel, und wie man diesen zumauerte, um jenen durch Hunger zu tödten, bei Cornel, auch nach dem christlich-kanonischen Rechte,) eine Freistatt selbst des Verbrechens war. So befiehlt Schelomoh den Joab, der den Altar umfaßt hatte, trotzdem zu tödten, weil er Abner mit Hinterlist getödtet hatte, (also ganz nach unserm V. 1 K. 2, 18—34.). Also selbst der Altar des Herrn sollte der Vergeltung für vorsätzlichen Mord kein Hinderniß in den Weg legen; wie sehr hierdurch auch priesterlicher Unfug hintertrieben wurde, ist einsichtlich. — 15—17. Es werden hier gleich drei Verbrechen angeführt, die mit dem Tode ebenfalls bestraft werden sollten, also vorsätzlichem Morde gleich gestellt wurden; 1) Eltern schlagen (s. Anm. zu 20, 12. nach der Trad.: sobald eine sichtliche Verletzung bewirkt wurde Sanhedr. 85. 2. Midr., מות יומת stets „erdrosseln," wenn keine nähere Bestimmung); 2) einen Menschen stehlen, s. zu V. 37.; 3) Eltern fluchen (s. Anm. zu 20, 12. nach der Trad. selbst nach dem Tode der Eltern; ausgenommen ein Unmündiger, darum 3 M. 20, 9. איש איש; weil eben daselbst דמיו בו dabei steht, dies aber immer „steinigen" bedeute, auch hier diese Todesstrafe. Sanhedr. 85. 2 ff.). — 18. „Er fällt auf's Lager," er wird krank in Folge der Schläge. — 19. „So ist der Schläger frei," nach Raschi, Rabe u. A. er wird aus dem Gefängnisse entlassen, in welches er unterdeß gebracht worden, der Midr. aber „er ist frei von der Todesstrafe." — 20. 21. S. Anm. zu V. 2. נקם ינקם nach der Trad. mit dem Schwerte hingerichtet, und daß es auch eine Todesstrafe bezeichnet, ist aus dem Gegensatze klar. — 22—25. Die Einmischung der Frauen in den Streit der Männer, um sie auseinander zu bringen, oder um zu helfen, wird auch 5 M. 25, 11. 12. vorausgesetzt. Hier wird für die Schonung einer schwan-

Figure 9. Exodus 21:15–25 from the second edition of Ludwig Philippson, *Mikra Torah Nevi'im Ketuvim: Die Israelitische Bible; Hamishah Humshei Torah: Der Pentateuch* (1844; Leipzig: Baumgarten, 1858), 428.

243 שמות כא משפטים

24. Auge Ersatz für Auge, Zahn Ersatz für Zahn; Hand Ersatz für Hand, Fuß Ersatz für Fuß.

25. Brand Ersatz für Brand, Wunde Ersatz für Wunde; Geschwulst Ersatz für Geschwulst.

24. עַיִן תַּחַת עַיִן שֵׁן תַּחַת שֵׁן יָד
תַּחַת יָד רֶגֶל תַּחַת רָגֶל׃

25. כְּוִיָּה תַּחַת כְּוִיָּה פֶּצַע תַּחַת
פָּצַע חַבּוּרָה תַּחַת חַבּוּרָה׃ ס

In allen solchen Fällen müßte es zweifelsohne: ולקחת heißen, daß dem Mörder das verwirkte Leben genommen werde. ונתתה läßt die Strafe geradezu als „Restitution" begreifen, sei es nun der Gerechtigkeit, des Gesetzes, der im Ermordeten verletzten Menschenwürde, oder aller dieser ohnehin in einander fallenden Momente zusammen. Die Gesamtheit hat den durch das Verbrechen verletzten Momenten das Leben des Verbrechers hinzugeben. In diesem Ausdruck liegt zugleich, daß das Leben des Einzelnen Gott und der Gesamtheit angehöre, und daß mit jedem Tode, auch mit dem des Mörders, die Gesamtheit einen Verlust erleide, der aber von der Pflicht der Restitution überwogen wird.

V. 24. Die in diesem Verse genannten Fälle sind Verstümmelungen, Beraubungen eines Organes, und zwar sind die Repräsentanten der verschiedensten Thätigkeiten genannt: das Auge: Organ der Sinnesthätigkeit, Zahn: der Körpererhaltung (Verdauung), auch des Sprechens, Hand: der produktiven Thätigkeit, Fuß: der Bewegung, und zwar hebt der Verlust eines Auges und eines Zahnes nicht die entsprechende Thätigkeit ganz auf, sondern schwächt sie nur, während der Verlust einer Hand und eines Fußes in der Regel eine bis dahin möglich gewesene Thätigkeit völlig aufhebt. Der durch solche Verstümmelung dem Beschädigten gebrachte bleibende Verlust wird unter den gesetzlichen Begriff: נזק, Schaden, gefaßt. —

V. 25. Die in diesem Verse besprochenen Beschädigungen sind: Verwundungen ohne bleibende Verstümmelung. כויה, Brand, wird (B. K. 84 b) als Repräsentant des einfachen Schmerzes, צער, gefaßt. Es ist dafür „Brennen" gewählt, weil sich damit, z. B. durch Führen eines glühenden Eisens über den Fingernagel, die Bewirkung eines Schmerzes ohne jede Verletzung darstellen läßt. פצע (verwandt mit פצה, פצח, öffnen) ist die klaffende Wunde. חבורה, (von חבר, verbunden sein) weist auf die geschlossene Wunde hin. Es kommt jedoch in Verbindung mit פצע vor: חברות פצע תמרוק ברע (Prov. 20, 30), und danach scheint es die weiterreichenden Folgen einer Wunde, somit Entzündung, dem Worte nach: Geschwulst zu bedeuten. (מרק, verwandt mit מרג, Dreschgerät, heißt: tief eindringen, daher ומרק ושטף מריקה בחמין שטיפה בצונן Sebachim 97 a. תמרוקי נשים: eindringliche Hautpflege.) Es heißt dort: „Nicht die offene Wunde, die dadurch hervorgerufenen Entzündungsgeschwülste sind das mit Gefahr Eindringende." Demgemäß hätten wir hier die Verwundung in ihren drei aufeinander folgenden Fortschritten: der Schmerz, der Schnitt, die Entzündung.

עין תחת עין וגו' וגו'. Die Konsequenzen, welche die buchstäbliche Auffassung dieses Rechtskanons in dem Sinne, daß dem Beschädiger eines Auges das Auge u. s. w. geschädigt werde, zu einer moralischen Unmöglichkeit machen würden, wie z. B. wenn ein Einäugiger einem Zweiäugigen ein Auge ausgeschlagen, wie der Bestrafte an einer Verwundung sterben könne, die dem Beschädigten nur den Verlust eines Gliedes gebracht, sind schon B. K. 83 b f. hervorgehoben. Es ist ebenso bereits bemerkt worden, wie schon die oben V. 18 u. 19 gegebene Bestimmung, daß bei Verletzungen, die bettlägerig machen und ärztliche Behandlung erfordern, Versäumnis und Heilung ersetzt werden sollen, die Auffassung des עין תחת עין וגו' פצע תחת פצע וגו' als jus talionis zurückweisen müsse, da ja die gleiche Wiederverletzung des Beschädigers diesen ebenfalls bettlägerig und ärzt=

16*

Figure 10. Exodus 21:24–25 from the third edition of Samson Raphael Hirsch, *Hamishah Humshei Torah: Der Pentateuch* (1869; Frankfurt am Main, 1899), 243.

so viel ihm auflegt der Ehemann des
Weibes, und er es geben durch die
Richter[4]. 23. Wenn aber ein Unfall[1]
entsteht, so gieb Leben um Leben[2], 24.
Auge um Auge, Zahn um Zahn, Hand
um Hand, Fuß um Fuß[1], 25. Brandmal um Brandmal, Wunde um Wunde,
Beule um Beule[1]. 26. Und wenn
Jemand schlägt ins Auge seines Knechtes oder ins Auge seiner Magd, und
verderbt es, so soll er ihn zur Freiheit entlassen für sein Auge[1]. 27. Und
wenn er den Zahn seines Knechtes
oder den Zahn seiner Magd ausschlägt,
so soll er ihn zur Freiheit entlassen
für seinen Zahn. 28. Und wenn ein
Ochse[1] stößt einen Mann oder ein
Weib, daß er stirbt: so werde der
Ochse gesteinigt[2] und sein Fleisch nicht
gegessen[3], aber der Herr des Ochsen
bleibt ungestraft. 29. Wenn es aber
ein stößiger Ochse war von gestern
und ehegestern, und sein Herr ist gewarnt[1] worden und er wollte ihn nicht
hüten, und er tödtet einen Mann oder
ein Weib, so soll der Ochse gesteinigt
werden, und auch sein Herr soll sterben[2]. 30. Wenn ihm eine Sühne auf-

יָשִׁית עָלָיו בַּעַל הָאִשָּׁה וְנָתַן
בִּפְלִלִים׃ כג וְאִם־אָסוֹן יִהְיֶה
וְנָתַתָּה נֶפֶשׁ תַּחַת נָפֶשׁ׃ כד עַיִן
תַּחַת עַיִן שֵׁן תַּחַת שֵׁן יָד תַּחַת
יָד רֶגֶל תַּחַת רָגֶל׃ כה כְּוִיָּה
תַּחַת כְּוִיָּה פֶּצַע תַּחַת פָּצַע חַבּוּרָה
תַּחַת חַבּוּרָה׃ ס כו וְכִי־
יַכֶּה אִישׁ אֶת־עֵין עַבְדּוֹ אוֹ־אֶת־
עֵין אֲמָתוֹ וְשִׁחֲתָהּ לַחָפְשִׁי
יְשַׁלְּחֶנּוּ תַּחַת עֵינוֹ׃ כז וְאִם־שֵׁן
עַבְדּוֹ אוֹ־שֵׁן אֲמָתוֹ יַפִּיל לַחָפְשִׁי
יְשַׁלְּחֶנּוּ תַּחַת שִׁנּוֹ׃ פ
כח וְכִי־יִגַּח שׁוֹר אֶת־אִישׁ אוֹ
אֶת־אִשָּׁה וָמֵת סָקוֹל יִסָּקֵל הַשּׁוֹר
וְלֹא יֵאָכֵל אֶת־בְּשָׂרוֹ וּבַעַל הַשּׁוֹר
נָקִי׃ כט וְאִם שׁוֹר נַגָּח הוּא
מִתְּמֹל שִׁלְשֹׁם וְהוּעַד בִּבְעָלָיו וְלֹא
יִשְׁמְרֶנּוּ וְהֵמִית אִישׁ אוֹ אִשָּׁה
הַשּׁוֹר יִסָּקֵל וְגַם־בְּעָלָיו יוּמָת׃
ל אִם־כֹּפֶר יוּשַׁת עָלָיו וְנָתַן פִּדְיֹן

22. [1] ינצו s. zu 2, 13. [2] Der Frau. [3] Für die Kinder. [4] Die Richter sollen diese Geldstrafe gutheißen, oder mildern.

23. [1] Der Frau. [2] N. E. heißt dies eigentlich das Leben, n. A. soll er nur den Werth des Lebens ersetzen, da er die Frau doch nicht absichtlich tödtete (Talm. Sanh. 79.).

24. [1] Da ausdrücklich nur beim Mörder untersagt ist, ihn bloß mit Erstattung des Werthes des Umgebrachten zu strafen 4 M. 35, 31., so ist hier wahrsch. kein eigentliches Wiedervergeltungsrecht (Talion) gemeint, zumal es meist unmöglich ist, z. B. wenn ein Blinder ein Auge ausschlägt; es ist daher (n. Talmud Babakama 83, Ebn Esra u. Raschi) der Sinn: Er muß den Werth der beispielsweise genannten, und ebenso überhaupt aller verletzten Glieder der Frau bezahlen, was auch aus 3 M. 24, 18. erhellt. Solchen Schadenersatz haben die Richter zu bestimmen.

25. [1] In allen diesen Fällen hat er nach dem Talmud den Schaden, die Versäumniß, die Heilung, die Schande und den Schmerz (נזק שבת רפוי בשת וצער) zu zahlen.

26. [1] Nach talmud. Erklär. gilt dies nur für den nicht-israel. Sklaven. Dem israel. Sklaven muß er wie dem freien Mitbürger die zu V. 25. genannten Dinge vergüten, wogegen jener aber keine Freiheit hierdurch erhält, da sie ihm nach dem 6. oder mit dem Jobeljahr wird. Dasselbe gilt bei der israel. Sklavin. Auge u. V. 27. Zahn sind beispielsweise als die stärksten und geringsten Verletzungen genannt.

28. [1] Der Ochse ist nur beispielsweise genannt, weil es bei ihm gewöhnlich war, es gilt dasselbe aber eben so bei jedem Thiere. [2] Am unvernünftigen Thiere wird das Menschenblut gerächt, um den Menschen den Mord desto abscheulicher darzustellen, wie daher auch andere alte Gesetzgeber Thiere und selbst leblose Werkzeuge des Mordes verurtheilten. Aus demselben Grunde soll [3] (nach Philo) des Ochsen „Fleisch nicht gegessen" werden, das n. d. Talm. nicht einmal wie sonst ein Aas den Hunden gegeben od. irgend benutzt werden durfte.

29. [1] הועד d. h. es sind Zeugen der Verwarnung da. Von diesem Ausdrucke heißt im Talmud ein solcher Ochse: מועד, der nichtstößige des vorigen V. aber תָּם. [2] Nach

Figure 11. Exodus 21:23–30 from the second edition of Salomon Herxheimer, *Torah Nevi'im Ketuvim: Die vier und zwanzig Bücher der Bible*; *Torah: Der Pentateuch oder die fünf Bücher Mose's* (1840; Bernberg: F.W. Gröning, 1854), 287.

nur sein Feiernmüssen ersetze er und lasse ihn heil
ausheilen.

Wenn jemand seinen Knecht oder seine Magd mit dem
Stock schlägt und er stirbt unter seiner Hand,
sühngerecht werd es gesühnt;
besteht ers aber noch einen Tag oder zwei Tage,
werde es nicht gesühnt, denn sein eigen Geld ists.

Wenn sich Männer raufen und treffen ein schwangres
Weib, daß ihr die Kinder abgehn, aber es geschieht
nicht das Ärgste,
wird er mit Bußgeld gebüßt, wie der Gatte des Weibs
ihm ansetzt, doch gebe er nur nach Schiedspruch.
Geschieht das Ärgste aber,
dann wende an: Leben statt Leben –
Auge statt Auge, Zahn statt Zahn, Hand statt Hand,
Fuß statt Fuß, Brandmal statt Brandmal, Wunde
statt Wunde, Strieme statt Strieme.

Wenn jemand das Auge seines Knechts oder das Auge
seiner Magd schlägt und verdirbt es,
entlasse er ihn in die Ledigung anstatt seines Augs;
bricht er den Zahn seines Knechts oder den Zahn seiner Magd ab,
entlasse er ihn in die Ledigung anstatt seines Zahns.

Wenn ein Ochs einen Mann stößt oder ein Weib, daß
es stirbt,
gesteinigt werde, gesteinigt der Ochs, sein Fleisch werde nicht gegessen,

Figure 12. Exodus 21:19–28 from Martin Buber and Franz Rosenzweig, *Die Schrift: Die fünf Bücher der Weisung: Das Buch Namen* (Berlin: Lambert Schneider, 1926), 86.

125 תהלים כב

2. Mein Gott mein Gott! Wozu hast du mich verlassen, sind fern von meiner Hilfe die Worte meines Angstgeschrei's!

3. Mein Gott! Ich rufe Tages und du antwortest nicht, Nachts und keine Beruhigung wird mir.

2. אֵלִי אֵלִי לָמָה עֲזַבְתָּנִי רָחוֹק מִישׁוּעָתִי דִּבְרֵי שַׁאֲגָתִי׃

3. אֱלֹהַי אֶקְרָא יוֹמָם וְלֹא תַעֲנֶה וְלַיְלָה וְלֹא־דוּמִיָּה לִי׃

---

seins (von ליל, לולאה), die Zeit bedeutet, in welcher die Gegenstände ununterscheidbar,
ungeschieden für die Erkenntniß sind, dagegen בקר die Zeit der Unterscheidung (לא יבקר
בין טוב לרע 3. B. M. 27, 33), ist שחר die Zeit des Tagesanbruchs, der Morgendämmerung,
die Zeit des „Suchens" (שוחר טוב Prov. 11, 27), in welcher sich die Gegenstände noch
nicht von selbst dem Blick klar geschieden darstellen, in welcher man sie jedoch bereits in
Folge „suchenden" Bemühens erkennen kann. (Siehe Pent. 1. B. M. S. 312). Dieser
Psalm spricht die Stärkung aus, die das Bewußtsein des bald anbrechenden Morgens
dem noch von tiefer Nacht Umfangenen gewährt. Es ist Israel, Israel in tiefster Galuthnacht, dessen Gedanken und Gefühlen dieser Psalm Ausdruck verleiht. Die Leidensnacht
umfängt es in tiefster, mitternächtlicher Schwärze des drohendsten Untergangs, B. 7–17.
Es fühlt sich von Gott verlassen, B. 1–3; trägt gleichwohl das Bewußtsein in sich, daß
seine Beziehung zu Gott nicht aufgehört, B. 4; und wie es sich B. 5. 6. des Beistands
erinnert, den seine Väter in allen Nöthen von Gott gefunden, so pflegt es B. 18 mitten
im Anblick seiner Feinde das Gedächtniß alles Dessen, was bis dahin seine Stärke und
seine Stütze gebildet, und das giebt ihm, B. 19—22, die alle äußern Verluste verschmerzende
Kraft und Zuversicht auf die kommende Rettung von Gott, und es feiert dann B. 23–32
die es erhebende Aussicht, wie es eben durch Gottes-Erfahrung in solchen Leiden befähigt
wird, Gott-Verkünder für die Folgegeschlechter seines eignen engern Kreises, so wie für
die Zukunft der Gesammtmenschheit zu werden, die, zur Huldigung der Gottesherrschaft
gebracht, in dieser Selbstunterordnung unter Gottes Willen erst zu dem Genusse der auf
Erden zu erreichenden Glückseligkeit und des wahren Lebens gelangen wird. Diese Ahnung
der aus der jüdischen Galuthnacht sich entwickelnden lichtvollen Zukunft ist der שחר, ist
die ahnungsreiche Morgendämmerung, welche die vorausgeworfenen Strahlen des
kommenden jüdischen und Völker-Tages bewirken.

B. 2. אלי אלי, den ich als Quelle meiner Kraft (זה אלי ואנוהו), erkannt und der sich
mir auch als solche bewährt hat. לָמָּה: zu welchem Zwecke, nicht לָמָּה: aus welchem
Grunde (siehe Pent. 2. B. M. 32, 11. 12). Es ist nicht die Frage „Warum?" Israel's
Pflichtvergessenheit ist hinreichender Grund. Allein Gottes Verheißung ואף גם זאת וגו׳
(3. B. M. 26, 44), daß demungeachtet Gottes Bund mit Israel und die darauf ge-
gründeten Ziele nicht aufhören werden, rechtfertigt die Frage nach dem Zweck der gänz-
lichen Verlassenheit, in welcher Israel in gesteigertem Galuthleiden sich fühlt. רחוק וגו׳,
das למה bezieht sich auch auf diesen zweiten Satz. Da das Prädikat רחוק vor dem Subjekt
דברי steht, so ist die Einzahl nicht auffallend. Es kann auch מקור sein, und wäre dann
soviel als ירחקו. Wozu bleiben die Worte meines Schreiens fern von der ersehnten Hilfe?
B. 3. אלדי וגו׳. Ich rufe Tages und sehe keine Spur der Erhörung in den Ereignissen
des Tages, ich rufe Nachts und gewahre keine Wirkung meines Emporrichtens zu dir in

Figure 13. Psalm 22:2–3 from the first edition of Samson Raphael Hirsch, *Sefer Tehilim: Die Psalmen* (Frankfurt am Main: J. Kauffmann, 1882), 125.

וַיֹּאמֶר מֶה עָשִׂיתָ קוֹל דְּמֵי אָחִיךָ צֹעֲקִים אֵלַי מִן־הָאֲדָמָה׃

Figure 14. Genesis 4:10 with Masoretic notation.

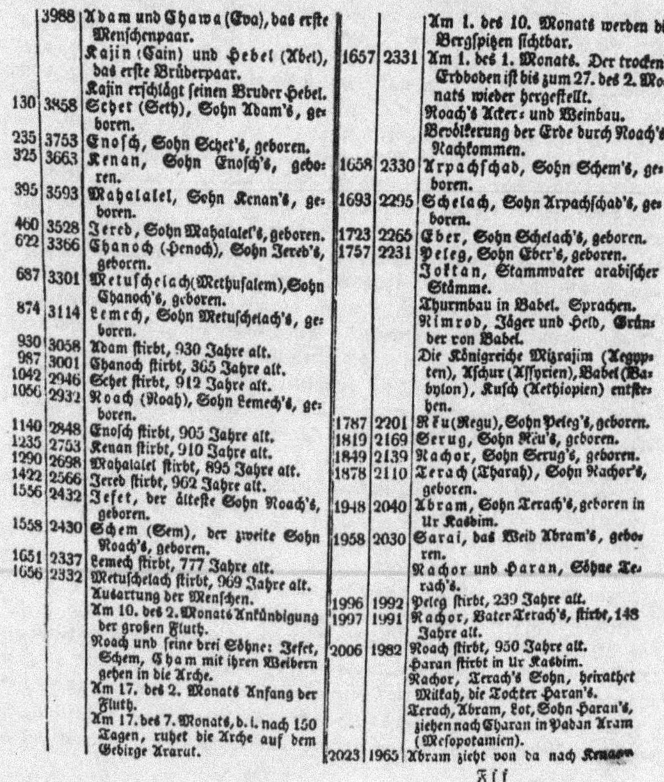

Zeittafel

über die gesammte heilige Schrift,

von Dr. Zunz.

Anmerkung. Die Zahlen in der ersten Columne bezeichnen die Jahre seit der Schöpfung; die in der zweiten die Jahre vor dem Anfang der üblichen Zeitrechnung.

	3988	Adam und Chawa (Eva), das erste Menschenpaar.
		Kajin (Cain) und Hebel (Abel), das erste Brüderpaar.
		Kajin erschlägt seinen Bruder Hebel.
130	3858	Schet (Seth), Sohn Adam's, geboren.
235	3753	Enosch, Sohn Schet's, geboren.
325	3663	Kenan, Sohn Enosch's, geboren.
395	3593	Mahalalel, Sohn Kenan's, geboren.
460	3528	Jered, Sohn Mahalalel's, geboren.
622	3366	Chanoch (Henoch), Sohn Jered's, geboren.
687	3301	Metuschelach (Methusalem), Sohn Chanoch's, geboren.
874	3114	Lemech, Sohn Metuschelach's, geboren.
930	3058	Adam stirbt, 930 Jahre alt.
987	3001	Chanoch stirbt, 365 Jahre alt.
1042	2946	Schet stirbt, 912 Jahre alt.
1056	2932	Noach (Noah), Sohn Lemech's, geboren.
1140	2848	Enosch stirbt, 905 Jahre alt.
1235	2753	Kenan stirbt, 910 Jahre alt.
1290	2698	Mahalalel stirbt, 895 Jahre alt.
1422	2566	Jered stirbt, 962 Jahre alt.
1556	2432	Jefet, der älteste Sohn Noach's, geboren.
1558	2430	Schem (Sem), der zweite Sohn Noach's, geboren.
1651	2337	Lemech stirbt, 777 Jahre alt.
1656	2332	Metuschelach stirbt, 969 Jahre alt.
		Ausartung der Menschen.
		Am 10. des 2. Monats Ankündigung der großen Fluth.
		Noach und seine drei Söhne: Jefet, Schem, Cham mit ihren Weibern gehen in die Arche.
		Am 17. des 2. Monats Anfang der Fluth.
		Am 17. des 7. Monats, d. i. nach 150 Tagen, ruhet die Arche auf dem Gebirge Ararat.
		Am 1. des 10. Monats werden die Bergspitzen sichtbar.
1657	2331	Am 1. des 1. Monats. Der trockene Erdboden ist bis zum 27. des 2. Monats wieder hergestellt.
		Noach's Acker- und Weinbau.
		Bevölkerung der Erde durch Noach's Nachkommen.
1658	2330	Arpachschad, Sohn Schem's, geboren.
1693	2295	Schelach, Sohn Arpachschad's, geboren.
1723	2265	Eber, Sohn Schelach's, geboren.
1757	2231	Peleg, Sohn Eber's, geboren.
		Joktan, Stammvater arabischer Stämme.
		Thurmbau in Babel. Sprachen.
		Nimrod, Jäger und Held, Gründer von Babel.
		Die Königreiche Mizrajim (Aegypten), Aschur (Assyrien), Babel (Babylon), Kusch (Aethiopien) entstehen.
1787	2201	Reu (Regu), Sohn Peleg's, geboren.
1819	2169	Serug, Sohn Reu's, geboren.
1849	2139	Nachor, Sohn Serug's, geboren.
1878	2110	Terach (Tharah), Sohn Nachor's, geboren.
1948	2040	Abram, Sohn Terach's, geboren in Ur Kasdim.
1958	2030	Sarai, das Weib Abram's, geboren.
		Nachor und Haran, Söhne Terach's.
1996	1992	Peleg stirbt, 239 Jahre alt.
1997	1991	Nachor, Vater Terach's, stirbt, 148 Jahre alt.
2006	1982	Noach stirbt, 950 Jahre alt.
		Haran stirbt in Ur Kasdim.
		Nachor, Terach's Sohn, heirathet Milkah, die Tochter Haran's.
		Terach, Abram, Lot, Sohn Haran's, ziehen nach Charan in Padan Aram (Mesopotamien).
2023	1965	Abram zieht von da nach [illegible]

Fff

Figure 15. *Zeittafel* (chronological table) from the twelfth edition of Leopold Zunz (ed.), *Torah Nevi'im Ketuvim: Die vier und zwanzig Bücher der Heiligen Schrift* (1838; Frankfurt am Main: J. Kauffmann, 1889), 1.

Figure 16. Photo of Raphael Hirsch (1777–1857) and Gella Hirsch (née Herz) (1786–1860) found in *Samson Raphael Hirsch-Jubiläums-Nummer* (Frankfurt am Main: Verlag des '"Israelit," 1908), 7.

Figure 17. Portrait of Isaac Bernays (1792–1849) by Siegfried Bendixen, Courtesy of Leo Baeck Institute, New York.

Figure 18. Portrait of Friedrich Schleiermacher (1768–1834) by Ernst Hader found in *The German Classics of the Nineteenth and Twentieth Centuries; Masterpieces of German Literature* vol. 5, edited by K. Francke, W. Howard, I. Singer (Albany: J.B. Lyon Company, 1913), p. 21.

Figure 19. Portrait of Jacob Ettlinger (1798–1871) by C. Fuchs, courtesy of Kedem Auction House, Ltd.

Figure 20. Portrait of Samson Raphael Hirsch as District Rabbi in Oldenburg (1830–1841), by N. Gordon, *The National Library of Israel, Abraham Schwadron Collection, ZR-0002.*

Figure 21. Portrait of Samson Raphael Hirsch as Rabbi of the Orthodox Congregation in Frankfurt am Main (1851–1888), *The National Library of Israel, Abraham Schwadron Collection, AR-0005.*

dert seien die Wasser von der Erde. 12. Und
er harrete noch sieben andere Tage, und entsandte
die Taube, aber sie kehrte nicht wieder zu ihm zurück.
13. Da war es im sechshundert und ersten Jahre,
im ersten Monat, am ersten des Monats, waren ver-
trocknet die Wasser von der Erde, und Noach that
die Decke der Arche hinweg, und schauete hin, und
siehe, getrocknet war die Fläche des Erdbodens.
14. Und im zweiten Monat, am sieben und zwan-
zigsten Tage des Monats war die Erde gänzlich
trocken. 15. Da redete Gott zu Noach und sprach:
16. Gehe aus der Arche, du und dein Weib und
deine Söhne und die Weiber deiner Söhne mit dir.
17. Alle Thiere, die bei dir sind, von allem Fleische,

כפיה וירא נח כי־קלו המים מעל הארץ׃
(יב) וייחל עוד שבעת ימים אחרים
וישלח את־היונה ולא־יספה שוב־אליו
עוד׃ (יג) ויהי באחת ושש־מאות שנה
בראשון באחד לחדש חרבו המים מעל
הארץ ויסר נח את־מכסה התבה וירא
והנה חרבו פני האדמה׃ (יד) ובחדש
השני בשבעה ועשרים יום לחדש יבשה
הארץ׃ ס [רביעי] (טו) וידבר אלהים
אל־נח לאמר׃ (טז) צא מן־התבה אתה
ואשתך ובניך ונשי־בניך אתך׃ (יז) כל־

Schrift vorkommende Namen „Ararat" bezeichnet eine Landschaft und einen Bergzug im asiatischen Hochland Armenien, die jetzt zur persischen Landschaft Erivan gehören. Die Einheimischen bezeichnen noch heute diesen Berg, wo die Arche

Berg Ararat

Noach's stehen blieb, und auf Persisch heißt er noch jetzt Kuhi Nuch (Berg Noach's). Dieser Berg ist gelegen N. B. 39° 30′ und Oe. L. 44° 30′ in der Kette des Taurus. Seine Spitze erhebt sich 17,260 F. über das Niveau des Meeres, immer mit Schnee bedeckt, von Wolken eingehüllt, Mörgens und Abends mit zaubrischem Sonnenlichte übergossen, erst ganz vor Kurzem zum ersten Male erstiegen; der Berg, wie er isolirt und entfernt von allen anderen, sich einzeln erhebt, um ihn, wie Hütten, nur kleine Hügel, bietet den prächtigsten Anblick dar; dennoch hat er zwei Spitzen, die man

Figure 22. Mount Ararat from Genesis 8:12–17 from the second edition of Ludwig Philippson, *Mikra Torah Nevi'im Ketuvim: Die Israelitische Bible; Hamishah Humshei Torah: Der Pentateuch* (1844; Leipzig: Baumgarten, 1858), 37.

PART III

NEO-ORTHODOXY

The Samson Raphael Hirsch Enigma

5
A Man of No Party

Hirsch's *Nineteen Letters on Judaism* as Bible Translation

Samson Raphael Hirsch was the most important nineteenth-century defender of German Orthodoxy. But his place on the Jewish religious spectrum has been much contested. Rabbi Hayim Ozer Grodzensky (1863–1940), an outstanding representative of Lithuanian Ultra-Orthodoxy, wrote of him in 1913:

> The great name of the genius (*hagaon*), the righteous (*hatzadik*), our teacher and rabbi, head of the rabbinical court (*av beit din*) of the Jeschurun community in Frankfurt am Main, Rabbi Samson Raphael Hirsch, may his memory be for a blessing, is known throughout Judah and Israel . . . People learned to strengthen the foundations of Judaism in Germany from him. The spirit of God was with him to prevent the entrenchment of Reform, to build a fence and stand in the breach, to rebuild what had been destroyed and to restore paths . . . Through his fiery sermons and wondrous essays many returned from sin and if his beginnings were meager, his end was very great. As one who made the public righteous, his name should be extolled from generation to generation.[1]

For the Eastern European Ultra-Orthodox Rabbi Grodzensky, Hirsch was a kindred spirit who returned Jews to the authority of halakhah by battling Reform. Yet five years earlier Rabbi Kaufmann Kohler, a radical Reformer and President of Hebrew Union College, had also extolled Hirsch:

> Samson Raphael Hirsch liberated me from the thralldom of blind authority worship and led me imperceptibly away from the old mode of thinking or rather of not thinking into the realm of free reason and research. His

[1] Grodzensky, "Approbation to *Meitav Higayon*" (Vilna, 1913), reprinted in Hirsch, *Sefer Shemesh Marpeh*, 334–335.

The Jewish Reformation. Michah Gottlieb, Oxford University Press (2021). © Oxford University Press.
DOI: 10.1093/oso/9780199336388.003.0006

> method of harmonizing modern thought with ancient thought, however fanciful, fascinated me. His lofty idealism impressed me. He made me, the yeshiva *bocher* from Mayence and Altona, a modern man. The spirit of his teachings electrified me and became a lifelong influence on me.[2]

For the radical Reformer Kohler, Hirsch was a liberator from blind submission to religious authority and a guide to modernity.[3] Who was correct? Was Hirsch closer to Ultra-Orthodoxy or to Reform? Robert Liberles expressed the difficulty of categorizing Hirsch when he wrote that "Hirsch was a puzzle for his contemporaries and has remained so for later scholars seeking to unravel the complex components of his personality."[4]

Over the next four chapters, I will unravel the enigma of Samson Raphael Hirsch. In this chapter, I will focus on the young Hirsch through the publication of his 1836 masterpiece *Nineteen Letters on Judaism* (*Neunzehn Briefe über Judenthum*). I will argue that in this period Hirsch puzzled his contemporaries because he was a self-described "man of no party" who created a new vision of German Judaism through critical dialogue with the four main German Jewish ideologies of the time: Haskalah, *Wissenschaft*, Reform, and traditionalist Judaism, and I will show how he presented this vision as a *translation* of central concepts of the Bible.

In Chapters 6, 7, and 8, I will argue that in his later career Hirsch was a puzzle because in reaction to Reform attempts to historicize the Bible and rabbinic literature, he created a sectarian Orthodox vision of Judaism that was more novel and untraditional than Mendelssohn's or Zunz's, which he expressed through his Pentateuch translation and commentary.

To understand Hirsch's early concept of Judaism, it is useful to begin with his family background and education.

Enlightened religious

In an important autobiographical passage from the *Nineteen Letters*, Hirsch writes: "You know . . . that I was educated by enlightened religious parents

[2] Kohler, "Response to Rabbi Max Heller," 211.

[3] Kohler studied with Hirsch in Frankfurt. On Kohler's relation to Hirsch, see Haberman, "Kaufmann Kohler and His Teacher Samson Raphael Hirsch."

[4] Liberles, *Religious Conflict in Social Context*, 113. Also see Katz, "Rabbi Samson Raphael Hirsch: To the Right and to the Left," 18.

(*erleuchtet religiösen Eltern*)."[5] Hirsch is here indicating that he was raised in a family committed to Mendelssohn's vision of *Haskalah*, with many members personally connected to Mendelssohn and his associates.

A key figure for Hirsch was his paternal grandfather Mendel Frankfurter (1742–1823). Frankfurter studied in the yeshiva of the legendary Rabbi Jonathan Eybeschütz (1690–1764) while also acquiring "secular knowledge and modern *Bildung*."[6] After serving as a teacher in Stuttgart, he became a merchant but remained involved in Jewish education, helping found a Talmud Torah for poor boys in Hamburg in 1805 that followed moderate maskilic educational principles. According to the school's charter, its goal was to raise pious children who would be self-supporting.[7] A report written by Frankfurter in 1812 states that the school's curriculum included instruction in Hebrew grammar, Bible with commentaries, Talmud with commentaries, orthography, arithmetic, French, and German.[8] Priority was given to study of the Bible, with only exceptional students being taught Talmud, and only after age thirteen.[9]

Frankfurter's connection with the Berlin Haskalah was more than ideological; it was personal. He had lived in Berlin and befriended Moses Mendelssohn, with whom he studied weekly, and Frankfurter prayed in Mendelssohn's home on the Sabbath.[10] Frankfurter's commitment to the "enlightened religious" path can be seen from an ethical will that he wrote for his children in 1815 at a time when Reform was stirring.

Frankfurter enjoins his children to keep his grandchildren away from the works of the "modernizers" that lead "the heart of the youth away from

[5] Hirsch, *Neunzehn Briefe über Judenthum* (henceforth; *NB*), Brief 2, 5; *The Nineteen Letters about Judaism* (henceforth: *NL*), Letter 2, 13. For the German I cite the first edition from 1836 unless otherwise indicated. I use Karin Paritzky's English translation, which I will emend frequently. On the moniker "enlightened religious," see Rosenbloom, *Tradition in an Age of Reform*, 44–56.

[6] See "Samson Raphael Hirsch: Ein Lebensbild," 7.

[7] This involved educating the children in "Torah, ethics (*mussar*), wisdom, good character traits (*midot yesharot*), and *derekh eretz*" as well as in "orthography, writing, and arithmetic," which are "greatly needed for earning a livelihood." See Assaf, *A Source Book*, 1:306, 311; Eliav, *Jewish Education*, 160. On the concept of *derekh eretz*, see pp. 276–287 of this volume.

[8] See Duckesz, "Zur Genealogie S.R. Hirsch's," 119–120. Yiddish writing was also taught. See Assaf, *A Source Book*, 1:311.

[9] Assaf, *A Source Book*, 1:308–309. The school's curriculum reflected the changing approach to education among Ashkenazim in Hamburg at the time (Hamburg also had a significant Sephardic community). In 1732, Ashkenazi Jewish education in Hamburg was administered in thirty-nine private *hadarim*, of which fourteen taught only Talmud, while the others also taught "reading and writing, Pentateuch (*Humash*), and Prophets and Writings (*Nach*). Only one *heder* taught French. See Assaf, *A Source Book*, 1:302. A report about the state of Jewish education in Hamburg at the end of the eighteenth century states that "the Polish teachers who teach only Talmud have almost disappeared." See ibid., 1:305.

[10] See Hamburger, *Pnei Tevel*, 234.

righteousness and truth." But he specifically exempts what he calls the "unimpeachable" (*unantastbar*) works of the Maskil Naphtali Herz Wessely.[11] Noah Rosenbloom correctly observes that "only an ardent admirer of the Haskalah would consider such a provision important enough to include in so important a document."[12]

Another important figure for Hirsch was his uncle Moses Hamburger (1782–1861). This uncle had adopted the name "Moses Mendelssohn Hamburger" in tribute to Mendelssohn.[13] In his work *Pnei Tevel* (*Face of the Earth*), published posthumously in 1871, Hamburger lavishes praise on Mendelssohn and Wessely, extolling their role in preserving Judaism: "Two sages Ramad [Rabbi Moses Dessau—Mendelssohn] and Ran [Rabbi Naphtali—Wessely] were pillars of their generation in Torah and wisdom and were it not for them the entire nation would have been covered in darkness."[14]

Hamburger notes that in Mendelssohn's time many rabbis considered those with any secular knowledge to be heretics, and traditional learning was in a lowly state because of the predominance of *pilpul*, the widespread ignorance of Hebrew grammar, and the fact that Bible was taught by ignorant Polish teachers.[15] According to Hamburger, Mendelssohn opened the gates of wisdom to Jews by composing his commentary on Maimonides's *Treatise on Logic* as a remedy for *pilpul* and the *Be'ur* to restore a proper understanding of the Bible. Hamburger writes that the rabbis who opposed Mendelssohn did not understand him: "Through Moses [Mendelssohn] and his translation, the crown was restored to its former glory. Had the rabbis of his day understood this, then instead of banning the translation they would have blessed and loudly praised it."[16]

Hamburger did not know Mendelssohn personally, as Mendelssohn died when he was a young child. But he knew Wessely well, reporting that he "sat before him as a student before his master for several years before his death."[17] Under Wessely's tutelage Hamburger became a prolific Hebrew poet and translator into Hebrew.[18] Hamburger's nephew Samson Raphael Hirsch

[11] Duckesz, "Zur Genealogie S.R. Hirsch's," 120–122.
[12] Rosenbloom, *Tradition in an Age of Reform*, 50.
[13] See Breuer, "Samson Raphael Hirsch," 265.
[14] Hamburger, *Pnei Tevel*, 241.
[15] Ibid., 228–230.
[16] Ibid., 230.
[17] Ibid., 239.
[18] Duckesz, "Zur Genealogie,"123. Hamburger translated Joachim Heinrich Campe's *Die Entdeckung von Amerika* (*The Discovery of America*) into Hebrew. See Rosenbloom, *Tradition in an Age of Reform*, 414, note 67.

shared his uncle's great esteem for Wessely, and according to Hamburger, Hirsch possessed several of Wessely's unpublished manuscripts.[19] Hirsch's esteem for Wessely can be discerned from his Pentateuch commentary. While Hirsch rarely cites modern commentators, he cites Wessely's commentary on Leviticus fifteen times, never disagreeing with it.[20] In Hirsch's first two citations of Wessely (Leviticus 2:12 and 3:3–5), he calls him "Rabbi Naphtali Herz Wessely נ"ע." The acronym נ"ע stands for *noho eden* (his repose be in heaven).

Writing in 1847, Hamburger recalls that in 1809 he saw German Judaism's main problem as ignorant, obscurantist Jewish traditionalists, and he had great hope that the "new generation" (*dor hadash*) pursuing secular knowledge and establishing new schools would become a "generation of knowledge" (*dor de'ah*) that would redeem German Jews. But Hamburger came to see his hope as misplaced. "Modernizers" (*mehadshim*) used their newly acquired secular knowledge not to redeem Judaism but to "blind the masses" and lead them away from the path of Torah.[21] Hamburger contrasts Reformers with Maskilim, writing that "[Mendelssohn and Wessely] sought to restore the crown of Torah and wisdom to its ancient glory and not to make a name for themselves . . . or destroy the foundations of faith as do the modernizers in our day who possess neither wisdom nor Torah."[22]

Hamburger is relentless in his criticism of Reform. He assails the Reform scholar Michael Creizenach (1789–1842) for seeking halakhic justification for radical reforms, including eliminating most Sabbath restrictions, denying the continued validity of the requirement of putting on phylacteries (*tefillin*), and permitting intermarriage, in his four-volume work *Schulchan Aruch*.[23] Hamburger's denigration of Reform culminates in his recounting a dream.[24] It is worth exploring this dream since dreams figure prominently in Hirsch's religious self-development, as we will see.[25]

[19] See Hamburger, *Pnei Tevel*, 241.

[20] See Hirsch's comments to Leviticus, 2:12; 3:3–5; 11:3; 13:4; 13:6; 13:9; 13:11; 14:41; 14:44; 20:10; 21:23; 23:11; 25:1; 27:11–12. Hirsch also begins his commentary to the rabbinic work *Pirkei Avot* by citing Wessely. See Hirsch, *Israels Gebete*, 416. Yonah Emanuel has shown that Wessely is by far the modern Bible commentator that Hirsch most often mentions. See Emanuel, *Modern Commentators and Decisors*.

[21] Hamburger, *Pnei Tevel*, 208.

[22] Ibid., 227.

[23] Ibid., 209. The four volumes of Creizenach's *Schulchan Aruch* were published between 1833 and 1840.

[24] Hamburger, *Pnei Tevel*, 213–216. Hamburger's dream recalls the work *Hatophet Vehaeden* (*Hell and Heaven*) by the thirteenth-century Italian Jewish poet Immanuel of Rome.

[25] See pp. 241–243, 297–301 of this volume.

Hamburger's dream begins with his having a vision of angels and feeling the "divine spirit" (*ru'ah elohim*) pass over him.[26] An angel then takes Hamburger by the hand, telling him that he will show him heaven and hell, and asks him where he would like to begin. Hamburger responds that he would like to first see heaven. Passing through various sections of heaven, he eventually encounters his father Mendel Frankfurter, whose "crown shone above all others."[27] Hamburger is then shown hell, which he finds populated by Reformers.

The angel next brings Hamburger to a battlefield. He hears a shout and sees an army of youths led by Creizenach holding his *Schulchan Aruch*. An opposing army rises to meet Creizenach, led by a traditionalist rabbi called "Rabbi Arsela," who is holding a Torah. Creizenach shouts at Rabbi Arsela, calling him "a sage (*talmid hakham*) without knowledge,"[28] whose Torah is all "vain pilpul." Holding up his *Schulchan Aruch*, Creizenach declares that he will use it to gouge out Rabbi Arsela's eyes and decapitate him. Rabbi Arsela responds by confessing, "I have done evil in Judah, my *hilukim*[29] are fearful, my *derashot* are empty and untrue, and it would be better had I been silent." Nevertheless, he declares that he learned true Torah and feared the word of God while Creizenach is a liar, whose book is heresy, and whose Torah is worthless. Hamburger recounts that the two armies then engaged in a heavy battle where "rivers of blood flowed like spilled water" and corpses were strewn everywhere. Creizenach was killed and his body dismembered, and only Rabbi Arsela remained, though his clothes were tattered, and his books ripped and scattered. As Hamburger moved to raise him up, he awoke.[30]

In addition to his grandfather and uncle, mention should be made of Hirsch's parents, to whom he dedicated his 1837 work *Horeb*, thanking them in the third person as "the guardians of his childhood, the guides of his youth and the friends of his mature years."[31] Hirsch's father Raphael was neither a scholar nor a poet, but a merchant. In 1807, he married Gella Hertz, and a year later Samson was born in Hamburg. Raphael's religious orientation

[26] Hamburger, *Pnei Tevel*, 213.

[27] Ibid.

[28] As we have seen, this is a rabbinic phrase from *Leviticus Rabbah* 1:15, "a carcass is better than a sage without knowledge," which Wessely provocatively used to criticize traditionalist rabbis in *Divrei Shalom Ve'emet* and which provoked a furious outcry. See pp. 84–85 of this volume.

[29] *Hiluk* is another term for *pilpul*.

[30] Hamburger, *Pnei Tevel*, 216.

[31] Hirsch, *Horev*, v.

seems to have been quite similar to his brother's and father's. As a moderate Maskil, he devoted himself primarily to studying Bible rather than Talmud, with Samson testifying that "The Bible (*Tanakh*) was a second soul (*zweite Seele*)" within him.[32] In a photo, Raphael Hirsch is shaven, a mark of maskilic tendencies, and like his brother and father he was a staunch opponent of Reform.[33] The Hamburg Reform Temple opened in 1818 when Samson was ten years old, and he later recalled that opponents of the Reform movement frequently met in his childhood home to plot strategy.[34]

Hirsch shared much of his family's evaluation of both traditionalist Judaism and Reform, though we will see that in the *Nineteen Letters* his attitude toward Reform Judaism was considerably more positive than his grandfather's and uncle's had been.

Class and Hirsch's early education

We have scant information about Hirsch's early education, but we know that he did not attend a *heder* focused on Talmud. In an autobiographical passage from the *Nineteen Letters* he writes that "from early on the tones of the Bible (*Tanakh*) spoke to my soul (*Gemüthe*) and as my intellect matured this led me from a free desire (*aus freier Lust*) to Gemara" (emphasis mine).[35] This passage shows Hirsch's early maskilic orientation in two respects. First, like the Maskilim, Hirsch's early Jewish education focused on the Bible and only later turned to Talmud. Second, Hirsch emphasizes his intellectual autonomy, noting that he only studied Gemara, "from a free desire."

The elementary school that Hirsch attended is the subject of some confusion. Rosenbloom and Grunfeld write that he studied at a German grammar school.[36] Breuer, however, writes that he attended a Jewish school led by "J.A. Isler, a competent talmudist who did most of the teaching himself including some secular subjects."[37] Breuer's source is a memoir penned by Isler's son, Meyer.[38] Meyer Isler recounts that his father Jisroel Abraham was born in

[32] Hirsch, *Gesammelte Schriften* (henceforth: GS) 1:324; *The Collected Writings* (henceforth: *CW*), 4:259.

[33] See Figure 16.

[34] Liberles, *Religious Conflict*, 115.

[35] Hirsch, *NB*, Brief 2, 5; *NL*, Letter 2, 13.

[36] Rosenbloom, *Tradition in an Age of Reform*, 53–55; Grunfeld, "Samson Raphael Hirsch: The Man and His Mission," xxiii.

[37] Breuer, "Review of *Tradition in an Age of Reform*," 141.

[38] Zimmerman, "Errinerungen des Hamburgers Bibliothekars Meyer Isler," 48–62.

1763 in Hamburg, where he received a traditional German Jewish education of near-exclusive study of Talmud with no general studies.[39] But under the influence of Maskilic ideas his father began to pursue secular knowledge with "unbelievable zeal" (*unglaublichem Eifer*) and became an autodidact, teaching himself German, French, and arithmetic. Hired as a private Hebrew tutor, he would stay to hear the lessons his students received on general subjects.[40] In 1793, Jisroel Isler opened a school. It was only the second Jewish school in Hamburg to incorporate general studies into the curriculum and his son attended it. Meyer recalls being taught arithmetic, German, French, and English in the school and receiving additional private instruction in algebra, Latin, and music.[41] He mentions nothing of the Jewish subjects taught, but it stands to reason that the school followed the maskilic model of focusing on the Bible, Hebrew, principles of religion, and ethics. We know that Hirsch attended this school because Meyer Isler tells us that one of his "best friends" from school was "Samson Hirsch now Rabbi of the separatist community in Frankfurt am Main."[42] Hirsch also received supplemental instruction from Rabbi Natan Nota Ellingen, whom Mendel Frankfurter had brought to Hamburg in 1809 to give students lessons in halakhah.[43] Hirsch studied with Rabbi Ellingen until age thirteen at the latest. For in 1821 Ellingen left Hamburg because he did not want to be subject to the city's new Chief Rabbi, Hakham Isaac Bernays, who was twenty years his junior.[44]

Why did Hirsch not attend the Talmud Torah founded by his grandfather Mendel Frankfurter? For the same reason that Mendelssohn did not send his children to the *Jüdische Freischule* in Berlin. Frankfurter established the Talmud Torah with the express purpose of helping poor students. While some wealthier families sent their children to the school, many saw doing so as a stigma, a problem that, as we have seen, Zunz sought to remedy.[45]

When Hirsch was fourteen his family apprenticed him as a merchant to groom him for a business career. But Hirsch did not find satisfaction in business and after a year enrolled in a German grammar school.[46] Though we lack explicit evidence, it is likely that he attended the St. Johannis school in

[39] Ibid., 48.
[40] Ibid., 49.
[41] Ibid., 60.
[42] Ibid., 61.
[43] See Hame'assef, "Letter from a Native of Hamburg," 28; Duckesz, *Chachme AHW*, 109–110.
[44] See Duckesz, *Chachme AHW*, 110.
[45] See p. 174 of this volume.
[46] See "Samson Raphael Hirsch: Ein Lebensbild," 8.

Hamburg because we know that in 1826 at age 18 he entered the Hamburg *Akademische Gymnasium*, which has been described as "merely a select class of the St. Johannis school," having the same mission, administration, and teachers.[47] The *Akademische Gymnasium* had a wide-ranging curriculum that included arithmetic and mathematics, history, geography, German rhetoric and poetry, French, and English. In addition, the school emphasized the study of classical languages, which included not only Greek and Latin, but also Hebrew, which the school's headmaster Johannes Gottfried Gurlitt taught using H.F.W. Gesenius's Hebrew grammar.[48] Hirsch studied at the *Akademische Gymnasium* until 1828, though he apparently did not graduate.[49]

Hirsch's guiding star

Hirsch's advanced Jewish education began in 1824 when at age sixteen he began studying with Hakham Bernays.[50] Hirsch's relationship to Bernays was formative, so a few words about Bernays are in order. Bernays was appointed the community rabbi of Hamburg in 1821 in a bid to quell the controversy over the Hamburg Reform Temple that had been dedicated three years earlier. The Hamburg Temple had introduced several innovations into the synagogue service, including prayers in the vernacular, liturgical changes, a German sermon, and choral singing accompanied by an organ played by a Gentile. These innovations led to a furious response from traditionalists, who solicited twenty-two halakhic responsa from leading rabbis all over Europe condemning the Temple's innovations.[51] Reformers responded with their own responsa defending their changes.[52] Moderate traditionalists in Hamburg then stepped forward and pushed the appointment of Bernays as community rabbi of Hamburg in the hope of stemming Reform's momentum.[53]

47 See Tasch, *Samson Raphael Hirsch*, 36. Raphael Breuer writes that Hirsch entered the academic gymnasium on April 16, 1826, with the intention of focusing on theological studies. See Breuer, *Unter seinem Banner*, 213.

48 See Tasch, *Samson Raphael Hirsch*, 37–39.

49 Tasch, *Samson Raphael Hirsch*, 48; Breuer, "Chapters in the Life of Rabbi Samson Raphael Hirsch: In Rabbi Jacob Ettlinger's Yeshiva," 56.

50 See Klugman, *Samson Raphael Hirsch*, 35.

51 These collected responsa were published in Altona 1819 under the title *Eleh Divrei Habrit* (*These are the Words of the Covenant*). A short selection from this work can be found in *JMW*, 187–189.

52 One of the most significant was Meyer Israel Bresslau's satirical *Herev Nokemet Nekam Brit* (*The Sword Which Avenges the Covenant*), which was published in Hamburg in 1819. For an excerpt, see *JMW*, 192–195.

53 Meyer, *Response to Modernity*, 53–61.

Bernays combined an outstanding talmudic education with a first-rate general education. At age seven, he knew an entire tractate of the Talmud by heart, and he later studied at the famed yeshiva of Rabbi Abraham Bing in Würzburg. He also attended the Universities of Würzburg and Munich where he studied philology, oriental studies, and philosophy. Bernays was particularly impacted by lectures he heard from the German Idealist philosopher F.W.J. Schelling.[54]

In Hamburg, Bernays fiercely opposed Reform but was willing to introduce religious reforms that he deemed halakhically permissible. He transformed the curriculum of the Hamburg Talmud Torah, greatly expanding general studies. Previously general education in the Talmud Torah had focused on reading, writing, arithmetic, and contemporary languages to prepare students for a career in commerce, but Bernays modelled the curriculum on a *Realschule*, including subjects such as science, geography, and history with the aim of preparing students to enter the professions.[55] Bernays introduced a vernacular sermon into the synagogue service, and his learned sermons included references to European philosophy, literature, and ancient mythology.[56] He wore the robes of a Protestant minister while preaching though he wore a black collar rather than a white one.[57] When, however, Bernays saw a Reform innovation as violating halakhah, he was unbending in opposing it.[58]

Hirsch studied with Bernays for four years before he left Hamburg in 1828. Two years later Bernays wrote a letter recommending Hirsch for his first rabbinic post in Oldenburg. In the letter Bernays stresses Hirsch's rabbinic credentials, writing that Hirsch attended his lectures on Talmud and practical legal religious texts (most probably the *Shulhan Arukh*), and that Bernays granted Hirsch rabbinic ordination.[59] This, however, does not give a full account of what Hirsch learned from Bernays. Hirsch attended Bernays's weekly Sabbath sermons, which often focused on linguistic analyses of the Bible and symbolic interpretations of Jewish laws and customs. He also

[54] See Bach, "Isaac Bernays," 533.

[55] See Tasch, *Samson Raphael Hirsch*, 46; Eliav, *Jewish Education*, 232–233.

[56] Bernays's congregants did not, however, always understand his references. Once Bernays mentioned the Roman God Jupiter in one of his sermons. One of the listeners asked a fellow congregant "Who is this Jupiter?" and received the reply, "I don't know, but since the Hakham mentioned him in his sermon, he must have been a distinguished Jew." See Heinemann, "The Relationship between S.R. Hirsch and His Teacher Bernays,"48–49.

[57] See Figure 17. Figure 18 is a portrait of the Protestant theologian and preacher Friedrich Schleiermacher wearing the white collar.

[58] See Heinemann, "The Relationship between S.R. Hirsch and His Teacher Bernays," 51–56.

[59] See Breuer, *Unter seinem Banner*, 218; "Hirsch Testimonial for the British Chief Rabbinate," item #3.

participated in Bernays's lectures on the Psalms and Judah Halevi's *Kuzari*, and he helped Bernays publish a new edition of the *Kuzari*.[60]

Describing his spiritual development in the *Nineteen Letters*, Hirsch employs the maskilic trope of autonomous self-formation while also mentioning his debt to Bernays: "I had to find the road to the reconstruction of Judaism as a science (*Wissenschaft*) almost entirely by myself . . . *only one star* (Stern) *hovered above me at the beginning to guide me*" (emphasis mine).[61] Most scholars agree that this "one star" is Bernays.[62]

Hirsch's countercultural decision to attend yeshiva

After leaving the *Akademische Gymnasium* in late spring 1828, Hirsch decided to attend Rabbi Jacob Ettlinger's yeshiva in Mannheim. He set out for Mannheim at the end of June but before arriving there spent twelve days traveling in and around Frankfurt. He visited the Orthodox Rabbi of Hanau, Moses Tuvia Sondheim, and the noted Hebraist Rabbi Wolf Heidenheim in Rodelheim. He dined with Baron Anselm von Rothschild and attended a meeting of Jewish Freemasons in Frankfurt. He also visited the Reformer Michael Creizenach, who had been friends with Bernays in their younger years. It was in Creizenach's home that Hirsch first met Abraham Geiger.[63] The radically different people Hirsch visited suggests that he was seeking to clarify his own religious position and was open to a wide range of viewpoints.

Hirsch arrived in Mannheim on July 12, 1828. Studying in a yeshiva was a somewhat unusual and even countercultural choice at the time. Since the

60 See Bach, "Isaac Bernays," 537; Duckesz, "Zur Biographie des Chacham Isaak Bernays," 307; "Samson Raphael Hirsch: Ein Lebensbild," 8. The new edition was published in Hanover in 1838.

61 Hirsch, *NB, Brief* 19, 106; *NL*, Letter 19, 333.

62 See Heinemann, "Samson Raphael Hirsch: The Formative Years," 30–31; Horwitz, "On Kabbala and Myth," 159; Elias, "Editor's Notes," 339. In Geiger's 1837 review of Hirsch's *NB*, he identifies the "star" as the author of *Der Bibelsche' Orient*, whom he took to be Bernays. See Geiger, "Recension der Briefe (3)," 77–78. Rosenbloom disagrees with Geiger's interpretation, but his reasons are unconvincing. See Rosenbloom, *Tradition in an Age of Reform*, 57–58. In a journal entry penned in 1832 Geiger noted Bernays's influence on Hirsch, writing that "Hirsch was moved by Bernays in Hamburg in a strange direction, and received from him excessive (*übermassig*) esteem for the Bible and absurd philology (*Afterphilologie*)." See Geiger, *Nachgelassene Schriften*, 5:18. Thirty years later, Hirsch sought to downplay Bernays's influence on him, writing that his commentary on the Pentateuch "had no immediate relationship to what I was fortunate to learn through my instructive and inspiring contact with Bernays." Instead, Hirsch claimed that what he gained from Bernays was simply "stimulation in general, and the striving to enter the halls of Torah thirsting for knowledge." See Hirsch, "Die Distellese des Herrn Kirchheim," 133.

63 See Breuer, "Chapters in the Life of Rabbi Samson Raphael Hirsch: In Rabbi Jacob Ettlinger's," 56–57; Heinemann, "Samson Raphael Hirsch: The Formative Years," 33. Hirsch mentions the visit with Creizenach in his 1838 work *Naftulei Naftali*, though he claims that he only spent a "quarter of an hour" with him. See Hirsch, *Erste und zweite Mitteillung*, iii; *CW*, 9:4.

end of eighteenth century, German yeshivot were in steep decline, with an astonishing number closing. In 1819, David Friedländer observed that important yeshivot had recently closed in Metz, Frankfurt, Fürth, Hamburg, Halberstam, and Prague, among other places.[64]

Illustrious yeshivot still existed, most notably Rabbi Akiva Eiger's yeshiva in Posen and Rabbi Abraham Bing's yeshiva in Würzburg. Both were large yeshivot with hundreds of students led by senior rabbis at the height of their fame.[65] But Hirsch opted to study with Rabbi Jacob Ettlinger, who was only thirty years old at the time and headed a small yeshiva with only about seventy students.[66] Why did Hirsch choose to study at Ettlinger's yeshiva? Rosenbloom speculates that Hirsch was worried that if he attended a large, established yeshiva he risked being embarrassed due to his "weak foundation in Talmud."[67] Far more likely is that studying with Ettlinger was simply a better fit. Ettlinger was both an outstanding Talmud scholar and university educated. He was a close friend of Isaac Bernays, having studied at R. Abraham Bing's yeshiva and at the University of Würzburg.[68] Ettlinger began writing talmudic novellae in his early twenties and his approach involved seeking *peshat* and rejecting *pilpul*, which likely would have appealed to Hirsch's maskilic sensibilities.[69] Like Bernays, Ettlinger was a fierce opponent of Reform but was willing to countenance ritual changes that did not conflict with halakhah.[70] Ettlinger wore the robes of a Protestant minister (even wearing a white collar like Protestants), preached in German, and prepared some prayers in German.[71] He also introduced Jewish educational reforms. The school he founded incorporated secular studies for both boys and girls, employed Christian teachers, and included the teaching of Hebrew

[64] See Friedländer, *Über die Verbesserung der Israeliten in Polen,* 11, cited in Eliav, *Jewish Education,* 149.

[65] The largest yeshiva in Germany was Rabbi Akiva Eiger's. See Eliav, *Jewish Education,* 151. Judith Bleich calls Bing's yeshiva "one of the most significant centers of Torah in Germany." See Bleich, *Rabbi Jacob Ettlinger,* 13.

[66] Bleich, *Rabbi Jacob Ettlinger,* 25; Klugman, *Rabbi Samson Raphael Hirsch,* 40–41.

[67] Rosenbloom, *Tradition in an Age of Reform,* 57.

[68] Bleich, *Rabbi Jacob Ettlinger,* 13. On the value of secular studies for Ettlinger, see ibid., 251–254.

[69] See Bleich, *Rabbi Jacob Ettlinger,* 19–20; Breuer, "Chapters in the life of Rabbi Samson Raphael Hirsch: in Rabbi Jacob Ettlinger's," 59. Rosenbloom, *Tradition in an Age of Reform,* 60. On Hirsch's attitude to *pilpul,* see pp. 262, 280, 303–304 of this volume.

[70] See Breuer, "Chapters in the Life of Rabbi Samson Raphael Hirsch: In Rabbi Jacob Ettlinger's," 60.

[71] See Figure 19 and compare to Figures 17 and 18. See Bleich, *Rabbi Jacob Ettlinger,* 12, 38. When Hirsch became a rabbi he followed Ettlinger in dressing like a Protestant minister, including wearing a white collar. See Figures 20 and 21. Note that in the Oldenburg portrait (Figure 20), it is not clear whether or not Hirsch is wearing a head covering.

grammar and medieval Jewish philosophy.[72] Ettlinger defended liberty of conscience, advocated for Jewish civil rights, and believed that Jews had a mission to improve humanity, ideas that became central for Hirsch.[73] He also shared the Hirsch family's esteem for Wessely, providing an approbation for Wessely's commentary on Genesis that appeared in 1842 despite the fact that many Orthodox rabbis deemed Wessely a persona non grata due to the controversy over *Divrei Shalom Ve'emet*.[74]

Hirsch's dream

About a month after arriving in Mannheim, Hirsch had a life-altering dream. He recounted it in a letter dated August 10, 1828, to his cousin Louise Mayer, who had just travelled to Denmark to be married. Hirsch began the letter by describing inner turmoil that he and his cousin shared:

> We both feel the magic of the foreign. The past stands before us with its wealth of images like a closed world. Now every trace of memory of home is precious to us. With every fiber of our soul we cling to the circle of our beloved ones whom we have left. Things we had assumed had been totally lost in the storm of times here return, live anew, and draw us in. To our surprise aspects of ourselves that were unknown to us come to light here. Only here do we find revealed to ourselves sparks of power and independence hitherto unknown. Only here do we know ourselves and our small world whose boundaries are nature, friendship, and religion. Only now are we cognizant of the great treasures we possess that we enjoyed before, but did not realize we were enjoying. The new path of life that I now find myself on has illuminated this to me with great power.[75]

72 See Breuer, "Chapter in the Life of Rabbi Samson Raphael Hirsch: In Rabbi Jacob Ettlinger's," 60; Bleich, *Rabbi Jacob Ettlinger*, 12, 264. Bleich notes that in his later years Ettlinger appears "to have been wary of the influence of secular studies on impressionable youngsters." See ibid., 12.

73 Bleich, *Rabbi Jacob Ettlinger*, 256–261.

74 In his approbation Ettlinger calls Wessely "the well-known poet, scholar, and advocate who is famous and praised *among all camps of Israel*" (emphasis mine). See Breuer, "Chapters in the Life of Rabbi Samson Raphael Hirsch: In Rabbi Jacob Ettlinger's," 60. Ettlinger surely knew that this description of Wessely's acceptance within the Jewish community was more aspirational than real.

75 The original letter has never been published. I translate from a partial Hebrew translation found in Breuer, "Chapters in the Life of Rabbi Samson Raphael Hirsch: In Rabbi Jacob Ettlinger's Yeshiva," 57–59. Breuer wrote that he was in possession of the German original and provided a copy of it to Eliyahu Meir Klugman, who published his own partial Hebrew translation in Klugman, *Sefer Shemesh Marpeh*, 277–278, and a partial English translation in Klugman, *Rabbi Samson Raphael Hirsch*, 36–39. I have been unable to locate the original.

Hirsch is speaking of a process of self-discovery emerging from the encounter between his past and the "sparks of power and independence" emerging within himself. While previously he had taken his Jewish upbringing for granted, living in a foreign environment he is coming to newly appreciate his past and seeks to understand the "great treasures" he has been bequeathed.

Hirsch then recounts a strange episode. He was riding along the Rhine in a lovely area of woods, orchards, vineyards, and fields. But seeing this beautiful sight, he began to feel dread. He reflected on the fact that every plant naturally fulfilled its divine purpose but wondered, how would he fulfill *his* purpose?[76] Hirsch writes that he then fell asleep. An old man appeared before him who had a serious demeanor and striking blue eyes that were joyous and kind. Seeing Hirsch so anxious, the man asked him what was the matter. Hirsch recounted his dread, and the man responded that he was surprised that "someone from your family would be struck by such despondency." He then told Hirsch that Hirsch had many supports whom he could rely upon, including the example of many of his family members. He could also seek role models from his own generation.[77]

Hirsch sighed, saying that he did not know whom among his generation to follow. So the man took Hirsch to the top of a hill and showed him three groups of people. The first was a group of elderly men. They held large, heavy staffs for support, but their staffs were old and covered with the dust. Next, he showed Hirsch a group of happy, carefree youths dancing in a circle. They each held a thin, pretty stick with which they played games. The elders offered the youths their staffs, but the youths refused them, figuring that since the staffs were heavy and dusty they would just slow them down. But when the youths encountered obstacles along their path and used their sticks to try to pass them, their sticks snapped and they stumbled. Finally, the man

[76] See Breuer, "Chapters in the Life of Rabbi Samson Raphael Hirsch: In Rabbi Jacob Ettlinger's," 58. Hirsch apparently drew the idea that human beings should follow plants in fulfilling their divine purpose from Friedrich Schiller's 1795 epigram "The Highest" (*Das Höchste*): "Do you search for what is highest and greatest? Every plant can teach it to you. What it is without a will of its own, you must be willingly—that's it!" Hirsch conveyed this idea in an admonitory message he placed on the synagogue in Wildehausen in 1834 while serving as District Rabbi in Oldenburg, and he uses it in the *Nineteen Letters*. See Heinemann, "Samson Raphael Hirsch: The Formative Years," 35–36 and see p. 267 of this volume.

[77] Breuer, "Chapters in the Life of Rabbi Samson Raphael Hirsch: In Rabbi Jacob Ettlinger's Yeshiva," 57–58.

showed Hirsch a group of individuals who took the heavy staffs from the elderly, but polished them and were then able to walk confidently and joyously to their destinations overcoming any obstacles. The man then asked Hirsch whether he knew what the staffs were but Hirsch blushed, confused. So the man took a staff and gave it to Hirsch, at which point it changed into a Torah scroll. The man told Hirsch to take the Torah, as it would guide him along his life path.[78]

Hirsch's dream is significant for several reasons. First, it reflects the angst that the young man felt at the time. On the eve of his entry into yeshiva, the twenty-year-old Hirsch was troubled about how he would fulfill his life purpose and understood that though he could look to others for guidance, the burden of figuring things out fell to him alone. He came to understand his life purpose as restoring the glory to the Torah by finding a middle path between the old-style traditionalists and the new Reformers. This would involve "sweeping the dust" off the Torah, thereby restoring its luster.[79] Hirsch's moderate maskilic ancestors had shown the way, and there were contemporary individuals such as Rabbis Bernays and Ettlinger who could guide him. But Hirsch understood that he would ultimately have to find the path to restoring the Torah's glory by himself.

Hirsch's sense of isolation becomes evident from the end of the letter. He closes by telling his cousin that he is pouring his heart out to her because "Here no one understands me for they are all *in the house* and so think entirely differently [than me]" (emphasis in original). Hirsch continues, "And what will you say about the fact that I am now reading the writings of Tasso and, of course, in the original?"[80] Hirsch understood that most of his fellow yeshiva students did not experience his existential anxiety and could not appreciate his desire to find a synthesis between Torah and modern European culture.

[78] Ibid., pp. 58–59.

[79] Hirsch alludes to this image in *Nineteen Letters*. Addressing Reformers, he writes, "Stay the hand you have raised to tear down, and first test whether you are not about to destroy an edifice that contains things sacred, eternal, filled with life and truth, which it appears to you worthy to ax merely because it is unrecognizable due to its being *covered with the dust of centuries* (*Staub der Jahrhunderte*)." Hirsch then refers to himself as "We to whom the mild times have given the task of *removing the dust* (*abzuwischen den Staub*) . . ." (emphasis mine). See Hirsch, *NB*, Brief 18, 101; *NL*, Letter 18, 276–277.

[80] Breuer, "Chapters in the Life of Rabbi Samson Raphael Hirsch: In Rabbi Jacob Ettlinger's," 59. Torquato Tasso (1544–1595) was an Italian poet. Hirsch refers to Tasso in the *Nineteen Letters*. See Hirsch, *NB*, Brief 1, 3; *NL*, Letter 1, 5.

Befriending Abraham Geiger

After completing his year at Ettlinger's yeshiva, Hirsch enrolled at the University of Bonn in 1829. Hirsch and Geiger had stayed in touch while Hirsch was in Mannheim and Geiger was studying at the nearby University of Heidelberg. The same year that Hirsch entered the University of Bonn, Geiger transferred there.[81] The two would run into each other often but did not grow close until one day after a lecture when they began an intense conversation about Goethe's autobiography *Truth and Poetry* (*Wahrheit und Dichtung*). They turned to talking about university life, commiserating about the sense of isolation felt by the *jüdische Theologen*, the Jewish students studying at the university with the intent of entering the rabbinate. After several conversations, they decided to form a homiletical society where these Jewish students could practice preaching.[82]

Hirsch and Geiger became study partners (*hevrutot*), learning the talmudic tractate *Zevahim* together, and Geiger writes that "mutual love and respect developed." This does not mean that that they were always in agreement. Geiger recounts that they often argued over religious issues. Nevertheless, Geiger says that he "admired his [Hirsch's] outstanding mental gifts, rigorous virtue . . . and good heart," and that Hirsch "respected my glowing plans, which were not altogether objectionable to him, loved my openness, and my youthful cheerfulness."[83]

Hirsch studied at Bonn for two semesters from 1829 to 1830. Majoring in philology and history, his work was recognized as "excellent" (*vorzüglich*).[84] His courses included: Juvenal taught by Carl Friedrich Heinrich[85]; Non-Roman Ancient History taught by Barthold Georg Niebuhr[86]; Experimental Physics taught by Karl Dietrich von Münchow[87]; and Logic

[81] See Geiger, *Nachgelassene Schriften*, 5:18.

[82] Ibid, 19.

[83] Ibid.

[84] This is found in a document dated March 28, 1830, signed by Professor Christian August Brandis. I am grateful to Tova Ganzel for sharing a copy of the original with me. The document is mentioned in "Hirsch Testimonial for British Chief Rabbinate," #7.

[85] "Hirsch Testimonial for British Chief Rabbinate,"#8; Breuer, *Unter seinem Banner*, 214. Juvenal was an ancient Roman satirist.

[86] "Hirsch Testimonial for British Chief Rabbinate," #10. Geiger reports that the course focused on non-Roman history. See Geiger, *Nachgelassene Schriften*, 5:23. Niebuhr's lectures from 1829 to 1830 were subsequently published. I discuss them on pp. 253–254 of this volume.

[87] "Hirsch Testimonial for British Chief Rabbinate," #6; Breuer, *Unter seinem Banner*, 213–214.

and the Philosophical Systems of Kant and Fichte taught by Christian August Brandis.[88]

In March 1830, Hirsch was offered the position of District Rabbi of the Grand Duchy of Oldenburg and he left Bonn to pursue his rabbinical career. Hirsch's professional responsibilities in Oldenburg were relatively light, and he was able to devote much of his time to reading, thinking, and writing. In 1836, he published אגרות צפון: *Neunzehn Briefe über Judenthum* (*Nineteen Letters on Judaism*), which became the manifesto of German Neo-Orthodoxy. Translation is at the center of this book.

The *Nineteen Letters* as translation project

Hirsch published the *Nineteen Letters* under the pseudonym Ben Uziel. The book's literary conceit is that Ben Uziel is publishing a correspondence that he found in the literary estate of a "dear friend" because it treats many subjects of "great importance" from "new perspectives."[89] The correspondence is between Benjamin, an alienated young Jew raised in a traditionalist home, and a young rabbi, Naphtali, who gradually convinces Benjamin to return to Jewish observance. The *Nineteen Letters* consists of a first letter authored by Benjamin and eighteen subsequent letters by Naphtali, with Benjamin's side of the correspondence not included. Hirsch generally uses Naphtali to express his own views. This is evident from the fact that the Bible refers to Naphtali as a deer (see Genesis 49:21) and *Hirsch* means "deer" in German.

A talmudic quote on the book's title page makes clear why Hirsch chose the pseudonym Ben Uziel and further elucidates the book's purpose. The quote, which Hirsch cites in the original Hebrew, reads, "It is fully known to you that I have not done this for my own honor or for the honor of my father's house, but solely for your honor that dissension may not increase in Israel (Babylonian Talmud, Megillah 3a)."

The context of the talmudic passage is a discussion of *Bible translation*. The Talmud states that Onkelos composed his Aramaic Pentateuch translation, "from the mouths" of the tannaitic rabbis Eliezer and Joshua, while

[88] "Hirsch Testimonial for British Chief Rabbinate," #9. The testimonial does not state who taught the course or which philosophical systems were taught, but Geiger states that it was taught by Brandis and focused on Kant and Fichte. See Geiger, *Nachgelassene Schriften*, 5:23.

[89] Hirsch, *NB*, iii.

Jonathan Ben Uziel composed his Aramaic translation of the Prophets "from the mouths" of the prophets Haggai, Zachariah, and Malachi. Stating that prophets were behind Jonathan Ben Uziel's translation, the Talmud seems to provide it with a more elevated status than Onkelos's, which was only received from rabbis. This impression is reinforced by the Talmud relating that when Jonathan Ben Uziel produced his translation an area of the Land of Israel, "four hundred parasangs by four hundred parasangs" quaked, and a heavenly voice (*bat kol*) called out asking, "who is this that has revealed my secrets to humankind?" The Talmud then states that Jonathan Ben Uziel arose and proclaimed the statement Hirsch quotes.

By citing this talmudic passage, Hirsch is presenting himself as a new Jonathan Ben Uziel and the *Nineteen Letters* as a translation of central concepts of the Torah into German, which will reveal notions about Judaism hitherto concealed from the public.[90] This may one of the reasons that he gives his book the unvocalized Hebrew title אגרות צפון, which can be translated as *Letters Concerning Concealed* Matters, reading the second word of the title as *tzafun*.[91] Hirsch clearly recognizes that the conception of Judaism he presents might prove controversial, as illustrated by God's causing the earth to shake and demanding who is revealing God's secrets to humanity.[92] But Hirsch justifies himself by claiming that he is presenting these teachings not for personal or familial prestige, but solely to redeem God's honor.

Like Jonathan Ben Uziel Hirsch aims to heal Jewish divisions by publishing a work of translation ("that dissension may not increase in Israel"). Through his *Nineteen Letters*, Hirsch seeks to unify German Jewry by offering a grand vision of Judaism. Hirsch expresses his independent, nonpartisan attitude in the last of the letters, where he writes, "In an age where opposites

[90] Rosenbloom's speculation that Hirsch chose the pseudonym Ben Uziel to connect with the Levitical prince Elitzaphan ben Uziel, mentioned in the Book of Numbers, is far-fetched and without basis. See Rosenbloom, *Tradition in an Age of Reform*, 140–142.

[91] The meaning of the title אגרות צפון is much disputed. Rosenbloom argues that it should be vocalized as *Igrot Tzafon* (*Northern Letters*) because Hirsch sees his work as a northern parallel to Maimonides's medieval letter to Yemen known as *Igeret Teiman* (*Southern Letter*), as both were written to restore the faith of Jews. One might add that Oldenburg is in northern Germany. Breuer argues that the title should be vocalized as *Igrot Tzafun* (*Letters of the Concealed One*), as it refers to the fact that Hirsch published the work under a pseudonym. See Rosenbloom, *Tradition in an Age of Reform*, 125; Breuer, "Review of Rosenbloom," 146. There is an interesting discussion of this issue on the blog *On the Main Line*, which observes that Samuel David Luzzatto read the title as *Igrot Tzafon* (*Northern Letters*). See http://onthemainline.blogspot.com/2011/06/shadal-series-2-on-hirschs-19-letters.html. M.Z. Ahronson's 1890 Hebrew translation also vocalizes the title as *Igrot Tzafon*. While I have offered a third suggestion, Hirsch may have had multiple intentions in selecting this title.

[92] See Hirsch's letter dated March 7, 1836, to his friend Gershon Josaphat, where he writes, "In publishing my *Letters*, I was prepared more for condemnation, opposition, and obloquy than for agreement from any side." A Hebrew translation of the letter is found in Hirsch, *Sefer Shemesh Marpeh*, 219.

confront each other and truth is on neither side, *a man who belongs to no party* (*der keiner Parthei angehörig*), who has only the matter itself before his eyes and serves it alone cannot expect agreement on either side" (emphasis mine).[93]

In the *Nineteen Letters* Hirsch analyzes four major German Jewish ideologies of his time: Haskalah, *Wissenschaft*, Reform, and Jewish traditionalism. Identifying the merits and shortcomings of each, he synthesizes what he finds of value in each into a new vision of German Judaism.[94]

Hirsch on Mendelssohn and the Haskalah

Benjamin's complaint about Judaism proceeds from basic assumptions about life's purpose. He writes, "I believe that every religion should bring a person nearer to his purpose. What else can this purpose be but the attainment of happiness (*Glückseligkeit*) and perfection (*Vollkommenheit*)?" But, Benjamin continues, by these criteria Judaism is a total failure.[95] Not only does it fail to promote fulfilling life's purpose, Benjamin enumerates several ways in which the Torah *prevents* one from achieving it: the Torah isolates Jews, which arouses Gentile mistrust and hostility; its numerous halakhic obligations bend the Jew's spirit into quiet submissiveness, which invites Gentile contempt; the Torah impedes the acquisition of culture and rational thought by forbidding the visual arts, commanding principles of faith, and

93 Hirsch, *NB*, Brief 19, 105–106; *NL*, Letter 19, 332.

94 Hirsch's synthetic approach is suggested by his selecting the name *Naphtali* for his Jewish apologist. Genesis 30:8 describes Rachel's choice of the name *Naphtali* for the son born to her maidservant Bilhah with the words *naftulei elohim niftalti im ahoti gam yakholti*. In his Pentateuch translation, Hirsch follows Rashi in interpreting the root of the name *Naphtali*, פ.ת.ל, as referring to struggle and wrestling, translating the phrase as "I have engaged in a divine wrestling match (*naftulei elohim, göttlichen Ringkampf*) with my sister and prevailed." In his commentary, Hirsch glosses the expression *naftulei elohim* as a "divine wrestling match of which . . . one should not be ashamed" and provides an explanation of the word-root *Naphtali* that conveys a sense of the nature of this struggle. He also explains that the root פ.ת.ל is connected to the root ב.ד.ל, which means "to separate." Hirsch then links this to an etymology that Rashi attributes to Menahem ben Saruk, who explains that the root פ.ת.ל is connected to the word פתילה, meaning "cord." Hirsch explains that in a cord "different strings form an independent whole." In the same vein, in the *Nineteen Letters* Hirsch adumbrates a new vision of Judaism by taking what is valuable in the major contemporary German Jewish ideologies of his time and weaving it into a new synthesis. See Hirsch, *Der Pentateuch,* 1:443; *The Hirsch Chumash,* 1:622 (Commentary to Genesis 30:8). This aspect of Hirsch's project recalls Hegel. Rosenbloom presses the connection between Hirsch and Hegel but goes too far. See Rosenbloom, *Tradition in an Age of Reform*, and the many references to "Hegel, G.W.F. and Hirsch" in the index, p. 473.

95 Hirsch, *NB*, Brief 1, 2; *NL*, Letter 1, 4.

enjoining Jews to study the "tasteless" (*geschmacklosen*) writings of the "Old Testament" and the "illogical" (*begriffswidrigen*) Talmud; the Torah's concern with halakhic obedience "shrivels the heart" by instilling anxiety over the observance of meaningless trifles; the authoritative Jewish code of law, the *Shulhan Arukh*, promotes a monklike Jewish existence devoted to fasting, praying, and observing holidays.[96]

Benjamin's critique of Judaism is informed by four maskilic assumptions: *first*, that inner conviction is of crucial importance to religion; *second*, that the individual has the right to judge for herself whether or not to accept religion based on rational judgment; *third*, that life's purpose is the attainment of happiness and perfection; and *fourth* that the utility of a religion in promoting this aim provides the basis for accepting or rejecting it.

Hirsch has a mixed attitude toward these assumptions. He accepts Benjamin's first assumption, stressing throughout the *Nineteen Letters* the importance of inner conviction in religion. Explaining his decision to become a rabbi, Naphtali writes that he was motivated "not by external necessity (*äußeres Bedürfnis*)" (i.e., the need to make a living) "but because of an inner life plan (*innerer Lebensplan*)."[97] Later, he refers to an "inner voice" (*innere Stimme*) that leads him along his unique religious path and that he expects will arouse opposition from both Reformers and traditionalists.[98] Hirsch's belief in the centrality of inner conviction for religious practice is evident from the fact that his 1838 *Horeb* is devoted to finding reasons for the commandments.[99] Naphtali also displays a clear maskilic sensibility by stressing that he formed his concept of Judaism *on his own* without relying on teachers, as we have seen.[100]

Hirsch also accepts Benjamin's second maskilic assumption, namely, that the basis for deciding whether or not to accept religion must be rational considerations. In the second letter, Naphtali asks Benjamin to refrain from "casting stones" (*den Stein darauf werfen*) on Judaism before he has fully understood it.[101] This implies that Hirsch accepts that Benjamin has the right to accept or reject Judaism once he has understood it. In the penultimate letter, Hirsch pens a moving paean to freedom of inquiry, writing, "I bless the fact

[96] Hirsch, *NB*, Brief 1, 3; *NL*, Letter 1, 5.
[97] Hirsch, *NB*, Brief 2, 5; *NL*, Letter 2, 13.
[98] Hirsch, *NB*, Brief 19, 106; *NL*, Letter 19, 332–333.
[99] See Hirsch, *Horev: Versuche über Jissroels Pflichten in Der Zerstreuung*; *Horeb; a Philosophy of Jewish Laws and Observations*.
[100] See p. 239 of this volume.
[101] Hirsch, *NB*, Brief 2, 8; *NL*, Letter 2, 16.

that now the scales are swaying entirely free, held by God alone and that only intellectual efforts (*Geistesbestrebungen*) can tip the balance, no force exerted on them being able to impede their movement . . . Let the scales swing! The more freely they swing, the more reliably they will weigh truth and life in the end."[102] For Hirsch, liberty of thought is the key to the individual being capable of weighing the truth of Judaism for herself, which is needed for Judaism to be accepted freely from rational conviction.

But Hirsch adopts a more critical attitude toward Benjamin's third and fourth assumptions. In the second letter, Naphtali questions Benjamin's assertion that attaining happiness is the goal of life and that Judaism should be judged by how well it promotes this aim. Naphtali observes that Benjamin's rejection of Judaism is based on the assumption that there is an objective standard of happiness. Naphtali questions this, noting that a drunkard delights in his intoxication and the sociopath enjoys crime. He asks, "Is not every individual entitled to decide his own measure (*Maßstab*) of happiness? After all, if happiness has to conform to an external measure (*Maßstab*) it can no longer be called happiness!" Naphtali concludes that if traditionalist Jews are happy in their religious practices, Benjamin has no grounds for criticizing them. At most, Benjamin may declare that *he* does not enjoy these practices, but he is not justified in issuing a blanket indictment of their Judaism.[103]

Naphtali then criticizes Benjamin's assumption that Judaism should be judged by whether or not it promotes perfection. He asks whether "intellectual perfection" (*Geistesvollkommenheit*) can properly be considered life's purpose since relatively few people are disposed to intellectual pursuits and even fewer attain truth, as evidenced by the fact that even great minds disagree about it. Naphtali further asks whether a person can be considered *obligated* to achieve perfection since failing to do so is ultimately only "a sin against oneself." This problem is especially acute in the case of morality, as in the maskilic view moral responsibility is grounded in the fact that ethical virtue is a central component of human perfection. But, notes Naphtali, if my moral responsibility to another derives from the fact that acting morally furthers *my own* perfection, then I am only accountable to myself for my (non-criminal) immorality. What then will motivate me to act morally, if I choose not to hold myself accountable?[104]

102 Hirsch, *NB*, Brief 18, 102–103; *NL*, Letter 18, 278.
103 Hirsch, *NB*, Brief 2, 6; *NL*, Letter 2, 14.
104 Hirsch, *NB*, Brief 2, 6; *NL*, Letter 2, 14.

Naphtali detects a more fundamental problem with Benjamin's maskilic assumptions. In making happiness and perfection the basis for judging Judaism, Naphtali sees Benjamin as seeking to judge Judaism by criteria that are *external* to it. Naphtali writes: "Let us put aside the yardstick (*Maß*) and first obtain an idea of the object we wish to measure (*messen*): Judaism according to its destiny and teachings (*nach Geschick und Lehre*)."[105] For Naphtali, rather than judge Judaism by whether it conforms to external standards, one must first understand its purpose according to its *internal* self-conception. Failing to do so risks misunderstanding Judaism, which violates the maskilic demand for intellectual honesty. In making this argument, Hirsch echoes historicist arguments against Enlightenment rationalism put forward half a century earlier by thinkers like Herder, who in *The Spirit of Hebrew Poetry* wrote:

> In order to judge of a nation, we must live in their time, in their own country, must adopt their modes of thinking and feeling, must see how they lived, how they were educated, what scenes they looked upon, what were the objects of their affection and passion, the character of their atmosphere, their skies, the structure of their organs, their dances and their music. All this too we must learn to think of not as strangers or enemies, but as their brothers and compatriots.[106]

For Hirsch, Mendelssohn and the Maskilim were not the first to err in judging Judaism by external concepts. Centuries earlier, Maimonides deemed intellectual perfection the goal of life and sought to explain the purpose of the Torah's commandments as a function of how they contributed to this end. While praising Maimonides for "preserving practical Judaism until this day" through his great legal code, the *Mishneh Torah*, Hirsch criticizes Maimonides's approach to giving reasons for the commandments. For Hirsch, Maimonides's conception of life was "Arab-Greek," and he approached Judaism "from without" (*von außen*), interpreting Judaism in light of philosophical concepts that were alien to it, which resulted in an incorrect, inauthentic understanding of Judaism.[107]

[105] Hirsch, *NB*, Brief 2, 7; *NL*, Letter 2, 15.

[106] See Herder, *Vom Geist*, 1:5–6; *On the Spirit*, 1:27–28. Herder already expressed this view nearly a decade earlier in his 1774 *Yet Another Philosophy of History*. See Herder, *Against Pure Reason*, 41–44. On Herder's significance for Hirsch in the *Nineteen Letters*, see Gottlieb, "Orthodoxy and the Orient," and pp. 281–282, 355–356 of this volume.

[107] Hirsch, *NB*, Brief 18, 89; *NL*, Letter 18, 265.

Hirsch finds evidence of the inadequacy of Maimonides's account of Judaism in the fact that many of his successors either became lax in halakhic observance or dropped it completely, reasoning that if the goal of Judaism was intellectual perfection, the commandments were dispensable.[108] For Hirsch, two specific shortcomings in Maimonides's approach to giving reasons for the commandments contributed to the abandonment of halakhah: first, Maimonides based his explanations only on the Written Law, providing no reasons for observing rabbinic interpretations of the law; second, Maimonides explained the reasons for the commandments *in general* but did not provide reasons for their particular details, which therefore came to be seen as unimportant.[109]

Hirsch then turns to Mendelssohn, whom he calls a "most brilliant (*hochverglänzende*) and most respected (*höchst achtbare*) personality whose commanding influence has led the development [of Judaism] to this day."[110] Hirsch does not regard Mendelssohn's error as identical to Maimonides's. To be sure, he claims that Mendelssohn derived most of his "free intellectual development" from philosophy rather than Judaism. But Hirsch describes Mendelssohn not as seeking to create a synthesis between Judaism and philosophy but, rather, as assigning the two to non-overlapping spheres. According to Hirsch, while Mendelssohn saw metaphysics and ethics as *rational and universal*, he saw Judaism as defined by obedience to ceremonial law that was *specific* to Jews and had *no connection* to universal truths of reason. Hirsch claims that Mendelssohn developed this concept of Judaism because he formulated it in an apologetic context. Responding to Christian charges that Judaism was irrational and immoral, Mendelssohn claimed that what was unique to Judaism was its statutory ceremonial law that could never conflict with rational, universal moral and religious truth. Similarly, Hirsch asserts that Mendelssohn defended the Bible by contending that its value was purely aesthetic as a great work of literature.[111] Hirsch's interpretation of Mendelssohn is encapsulated in his famous remark that while Mendelssohn "personally [was] a practicing religious Jew, he showed his brethren and the world that it was possible to be a strictly religious Jew *and yet* to shine, highly

[108] Hirsch, *NB*, Brief 18, 90; *NL*, Letter 18, 266.

[109] Hirsch, *NB*, Brief 18, 95; *NL*, Letter 18, 271. Hirsch cites Maimonides, *Guide of the Perplexed*, part III, chs. 26 and 41, in support of this interpretation.

[110] Hirsch, *NB*, Brief 18, 93; *NL*, Letter 18, 268.

[111] Hirsch, *NB*, Brief 18, 93; *NL*, Letter 18, 269.

respected as the German Plato."[112] For Hirsch, Mendelssohn strictly segregated the human being and the Jew in himself.[113]

But Hirsch is a careful enough reader to recognize that this description of Mendelssohn is not fully accurate. In an important footnote, he writes:

> Do not misunderstand me. I am here speaking only of his work for Judaism in a general sense. His *Jerusalem,* which defends freedom of thought and belief and also vindicates these ideas on the basis of Judaism stresses in contradistinction to the *Moreh* [*The Guide of the Perplexed*] that the essence of Judaism is practice (*practische Wesenheit des Judenthums*) and expresses a view of the *Edot* that might have given a different direction to the period that followed had it been developed further by him or his successors. But neither the one thing nor the other occurred: the science of Judaism (*Wissenschaft des Judenthums*) was not developed further by him; and his successors, lacking their master's religious sentiment, were not content to stress the eternally binding nature of the law as the divine dictum, and they found no other way to form an intellectual conception of [the law] other than by embracing Maimonides's synthesis.[114]

Hirsch here qualifies his earlier interpretation of Mendelssohn in a way that cancels it. According to Hirsch, Mendelssohn viewed practice as the essence of Judaism and considered halakhah "eternally binding" in light of its origin as "divine dictum." In *Jerusalem*, Mendelssohn began to develop a concept of halakhah as *Edot.* Earlier in the *Nineteen Letters* Hirsch had defined *Edot* as rituals that serve as "monuments of foundational truths . . . represented in words and symbolic acts." So Hirsch understood that Mendelssohn saw the ceremonial law as a way of embodying religious truths in life through symbolic actions.

Hirsch observes that while Mendelssohn presented the outlines of this understanding of halakhah in *Jerusalem,* he did not explain it in detail. Hirsch speculates that had Mendelssohn done so he might have prevented much of the later defection from halakhic practice. But lacking this explanation of halakhah, many of Mendelssohn's followers recurred to Maimonides's

112 Ibid.

113 Four years later the Reformer Salomon Ludwig offered a similar interpretation of Mendelssohn, calling him "a heathen in his brain and a Jew in his body." See Steinheim, *Moses Mendelssohn und seine Schule,* 37, cited in Meyer, *Response to Modernity,* 69. Nearly a century later Rosenzweig repeated a similar criticism of Mendelssohn. See p. 414 of this volume.

114 Hirsch, *NB,* Brief 18, 93; *NL,* Letter 18, 269.

approach to the commandments, seeing them as means to acquire intellectual perfection, which led them to consider the ritual laws dispensable.[115]

Like Zunz, Hirsch worries that maskilic ideals came to be used to justify materialistic selfishness. He notes that while for Mendelssohn and the early Maskilim happiness involved perfecting one's faculties especially one's moral capacity, later generations interpreted happiness as comfort and pleasure. Discarding Jewish laws they regarded as impeding their materialistic pursuits, Haskalah become a code word for self-satisfied selfishness that mocked Jewish tradition and sought liberation from halakhah for the sake of self-gratification.[116] But Hirsch observes that a curious thing happened on the way to happiness. Maskilim discovered that "mocking what had hitherto been held sacred in Judaism" and "slackening its burdens" not only did not increase happiness, it led to misery. For while Judaism had provided life meaning by demanding sacrifices to a great cause, making selfish self-gratification the ultimate goal of life made life pedestrian and empty.[117]

It would be wrong, however, to think that Hirsch completely rejects Benjamin's criticisms of traditionalist German Judaism. As we will see, he regards Benjamin's criticisms as generally on target. But for Hirsch the problem is not with Judaism but, rather with the way the Jewish traditionalists have understood or, rather, misunderstood it. For Hirsch, a proper understanding of Judaism requires a proper methodological approach. He sketches such an approach through his engagement with *Wissenschaft des Judentums*.

Hirsch on *Wissenschaft des Judentums*

Hirsch was very familiar with *Wissenchaft* methods of studying history. As we noted, he majored in philology and history at the University of Bonn, and his courses included one on non-Roman Ancient History with the renowned historian Barthold Georg Niebuhr. Niebuhr's lectures from the course

[115] Yitzhak Baer notes that this reasoning led some medieval Jewish Maimonideans to justify "extreme liberalism" that "put rational understanding ahead of the observance of the commandments." See Baer, *A History of the Jews in Christian Spain*, 1:97, 297. The most famous radical Maskil who adopted this approach was Salomon Maimon. See Maimon, *Salomon Maimons Lebensgeschichte*, 163; Maimon, *The Autobiography of Solomon Maimon*, 80–81. For discussion of Maimon in relation to Hirsch, see Gottlieb, *Faith, Reason, Politics*, 163–165.

[116] Hirsch, *NB*, Brief 16, 82; *NL*, Letter 16, 227. See pp. 173–174 of this volume

[117] Hirsch, *NB*, Brief 18, 93; *NL*, Letter 18, 271.

were later published, and it is evident that Hirsch appropriates many methodological elements Niebuhr presented in his lectures while giving them a distinctive twist.[118]

In the introductory lecture, Niebuhr writes that every nation has a distinct national character that can be known through its history.[119] Like Zunz, Niebuhr adopts a text-centered approach in which history is studied "mainly as a branch of philology or as a means of interpretation and of philological knowledge."[120] Niebuhr stresses the need to distinguish historical facts from anachronistic ideas projected onto the past.[121] Similar to Niebuhr, throughout the *Nineteen Letters* Hirsch calls Jews a "nation" (*Volk*) that must be understood historically and stresses that this history must be based on philological study.[122] And we have just seen that Hirsch criticizes Maimonides and the Maskilim for projecting alien concepts onto Judaism rather than seeking to understand its teachings from within as they were originally intended.[123]

Hirsch's regard for *Wissenschaft* is evident by his repeatedly calling for a new *Wissenschaft des Judentums*.[124] But while Hirsch's adopts the watchword *Wissenschaft*, his understanding of what it involves differs greatly from how it is understood by its self-described practitioners. Specifically, Hirsch thinks

[118] The lectures were published in English translation in 1852. In the preface, the translator Leonhard Schmitz states that the translation is from a "literal transcript" of the lectures that Niebuhr delivered in the 1829–1830 winter session at the University of Bonn. See Niebuhr, *Lectures on Ancient History*, 1:vii, x.

[119] Niebuhr, *Lectures on Ancient History*, 33–35.

[120] Ibid., 37.

[121] This principle is implicit throughout Niebuhr's book. See, for example, his discussion of the Ionic migration into Attica, where he argues that while ancient historians claimed that it involved "a friendly reception of exiles," it actually occurred by force. Niebuhr then observes that "many things, even such as belong to a later period, are fabrications; national vanity has often been guilty of fabrications." Niebuhr, *Lectures on Ancient History*, 231.

[122] Hirsch writes that "Israel is an historical phenomenon (*geschichtliche Erscheinung*) among all others." See Hirsch, *NB*, Brief 3, 9; *NL*, Letter 3, 27. For places where Hirsch calls Jews a *Volk* in the *NB*, see Hirsch, *NB*, Brief 2, 7; Brief 7, 35–36; *NB*, Brief 8, 41; *NL*, Letter 2, 15; Letter 7, 105, 106; Letter 8, 114. Breuer observes that "Hirsch thoroughly loved the expression 'nation' as he perceived it with respect to Judaism, and he used it in innumerable instances in his writings, with all possible derivatives and lexical combinations." See Breuer, *Modernity within Tradition*, 288–289, 294–296.

On Hirsch's emphasis on philology as the foundation for understanding the Jewish nation, see Hirsch, *NB*, Brief 2, 7; *NL*, Letter 2, 15. Also see his 1861 essay "Jüdische Welt- und Lebensanchauungen" ("Jewish Outlook on World and Life"), where he writes that "the sole sources for understanding a people's outlook on life and the world are its language and literature. For word and speech are the sole elements which bear the imprint of that people's spirit (*Geist*) and feelings." See Hirsch, *GS*, 5:144; *CW*, 8:22.

[123] See Hirsch, *NB*, Brief 2, 9; *NL*, Letter 2, 16–17. See pp. 250–251 of this volume.

[124] See, for example, Hirsch, *NB*, Brief 19, 106; *NL*, Letter 19, 333; Hirsch, *NB*, Brief 18, 97–98; *NL*, Letter 18, 273.

that contemporary *Wissenschaft des Judentums* is practiced in a distinctly *unwissenschaftlichen* way.

In an important footnote to Letter 18 of the *Nineteen Letters*, Hirsch compares the scientific study of the Torah to the scientific study of nature. For Hirsch, a scientific understanding of nature is epitomized by experimental physics.[125] Hirsch notes that the scientific study of nature seeks laws that govern "facts" (*Facta*). Beginning with the facts, the scientist hypothesizes laws "backward (*rückwärts*) from the phenomena" that explain how the facts of nature are governed. One then tests the hypothetical law against the phenomena to see if they act in accordance with it. A single "contradicting phenomena" disproves the hypothesized law. But regardless of whether or not one is able to discover a law that describes the interrelation among phenomena, "the phenomenon itself remains a fact."[126]

Hirsch takes this approach as a model for proper *Wissenschaft des Judentums*, writing that the method of "research (*Forschung*) into the Torah is entirely the same." He provides a theological basis for comparing the study of nature to the study of Torah, writing that nature and the Torah are both divine "revelations."[127] Just as God is the ultimate "cause" (*Grund*) of nature, so God is the "cause" (*Grund*) of the Torah. For Hirsch, a *wissenschaftlichen* approach to Torah research involves seeking to understand the "determinations" (*Bestimmungen*) of the Torah, which Hirsch applies to the study of Jewish law. While in the science of nature one begins with facts and hypothesizes laws that explain their interrelation, in Torah research the laws of the Torah are facts, and one seeks to explain the interrelation among them by hypothesizing reasons for them that connect the laws to one another. Just as in the science of nature, one must then test one's hypothesized laws by verifying that they accurately describe the facts, so in Torah research one must test one's hypotheses concerning the reasons for the laws against the laws themselves. Finally, just as in the science of nature, facts have priority over hypothesized laws, with a single fact able to

125 This is not surprising, as experimental physics was the only natural science that Hirsch studied at university. See p. 244 of this volume.

126 Hirsch, *NB*, Brief 18, 96; *NL*, Letter 18, 271–272.

127 The idea that one can compare study of nature to the study of Scripture has its roots in Psalm 19, but was first developed by the Church Fathers. See Hess, "The Two Books." As we have seen, both Mendelssohn and Spinoza use this analogy. For a discussion of how Spinoza, Mendelssohn, and Hirsch, deploy this analogy, see Gottlieb, "The Study of Scripture and the Study of Nature: Spinoza and Modern Jewish Thought."

disprove the most elegant hypothesis so the laws of the Torah have priority over the hypothesized reasons for them, with a contradiction between the reason and the law always invalidating the hypothesized reason, but never the law itself.[128]

Hirsch criticizes the methods that self-proclaimed *Wissenschaft* scholars use to study the Torah as unscientific. We have seen that he accepts the *wissenschaftlichen* principle that texts should be understood as they were originally intended. But while *Wissenschaft* scholars deploy this principle to oppose how traditionalist Jews understand the Torah, Hirsch argues that naïve Jewish traditionalists are *closer to this scientific ideal than Wissenschaft scholars.* He notes that the Hebrew word *Torah* literally means "instruction" (*Unterweisung*).[129] According to Hirsch, the Torah presents itself as a revelation from God to the Israelites that explains their place and responsibilities in the world. To understand the Torah as it was originally intended, a Jew must therefore read it in a spirit of engagement as a personal address from God teaching one how to live.[130] By contrast, Hirsch sees prevailing *Wissenschaft* approaches to the Torah as marked by antiquarian interests, where the ideal is impartial scholarship. Scholars may read the Torah to glean information about ancient Israel, the geography of Palestine, and ancient Semitic languages, or aesthetically as a work of literature.[131] But in doing so they necessarily misunderstand the Torah's original intent as God's prescriptions for living.[132]

[128] Hirsch, *NB*, Brief 18, 96; *NL*, Letter 18, 271–272. Hirsch notes that only the practice of *Edot*, which he defines as rituals whose aim is to convey ideas that impact one emotionally, remains "imperfect" without understanding the reasons for it. See ibid. Hirsch's approach explains why the subtitle of *Horeb*, his great work on the reasons for the commandments, is "***Versuche** über Jissroël, und über Jissroëls Pflichten in der Zerstreuung,*" namely, "essays" or "attempts" to provide explanations for a Jew's duties in the diaspora.

[129] Hirsch, *NB*, Brief 2, 7; *NL*, Letter 2, 15.

[130] Hirsch, *NB*, Brief 2, 7–8; *NL*, Letter 2, 15–16. Buber and Rosenzweig later make a similar point as they gave their translation of the Pentateuch known in Hebrew as *Hamishah Humshei Torah* the German title *Die fünf Bücher der Weisung*, where *Weisung* (instruction) translates *Torah*. Also see Buber's essay "People Today and the Jewish Bible" in Buber and Rosenzweig, *Die Schrift und Ihre Verdeutschung*, 20; *Scripture and Translation*, 8.

[131] Hirsch, *NB*, Brief 18, 97–98; *NL*, Letter 18, 273.

[132] Hirsch extended his attack on *Wissenschaft des Judentums* in later writings, most notably his 1861 essay "How Does Life Benefit from Our *Wissenschaft*?" See Hirsch, *GS*, 2:424–433; *CW*, 7:36–45. A similar sentiment was later echoed by the eminent Jewish studies scholar Solomon Schechter. In his 1902 lecture "The Emancipation of Jewish Science," he writes: "You will agree with me, I think, that our grandmothers and grandfathers, who did read the Psalms and had a good cry over them, understood them better than all the professors." See Schechter, *Seminary Addresses*, 4.

Hirsch on Reform Judaism

The third major ideology that Hirsch considers is Reform Judaism. Were the *Nineteen Letters* Hirsch's only literary legacy, he would never have been considered an implacable foe of Reform. While Hirsch is clearly critical of Reform Judaism, he also displays a remarkable sympathy for it, even adopting the label for himself, though, as with *Wissenschaft*, he gives it a distinct interpretation.

Many of Benjamin's complaints about Judaism reflect criticisms commonly leveled by Reformers. But somewhat surprisingly, Benjamin rejects what he calls "the current efforts to reform Judaism." Specifically, he considers Reformers' attempts to harmonize Judaism with modern German culture misguided. In seeking to preserve elements of Judaism that are consistent with German culture while cutting out those that are inconsistent with it, Benjamin contends that Reformers create "an arbitrary patchwork" (*willkürliches Stückwerk*) of Judaism and German culture that is inadequate to both. Benjamin reasons that since Reformers regard German culture as clearly superior to Judaism, it makes more sense for them embrace it completely and abandon Judaism.[133]

Benjamin also worries that Reformers undermine Jewish unity. Lacking the authority of central legislative bodies, Reformers relate to halakhah in wildly different ways, with some seeking to "tear down" halakhah and others "to hold fast to it." As there is no consensus on what to preserve and what to discard, Benjamin criticizes Reformers for sowing religious anarchy.[134]

Naphtali discusses Reform in Letter 17. Evincing great sympathy for Reformers' aims, he notes that they get much right in their critique of contemporary Judaism and effusively praises their motives, writing:

> Do not be angry with anyone. Respect all of them. For they all sense a defect: they all desire the good as it is known to them: they all seek the welfare of their brethren. If they have not recognized the good, if they have failed to grasp the truth it is not *they* who must chiefly bear the blame; the entire past must shoulder it with them. Therefore, respect their intentions.[135]

[133] Hirsch, *NB*, Brief 1, 4; *NL*, Letter 1, 6.

[134] Ibid. Four years earlier, Zunz had raised concerns about the chaotic attempts to introduce synagogue reforms. See Zunz, *Vorträge*, 458.

[135] Hirsch, *NB*, Brief 17, 85; *NL*, Letter 17, 243. Hirsch's expression recalls what the angel tells the pagan king in the opening lines of Judah Halevi's *Kuzari*: "Your intentions are pleasing to the Creator but not your actions." See Halevi, *Kuzari*, 1:1, 24.

For Hirsch, Reformers correctly sense problems in traditionalist Judaism and honestly seek to advance Jewish emancipation and improve the cultural and intellectual state of their coreligionists. The problem is not the Reformers' *motives*, but their lacking a correct understanding of Judaism. Failing to find the "spirit" in traditionalist Judaism, they come to regard it as "a spiritless (*geistlose*) phenomenon, belonging to a time long past and buried," and so seek to change it. The problem, for Hirsch, is that in discarding important elements of Judaism, Reformers risk severing Judaism's "last nerve."[136]

For Hirsch, Reformers do not err because they probe Judaism too deeply, but because they do not probe it deeply enough. They focus on changing the synagogue service. But in doing do they fetishize externals of the service such as playing an organ, maintaining decorum, having the rabbi dress in Protestant attire, shortening or eliminating prayers, etc. Their concern is to make the synagogue service "conform to the demands of the sentimentalities of the age."[137] While Hirsch does not consider concern with the "external form" (*äußere Erscheinung*) of the synagogue service unimportant, he sees Reformers as failing to provide an encompassing, inspiring philosophy of Judaism.[138] So while Reformers complain that Judaism is "spiritless," their focus on changing the externals of Judaism cannot remedy the problem.[139]

Hirsch claims that Reformers seek to relax elements of halakhah that they see as impeding a "comfortable life" and the "pursuit of possessions and enjoyment" in the name of high-sounding ideals like "progress" (*Fortschritt*) and "civilization" (*Zivilisation*).[140] But he thinks that they commit a grievous error in imagining that "trimming" Jewish law will inspire greater Jewish commitment.[141] Changing halakhah to make life easier and to better conform with German cultural sensibilities merely engenders complacency and indifference. Co-opting the motto of Reform, Hirsch writes:

[136] Hirsch, *NB*, Brief 18, 97; *NL*, Letter 18, 272–273.

[137] Hirsch, *NB*, Brief 17, 85; *NL*, Letter 17, 243.

[138] Ibid. Hirsch was open to changing external forms of the synagogue to increase devotion as long as doing so did not violate halakhah. In Oldenburg, he dressed like a Protestant minister, preached a German sermon, stressed decorum, introduced a male choir, and even eliminated *Kol Nidre*. See Meyer, *Response to Modernity*, 77–78. Breuer shows that Hirsch only eliminated *Kol Nidre* for one year in 1839 before reinstating it. See Breuer, "Chapters in the Life of Rabbi Samson Raphael Hirsch: On the Elimination of *Kol Nidre*"; idem, *Modernity within Tradition*, 32.

[139] As we have seen, Zunz expressed a similar concern; see p. 159 of this volume.

[140] See Hirsch's 1854 essay "Religion Allied to Progress," where addressing a Reformer's call to ease Sabbath restrictions to make Judaism accord with "progress" and "civilization," Hirsch wryly remarks that apparently "the smoldering tobacco leaf also belongs to civilization." See Hirsch, *GS*, 3:498; *CW*, 6:118.

[141] Hirsch, *NB*, Brief 16, 82; *NL*, Letter 16, 227.

> Therefore: Reform! Let us work with all our powers, with exertion of all goodness and nobility to reach this ideal. Reform! But this goal can be nothing other than the actualization of Judaism by Jews in our time; the actualization of each eternal ideal in relation to the particular age and by using the specific circumstances that it provides. Education and elevation of the time to the Torah, not lowering the Torah to the times and reducing its lofty peaks to the shallowness of our life. We *Jews need reform*, through renewed attention to Judaism, intellectually (*geistig*) understood and actualized with all powers of actions. The eternal set up as a model for all times by the God of all ages does not need reform, as advocated by the children of our time who desire an easier life. The Torah means to elevate us to its heights: should we drag it down to us? (emphasis mine)[142]

For Hirsch, the key to inspiring Jewish youth is to provide a compelling vision of a *demanding* Judaism. True reform involves reforming Jews by elevating them to the lofty ideals of the Torah "intellectually" (*geistig*) understood. So for Hirsch the key to inspiring renewed commitment to Torah is education.

Hirsch recognizes that Reformers did not neglect Jewish education. Many sought to establish supplemental religious schools for Jewish students centered on a religion textbook. While David Friedländer's *Reader for Jewish Children* was the first such textbook, over the next century Maskilim and Reformers published over 160 such works. They were often written as catechisms that sought to instill Judaism's central theological and moral principles.[143]

Hirsch mounts a scathing critique of these religion textbooks. In using a catechism to present Judaism as a creed, Hirsch sees these textbooks as weak imitations of Protestant religion textbooks.[144] For Hirsch, the fact that the religion textbooks often based Judaism's theological principles on Maimonides's Thirteen Principles and Judaism's moral principles on the Ten

[142] Hirsch, *NB*, Brief 17, 83–84; *NL*, Letter 17, 241–242. Zunz uses similar language nine years *later* in an 1845 letter to Geiger when he writes, "It is not religion, but ourselves that we must reform." See Geiger, *Abraham Geiger and Liberal Judaism*, 115–116. One wonders whether Zunz drew this expression from Hirsch.

[143] On Friedländer's *Reader*, see p. 83 note 29 of this volume. While Maskilim and Reformers authored the vast majority of the religion textbooks, there were also Orthodox versions. Salomon Plessner produced the first Orthodox religion textbook in 1838, two years after the appearance of the *Nineteen Letters*. For a classic discussion of the nineteenth-century Jewish religion textbook, see Petuchowski, "Manuals and Catechisms."

[144] The Protestant context of these works is reinforced by the fact at least thirty-five were produced for use in confirmation ceremonies introduced into Reform synagogues that were modelled on the Protestant confirmation ceremony. See Petuchowski, "Manuals and Catechisms," 47.

Commandments does not detract from the fact that this way of presenting Judaism is fundamentally inauthentic.[145] Hirsch expresses special concern about the cursory treatment of the ritual laws, which are often not mentioned at all, mentioned very briefly, or relegated to an appendix in the textbooks. For Hirsch, learning a religious catechism, even if it is based on Maimonides's Thirteen Principles and the Ten Commandments, cannot inspire love and fervor for Judaism. It is a way of burying Judaism, not revitalizing it.[146]

Once again Hirsch presents the intentions of Reformers as praiseworthy. They seek to provide a reasonable, edifying account of Judaism. But for Hirsch the way to achieve this is not by introducing mechanical catechisms, paring away inconvenient rituals, or bringing the synagogue more into accord with German cultural sensibilities, but by articulating an inspiring moral vision of the world and a Jew's task within in it as it emerges from reading the Torah itself. Hirsch seeks to provide this in the *Nineteen Letters.*

Despite Hirsch's criticisms of Reform, he does not fully embrace Benjamin's charges against it. Specifically, he does not see Reformers' undermining Jewish unity as all bad. Noting the great variety of synagogue services that have emerged in Germany, Hirsch writes, "Can you not see that this too has a good side? I am convinced that not one of us now living conceives Judaism in its purity and truth. Because of the differences of opinion, which are quite natural, nearly every Rabbi is obliged to find his own path and no school guides him."[147] For Hirsch, the breakdown of a unified community liberates individuals to find their own path, which fosters honest searching for truth yielding free conviction, which is crucial for religious practice.

Hirsch on Jewish traditionalism

The fourth major ideology that Hirsch discusses is the traditionalist form of German Judaism that predated the Enlightenment and survived it. While Hirsch does not give it a specific name, I call it "Jewish traditionalism." As

[145] As we have seen, Friedländer's *Reader* contained a rendering of Maimonides's Thirteen Principles and a translation of the Ten Commandments by Mendelssohn. See p. 83 note 29 of this volume. Many of the textbooks do not follow Maimonides's Thirteen Principles but, rather, Albo's reduction of Judaism to three principles, often adjusting Albo's principles to reflect Reform sensibilities. See Petuchowski, "Manuals and Catechisms," 57.

[146] Hirsch, *NB*, Brief 17, 86; *NL*, Letter 17, 244. See Breuer, *Tradition within Modernity*, 99–100.

[147] Hirsch, *NB*, Brief 18, 102; *NL*, Letter 18, 277.

with Haskalah, *Wissenschaft*, and Reform, Hirsch has a complex attitude toward it.

At first glance, Hirsch's stance toward Jewish traditionalism is highly negative. Near the beginning of his complaint, Benjamin recalls that he had previously expressed dissatisfaction with Judaism to Naphtali, who responded that Benjamin's objections stemmed from a distorted view of Judaism deriving from his "habitual parental education, and mindless instruction in Bible and Talmud from Polish teachers."[148] In worrying about Jewish traditionalism engendering a lack of understanding of Judaism through instruction by Polish teachers, Hirsch repeats a stock maskilic complaint that we have encountered in Wessely and Zunz.[149]

Throughout the *Nineteen Letters*, Hirsch holds Jewish traditionalism responsible for the contempt with which many young Jews regard Judaism.[150] But Hirsch does not simply condemn Jewish traditionalism. Rather, he seeks to explain *why* such a cloistered, uncomprehending Judaism developed. For Hirsch, centuries of Christian persecution are to blame. Excluded from broader culture and oppressed by their neighbors, many Jews came to view the cultural world outside Judaism negatively. Despairing of this world, they focused on the "external forms" of Judaism, finding "inspiration only in prayer, and consolation in a contemplative life" devoted to Torah study. Hirsch uses language suffused with morbid imagery to express the depths to which Jewish traditionalism had sunk: "a mindless spirit (*geistloser Geist*) encompassed those laws full of life (*lebensvollsten*) and turned them into mummies (*Mumie*) from fear of errors in intellectual inquiry just as birds of prey chase the spirit (*den Geist*) from a beloved corpse."[151]

In blaming Christian persecution for premodern Ashkenazic Jewry's insularity, Hirsch's analysis of Jewish traditionalism sounds very similar to Zunz's.[152] But unlike Zunz, Hirsch does not limit his diagnosis of the problem to post-Reformation Christian persecution. Rather, he sees *intra-Jewish* dynamics going back to Maimonides as also contributing to it. We have seen Hirsch's claim that for Maimonides's the purpose of halakhah was to

[148] Hirsch, *NB*, Brief 1, 102; *NL*, Letter 1, 3.

[149] See pp. 94–95, 169–170 of this volume.

[150] As Hirsch put it in his discussion of Reform, "If they have not recognized the good, if they have failed to grasp the truth, it is not *they* who must chiefly bear the blame; the entire past must shoulder it with them." Hirsch, *NB*, Brief 17, 85; *NL*, Letter 17, 243.

[151] Hirsch, *NB*, Brief 10, 50; *NL*, Letter 10, 143–144.

[152] See 148–149, 155–156 of this volume. As we have seen, Mendelssohn also made this claim; see pp. 100 and 2 note 7 of this volume.

promote intellectual perfection caused many of his successors either to become lax or defect from halakhah entirely.[153] According to Hirsch, Maimonides' approach provoked a reaction from Jewish traditionalists. At first the traditionalists saw philosophy as the cause of Maimonides's error and turned against the study of it. But gradually they became more extreme, opposing any attempt to "to offer an intellectual understanding" of reasons for the commandments relying on what Hirsch calls "misunderstood" talmudic expressions.[154] While study of Torah remained central, the only questions deemed worthy of study were questions of *fact* ("what is stated here?") while questions of *value* ("why is it stated here?") were considered out of bounds. This was true even with the *Edot*, which are meant to bring Jewish concepts to life.[155]

Hirsch then offers a genealogy of talmudic *pilpul.* He notes that the Bible presents the Torah's vision of the world and the Jews' place within it. But as Jewish traditionalists came to focus only on understanding *how* to practice laws, which was determined by the talmudic interpretation of these laws, they came to reject the study of the Bible, again relying on a "misunderstood" talmudic passage.[156] But, Hirsch observes, the intellect will not rest. As oppression and persecution robbed Israel of its "living outlook on the world and life" and the Talmud became the sole focus of study, the intellect sought an outlet and "went astray occupying itself with dialectical subtleties (*Spitzfündigkeit*)."[157] Studying the practical law derived from the Talmud was not emphasized, instead engaging talmudic dialectic through *pilpul* was. For Hirsch, *pilpul* is completely at odds with true Judaism, which emphasizes inculcating *practical action* informed by an understanding of Jews' task in the world rather than theoretical, intellectual rumination. In this sense, Hirsch sees *Wissenschaft* antiquarianism and Jewish traditionalism's devotion to *pilpul* as different expressions of the same problem. Both see study as an end in itself rather seeking practical knowledge focused on purposeful action in the world.[158]

Hirsch is aware that many Jewish traditionalists did not see themselves as neglecting seeking the purpose of halakhah. For this, they turned to what they regarded as a native Jewish tradition, namely, kabbalah. Hirsch agrees that kabbalah contains important teachings regarding the "spirit" of Judaism. He even used a copy of the *Zohar* gifted to him by his grandfather Mendel

153 See Hirsch, *NB*, Brief 18, 90; *NL*, Letter 18, 265–266. See p. 253 note 115 of this volume.

154 Hirsch cites *Genesis Rabbah* 44:1 and *Sifra*, 13:9. See Hirsch, *NB*, Brief 18, 90–91, note; *NL*, Letter 18, 266–267, note.

155 Hirsch, *NB*, Brief 18, 90–91; *NL*, Letter 18, 266–267.

156 Hirsch, *NB*, Brief 18, 91; *NL*, Letter 18, 267. Hirsch cites Tosefot on Babylonian Talmud Sanhedrin 24a, s.v. *belulah*.

157 Hirsch, *NB*, Brief 18, 91; *NL*, Letter 18, 267.

158 See p. 99 note 98 of this volume.

Frankfurter in composing *Horeb*.[159] But for Hirsch kabbalah became corrupted, as it came to interpret halakhah as a "magical mechanism, a way of influencing theosophical worlds or protecting against demonic dream worlds (*Traumwelten*)."[160]

Some Jews in Hirsch's day saw the growing Hasidic movement as a remedy for failures of Jewish traditionalism. Hirsch does not agree. He writes that in rabbinic literature the term *hasid* refers to someone who lives in the world by devoting himself entirely to others.[161] By contrast, Hirsch contends that contemporary Hasidim misuse the term, interpreting a *hasid* as one who lives "a life of seclusion, contemplation, and prayer." For Hirsch, this mistaken understanding derives from interpreting the term *hasid* according to concepts "from outside" Judaism, namely, in accordance with monastic Catholic ideals of piety.[162]

Despite these criticisms of Jewish traditionalism, Hirsch thinks that it preserves crucial Jewish truths. Hirsch claims that in regarding themselves as personally addressed by the Torah and responsible for fulfilling its commandments regardless of whether these commandments contribute to personal happiness, the traditionalist Jew better understands the intention of the Torah than Maskilim, Reformers, or adherents of *Wissenschaft*.[163] And Hirsch thinks that Jewish traditionalists' unwavering commitment to halakhic practice preserves an insight that many Jewish modernizers have lost, namely, that willingness to sacrifice "life, possessions and pleasures" to a higher cause gives meaning and joy to one's life that can never be matched by those who make maximizing personal pleasure their conscious goal.[164] While Hirsch thinks that Jewish traditionalists have largely adopted an uncomprehending attitude toward Judaism, they prepare the soil for a reasonable Judaism by sustaining a community strictly committed to obeying the laws of the Torah.

In sum, when Hirsch describes himself as belonging to "no party," he is referring to his belief that each major group within contemporary German Judaism possesses elements of truth and error. Hirsch sees it as his task to weave together the partial truths grasped by each group into an inspiring,

159 See Breuer, "Aus den Vorarbeiten zum Horeb," 143–144.

160 Hirsch, *NB*, Brief 18, 92; *NL*, Letter 18, 267–268.

161 Hirsch notes that David, "a man who from his earliest youth labored ceaselessly for the spiritual and material welfare of his people," was called a *hasid*. See Hirsch, *Die Psalmen*, 2:80; *The Psalms*, 2:107–108 (commentary on Psalm 86:2). Hirsch similarly cites *Pirkei Avot* 5:10, which calls a *hasid* a person who lives by the principle "what is mine is yours and what is yours is yours." See Hirsch, *NB*, Brief 15, 73; *NL*, Letter 15, 202.

162 Ibid.

163 See p. 256 of this volume.

164 See pp. 258–260 of this volume, Hirsch, *NB*, Brief 4, 20–22, Brief 18, 91–92, 95; *NL*, Letter 4, 58, Letter 18, 267, 271.

authentic vision of Judaism for contemporary German Jews. Hirsch claims to derive this new vision not from independent philosophical or theological reasoning, but from a direct reading of the divinely revealed Torah, both Written and Oral.

Hirsch on the Written Torah's relation to the Oral Torah

Hirsch's conception of the Written Torah's relation to the Oral Torah in his early writings draws on elements found in both Mendelssohn and Zunz. In an important passage in Letter 18 of the *Nineteen Letters*, he outlines the relationship between the Oral Torah and Written Torah:

> Originally only the fundamental principles (*Grundnormen*) of Israel's *Wissenschaft* were recorded in writing, the Written Torah *(Torah shebikhtav)*, but the detailed explanation and above all the spirit (*Geist*) which is its life (*Leben*) could only be preserved in the living word (*lebendingem Wort*), Oral Torah (*Torah she-b'al peh*). The pressures of the times and the dispersion threatened the destruction of our *Wissenschaft*, so the *Mishnah* was recorded in writing leaving the spirit to the oral word. The pressure of the times demanded more: the spirit (*Geist*) of the *Mishnah* was written but only in its practical expression in the *Gemara*; the *Gemara's* spirit (*Geist*) remained an oral teaching. The pressure of the times demanded more: the spirit (*Geist*) of *Tanakh* and *Gemara* were written in *Aggadot*, but again only in veiled form, so that one must actively penetrate them [the *Aggadot*] and reveal its spirit (*Geist*), assisted by [teachings] passed down orally (emphasis in original).[165]

For Hirsch, the Written Torah contains Judaism's "fundamental teachings," while the Oral Torah contains two elements: (1) "the detailed explanation" of the Written Torah and (2) "the spirit" (*Geist*) of the Written Torah. In a later passage in the *Nineteen Letters*, Hirsch identifies the first element primarily with *halakhah* and the second with *aggadah*.[166] Like Mendelssohn, Hirsch sees the Oral Torah as having two main tasks: to supply the details, which are not elaborated in the Bible, especially regarding how to practice law, and to explain the deeper meaning and purpose, i.e., the "spirit," of the Bible.[167] But

165 Hirsch, *NB*, Brief 18, 88; *NL*, Letter 18, 263.
166 See Hirsch, *NB*, Brief 18, 98; *NL*, Letter 18, 273.
167 For Mendelssohn's view, see pp. 114–116 of this volume.

in *Horeb*, Hirsch offers a fuller account of the difference between halakhah and aggadah, which is similar to Zunz's account in important respects.

Hirsch notes that the Oral Torah includes legal traditions that were transmitted from generation to generation orally, which is why the laws of the Oral Torah are called *shmateta* (from the Hebrew root *shma* meaning to be heard). These traditions came to an end with the completion of the Gemara.[168] Hirsch defines *aggadeta* as "ideas, which arose from the spirit (*Geist*) of each individual, which the individual spoke (*hegid*)." As such, the "sphere of aggadah" is "free and capable of enlargement at all times." Hirsch concludes that since *shmateta* "emanates from the authority which has the power to bind," it is "obligatory" while *aggadeta*, which "represents only the views of individuals . . . has no power to bind."[169] For both Hirsch and Zunz the Oral Torah is "oral" in two distinct senses. With halakhah, it is oral in the sense that the details of the commandments were passed down orally from generation to generation. But for aggadah, it is oral in the sense that it involves free insights of the individual that were communicated orally.

The Jewish task

We have seen that the *Nineteen Letters* can be understood as Hirsch's attempt to translate biblical teachings for contemporary German Jews. In Letters 3–9 he lays out a vision of Judaism, which he sees emerging from reading the Torah as a revelation from God. Since Hirsch regards the Bible, especially the Pentateuch, as containing the Torah's basic concepts, these letters focus on a theological exposition of the Pentateuch with most attention given to the first twelve chapters of Genesis. Hirsch often concludes the chapter with a long translation, usually from the Prophets or the Writings, that he sees as supplementing the basic concepts he derives from the Pentateuch.[170] Hirsch also cites aggadic

[168] See *Horev*, x; Hirsch, *Horeb*, clviii. The term *shmateta* is talmudic. See *JT*, Yebamot, 50a. Also see *BT*, Eruvin, 9b, 65a; Kiddushin, 50b; Berakhot, 33a, 42a; Sotah, 21b, Sanhedrin, 38b, Baba Kamma, 60b.

[169] See Hirsch, *Horev*, x; *Horeb*, clvii–clviii. Compare Zunz's view on pp. 151–155 of this volume. Hirsch adds, however, that while *aggadeta* is not binding, one must "welcome the confirmation of any views which show agreement with those of our sages." This is because the rabbinic sages were "much nearer to the origin and the early tradition." Hirsch, *Horev*, xi; *Horeb*, clviii–clvix. Hirsch maintained that *aggadeta* was not binding throughout his life. In an 1876 letter to Rabbi Hille Wechsler, Hirsch wrote that rabbinic statements that contradicted science need not be believed because they were within the realm of *aggadeta*, not *shmateta*. See Hirsch, *CW*, 9:201–215.

[170] I will discuss an example in the next chapter. See pp. 292–294 of this volume.

statements to elucidate the "spirit" of these basic concepts. The following chart summarizes the subject matter of Letters 3–9 and the passages from the Written Torah and Oral Torah that Hirsch translates or cites:

Letter	*Subject*	*Passage from Pentateuch that is basis of chapter*	*Biblical sources translated*	*Rabbinic passages cited*
3	Creation of the world	Genesis 1:1–25	Psalm 29 Job 37 Psalm 104: 2–4 Isaiah 55:10–11	*Yalkut Shimoni,* Genesis 5 *Yalkut Shimoni,* Psalms 857 *Pirkei Avot,* 5:1 *Genesis Rabbah* 12:2
4	Creation of human beings	Genesis 1:26–27 Genesis 2:4–25	Psalm 103:1–6; 15–22	Yalkut Shimoni, Jethro 227 *BT,* Nidah, 16b
5	Origins of idolatry and human suffering	Genesis 1:28 Genesis 2:16–17 Genesis 3:1–8:1		*BT*, Sanhedrin, 56a
6	Beginning of human history	Genesis chs. 9–11	Isaiah 2 Ecclesiastes 1:2–15 and 12:13 Psalm 90:1–7 Psalm 67 II Samuel 23:1–7	
7	Jews' task in the world[171]		Deuteronomy 33:2–4	
8	Creation of Jewish people	Genesis chs. 12– end of Deuteronomy	Psalms 105:13–15 Isaiah 19:1 Numbers 24:5–7 Numbers 23:21–23	
9	Jewish exile		Jeremiah 2:28 Isaiah 40:3–5 Isaiah 52:11–56:7	

[171] This chapter is unlike the others. It does not follow a specific passage from the Pentateuch (Chapter 9 also does not follow a Pentateuchal passage, but this is to be expected since it describes post-Pentateuchal Jewish history). It is also seemingly out of place as one would have expected it to follow Chapter 8, which deals with the creation of the Jewish people. This placement may indicate Hirsch's view that the Jewish people is defined by its mission and has no *raison d'être* without it.

For Hirsch, the Bible teaches that the Jews' task in the world is inextricably linked to humanity's. It therefore begins by describing God's relation to the world. Everything in the universe is the creation of a single, unique God with all of nature forming a perfectly ordered "harmonious system."[172] God sets down laws of nature, and since all nonhuman creatures naturally comply with these laws, they can be described as God's perfectly obedient servants.[173]

According to Hirsch, Genesis describes the world as composed of opposites that it calls "light and dark." Light is a positive principle of matter and energy associated with love and life, while darkness is a negative principle of limits and boundaries associated with justice and death.[174] God, whom Hirsch calls the "Unique-One-Unifying All" (*Alleine*),[175] is the "mediator of opposites" who joins these two principles.[176] Hirsch writes that Genesis further describes everything in nature as united in "one great bond of love."[177] This great bond involves receiving in order to give in a perpetual cycle. For example, the seed is received by the earth, which then produces a tree with fruit. This fruit contains seeds, which will then be given to the ground so that the cycle can repeat itself.[178]

Hirsch then moves to God's creation of human beings as described in Genesis 1 and 2. Like all else in nature, humans are God's servants who must obey God's laws. The difference is that while all other beings comply with God's laws from *necessity*, human beings alone can *freely* choose whether or not to obey God.[179] As with the laws governing the natural world, the laws governing human conduct bring harmony to the world when followed. But when human beings rebel against God and disobey, they bring chaos and destruction to the world.[180]

[172] Hirsch, *NB*, Brief 3, 12; *NL*, Letter 3, 29.

[173] Hirsch, *NB*, Brief 3, 14–15; *NL*, Letter 3, 32.

[174] Hirsch, *NB*, Brief 3, 12; *NL*, Letter 3, 30.

[175] It is difficult to translate the term *Alleine*, which Hirsch repeatedly uses to describe God. *All* means "all," *eine* is "one," while *allein* is "unique." Hirsch explains the term by noting that God "unifies (*einet*) a myriad into an all (*zum All*)." I therefore translate *Alleine* as "Unique-One-Unifying-All." In his commentary on the Pentateuch, Hirsch translates God being *ehad* (one) as *einzig Eine*, that is, the "Unique One." See Hirsch, *Der Pentateuch* 5:79; *The Hirsch Chumash*, 5:106 (Deuteronomy 6:4).

[176] Ibid.

[177] Hirsch, *NB*, Brief 3, 16; *NL*, Letter 3, 33.

[178] As Hirsch puts it, "Everything receives strength and resources not for itself but merely in order to give and thereby attain fulfillment of the purpose of its existence . . . Everything in nature breathes 'love' to you." See Hirsch, *NB*, Brief 3, 16; *NL*, Letter 3, 34.

[179] Hirsch, *NB*, Brief 4, 18; *NL*, Letter 4, 56. For the source from which Hirsch drew this idea, see p. 242 note 76 of this volume.

[180] Hirsch, *NB*, Brief 5, 24–25; *NL*, Letter 5, 76–77.

In defining the purpose of human life, Hirsch engages in an implicit polemic with the maskilic/Mendelssohnian outlook. We have seen that for Mendelssohn God created the world to benefit human beings by providing a context in which they could achieve happiness and perfection through *Bildung*.[181] Mendelssohn considers human beings the pinnacle of creation, with everything on earth existing to promote human happiness.[182] He interprets the creation of human beings in God's image to mean that like God human beings are *ends in themselves* who *know truth* and *rule the earth* through their *intellects*.[183]

Hirsch rejects this line of thinking. For Hirsch, humans being created in God's image (*tzelem elohim*) means not that their happiness is the purpose of creation but, rather, that they are tasked with imitating God's justice and love by freely fulfilling God's moral will. The world does not exist to serve human beings—human beings exist to serve the world.[184] *Bildung* is not the *goal* of life, but a *means* to fulfill one's divinely appointed task.[185]

Hirsch interprets the command given to Adam in the Garden of Eden not to eat from the Tree of Knowledge of Good and Evil as meaning that humans are supposed to obey God's will not because "it strikes us as being right, wise and good," but "merely because it is God's will." For fulfilling God's will only because it makes sense to us is not *obedience to God*, but "*obedience to oneself*."[186] This may seem like a bleak view. But Hirsch writes that one of life's secrets is that sacrificing happiness for the sake of obeying God does not *increase* suffering, but *decreases* it. By focusing one's attention on serving God, a person "transcends life's vicissitudes," finding equanimity by seeing "in every new blessing, as in every loss, merely another challenge to tackle anew the same unchanging task." This, Hirsch writes, is the meaning of the rabbinic teaching of *simhah shel mitzvah* (joy in performing commandments).[187]

[181] See pp. 99–100 of this volume.

[182] See p. 100 note 101 of this volume.

[183] See Mendelssohn, *JubA*, 15.2, 13 (Commentary on Genesis 1:26). Also see ibid., 14 (Commentary on Genesis 1:28) s.v. *vekivshu'a*, where Mendelssohn writes, "[God] gave the human being power and dominance on the land to *do as he desires* (*la'asot kirtzono*) with animals, with those which swarm, and with everything which crawls on the land, and to build, plant, uproot, dig etc. to establish a political community" (emphasis mine).

[184] See Hirsch, *NB*, Brief 4, 17–18; Hirsch, *NL*, Letter 4, 55–56; *NB*, Brief 5, 24; *NL*, Letter 5, 76. In her memoirs, Glikl presents a similar idea. See Glikl, *Memoirs*, 51.

[185] Hirsch, *NB*, Brief 4, 19; *NL*, Letter 4, 57.

[186] Hirsch, *NB*, Brief 5, 25; *NL*, Letter 5, 78.

[187] Hirsch, *NB*, Brief 4, 20–21; *NL*, Letter 4, 58. See Hirsch, *Der Pentateuch*, 1:366–367; *The Hirsch Chumash*, 1:510–511 (Commentary to Genesis 24:1 s.v. *berakh et Avraham bakol*).

For Hirsch, Adam and Eve's sin in eating from the Tree of Knowledge of Good and Evil involved their seeking to judge good and evil for themselves *independently* of the divine will. In defining good and evil for oneself, the natural tendency is to understand good as what "tastes sweet" to me and evil as "what tastes bitter" to me. That is, I define as "good" what I perceive contributes to my happiness and "evil" as what I perceive detracts from it.[188] In setting personal happiness above responsibility to God, Adam and Eve violated their purpose and thus "forfeited (*verwirkt*) any claim to presence [on earth]" and so deserved to die.[189] But God did not wish to inflict this punishment but, rather, to educate them.[190] So God instead informed Adam and Eve that they would be expelled from their pain-free existence in the Garden of Eden and experience suffering in the world. Hirsch explains this psychologically. Prior to the sin, Adam and Eve's desires were moderate and "nature accorded with their wishes." But when they prioritized pleasure, they increased desires, creating "demands greater than could be fulfilled" and thus experienced much disappointment and pain.[191] Before their sin, Adam and Eve had no need for "renunciation" (*Entsagung*), but after the sin it became necessary. Increased needs and desires meant that Adam could now only earn his bread through hard work. Hirsch explains Eve's renunciation as even greater. With greater needs and desires, raising children became much more difficult, and woman now needed to sacrifice to raise her children. As Hirsch puts it, "There is no greater happiness for a woman than having children, but this greatest happiness can only be purchased through the greatest renunciation." For Hirsch, these increased desires were also the source of inequality between the sexes. With increased needs woman "became dependent on her husband as the primary breadwinner," which "compromised men and women's original equality."[192]

Hirsch sees Adam's and Eve's punishment ultimately as benefitting humanity, since learning renunciation is the key to self-development. As he puts it, "Renunciation makes a person free (*frei*), it brings out a self which is

[188] Hirsch, *NB*, Brief 5, 26; *NL*, Letter 5, 78. See Hirsch, *Der Pentateuch*, 1:58–59; *The Hirsch Chumash*, 1:76–78 (Commentary to Genesis 2:9); this is very close to Spinoza's conception of good and evil. See Spinoza, *Ethics*, Part 3, Proposition 9, Scholia; Part 4, Definitions 1–2.

[189] Hirsch, *NB*, Brief 5, 26; *NL*, Letter 5, 78.

[190] Hirsch, *NB*, Brief 5, 26–27; *NL*, Letter 5, 78–79.

[191] See Hirsch, *Der Pentateuch*, 1:80; *The Hirsch Chumash*, 1:108–109 (Commentary to Genesis 3:16).

[192] For Hirsch, this is the meaning of God telling Eve that "he [Adam] will rule over you" (Genesis 3:16). See ibid.

better, nobler, and more devoted to God. It makes a person independent of external things, of what the earth offers and refuses. A person's sense of self-worth springs from being true to his duties to God, and in this he also finds undisturbed felicity."[193]

Continuing his reading of Genesis, Hirsch notes that following Adam's and Eve's expulsion from Eden, idolatry emerged. The Bible teaches that idolatry involves worshipping forces of nature by regarding these forces not as ruled by God, but as independent powers, each seeking their own "possessions, enjoyment, and domination." In other words, it involves worshipping *creatures* rather than the *Creator*. Seeing nature this way, the individual seeks to imitate these self-seeking forces and worships them with the hope of currying their favor to advance her own enjoyment. Since these forces, which were deified, were regarded as selfish, striving to indulge one's desires came to be regarded as "a divine goal." For Hirsch, the subsequent story of the flood teaches that when everyone prioritizes their own enjoyment above all else, this creates widespread immorality that culminates in disaster.[194]

Hirsch notes that the Written Torah does not contain an account of the moral commandments that God reveals to humanity. He explains that this is because the Written Torah is a book of instruction directed to Israel, and the Jews were later given a revelation on Mount Sinai that superseded the earlier one given to humanity. But Hirsch explains that the Oral Torah (*BT*, Sanhedrin, 56a) preserves "an indication" (*Nachhall*) of God's revelation to humanity in the form of the seven Noahide Commandments, which he distills to three "basic principles": (1) acknowledging God as the "Unique-One-Unifying All," (2) commandments of justice "guided by the inner revelation of human conscience," and (3) control of "bestial drives" and "protection against bestial degeneration." Hirsch notes, however, that the Noahide Commandments do not contain demands based on "lovingkindness."[195]

Turning to the story of the Tower of Babel (Genesis 11), Hirsch writes that following the flood humans developed technological prowess, allowing them

[193] Hirsch, *Der Pentateuch* 1:82; *The Hirsch Chumash*, 1:110 (Commentary to Genesis 3: 17).
[194] Hirsch, *NB*, Brief 5, 27–28; *NL*, Letter 5, 79–80.
[195] Hirsch, *NB*, Brief 5, 25; *NL*, Letter 5, 77. See Hirsch's more elaborate discussion of the Noahide laws in his commentary on the Pentateuch in Hirsch, *Der Pentateuch*, 1:61–63; *The Hirsch Chumash*, 1:80–83 (Commentary to Genesis 2:16).

to control nature. This led them to think that they "could dispense with God." God therefore dispersed the people, separating them into nations so that "corruption festering at one end [would no longer] quickly infect the whole."[196] This began the cycles of history in which nations arise, each striving to amass possessions and luxuries before "crashing into ruin" and "making way for a new generation to try the same." Hirsch writes that when enough of these cycles occur, humanity will ultimately realize that "all efforts to secure lasting happiness through wealth and self-gratification have failed" and appreciate that only pursuing "God-revering efforts on behalf of justice and love will endure forever."[197]

Hirsch then turns to Jewish history. He notes that the nation of Israel has a unique educational mission to the world. While the rest of humanity is taught knowledge of God by "experience and fate," God introduced one people to show by its "destiny and life" that "God, the Unique One-Unifying-All, is the sole foundation of life and that life's only purpose is the fulfillment of His will."[198] Hirsch characterizes the Jews as a nation defined solely by its duties to God.[199] To educate humanity, the Jews had to be poor in material possessions and politically weak. This would teach them and the world that their survival was solely the result of their dependence on God. Furthermore, to show themselves a people exclusively committed to obeying God, God gave the Jews an elaborate set of duties that they had to devote all their resources to fulfilling. In these ways, the Jews teach humanity that everything depends on God and that the purpose of life is to fulfill God's ethical will.[200]

Hirsch explains that the Bible presents Abraham as the progenitor of Israel. Reared among idolaters, Abraham sought out the "Unique-One-Unifying All." When God called him, Abraham willingly gave up "his fatherland, his birthplace, his family, and his parental home (*Elternhaus*)" and wandered, dependent on God. He expressed his "love" (*ahavah*) for God by "*loving God's children*, his fellowmen" (emphasis in original). To this love was joined

196 Hirsch, *NB*, Brief 6, 28–29; *NL*, Letter 6, 91.

197 Hirsch, *NB*, Brief 6, 28–29; *NL*, Letter 6, 92.

198 Hirsch, *NB*, Brief 7, 35; *NL*, Letter 7, 105.

199 Ibid. In several other places in the *NL*, Hirsch repeats this idea. See Hirsch, *NB*, Brief 18, 87; *NL*, Letter 18, 263, "Israel's entire essence (*Wesen*) rests on the Torah. It is its ground, goal and lifeblood in its veins"; Hirsch, *NB*, Brief 16, 79; *NL*, Letter 16, 224, "The bond of Israel was never land and soil, but only the common tasks of the Torah."

200 Hirsch, *NB*, Brief 7, 35–36; *NL*, Letter 7, 105–106.

firm "trust" (*emunah*) in God and readiness to surrender to God without complaint "all that is most precious (*yirah*)."[201]

Abraham bequeathed these qualities to his son Isaac and to his grandson Jacob. With Jacob the family formed into a nation devoted to God that had to attain its "nationhood" (*Volkstühmlichkeit*) through suffering. Egypt was the crucible of this suffering as Jacob's descendants were slaves there until God redeemed them. Israel then received the Torah from God on Mount Sinai and wandered in the desert for forty years, again dependent on God alone. In this way, they became what the Torah calls a " kingdom of priests" (*mamlekhet kohanim*), which Hirsch glosses as a "guardian of God's word in the midst of humanity like a priest among a people" and a "holy nation" (*goy kadosh*) which Hirsch explains as a nation "standing apart in holiness, never entering into the drives and aspirations of other nations."[202]

The nation of Israel was therefore removed from history, existing as a powerless, stateless people utterly dependent on God as they wandered through the desert. But they entered history as a nation among nations when God led them to conquer Canaan. God's purpose was to show the nations of the world that the blessings they most prized, namely, "land, prosperity, and the *institutions of statehood*" (emphasis in original) could be used to fulfill God's will.[203]

But Israel failed. Rather than fulfilling the Torah amidst prosperity, it instead turned to materialism and idolatry. God therefore had to lead Israel into exile. Since Jewish nationhood was never dependent on a land or material things, but solely on their religious mission as defined by the Torah, Jews retained their nationhood in exile.[204] For Hirsch, exile had a positive, constructive dimension. It helped perfect the Jews by teaching them the disastrous consequences of worshipping "wealth and power." In exile, Jews learned obedience and willingness to sacrifice themselves to serve God. That

201 Hirsch, *NB*, Brief 8, 37–38; *NL*, Letter 8, 113–114. Hirsch's understanding of *emunah* (faith) not as propositional belief but as "trust" (*Vertrauen*) in God is very similar to Mendelssohn's view. See p. 59 of this volume.

202 The expressions "kingdom of priests" and "holy nation" appear in Exodus 19:6. See Hirsch, *NB*, Brief 8, 38–40; *NL*, Letter 8, 114–115.

203 Hirsch, *NB*, Brief 8, 40; *NL*, Letter 8, 116.

204 Hirsch, *NB*, Brief 9, 40; *NL*, Letter 9, 125. As Hirsch puts it, when Israel lost its land its mission was not "cancelled" (*aufgehoben*). This is an implicit rejoinder to the Spinozistic line of thinking, which sees Judaism as a political religion and Jewish nationhood and election as dependent on statehood. See Spinoza, *Tractatus Theologico-Politicus*, ch. 3.

is why when Christians dangled "earthly happiness" before Jews if they renounced Judaism, most Jews resisted even when this cost them their lives. As Hirsch put it, "the entire history of *Galut* (exile) is an altar on which it [Israel] sacrificed everything that men desire and love for the sake of acknowledging God and His Torah (*Lehre*)."[205] For Hirsch, the exile is not just of value for educating Jews; it also helped the Jewish people fulfill its priestly mission to educate humanity. For when Gentile nations witnessed Jews willing to let themselves be murdered out of devotion to God and Torah, this made a great impression on them.[206]

Hirsch then addresses contemporary Jews' task in light of emancipation. Citing Jeremiah 29:5–7, Hirsch stresses Jews' halakhic duty to be loyal citizens.[207] In *Horeb*, Hirsch devotes an entire chapter to this principle, enumerating several duties a Jew owes to the state, including: (1) establishing a home and maintaining it, which is a civic duty since the state flourishes through "countless individual homes united in honest endeavor"; (2) obeying all the laws of the state; (3) contributing one's money, energy, wisdom, and even one's life to the state; (4) being loyal to the state "with heart and mind" and protecting its honor with "love and pride"; (5) promoting truth, justice, and peace within the state.[208]

In *Horeb*, Hirsch implicitly rejects what later became Zionism by emphasizing that it is absolutely forbidden for Jews to seek to regain their ancestral land "by any external means."[209] He also notes that Jews' duty to the states in which they reside is not dependent on how the state treats them and must be fulfilled "even should they [the state] deny your right to be a human being."[210] In support of these doctrines, Hirsch cites, in addition to the passage from

[205] Hirsch, *NB*, Brief 9, 44; *NL*, Letter 9, 127.

[206] As Hirsch puts it, "Is it conceivable that these [nations] learned nothing from all this? Could they fail to learn that amidst such a fate, something higher, the Unique-One-Unifying All preserved [Israel] in its faithfulness, which is the human calling?" See Hirsch, *NB*, Brief 9, 44; *NL*, Letter 9, 128.

[207] Hirsch, *NB*, Brief 16, 79; *NL*, Letter 16, 224.

[208] See Hirsch, *Horev*, Kap. 96, #609, 617–618; *Horeb*, ch. 96, #609, 462.

[209] Hirsch, *Horev*, Kap. 96, #608, 617; *Horeb*, ch. 96, #608, 461. Zionism arose later in Hirsch's lifetime, and when the proto-Zionist Rabbi Zvi Hirsch Kalischer tried to enlist Hirsch's support for it, Hirsch forcefully rebuffed him. On Hirsch's attitude to Zionism, see Hirsch, *Sefer Shemesh Marpeh*, 211–217; Hildesheimer, "Rabbi Zvi Hirsch Kalischer and Rabbi Samson Raphael Hirsch."

[210] See Hirsch, *Horev*, Kap. 96, #609, 618; *Horeb*, ch. 96, #609, 462. Japhet notes that Hirsch sometimes rendered the famous passage from Isaiah 2:3, "For out of Zion shall go the Torah and the word of God from Jerusalem", as "from where the Torah emanates, there is my Jerusalem." See Japhet, "The Secession from Frankfurt," 106.

Jeremiah, the rabbinic concept of *dina demalkhuta dina* (the law of the land is the law).[211]

Hirsch also addresses the question of whether Jewish emancipation is desirable in light of Jews' task in the world. He embraces emancipation for three reasons.[212] First, he "blesses" it as a means of furthering the development of the Jewish "spirit" (*Geistes*). As we have seen, Hirsch thinks that as a result of social and political inequality, Jews turned inward, retreating from the world and taking refuge in *pilpulistic* Talmud study. Hirsch sees emancipation as fostering Jews' engagement with western culture enabling "the free unfolding of its [Israel's] noble character" by both promoting an intellectual understanding of Judaism, and encouraging Jewish moral activity in the world.[213]

Second, Hirsch sees emancipation as helping the Jewish people fulfill its educational mission to humanity. As he puts it:

> If amidst a society idolizing possessions and pleasure, Israel were to live its life calmly in justice and love; if all around it families were declining through sensuality and debauchery, but the sons and daughters of Yisrael were to bloom in the powerful youthful ornament of pure morality and innocence: if everywhere families should no longer raise in the nursery, pure sprouts suffused by God, but every home of Israel were to be a temple raising [children] to fear, love, and trust God . . . If Israel so dispersed were to flourish as priests of God and pure humanity . . . what a mighty lever for the ultimate goal of human education![214]

211 Hirsch, *Horev*, Kap. 96, #609, 618; *Horeb*, ch. 96, #609, 462. Hirsch's concept of loyalty to the state bears strong affinities to Lutheran concepts of political loyalty as religious duty. The *Augsburg Confession* emphasizes that Christians have an obligation to obey the laws of the state as long as this does not infringe on their religion and rejects the Catholic tendency to "annul or disrupt secular law and obedience to political authority." See *The Book of Concord*, "The Augsburg Confession," #16, 50–51, #28, 92. Of course, there are differences between Hirsch's position and the Augsburg Confession. The Augsburg Confession is primarily concerned about the Catholic Church intervening in politics and seeking to control it. By contrast, Hirsch is primarily concerned about Jews who feel enmity toward the state and therefore do not to feel the need to be loyal to it, contribute to it, or obey its laws.

212 Many traditionalist Orthodox rabbis had a negative or at least conflicted view of Jewish emancipation, seeing it as threatening the dissolution of Judaism. See Breuer, *Modernity within Tradition*, 74–75.

213 Hirsch, *NB*, Brief 16, 81; *NL*, Letter 16, 226.

214 Hirsch, *NB*, Brief 9, 44–45; *NL*, Letter 9, 128

For Hirsch, emancipation can further the Jews' mission by enabling them to model obedience to God even when given the opportunity to pursue materialistic ends. Hirsch describes preserving obedience to God and the Torah in the context of emancipation as a "greater test" (*noch größere Prüfungsschule*) than preserving such obedience in pre-emancipation society and thus of having a greater potential impact on society.[215] In *Horeb,* he amplifies the significance of this task in halakhic terms by expounding on the significance of the Jews being a "priestly nation." Just as a priest upholds the "vision of God and humanity" among his people through his irreproachable ethical conduct, so the Jews must uphold the divine vision among the nations by "being a holy nation, raised above every injustice, profaneness, and hardheartedness."[216] This requires that a Jew live committed to the Torah, treating all creatures with justice and love. Because of the Jews' educational mission, Hirsch stresses that it is particularly important for a Jew to be ethically unimpeachable in her dealings with Gentiles and avoid giving even a *semblance* of dishonesty. For this reason, he notes that the rabbinic sages stated that stealing from Gentiles was *worse* than stealing from Jews. For with a Jew there is simply the transgression of stealing while with a Gentile there is also the transgression of profaning the divine name, a sin so great that, it is impossible to atone for except through death.[217]

Finally, Hirsch writes that Jews should celebrate emancipation because it reflects a deep moral impulse within modern civilization namely "a regard . . . for human rights (*Menschenrechts*)." Hirsch makes clear, however, that emancipation is of value only if it helps Jews further their moral mission to humanity. He writes that he would "grieve" (*trauerte*) if "Israel were to idolize emancipation as just a means to a comfortable life and greater opportunity to acquire possessions and pleasures." If this were the case, emancipation would prove a curse rather than a blessing.[218]

215 Hirsch, *NB,* Brief 16, 80; Hirsch, *NL,* Letter 16, 225.

216 Hirsch, *Horev,* kap. 97, #613, 622; *Horeb,* ch. 97, #613, 465.

217 Hirsch, *Horev,* kap. 97, #613, 625–626; *Horeb,* ch. 97, #613–614, 466–468. On the prohibition of profaning the divine name, Hirsch cites Leviticus 22:31–33; *Pirkei Avot* 4:5, *BT,* Yoma, 86a, and *BT,* Kiddushin, 40a. On stealing from a Gentile being worse than stealing from a Jew, Hirsch cites the thirteenth-century halakhic work by Moses of Coucy, *Sefer Mitzvot Gadol* (*Great Book of Commandments*), Prohibition II, # 151.

218 Hirsch, *NB,* Brief 16, 82; Hirsch, *NL,* Letter 16, 226–227. Hirsch's position bears an affinity to Mendelssohn's. See p. 118 of this volume.

Hirsch's notion of exile having a positive educational value has precedents within the Jewish tradition, most notably in Judah Halevi's medieval work the *Kuzari*.[219] It is also clearly connected to Mendelssohn's doctrine of Jewish witness. But while Mendelssohn focuses on the Jews' role in teaching metaphysical *concepts*, most notably the unity of God, Hirsch's focuses on the Jews' role in teaching ethical principles, namely, *obedience* to God's moral will.[220]

Family, gender, and class in Hirsch's vision of Jewish education

For Hirsch, education is the key to Jews coming to know their task in the world. Throughout his life, Hirsch was deeply concerned with Jewish education. In 1853, two years after being appointed rabbi of the Orthodox congregation in Frankfurt, he founded a co-educational school there. But a decade and a half earlier, Hirsch had already outlined central elements of his philosophy of education in the *Nineteen Letters* and *Horeb*.

Two concepts are key. The first is Hirsch's designation of the Jew as a *Mensch-Jissroël* (human being–Israelite), which he first used in *Horeb*.[221] It is significant that Hirsch puts human being *before* Israelite for in doing so he signals that being a good Jew is not a goal *separate* from being a good human being but, rather, its *fullest actualization* as it involves supererogatory moral responsibility.[222] The second major educational concept is encapsulated in Hirsch's slogan *torah im derekh eretz* (Torah with the Way of the World). Although Hirsch did not use the slogan in the *Nineteen*

219 Halevi, *The Kuzari*, 4:23, 226–228.

220 To be sure, metaphysical truth is deeply connected to ethics for Mendelssohn, as we have seen. See pp. 102–104 of this volume. Nevertheless, the difference in how Mendelssohn and Hirsch describe the Jewish mission to humanity is striking.

221 See Hirsch, *Horev*, Kap. 1, #4, 5; Kap. 17, #126–127, 81; Kap. 21, #140, 92; Kap. 36, #268, 227; *Horeb*, Ch. 1, #4, 4; ch. 17, #126–127, 54–55; ch. 21, #140, 63; ch. 36, #268, 172.

222 See Hirsch's "Outline of Jewish Symbolism," where he writes that "the highest Jewish perfection is nothing but the highest fulfillment of human destiny." See Hirsch, *GS*, 3:335; *CW*, 3:128. See Hirsch, *Der Pentateuch*, 1:276; *The Hirsch Chumash*, 1:379 (commentary to Genesis 1:1). In several places Hirsch discusses what Jews' supererogatory moral responsibility involves. In the *Nineteen Letters* he claims that the moral law for humanity exemplified by the Noahide laws only includes observing dictates of justice, but not lovingkindness, while halakhah also includes dictates of lovingkindness. See Hirsch, *NB*, Brief 5, 25; Hirsch, *NL*, Letter 5, 77. In his "Outline of Jewish Symbolism," Hirsch writes that the Jews' greater actualization of humanity involves halakhah's special emphasis on sensual restraint. See Hirsch, *GS*, 3:329–332; *CW*, 3:123–125. In his commentary on Genesis 17:1, Hirsch

Letters or *Horeb*, the concept suffuses these early writings.[223] *Torah im derekh eretz* is a rabbinic concept found in *Pirkei Avot*, and Mordechai Breuer has shown that it was a guiding principle in Jewish education prior to Hirsch.[224] As we have seen, Hirsch's grandfather Mendel Frankfurter included *derekh eretz* among the educational goals of the school that he helped found in 1805.[225] But Hirsch elevated the importance of *torah im derekh eretz*, making it his guiding motto. He had the phrase engraved on the foundation stone of the community synagogue in Frankfurt and embroidered it in gold letters on the banner of the school he founded there.[226] Hirsch also gave the slogan his own distinctive interpretation. In his 1852 proposal for the Frankfurt school, Hirsch defined *torah im derekh eretz* as follows:

> [The school] is based on the ancient and sacred principle of Judaism that social knowledge and life (*sociales Wissen und Leben*) and religious knowledge and life not only do not exclude one another but rather condition, complete, and fulfill one another, and that the closest connection and interpenetration of the two produces welfare towards which we strive throughout our life on earth. *Social knowledge and life finds its first ground and consecration in the religious and the religious finds its first confirmation and actualization in the social.* (emphasis mine)[227]

For Hirsch "religious knowledge and life" refers to Torah while "social knowledge and life" refers to *derekh eretz. Derekh eretz* involves knowledge and actions that benefit both the individual and society. Elsewhere Hirsch makes clear that it includes earning a living, contributing to social order, propriety and courtesy, *Kultur*, and *Bildung*.[228]

contends (perhaps thinking of Kant) that while for humanity at large good intentions (what he calls "goodness of heart" [*guten Herzens*]) bestow moral worth, for Jews good intentions are not enough—intentions must be followed by deeds. See Hirsch, *Der Pentateuch*, 1:279: *The Hirsch Chumash*, 1:384.

223 To the best of my knowledge, Hirsch first used the slogan in an educational context in 1845 in his response to the Reform rabbinical assembly in Braunschweig. See Hirsch, *Sefer Shemesh Marpeh*, 194.

224 Breuer, *The Torah im Derekh Eretz*, 11–13.

225 See p. 231 note 7 of this volume.

226 See Breuer, *The Torah im Derekh Eretz*, 16.

227 See Sulzbach, "Zur Geschichte der Schulanstalten," 34–35, 44–45. This quote is found on p. 34.

228 See Hirsch, *Israels Gebete*, 436; *Chapters of the Fathers*, 22 (Commentary on *Pirkei Avot* 2:2); Hirsch, *Der Pentateuch*, 1:90; *The Hirsch Chumash*, 1:121 (Commentary on Genesis 3:24).

For Hirsch, Torah and *derekh eretz* mutually support one another. *Derekh eretz* promotes the Torah's values in several ways. Hirsch sees modern society's moving toward embracing the ideals of civil equality and emancipation as an expression of *derekh eretz* that helps actualize the Torah's concept of human equality.[229] Hirsch also sees Jews' participation in the world as helping them fulfill their divine mission. As the Jewish mission to humanity involves modeling a life of ethical obedience to God by living as dignified, middle-class German citizens, this requires that Jews be economically independent, cultured, well-mannered, loyal citizens, which means acquiring *derekh eretz*.

We have already seen that for Hirsch the Torah supports *derekh eretz* by accounting the duty to be loyal to the state as a religious duty and stressing the necessity for a Jew to act according to the highest ethical standards, especially in relation to her non-Jewish neighbors. But for Hirsch the lynchpin of *torah im derekh eretz* is the family.

Hirsch describes the founding of a home as "the highest task of life" since "the welfare of the people and humanity flowers in and through [it]."[230] The family is of great importance to the state as families train children to be honest, productive, loyal members of society. Hirsch's account of the family reflects many elements of the bourgeois sensibility of the post-Napoleonic Restoration period, especially in its account of male and female gender roles.[231]

For Hirsch, the Torah teaches that the husband's role is to amass wealth, protect the family, represent it to the outside world, and provide its general moral and religious direction.[232] Hirsch calls the husband the "sole representative and head of the household."[233] The wife who "gives herself up" to the husband's lead is responsible for "deploying and administering" the financial resources that the husband supplies and supervising family members to

[229] See p. 275 of this volume. Hirsch describes human equality as a central principle of the Torah. In his 1873 essay "The Educational Value of Judaism," he writes that "The perception of mankind in which all members are equal had its origin in Judaism." See *CW*, 7:266. In his commentary on Exodus 1:14, Hirsch writes that "*Complete equality of the stranger* with the *native-born* is a basic characteristic of Jewish law" (emphasis in original). See Hirsch, *Der Pentateuch*, 2:9; *The Hirsch Chumash*, 2:10. For an example of Hirsch enunciating this principle in his early writings, see Hirsch, *Horev*, Kap. 51, #379, 343; *Horeb*, ch. 51, #379, 255–256.

[230] Hirsch, *Horev*, Kap. 81, #530, 524; *Horeb*, ch. 81, #530, 395.

[231] For good discussions of bourgeois German constructions of gender and the family in the late eighteenth and early nineteenth centuries, see Frevert, *Women in German History*, 11–72; Hausen, "Family and Role Division."

[232] Hirsch, *Horev*, Kap. 80, #527, 522; *Horeb*, ch. 80, #527, 394.

[233] Hirsch, *Horev*, Kap. 81, #533, 526; *Horeb*, ch. 81, #533, 397

make sure they fulfill their responsibilities in the world.[234] Hirsch waxes poetic when describing the Jewish wife, calling her the "priestess of the home" (*Priesterin des Hauses*). He stresses that the husband is obliged to honor and protect his wife as his "holiest possession," while she "perfects his humanity" (*Menschthum*) by elevating him morally, as women possess special attunement to the good.[235] Both husband and wife are to be entirely devoted to one another and monogamy is expected on both sides. But Hirsch puts special emphasis on the need for female modesty, writing that a woman "should only adorn herself for her husband" and that "her home should be the fairest field of her activity."[236]

While the woman's sphere is the home, the man is not exempt from responsibility there. For Hirsch, the Torah dictates that it is the father's responsibility to educate the children, though in practice the father usually outsources this duty to the school.[237] The goal of Jewish education is "practical," namely, to learn the correct "way of life."[238] Education must help both male and female children achieve "independence" (*Selbstständigkeit*), which happens when they "set up their own home."[239] Focusing on male education, Hirsch writes that independence is promoted by cultivating three "capacities."[240]

234 See Hirsch, *Horev*, Kap. 80, #527, 522; Kap. 81, #533, 526; *Horeb*, ch. 80, #527, 394; ch. 81, #533, 397. See Hirsch, *GS*, 4:165; *Judaism Eternal*, 2:54.

235 See Hirsch, *Horev*, Kap. 81, #540, 532–533; *Horeb*, ch. 81, #540, 401. See Hirsch's comment on Proverbs 18:22, "He who has found a woman has found good," where Hirsch remarks that "the concept of 'woman' incorporates good." Hirsch, "Die Ehe," 51. The description of the woman as a "priestess" of the home is found in Christian Wilhelm Spieker's 1808 work, *Emiliens Stunden der Andacht*, where he writes that a woman's vocation "like the Priestess of Vesta, [is to] administer the quiet worship of innocence and virtue in the interior of the house." The passage is cited in Baader, *Gender, Judaism, and Bourgeois Culture*, 23. On the idea of women as naturally more moral than men, see Hirsch, *GS*, 4:163; *Judaism Eternal*, 2:51–52; Hausen, "Family and Role Division," 54–55.

236 Hirsch, *GS*, 4:163; *Judaism Eternal*, 2:51–52.

237 See Hirsch, *Horev*, Kap. 84, #548, 539–540; #556, 552; *Horeb*, ch. 84, #548, 406–497; #556, 415.

238 See *Horev*, Kap. 75, #492, 488; *Horeb*, ch. 75, #492, 370. As Hirsch explained in the plan for his school in Frankfurt, "We are not educating all our children to be theologians (*Theologen*), but we may not leave the religious sphere unknown to them. All should attain knowledge that befits honorable Jewish males and whose best possible attainment it is our religious duty to promote." See Sulzbach, "Zur Geschichte der Schulanstalten," 35. Hirsch's claim that Jewish education is not to educate "theologians" recalls Wessely's claim in *Divrei Shalom Ve'emet* that "we were not all created to become talmudic masters and to occupy ourselves with the depths of religion and to teach." See p. 84 of this volume. Hirsch's concepts of *Mensch-Jissroël* and *torah im derekh eretz* bear important affinities with Wessely's conception of the relation of *torat hashem* to *torat ha'adam*. On Hirsch's esteem for Wessely, see pp. 232–233 of this volume. An in-depth comparison of Hirsch's and Wessely's views on education remains an important scholarly desideratum.

239 Hirsch, *Horev*, Kap. 84, #552, 546; *Horeb*, ch. 84, #552, 411.

240 Hirsch, *Horev*, Kap. 84, #550, 541; *Horeb*, ch. 84, #550, 408.

The first capacity to be cultivated is a boy's *physical powers*. This requires providing proper food, clothing, and housing, and making sure that the child's environment is "kept tidy and clean." Boys should also be given exercise, and taught proper articulation and diction.[241] Second, the boy's *mental capacities* are to be developed. Hirsch describes the Torah as the "root and crown of [a Jew's] knowledge."[242] Like Mendelssohn and Zunz, he is harshly critical of the near exclusive emphasis on Talmud study for boys and the predominance of *pilpul* in traditionalist Orthodox education. Criticizing *pilpul*, Hirsch writes that "the spirit of the recent time has been dominated by the spirit of rumination (*Grübelgeist*)."[243] For Hirsch, the main problem with *pilpul* is that it distracts the student from the true purpose of the Torah, which is *fulfilling one's halakhic duties in the world with understanding and a sense of purpose*. He laments that the study of the Bible has been neglected or relegated to secondary status, writing that such an approach "is not the genuine way of Judaism."[244]

Hirsch explains that the Bible (*Tanakh*) must have educational priority because it contains the fundamental "concept of Judaism" in its narrative account of God's relation to the world and the Jews' task within it.[245] Only after understanding these fundamental concepts should the Talmud be studied.[246] In *Horeb*, Hirsch provides a more detailed account of the aims and course of study for boys, writing that a boy should begin by studying the Pentateuch, then the Prophets, and finally, the Writings. From the Pentateuch and the Prophets, the boy learns to understand God's relation to the world, human beings' place in the world, Jews' place among the nations, and the Jews' early struggles to fulfill their divine mission. From the Writings, the boy learns wisdom and poetry that can help support him spiritually through the struggles of life.[247] Understanding the mission of Israel, the boy is then introduced to his halakhic duties drawn from the Written Torah and from the "practical codes of the Oral Torah," especially Maimonides's *Mishneh Torah* and Joseph Karo's *Shulhan Arukh*.

[241] Ibid.
[242] See *Horev*, Kap. 84, #551, 542; *Horeb*, ch. 84, #551, 408.
[243] Hirsch, *NB*, Brief 15, 72; *NL*, Letter 15, 201. See p. 262 of this volume. Also see Hirsch's Letter to Z.H. May of April 13, 1835, found in Hirsch, *Horeb*, cxliii.
[244] Hirsch, *NB*, Brief 15, 72; *NL*, Letter 15, 201.
[245] Ibid.
[246] Hirsch, *NB*, Brief 18, 97–98; *NL*, Letter 18, 273.
[247] See Hirsch, *Horev*, Kap. 75, #494, 489; *Horeb*, ch. 75, #494, 371.

Hirsch notes that a boy is to be introduced to Mishnah and Gemara only at an older age and only if "his thirst for knowledge is aroused and if you have the opportunity."[248] Like Mendelssohn and Wessely, Hirsch claims that this order of Jewish education is the authentic one as attested to by rabbinic texts, while the traditionalist Ashkenazic emphasis on Talmud study from an early age is a dangerous deviation from Jewish tradition. He cites Pirkei Avot 5:25, which he explains to mean that study of Bible and Hebrew should begin at age five; Mishnah, which he glosses as "knowledge of one's religious duties" and "the rudiments of the Oral Torah," at age ten; and Gemara, which he defines as "deeper penetration into the science of Torah," only at age fifteen. Commenting that this order is "the natural way which leads to truth and life (*zur Wahrheit und zum Leben*)," Hirsch asks, "Why has this system been abandoned? Why has it been perverted?"[249]

For Hirsch, the Bible should be taught in the original Hebrew, which requires grammatical knowledge of the language. In the *Nineteen Letters* Hirsch writes that a boy should study Hebrew in order to understand the Bible "according to the *spirit* (*Geist*) of this language" (emphasis mine). Hirsch apparently has Herder in mind as in *The Spirit of Hebrew Poetry*, Herder had stressed that the key to understanding the ancient Hebrews was

[248] See Hirsch, *Horev*, Kap. 84, #551, 543–545; *Horeb*, ch. 84, #551, 409–410. Hirsch's lack of enthusiasm for the yeshiva, which focuses on Talmud study, is clear from his never having attempted to established one in Frankfurt despite the fact that his community, the *Israelitische Religionsgesellschaft*, gave him a mandate to do so. It was only Hirsch's successor, his son-in-law Salomon Breuer, who established a yeshiva in Frankfurt, and this move aroused much opposition from community members who saw it as deviating from Hirsch's approach. See Katz, "Rabbi Samson Raphael Hirsch: To the Right and to the Left," 26; Breuer, *Modernity within Tradition*, 114–115.

[249] Hirsch, *Horev*, Kap. 84, #551, 543–545; *Horeb*, ch. 84, #551, 409–410. See Hirsch, *NB*, Brief 15, 72; *NL*, Letter 15, 201; Hirsch, *Israels Gebete*, 513; *Chapters of the Fathers*, 95 (Commentary on *Pirkei Avot* 5:25). In his 1852 plan Hirsch proposed the following Judaic curriculum. There would be four classes, each lasting two years for students ages seven to fifteen. In the first class, which a child would enter at age seven, Genesis and Exodus would be studied along with some Proverbs. In the second class, which would begin at age nine, Leviticus and Numbers would be studied, while Genesis and Exodus would be reviewed. The child would also study the books of Joshua and Judges and a selection from the Mishnah. In the second year of the second class, "capable" students would be introduced to selections from the Talmud. In the third class, begun at age eleven, Deuteronomy would be studied and Leviticus and Numbers reviewed. Students would also learn a selection from Rashi's commentary on the Pentateuch and the books of Samuel, Kings, and Psalms. Mishnah would be continued, and capable boys would study Talmud. In the final class begun at age thirteen, the entire Pentateuch would be reviewed, and Isaiah, a selection from the other prophets, and the book of Job would be studied. Mishnah would be continued, an anthology of rabbinic parables and ethical adages would be introduced, and students would learn a selection from the legal codes of Maimonides and Joseph Karo. Advanced students would study Talmud instead of Mishnah, rabbinic parables and ethical adages, and legal codes. See Sulzbach, "Zur Geschichte der Schulanstalten," 44–45. It is significant that Hirsch recommends studying the Pentateuch independently of Rashi's commentary, which is only introduced in the third year. On the centrality of Rashi's commentary in early modern Ashkenazic Jewish education see p. 93 of this volume.

understanding their language.[250] In Letter 2 of the *Nineteen Letters* Hirsch describes two features of Hebrew. First, he notes that Hebrew words are composed of "word roots" (*Wortwurzeln*) that are "rich with meaning, depicting the object in words," resulting in Hebrew being a "quasi semi-symbolic writing."[251] Second, Hirsch notes that Hebrew is a parsimonious language, where "nothing is explained in detail" and many "assumptions" are omitted that the reader must supply through her "own effort." As such, reading Hebrew requires "an alert eye and ear, with a soul awakened to self-activity."[252]

In an important 1866 essay titled "Some Suggestions Regarding the Role of Hebrew Instruction in General Education," Hirsch argues that the Torah supports *derekh eretz* by promoting *Bildung* and *Kultur*. He notes that while *Bildung* and *Kultur* are often associated with wearing stylish clothes, elegant manners, and knowing "stock phrases borrowed from current literature," true *Bildung and Kultur* involve cultivating one's intellectual, affective, and linguistic capacities in service of the true and good.[253] The first and most obvious way that the Torah promotes *Bildung* and *Kultur* is by cultivating moral obedience through its commandments, historical narratives, and moral wisdom.[254] But Hirsch also notes other ways that Torah contributes to *Bildung*. He observes that Jews were traditionally known as a "nation of students" (*Studentenvolk*) because the duty to study Torah promoted a "thirst for knowledge," not for economic ends but for the "ennoblement and enrichment of the mind and heart."[255] Hirsch further remarks that Jewish education promotes knowledge of German since an important component of Jewish education is studying Hebrew, and learning a foreign

[250] Hirsch, *NB*, Brief 2, 8; *NL*, Letter 2, 16. It is often asserted that the *Nineteen Letters* is modelled on Judah Halevi's medieval dialogue the *Kuzari*, which is an apology for Judaism. It is, however, also likely that Hirsch used Herder's *The Spirit of Hebrew Poetry* as a model since Herder's work is a defense of the value of studying Hebrew in dialogue form. It begins with a youth named Alciphron dismissing Hebrew, which he calls "a poor and barbarous language," and complaining about having been forced to study it. In response, his interlocutor Euthyphro argues that Alciphron has been miseducated about Hebrew and Euthyphro tries to demonstrate Hebrew's beauty and richness and the need to understand its character to properly appreciate the Bible. See Herder, *Vom Geist*, 1:viii–ix, 2; *On the Spirit*, 1:18, 25–26. Geiger immediately noted the similarities between Herder's work and the *Nineteen Letters*. See Geiger, "Recension der *Neunzehn Briefe über Judenthum* (1)," 353. For a more detailed examination of the relationship between the *Nineteen Letters* and Herder's *The Spirit of Hebrew Poetry*, see Gottlieb, "Orthodoxy and the Orient."

[251] See Hirsch, *NB*, Brief 2, 8; *NL*, Letter 2, 16. This recalls, *mutatis mutandi*, Mendelssohn's claim that the Hebrew letters originated as imitative symbols. See Mendelssohn, *JubA*, 8: 176; *Jerusalem*, 110.

[252] Hirsch, *GS*, 2:440; Hirsch, *CW*, 7:70–71. I will explore these points in greater detail in chapter 7. See pp. 355–358 of this volume.

[253] Hirsch, *GS*, 2:437–438; *Judaism Eternal*, 1:191–193.

[254] See Hirsch, *GS* 2:444–447, *Judaism Eternal*, 1:198–200.

[255] Hirsch, *GS*, 2:439–440; *Judaism Eternal*, 1:193–194.

language is "the best means of obtaining mastery and ready command of one's own mother tongue." This is because while one is not usually attentive to the grammar and vocabulary of one's native language, one becomes more attuned to this by studying the grammar and vocabulary of a foreign language.[256]

In addition to the value of studying the Bible and Hebrew, Hirsch notes several ways in which Talmud study promotes discernment and logical thinking. He observes that talmudic texts contain no vowels or punctuation marks, which must be supplied by the student. This stimulates "alacrity of thought, closeness of attention, and shrewdness of conjecture."[257] Hirsch also observes that the Talmud often presents matters extremely tersely, as it frequently begins by discussing a topic in the middle, relying on the student to supply the premises and legal concepts operative in the case. Hirsch also notes that the Talmud will often take "synthetically given" laws found in the Bible and "analytically" abstract the legal principle behind them before applying them to new cases. For these reasons, Hirsch calls Talmud study "the finest school for forming logical and ethical judgments."[258]

In Hirsch's plan for his school, he makes clear that Torah and general studies should be undertaken with "equal seriousness and care."[259] He sketches a curriculum in which approximately forty percent of studies are devoted to Jewish subjects.[260] Hirsch's valuing both Jewish and general education is connected to his view of the unity of truth. As he puts it in an 1867 essay, "It is the Jewish view that truth like God its source is one and indivisible and that therefore the knowledge of it can only be one and indivisible. It knows nothing of a requirement to subject reason to faith."[261] For Hirsch, given the harmony between the revelation of nature and the revelation of Torah, knowledge of each is complementary.[262]

In *Horeb*, Hirsch writes that general studies include knowledge of the vernacular, writing, arithmetic, world history, and "nature and humanity,"

256 Hirsch, *GS*, 2:440; *Judaism Eternal*, 1:194. For a more detailed account of how Hirsch thinks that Hebrew's promotes mental perfection see pp. 355–356 of this volume.

257 Hirsch, *GS*, 2:447–448; *Judaism Eternal*, 1:201.

258 Hirsch, *GS*, 2:447; *Judaism Eternal*, 1:201–202. See p. 81 note 19 of this volume.

259 Sulzbach, "Zur Geschichte der Schulanstalten," 34.

260 See Sulzbach, "Zur Geschichte der Schulanstalten," 44–45. In practice, due to government regulations the curriculum was never more than one-third Jewish subjects and declined to less than a quarter over the years. See Breuer, *Modernity within Tradition*, 111.

261 Hirsch, *GS*, 2:454; *Judaism Eternal*, 1:207–208.

262 See pp. 255–256 of this volume.

which includes natural history, physics, geography, psychology, and anthropology.[263] For Hirsch, history and the study of nature should be taught concurrently with Bible because the history of the Jewish people is closely connected with other nations in respect to its "origin and goal" (*Ursprung und Ziel*).[264] Hirsch's sense of the religious significance of general knowledge is illustrated by the fact that, unlike his mentor Bernays, who employed Christian teachers to teach general subjects, Hirsch recommended employing Orthodox Jewish teachers for these studies.[265]

Hirsch recognizes that there can be contradictions between the Torah and general education. Given that the Torah provides the meaning and context for general education, deciding which general subjects to study must be done carefully. Hirsch stresses that literature that "stokes animalistic fantasies" or subjects that undermine central tenets of Judaism such as the biblical criticism should not be studied.[266]

Finally, Hirsch writes that education should provide the boy with *the capacity to earn a living and be self-supporting*. To this end, he should learn writing and arithmetics and be taught a craft, trade, or profession. In the plan for his school Hirsch also stresses the need to learn Yiddish, English, and French for this purpose. For Hirsch, a person's choice of occupation does not matter as long as it is "honest and upright, approved by God and permitted

[263] Hirsch, *Horev*, Kap. 84, #553, 546–547; *Horeb*, ch. 84, #553, 411–412. In his 1852 plan, Hirsch specifies these contents more precisely. Knowledge of vernacular includes learning English and French as well as German and seeks to inculcate the skills of thinking and speaking well, grammar, reading, and writing. In his plan, Hirsch also includes several subjects not mentioned in *Horeb*, namely, writing German in Hebrew characters, technology, popular astronomy, geometry, algebra, drawing, and singing. See Sulzbach, "Zur Geschichte der Schulanstalten," 34–35, 44.

[264] Hirsch, *Horev*, Kap. 75, #494, 490–491; *Horeb*, ch. 75, #494, 372. In Hirsch's school general and Jewish history were studied together, but he paired them in a peculiar way. Ancient world history was studied together with Jewish history prior to the Babylonian exile (586 BCE); medieval history was studied together with Jewish history during the Second Temple period (516 BCE to 70 AD), and modern and contemporary history was studied with Jewish history post destruction of the Second Temple (70 AD). See Sulzbach, "Zur Geschichte der Schulanstalten," 44.

[265] Breuer, *Modernity within Tradition*, 119.

[266] See Hirsch, *NB*, Brief 15, 71–72; Hirsch, *NL*, Letter 15, 200–201. In the introduction to *Horeb* Hirsch makes clear that he considers the divinity of the Torah axiomatic to Judaism and that denying it places one "outside of Judaism." See Hirsch, *Horev*, xiv; *Horeb*, clxi. On Hirsch's concern about teaching literature that arouses sensuality, see Hirsch, *Der Pentateuch*, 1:90; *The Hirsch Chumash*, 1:121 (Commentary on Genesis 3:24). In a famous comment in his commentary on Leviticus, Hirsch describes the Torah as the "absolute and unconditional . . . standard by which to measure all the results obtained in other branches of knowledge"; see Hirsch, *Der Pentateuch*, 3:368–369; *The Hirsch Chumash*, 3:570 (Commentary on Leviticus 18:4–5). This does not mean that Hirsch opposed teaching scientific doctrines that ostensibly contradicted the Bible such as heliocentrism and evolution. I will discuss Hirsch's approach to contradictions between natural science and Torah in the next chapter.

by the law of the land."[267] Hirsch's concept of education most closely approximates the German *Realschule*, which was not an academic gymnasium that taught classical languages such as Greek and Latin, nor a trade school, but rather, a school whose purpose was to train students to enter the professions. Like Zunz, Hirsch did not wish the school to be directed to poor children but envisioned a school for the wealthy and poor alike.[268]

Like Zunz, Hirsch advocates female Jewish education. We have seen that Mendelssohn's neglect of female Jewish education was informed by his view that there was no halakhic obligation to teach one's daughter Torah as expressed in the Talmud's interpretation of Deuteronomy 11:19 (you should teach beneikhem to speak of them), where beneikhem is understood to mean "sons." In line with this, Mendelssohn translated Deuteronomy 11:19 as "Teach your *sons* (*Söhne*) to always speak of them."[269] By contrast, Zunz considered it important to teach girls Torah and thus translated the verse as "And you should teach your *children* (*Kinder*) to speak of them."[270] Like Mendelssohn, Hirsch translates Deuteronomy 11:19 in accordance with the talmudic interpretation as "and teach your *sons* (*Söhne*) to speak of them." But in his commentary Hirsch explains that the Talmud understood the verse to mean that fathers were only exempt from teaching their daughters certain forms of Torah knowledge, namely, "Torah erudition (*Gelehrsamkeit*) that leads to scientific knowledge of the law (*wissenschaftlichen Gesetzeskunde*)," namely advanced Talmud study.[271]

Hirsch emphasizes the importance of female Jewish education writing that it is crucial that "our daughters no less than to our sons" be given an "understanding of Jewish literature" and knowledge of the commandments.[272] For Hirsch, Bible study is a crucial component of female Jewish education. He forcefully rejects commentators who interpret the Talmud (*BT*, Nedarim, 35b) to mean that there is no commandment to teach one's daughters the Bible, noting that in addition to contradicting the Gemara two pages later (Nedarim, 37b), the idea is belied by the large literature in "Yiddish" (*jüdisch*

[267] See Hirsch, *Horev*, Kap. 80, #524, 519–520; *Horeb*, ch. 80, #524, 392. Also see Hirsch, *Horev*, Kap. 84, #552, 545; Kap. 84, #552, 410.

[268] See Breuer, *Modernity within Tradition*, 104. As we saw previously, Bernays also modelled his school on the *Realschule*. See p. 238 of this volume.

[269] See p. 87 of this volume.

[270] See p. 175 of this volume.

[271] Hirsch, *Der Pentateuch*, 5:164; Hirsch, *The Hirsch Chumash*, 5:225 (Commentary to Deuteronomy 11:19).

[272] Ibid.

deutsch) aimed at teaching females the Bible.[273] For Hirsch, it is essential that girls be taught Torah since women are guardians of Judaism within the home and the perpetuation of Judaism depends on Jewish women being educated.[274]

Hirsch went much further than Zunz in advocating girls' education. In *Horeb*, which he addressed to "Israel's thinking young men *and women*" (emphasis mine), he wrote that girls should pursue the same "general course" (*Allgemeine Weg*) of study as boys, and unlike Zunz, Hirsch advocated a coeducational school.[275] In practice, however, in his early writings Hirsch did not advocate equality for girls' education. In *Horeb*, he wrote that while girls should study Hebrew, the vernacular, the Bible, natural history, physics, geography, psychology, anthropology, world history, writing, and arithmetic, it should be in a "simplified" form, though Hirsch does not clarify exactly what this simplification involves.[276] In addition, while boys are to focus on understanding their religious duties from the standpoint of being a "*Mensch-Jissroël* and citizen," girls are to focus on their religious duties from the standpoint of "domestic life." Finally, whereas boys are taught professional job skills, girls are taught needlework and house management.[277]

Over time, however, Hirsch came to increasingly stress the equality of male and female education in practice. In his 1852 plan for the Frankfurt school, Hirsch recommends that boys and girls follow identical courses of general education and Torah study for the first four years (ages 7–10). The main difference in boys' and girls' education is that from ages 10 to 14 Hirsch recommends that during a portion of the Hebrew studies (presumably Talmud study) girls would learn needlework; when studying halakhah, boys and girls would focus on their gender-specific duties, and that girls would learn needlework instead of professional studies.[278]

[273] Hirsch, *Der Pentateuch,* 5:165; *The Hirsch Chumash,* 5:226 (Commentary to Deuteronomy 11:19).

[274] See Hirsch, *Horev,* Kap. #494, 489; *Horeb,* ch. 75, #494, 371; Hirsch, *GS,* 3:459–460 *CW,* 7: 394–395.

[275] See Hirsch, *Horev,* Kap. 84, #553, 547; *Horeb,* ch. 84, #553, 412.Initially the lower grades even held mixed classes, though this was eventually abandoned. See Breuer, *Modernity within Tradition,* 123.

[276] Hirsch, *Horev,* Kap. 84, #553, 547; *Horeb,* ch. 84, #553, 412.

[277] Ibid.

[278] See Sulzbach, "Zur Geschichte der Schulanstalten," 45. Hirsch's rhetoric also increasingly moved toward stressing male and female equality. In his 1864 essay "The Jewish Woman," he wrote of the "complete spiritual/intellectual (*geistige*) equality" of men and women, and in his 1867 commentary on Genesis he wrote of the "complete equality and equal independence" of men and women. See Hirsch, *GS,* 4:207; *Judaism Eternal* 2:95; Hirsch, *Der Pentateuch,* 1:64; *The Hirsch Chumash,* 1:85 (Commentary to Genesis 2:18).

By increasing the amount and intensity of girls' study of the Bible while decreasing the amount and intensity of boys' study of the Talmud, Hirsch took great steps toward equalizing male and female Jewish education.[279] Given that in traditionalist German Jewish settings Talmud study was greatly prized and formed a foundation of male superiority in Torah knowledge, while females mostly studied the Bible, Hirsch's educational turn to the Bible and away from the Talmud for both boys *and* girls was an important step toward gender equality that can be seen as a "feminizing" of Jewish education.[280] Nevertheless, Hirsch retained a bourgeois German conception of gender roles, with males responsible for supporting the family and females for raising children at home.

Conclusion

In the *Nineteen Letters*, Hirsch seeks a reformation of German Judaism by translating biblical concepts into an inspiring religious vision. This vision synthesizes what he sees as the partial truths of the four major ideologies of the time, Haskalah, *Wissenschaft*, Reform, and Jewish traditionalism, while critiquing their errors. Like Mendelssohn and Zunz, Hirsch seeks to unite German Jewry through a new vision of Judaism that would nurture the emergence of middle-class German Jews, loyal both to the Torah and the German state, who see in the practice of Judaism a means of promoting both their own *Bildung* and that of their German Christians neighbors. And like Mendelssohn and Zunz, Hirsch seeks to implement his vision by reforming German Jewish education, emphasizing Bible study, and reducing the time spent studying Talmud. Hirsch goes even further than Zunz in advancing gender equality in education, though he preserves bourgeois gender roles.

While Hirsch embraces the ideal of *Bildung* that Mendelssohn and Zunz had placed at the center of Judaism, his emphasis is different. For Mendelssohn, cultivating *Bildung* is a spiritual enterprise that serves God because God created the world to enable people to perfect themselves. Jews

[279] See Breuer, *Modernity within Tradition*, 123.
[280] See p. 9 of this volume.

model the theological truths that promote *Bildung* for humanity by adhering to the Torah Hirsch criticizes the maskilic ideal of self-perfection and happiness as the goal of life. Instead, he sees *Bildung* as a means of serving God by enabling Jews to obey God's commandments as found in the Torah with a proper understanding and attain respectability among German Christians thereby helping them implement God's moral law in the world and model it for the benefit of humanity.

Hirsch's endeavor to seek a new German Jewish consensus ultimately failed and he abandoned it in favor of Orthodox sectarianism, which he anchored in his new Pentateuch translation and commentary. But Hirsch's move from seeking German Jewish consensus to Orthodox sectarianism was gradual. The next chapter will trace this process.

6
The Road to Orthodoxy
Hirsch in Battle

One of Hirsch's best-known claims is that the Torah is timeless and unchanging, existing outside the vicissitudes of history.[1] We will discuss this claim later in the chapter. But it is noteworthy that even scholars who reject Hirsch's view of the Torah as unchanging still accept the notion that *Hirsch's own ideas did not change.* Consider the judgment of Isaac Heinemann, professor at the Jewish Theological Seminary in Breslau, and the penultimate editor of the flagship journal of the Positive-Historical school, the *Monatsschrift für die Geschichte und Wissenschaft des Judentums*: "In his conceptual principles that is in his worldview and in his view of Judaism, [Hirsch] maintained the same ideas that he formulated in the *Nineteen Letters* throughout his life. *They are primary and the rest is interpretation*" (emphasis mine).[2] Heinemann is not alone in this judgment. It is repeated by leading scholars of Orthodoxy such as Mordechai Breuer and Moshe Samet.[3]

In the last chapter I argued that in the *Nineteen Letters* Hirsch aims to unify German Jewry by weaving together the partial truths expressed by the four major German Jewish ideologies of his time into a compelling new vision of Judaism that he translates from the Bible. I showed that in the *Nineteen Letters* Hirsch expresses great sympathy for Reform Judaism, even appropriating the motto "Reform" for himself. But Hirsch's later career is marked by bitter polemics with the movement. How did this transformation happen? In this chapter I will show that this was a gradual process that started almost

[1] Jacob Breuer titled a collection of Hirsch's writings *Timeless Torah.* I am not aware of Hirsch ever using the German equivalent of this phrase, but he certainly expressed the idea underlying it. See, for example, Hirsch, *GS*, 6:111; *CW*, 1:276–277.

[2] Heinemann, "The Relationship between S.R. Hirsch and His Teacher Isaac Bernays," 44.

[3] Breuer writes, "To the *Nineteen Letters* one may apply the famous words, 'This is the entire Torah of Samson Raphael Hirsch and as for the remainder, go and study.'" Breuer, "Samson Raphael Hirsch," 270–271. Samet likewise opines: "Hirsch formulated his ideological system in his well-known works *Nineteen Letters on Judaism* and *Horeb*, published in the 1830s, but did not succeed in putting it into practice in the communities which he served before coming to Frankfurt." See Samet, "The Beginnings of Orthodoxy," 264.

The Jewish Reformation. Michah Gottlieb, Oxford University Press (2021). © Oxford University Press.
DOI: 10.1093/oso/9780199336388.003.0007

immediately after the publication of the *Nineteen Letters*. Hirsch's increasingly hostile attitude toward Reform Judaism emerged from his growing concern that Reformers were historicizing the Bible and Talmud as a means of introducing radical halakhic changes. Tracing the evolution from the early, inclusive Hirsch to the later, polemical Hirsch is crucial for understanding his magisterial Bible translation and commentary.

Geiger counters

Hirsch's hope that Reformers would be receptive to the vision he outlined in the *Nineteen Letters* was swiftly dashed. Within a year of the book's appearance, Hirsch's university friend Abraham Geiger published the first of three reviews of it.[4] These reviews, which ran to fifty-five pages, were nearly half the length of Hirsch's original book.[5] They amounted to a searing rejection of Hirsch's vision for German Jewry. At the heart of Geiger's attack is a critique of Hirsch's reading of the Bible.

Geiger begins his first review with considerable sympathy for Hirsch. He describes the anonymous author of the *Nineteen Letters* as a man of "clarity and sharpness, fiery zeal, tough love, and independent power" who seeks to "save this sick and wounded generation from the confusions and gnawing contradictions" that plague it.[6] Geiger notes that the author does this not through "cold, systematic instruction" but through "warmth and intimacy," using the attractive literary device of a correspondence between friends.[7] That Hirsch had crafted his work as a correspondence between two young men must have reminded Geiger of his own intimate conversations with Hirsch during their university days. But while Benjamin is Hirsch's spokesman for skeptical youth, Geiger does not see him as an adequate representative:

> Would such a man [Benjamin] never have questioned the obligatory nature of Judaism? Would a man to whom was entrusted so much biblical and talmudic knowledge . . . never have had doubts about whether the

[4] Geiger's reviews appeared in the *Wissenschaftliche Zeitschrift für jüdische Theologie* (*Scientific Journal for Jewish Theology*) (henceforth: *WZJT*) in vol. 2.2 (1836), pp. 351–359; vol. 2.3, pp. 518–548; and vol. 3.1 (1837), pp. 74–91.
[5] Hirsch's book was 111 pages.
[6] See Geiger, "Recension der *Briefe über Judenthum* (1)," 351–352.
[7] Ibid., 352–353.

Bible, Talmud, and later rabbinic writings were all written in a single spirit (*in einem Geist geschrieben*), whether they form parts of a single indivisible whole? Would it never have occurred to him that at times a spirit that speaks through the whole of Judaism stands in the most glaring contradiction with many of its particulars? Why does he [Benjamin] withhold these doubts from the friend to whom he opens his heart with complete confidence?[8]

For Geiger, Benjamin cannot adequately represent the doubts and confusions of German Jewish youth as long as he does not question the divinity of the Bible and Talmud and whether they form a whole. As long as Benjamin does not express these doubts, Naphtali's response, however eloquent, cannot satisfy skeptical, intelligent youths. Geiger further claims that Benjamin's concerns over halakhic practice only makes sense on the assumption that he harbored doubts about the divinity of the Torah. Had Benjamin truly believed that all the laws of the Bible and Talmud were divinely revealed, he could not have doubted the importance of observing them, since God's reward for obedience must surely outweigh any worldly inconveniences. Why then does Hirsch not have Benjamin voice doubt about the Torah's divinity?[9]

In the third review Geiger presses his point further, criticizing Hirsch's defense of the divinity of the Torah as completely inadequate. He notes that Hirsch compares the study of Torah to the study of nature, claiming that one must read the Torah without prior assumptions, considering it a fact of nature no different from heaven and earth. According to Hirsch, one must study the Torah's laws in the same way that a scientist studies nature, namely, by seeking hypotheses that explain the data while never questioning the validity of the data itself. Geiger argues that Hirsch completely misunderstands the scientific method. When a scientist observes a flower, she does not consider the flower in isolation from all other natural phenomena, bracketing assumptions about its place in the natural order. Rather, she begins with the assumption that nature operates according to *causal laws* and seeks to understand how the flower develops from prior phenomena in accordance with these laws. In the same way, the scholar who studies the Torah must not treat it in isolation from all other phenomena in history. Rather, she must assume that

[8] Ibid., 354.
[9] Ibid., 355.

history operates according to natural causes and seek to discover the developmental process by which the Torah came into being and was transmitted.[10]

Geiger objects that Hirsch simply assumes that the Torah is a timeless, unchanging unit consisting of the Bible (the Written Torah) and the Talmud (the Oral Torah). He finds the idea that the Talmud exists outside of history particularly bizarre since the Talmud itself testifies that it was preserved through human agents who transmitted it orally from generation to generation.[11] Geiger then turns to Hirsch's view of the Hebrew language and biblical interpretation, noting that Hirsch describes Hebrew as distinguished from all other languages by its ability to express abstract notions intuitively using metaphorical imagery that expresses several concepts using single words or expressions.[12] Geiger charges that on the basis of this view of Hebrew, Hirsch proposes interpretations of the Bible that show blatant disregard for fundamental rules of Hebrew grammar, syntax, and lexicography. While Hirsch claims to read the Bible without prior preconceptions he clearly imposes his own ideological assumptions upon it.[13]

To illustrate this problem, Geiger cites Hirsch's translation of the first eleven verses from the first chapter of Ecclesiastes, which occurs at the end of the sixth letter.[14] For Geiger, the meaning of these verses is perfectly clear. The author is teaching that everything on earth is fleeting while the four elements remain eternally such that nothing truly new ever happens. The four elements are alluded to in verses 4–7, which speak of the earth remaining the same forever (verse 4), the sun continually rising and setting (verse 5), the wind ever blowing (verse 6), and the streams always flowing into the sea (verse 7).[15] The problem is that Ecclesiastes's teaching contradicts Hirsch's view that the world is progressing toward a divinely ordained goal. Geiger claims that Hirsch therefore seeks to fit Ecclesiastes into the "arbitrary, procrustean bed" of his own ideas through a highly idiosyncratic translation. Compare the JPS translation of Ecclesiastes 1:3–4 with Hirsch's translation. The JPS translation reads:

[10] Geiger, "Recension der *Briefe über Judenthum* (3)," 74–77.
[11] Ibid., 77.
[12] Ibid., 78. See p. 282 of this volume.
[13] Ibid., 78–81.
[14] See Hirsch, *NB*, Brief 6, 32–33; *NL*, Letter 6, 94–95.
[15] Geiger, "Recension der *Briefe über Judenthum* (3)," 80.

> What real value (*yitaron*) is there for a man in all the gains he makes beneath the sun? One generation goes, another comes, but the earth remains the same forever (*vehaaretz leolam omadet*).

Hirsch, however, provides the following translation:

> What is the goal (*Ziel/yitaron*) of humanity in all of its efforts under the sun!? Generations go, generations come, and the developing earth continually awaits a hidden future (*die Erdentwickelung harrt immer neu verhülleter Zukunft entgegen/vehaaretz leolam omadet*).[16]

The Hebrew word *yitaron* is generally understood to mean a "benefit."[17] Hirsch, however, interprets it as related to the word *matarah*, meaning "goal" and thus translates it as *Ziel*, despite the fact that *yitaron* (יתרון) is spelled with a *tav* (ת) while *matarah* (מטרה) is spelled with a *tet* (ט). On this basis, Hirsch interprets the verse not as questioning the value of human beings' efforts on earth but, rather, as asking about the goal of humanity. Verse 4 is commonly understood to mean that while generations come and go, the earth remains the same, such that nothing truly new ever occurs. Hence, in the phrase *vehaaretz leolam omadet* the words *leolam omadet* mean "continually the same." Hirsch, however, translates the phrase as meaning that the "developing earth" (*Erdentwickelung*) is continually moving toward a "hidden future" (*verhülleter Zukunft*).[18] Hirsch reads the word *leolam* as related to the Hebrew root ע.ל.מ, meaning "hidden," with the word "future" being implied.[19]

Geiger is dumbfounded by Hirsch's translation. The talmudic tractate *Beitzah* focuses on the question of whether one may eat an egg laid on a holiday. Maskilim and Reformers used this as a paradigmatic example of talmudic hairsplitting. Comparing Hirsch's translation of Ecclesiastes to this talmudic question, Geiger remarks: "Whoever can find true exegesis here, can surely also find the highest religion in the question of an egg laid on a holiday."

16 Hirsch, *NB*, Brief 6, 32; *NL*, Letter 6, 94.

17 See the commentaries of Rashi, Metzudat David, and Metzudat Zion ad loc.

18 On Hirsch's reason for translating *eretz* as "developing earth," see Hirsch, *GS*, 5:161–163; *CW*, 8:33–34.

19 On the idea of *olam* (world) as related to *elem* (hiddenness), see *Midrash Lekah Tov* on Ecclesiastes 3:11. But the Midrash's comment draws on the fact that in Ecclesiastes 3:11 the word *haolam* is written defectively without a *vav* (העלם). In Ecclesiastes 1:4 the word *leolam* is written *plene* with a *vav* (לעולם).

For Geiger, Hirsch's exegetical approach renders the meaning of Scripture completely arbitrary. Geiger asks, "Is there anything Holy Scripture cannot become when such foundationless subjectivity rules?"[20]

Geiger sees the source of Hirsch's error in that he interprets the Bible through what Geiger calls a *Darschangeist* (homiletical spirit).[21] In speaking of Hirsch's *Darschangeist*, Geiger is not referring to Hirsch's recourse to specific midrashic interpretations, as many of Hirsch's interpretations are based on his own creative interpretations.[22] Rather, Geiger is claiming that Hirsch follows the midrashic method of translating the Bible using arbitrary interpretations that are alien to the Bible's original meaning. Geiger remarks on the irony that Hirsch attacks kabbalah and *pilpul* for deviating from the plain sense of the Bible and Talmud while doing the same thing himself.[23]

In this way, Geiger expresses a negative view of rabbinic Midrash. But near the end of his third and final review of the *Nineteen Letters*, Geiger presents a more sympathetic view of it writing:

> . . . we will nevertheless listen to the voices of the ancients in the Talmud, as the documents of a great and long history of Judaism. We seek the true Jewish spirit (*ächtjüdischem Geiste*). With a scrutinizing eye we will become acquainted with the excellent conduct of the teachers of the Talmud, particularly the ancient ones, who sought provisions and modifications *for their time.* Since they used forced interpretations of biblical phrases, later generations soon misunderstood their views. But we take this conduct equally as a model for ourselves who also seek *the spirit and not the letter* (*den Geist und nicht den Buchstaben*)." (emphasis mine)[24]

For Geiger, while Midrash deviates from the original meaning of the Bible, it served an important function, as the talmudic rabbis used it to modify the biblical letter to enable the biblical spirit to speak "for their time." This can be a model for contemporary Reformers who seek to make Judaism relevant for the present.[25] The problem with Hirsch is that he fails to distinguish between

[20] Geiger, "Recension der *Briefe über Judenthum* (3)," 81.
[21] Ibid., 83.
[22] To the best of my knowledge, many of Hirsch's interpretations of the first chapter of Ecclesiastes have little or no basis in rabbinic or medieval Jewish exegesis.
[23] Ibid., 88.
[24] Ibid., 90.
[25] In his early writings Geiger evinces an ambivalent attitude toward Midrash, expressing a negative view of it from a historical, scholarly perspective and a positive view of it from a pragmatic, religious perspective. In his later 1857 *Urschrift und Übersetzungen der Bibel* (*Original Text and*

peshat and *derash*, pretending that his homiletical midrashic interpretations are the plain meaning of the biblical text.

Hirsch's clever response

Hirsch was likely taken aback by his friend's forceful and often insulting review. But he recognized that Geiger had mounted substantive challenges to his vision of Judaism. One can find Hirsch's first response to Geiger in *Horeb*, which appeared in 1837 after Geiger's reviews had begun to appear. The main purpose of *Horeb* is to fulfill the vision of a true *Wissenschaft des Judentums* that Hirsch had sketched in the *Nineteen Letters* by providing a detailed account of the reasons for the Torah's commandments and how they relate to one another. As in the *Nineteen Letters*, Hirsch emphasizes that his *wissenschaftlichen* method seeks to understand the Torah as it was originally intended, namely, as a guide to life. Hence, the first chapter of *Horeb* begins: "Let the flower of knowledge be life."[26]

As we just saw, Geiger criticized Hirsch for presenting himself as addressing the perplexed youth but assuming that the Torah, both Written and Oral, is divinely revealed. In the preface to *Horeb*, Hirsch addresses Geiger without naming him, writing that the book will not attempt to prove the divinity of the Torah's commandments "since the very thought of such an attempt would appear to me as a denial of their divine origin and consequently as lying outside of Judaism."[27] Whereas for Geiger the question of whether the Torah is divinely revealed must be resolved through *historical inquiry*, for Hirsch the very *asking of this question* involves an implicit denial of the Torah's divine origin and thus places one "outside of Judaism." As Hirsch addresses his book to the "thinking young men and women of Israel," that is, for Jews who identify with Judaism but seek a deeper understanding of it, he deems it necessary to assume that the Torah is divine.

In 1839, Geiger published a lengthy review of *Horeb*. The review is filled with sarcasm alongside a few substantive points of criticism. But for

Translations of the Bible), Geiger's attitude toward Midrash is more uniformly positive. For discussion of Geiger's view of Midrash, see Harris, *How Do We Know This?*, 157–165; Heschel, *Abraham Geiger and the Jewish Jesus*, 25–26; Koltun-Fromm, *Abraham Geiger's Liberal Judaism*, 40–63.

26 Hirsch, *Horev*, 3; *Horeb*, 3.
27 Hirsch, *Horev*, xiv; *Horeb*, clxi.

our purposes, I would like to focus on the beginning of the review. Geiger is flabbergasted that Hirsch has the audacity to address *Horeb* to the "thinking" (*denkende*) Jewish youth and then dogmatically assert that a person must believe that the Torah is divinely revealed.[28] For Geiger, this epitomizes Hirsch's unscientific dogmatism. As Geiger puts it, "all thinking and *wissenschaftlichen* readers" must "protest against this entirely unreasonable demand."[29] Geiger concedes that questioning the divinity of the Torah *places one outside of Judaism*, but he nevertheless considers it necessary, writing, "I must first place myself outside of Judaism in order that I may then return to it with greater reverence."[30]

Hirsch responded to Geiger in an 1840 pamphlet titled "Postscripta." Addressing Geiger's claim that his approach excludes all "thinking and *Wissenschaft*," Hirsch retorts that this statement is "testimony to the greatest scientific poverty (*wissenschaftlichen Armuth*)" of Geiger's perspective.[31] For Hirsch, the Torah can be studied through two *equally scientific* methods. Geiger favors a method that understands the development of the Torah *within* history as the product of human authors subject to historical forces. But an equally valid method treats the Torah's laws phenomenologically as a divinely revealed unit that is accepted and practiced by a community of believers, and it seeks to understand the rationale behind individual laws, how they relate to one another, and how they inform life.

In the *Nineteen Letters*, Hirsch writes that any *wissenschaftlichen* method of studying the Torah must treat it as "appearance" (*Erscheinung*).[32] Kant had used the term *Erscheinung* to refer to the realm of *phenomena*, which he contrasted with *noumena*, the realm of the "thing in itself" (*Ding an Sich*), which is inaccessible to the understanding.[33] By asserting that *Wissenschaft* treats the Torah as *Erscheinung*, Hirsch is claiming that reason is incapable of answering the question whether the Torah is divinely revealed or humanly composed.

Hirsch contends that in the *Nineteen Letters* and *Horeb*, he analyzed the Torah as *Erscheinung* using a *wissenschaftlichen* method that relied on the unprovable assumption that the Torah is divinely revealed. While Geiger dismisses this approach as dogmatic and unscientific, Hirsch asserts that this

28 Geiger, "Recension der Hirsch's *Versuche*," 355–381.
29 "Recension der Hirsch's *Versuche*," 356.
30 Ibid.
31 Hirsch, *Postscripta*, 34.
32 See Hirsch, *NB*, Brief 18, 96; *NL*, Letter 18, 271–272.
33 See Kant, *Critique of Pure Reason*, 347-351 (part 2, division 1, book 2, chapter 3).

dismissal reflects Geiger's own dogmatism and unscientific assumptions. For when Geiger analyzes the *Erscheinung* of the Torah using the historical-critical method, he implicitly relies on his own unprovable assumption, namely, that the Torah is of human origin. Hirsch later expressed the difference between Geiger's historical-critical view of the Torah and what he saw as the authentic Jewish view: "*Theology* comprises the thoughts of *human beings* about *God* and *divine things*. But the *Torah* comprises the thoughts of *God* about *human beings* and *human* things."[34] Or, as he put it pithily, the Torah "is not so much human theology (*menschliche Theologie*) as divine anthropology (*göttliche Anthropologie*)."[35]

For Hirsch, what motivates Geiger's method and criticism of Hirsch is not dispassionate rational considerations but, rather, a *practical* interest, namely, the desire to adapt Judaism to the needs of the time. For if the Torah is a human document that develops throughout history in response to shifting social and political circumstances, this legitimates *continuing* its development in the present.[36]

Hirsch's nightmare

As we have seen, Hirsch's attitude toward Reform was quite restrained in the *Nineteen Letters*. But two years later, in 1838, he wrote a follow-up to the work in which he presented a much harsher view of Reform. This much lesser-known work was titled *Naphtulei Naphtali: First Communications from Naphtali's Correspondence* (*Naphtulei Naphtali: Erste Mitteilungen aus Naphtali's Briefwechsel*).[37] Like the *Nineteen Letters*, *Naphtulei Naphtali* is presented as a correspondence edited by an anonymous editor named Ben Uziel between a young rabbi named Naphtali and a disaffected Jewish young man. But unlike the *Nineteen Letters*, *Naphtulei Naphtali* contains no complaint, and Naphtali's side of the correspondence appears in five letters. The addressee is no longer Benjamin, but a man named Simeon. The

[34] See Hirsch, *GS* 1:89; *CW*, 1:189.

[35] See Hirsch's 1866 essay "The Role of Hebrew Study in General Education" in Hirsch, *GS*, 2:434; *CW*, 7:64. Abraham Joshua Heschel later employed Hirsch's contrast, though he did not endorse Hirsch's view of the Bible's origin, writing, "This is why the Torah is divine anthropology, not human theology." See Heschel, *God in Search of Man*, 412.

[36] Ibid., 34–35.

[37] *Naphtulei Naphtali: Erste Mittheillungen aus Naphtali's Briefwechsel* (Altona: Hammerich, 1838). I will cite the 1920 edition, which includes both the *Erste* and *Zweite Mitteilungen*; see Hirsch, *Erste und Zweite Mitteilung*.

main purpose of the work is to discuss troubling ideas that Hirsch found in Geiger's journal, the *Wissenschaftliche Zeitschrift für jüdische Theologie*.[38]

The first letter opens with Naphtali describing passing the room of a young lodger living in his home named Peretz while on the way to bed.[39] Naphtali noticed that Peretz's lamp was still on and put it out. Entering Peretz's room, Naphtali saw him asleep on his table with volumes of Geiger's journal open in front of him. Napthali's eyes fell on a piece of paper in Peretz's handwriting that contained a harsh attack on the Talmud in the name of *Wissenschaft*, which read:

> O century of *Wissenschaft*! At long last Judaism will also become *Wissenschaft*. Formerly, darkness! Formerly, one believed that Judaism must be known and built out of Judaism (*Judentum aus Judentum erkennen und aufbauen*) and into one's old age one would sit bent over folios of Talmud, which made one so foreign, so dull, so dead! Our Judaism will no longer grow from this harebrained scholasticism (*scholastischen Mistbeet*) from such codgers and poisonous men. Our theology is born in the bright halls of German philosophy, nurtured with European dogmatics, ecclesiastical history, philosophy of religion, and pastoral theology! This affords one a completely different outlook! If we compare this with that cumbersome Talmud of the Middle Ages, we find it all to be illogical nonsense. One cannot fool us so easily anymore.[40]

Peretz draws a distinction between studying Judaism using intellectually honest, logical, modern academic methods, and deceptive, illogical, medieval talmudism, which claims to "know Judaism out of Judaism" (*Judentum aus Judentum erkennen*). This phraseology is clearly reminiscent of Hirsch's assertion in the *Nineteen Letters* that Judaism must be studied "out of itself" (*aus sich selber*) and suggests that Peretz is linking Hirsch's approach with

[38] In *Naphtulei Naphtali*, Hirsch dispenses with the anonymity of the *Nineteen Letters*, signing the preface in his own name.

[39] Peretz is likely based on Heinrich Graetz, who came to live with Hirsch in 1837. As we will discuss shortly, Graetz later became one of the leading figures of Positive-Historical Judaism and Hirsch crossed swords with him. See pp. 324–328 of this volume. That Peretz stands for Graetz is suggested by the phonetic similarity between the names. Hirsch may also have chosen the name because Peretz means "to break forth" and Hirsch saw Graetz as breaking the boundaries of Judaism. But according to the Bible, Peretz was also a direct ancestor of the Davidic Messiah, which may express Hirsch's hope that Graetz could still become a redemptive force for German Jewry.

[40] Hirsch, *Erste und Zweite Mitteilung*, 1–2; *CW*, 9:6.

medieval talmudism.[41] Peretz ends his piece by comparing liberation from the Talmud to the storming of the Bastille: "Just look at the crowds of fighters for light and truth! They all carry the banner of reason! They rush over to me! They call out to me! And I stand at their head, marching forward *to storm the talmudic Bastille* (*stürmen die talmudische Bastille*!)" (emphasis mine).[42]

Naphtali recounts that after reading Peretz's call to arms he quietly moved him to his bed, gathered up the volumes of Geiger's journal, and put out the lamp. He then went to his room and fell asleep. That night Naphtali had a terrible nightmare. He saw Peretz and his friends marching toward the Temple Mount with torches. At the summit of the Temple stood the "divine law," and the mountain was populated with countless people who had taught, observed, fought, and died for the law. When these people saw Peretz and his friends approaching the Temple, they hid their faces in shame, as they were used to being attacked by outsiders, but not by Israel's own children. As Peretz and his friends moved closer to the Temple, they set fire to mounds of sacred books and burned the beards of aged men. They wished to spare the Temple itself, but the fire raged out of control and the Temple along with all its sacred objects were incinerated.

Peretz lay on the ground holding a torch and laughing madly, looking to see if anything was spared from the flames. Surveying what he had burned, he was delirious with delight. But with nothing left to burn, the fired consumed Peretz himself. When the sun came up, Naphtali saw Israel's elders, judges, prophets, talmudic sages, and rabbis all clothed in white. At their head stood Moses, who held the Menorah,[43] the only thing saved from the Temple. Light shone from the Menorah and the Temple rose again.[44]

For Hirsch, the Temple represents the "divine law," that is, the Torah.[45] In describing Peretz and his friends as wishing to set fire to the books and aged men within the Temple without destroying the Temple itself, Hirsch is suggesting that some Reformers wish to attack the Oral Torah while preserving the Written Torah. But for Hirsch this is impossible. Attacking the Talmud leads to the destruction of the Torah as a whole, as the Bible cannot

41 See p. 250 of this volume. See Hirsch, *NB*, Brief 2, 8; Brief 18, 96, 100, 101, 106; *NL*, Letter 2, 16; Letter 18, 267, 268, 271.

42 Hirsch, *Erste und Zweite Mitteilung*, 2; *CW*, 9:6 (emphasis mine).

43 The Menorah is a seven-branched candelabra that was lit in the Temple. See Exodus 25:31–40.

44 Hirsch, *Erste und Zweite Mitteilung*, 2–4; *CW*, 9:6–8. Elsewhere Hirsch explains that the Menorah symbolizes timeless wisdom that illuminates one's task in life. See Hirsch, *GS*, 3:421–428; *CW*, 3, 212–216.

45 On this symbolism, see Hirsch, *GS*, 3:369–372; *CW*, 3:161–163.

be preserved without the Talmud. And without the Torah, Peretz himself is consumed as the Jewish people cannot persist without it.

In the subsequent letters of *Naphtulei Naphtali*, Hirsch criticizes various Reformer authors who, in the pages of Geiger's journal, denigrate the Talmud and/or consider the Bible of human authorship. He cites Rabbis Abraham Kohn, Joseph Aub, and Leopold Stein, who claim that the talmudic sages had a poor grasp of Hebrew;[46] the radical Reformer Rabbi Moses Brueck, who calls the talmudic rabbis "eccentrics who want nothing more than to spread illusions" and who declares that Moses, not God, authored the Pentateuch;[47] and Rabbi Michael Creizenach, whom Hirsch ironically dubs "a second Luther" (*ein zweiter Luther*) for "satirizing the Talmud" and claiming that it is not necessary to follow it anymore.[48]

Comparing Hirsch's dream of 1828 with his nightmare a decade later, we can see his attitude toward Reform shifting. In 1828, Hirsch portrays Reformers as carefree youths with good intentions who stumble because they do not give proper attention to rabbinic tradition. Hirsch holds out hope that they can be corrected. By 1838, however, Hirsch portrays Reformers as dangerous arsonists who, left unchecked, will annihilate Judaism.

Yet in *Naphtulei Napthali*, Hirsch's attitude toward Reformers is still not entirely negative. He acknowledges that Reformers are inconsistent in their views of the Bible and Talmud, oscillating between seeing the Torah as divine and human.[49] He also notes that Reformers do not universally denigrate the Talmud, with some seeing the "talmudic principle" (*talmudischen Prinzips*) as playing a positive role in preserving Judaism.[50] And as in the *Nineteen Letters*, Hirsch acknowledges that many Reformers are guided by a sincere

[46] Hirsch, *Erste und Zweite Mitteilung*, 34; *CW*, 9:33. Abraham Kohn (1806–1848) was a Reform rabbi in Hohenems who later became a rabbi in Lemberg and was murdered. See Stanislawski, *A Murder in Lemberg*. Joseph Aub (1804–1880) was a Reform rabbi in Bayreuth who later become a rabbi in Berlin. Leopold Stein (1810–1882) was a Reform rabbi in Frankfurt.

[47] Hirsch, *Erste und Zweite Mitteilung*, 53, 59; *CW*, 9:47, 53. Moses Brueck (1812–1849) was author of two important early Reform works.

[48] Hirsch, *Erste und Zweite Mitteilung*, 14–15; *CW*, 9:17. Hirsch notes that when Creizenach saw that his approach was not gaining traction, he changed his attitude toward the Talmud and sought to justify reforms on its basis. On Hirsch's relationship to Creizenach, see p. 239 of this volume.

[49] Hirsch writes, "For the past three or four years, I have diligently studied and followed most of the writings of these men. I have tried to connect their diverse statements to uncover their system. But their statements strike me as constantly contradictory; sometimes Jewish, sometimes non-Jewish; here based on the Torah, there on philosophy; here seeing the Torah as divine (*Thora göttlich*), there the Torah as human (*Thora menschlich*); here seeing Moses as a divine [agent] (*göttlicher Moses*), there seeing God as the [creation] of Moses (*mosaicher Gott*). They are not sure what they hold, what their basic premise is." Hirsch, *Erste und Zweite Mitteilung*, 6; *CW*, 9:9.

[50] We have seen that Geiger expressed this view. See pp. 294–295 of this volume. See Hirsch, *Erste und Zweite Mitteilung*, 75; *CW*, 9:65.

desire to improve Judaism, though his appreciation of these intentions is now much more circumspect.[51]

While in *Naphtulei Naphtali* Hirsch is becoming increasingly concerned about the direction of Reform, he makes clear that vilifying Reformers is not helpful. Rather, Jews who seek to live according to the Torah's laws should lead by example, acting virtuously, and raising a pious family.[52] As in the *Nineteen Letters*, Hirsch affirms the right of everyone to hold their own opinions. But this means not only respecting *others' rights* to live by their convictions and express them, but also affirming these rights *for oneself*. As Hirsch puts it, "Let everyone have the right to their opinion, but truly express your own . . . Do not oppose the right of anyone to live as he wants but guard carefully your right to live freely and openly according to the law of God . . . Let everyone educate his children as he sees fit, but educate your children as you see fit."[53]

Hirsch on Reform pilpul

In 1841, Hirsch was installed as Chief Rabbi of East Friesland in the city of Emden. This post was more prestigious than the one he had held in Oldenburg but was also more demanding, and Hirsch had much less time to publish. He was, however, prompted to write a follow-up to *Naphtulei Naphtali*. The occasion was the appearance of a radical Reform treatise by the Chief Rabbi of Mecklenburg-Schwerin, Samuel Holdheim.

Born in Kempno in 1806, Holdheim received a traditional Ashkenazi education focused almost exclusively on Talmud study. He became known as a talmudic prodigy (*illui*) and married the daughter of Rabbi Joseph Shapiro, the head of the rabbinical court in Kornik.[54] In his twenties, Holdheim moved to Prague to attend university and continue his rabbinical training under Rabbi Samuel Landau, who later ordained him.[55]

[51] Hirsch writes, "My dear Simeon, it is true that new developments in Judaism based on the so-called 'spirit of the times' (*Zeitgeist*) are dismal, but they are not the worst. These are convulsions, seizures, an illness perhaps dangerous yet which reflects movement, stirring, arousal, and life, even if it is a diseased stirring." Hirsch, *Erste und Zweite Mitteilung*, 75; *CW*, 9:66.

[52] Hirsch, *Erste und Zweite Mitteilung*, 78; *CW*, 9:68.

[53] Ibid.

[54] See Ritter, "Samuel Holdheim, the Jewish Reformer," 202; Philipson, "Samuel Holdheim: The Jewish Reformer," 309; Meyer, "Most of My Brethren," 8.

[55] See Meyer, "Most of my Brethren," 8. Holdheim had several other rabbinic ordinations as well. See Tänzer, "Samuel Holdheim als Rabbinatskandidat," 19; Petuchowski, "Abraham Geiger and

In 1836, Holdheim received his first rabbinical appointment in Frankfurt-on-Oder, which he secured on the basis of several recommendations, including a glowing one from Rabbi Moses Sofer, the famed architect of Ultra-Orthodoxy.[56] While in Frankfurt, Holdheim remained completely committed to traditionalist Jewish thought and practice.[57] But in 1840 he was appointed Chief Rabbi of Mecklenburg-Schwerin and began to adopt increasingly radical reforming tendencies, which he expressed in his landmark 1843 book *On the Autonomy of the Rabbis and the Principle of Jewish Marriage* (*Ueber die Autonomie der Rabbinen und das Prinzip der juedischen Ehe*).

David Ellenson has argued that *On the Autonomy of the Rabbis* must be understood against the background of Bruno Bauer's influential book, *The Jewish Question* (*Die Judenfrage*).[58] Bauer argued that Judaism was responsible for anti-Jewish oppression. Judaism set Jews "against the wheel of history" by teaching Jews to regard themselves as a separate nation, which naturally provoked an anti-Jewish response from Christians.[59] For Bauer, as long as Jews clung to their religion, it was impossible for them to change due to the immutable, "oriental" character of their religion.[60] He concluded that the only way a Jew could be eligible for emancipation was by divesting himself of Judaism. As Bauer put it, "Can the Jew really possess human rights as long as he lives as a Jew in perpetual segregation from others, as long as he therefore must declare that others are not really his fellowmen?"[61] Bauer did not single out particular Jewish texts as responsible for Jewish self-segregation, seeing both the Old Testament and the Talmud as promoting it.[62]

For Holdheim, Bauer's assertion that Judaism caused Jews to be segregated from Christians was not solely Jews' fault. It was also promoted by

Samuel Holdheim," 143, note 11. Rabbi Samuel Landau was the son of Mendelssohn's critic Rabbi Ezekiel Landau. See p. 17 of this volume.

[56] See Wilke, "Holdheim's Seven Years in Schwerin," 85, note 21. Also see Geiger, "Nachrichten," 450, where it is reported that Rabbi Sofer praised Holdheim's talmudic knowledge by paraphrasing Exodus 18:26 writing, *kol hadavar hakasheh yevi'un eilav* ("every difficult matter should be brought to him"). See Petuchowski, "Abraham Geiger and Samuel Holdheim," 143, note 11. On Sofer, see Katz, *Divine Law in Human Hands,* 403–443.

[57] See Meyer, *Response to Modernity,* 81.

[58] See Ellenson, "Samuel Holdheim and Zacharias Frankel," 201–202. I will cite from Helen's Lederer's English translation of this work found in *JMW.*

[59] See *JMW,* 297.

[60] See ibid., 298. On the widespread assumption among scholars in the eighteenth and nineteenth century that the Orient did not change, see Hess, *Germans, Jews and the Claims of Modernity,* 51–52, 58–79.

[61] Ibid.

[62] See Katz, *From Prejudice to Destruction,* 166–168.

governmental regulations. In Mecklenburg-Schwerin, the government recognized Jewish marriage, divorce, and inheritance law as authoritative, and in Prussia, a law was being discussed that would make membership in the local Jewish community mandatory. This law was enacted in 1847, four years after the appearance of Bauer's book.[63]

In *On the Autonomy of the Rabbis* Holdheim defends three theses: *First*, halakhah has no civil authority, and the rabbis should have no legal autonomy. In all cases of conflict between halakhah and state law, state law must supersede halakhah. *Second*, Judaism only deemed religious and civil law united when Jews had an independent state during the First Temple. With the destruction of the First Temple in 586 BCE and the fall of an independent Jewish state, Judaism came to be *solely a religion* with *no distinct national/political identity*. *Third*, Judaism regards marriage as a civil, not religious act.[64] The upshot of Holdheim's argument is that since Jews have no national Jewish identity, there is no impediment to their regarding themselves as members of the same nation as their German Christian brethren. There can be no conflict between loyalty to halakhah and adherence to civil law since *Judaism itself* mandates obedience to civil law in cases of conflict. In this way, Holdheim counters Bauer's contention that Judaism is an immutable, oriental religion, arguing that Judaism has the *internal resources* needed to reform itself in light of progressive, occidental ideas.

A year after Holdheim's book appeared, Hirsch responded to it in a sequel to *Naphtulei Naphtali* titled *Second Reports from a Correspondence Concerning the Most Recent Jewish Literature: A Fragment* (*Zweite Mitteilungen aus einem Briefwechsel über die neueste jüdische Literature: Ein Fragment*).[65] Surprisingly, the book opens with a discussion of *pilpul*:

> How I wish we lived in those times of *Blauser*,[66] of false *hilukim*,[67] of peripatetic Torah *bon-mots*! You think those were bad times for *Wissenschaft*

[63] See Ritter, "Samuel Holdheim," 207; Schreiber, *Reformed Judaism and Its Pioneers*, 194–195; Baron, "Freedom and Constraint," 11–12.

[64] See Ritter, "Samuel Holdheim," 208; Philipson, "Samuel Holdheim," 306.

[65] While this work was a sequel to his 1838 *First Reports*, Hirsch dropped many of the literary devices of that work. Unlike the *First Reports*, the *Second Reports* no longer purports to be a selection from Naphtali's correspondence edited by the pseudonymous Ben Uziel and does not bear the Hebrew title *Naphtulei Naphtali*. Hirsch is identified as the author on the title page, and the entire work consists of a single letter from Samson to Philipp that critically discusses Holdheim's *On the Autonomy of the Rabbis*. It is not clear to me why Hirsch uses Philipp for his addressee.

[66] *Blauser* is a German transliteration of a pilpulistic method known as *belo zeh*. See Katz, "Hirsch: To the Left and to the Right," 22. On this method, see Dimitrovsky, "On the Method of Pilpul," 145–149.

[67] As mentioned in the previous chapter, *hiluk* is another term for *pilpul*.

des Judentums? They were fortunate times, dear Philipp, when compared with the appearances of the present. True, there were sophisms, intellectual bull-fights (*Geistesstiergefechte*), witticisms (*Witzeleien*), and clownish pantomime (*Harlequinaden*), but everyone knew what they were and took the sophisms, wrestlings, and play for exactly what they were: entertainment and mental training. Untruth did not penetrate into the marrow of life. Mental training and amusement were strictly distinguished from the serious matters of life. The *wissenschaftliche* temple of practical life remained pure and dedicated to honesty and truth, undefiled by jokes that resound without penetrating deeply, by the glitzy light of sophistry that glitters but does not enlighten.[68]

In the last chapter, we saw that Hirsch criticized Jewish traditionalists for prioritizing *pilpul* over a straightforward reading of Jewish texts focused on practical life. But in the eight years since publishing the *Nineteen Letters*, Hirsch's concerns have changed. He now sounds wistful for a time when talmudic *pilpul* was his chief worry. Whatever their shortcomings, those employing *pilpul* at least understood that it was a mental game. They never imagined that *pilpulistic* methods would impact halakhic practice. For Hirsch, Holdheim's treatise marks a new, more dangerous stage of *pilpul* since he uses these sophistical methods to undermine halakhic authority and justify introducing major reforms to Judaism. For Hirsch, it is no accident that the most radical Reformer was trained as a Polish *lamdan* (talmudic scholar).

To unmask Holdheim's Reform *pilpul*, Hirsch begins by exposing the theoretical substructure undergirding his treatise. He cites Holdheim's own methodological statement in *On the Autonomy of the Rabbis*:

> Our guiding principle, which we share with so many contemporaries is to strive to act in accordance with the spirit of the rabbis (*Geist der Rabbinen*). That means to bring the letter of the law (*Buchstaben des Gesetzes*) into agreement with current conditions (*Zeitverhältnissen*) so that the letter of the law becomes a testimony to progress. *As long as* the letter of the law is a means to modern progress, Judaism will be brought to a *higher state*. Through a free and independent grasp of the religious spirit (*religiösen Geistes*) revealed in the Bible, Judaism will be elevated above the core views

[68] Hirsch, *Erste und Zweite Mitteilung*, 83; *CW*, 9:71.

of the rabbis themselves. In this way, Judaism will advance further than what was achieved by the Talmud (emphasis in original).[69]

Holdheim here elaborates an approach bearing important similarities to the one Geiger expressed in his reviews of Hirsch. For Holdheim, the talmudic rabbis sought the spirit of the Bible, which they applied to their time by creatively interpreting the biblical letter. Contemporary rabbis should follow their talmudic predecessors by inventively interpreting the biblical and talmudic letter to meet the needs of their time.

Hirsch thinks that if Holdheim's view of Midrash is correct, it amounts to a devastating indictment of the talmudic rabbis. Hirsch accuses Holdheim of claiming that the rabbis "deliberately deceived their people regarding what was most sacred to them" by imposing their own views on the Bible and then claiming that this was the true meaning of the divinely revealed Bible. For Hirsch, if this is correct the rabbis should not be celebrated as heroes but, rather, denounced as "scoundrels" (*Schufte*), and one should be willing to "consign the old tomes [of the Talmud] to the flames."[70] As Hirsch puts it, "it is better to be led to eternal damnation by the hand of truth than to have the gates of heaven opened by lies."[71]

Before turning to specific examples of how Holdheim misrepresents Jewish sources, Hirsch asserts that there is a core principle that guides Holdheim's distorted portrayal of Judaism, namely, the *separation of church and state*. Hirsch notes that Christians developed this doctrine in response to the long religious wars between Catholics and Protestants following the Reformation. It was hoped that by assigning church and state different functions and domains the wars of religion could be ended. The function of the state was to unite people for the sake of their "earthly well-being" (*irdische Wohlfahrt*) by applying principles of "justice and humanity" (*Rechts und Humanität*). As such, the state's primary concern was with people's *actions*, while *convictions* were only of interest insofar as they could impact earthly well-being. By contrast, the function of the church was to unite people for the sake of their "heavenly well-being" (*himmlische Wohlfahrt*) by imbuing them with salvational *beliefs*. The primary concern of the church

[69] Hirsch, *Erste und Zweite Mitteilung*, 84; *CW*, 9:72, citing Holdheim, *Ueber die Autonomie*, 165.
[70] Hirsch is here obliquely referring to the many times that the Talmud was burned in Christian Europe.
[71] Hirsch, *Erste und Zweite Mitteilung*, 85; *CW*, 9:72–73.

was therefore with "thoughts, feelings, and convictions," with actions only deemed significant to the extent that they expressed beliefs. Since church and state occupied separate, non-overlapping domains, religion should play no role in politics.[72]

But Hirsch claims that the separation of church and state is inapplicable to Judaism, which regards *action in the world, not belief* as the key to salvation. The only way that Holdheim can make Judaism fit this Christian schema is through *pilpul.* Hirsch notes that Holdheim divides halakhah into two categories: (1) laws of an "absolute religious nature" that concern "pure religious forms" and (2) laws that deal with "political, judicial, and civil" matters.[73] For Holdheim, religious laws concern human beings' *relation to God* and are "commanded for all time," while the civil laws concern *interpersonal relations* and were only valid when the Jews had an independent state. Lacking an independent state, Jews are bound solely by the civil laws of the states in which they live.[74]

Hirsch charges that Holdheim's division of halakhah is arbitrary, confusing, and inadequately grounded in Jewish sources. He asks: if religious laws concern relations between the individual and God while the civil laws concern interpersonal relations, in what category do the dietary laws fall? Presumably they would be religious laws since they regulate a person's relation to God. But, Hirsch notes, Holdheim holds that religious laws are always binding while it is only the civil laws whose validity is limited to the time when the Jews had a state. Why, then, does Holdheim claims that the dietary laws are no longer binding?[75] Similarly, Hirsch asks how Holdheim regards laws in the Torah, like not stealing or having incestual relations? As they govern interpersonal relations, they would seem to be civil laws. Referring to Xenophon's claim that in ancient Sparta boys would be kept hungry so that they learned how to steal, and that in ancient Greece it was permissible to marry one's sibling if she was from a different mother, Hirsch asks whether

72 Hirsch, *Erste und Zweite Mitteilung,* 87; *CW,* 9:74.

73 Hirsch, *Erste und Zweite Mitteilung,* 88; *CW,* 9:74, citing Holdheim, *Die Autonomie,* 49–50.

74 Ibid. As several scholars have observed, Holdheim's view is clearly indebted to Spinoza's *Theological-Political Treatise* and Mendelssohn's *Jerusalem.* This is not the place to explore this connection.

75 Hirsch, *Erste und Zweite Mitteilung,* 91; *CW,* 9:76. Of course, Spinoza had claimed that ritual laws were civil laws whose only purpose was creating a social bond among the ancient Jews. Holdheim seems to adopt this view in his later 1845 work *The Ceremonial Laws in the Messianic Kingdom* (*Das Ceremonialgesetz im Messiasreich*). See Ellenson, "Antinomianism and Its Responses," 270.

Holdheim would claim that the Torah would permit a Jew living in Sparta to steal or a Jew living in ancient Greece to marry his sister?[76]

Hirsch notes that Holdheim seeks to ground his division of halakhah in biblical texts, but he claims that the texts themselves belie his argument. Holdheim asserts that the Bible "expressly" states that Jewish civil laws are only applicable when the Jews have a state, and Hirsch surmises that he is referring to laws such as the appointment of a king (Deuteronomy 17:14–15) or the execution of an idol worshipper (17:2–5), which are prefaced by phrases implying that the Hebrews would implement these laws while ruling Palestine.[77] The problem, Hirsch points out, is that many other biblical laws contain similar descriptions, and Holdheim would surely not limit their validity to a time when Jews ruled Palestine. Concerning the poor, Deuteronomy 15:7 states, "If there is a needy person among you, one of your kinsmen *in any of the settlements in the land that the Lord your God is giving you* do not harden your heart and shut your hand against your needy kinsman" (emphasis mine), while the Fifth Commandment of the Decalogue states, "Honor your father and mother as the Lord your God has commanded that you may long endure and fare well *in the land that the Lord your God is assigning you*" (Deuteronomy 5:16). Surely Holdheim would not want to say that it is only incumbent on a Jew to help the poor or respect her parents in the ancient Hebrew state![78]

Hirsch also charges Holdheim with misreading rabbinic sources. For example, Holdheim claims that the Talmud explicitly states that many civil/political laws in Judaism are not practiced when there is no Hebrew state and/or no Temple, such as the laws pertaining to sacrifices, kings, or capital punishment.[79] But, Hirsch responds, the reason that these laws are not practiced is

[76] Hirsch, *Erste und Zweite Mitteilung*, 95; *CW*, 9:79. On Xenophon's claims about Sparta, see Ducat, *Spartan Education*, 9–10. On marriage between half-siblings in ancient Greece, see Huebner, "Brother-Sister Marriage in Roman Egypt." Huebner notes that in Roman Egypt marriage between full siblings was legally condoned and about a sixth of all documented marriages of the time were between full siblings.

[77] The law concerning the appointment of a king states: "*When you have come into the land that the Lord your God is giving you, and have taken possession of it and settled in it*, and you say, 'I will set a king over me, like all the nations that are around me,' you may indeed set over you a king whom the Lord your God will choose" (Deuteronomy 17:14–15). The law concerning the execution of an idolater states: "If there is found among you, *in one of your towns that the Lord your God is giving you*, a man or woman who does what is evil in the sight of the Lord your God, and transgresses his covenant by going to serve other gods and worshiping them . . . then you shall bring out to your gates that man or that woman who has committed this crime and you shall stone the man or woman to death" (Deuteronomy 17:2–5).

[78] Hirsch, *Erste und Zweite Mitteilung*, 90; *CW*, 9:75–76.

[79] Hirsch, *Erste und Zweite Mitteilung*, 93; *CW*, 9:77–78, citing Holdheim, *Ueber die Autonomie*, 44–45.

not that they have *ceased to be valid* but, rather, that the *Jews lack the institutions to fulfill them*. Just as a person is only bound to honor his parents as long as they are still alive, so he is only bound to offer sacrifices as long as there is a Temple.[80]

While Holdheim asserts that he is following the spirit of the Bible, which separates religion and state, for Hirsch, intellectual honesty demands recognizing that the Torah makes no distinction between religious and civil law. Indeed, Hirsch observes that biblical Hebrew does not even have words for "religion" and "state."[81]

Hirsch's anxiety over Reform's radicalization

We saw in the last chapter that in the *Nineteen Letters* Hirsch complained that Reformers were sowing religious anarchy as individuals were implementing reforms haphazardly.[82] Geiger seems to have taken this criticism to heart, for in May 1837 he published an open letter in his journal titled "The Rabbinical Assembly: Letter to a Friend of the Jewish Ministry." In this letter, Geiger called for organizing a convention of progressive rabbis to generate a coherent program of reform.[83] Three months later, he convened an assembly attended by fourteen rabbis in Wiesbaden, though the Wiesbaden assembly accomplished little.[84]

In 1844 Ludwig Philippson convened the first official Reform rabbinical assembly in Brunswick.[85] Lasting from June 12 to June 19, the Brunswick assembly brought together many of the leading Reform-minded rabbis of the time, including Geiger and Holdheim as well as Samuel Hirsch, Gotthold Salomon, and Salomon Herxheimer.[86] The assembly protocols were published shortly after it concluded and revealed that while there was

[80] Hirsch, *Erste und Zweite Mitteilung*, 93; *CW*, 9:78.

[81] Hirsch, *Erste und Zweite Mitteilung*, 90; *CW*, 9:77. As we have seen, Mendelssohn pointed out that Hebrew has no word for "religion." See p. 29 of this volume.

[82] See p. 257 of this volume.

[83] See Philipson, *The Reform Movement in Judaism*, 197.

[84] Michael Meyer observes, "By the early forties the course of reform seemed chaotic. In some communities there had been considerable change, at least in the synagogue atmosphere; in others very little. There was no central authority to lay down criteria and provide links between theoretical conceptions of Judaism, the results of scholarly research, and practical reforms." See Meyer, *Response to Modernity*, 132. Also see Philipson, *The Reform Movement in Judaism*, 198–199.

[85] Meyer, *Response to Modernity*, 132; Philipson, *The Reform Movement*, 200–201.

[86] See Meyer, *Response to Modernity*, 132–134; Lowenstein, "The 1840s and the Creation of the German Jewish Religious Reform Movement," 275–279.

considerable disagreement, four important decisions were agreed upon: (1) a Jew must regard the state in which he lives as his fatherland and be committed to defending it and obeying all of its laws;[87] (2) the *kol nidre* prayer, which annuls vows, should be eliminated from the Yom Kippur liturgy;[88] (3) the ritual of sucking blood from the wound of a baby being circumcised, known as *metzizah befeh*, should be abolished;[89] (4) intermarriage between Jews and Christians or other monotheists was not halakhically prohibited as long as the children born could also be raised as Jews.[90]

The first decision was not controversial, but the latter three, particularly the last one, provoked outrage. In Altona, Hirsch's teacher Rabbi Jacob Ettlinger circulated a manifesto protesting the assembly that was signed by seventy-seven traditionalist rabbis, including Hirsch.[91] In Holland, a layman, Zvi Hirsch Lehren, sought out responsa from leading traditionalist rabbis objecting to the assembly, and in 1845 he published a collection of thirty-seven Hebrew responsa, which he titled *The Law of Zealotry* (*Torat Hakena'ot*).[92] The collection included a long responsum by Hirsch.[93]

In his responsa, Hirsch does not limit himself to discussing the particular decisions arrived at by the assembly. Rather, he seeks to uncover the *root* of the problem, which he identifies as an *open disregard for talmudic authority* and a *veiled disregard for biblical authority*. Hirsch finds *open disregard for talmudic authority* in the opinion of a rabbi who claims that a Jew is free "to depart from the Talmud only where the consciousness of the time (*Bewusstsein der Zeit*) has already departed from it."[94] While acknowledging that the assembly did not officially adopt this statement as a guiding principle, Hirsch sees it as clearly assumed in a number of the participants' statements, such as one rabbi who claims that one need not follow rabbinic interpretations of the Sabbath laws and another who claims that rabbinic decrees (*gezerot*) are not binding.[95] Hirsch finds *veiled disregard for biblical*

87 Philipson, *The Reform Movement*, 212.

88 Meyer, *Response to Modernity*, 134.

89 Katz, *Divine Law in Human Hands*, 234–235, 373. For discussion of the ritual and the controversy surrounding it in the nineteenth century, see ibid., 357–402.

90 Meyer, *Response to Modernity*, 135; Philipson, *The Reform Movement*, 211–212.

91 Signatories continued to be gathered, and eventually three hundred rabbis signed the protest. See Bleich, *Jacob Ettlinger*, 186–191; Philipson, *The Reform Movement*, 225–229; Katz, *Divine Law in Human Hands*, 231–232.

92 A play on Numbers 5:29.

93 See Katz, *Divine Law in Human Hands*, 236–241.

94 Holdheim made this statement. See *Protocolle der ersten Rabbiner-Versammlung*, 66; Hirsch, *Sefer Shemesh Marpeh*, 190.

95 Hirsch, *Sefer Shemesh Marpeh*, 191, citing *Protocolle*, 90, 91.

authority in Reformers distinguishing between the moral laws of the Bible whose authority is absolute and the ritual laws whose authority is questionable.[96] Hirsch notes that the assembly even failed to declare itself in favor of the biblical commandment of circumcision.[97]

Hirsch draws extreme conclusions about Reformers' relationship to Judaism. Asserting that obedience to the Torah, both Oral and Written, is foundational to Judaism, Hirsch writes that "the words of the participants in this assembly show that they are *of a different religion* (*benei dat aheret*)" (emphasis mine).[98] For Hirsch, Reformers' deviation from historical Judaism is so radical that they threaten to provoke a religious schism in Judaism. Still, Hirsch does not see this schism as inevitable, and near the end of the responsum he reproves Reformers in the hope that Jewish unity can be preserved if Reformers pull back from their more radical positions:

> You children of the nation, whose assembly has caused all this [protest] . . . Do your eyes not see that evil and bitterness will follow the path on which you have begun? Do you not know and understand that if your words bear fruit, *the house of Israel will be torn into two*? . . . for when those who listen to you follow your words, transgressing talmudic law by permitting foods and marriage that are forbidden to us, our shared covenant cannot endure and with tears we will separate from one another. Do you not know and understand that by removing faith in the Talmud and the traditions of our Sages, may their memory be for blessing, the foundation on which our [communal] life rests will be removed?[99] (emphasis mine)

For Hirsch, once Reformers deny the legal authority of the Talmud and reject and/or radically change basic Jewish laws such as the dietary and marriage laws, the basis for Jewish unity will dissolve.

While in his 1844 responsum Hirsch still hoped that German Jewish unity could be salvaged, a decade later he would conclude that this was no longer possible.[100]

96 Hirsch, *Sefer Shemesh Marpeh*, 191, citing *Protocolle*, 37, 52, 53, 69, 90, 91.

97 Hirsch, *Sefer Shemesh Marpeh*, 191, citing *Protocolle*, 80. On the controversy among Reformers over circumcision in the 1840s, see Katz, *Divine Law in Human Hands*, 320–356.

98 Hirsch, *Sefer Shemesh Marpeh*, 190.

99 Ibid., 195–196.

100 See Hirsch, *GS*, 1:216–217; *CW*, 6:16.

From Chief Rabbi to separatist leader: How Hirsch became Orthodox

In 1847, Hirsch left his post in Emden to assume the prestigious position of Chief Rabbi of Moravia. His appointment was both unusual and controversial since Moravian Jews were averse to appointing a foreigner to this position.[101] But as Michael Miller has shown, a primary consideration in selecting a new Chief Rabbi was to address the looming schism in Moravian Jewry between Orthodoxy and Reform.[102] Hirsch seemed like a perfect choice given that he was a traditionalist who wore the robes of a Protestant minister (including a white collar),[103] preached in flawless German, advocated aesthetic, but not liturgical, reforms in the synagogue, and stressed the need to combine secular education with intensive Torah study.

In Moravia, Hirsch sought to unify Moravian Jewry by creating a centralized religious authority, which would exert control over Moravia's many distinct Jewish communities. But several of these communities resented a foreigner seeking to set aside local customs and strip local communities of their autonomy.[104] Following the 1848 revolutions, Hirsch was able to rally Moravian Jewry behind him through his vigorous advocacy for Jewish civil rights.[105] But after the revolutions, he again felt frustrated as his attempts to form a centralized religious community met resistance. So when Hirsch was offered the position of rabbi of a small Orthodox congregation in Frankfurt in 1851, he accepted.[106]

The change from Moravia to Frankfurt could not have been more dramatic. In Moravia Hirsch was the Chief Rabbi of some forty thousand Jews, while in Frankfurt he was the rabbi of a small congregation of thirty-four families.[107] But the move was to Hirsch's advantage. Moravian Jews were divided into fifty-two communities with diverse traditions and significant autonomy, which is why they resented Hirsch's attempt to subordinate them

101 See Miller, *Rabbis and Revolution*, 173–175. Miller notes that the Moravian *Gubernium*, which had to approve the appointment of the Chief Rabbi, originally rejected Hirsch's appointment because he was not Moravian.

102 See ibid., 140–142.

103 See Figure 20.

104 Miller, *Rabbis and Revolution*, 180–189.

105 Ibid., 189–218.

106 Ibid., 290–309, 313–320; Liberles, *Religious Conflict*, 111–112. Miller and Liberles discuss several reasons that Hirsch may have decided to leave Moravia for Frankfurt. See Liberles, *Religious Conflict*, 133–135; Miller, *Rabbis and Revolution*, 314–315.

107 On the number of Moravian Jews, see Miller, *Rabbis and Revolution*, 350. On the number of Frankfurt Jews in Hirsch's congregation in 1851, see Liberles, *Religious Conflict*, 95–98.

to his authority and religious vision. By contrast, in Frankfurt Hirsch was rabbi of the *Israelitische Religionsgesellschaft* (Israelite Religious Society), a small, separatist congregation that had recently broken from the community because they opposed its control by Reformers, though they remained tax-paying members of the Frankfurt Jewish community as mandated by state law. As a minority group of religious dissenters, the group was tight knit, highly energized, and ideologically driven, and they welcomed a forceful leader like Hirsch who would articulate a clear religious vision and boldly implement it.[108] Here Hirsch took the final step that would determine the remainder of his career. Relishing the freedom that came from being the leader of an embattled minority, Hirsch sought to create an ideologically pure, model community, whose principles he would defend through skilled polemics.

Rhetoric is an important element of any religious ideology, and it is highly significant that shortly after his arrival in Frankfurt, Hirsch first adopted the moniker "Orthodox" for himself. Scholars have long noted the significance of this term. In his seminal 1986 article, Jacob Katz offered an expansive, sociological understanding of Orthodoxy, noting that Orthodoxy is not a seamless continuation of "tradition-bound," pre-Enlightenment Judaism. For Katz, while "tradition-bound" Jews practice Judaism unselfconsciously, Orthodoxy is defined by its vigorous opposition to rival trends within Judaism that it sees threatening tradition. As Katz puts it, Orthodoxy "oppose[s] . . . the relinquishing of traditional Jewish customs" in conscious "awareness of other Jews' rejection of tradition."[109]

More recently, Jeffrey Blutinger has investigated how Jews employed the term "Orthodox" in the eighteenth and nineteenth centuries. He concludes that the meaning of the term "Orthodox" shifted between the centuries.

[108] See Liberles, *Religious Conflict*, 93–102.

[109] Katz, "Orthodoxy in Historical Perspective," 3–4. Michael Silber follows Katz's understanding of Orthodoxy and provides a nice summary of this view: "Orthodoxy in all its variety is characterized by a firm ideological stance, defining itself in relation to rival trends within Judaism. It implies more than an adherence to traditional forms of religious observance; rather, it is an ideology committed to the preservation of tradition . . . As such, it is a relatively new phenomenon, a consequence of the challenges posed to tradition by modern ideologies . . . . With the authority of tradition no longer taken as self-evident, it has had to be consciously defended and justified, augmented and amplified. Orthodoxy thus emerged in response to ideologies that challenged tradition and presented themselves as legitimate alternatives. It did not arise in the absence of ideological confrontation even where there was noticeable erosion of tradition associated with modernization." See Silber, "Orthodoxy." Moshe Samet provides a more restrictive definition of Orthodoxy, distinguishing between factors shared by Ultra-Orthodoxy and Neo-Orthodoxy and factors that distinguish the two. See Samet, "The Beginnings of Orthodoxy," 249–250.

In the eighteenth century "Orthodoxy" referred to Jews who opposed the Enlightenment, but in the nineteenth century it came to refer to Jews who opposed Reform.[110] Hirsch's embrace of the moniker fits Blutinger's thesis nicely.

In 1854 an anonymous pamphlet appeared titled "The Religious Confusions in the Jewish Community of Frankfurt am Main" (Die religiösen Wirren in der Israelitischen Gemeinde zu Frankfurt am Main). The pamphleteer attacked Frankfurt traditionalists in harsh terms, seeing them as part of a broader European phenomenon that he called "Orthodoxy":

> [The Orthodox] are people who claim to have a monopoly on religion and piety . . . who believe themselves relieved of all duties of love and justice towards those whose viewpoints diverge from their own one iota; who imagine themselves or [at least] wish to convince others that they are acting in God's name when they sow the dragon seed of hatred and dissension in peaceful communities; who seek to turn back the wheel of history and return the nineteenth century to the cultural level of the fifteenth. Such Orthodox or rather Pseudo-Orthodox have also always existed in the Jewish community.[111]

For the pamphleteer, Ultramontane Catholics who seek to reverse modern progress by returning society to the pre-Reformation Dark Ages under a tyrannical Pope typify "Orthodoxy." He presents Orthodox Jews, whom he calls the "party of darkness" (*Dunkelpartei*), as the Jewish equivalent of these Catholic reactionaries and contrasts Orthodox hate with Reform love.[112]

Hirsch responded with a pamphlet of his own to which he gave the ironic title "Religion Allied to Progress" ("Religion im Bunde mit Fortschritt").[113] Near the beginning of his pamphlet, Hirsch reappropriates the label "Orthodox":

> In point of fact, it was not "Orthodox" Jews who introduced the name "Orthodoxy" into Jewish circles. It was the modern "progressive" Jews who first applied this name to their "old" retrograde brothers to differentiate "the Orthodox" from themselves in a deprecating manner. The old Jews at

110 Blutinger, "So-Called Orthodoxy," 320.

111 *Die Religiösen Wirren*, 3.

112 Ibid., 5.

113 The pamphleteer had used this expression to describe his own religious outlook. See *Die Religiösen Wirren*, 4.

> first saw this designation as an insulting name and rightly so. "Orthodox" Judaism does not know any varieties of Judaism. Judaism is one and indivisible. It does not know a Mosaic, Prophetic, and Rabbinic Judaism, nor an Orthodox and Neological Judaism.[114] It knows only Judaism and non-Judaism . . . It does indeed know conscientious and frivolous Jews, good Jews, bad Jews or baptized Jews. Nevertheless, all are Jews with a mission which they cannot abrogate. They are only distinguished to the extent they fulfill or do not fulfill their mission.[115]

Hirsch is observing that the label "Orthodox" has an extremely negative connotation. At first applied to reactionary Catholics, it connotes retrograde religious types. In this sense, Orthodoxy represents the opposite of the pamphleteer's "Religion Allied to Progress." Hirsch notes that when they were given this name by their opponents, the so-called "Orthodox" Jews resented this label, but not merely because of its negative implications. What most disturbed them was that the label implied that Judaism comprises denominations. Orthodox Jews do not, however, regard themselves as members of a sect *within* Judaism but, rather, as the authentic perpetuators of historical Judaism as it existed from time immemorial. To them, Reformers are not members of a rival sect, but simply wayward Jews. Hirsch recognizes, however, that for the foreseeable future Orthodox Jews will be a minority group that must battle to protect its integrity and he embraces the Orthodox moniker.[116]

Hirsch turns Mendelssohn Orthodox

We have seen that in the *Nineteen Letters* Hirsch expressed a mixed attitude toward Mendelssohn, combining praise with criticism.[117] But when

[114] Hirsch uses the term "Neology" to include both radical Reformers and more moderate reformers who in Germany adopted the moniker "Positive-Historical." See p. 403 of this volume.

[115] Hirsch, *GS*, 3:494; *CW*, 6:114.

[116] Hirsch's acute consciousness of being a member of a sectarian minority group is reflected in an essay he published three years after "Religion Allied to Progress," titled "Die Minorität" ("The Minority") in which he used the stories of the Maccabees to reflect on the dynamics of being a minority within the Jewish community. The essay is found in Hirsch, *GS*, 4:28–49; *CW*, 2:233–248. Also see Hirsch's 1862 essay " "How should a minority loyal to the law act in relation to the will of a Neological majority?" The essay is reprinted in Hirsch, *GS*, 2:358–374. Meyer makes clear how from the 1830s to the 1850s Hirsch's traditionalism went from being a majority position to being a minority one, writing, "Although in his earlier years, Hirsch had boasted that the mass of German Jewry was on his side, during the second half of the century his position became that of a diminished minority." See Meyer, *Response to Modernity*, 79.

[117] See pp. 247–253 of this volume.

Hirsch became Orthodox his criticisms of Mendelssohn disappeared, and he deployed Mendelssohn as a cudgel to beat back Reform. Reformers had often looked to Mendelssohn as their model. The pamphleteer noted that in rejecting the idea that Judaism contains articles of faith, Mendelssohn had demonstrated that the "concept of Orthodoxy (*Orthodoxie*), that is, orthodox belief (*Rechtgläubigkeit*)," is inapplicable to Judaism.[118] The pamphleteer presented Mendelssohn as the most recent in a series of progressive Jewish thinkers persecuted by Orthodox Jews. Just as twelfth-century French rabbis had attacked Maimonides as an "ungodly renegade" and seventeenth-century Dutch rabbis had excommunicated Spinoza and "committed his soul to the devil," more recent "pharisaic" Orthodox Jews had persecuted the "God-forsaken" (*gottvergessenen*), "unorthodox" (*unrechtgläubig*) Mendelssohn for having the audacity to translate the Bible into German.[119]

In response, Hirsch turned Mendelssohn into an Orthodox Jew. Addressing the pamphleteer's claim that Mendelssohn's denial that Judaism has articles of faith separates him from Orthodoxy, Hirsch observes that Mendelssohn made this claim because he saw the religious doctrines at the heart of Judaism as universal while maintaining that the distinctiveness of Judaism rested on its commitment to ritual law.[120] Pointing to changes Reformers have introduced into the synagogue service, dietary, and Sabbath laws, Hirsch asks Reformers whether they think Mendelssohn would "rejoice in your 'true progress'?"[121] Hirsch then cites a long passage from the end of *Jerusalem* in which Mendelssohn affirms that all the "personal commandments" of the Torah must "be observed strictly according to the words of the law."[122]

Hirsch's use of Mendelssohn runs deeper. Throughout "Religion Allied to Progress," Hirsch accuses Reformers of using the high-minded term *progress* to mask baser reasons for loosening halakhic rituals, namely, because observing ritual restrictions such as the Sabbath and dietary laws threaten economic opportunity and impede their ability to indulge their lusts.[123]

118 *Die Religiösen Wirren*, 3.

119 Ibid., 4–5.

120 Hirsch, *GS*, 3:493; *CW*, 6:114–115. Hirsch cites Mendelssohn's claim in *Jerusalem* that "laws cannot be abridged. In them everything is fundamental and in this regard we may rightly say: to us all words of Scripture, all of God's commandments and prohibitions are fundamental." See Mendelssohn, *JubA*, 8:168; *Jerusalem*, 101–102.

121 Hirsch, *GS*, 3:504; *CW*, 6:125.

122 Hirsch, *GS*, 3:507; *CW*, 6:128–129. See Mendelssohn, *JubA*, 8:199; *Jerusalem*, 134.

123 Hirsch, *GS*, 3:496; *CW*, 6:116.

But Hirsch recognizes that there is another motive driving Reform efforts to ease halakhic restrictions. Many Reformers feel *embarrassed* when practicing Jewish rituals in front of Christians.[124] They assume that to be respected by Christians, they must eliminate ritual laws that create barriers to sociability. For Hirsch, this reflects a deep misunderstanding of human psychology. He observes that the Jew who is willing to "sacrifice his inclinations and prospects of material gain to obey God's holy will" displays "far greater moral strength" than the one who abandons halakhah to be accepted and therefore embodies "true *Bildung*."[125] While Reformers think that rituals create barriers that make full participation in "civic and public life" impossible, Hirsch predicts that when Christians see Jews unwilling to bend their religious laws for social acceptance, this commitment to conscience will impress them and "enlightened governments and nations" will "gladly accommodate" Jews' religious restrictions. For Christians will regard this commitment to conscience as "a not inconsiderable contribution by Jewish citizens to the society in which they live" given the social value of moral restraint.[126]

Hirsch claims that Mendelssohn understood this point when in *Jerusalem* he advised his fellow Jews to "adapt yourselves to the morals and the constitution of the land to which you have been removed but hold fast to the religion of your fathers too."[127] Mendelssohn made clear that if civil rights could only be obtained by abandoning halakhic observance, then Jews must refuse civil rights.[128]

In sum, Hirsch's attitude toward Mendelssohn shifted as he became Orthodox. When Hirsch sought to present a new German Jewish synthesis that combined the partial truths embedded in the major Jewish trends of his time while criticizing their deficiencies, he expressed a mixed attitude

[124] David Friedländer offers a striking expression of German Jewish embarrassment over practicing the ritual laws in his 1799 *Open Letter to Provost Teller* in which he proposes conversion to enlightened Christianity. The wealthy Friedländer recounts feeling embarrassed practicing Jewish rituals even in front of his Christian domestic servants. As he puts it, "The ceremonial laws were observed with worrysome precision in the paternal household. They alienated us in the circle of everyday life; as empty customs without any further influence on our other preoccupations, they had no other effect than that their observance in the presence of people of a different religious persuasion, even domestic servants made us shy, embarrassed, and often restless." See Friedländer, *A Debate on Jewish Emancipation and Christianity in Old Berlin*, 42.

[125] Hirsch, *GS*, 3:500; *CW*, 6:121.

[126] Hirsch, *GS*, 3:503; *CW*, 6:124.

[127] Hirsch, *GS* 3:507–508, citing Mendelssohn, *JubA*, 8:198; *Jerusalem*, 133.

[128] See Mendelssohn, *JubA*, 8:200; *Jerusalem*, 135. See p. 118 of this volume. See Scholem, *On Jews and Judaism in Crisis*, 76.

toward Mendelssohn, the maskilic hero. But once Hirsch embraced sectarian Orthodoxy, he found it most effective to enlist Mendelssohn against Reformers and his criticisms of Mendelssohn disappear.

Hirsch's use of Protestantism and Catholicism as rhetorical tropes

We have seen that Mendelssohn and Zunz both associate Protestantism with individual freedom, interiority, intellectual honesty, and egalitarianism while Catholicism represents despotism, empty religious forms, superstition, intellectual deception, and hierarchy. Not surprisingly, both Mendelssohn and Zunz seek to align their visions of Judaism with Protestantism and attack their opponents for acting like Catholics.

Hirsch, however, is not averse to sometimes identifying as a Catholic and deriding his opponents as Protestants, if only for ironic effect. For example, we have seen that the author of "The Religious Confusions" links Orthodoxy with Catholic reaction. In "Religion Allied to Progress," not only does Hirsch adopts the moniker "Orthodox" for himself, he embraces the Catholic reactionary undertones of the term by subtitling the essay *von einem Schwarzen*. The term *Schwarzen* with its connotations of darkness and evil evoked the image of despotic Catholicism, and Hirsch embraces the slur with a dollop of irony.[129]

Hirsch also sometimes stresses the extreme Protestantism of his opponents to subtly mock them. For example, we have seen that Hirsch calls the Reformer Michael Creizenach "a second Luther" for belittling the Talmud and seeking to base Judaism on the Bible alone.[130] For Hirsch, the Ultra-Protestant Creizenach deforms Judaism by negating talmudic texts and traditions that are central to Judaism.

But, in general, Hirsch follows Mendelssohn and Zunz by aligning himself with Protestantism and deriding his opponents as Catholics. An important reason for Hirsch's negative view of Catholicism is that Ultramontane Catholics were leading opponents of Jewish civil rights. In December 1864, Hirsch published an essay titled "The Mainz Journal and the Ideas of Nationality, Humanity, Civilization, and Freedom." Calling the *Mainz*

[129] Hirsch, *GS*, 3:488; *CW*, 6:107.
[130] See p. 300 of this volume.

Journal the "vanguard of south German Ultramontanism," Hirsch responded to an article attacking the campaign for Jewish civil rights. He noted that the author had argued that Jewish civil rights were being demanded on the basis of "fashionable, frivolous, abstract ideals" of "nationality, humanity, civilization and freedom," which were undermining the "true goods" of "monarchic, Christian, and German" values.[131] Calling for "Christians to band together against Jews the same way that Jews band together against Christians," the author attacked Jews for stealing business from Christians and argued that German Christians should be granted economic, professional, and religious privileges.[132]

In his essay, Hirsch appealed to *Christian self-interest*, arguing that granting privileges to Christians ultimately did not benefit them.[133] Economic privileges bred laziness, resulting in loss of skills that would ultimately impoverish society. Professional privileges such as excluding Jews from university positions would cause research to suffer. Religious privileges such as the state granting favored status to Christianity engendered spiritual and moral complacency as members of the privileged religion would be convinced of their "holiness," "mercy," and "spirituality" and so feel no need to actually sanctify their life, show compassion for others, and perfect their souls.[134]

For Hirsch, *meritocracy* and *state neutrality in matters of religion* are the best ways for society to flourish.[135] Addressing Ultramontane Catholics, Hirsch presents Orthodox Jews as their opposite: "There is no greater contradiction than between you and the old, indeed the oldest religion the one called 'Orthodox Judaism' for there is no greater enemy of privileged holiness than this." Hirsch quotes a striking statement from the rabbinic text *Tanna Debei Eliyahu*: "I testify before you with heaven and earth, that between man and woman, Gentile and Jew, male and female slave, that the holy spirit descends on a person only according to their *acts*" (emphasis in original).[136] While Ultramontane Catholics advocate granting privileges on the basis of *religious affiliation*, Judaism emphasizes that a person's merit is based solely on *how they act*. Hirsch ends his essay by noting that whereas Ultramontane Catholics oppose the ideals of *nationality*, *humanity*, *civilization*, and *freedom*

[131] Hirsch, "Das Mainzer Journal," 90.
[132] Ibid., 89–90.
[133] Ibid., 91.
[134] Ibid., 91.
[135] Ibid., 91.
[136] *Tanna Debei Eliyahu*, 9. See Hirsch, "Das Mainzer Journal," 92–93.

deeming them "chimerical [and] abstract," Judaism cherishes these ideals as "the truest goods."[137]

The first time Hirsch deploys Catholicism rhetorically for polemical purposes is in the *Nineteen Letters*. As we have seen, Hirsch claims that while kabbalah originally contained teachings that elucidate the "spirit" of Judaism, it came to interpret halakhah as a magical mechanism for manipulating higher worlds. Hirsch writes that kabbalistic concepts were used to conceive halakhah as a "spiritless (*geistlose*) *opus operatum*, or almost as amulets to protect against physical evil or build mystical worlds."[138] By claiming that kabbalists viewed halakhah as an *opus operatum*, Hirsch is invoking language used by Protestants to criticize Catholicism. Richard Muller explains that Protestants used the expression *opus operatum* or *ex opera operato* to describe the Catholic view that the correct performance of sacramental rites bestowed grace. By contrast, Lutherans and Reformed (Calvinists) held that what bestowed grace was not the mere *performance* of a sacramental rite but, rather, the *faith* present while performing it. Like these Protestant critics, Hirsch does not reject ritual per se but holds that intention is essential and that the performance of rituals does not magically transform reality. In this respect, he presents true Judaism as anti-Catholic.[139]

We have seen ways that Reformers often aligned themselves with Protestants and attacked their Orthodox opponents for acting like Catholics.[140] Hirsch does the same, connecting Orthodoxy with Protestantism and Reform with Catholicism. For example, in his attack on Holdheim, Hirsch links Holdheim's *pilpulistic* approach with hypocritical Jesuitism, writing, "Sacred God of truth, save us from this modern Jewish Jesuitism."[141] Similarly for Hirsch, Reformers' idea that the rabbis used Midrash to bring Judaism up to date by attributing novel doctrines to Scripture and that contemporary Reformers should do the same is nothing but "pious priestly fraud" (*frommer Priesterbetrug*) through which

[137] Ibid., 93.

[138] Hirsch, *NB*, Brief 17, 84; *NL*, Letter 17, 242. The second edition of the *Nineteen Letters*, which incorporates Hirsch's handwritten notes on his copy of the first edition, softens this criticism of kabbalah slightly. Instead of definitively declaring that kabbalah was used to interpret halakhah as a spiritless *opus operatum*, Hirsch writes that kabbalah was "often" (*oft*) employed this way. See Hirsch, *Neunzehn Briefe über Judentum zweite Auflage*, Brief 17, 92.

[139] See Muller, *Dictionary of Latin and Greek Theological Terms*, 108. Article 13 of the *Augsburg Confession* employs the expression *ex opere operato* to criticize Catholic views of the sacraments. See *The Book of Concord*, 46.

[140] For Reform valorizations of Luther through the 1860s, see Wiese, "'Let His Memory be Holy to Us!': Jewish Interpretation of Luther from the Enlightenment to the Holocaust," 106–111.

[141] Hirsch, *Erste und Zweite Mitteillung*, 85; *CW*, 9:72.

Reformers seek to "impose their views on the people by claiming it to be the received word of God."[142]

Hirsch frequently emphasizes that Judaism is founded on the egalitarian principle that each person can be their own priest, accessing God directly by studying sacred texts without the need for religious intermediaries. Hirsch sees this view expressed by the biblical idea that God designated the Israelites as a "kingdom of priests" (Exodus 19:6).[143] In this way, Hirsch aligns his conception of Judaism with Luther, who had criticized the Catholic hierarchy in favor of a "priesthood of all believers."[144]

For Hirsch, the idea of Jews being a "kingdom of priests" involves two elements. *First*, by making Torah study a supremely important commandment, Jews are enjoined to access the word of God directly.[145] *Second*, worship of God does not occur primarily in the *synagogue* through the *mediation of a rabbi*, but through the *individual Jew* practicing the Torah's commandments in *all aspects of life*. Since every Jew can worship God directly by performing the commandments, he can be his own priest.[146]

Hirsch criticizes Reformers for turning away from these egalitarian dimensions of Judaism in favor of hierarchical, Catholic approaches. As we have seen, in the *Nineteen Letters* he criticizes Reformers for replacing traditional Jewish educational methods that taught students how to read the original texts of the Torah on their own with teaching Judaism through religion textbooks that include a paltry selection of Torah texts in translation and

142 Hirsch, *GS*, 1:153; *CW*, 8:4.

143 See Hirsch, *GS*, 1:289; *CW*, 7:54–55: "From the very beginning the aim of the institutions ordained by Bible was not to establish a priestly hierarchy (*hierarchisch von Priestern*) but to establish a kingdom 'consisting entirely of priests and a holy people' (Exodus 19:6). This statement makes clear that the Torah expects everyone to acquire a priestly education and moral sanctity the one being dependent on the other. It is therefore clear that God did not make His covenant with priests, elders, or leaders, but that he established it on a fully equal basis (*in völliger Parität*) with everyone directly and without intermediaries, down to the 'woodcutters and drawers of water'" (see Deuteronomy 29:10).

144 Luther did not use this precise expression. In his 1520 essay "To the Christian Nobility," he wrote, "we are all consecrated priests through baptism," while in his 1520 essay "On the Babylonian Captivity of the Church," he wrote, "we are all equally priests." For a history of the doctrine of the "Priesthood of all Believers" see Eastwood, *The Priesthood of All Believers*.

145 As Hirsch puts it, "The belief system to be taught does not primarily involve faithfully accepting and believing tradition, but first and foremost demands that each and every one of its adherents should be taught to draw from the original sources on his own, *to become his own priest* (*Hierophant*), as it were" (my emphasis). See Hirsch, *GS*, 2:434; *CW*, 7:64.

146 As Hirsch writes, "A Jew living in complete isolation can still be a Jew; he can do this even without a community, without a synagogue and without a rabbi . . . [*Mitzvot*] transform his hovel into a temple (*Tempel*), his table into an altar (*Altare*), his bread into an offering, his entire life into a hallowed life of priesthood (*Priesterleben*), a life which, if *necessary*, he is able to carry even when he has no contact with his brethren or with 'priests' ('*Priestern*')." See Hirsch, *GS*, 1:213; *CW*, 6:13.

theological catechisms to be memorized and recited. Comparing Reform teachers to Catholic priests who dispense communion wafers, Hirsch writes: "The religious literature of Judaism is not entrusted to a special class of theological scholars to extract catechisms from and throw them to the laity as crumbs from the bread of eternal life (*das Brod des ewigen Lebens*)."[147]

According to Hirsch, Reform leaders do not teach young Jews the skills to read the Torah in Hebrew on their own so that they can despotically control access to the Torah and elevate their own "priestly" status as indispensable intermediaries to God.[148] Hirsch therefore sees reviving Jews' ability to study the Torah in Hebrew on their own as the key to the Jewish masses overthrowing the hierarchical governing boards of communities in which Reformers have taken control. By understanding the true teachings of the Torah, the majority of Jews will reject Reformers' distortions of the Torah's teachings.[149]

Hirsch similarly derides Reform attempts to determine Judaism through rabbinical assemblies, which he compares to Catholic papal conclaves. Reflecting on Geiger's 1837 Wiesbaden assembly, Hirsch remarks, "And then came the hour of the Wiesbaden synod (*Synode*). All eyes were riveted on this ominous conclave (*Conclave*)." Remarking on the failure of Geiger's assembly, Hirsch concludes, "To date, the little baby has not appeared, perhaps it has not been baptized yet (*noch nicht getauft*)."[150]

We have seen that in the *Nineteen Letters* and *Naphtulei Naphtali*, Hirsch expresses sympathy with Reformers' intentions. But by the time he comes to Frankfurt, this sympathy has entirely evaporated. We have mentioned Hirsch's interpreting the Reform slogan "Religion Allied to Progress" as involving sacrificing Judaism to base motives such as pleasure seeking, social climbing, and money grubbing.[151] He also links this slogan with Catholic superstition

[147] Hirsch, *GS*, 1:219; *CW*, 6:19–20. Also see Hirsch, *GS*, 1:270–275; *CW*, 7:14–19. See pp. 259–260 of this volume.

[148] As Hirsch puts it, "They have accustomed him [the student] for the rest of his life to use the teacher of religion (*Religionslehrer*) as an intermediary between himself and the Word of God, to look upon the teachers of religion as his 'priests' (*Priestern*) and 'clergymen' (*Geistlichen*), to regard them as privileged individuals who alone are entitled to draw near to the Word of God as to the Holy of Holies (*Allerheiligsten*) and to impart whatever they choose from to those who will listen." See Hirsch, *GS*, 1:275; *CW*, 7:18.

[149] See Hirsch, *GS*, 3:509–510; *CW*, 6:130–131. Rosenzweig repeats a similar charge, criticizing liberal Judaism for establishing rabbis as priests who mediate God's word while Judaism regards each Jew as his or her own priest who can access God's word directly through the Torah. See Rosenzweig, *On Jewish Learning*, 43–44; *Zweistromland*, 121.

[150] Hirsch, *Erste und Zweite Mitteilung*, 6; *CW*, 9:10.

[151] See Hirsch, *GS*, 3:496; *CW*, 6:116.

and hypocrisy, writing, "The prophet of the new gospel (*neuen Botschaft*) appeared with the slogan, 'Religion Allied to Progress' . . . With this one magic spell (*Zauberspruch*) he made irreligion appear as godliness, apostasy as priestliness (*Priestertum*), sin as merit, frivolity as virtue, weakness as strength, shallowness as deep thought."[152]

Hirsch presents the Reform endeavor to center Jewish religious life on the recitation of catechisms and a weekly synagogue service led by a rabbi as an attempt to mirror Christian views of "religion" that emphasize belief and center religious life on a weekly church service.[153] He contends that this view is completely alien to Judaism, for the Torah is "*no 'religion'*" (emphasis in original). Rather, Hirsch calls the Torah "a 'law,' a 'fiery law,' intended to permeate, enliven, enlighten, warm, and shape, *every* aspect of life . . ." (emphasis in original).[154]

In denying that Judaism is a religion, Hirsch's critique of Reform appears similar to contemporary scholars such as Talal Asad and Saba Mahmood, who claim that a Protestant view of religion as centered on private belief separate from law, politics, and science dominates the modern West and results in a distorted perspective on religions that do not conform to this model such as Islam.[155] Hirsch, however, sees the emphasis on belief not as Protestant but, more generally, as Christian. Furthermore, Hirsch does not see Christianity as relegating religion to the private sphere. Rather, he sees it as centering religion within specific *public* spaces like the Church.

[152] Hirsch, *GS*, 3:489; *CW*, 6:109.

[153] Hirsch, *GS*, 1:85–86; 91; *CW*, 1:186–187, 190–191. See Hirsch, *GS*, 1:216; *CW*, 6:16. For Hirsch, there is a deep irony in Reformers using the pejorative "Orthodox," meaning "right-believing," to define their opponents. For it was Reformers who replaced traditional study of Bible and Talmud with the recitation of catechisms, making catechisms the central component of the confirmation ceremonies that replaced the traditional Bar Mitzvah ceremony. See Hirsch, *GS*, 3:493; *CW*, 6:114.

[154] Hirsch, *GS*, 1:235–236; *CW*, 6:35. See Hirsch, *GS*, 1:92–94; *CW*, 1:192–193. Also see Hirsch's 1835 letter to Z.H. May, where he laments the fact that the standard Jewish code of law, the *Shulhan Arukh*, appeared in four parts. This gave the impression that ritual law could be separated off from civil law and moral law. See Hirsch, *Horeb*, cxli. In his Pentateuch commentary Hirsch remarks that Hebrew has no word for "religion." He explains that part of the reason for this is that "religion" implies something that belongs to one sphere of life that can be separated from the other spheres. By contrast, Judaism considers all of life as informed by "religious" considerations. See Hirsch, *Der Pentateuch*, 1:201–202; *The Hirsch Chumash*, 1:275 (Commentary on Genesis 11:7). Buber and Rosenzweig also reject the view that religion should be limited to one sphere of life. See Buber's essay "People Today and the Jewish Bible" in Buber and Rosenzweig, *Scripture and Translation*, 5–6, and Rosenzweig, *On Jewish Learning*, 56–57, 75.

[155] See Asad, *Genealogies*, 28; Mahmood, "Religious Reason and Secular Affect," 71–72, 87; *Religious Difference in a Secular Age*, 174–175.

Facing historicism

It was not only his position in Frankfurt that led Hirsch to identify himself as a member of an embattled minority faction. As Meyer has noted, by the 1850s Orthodoxy had suffered severe demographics losses throughout German lands and become a "diminished minority."[156] But Hirsch understood that the problem was not simply demographic. Orthodoxy faced serious intellectual challenges.

Not debating Geiger

In 1857, Geiger published his path-breaking *Original Text and Translations of the Bible in Their Dependence on the Inner Development of Judaism* (*Urschrift und Übersetzungen der Bibel in ihrer Abhängigkeit von der innern Entwicklung des Judenthums*). We have seen that in his critique of the *Nineteen Letters* some twenty years earlier, Geiger had argued that the talmudic rabbis reinterpreted the Bible to fit contemporary concerns. But in *Original Text* he went much further, arguing that different schools of Judaism *rewrote the Bible* to fit their needs. In this way, Geiger called into question the textual integrity of the Masoretic Bible. Like Mendelssohn, Hirsch understood that textual criticism of the Bible undermined the authority of much of halakhah, which was grounded in precise midrashic exegesis of biblical texts.[157]

Hirsch did not, however, respond to Geiger's book. Geiger was a leader of the Reform camp and no Orthodox Jew would imagine that he spoke for him. Furthermore, as we have seen, Hirsch thought that Reform and Orthodoxy rested on such different premises that debate between them was impossible.[158] But while Hirsch did not engage with Geiger after becoming Orthodox, he launched severe attacks on two ostensible allies of Orthodoxy, both of whom Hirsch regarded as wolves in sheep clothing who were doing irrevocable damage to Judaism.

156 See Meyer, *Response to Modernity*, 79.

157 For discussion of Geiger's work on the Bible, see Heschel, *Abraham Geiger and the Jewish Jesus*, 76–83, 121–122; Koltun-Fromm, *Abraham Geiger's Liberal Judaism*, 44–50; Sarna, *Studies in Biblical Interpretation*, 161–172.

158 The extent of Hirsch's non-engagement with Geiger is remarkable. In 1863, twelve years after Hirsch's arrival in Frankfurt, Geiger became rabbi of the official Jewish community which Hirsch's separatist congregation paid taxes to. Geiger remained in Frankfurt until 1870. Yet I have found no evidence of any communication between the former best friends while they lived in the same city.

Deconstructing Graetz's *History of the Jews*

In 1853, a budding thirty-six-year-old scholar destined to become the preeminent nineteenth-century Jewish historian published the first volume of his landmark *History of the Jews* (*Geschichte der Juden*). His name was Heinrich Graetz.[159] By the time Graetz published his book, he and Hirsch already had a long history together. Seventeen years earlier, Graetz had written to Hirsch in excited tones. A disillusioned nineteen-year-old yeshiva student in Wollstein, Graetz read the *Nineteen Letters* and was deeply moved.[160] He described "devouring every word" of Hirsch's book, which "reconciled [him] to the Talmud as to a mistress deemed faithless but proved true."[161] Discovering that Hirsch was the anonymous author of the work, Graetz addressed him in reverential terms as "the Ezra of our spiritual exile." Graetz confessed that every line of Hirsch's "divine letters" (*göttliche Epistel*) had melted the icy skepticism freezing his heart, and he entreated Hirsch for the privilege of coming to Oldenburg to study with him.[162]

Hirsch responded by inviting Graetz to live with him in Oldenburg.[163] Arriving in 1837, Graetz lived in Hirsch's home for three years, studying with him every day. Their study schedule was intense. The day began at 4 am, with two hours devoted to Talmud and halakhah; from 6 to 8 am were prayers, Bible study, and breakfast; from 8 to 10 am, more Talmud; and from 10 am to 12 pm they studied Greek. After an hour break for lunch, study resumed at 1 pm, with two hours devoted to Greek, Latin, or physics; from 3–5 pm they studied mathematics and geography. After an hour for dinner, they studied the Bible with much attention given to Psalms, and from 6 to 8 pm they studied legal responsa. The day ended with two hours of reading texts in German, Hebrew, French, and Latin from 9 to 11 pm.[164]

[159] Graetz, *Geschichte der Juden vom Untergang des jüdischen Staat bis zum Abschluß des Talmuds* (*History of the Jews from the Fall of the Jewish State to the Conclusion of the Talmud*). Graetz began his history in the middle, and the first volume he published eventually became the fourth volume of an eleven-volume history.

[160] Bloch, *Heinrich Graetz: A Memoir*, 6–7.

[161] Bloch, *Heinrich Graetz*, 12–13.

[162] See Brann, "Aus H. Graetz Lehr-und Wanderjahren (1)," 258–259, cited in Rosenbloom, *Tradition in an Age of Reform*, 71.

[163] Bloch, *Heinrich Graetz*, 16.

[164] Brann, "Aus H. Graetz Lehr-und Wanderjahren (2)," 46. See Rosenbloom, *Tradition in an Age of Reform*, 72.

But Graetz's skepticism about the Talmud soon returned, and he grew disaffected with Hirsch. Graetz criticized Hirsch's legalism, which he called "narrow Shulhan Arukhinism" (the *Shulhan Arukh* being the standard code of Jewish law). He complained about Hirsch's punctilious observance of halakhah, including his only drinking black coffee while traveling to avoid violating the Jewish dietary laws. And Graetz mocked the enormous amount of time he found Hirsch studying Talmud, complaining that he acted like "a Polish *lamdan* (talmudic scholar)."[165]

In 1840, Graetz left Oldenburg, and after working for two years as a private tutor in Ostrow enrolled at the University of Breslau. Geiger was then rabbi of the liberal community in Breslau, and Graetz accused him of covertly seeking Judaism's destruction while posing as a pious Jew. When Geiger published a textbook for the study of the Mishnah, Graetz excoriated it as an error-laden work marred by blatant ideological motivations.[166]

Despite his misgivings about Hirsch, Graetz remained attached to him and sympathized with his attacks on Reform. This was reflected in his dedicating his first book *Gnosticism and Judaism* (1846) to "the most honorable, District Rabbi, Samson Raphael Hirsch, the spirited fighter for historical Judaism, the unforgettable teacher and paternal friend, with love and gratitude."[167] A year later when Hirsch was appointed Chief Rabbi of Moravia, he invited Graetz to become a teacher in the local Jewish school and lecture the yeshiva students about Jewish history in the talmudic period.[168] But for reasons that are not entirely clear, in 1850 Graetz precipitated a final break with Hirsch by snubbing him and asking Hirsch's rival and harsh critic Hirsch Fassel to officiate at his wedding.[169]

Graetz published the first volume of his *History of the Jews* three years after his rift with Hirsch, and in October 1855, Hirsch published the first of what became a twelve-part review of the work.[170] Hirsch begins his review

[165] See Brann, "Aus H. Graetz Lehr-und Wanderjahren (3)," 356–357, 360, cited in Rosenbloom, *Tradition in an Age of Reform*, 73–74. Hirsch recognized Graetz's alienation early on. As I argued previously, the character Peretz in his 1838 *Naphtulei Naphtali* was likely based on Graetz. See p. 298 note 39 of this volume.

[166] See Bloch, *Heinrich Graetz*, 28–29; Meyer, "From Combat to Convergence," 147–148.

[167] Graetz, *Gnosticismus und Judenthum*, iv.

[168] See Breuer, "Chapters in the Life of Rabbi Samson Raphael Hirsch: Graetz," 46; Bloch, *Heinrich Graetz*, 40–41.

[169] Breuer, "Chapters in the Life of Rabbi Samson Raphael Hirsch: Graetz," 46. On Fassel's rivalry with Hirsch, see Miller, *Rabbis and Revolution*, 138–176.

[170] The articles are reprinted in Hirsch, *GS*, 5:318–509; *CW*, 5:3–208.

with the words: "I once had a young friend who was a deaf-mute."[171] Hirsch recounts that this deaf-mute friend was an artist who would paint unnaturally large portraits with greatly exaggerated features. He did so because he did not represent the "objective reality" (*objective Wirklichkeit*) of his subjects, but rather, the "subjective impression" (*subjektiven Eindruck*) that their personalities made upon him.[172] Hirsch notes that the tendency to amplify certain features of a person commonly occurs when emotional factors color the way we see them.[173] Among artists it is especially common that their subjective likes and dislikes and momentary moods unconsciously guide their artwork such that accidental features or traits of the subject become "a basis for interpreting an entire personality."[174]

Hirsch compares Graetz's history to the portraits of his deaf-mute artist friend. Like the work of the deaf-mute artist, Graetz's history centers on narrative portraits of individual talmudic sages. And like the deaf-mute artist, Graetz interprets these personalities by inflating the importance of their accidental features, guided by his own subjective interests. But, Hirsch claims, while the deaf-mute artist's portraits were larger than life, Graetz's historical portraits are smaller than life.[175] Rather than draw complex character sketches of the rabbis, Graetz presents them in simplistic two-dimensional fashion, often reducing their character to a single dominant trait. And instead of a rich discussion of the reasoning behind their legal rulings, Graetz reduces these rulings to "individual temperaments, psychological traits, and all too often egoistic, hierarchical, and political motives."[176] According to Hirsch, a tacit aim of Graetz's *History* is to convince the reader that the talmudic rabbis were "not the *bearers* of [divine] tradition, but rather its *creators*" (emphasis in original).[177]

Hirsch does not just focus on unmasking Graetz's methodological approach. Instead, he seeks to show the *inadequacy* of Graetz's history on scholarly grounds.[178] Hirsch asserts that Graetz's claims are, for the most part, based on scant textual evidence that has been distorted through "hasty judgment or

[171] Hirsch, *GS*, 5:318; *CW*, 5:3. See Breuer, "Chapters in the Life of Rabbi Samson Raphael Hirsch: Graetz," 47.
[172] Hirsch, *GS*, 5:318; *CW*, 5:3.
[173] Hirsch, *GS*, 5:319; *CW*, 5:3.
[174] Hirsch, *GS*, 5:318; *CW*, 5:3–4.
[175] Hirsch, *GS*, 5:319–320; *CW*, 5:4.
[176] Hirsch, *GS*, 5:322; *CW*, 5:6.
[177] Ibid.
[178] Hirsch, *GS*, 5:321; *CW*, 5:5.

misinterpretation." Hirsch concludes that Graetz's history is "more fiction than truth" (*mehr Dichtung als Wahrheit*).[179]

An example will illustrate Hirsch's critique. Graetz opens his history with the Roman siege of Jerusalem. He describes the argument between Jewish zealots who wished to fight the Romans and the sage Rabbi Yohanan ben Zakkai whom Graetz calls a man of "peaceful character" (*friedfertigen Charakters)*, who urged the people to "surrender Jerusalem and submit to the Romans."[180] Graetz recounts that when R. Yohanan recognized that the zealots would not listen to his warnings, he escaped to the Roman camp where he met Vespasian, the Roman general laying siege to Jerusalem. Vespasian welcomed R. Yohanan and granted him a request, whereupon R. Yohanan asked for permission to establish a school in Yavne.[181]

Shortly thereafter the Romans burned the Temple. Graetz asserts that R. Yohanan recognized that Judaism was in crisis and so sought to establish it on a new foundation by transferring the main worship of God from sacrifices to acts of charity and prayer. The supreme Jewish judicial body, the Sanhedrin, had met in the Temple. Opposing the widespread view that the Sanhedrin "could only possess competent authority within the hall of the Temple (*lishkhat hagazit*)," R. Yohanan ordained that the Sanhedrin be relocated to Yavne.[182] Graetz concludes that by doing so R. Yohanan "removed the soul from the Temple and infused it in a different body."[183]

Hirsch begins his review by posing a simple question. Graetz asserts that R. Yohanan had opposed the Jewish zealots because he was a man of "peaceful character." But, asks Hirsch, how does Graetz know this? Hirsch notes that Graetz supports his contention by citing a Midrash in which R. Yohanan explains that the Bible prohibits using iron tools in building the Temple altar because iron symbolizes war and strife while the altar symbolizes peace and atonement.[184] But Hirsch claims that this source is completely inadequate to support Graetz's claim about R. Yohanan's character since praising peace is a typical teaching of rabbinic sages. Hirsch cites teachings on peace ascribed to figures such as R. Eliezer Hagadol and R. Meir, whom Graetz elsewhere

179 Hirsch, *GS*, 5:320- 321; *CW*, 5:4–5. In using this phrase, Hirsch is, of course, alluding to the title of Goethe's autobiography. See p. 244 of this volume.

180 Graetz, *Geschichte der Juden*, 11; *History of the Jews*, 2. See Hirsch, *GS*, 5:323; *CW*, 5:7.

181 Graetz, *Geschichte*, 11–13; *History of the Jews*, 2–3.

182 Graetz, *Geschichte*, 11–15; *History of the Jews*, 2–4.

183 Graetz, *Geschichte*, 14.

184 Hirsch, *GS*, 5:323–324; *CW*, 5:8, citing Graetz, *Geschichte der Juden*, 19; *History of the Jews*, 8. The reference is to *Mekhilta*, Jethro, parashah 5, commentary to Exodus 20:22.

describes as contentious individuals.[185] Hirsch further questions Graetz's ascribing R. Yohanan's opposition to rebelling against the Romans to his peaceful character. Hirsch claims that it just as likely stemmed from cold pragmatic considerations, namely, his recognizing that waging rebellion was futile and that "*political* independence would have to be sacrificed for *religious* independence" (emphasis in original).[186]

Hirsch also takes issue with Graetz's claim that by transferring the Sanhedrin to Yavne, R. Yohanan adopted a creative halakhic response to an unprecedented new reality, namely, the loss of the Temple. Hirsch notes that according to the Talmud, forty years *before* the destruction of the Temple, the Sanhedrin had already been removed from the Temple.[187] Similarly, Hirsch writes that there was precedent for Jewish religious life absent a Temple. After the destruction of the First Temple, Jewish leaders living in exile such as Daniel and Ezekiel had confronted this reality.[188]

Hirsch identifies a clear ideological motivation behind Graetz's portrayal of R. Yohanan as a "reformer" of Judaism, namely, Graetz's desire to present R. Yohanan as a contemporary religious model.[189] For Graetz, just as R. Yohanan met the spiritual crisis precipitated by the loss of the Temple by recasting tradition in novel ways, so must German rabbis meet the spiritual crisis wrought by modernity by recasting tradition in novel ways. Hirsch charges that while Graetz claims to be writing an objective *wissenschaftlichen* history, he has actually produced a subjective, ideologically-driven modern myth.

Exposing Frankel's humanization of the Oral Law

In 1845, the year after the first Reform assembly in Brunswick, Reformers held a second assembly in Frankfurt. The Chief Rabbi of Dresden, Zacharias Frankel, had not attended the Brunswick assembly, but the self-described "moderate (*gemäßigte*) Reformer" did attend the Frankfurt assembly.[190]

185 Hirsch, *GS*, 5:324; *CW*, 5:8. Hirsch cites Graetz, *Geschichte der Juden*, 52, 225.

186 Hirsch, *GS*, 5:324–325; *CW*, 5:9.

187 Hirsch, *GS*, 5:329–331; *CW*, 5:13–15. Hirsch cites *BT*, Abodah Zarah, 8b.

188 Hirsch, *GS*, 5:333; *CW*, 5:17.

189 Graetz himself does not use the term *reformer* to refer to R. Yohanan, but Hirsch repeatedly uses this term to describe Graetz's characterization of him. See Hirsch, *GS*, 5:327, 330; *CW*, 5:12, 14.

190 On this label, see Frankel, "Über Reformen im Judenthume," 27.

When the Frankfurt assembly adopted a resolution stating that Hebrew was not an essential part of the prayer service, Frankel walked out.[191] Frankel's action galvanized like-minded Jewish religious conservatives, and a year later he sought to organize his own assembly to solidify this group.[192]

At the Frankfurt assembly Frankel labelled his religious position "positive, historical Judaism" and provided a meandering explanation of it.[193] His conviction was that one must look to the past to address the needs of the present. For Frankel, "the positive forms of Judaism" (*Die positiven Formen des Judenthums*) have a deep connection with the inner essence of Judaism and so should not be "coldly and heartlessly" discarded. But what should one do when these religious forms no longer speak to us? Frankel begins by reviewing several approaches that he thinks are *not* appropriate. Given the historical nature of Judaism, one should not seek to create a rational Judaism *de novo* like "Minerva emerging from Jupiter's head." It is also impossible to return to the "letter of Scripture" (*Buchstaben der Schrift*) since there is too great a gap between the literal meaning of the Bible and contemporary life. Reforming Judaism by offering fanciful new "interpretations" (*Exegese*) of Scripture is likewise unacceptable because it violates *Wissenschaft's* demand for intellectual honesty. Finally, one cannot simply recast Judaism in line with the "spirit of the time" (*Geiste der Zeit*) since the *Zeitgeist* is always changing and so cannot bring "satisfaction, comfort, calm, and happiness."[194]

Frankel outlines proper parameters for introducing reforms into Judaism. For Frankel only the *laws* of Judaism are subject to evolution not its *beliefs*. So any reform of Judaism must apply only to *halakhah*. As halakhah exerts great power over the "people," one's aim must be to *strengthen its power*. In undertaking reforms, concern must be directed to the needs of the people *as a whole* not to the needs of isolated individuals. A primary concern must be to "prevent any split (*Zerspaltung*)" in Judaism and to avoid creating new factions, but instead seek to unify existing factions. Finally, any reforms

[191] See Meyer, *Response to Modernity*, 136–138; Bloch, *Heinrich Graetz*, 36.

[192] Though originally forty individuals indicated their intent to attend Frankel's assembly, including Solomon Rapaport, the Chief Rabbi of Prague, and Rabbi Michael Sachs of Berlin, most withdrew due to Orthodox opposition, and the assembly was postponed and eventually cancelled. See Meyer, *Response to Modernity*, 140–141; Bloch, *Heinrich Graetz*, 34–37. On Frankel's break from Reform and his attempt to unify conservatives, see Brämer, *Rabbiner Zacharias Frankel*, 225–254.

[193] *Protokolle und Aktenstücke der zweiten Rabbiner-Versammlung*, 19. On the meaning of the term "Positive-Historical Judaism", see Meyer, *Response to Modernity*, 86; Schorsch, *From Text to Context*, 256–257; Brämer, *Rabbiner Zacharias Frankel*, 157–176.

[194] *Protokolle und Aktenstücke der zweiten Rabbiner-Versammlung*, 19–20.

of Jewish law must be undertaken on the basis of the highest standards of *Wissenschaft*.[195]

A careful examination of Frankel's statement reveals that he emphasizes two components of reform that are not obviously connected with each other and can easily be in tension. First, reforms must pay due attention to texts and history, treating them in a responsible, scholarly way. Second, regard must be given to the spiritual health of the people and avoiding factional splits.[196]

In 1854, Frankel was appointed director of the newly established *Jewish Theological Seminary* (*Jüdisch-Theologisches Seminar*) in Breslau, the first modern rabbinical seminary in German lands.[197] The seminary's task was to produce rabbis who would serve in all German Jewish communities *including Orthodox ones*. Hirsch had been concerned about Frankel's religious direction for at least a decade. After the 1844 Reform assembly in Brunswick Frankel had been asked to join the many rabbis who condemned it, but he pointedly refused to do so.[198] With the establishment of a rabbinical seminary under Frankel's leadership whose goal was to produce rabbis who would also serve in Orthodox communities, Hirsch perceived a threat. So, in April 1854, four months before the Breslau seminary was inaugurated, Hirsch had an anonymous open letter published.[199] The letter challenged Frankel to publicly declare how the new seminary would teach four questions.[200]

The first issue concerned *revelation* (*Offenbarung*). The letter declares that Orthodox Jews understand revelation to mean that the unique, personal God reveals God's word directly to human beings. When the Bible states "God spoke to Moses," this refers to a supernatural act of speaking analogous to how one person speaks to another. What would the new seminary teach about revelation?

The second matter concerned the *Bible*. The letter states that Orthodox Jews believe in the "divine authenticity" of the entire Bible and reject the idea that different authors composed the Pentateuch or Isaiah, or that certain Psalms dated to the Second Temple period. How would the new seminary address biblical authorship?

195 Ibid., 20.

196 Ibid.

197 Schorsch, *From Text to Context*, 255. On Frankel's tenure at the *Jüdisch-Theologisches Seminar*, see Brämer, *Rabbiner Zacharias Frankel*, 318–414.

198 See Schorsch, *From Text to Context*, 262.

199 The letter was signed "Association of Friends of Truth and Orthodox Judaism."

200 Bloch, *Heinrich Graetz*, 53. Though the letter was published anonymously, Hirsch was clearly the driving force behind it. The *AZJ* states that it was sent from Frankfurt. See Brämer, *Rabbiner Zacharias Frankel*, 337.

The third issue concerned *Jewish tradition*. The letter asserts that Orthodox Jews understand Jewish *tradition* to include both the written word of God (the Bible) and everything that the Talmud indicates is of "biblical authority" (*de'oraita*) even if it is not found explicitly in the Bible. Orthodox Jews reject the idea of a historically developing tradition that expands law. What would the new seminary's position be on tradition?

The fourth issue concerned the meaning of *rabbinic law* (*derabbanan*) and *religious custom* (*minhag*). The letter states that Orthodox Jews deem rabbinic law fully binding, seeing its authority as deriving from the biblical injunction not to deviate from the rulings of the rabbis. Orthodox Jews also consider religious customs as having the status of binding communal oaths.[201] What would the new seminary teach about rabbinic law and custom?[202]

Frankel ignored the open letter. Five years later in 1859, he published his landmark *Darkhei Hamishnah* (*Methods of the Mishnah*), in which he presented his views on the origin and methods of the Mishnah and early rabbinic literature.[203] This gave Hirsch the opportunity to press his attack.[204]

Hirsch's polemic centered on the charge that in *Darkhei Hamishnah*, Frankel had presented the Oral Torah as being of human origin. Hirsch's attack had three parts. In January 1861, he published a critique of Frankel's work by the Hungarian lay scholar Gottlieb Fischer in his monthly *Jeschurun*. Originally written in Hebrew, Hirsch translated Fischer's three-part essay into German.[205] Hirsch then supplemented Fischer's attack on Frankel with his own.[206] Finally, Hirsch composed three additional essays responding to defenses of Frankel and attacks on himself.[207] Taken as a whole, Hirsch's polemic against Frankel was over a hundred pages.[208]

201 Hirsch expressed this view of religious custom years earlier in *Horev*. See Hirsch, *Horev*, #474, 461; *Horeb*, #474, 351–352.

202 "Offene Anfrage," 244–246.

203 After the Hebrew title page, there is a Latin title page that gives the title as *Hodgetica in Mischnam*. Elsewhere Frankel renders the title in German as *Hodegetik in die Mishna*. "Hodegetic" literally means "indicator of the way" in Greek, and in nineteenth-century German it connoted the idea that understanding the method of a work helps elucidate its content. See Moynahan, *Ernst Cassirer and the Critical Science of Germany*, 18.

204 On *Darkhei Hamishnah* and the debate over it, see Brämer, *Rabbiner Zacharias Frankel*, 355–381.

205 Fischer's essays appeared in *Jeschurun* 7:4, 196–214; 7:5, 241–252; 7:9, 470–491.

206 Hirsch's essay titled "Anmerkung der Redaktion" ("Editor's Note") was the article immediately following the second of Fischer's essays. It appeared in *Jeschurun* 7:5, 252–269.

207 These were "Provisional Statement of Accounts" ("Vorläufige Abrechnung"), *Jeschurun* 7:7 (April 1861), 347–377; " "Dr. Frankel's Clarification" (Dr. Frankel's Erklärung"), *Jeschurun* 7:8 (May 1861) 437–444; "Chief Rabbi Rapaport's *Divre Schalom Ve'emet*" *Jeschurun* 7:10 (July 1861), 544–560.

208 These essays were gathered and republished in Hirsch's *Gesammelte Schriften*. See Hirsch, *GS*, 6:322–418; *CW*, 5:211–314.

In a statement defending his intentions in *Darkhei Hamishnah*, Frankel declared that he had consistently sought to demonstrate the "scientific form" of the Mishnah and always treated the Oral Torah with the greatest reverence. On the question of whether he regarded rabbinic tradition as of divine or human origin, Frankel stated that this was a question of theological "dogma" (*Dogmatisches*), which "academic research" (*wissenschaftlichen Forschung*) could not address. Academic research could, at best, prove the antiquity of many of laws that the rabbis described as revealed to Moses, but not whether their origin was divine or human.[209]

At the center of Hirsch's attack on Frankel is his claim that Frankel is disingenuous in presenting his book as a work of pure scholarship that does not take a stand on theological questions. On three separate occasions Hirsch states what he sees as Frankel's position: "*God gave Moses on Sinai nothing more than the Written Law (das schriftliche Gesetz), the Five Books of Moses. Everything else emerged through human interpretations of this law or from human thought processes independent of these interpretations*" (emphasis in original).[210] For Hirsch, Frankel is far from agnostic on theological questions but, rather, assumes that only the Pentateuch is the revealed word of God, while he regards the Oral Torah as the product of human activity.

Fischer identifies three elements of the Oral Law that Frankel ascribes to human rather than divine origin. The first involves *interpretations of biblical commandments* (*perushei hamitzvot*). Many of the commandments in the Pentateuch are stated in general terms without specifying exactly how to practice them. For example, the Pentateuch states that it is prohibited to do *melakhah* (often translated as "labor") on the Sabbath but provides very little guidance about what constitutes *melakhah*. Fischer notes that according to Frankel the *soferim* or scribes, who were members of the so-called "Great Assembly" (*Knesset Hagedolah/Ecclesia Magna*) convened by Ezra in the fifth century BCE originated many of the interpretations of how to practice biblical law.[211]

[209] Frankel, "Erklärung," 159–160. Andreas Brämer has published private correspondence between Frankel and Bernhard Beer in which Frankel expressed his views on the controversy more forthrightly. Hirsch, of course, was unaware of these letters. See Brämer, "Revelation and Tradition: Zacharias Frankel on the Controversy Concerning the '*Hodegetica in Mischnam.*'"

[210] Hirsch, *GS*, 6:369–370; *CW*, 5:263. Hirsch repeats this description of Frankel's position nearly verbatim in "Vorläufige Abrechnung," Hirsch, *GS*, 6:407–408; *CW*, 5:303; and in "Dr. Frankel's Erklärung," Hirsch, *GS*, 6:418; *CW*, 5:314.

[211] Hirsch, *GS*, 6:326; *CW*, 215. Fischer cites Frankel, *Darkhei Hamishnah*, 5: "These great men [the Men of the Great Assembly] are identical with the sages known as the *soferim* who interpreted the law and attached their interpretations to the words of Scripture. These interpretations were not the product of any one of these men as individuals . . . rather these interpretations of the law were

The second element of the Oral Law that Frankel ascribes to human origin involves laws not found in the Pentateuch but that the rabbis describe as "law given to Moses on Sinai" (*halakhah lemosheh misinai*). Citing the thirteenth-century legal authority R. Asher ben Yehiel (Rosh), Frankel claims that the phrase *halakhah lemosheh misinai* does not mean that the law was literally given to Moses on Mount Sinai but, rather, is a metaphor indicating the law's great antiquity and widespread acceptance among the Jewish people.[212] The final element of the Oral Law that Frankel ascribes to human agency is laws that the rabbis derived from the Bible using the so-called "thirteen hermeneutical principles" (*shlosh esreh middot*). Fischer notes that Frankel claims that the rabbinic sages invented these principles.[213]

According to Fischer, while Frankel presents himself as a conservative who seeks to preserve historical Jewish tradition, his attributing various elements of the Oral Law to independent human activity contradicts the *unanimous* position of the major rabbinic commentators and legal decisors all of whom conceived the Oral Law as divinely revealed to Moses.[214] As such, Frankel's view places him outside rabbinic Judaism.[215] Indeed, Fischer asserts that Frankel's position most closely aligns with the Jewish sectarians, the Sadducees and Karaites, both of whom revered the Pentateuch as divinely revealed but saw the rabbinic sages as the human authors of the Oral Law.[216]

announced by the Men of the *Ecclesia Magna* after due deliberation and discernment." I follow Hirsch's translation of Frankel.

212 See Hirsch, *GS*, 6:339–340; *CW*, 5:229–230. Fischer cites Frankel, *Darkhei Hamishnah*, 20–21: "Aside from the laws that were derived from midrashic exegesis of the Bible and from the hermeneutical principles mentioned, there are other laws for which it is impossible to discern their reason, They were received and called a 'law given to Moses on Sinai. . . [this phrase] can only be explained in accordance with the words of R. Asher [meaning] a matter as clear as if it were given to Moses on Sinai. And it seems to me also that there are times when an old law which had spread amongst Israel from ancient days attained the name 'a law given to Moses on Sinai.'" Also see Hirsch's remarks on this passage. Hirsch, *GS*, 6:395–396; *CW*, 5:290–291.

213 Hirsch, *GS*, 6:349–350; *CW*, 5:241–242. Fischer cites Frankel, *Darkhei Hamishnah*, 19, which states: "Beyond the fact that they attached the halakhah to the biblical text they produced and expanded the halakhah by the light of their wisdom . . . and so that truth is not missing, [it must be pointed out] that they *established hermeneutical rules* (*hetzigu kelalim*) called *middot* on whose basis the Torah was to be interpreted." Hirsch preserves phrase *hetzigu kelalim* in the original Hebrew to highlight it. Like Fischer, Hirsch emphasizes that this passage shows that Frankel conceived the Oral Law as a human creation. See Hirsch, *GS*, 6:397–399; *CW*, 5:292–294.

214 In fact, the disagreement between Fischer/Hirsch and Frankel over the Oral Torah is reminiscent of, though not precisely the same, as a medieval argument between the Gaonim and Maimonides. On this dispute, see Halbertal, *Maimonides*, 100–107.

215 Fischer and Hirsch both attack Frankel's claiming support from R. Asher for his position on "a law given to Moses on Sinai," asserting that Frankel misuses R. Asher, who only claimed that *certain* laws described as "a law given to Moses on Sinai" are so described metaphorically. See Hirsch, *GS*, 6:340–348, 396; *CW*, 5:230–239, 290–291.

216 Hirsch, *GS*, 6:333–334; *CW*, 5:223–224.

For Fischer, the main difference between Frankel and these Jewish sectarians is that while the Sadducees and Karaites *openly disparaged* the rabbinic sages for deviating from the word of God expressed in the Bible, Frankel *professes great respect for them*. But Fischer claims that Frankel's "wrapping himself in the guise of a faithful believer in tradition (*treuen Traditionsgläubigen*)" makes him much *more dangerous* as it enables him to surreptitiously inculcate unsuspecting Orthodox students with his heretical doctrines.[217] Fischer concludes that Frankel's work constitutes such a radical break with Judaism that rather than titling it *Darkhei Hamishnah* (*The Methods of the Mishnah*), he should have titled it *Darkhei Hameshaneh* (*The Methods of the Changer*).[218]

Hirsch supplements Fischer's arguments. In addition to the three elements of Oral Law that Fischer presents Frankel as ascribing to human origin, Hirsch notes that, like Graetz, Frankel sees the origin of rabbinic lawmaking in *time-bound political interests* rather than in an *honest endeavor to preserve Jewish tradition*. For example, one of the few statements explicitly attributed to the Men of the Great Assembly is their injunction to magistrates to "be circumspect in judgment."[219] Frankel claims that this statement must be understood within its historical context. Living under Persian rule, Jews retained legal autonomy. The Men of the Great Assembly sought to preserve this autonomy and worried that if Jewish courts issued improper rulings, the aggrieved party might seek redress from Persian authorities, who might then interfere in internal Jewish affairs. For this reason, the Men of the Great Assembly instructed Jewish magistrates to be circumspect in judgment.[220]

For Hirsch, Frankel's claim to revere Jewish tradition and respect the authority of halakhah is a dodge that cannot mask the damage to halakhic

[217] See Hirsch, *GS*, 6:324–325, 334; *CW*, 5:213–214, 224. Hirsch also emphasizes the danger Frankel poses given that he is head of rabbinical seminary that will train rabbis who will serve in Orthodox communities. Hirsch, *GS*, 6:369; *CW*, 5:262.

[218] Hirsch, *GS*, 6:348; *CW*, 5:239. See Schorsch, *From Text to Context*, 262.

[219] *Pirkei Avot* 1:1.

[220] Hirsch, *GS*, 6:373–374; *CW*, 5:266–267. Hirsch cites Frankel, *Darkhei Hamishnah*, 4. Hirsch also quotes Frankel's earlier work for clear evidence that Frankel regards the Oral Law as a human creation. Hirsch cites Frankel's 1841 *Preliminary Studies on the Septuagint* (*Vorstudien zu der Septuaginta*), where Frankel writes: "Moreover many a law may have evolved into a norm without sanction from a higher authority. Once the practices of everyday life, the practices of folk piety had been elevated to the status of [communal] standards and took root, they attained binding force." See Frankel, *Vorstudien zu der Septuaginta*, xiii, cited in Hirsch, *GS*, 6:381; *CW*, 5:275. Hirsch also cites Frankel's 1851 *On the Influence of Palestinian Exegesis on the Alexandrian Hermeneutic* (*Über den Einfluß der palästinischen Exegese auf die alexandrinische Hermeneutik*) where Frankel writes: ". . . it would seem that much halakhic material should be regarded not so much as a result of speculation but rather as rules evolving from custom that were eventually elevated to the status of legal prescriptions . . . Many a practical observance that had been hallowed by time evolved into a legal norm." See Frankel, *Über den Einfluß*, 133, cited in Hirsch *GS*, 6:382; *CW*, 5:276.

authority wrought by his humanization of it. Frankel claims to be instilling reverence for halakhah by claiming that much of it is of great antiquity, with some laws dating back hundreds of years before the composition of Mishnah (ca. 200 AD). But for Hirsch this is like saying that the Bible should be revered because some elements of it precede Ezra.[221] As long as Frankel regards halakhah as a human creation arising in response to specific historical challenges, he undermines its binding authority no matter how old he considers it. As Hirsch puts it, "Frankel explains everything in times of time-bound needs and interests. Truly, if we were to perceive these men, our great *transmitters* (*Regenatoren*) of the Law whom Frankel considers its *generators* (*Generatoren*), the producers and creators of our practical religious law, then we [must] consider them as Machiavellians . . . [and] would not value anything they have taught us" (emphasis mine).[222]

While Frankel claims to be concerned with avoiding factionalism within Judaism, Hirsch claims that his approach is very divisive, writing, "If God placed into the hands of His people nothing more than the Written Law, the Five Books of the Pentateuch . . . it would mean that God entrusted the interpretation of His law to the views and insights of men in every age and generation . . . In that case Yannai would be entirely correct: 'The Torah is placed in a corner whoever wishes may take it.' "[223] Hirsch is referring to talmudic accounts of the Hasmonean King Alexander Yannai (126–76 BCE), who clashed with the Pharisees and sympathized with the Sadducees.[224] Hirsch sees Frankel's position as aligning with the Sadducean position, which critiques rabbinic interpretation as a purely human invention resulting in everyone having the authority to interpret how to practice Biblical law for themselves. The result is religious anarchy that that will "shatter the House of Israel into a thousand splinters."[225]

As in his critique of Graetz, Hirsch is not content with demonstrating how his opponent's position deviates from rabbinic tradition or damages halakhic authority. Rather, Hirsch seeks to prove the inadequacy of Frankel's argument on *scholarly* grounds. Hirsch asserts that Frankel does not (and, indeed,

221 Hirsch *GS*, 6:414; *CW*, 5:311.
222 Hirsch, *GS*, 6:374; *CW*, 5:267–268.
223 Hirsch *GS*, 6:415; *CW*, 5:311–312.
224 Hirsch is referring to a story recounted in *BT*, Kiddushin, 66a. After a clash with the Pharisees, one of Yannai's advisors, Eleazar ben Po'eira, recommended that the king crush the Sages. As the Pharisees taught Torah, Yannai grew concerned about how Jews would learn Torah. Eleazar responded, "The Torah is placed in the corner, whoever wishes may take it." In other words, there is no need for rabbinic sages as everyone can learn Torah on their own.
225 Hirsch, *GS*, 6:401; *CW*, 5:296.

cannot) provide evidence for his claim that the Oral Law is of human rather than divine origin. Instead, this ungrounded assumption "forms the basis and starting point of [his] entire work."[226] Similarly, Frankel cannot prove that the rabbis issued injunctions on the basis of time-bound political considerations rather than honestly seeking to preserve observance of God's law. For example, we have seen Frankel's claim that the Men of the Great Assembly charged magistrates to be "circumspect in judgment" to avoid Persian authorities infringing on Jewish communal autonomy. But, asks Hirsch, what is Frankel's evidence for this? As Frankel himself acknowledges, rabbinic literature only contains three statements attributed to the Men of the Great Assembly.[227] How can Frankel be certain that the charge to magistrates to be circumspect in judgment was not made simply to ensure that judges arrive at correct decisions in order to faithfully fulfill God's will?[228]

Conclusion

In the *Nineteen Letters,* Hirsch seeks to craft a new vision of German Judaism that will synthesize the partial truths of the Haskalah, *Wissenschaft*, Reform, and Jewish traditionalism. But he gradually came to regard the quest to create a unified German Jewish religious vision as futile. If Hirsch was confident that most German Jews were sympathetic to his views when he published the *Nineteen Letters* in 1836, with his appointment as leader of a small separatist Orthodox congregation in Frankfurt fifteen years later, it became clear to him that his views belonged to an embattled minority. Hirsch embraced this fact, seeing it as an opportunity to create an ideologically pure, model community, and he turned into a sharp polemicist, adopting the moniker "Orthodox" for himself for the first time.

Hirsch recognized that the key ideological split between Orthodoxy, Reform, and Positive-Historical Judaism was that while Orthodoxy regarded the entire Torah, both Written and Oral, as divine, Reform regarded both as human, while Positive-Historical Judaism deemed the Oral Torah to be human without explicitly declaring so. For Hirsch, the only way to preserve halakhic observance was to show the absolutely binding, timeless character of the entire Torah, both Written and Oral, grounded in divine revelation.

226 See Hirsch, *GS*, 6:369; *CW*, 5:262–263.
227 See Frankel, *Darkhei Hamishnah*, 5.
228 Hirsch, *GS*, 6:374; *CW*, 5:267.

This required demonstrating the inseparability of the Written Torah and Oral Torah. But Hirsch recognized that non-Orthodox Jews would never accept the revealed nature of the entire Torah, which could never be proven. So instead of seeking to create a unified German Jewish religious vision, he sought to consolidate and strengthen his own community. Education was key and Hirsch's educational centerpiece would be a sectarian Orthodox Pentateuch translation and commentary based on an innovative justification of the unity of the Oral and Written Torah.

7
The Innovative Orthodoxy of Hirsch's Pentateuch

We have seen that Graetz criticized Hirsch for spending excessive time studying Talmud, mocking him for behaving like a "Polish *lamdan*." But David Feuchtwang reports that during his tenure as the Chief Rabbi of Moravia some older rabbis chided Hirsch for neglecting Talmud study in favor of the Bible, remarking that "previously, one would study Talmud and recite Psalms, but now one recites Talmud and studies Psalms."[1] We have noted that defending the authority of the Talmud and rabbinic interpretation was a central concern of Hirsch's from his earliest writings. At the same time, he followed the Maskilim in placing the Bible at the center of the Jewish curriculum.[2]

Hirsch's literary activity centered on the Bible, and his *magnum opus* is undoubtedly his Pentateuch translation and commentary, which he published from 1867 to 1878.[3] But his Pentateuch commentary focuses on rabbinic, midrashic interpretations and pays considerably less attention to the medieval *peshat* commentators favored by the Maskilim. *Did Hirsch neglect rabbinic literature or emphasize it?*

Over the next two chapters, I will argue that a central aim of Hirsch's Pentateuch is showing the inseparability of the Oral Torah and the Written Torah as a way of providing an ideological anchor for his sectarian Orthodox community.

[1] Feuchtwang, "Samson Raphael Hirsch als Oberlandesrabbiner von Mähren," 21, cited in Rosenbloom, *Tradition in an Age of Reform*, 91.

[2] See chapters 5 and 6 of this volume.

[3] In addition to his Pentateuch translation and commentary, Hirsch published a two-volume translation and commentary on the Psalms that we will explore. He also published lectures on the Psalms and Isaiah that contain many translations.

The Jewish Reformation. Michah Gottlieb, Oxford University Press (2021). © Oxford University Press.
DOI: 10.1093/oso/9780199336388.003.0008

Hirsch's Pentateuch and Mendelssohn's *Be'ur*

A good entry point for understanding Hirsch's Pentateuch is to compare its formal features with Mendelssohn's *Be'ur*. Recall that Mendelssohn's *Be'ur* includes both a German translation in Hebrew characters facing the Hebrew original and a Hebrew commentary, which reflects both conservative and reformatory aims. Its conservative character is suggested by Mendelssohn reproducing the basic format of the traditional rabbinic Bible, the *Mikra'ot Gedolot*, and by his giving his Pentateuch a Hebrew title, *Sefer Netivot Hashalom* (*Book of the Paths of Peace*), but no German one. His reformatory aims are suggested by Mendelssohn's replacing the multiple Aramaic translations in the *Mikra'ot Gedolot* including the canonical Onkelos with his own German one, and by his replacing all commentaries including the canonical Rashi with his *Be'ur* commentary.[4]

One might assume that the founder of Neo-Orthodoxy would produce a *more traditional-looking* Pentateuch than the archetypical Maskil. But Hirsch's Pentateuch looks much *less traditional* than Mendelssohn's. Like Mendelssohn, Hirsch replaces Onkelos's Aramaic translation with his own German translation and Rashi's commentary with his own.[5] But unlike Mendelssohn's translation, which is in Hebrew characters, Hirsch's is in Gothic characters, and unlike Mendelssohn's commentary, which is in Hebrew, Hirsch's commentary is in German, though it includes a smattering of words and phrases printed in Hebrew. While Mendelssohn only gives his Pentateuch a Hebrew title, Hirsch gives his Pentateuch both German and Hebrew titles, which he places on separate pages-- *Der Pentateuch* in German and *Hamishah Humshei Torah* (*Five Fifths of the Torah*) in Hebrew.[6]

As with Zunz's Bible, it is clear that linguistic changes within German Jewry account, at least in part, for the differences between Hirsch's and Mendelssohn's Pentateuchs. While Mendelssohn wrote primarily for Yiddish-speaking Jews who had significant familiarity and comfort with Hebrew texts, Hirsch wrote for German-speaking Jews much less familiar with Hebrew texts. I will say more about why Hirsch chose the specific layout for his Pentateuch later in the chapter.

[4] See Figures 3 and 4 and pp. 92–93 of this volume.

[5] Modechai Breuer notes Hirsch's success in replacing medieval Jewish commentaries, noting that members of Hirsch's community "would skip all other commentaries on the Torah *including Rashi's* and study the Torah with the commentary of Rabbi Samson Raphael Hirsch" (emphasis mine). See Breuer, "Rabbi Samson Raphael Hirsch's Commentary on the Torah," 348–349.

[6] See Figures 4 and 10.

Moving to questions of content, the Hebrew *Be'ur* commentary is concise, and its primary aim is consistent with that of the classical medieval commentators Rashi, Rashbam, Ibn Ezra, and Nahmanides, namely, to determine the *peshat* of the Bible. The Be'urist will often quote or paraphrase one or more medieval commentators and introduce adjustments, interpolations, and critical comments as he sees fit. Given that seeking *peshat* is a priority, it is not surprising that Midrashim are quoted much less frequently. By contrast, Hirsch's German commentary is verbose and frequently homiletical. While he includes some *peshat* comments and evinces sensitivity to literary considerations his concerns are usually far from those of the medieval commentators.[7] When Hirsch cites prior interpretations, he almost always recurs to rabbinic texts, connecting their interpretations with the biblical text. Medieval commentators are discussed much less frequently. The medieval commentator whom Hirsch cites most often is Rashi, who himself usually paraphrases rabbinic texts. Hirsch will frequently present original homiletical interpretations of the biblical text to elaborate his vision of German Neo-Orthodoxy. Polemical comments occur quite frequently in which Hirsch contrasts what he considers the Torah's view on a question with ideas he deems problematic or heretical, though he almost never identifies his targets by name.

Hirsch's as anti-historicist Pentateuch

Hirsch included a brief preface to his Genesis volume that appeared in 1867. This preface must be read very carefully, as Hirsch writes that his comments are very compressed, only "hinting" (*andeuten*) at his goals in the work.[8] Describing the origin of his commentary, Hirsch writes that it grew out of lectures that he gave "for several years" to members of his community in Frankfurt. Community members took notes, which they shared with Hirsch, who then used them as a basis for his written commentary. Hirsch makes clear that his commentary having originated as lectures impacted its form, as he will not refrain from repeating himself so that each

7 Jonathan Jacobs has pointed to instances where Hirsch displays sensitivity to literary nuance. But he concedes that "large parts of Hirsch's commentary are distinctively midrashic and what a modern eye would accept as *peshat* is definitely in the minority." See Jacobs, "Rabbi Samson Raphael Hirsch as a Peshat Commentator," 199.

8 Hirsch, *Der Pentateuch*, 1:v; *The Hirsch Chumash*, 1:xv.

passage will be accompanied by the "fullest possible explanation."[9] Hirsch does not inform the reader when or how he composed the translation.

In essays published in the 1860s, Hirsch elaborates themes he first advanced in the *Nineteen Letters*, which elucidate goals of his Pentateuch. In an 1861 essay titled "Jewish Outlook on the World and Life," Hirsch stresses the centrality of philology for understanding a nation, writing that "language and literature" are the "the sole sources for understanding a people's outlook on life and the world."[10] Hirsch then contrasts two ways of understanding a nation's language and literature. As long as a nation "dwells in its language and its language dwells in it," the nation will be continually "educated or miseducated (*bildend oder verbildend*) by the. . . opinions which its forbearers expressed in its language and literature." By contrast, when a nation has become "separated from life," its language and literature become "objects for researchers" who seek to reconstruct "a composite picture of the outlook and true spiritual essence (*geistigen wahrhaftigen Wesens*)" of the lost nation.[11]

For Hirsch, the literature that defines the Jewish people is the Torah and its language is Hebrew.[12] In his 1866 essay "Some Suggestions Regarding the Role of Hebrew Instruction in General Education," Hirsch stresses that one must read a nation's literature in the original language, noting that "thoughts and emotions can be truly preserved and passed to posterity only [when]. . . *unspoiled by translation*" (emphasis mine). He advises Jewish parents to teach their children the Bible in Hebrew.[13] Hirsch further notes that for centuries the Jews were an unusual nation in that Hebrew remained a living force among them only as a *written language* for religious study. But he notes that contemporary political and intellectual upheavals have led a large segment of the Jewish nation to no longer study the Bible in Hebrew, hence the need for translation. Hirsch attacks *Wissenschaft* scholars for studying Judaism as an object of research belonging to the historical past. For Judaism to flourish, Jews must study the Torah in Hebrew as an eternally valid living text that shapes the life and destiny of the nation for the present and future.[14]

[9] Hirsch, *Der Pentateuch*, 1:vi; *The Hirsch Chumash*, 1:xvi.
[10] See Hirsch, *GS*, 5:144; *CW*, 8:22. See p. 254 of this volume.
[11] Hirsch, *GS*, 5:144–145; *CW*, 8:22. The English translation is particularly inaccurate.
[12] See Hirsch, *NB*, Brief 2, 7–8; *NL*, Letter 2, 15–16.
[13] Hirsch *GS*, 2:436; *CW*, 7:66.
[14] Hirsch, *GS*, 5:146–147; *CW*, 8:22–23. See p. 256 of this volume. Also see Hirsch's important 1861 essay "How does Life Benefit from our Wissenschaft?" in Hirsch, *GS*, 2:416–432; *CW*, 7:27–45. Buber and Rosenzweig also worry that *Wissenschaft des Judentums* alienates contemporary Jews from Judaism. See Buber and Rosenzweig, *Scripture and Translation*, 4–21, 22–25.

Hirsch pursues this point in the preface to his Pentateuch, writing that a primary aim of the work is to elucidate "the truths . . . upon which the Jewish outlook on the world and life is built" and that "constitute the norms of Jewish life for all time." Hirsch asserts that this method reveals the Pentateuch to be a coherent unit, informed by a "unified spirit" (*einheitlicher Geist*) that does not belong to the "antiquated past," but to the "living present," and that constitutes the "hope of all strivings of humanity for the future."[15]

In the introduction to his translation of the Psalms, which he published in 1882, Hirsch elaborates on this point, writing that the Pentateuch, which he calls the "Books of the Law" (*Bücher der Gesetzes*) "reveals our vocation (*Bestimmung*) as human beings and as Jews and the tasks by which we fulfill this vocation." It does so by beginning with the creation of the world and the early history of humanity, then detailing the history of the Israelite forefathers, leading to the founding of the Jewish people and their receiving the Torah before providing the "basic outline" (*Grundriß*) of their later destiny. By beginning with the creation of the world and humanity, the Pentateuch seeks to show that the purpose of the Jewish people is to promote the educational development of humanity.[16]

The exegetical method of Hirsch's Pentateuch

As in the *Nineteen Letters*, in the preface to his Pentateuch Hirsch makes clear that his aim is to "explain the biblical text from itself" (*Den biblischen Text aus sich selber zu erklären*). He explains that this will involve "draw[ing] this elucidation from the wording [of the Bible] in all its nuances (*Nüancen*)."[17] But how does Hirsch propose to discern and explain these nuances?

Hirsch does not explain this in the preface, but his commentary reveals at least seven considerations. These include: (1) Hebrew grammar,[18] (2) biblical cantillation marks,[19] (3) *plene* or defective word

[15] Hirsch, *Der Pentateuch,* 1:v; *The Hirsch Chumash* 1:xv.

[16] See Hirsch, *Die Psalmen,* 1:i; *The Psalms,* 1:xi. See pp. 271–276 of this volume.

[17] Hirsch, *Der Pentateuch,* 1:v; *The Hirsch Chumash,* 1:i.

[18] For an example of Hirsch using grammatical considerations, see his discussion of the Tetragrammaton on pp. 360–362 of this volume.

[19] Like Mendelssohn, Hirsch considers the cantillation marks a form of punctuation, and in his Psalms he includes an appendix discussing how the cantillation marks function in Psalms, Proverbs, and Job, which differ from how they function in other biblical books. His discussion relies on Wolf Heidenheim's 1825 work, *Siddur Safah Berurah*. See Hirsch, *Die Psalmen,* 1:viii–ix; *The Psalms,* 2:498–500. For some examples of Hirsch using the cantillation marks to interpret the Pentateuch, see

forms,[20] (4) cognate words and expressions found elsewhere in Scripture,[21] (5) conceptual etymology,[22] (7) literary context, and (8) rabbinic exegesis.[23] An example will illustrate important elements of Hirsch's approach.

Sending away the mother bird

Deuteronomy 22:6–7 details the law of sending away the mother bird before taking her young. Hirsch's translation reads:

> Wenn ein Vogelnest (*kan tzippor*) vor dir auf dem Wege betroffen wird, auf irgend einem Baum oder auf der Erde, Junge oder Eier, und die Mutter ruht auf den Jungen oder auf den Eiern, sollst du nicht die Mutter auf den Jungen nehmen. Freischicken sollst du die Mutter, die Jungen aber darfst du dir nehmen; darob wird es dir gut ergehen, und du wirst lange leben.
>
> If you happen upon a bird's nest on the way, in a tree or on the earth, [with] young or eggs and the mother is sitting on the young or on the eggs, you should not take the mother while on her young. You should send the mother free, but you may take the young, so that you will fare well and you will live long.[24]

Hirsch's commentary includes *peshat* interpretations. For example, commenting on the fact that the verse states that the mother is sitting on the young, Hirsch explains that this is to protect the young from cold. Hirsch explains that the mother is described as sitting on the eggs to indicate that she is incubating them.[25] Similarly, Hirsch notes that the Hebrew word *ken* (קֵן) is commonly understood to mean "nest." But citing Deuteronomy 32:11,

Hirsch, *Der Pentateuch,* 1:67, 158, 347; *The Hirsch Chumash,* 1:89, 217, 482 (Commentary to Genesis 2:23; 8:22; 22:1).

[20] See Hirsch, *Der Pentateuch,* 1:613; *The Hirsch Chumash,* 1:871 (Commentary to Genesis 49:10).
[21] See Hirsch, *Der Pentateuch,* 1:v; *The Hirsch Chumash,* 1:xv. Hirsch also includes linguistic comparisons to Hebrew words found in rabbinic works such as the Mishnah and the Talmud. Hirsch will even occasionally use rabbinic Aramaic to elucidate biblical Hebrew. I will discuss Hirsch's reason for doing this a little later. See pp. 371–372 of this volume.
[22] See p. 282 of this volume.
[23] Hirsch, *Der Pentateuch,* 1:v; *The Hirsch Chumash,* 1:xv.
[24] Hirsch, *Der Pentateuch,* 5:369–371; *The Hirsch Chumash,* 5:509–511.
[25] Hirsch, *Der Pentateuch* 5:370; *The Hirsch Chumash,* 5:510.

kenesher ya'ir ***kino***, which he translates as *Wie der Adler weckt zuerst sein* ***Nest*** (as the eagle first awakens its nest), Hirsch notes that in Deuteronomy 32:11 the word *ken* clearly refers to young birds in a nest, since a nest by itself cannot be awakened. By citing *another usage of the word in the Bible*, Hirsch infers that the word *ken* can mean both "nest" and "young birds in a nest."[26]

Hirsch uses *literary context* to provide deeper insight into the passage. He notes that the first five verses of Deuteronomy 22 contain several laws: to return one's neighbor's lost property, to help one's neighbor if his animal collapses, and the prohibition of cross-dressing. Hirsch infers that the first five verses of the chapter posit two "basic principles" that are to guide the Jewish nation as it establishes and develops its national life: *first*, the need to preserve solidarity with others by caring for their property and helping them in times of trouble, and *second*, the need to maintain gender differentiation. For Hirsch, both are crucial for societal stability as caring for others forms the basis of harmonious social relations and gender differentiation forms the foundation of home life.[27]

Hirsch then connects the law about sending away the mother bird to the law against a woman wearing men's clothes, which occurs in the verse immediately preceding it. For Hirsch, the purpose of the law forbidding a woman to wear men's clothing is to promote her dignity as the mother of the home.[28] Similarly, the reason that a person must send away the mother bird before taking her chicks or eggs is to instill respect for the female's role as mother.[29] When discussing the last part of the law, which promises long life to one who obeys it, Hirsch notes that there is only one other law in the Torah that promises a long life for its observance, namely, respecting one's parents (Exodus 20:12, Deuteronomy 5:16). Hirsch explains that this is not incidental but reflects that a person's present and future happiness depend on respecting motherhood.[30]

Hirsch's emphasis on gender differentiation is likely a response to Reformers who sought to level male and female gender roles in Judaism. In an 1837 article titled "The Position of Women in the Judaism of our Times," Geiger argued that Reformers should ameliorate Judaism's "oriental" view of women by discarding the rabbinic notion that women and men had different

[26] See Hirsch, *Der Pentateuch*, 5:370, 548; *The Hirsch Chumash*, 5:510, 759–760.

[27] Hirsch, *Der Pentateuch* 5:369–370; *The Hirsch Chumash*, 5:509 (Commentary to Deuteronomy 22:6).

[28] See pp. 278–279 of this volume.

[29] Hirsch, *Der Pentateuch* 5:369–370; *The Hirsch Chumash*, 5:509–510.

[30] Hirsch, *Der Pentateuch* 5:371; *The Hirsch Chumash*, 5:511.

halakhic obligations, which resulted in women being prohibited from taking public roles in the synagogue such as leading the prayer service. Geiger concluded his article: "Let there be from now on no distinction between the duties of men and women . . . no institution of the public service either in form or content which shuts the doors of the temple in the face of women."[31]

In his 1843 *On the Autonomy of the Rabbis*, Holdheim argued for abolishing distinctions between male and female roles in the Jewish marriage ceremony.[32] Two years later at the 1845 Reform rabbinical assembly in Frankfurt, Samuel Adler introduced a petition arguing that women should be "bound by equal duties and eligible for equal rights," and he included a fourteen-page Hebrew responsum in Hebrew defending his position.[33] The following year at the Reform rabbinical assembly in Breslau, David Einhorn presented a report recommending introducing six changes to ameliorate women's standing in Judaism, including: (1) regarding women as equally obligated to perform all the ritual commandments; (2) deeming women to have the same obligations toward their children as men;[34] (3) ruling that a man may not annul the vows of his mature daughter or wife;[35] (4) abolishing the daily benediction that men recite thanking God for not having made them a woman; (5) obligating women to participate in public worship and be counted in the traditional prayer quorum (*minyan*); (6) making the age of bar and bat mitzvah thirteen for both boys and girls.[36]

For Hirsch, the problem with the Reform approach is that rather than honor gender differences between men and women affirmed by the Torah, Reformers seek to turn women into honorary men on the basis of the abstract, rationalist Enlightenment principle of equality from fear that Judaism

[31] See Baader, *Gender, Judaism, and Bourgeois Culture,* 59. Baader notes that in 1788 David Friedländer had already called for equalizing male and female roles in Judaism. See ibid., 57.

[32] See Meyer, "Women in the European Jewish Reform Movement," 143–144. As we have seen, Hirsch critiqued this work in his 1844 *Zweite Mitteilungen.* See pp. 302–308 of this volume.

[33] Baader notes that while Adler recommended women be counted in the traditional prayer quorum (*minyan*), he still preserved the basic halakhic principle that women are exempt from positive, time-bound ritual obligations. See Baader, *Gender, Judaism and Bourgeois Culture,* 65–66.

[34] This likely attempts to undo the traditional halakhic notion that it is the father's duty to teach his children Torah. See pp. 87, 175, 185 of this volume.

[35] This law is found in Numbers 30:4–16 and is codified in the Mishnah, Talmud, and later halakhic works, including the *Shulhan Arukh.* See *Shulhan Arukh, Yoreh Deah,* 234.

[36] In classical halakhah girls come of age a year earlier at age twelve. On Einhorn's proposal, see Prell, "The Vision of Women in Classical Reform Judaism," 576–582; Baader, *Gender, Judaism and Bourgeois Culture,* 67–69. For the text of Einhorn's 1846 proposal, see Plaut, *The Rise of Reform Judaism,* 255. Given how closely Hirsch followed the Brunswick and Frankfurt assemblies, it is very likely that he read about Einhorn's proposal, and he was certainly familiar with Geiger's article. See Gottlieb, "Orthodoxy and the Orient."

will be perceived as primitive and oriental. But given the division of gender roles that was typical of the mid–nineteenth century German bourgeoisie, Hirsch is likely suggesting that Orthodoxy is, in fact, more in line with middle-class German values than Reform.[37]

Hirsch's indirect response to Reformers is characteristic of the way he deploys polemics in his Pentateuch. While Hirsch's commentary is deeply polemical, he almost never identifies his targets by name. This is because Hirsch does not wish to air opinions he deems dangerous in a biblical commentary meant for liturgical use and religious study. Those who are familiar with his opponents will understand his commentary as a response to them. But those with no knowledge of those heretical views will not be exposed to them. As we will see later in the chapter, Hirsch uses this strategy against biblical criticism in his Pentateuch.

Much of Hirsch's commentary on Deuteronomy 22:6–7 involves *connecting the biblical text to its rabbinic legal interpretation.* For example, Hirsch translates the first clause in Deuteronomy 22:6, which reads *ki yikareh kan tzipor lefanecha baderekh*, as *Wenn ein Vogelnest vor dir auf dem Wege betroffen wird* (If a bird's nest happens to be before you on the path). In his commentary, Hirsch cites the Talmud tractate *BT*, Hullin, 139a, which indicates that the accidental language of the verse indicates that the law only applies if a person has no prior connection with the nest and happens upon it. If, however, a person owns the bird's nest, the law of chasing away the mother bird does not apply. Similarly, Hirsch translates a later clause of the verse *vehaʾem rovetzet al haʾefrohim o al habeitzim* as *und die Mutter ruht auf den Jungen oder auf den Eiern* (and the mother is resting on the young or on the eggs). Citing the Talmud, *BT*, Hullin, 140b, Hirsch comments that the Bible draws a parallel between the young and the eggs to teach that just as the eggs require the mother to survive, so the law of chasing away the mother bird only applies to

[37] To be sure, Hirsch contributed to equalizing males and females by stressing the Bible as the foundation of both male and female Jewish education and outlining a very similar course of Jewish education for both sexes. See pp. 285–287 of this volume. Furthermore, Baader argues that Hirsch "regarded femininity as the highest form of Jewishness and as the essence of Judaism." Baader quotes a striking passage where Hirsch addresses the gender implications of his view explicitly: "The whole history of the Jews since the fall of Jerusalem is nothing but a triumph of the 'female' over the 'male'" (Hirsch, *GS*, 4:60; *CW*, 2:303). For Hirsch, the female represents the domestic realm, compassion, and humanity, while the male realm represents civil life, state power, and glory. With the fall of the Temple, Jews forsook "the male realm" in favor of the "female realm." See Baader, "Jewish Difference and the Feminine Spirit of Judaism," 54–58. Hirsch also saw the "female" as dominant in Judaism since Judaism stresses renunciation and sacrifice to God's law and he valences renunciation and sacrifice as female. See p. 269 of this volume.

young that cannot fly and need the mother to survive. If, however, the young can fly, the law does not apply.[38]

Hirsch's defending rabbinic interpretation might seem surprising given that in his preface he declared his intention to "explain the biblical text from itself." Is not rabbinic interpretation distinct from the biblical text? Hirsch's novel account of the relationship between the Written Torah and the Oral Torah, which he expresses in his Pentateuch, explains his answer this problem.

The Unity of the Torah in Hirsch's Pentateuch

As we have seen, in the *Nineteen Letters* Hirsch follows Mendelssohn and Zunz in claiming that the Talmud helps preserve the "spirit" (*Geist*) of the biblical "letter" (*Buchstabe*) by inculcating a living understanding of it.[39] But in his Pentateuch Hirsch abandons this conception of the relationship between the Oral Torah and the Written Torah in favor of an entirely new approach, which he explains most extensively in his commentary on Exodus 21. Noting that Exodus 21 contains "the civil and criminal code of a nation," Hirsch remarks on the oddity of the fact that the law code begins with the laws of buying and owning a male slave and selling one's daughter into slavery.

German Bible critics such as Heinrich Ewald had interpreted this fact as evidence that Exodus 21–23 was originally part of an older document that the biblical redactor cut and pasted into the Pentateuch.[40] But Hirsch turns this oddity to his advantage asserting that "to the unprejudiced mind, nothing could demonstrate the authenticity of the Oral Law as cogently." He then presents his understanding of the relationship between the Oral and Written Torah in a famous passage that is worth quoting in full:

> The relationship between Written Torah and Oral Torah is like that between brief written notes taken on a scientific lecture and the lecture itself. Students who attended the oral lecture require only their brief notes to recall at any time the entire lecture. They often find that a word, a question

[38] Hirsch, *Der Pentateuch* 5:370–371; *The Hirsch Chumash*, 5:510.
[39] See pp. 264–265 of this volume.
[40] Ewald presented this view in 1831. See Ewald, "Recension der *Kritische Untersuchungen über die Genesis*," 603.

> mark, an exclamation mark, a period, or the underscoring of a word is sufficient to bring to mind a whole series of ideas, observations, qualifications, and so forth. But for those who did not attend the instructor's lecture, these notes are not of much use. If they try to reconstruct the lecture solely from these notes, they will of necessity make many errors. Words, marks, and so forth that serve the students who listened to the lecture as most instructive guiding stars (*belehrendsten Leitsterne*) for the retention of the truths expounded by the lecturer appear to the uninitiated as silent sphinxes. The truths, which the initiated *reproduce* (*reproduciren*) from them (but do not *produce* [*produciren*] out of them) are smiled at by the uninitiated as a witty play of words and empty dreams without any real foundation. (emphasis in original)[41]

While for Bible critics like Ewald the fragmentary quality of certain passages in the Bible provides evidence for the Bible's compositional history, for Hirsch this fragmentary appearance testifies to the Oral Torah being primary revelation while the Written Torah is notes on the Oral Torah and hence secondary revelation. Without prior knowledge of the Oral Torah, the Written Torah is incomprehensible.[42]

Hirsch's account of the relationship between the Oral Torah and the Written Torah results in a paradox. On the one hand, his approach seems to *devalue* the Pentateuch as mere notes of the Oral Torah which is unintelligible without it. On the other hand, because the notes are so allusive and difficult to decipher, Hirsch must devote thousands of pages to his Pentateuch translation and commentary.[43]

[41] Hirsch, *Der Pentateuch,* 2:251; *The Hirsch Chumash,* 2:364. Hirsch also mentions this theory in his commentaries on Genesis 1:14–19 and 9:18, and Deuteronomy 31:26.

[42] Alan Levenson writes that for Hirsch "the Written Torah provided the CliffsNotes to the Oral Torah, which God taught to Moses on Mount Sinai." See Levenson, *The Making of the Modern Jewish Bible,* 50. While poignant, this analogy is somewhat misleading. The purpose of CliffsNotes is to provide a comprehensible summary that makes studying the original superfluous. By contrast, Hirsch contends that the Written Torah is *incomprehensible* without knowledge of the Oral Torah. In his commentary on Genesis 9:18 Hirsch makes clear that his theory applies to both the legal and narrative sections of the Bible. See Hirsch, *Der Pentateuch,* 1:171; *The Hirsch Chumash,* 1:235. Hirsch's applying this theory to the narrative sections of the Bible seems to be in tension with his understanding of Midrash Aggadah as personal interpretations of rabbis, not infallible divine revelation. See p. 265 of this volume.

[43] Hirsch's Pentateuch translation and commentary is about 3000 pages. The volumes of Hirsch's Pentateuch appeared as follows: Genesis (1867), Exodus (1869), Leviticus (1873), Numbers (1876), and Deuteronomy (1878). Hirsch published a second edition of the Genesis volume in 1883. He first published the beginning of his commentary on Genesis in February 1865. See Hirsch, "Beiträge zum Verständnis der ersten Blätter des Pentateuch," 141–154.

Creativity in defense of tradition and Orthodox hybridity

Jay Harris has noted that Hirsch's account of the relationship between the Oral Torah and the Written Torah in his Pentateuch is an innovation without precedent in rabbinic and post-rabbinic writings.[44] So while presenting himself as an Orthodox defender of tradition, Hirsch ends up adopting an approach to the Torah that is *much more novel* than that employed by the Maskil Mendelssohn, or the *Wissenschaft* scholar and Reformer Zunz. But while Harris is correct that Hirsch's doctrine is without precedent in rabbinic tradition, I have discovered an indirect source for it. It is none other than Hirsch's nemesis Zacharias Frankel.

In his 1861 attack on Frankel's *Darkhei Hamishnah*, Hirsch cites a passage in which Frankel discusses the Mishnah's oral quality. Frankel writes: "Even though the Mishnah was written down, it did not cease to be oral teaching. The Mishnah for the most part was written down with great brevity such that it was impossible to understand its statements or interpret them with certainty without a teacher to reveal their meaning and explain what is unclear . . . All that Rabbi [Judah the Prince, the author of the Mishnah--MG] intended was to write a work consisting of *notes to refresh the reader's memory. But the detailed explanation remained the function of the oral tradition as before*" (emphasis mine).[45]

Frankel describes the relationship between the Mishnah and the oral tradition in ways that are strikingly similar to Hirsch's explanation of the relation of the Pentateuch to the Oral Torah. He likens the Mishnah to brief mnemonic notes that cannot be understood without the oral teaching from which they are drawn. Frankel's description of the Mishnah clearly impacted Hirsch's conception of the relation of the Written Torah to the Oral Torah. For after citing Frankel's words, Hirsch comments: "This, by the way, is *entirely* the same relationship that Orthodox Judaism (*orthodoxen Judentum*) conceives the Pentateuch as having to the Sinaitic Oral Tradition!" (emphasis in original).[46] Hirsch transposes Frankel's teaching about the Mishnah's

[44] Harris, *How Do We Know This?*, 226–228. Benjamin Sommer claims that Hirsch's position has rabbinic antecedents such as *Exodus Rabbah* 47:1. See Sommer, *Revelation and Authority*, 156. I see things differently. *Exodus Rabbah* portrays Moses as receiving "Bible, Mishnah, Talmud and Aggadah" orally and then only writing down Scripture. On this schema, the Bible (Pentateuch) is still an independent, comprehensible text. For Hirsch, however, the Pentateuch is notes that are *incomprehensible* without knowledge of the Oral Torah.

[45] Hirsch, *GS*, 6:379; *CW*, 5:273. Hirsch cites Frankel, *Darkhei Hamishnah*, 218. I follow Hirsch's translation of Frankel.

[46] Hirsch, *GS*, 6: 379; *CW*, 5:273.

relation to the Oral Torah to the Pentateuch's relation to the Oral Torah. While Hirsch announces this view for this first time in his 1861, he only elaborates it in his Pentateuch.[47]

Through his novel account of the relationship between the Oral Torah and Written Torah, Hirsch makes several intellectual breakthroughs. First, he reconceptualizes the Protestant/Maskilic/Reform dichotomy between dead letter and living spirit. For Hirsch, the Written Torah is a *trace* of the Oral Torah. What makes the Oral Torah living spirit is not that it makes the Written Torah accessible to a new generation of students or that it brings biblical laws up to date, but that it constitutes the excess of the Written Torah that can never be contained in writing. As Hirsch puts it, "the whole meaning and living spirit (*lebendigen Geist*) of the Torah's content cannot be fixed in writing."[48] In this way, Hirsch points toward Walter Benjamin's claim that "in all language and linguistic creations there remains something in addition to what can be conveyed, something that cannot be communicated."[49]

Second, by casting the Oral Torah as the fundamental text of revelation, Hirsch offers a novel defense of Orthodox Judaism that undercuts the methodological assumption of historical criticism that through proper historical, philological, and linguistic work one can discern the original text and meaning of the Bible. Instead, Hirsch claims that one can only determine the meaning of the Bible in relation to *prior assumptions about its meaning.* In this way, he can be seen as pointing toward postmodern theories of textual indeterminacy and the role of reading communities in constituting the meaning of texts.

Finally, Hirsch's notion that the Oral Torah precedes the Written Torah paradoxically points toward some contemporary academic approaches to the origins of the Pentateuch. While late-nineteenth century *Wissenschaft* tended to give priority to written texts and sought to reconstruct

[47] In his 1855 review of Graetz's *History of the Jews*, Hirsch had not yet developed his novel account of the relationship between the Oral Torah and Written Torah. He writes that the Pentateuch contains the laws written as "general norms" (*allgemeinen Normen, klalim*) while the "detailed explanation" (*einzelnen Ausführungen*) of how to practice them were given orally and handed down through the Oral Torah. To ensure that the Oral Torah would not be forgotten, hermeneutic "rules" (*Regeln, midot*) were given whose primary purpose was to allow the derivation of the Oral Law from the Written Law. Hirsch also notes that there are a small number of laws that were given orally but not linked to the biblical text, which the Talmud calls "law given to Moses on Sinai" (halakhah lemosheh misinai). There is no indication that at this point Hirsch saw the Written Torah as fragmentary notes that are incomprehensible without the Oral Torah. See Hirsch, *GS*, 5:351; *CW*, 5:39.

[48] See Hirsch's commentary on Exodus 24:27 in Hirsch, *Der Pentateuch*, 2:570–571; *The Hirsch Chumash*, 2:819–820.

[49] See Benjamin, *Illuminations*, 79.

the original documents from which the Pentateuch was composed, contemporary Bible criticism tends to see oral tradition as preceding written documents.[50]

Objectivity and subjectivity: Hirsch's Pentateuch and Psalms

Like Mendelssohn, the Psalms is the only complete book of the Bible that Hirsch translated aside from the Pentateuch.[51] We saw that the audience and aim of Mendelssohn's Psalms translation was very different from that of the *Be'ur*. The *Be'ur* was directed to *Jews* and aimed to root a maskilic conception of Judaism in rabbinic and medieval Jewish sources. By contrast, Mendelssohn's Psalms was a non-confessional translation for *both Jews and Christians* that presented the biblical text as enlightened Hebrew lyric poetry. For Mendelssohn, *empathy* was key to understanding the Psalms, and he sought to enable readers to access the emotions conveyed by the Psalms through an immediate encounter with the translated text.

Mendelssohn's aims were reflected in the material features of his Psalms translation. Unlike the *Be'ur*, which looked like a rabbinic Bible and had a Hebrew title, his Psalms looked like a German book, containing only a translation in Gothic characters, a short German introduction, and a German title (*Die Psalmen*). The work contained no commentary or scholarly apparatus.[52]

At first glance, it seems that Hirsch's aims and methods in his Psalms translation and commentary are quite different from Mendelssohn's. Hirsch employs the *identical* format for his Psalms as for his Pentateuch.[53] The continuity between his Psalms and his Pentateuch seems confirmed by his giving his Psalms both Hebrew and German titles (*Sefer Tehillim*

[50] I owe this insight to conversations with Benjamin Sommer. See Sommer, *Revelation and Authority*, 154–156, 165–166, 168–170, and especially 322–323, note 98.

[51] Hirsch published his Psalms translation and commentary in 1882, six years after completing his Pentateuch. He first published a translation of several Psalms with a commentary from 1859 to 1867 in *Jeschurun* using his preferred literary device of a fictional correspondence. See "From a Correspondence about the Psalms" ("Aus einem Briefwechsel über die Psalmen") in Hirsch, *GS*, 1:324–414; *CW*, 4:257–401. Aside from the Psalms and the Pentateuch, Hirsch published a translation and commentary on a few chapters of Isaiah in *Jeschurun* from 1862 to 1863. See Hirsch, *GS*, 2:160–334; *CW*, 4:3–255. Hirsch also published a translation and commentary on selected chapters from Proverbs in *Jeschurun* from 1883 to 1885. These texts were collected and translated into English in 1976. See Hirsch, *From the Wisdom of Mishlé*.

[52] See Figures 2 and 4. See pp. 40–41 of this volume.

[53] See Figures 10 and 13.

meturgam umevo'ar/Die Psalmen übersetzt und erläutert) that parallel those he gave to his Pentateuch (*Hamishah Humshei Torah meturgam umevo'ar/ Der Pentateuch übersetzt und erläutert*). But appearances can be deceiving, and Hirsch's Psalms share much in common with Mendelssohn's.[54]

Hirsch opens the introduction to his Psalms, by stressing the Psalms' importance for Jews, writing that "next to the Pentateuch, the Psalms is the book of Scripture that has done the most to influence the *Bildung* of the Jewish spirit and mind (*Geistes und Gemüthes*)."[55] He makes clear the intimate connection between the Pentateuch and the Psalms, noting that "all the points contained in the Pentateuch form the foundation of the Psalms."[56]

For Hirsch, the Pentateuch sets out God's *objective* vision of humanity's task in the world, the task of Israel centered on obeying God's revealed law, and the mission of Israel to humanity. The Psalms assume this vision as its starting point but explore the *subjective* inner world of a person striving to fulfill their task.[57] The purpose of the Psalms is to "awaken people to consciousness of God" and to inspire them to "sing praises of God."[58] We saw earlier that for Hirsch the Pentateuch was "divine anthropology"—God's thoughts about human beings, not "theology"—human thoughts about God.[59] For Hirsch, the Psalms are human beings' thoughts and feelings about God, but not as theology. Rather, they are thoughts and feelings one experiences while striving to fulfill one's God-appointed task in the world.

Mendelssohn had presented the Psalms as poetically expressing universal enlightened religiosity. While Hirsch begins the introduction to the Psalms by stressing the Psalms importance for Jews, he then notes their universal import writing that David "confidently expected that his psalms would have an impact also upon the spirits and minds of all nations (*Völker*)."[60] Hirsch regards David as enormously successful in this endeavor, writing that the Psalms have become "the most universal book of humanity, producing an *enlightened* (*erleuchtendes*) and ennobling echo in the chest of the most varied

[54] Hirsch recounts his aims and methods for interpreting the Psalms in two works: the introduction to his 1859 "From a Correspondence about the Psalms" and the introduction to his 1882 translation and commentary on the Psalms.
[55] Hirsch, *Die Psalmen*, 1:i; *The Psalms*, 1:xi.
[56] Hirsch, *Die Psalmen*, 1:ii; *The Psalms*, 1:xii.
[57] Ibid.
[58] Hirsch, *GS*, 1:326; *CW*, 4:260–261.
[59] See p. 297 of this volume.
[60] Hirsch, *Die Psalmen*, 1:iv; *The Psalms*, 1:xiv.

people of every color, origin, age, and cultural level throughout time" (emphasis mine).[61]

Hirsch's claim that the Psalms aim to inspire people of every nation is reflected in an important difference in the *exegetical approach* he advocates for interpreting the Psalms as opposed to the Pentateuch. We have seen that an important goal of his Pentateuch is to show how the Pentateuch can only be understood in relation to the Oral Torah. But Hirsch makes clear that the Psalms can be understood independently of rabbinic tradition.[62] Hirsch's different approach to the Psalms is confirmed by comparing the content of his commentaries to the Psalms and the Pentateuch. While his Pentateuch commentary is suffused with references to rabbinic texts that Hirsch claims constitute the definitive interpretation of the biblical text, he rarely references rabbinic texts in his Psalms commentary and when he does reference them, he cites them not as the *authoritative* interpretation of the biblical text, but as illuminating literary aspects of it.[63]

In stressing that the Psalms can be understood through a direct reading of the text, Hirsch is stressing not only that *rabbinic tradition is unnecessary*, but also that *historical scholarship is not needed*. As he puts it, "Our sacred writings were not meant for a caste of scholars (*Gelehrtenkaste*) but are supposed to be a sacred treasure of our people without need for an auxillary apparatus (*Hülfapparates*)."[64] Like Mendelssohn, Hirsch sees *empathy* as the key to unlocking the meaning of the Psalms.[65] But unlike Mendelssohn, Hirsch stresses the need to understand the life and character of the author of the text, namely, David.[66] Hirsch makes clear that this knowledge does not

61 Hirsch, *GS*, 1:326; *CW*, 4:260.

62 Hirsch, *GS*, 1:327; *CW*, 4:262.

63 See, for example, Hirsch's commentary on Psalm 1, which references the *Yalkut* on Psalms. See Hirsch, his Psalms 1:1; *The Psalms*, 1:1. I think it is likely that Hirsch directed *Die Psalmen* for Jews given his use of Hebrew words in the commentary. But I cannot rule out the possibility that he may have also wished that Christians use his translation and commentary given his emphasis on the universal religious teachings of the Psalms, his claim that David intended his Psalms be read by Gentiles, and his assertion the Psalms can be understood without recourse to rabbinic teachings.

64 Hirsch, *GS*, 1:327; *CW*, 4:262.

65 As Hirsch puts it, "Our task is to find the core ideas underlying each Psalm and ponder them as vividly as they must have appeared in the singer's chest before he chose the precise words and sentences . . . with which to express them." See Hirsch, *GS*, 1:324–325; *CW*, 4:259–260. Compare this with Mendelssohn's statement in the introduction to his Psalms translation: "I carried it [a Psalm] around in my head throughout many different activities until I believed myself to be as intimate with the spirit of my poet as my abilities would allow. Writing it down was then a modest task." See Mendelssohn, *JubA*, 10.1: 6; *Moses Mendelssohn: Writings*, 183.

66 See Hirsch, *GS*, 1:327; *CW*, 4:262. In the introduction to his 1859 essays on the Psalms Hirsch acknowledges that David only authored "most of the Psalms" (*die Meisten Psalmen*). See Hirsch, *GS*, 1:326; *CW*, 4:260-261. The English translation inexcusably omits the word "most" (*Meisten*). In the introduction to his 1882 Psalms Hirsch makes clear that "inspired men of kindred spirit," including

require scholarly or historical research but can be obtained just by reading the Bible.[67]

According to Hirsch, several features of David's character and life help one understand the Psalms: (1) from his earliest youth David dedicated himself to serve God and his people; (2) David saw his task as defending and protecting his nation from external enemies but regarded his *greater* task as helping his nation understand their mission in the world and inspire them to fulfill it; (3) David's life was a constant struggle in which he "tasted all the bitterness . . . [that] can possibly be infused into a person's cup" through "ingratitude, envy, slander, and persecution"; (4) this bitterness was not only due to external circumstances but also due to David's imperfect character, which led him to sin and guilt; (5) David used every moment of both joy and suffering as an opportunity to come closer to God through ever-developing "clarity of thought" and "purity of resolve and conviction," which he often expressed through poetry and music; (6) David expected his songs and music not only to inspire Israel to its true mission but also to "impact the spirits and minds of all the other nations."[68]

Hirsch's emphasis on the need to appreciate David's life to understand the Psalms stands in marked contrast to his *not* seeing Moses' life as important for understanding the Pentateuch. The reason for this difference is clear. For Hirsch, the Pentateuch did not originate in Moses's mind but in God's, with Moses serving as a passive copyist. By contrast, Hirsch thinks that David composed the Psalms himself through divine inspiration.

While Hirsch considers the Psalms as humanly composed, he nevertheless rejects scholars' endeavor to supply textual emendations. For Hirsch, discerning the meaning of the Psalms requires a two-step process. We have seen that one begins by seeking to penetrate the "core ideas" (*Kerngedanken*) of the Psalm through empathetic identification with the state of mind of its author. By discovering these "core ideas" one seeks to understand the "necessity" of "every sentence, word, [and] literary nuance" in the psalm.[69]

descendants of Korah, Asaph, Heman, Ethan, Moses, and Solomon, authored several Psalms. See Hirsch, *Die Psalmen,* 1:vi; *The Psalms,* 1:xvi.

[67] Hirsch, *GS,* 1:327; *CW,* 4:262.

[68] Hirsch, *Die Psalmen,* 1:ii–v; *The Psalms,* 1:xii–xv.

[69] Hirsch, *GS,* 1:325; *CW,* 4:259–260. While Christians scholars had been declaring the biblical text corrupt and emending it since the eighteenth century, Hirsch may have been particularly concerned about the free approach to textual emendation being used by his former pupil Heinrich Graetz. By the 1860s Graetz was advocating textual emendations to the biblical text, and they are prominent

Hirsch's rejection of scholars' emendations of biblical texts recalls Mendelssohn's skepticism about textual emendation.[70] But Hirsch goes further than Mendelssohn. While in the case of the Pentateuch Mendelssohn rejected emendations completely, he allowed that some Psalms may be corrupt.[71] Hirsch makes no such concession.

Hirsch on Hebrew as mental trainer

We have seen that for Hirsch to understand the Bible, it must be read in Hebrew, understanding all the "nuances" of the original text. For Hirsch, this requires appreciating the distinctive qualities of Hebrew. An important function of both his Pentateuch and Psalms is to provide a translation and commentary that conveys these qualities.

Hirsch's conception of Hebrew is similar to Mendelssohn's but also differs from it. As we have seen, in *The Spirit of Hebrew Poetry* Herder emphasizes the poetic qualities of the Bible while denigrating its rationality.[72] Herder expresses this view by writing that the Hebrew Bible must be understood within its "oriental light" (*morgenländisches Licht*), noting that "for an abstract thinker the Hebrew language may not be best."[73] Mendelssohn responds to Herder by claiming that the Bible is, indeed, a poetic work, but also conveys rational metaphysical ideas, thereby connecting heart and mind.[74]

In his 1866 essay "Fantasies about the Jewish Calendar," Hirsch offers a response to Herder that is similar Mendelssohn's, writing that, "No more untrue

in his 1871 translations and commentaries on Ecclesiastes and the Song of Songs as well as in his 1882–1883 translation and commentary on the Psalms in which he denied Davidic authorship of *any* of the Psalms. See Schorsch, "In the Shadow of Wellhausen: Heinrich Graetz as Biblical Critic." Also see Zirkle, "Heinrich Graetz and the Exegetical Contours of Modern Jewish History." Regardless of whether or not Hirsch was able to read Graetz's translation and commentary on the Psalms while composing his own, he was certainly aware of Graetz's approach to the Bible and that Graetz was intending to apply it to the Psalms.

70 See, p. 58 of this volume.

71 As Mendelssohn put it in a 1771 letter to Johann Georg Zimmerman, "Some difficult Psalms are of such a nature that you can read into them what you want . . . because some passages are possibly corrupt." See Mendelssohn, *JubA*, 12.2:21–22 (Letter to J.G. Zimmerman, November 1771), as cited in Altmann, *Moses Mendelssohn,* 275.

72 See pp. 31–32 of this volume.

73 Herder, *Vom Geist,* 1:v, 9; *The Spirit,* 1:14, 30.

74 See 45–49 of this volume.

word was ever spoken than that the 'Spirit of the Hebrew Nation' '(*Geist des ebräischen Volkes*) belongs to the fantasy-rich Orient (*phantasiereichen Orient*), to the educational stage (*Bildungsstadium*) of thoughtless human intellectual development." Hirsch contends that the "creator of the Jewish nation" established the Jews as a "thinking people" who exemplified the unity of heart and mind noting that biblical imagery conveys rational concepts in emotionally stirring, concise ways.[75]

But Hirsch goes beyond Mendelssohn by seeking to identify *specific features* of Hebrew that stimulate rational thinking. Hirsch notes that Hebrew is written with extreme brevity. Printed Hebrew texts contain an enormous number of abbreviations, which the reader must decipher.[76] Hirsch observes that in any other language this would have rendered the text functionally unintelligible. But this did not cause Hebrew readers undue trouble because they were used to reading Hebrew without vowels, punctuation marks, and paragraph divisions. The fact that the Hebrew readers must decipher texts without these aids helps sharpen their minds by training them to become adept at "quickly identifying the author's trend of thought as if he were reading the words from his lips."[77]

In his 1866 essay, "Some Suggestions Regarding the Role of Hebrew Instruction in General Education," Hirsch expands on the link between the brevity of Hebrew and mental acuity by noting that Hebrew grammar is "a constant exercise of making the mind quickly seize the heart (*Kern*) of the matter and make the finest distinctions."[78] He explains that in Hebrew one can change a word's meaning by adding new syllables to word roots and introducing slight changes in vocalization. Hirsch gives the example of the Hebrew sentence *re'itihu va'ohavehu*. The first word's root is ר.א.ה, which means "to see," while the second word's root is א.ה.ב, which means "to love." Because Hebrew modifies words through prefixes, suffixes, and vocalization, it can convey in two words (*re'itihu va'ohavehu*) what would require eight

[75] Hirsch, *GS*, 3:532–533; *CW*, 8:236. Hirsch makes a similar point in the introduction to his 1859 correspondence on the Psalms; see Hirsch, *GS*, 1:325–326; *CW*, 4:260–261. Hirsch also emphasizes the rationality of the Bible's teachings about God and the task of humanity in the preface to his Pentateuch, where he calls the Bible a "seed of light and understanding (*Saat des Lichtes und der Erkenntniß*) for all who delve into it with seriousness." See Hirsch, *Der Pentateuch*, 1:vi; *The Hirsch Chumash*, 1:xv.

[76] Hirsch observes that printers used these abbreviations to save money on printing costs. See Hirsch, *GS*, 3:532–533; *CW*, 8:236.

[77] Hirsch, *GS*, 3:531–532; *CW*, 8:235–236.

[78] Hirsch, *GS*, 2:440; *CW*, 7:70.

words in German: *Ich habe ihn gesehen und habe ihn liebgewonnen* (I saw him and came to love him).[79]

Hirsch also notes that Hebrew promotes mental perspicacity because its words are built from roots that convey concepts that he calls "nuclei of ideas" (*Gedankenkerne*). For example, Hirsch claims that the Hebrew word *adam* (אדם), meaning "human being," is connected to the root *damah* (ד.מ.ה), meaning "likeness," as well as to the word *adamah* (אדמה), meaning "earth." This points to the fact that human beings are created both in the likeness of God and with an earthly form. Similarly, Hirsch notes that the word *adam* (אדם) is connected to *adom* (אדום), meaning "red." Hirsch explains that red light is the least refracted of all light, which represents that human beings are "the closest manifestation of the divine," and that through human beings "God's presence is revealed on earth." For Hirsch, Hebrew trains one to think about world in terms of conceptual relations.[80]

One of the most striking features of Hirsch's Pentateuch is his frequent use of the principle that "phonetic relationship" (*Lautverwandtschaft*) between Hebrew words relates their meaning.[81] For Hirsch, not only are different Hebrew letters with *identical phonetic sounds* related, but Hebrew letters that are articulated *in the same part of the mouth* are also related. Dividing Hebrew letters into the five categories of gutterals, palatals, dentals, labials, and sibilants, Hirsch claims that letters from the same category are cognate, and so the meanings of words containing these letters are connected.[82] While this approach has a basis in Rashi, Hirsch deploys it far beyond Rashi, identifying hundreds of related word roots.[83] Hirsch connects his attention to phonetic relationships with his conceptual etymology, claiming that Hebrew word roots that are related phonetically are also related conceptually.[84] For example, he explains that in the commandment to send away the mother

[79] Hirsch, *GS*, 2:440; *CW*, 7:70–71.

[80] Hirsch, *GS*, 2:441; *CW*, 7:71; Hirsch, *Der Pentateuch*, 1:30–31; *The Hirsch Chumash*, 1:39 (Commentary to Genesis 1:26). This point is similar to Mendelssohn's assertion that his early education in Hebrew disposed him to understand the world in a specific way. See pp. 28–29 of this volume. But Hirsch goes beyond Mendelssohn by applying this not just to Hebrew lexicography, but also to Hebrew word roots.

[81] Hirsch, *Der Pentateuch*, 1:vi; *The Hirsch Chumash*, xv. In his Psalms commentary, Hirsch uses the principle of *Lautverwandtschaft* much less often.

[82] Clark, *Etymological Dictionary of Biblical Hebrew*, xi.

[83] There is a list of all the roots that Hirsch uses in an index to Breuer's Hebrew translation of Hirsch's Pentateuch. A quick count reveals around 1,800 word roots. See Breuer, "Index of Roots." For the origin of this principle in Rashi, see Rashi's commentary to Leviticus 19:16, and Breuer, "Preface," 9–10. An important difference between Rashi's and Hirsch's use of letter interchange is that Rashi does not seek conceptual relations between words.

[84] Hirsch, *GS*, 2:441–443; *CW*, 7:71–75.

bird, the Hebrew word for "nest," *ken* (קן), derives from the root ק.נ.ן, which is related to the root ג.נ.ן., which means "protection." The Hebrew word *ken* therefore conveys the idea that the nest exists to protect the young.[85] Similarly, Hirsch notes that the word *adam* (אדם) is connected to *hadom* (הדום), meaning "footstool," since human beings are God's "footstools" on earth as they are the "agents and bearers" of God's glory on earth.[86]

In sum, like Mendelssohn Hirsch conceives the Bible as a work of poetic rationality. But he goes beyond Mendelssohn in describing how Hebrew trains the mind. Hirsch also breaks from Mendelssohn's account of the *substantive doctrines* that the Bible teaches. To appreciate these differences, it is instructive to compare Mendelssohn's and Hirsch's approach to three topics: (1) the relation between the Bible and scientific truth, (2) the Tetragrammaton, and (3) biblical anthropomorphism.

The Bible and scientific truth

We have seen that Mendelssohn does not seek to reconcile natural science with the Bible because he thinks that the Bible describes the natural world as the common person sees it. As such, one should not assume that the Bible is scientifically correct.[87] Hirsch adopts a similar, though somewhat different approach. Psalm 19, verses 5–7 describe the sun revolving around the earth. Hirsch's lengthy commentary on the passage is worth quoting in full:

> David like all the Holy Scriptures speaks in the language of human beings (*dibrah Torah kil'shon b'nei adam*). He speaks in the language of human beings to human beings in the same way that Copernicus, Kepler, and Newton did, as we now speak, and probably as will be spoken by every human tongue as long as men will be capable of speech. The language will remain the same even when, contrary to how things appear to us, the path of the earth around the sun will have attained the highest degree of probability and have the status of irrefutable certainty. *For it is not the aim of Holy Scriptures to teach astronomy, cosmology, or physics, but only to orient*

85 Hirsch, *Der Pentateuch*, 5:370; *The Hirsch Chumash*, 5:510 (Commentary to Deuteronomy 22:6).
86 Hirsch, *Der Pentateuch*, 1:30–31; *The Hirsch Chumash*, 1:39 (Commentary to Genesis 1:26).
87 See p. 47 of this volume.

> *human beings to fulfill their life's task within the framework of the constellation of their existence.* For this purpose it is irrelevant whether the course of the days and years is determined by the earth's revolutions around the sun or by the latter's orbit around the former. The Holy Scriptures will have achieved their purpose only if the human beings' spiritual ear will remain attuned to understanding the 'speech of heaven and earth.' The language speaks to the thinking man through the conformity of all these phenomena to a fixed set of laws which control all of nature from the paths of the infinite galaxies down to the microscopic development of the most minute one-celled organism. (emphasis mine)[88]

Hirsch makes three important points in this rich passage. *First*, like Mendelssohn, Hirsch claims that in describing nature the Bible speaks according to common understanding. But Hirsch goes beyond Mendelssohn by emphasizing that even the greatest scientists would describe nature this way. When speaking to a friend, even Stephen Hawking would say that the sun rises and sets despite the fact that every child today knows that the earth revolves around the sun!

Second, like Mendelssohn, Hirsch emphasizes that the Bible uses everyday language to describe nature because its aim is not to teach scientific truth. But while Mendelssohn stresses that the purpose of the Bible is to teach "matters of Torah and faith (*emunah*),"[89] which include metaphysical truths such as the immortality of the soul, Hirsch emphasizes that the purpose of the Torah is practical, namely, to teach a person her moral task in life.

Finally, unlike Mendelssohn, Hirsch does not simply assert that the Bible does not teach scientific truth. As we have seen, central to Hirsch's understanding of the Bible is that it teaches that nature obeys God's will by following laws that God instituted.[90] When Hirsch says that the Bible does not "teach astronomy, cosmology or physics," he means only that it does not specify the precise *content* of scientific laws.[91]

88 Hirsch, *Die Psalmen,* 1:109; *The Psalms,* 1:138.

89 See Mendelssohn, *JubA,* 15.2:11.

90 See p. 267 of this volume. Also see Hirsch, "On the Educational Value of Judaism" ("Vom dem pädagogischen Werte des Judentums"), 7–11; *CW,* 7:251–254.

91 In his essay "On the Educational Value of Judaism," Hirsch explains why the Bible does not describe scientific truths in detail. Were the Torah to teach scientific truths that had not yet been discovered, scientifically-minded individuals would reject these teachings. But were the Torah to teach scientific doctrines that are widely accepted, it would be rejected once those doctrines were rendered obsolete by scientific advances. See Hirsch, "Vom dem pädagogischen Werte," 13; *CW,* 7:257.

The Tetragrammaton

Hirsch discusses the Tetragrammaton at its first appearance in Genesis 2:4. He translates the verse as follows:

> *Dies sind die Erzeugnisse des Himmels und der Erde, die bereits in ihrer Erschaffung, mit dem Tage, an welchem* G o t t *Erde und Himmel gestaltete, gegeben waren.*
>
> These are the products of the heavens and earth, which had already been given in their creation on the day when G o d formed the heaven and the earth.[92]

Hirsch begins his commentary by acknowledging that the Tetragrammaton expresses the "deep essence" of God, which is unfathomable to human beings. But this deep essence is not his concern. Rather, he seeks to explain the meaning of the Tetragrammaton for contemporary Jews and harshly criticizes Mendelssohn's translation of the term without naming Mendelssohn. It is worth quoting the relevant passage in full:

> Our sages say that the Tetragrammaton refers to *midat harahamim*, the powerful love of God. This shows how far the concept of the "Eternal" (*Ewiger*) is from the true meaning of the Tetragrammaton. This concept [the Eternal], which people commonly use to express this name does not conform to the meaning of the Tetragrammaton in the least and flattens it. "Eternal" is a metaphysical, transcendental concept that has scarcely any practical relation to anything outside itself and is silent about our being and becoming. Eternity is a state of existence (*Dasein*) that is closed within itself. When predicated of a being the attribute of eternity reveals nothing to us about its subjective existence and contains nothing about its action and effects. The concept "Eternal" leaves our hearts cold; it has no meaning for our lives and so is unrelated to *midat harahamim*.[93]

[92] Hirsch, *Der Pentateuch* 1:48–49; *The Hirsch Chumash*, 1:63.
[93] Hirsch, *Der Pentateuch*, 1:49; *The Hirsch Chumash*, 1:64–65.

Hirsch grounds his interpretation of the Tetragrammaton in the rabbinic idea that the Tetragrammaton refers to God's mercy while the name *elohim* refers to God's justice.[94] In terms later echoed by Rosenzweig, Hirsch considers Mendelssohn's translation of the Tetragrammaton as "the Eternal" a cold, metaphysical translation that obscures God's relation to human beings. By contrast, the attribute of mercy involves the sense of God's deep love and care for the world, and Hirsch therefore deems "the Eternal" an inappropriate translation of the Tetragrammaton.[95]

Hirsch then undertakes a grammatical analysis of the Tetragrammaton to show that Mendelssohn's translation is incorrect. He writes that the Tetragrammaton is not a present, intransitive of the root ה.י.ה in the *kal* form but, rather, a future transitive *pi'el* or *hif'il* form of the root. As such, the Tetragrammaton does not denote "the one who exists" (*der Seiende*) but, rather, "the one who grants existence" (*der Sein Spendende*), or more specifically, "the one who is always ready to grant new existence."[96]

Hirsch elaborates that the Tetragrammaton does not refer to God as an "Ancient of Days" (Atik Yamin) who, having created the world, "retired to repose within the depths of His eternal being." Rather, God is "the living, eternally active God." This is a God who not only created the world in the past, but who is also ready to "bestow [existence] at each *future* moment." God's mercy is reflected in the fact that God "is willing to grant *new* existence (*Dasein*) at each moment even if the past has been tossed away." In other words, the Tetragrammaton does not refer to God as a necessary existent from which the world emerged but, rather, as an active force who is also ready to bestow and renew life at any moment.[97]

Hirsch then contrasts the Tetragrammaton with the name *elohim*. For Hirsch, *elohim* refers to the God of creation who establishes a natural world that operates according to necessary causal laws. He notes that the Sages express this idea by saying that *elohim* refers to the attribute of justice,

94 See *Genesis Rabbah* 33.

95 As we have seen, Rosenzweig's understanding of Mendelssohn is more complex. See pp. 21–22 of this volume.

96 Hirsch, *Der Pentateuch* 1:49–50; *The Hirsch Chumash*, 1:65–66.

97 See ibid. Hirsch's interpretation is also clearly directed against Maimonides, who suggests that the Tetragrammaton may refer to God's necessary existence. See Maimonides, *Guide of the Perplexed*, I:61, 147–148. In truth, Maimonides' position is not that far from Hirsch's, as he adopts the Avicennean view that God is constantly granting the cosmos new existence. Maimonideans, like Moses Narboni and Isaac Albalag, saw this view expressed by a phrase found in *BT*, Hagigah, 12b, and the phrase *hamehadesh betuvo tamid ma'aseh bereshit* (Who constantly renews the act of creation with goodness) was eventually inserted into the morning prayers.

which Hirsch interprets as involving "law and measure."[98] By contrast, the Tetragrammaton refers to God's relation to human beings, that is to God's providential moral guidance of human history through the attribute of mercy. The "correlate" (*Correlat*) of God's providential concern with human moral progress is a human being's *free* acceptance of God's kingship and subordinating herself to God's will. Hirsch notes that because of this, the Tetragrammaton, which cannot be pronounced, is vocalized as *adonai*, meaning "Lord."[99]

While Hirsch acknowledges that the Tetragrammaton is untranslatable, he informs the reader that he will translate both the Tetragrammaton and *elohim* as *Gott*. But to indicate that the Tetragrammaton denotes a "proper name" (*nomen proprium*) that stands in personal relationship to human beings, he will print the word *Gott* using "letter-spacing" (*gesperrter Schrift*) as *G o t t*, which indicates emphasis.[100] In printing the Tetragrammaton in a special way, Hirsch's approach recalls Luther, who had printed his translation of the Tetragrammaton using capital letters. But while Hirsch translates *elohim* as *Gott* and the Tetragrammaton as *G o t t*, Luther translates *elohim* as *Gott* but the Tetragrammaton as *der HERR* to signify that it refers to a different person of the Godhead, namely, Lord Jesus.

Hirsch's attack on Mendelssohn is based on a misrepresentation of Mendelssohn's view. It is true that for Mendelssohn "the Eternal" is not a proper name for God the way it is for Hirsch. But as we have seen, Mendelssohn makes clear that "the Eternal" includes God's providential concern for humanity.[101]

Biblical anthropomorphism

Hirsch's concern about describing God in an abstract, depersonalized, metaphysical fashion becomes even more evident in his discussion of biblical anthropomorphism. His main discussion of this is in his translation and commentary on Genesis 6:6, which describes God's regret and grief at having created humanity. Hirsch translates the verse as follows:

[98] See p. 267 of this volume.
[99] Hirsch, *Der Pentateuch,* 1:50–51, *Der Pentateuch,* 1:65, 67.
[100] Hirsch, *Der Pentateuch,* 1:51; *The Hirsch Chumash,* 1:67.
[101] See p. 22 of this volume.

> *da ward G o t t zur Aenderung seines Entschlusses, daß er den Menschen auf Erden geschaffen, veranlasst, und er betrübt sich um sein Herz.*
>
> Then G o d was induced to alter his decision to create human beings on earth and he grieved in his heart.[102]

In his commentary, Hirsch writes that he will "make a general remark about anthropomorphic expressions" in the Bible. He observes that there is a long tradition of "philosophizing" about anthropomorphic descriptions of God to avoid any semblance of divine corporeality. But, Hirsch claims, concern about anthropomorphism creates the danger of "blurring" and obscuring God's personality. He explains that God must have deemed it important to describe God's self in anthropomorphic terms in the Bible, since it would have been easy to avoid these expressions.[103] In his commentary on Genesis 8:21 Hirsch elaborates this point, writing that turning God into a "transcendental metaphysical concept" is a much greater danger than anthropomorphism since a primary goal of the Torah is to teach the moral duties that human beings receive from God and God's providential, loving concern for humanity. Both of these notions presuppose a personal God.[104]

In criticizing those seeking to eliminate anthropomorphism and turn God into an abstract concept, Hirsch seems to be primarily thinking of Maimonides, though he does not name him.[105] That he is thinking of Maimonides is evident because in his commentary on Genesis 6:6 Hirsch praises Rabbi Abraham of Posquières (Rabad), whom he calls a "distinctively Jewish thinker," for asserting that "the personality of God is more important than speculations about whether to attribute this or that predicate to God." Hirsch is referring to Rabad's famous gloss on Maimonides's *Mishneh Torah*, where he criticizes Maimonides for claiming that one who ascribes to God a body or physical form is a heretic, claiming that "people greater and better than he [Maimonides] have followed this opinion based on what they found in Scriptural texts."[106] By calling Rabad a "distinctly Jewish thinker," Hirsch is repeating the view he expressed in the *Nineteen*

[102] Hirsch, *Der Pentateuch*, 1:125; *The Hirsch Chumash*, 1:169.

[103] Hirsch, *Der Pentateuch*, 1:126; *The Hirsch Chumash*, 1:171.

[104] As Hirsch puts it, "The belief in God's personality and his close relation to every person on earth is more important than any speculation on transcendental concepts such as God's eternity, incorporeality etc., for these concepts have as little relation to our moral life (*sittlichen Leben*) as do algebraic codes." See Hirsch, *Der Pentateuch*, 1:155; *The Hirsch Chumash*, 1:212.

[105] See p. 361 note 97 of this volume.

[106] See Rabad's commentary on Maimonides, *Mishneh Torah*, "Laws of Repentance," 3:7.

Letters that Maimonides distorted Judaism by imposing foreign "Arab-Greek" philosophical concepts on it. But while Hirsch may be primarily thinking of Maimonides, his criticisms of Mendelssohn's translation of the Tetragrammaton indicate that he probably also has Mendelssohn in mind.

For Hirsch, the anthropomorphic expressions in Genesis 6:6 convey two important truths, namely, God's freedom and human freedom.[107] God's freedom is expressed by God's altering God's original decision to create human beings in response to human sinning, while human freedom is expressed by God's seeing that human beings had become wicked, which grieved God.[108]

Once again, inspection reveals that Hirsch's charge that Mendelssohn seeks to downplay God's personality is highly questionable. Mendelssohn preserves the anthropomorphic descriptions in Genesis 8:21 *more clearly* than Hirsch. While Hirsch translates *vayinahem YHWH* in the verse as *da ward G o t t zur Aenderung seines Entschlusses* (G o d was induced to alter his decision), Mendelssohn translates it literally as *Da bereute der Ewige* (the Eternal regretted). And Mendelssohn translates *vayitatzev* in the verse as God feeling "vexation" (*Verdruß*), explaining in his commentary that ascribing vexation to God is entirely appropriate, as we have seen.[109]

Hirsch's translation provides deeper insight into his exegetical method. In his commentary on Genesis 5:29, he claims that the Hebrew root נ.ח.מ has three meanings: (1) comfort, (2) altering one's decision in response to something that happened, and (3) regretting having done something. For Hirsch, the "fundamental meaning" (*Grundbedeutung*) of the word root is "changing one's mind (*Sinn*)." While this is evident for the last two meanings, he claims that this also explains the meaning of "comfort," since providing comfort changes the mood of the person grieving.[110] In the case of Genesis 6:6, clearly the word *vayinahem* cannot mean comfort. So why does Hirsch choose "alter His decision" rather than "regret"? It seems that Hirsch is driven by his commitment to divine freedom, seeing God changing God's decision in response to human sin as expressing God's freedom, while regret does not. It is therefore evident that Hirsch's *theological commitments* sometimes drive his translation choices even as he seeks to provide a *philological basis* for them.

[107] These expressions are really anthropopathic. Hirsch does not seem to distinguish between anthropomorphism and anthropopathism.

[108] Hirsch, *Der Pentateuch,* 1:126; *The Hirsch Chumash,* 1:171.

[109] See p. 49 of this volume.

[110] See Hirsch, *Der Pentateuch,* 1:20; The Hirsch Chumash, 1: 161–162 (Commentary on Genesis 5:29).

Hirsch on the cultural value of translation

We have already seen that Hirsch deems translation important given the severe decline in knowledge of Hebrew and the Bible among German Jews.[111] But in his essay "Some Suggestions on the Role of Hebrew," he offers more general comments on the value of translation. Hirsch asks the reader to consider a German national living in America who wishes to transmit a sense of "German ideas, aspirations, character, worldview, spirit and the heart" to his children. For Hirsch, this is of value not merely to inculcate an awareness of German "cultural heritage for its own sake"; it also benefits the "the moral and spiritual welfare of [the German's] new fatherland," namely, America. Echoing Mendelssohn's defense of translation and cultural pluralism, Hirsch writes that teaching a German child living abroad about his heritage benefits the host country since "the welfare (*Heil*) of all nations and humanity" is enriched through exposure to the "rich variety of personal and national individualities that live on earth."[112] Hirsch uses chromatic imagery to express this idea, noting that light is "composed of seven colors blended into one." He explains that visual and auditory harmony result not from uniformity but from "the greatest possible multiplicity."[113] Hirsch then applies this principle to German Jews. Just as a German American makes his child a better *American* by teaching her German language and literature, so a German Jew makes her child a better *German* by teaching her Jewish language and literature.

Hirsch sees the Torah itself as valuing translation. Deuteronomy 27:8 describes God commanding Moses to write the Torah on stones on the eve of the Israelites entering Canaan. Hirsch translates the verse as follows: *und schreibst auf die Steine alle Worte dieser Lehre zu hinlänglichem Verständniß* (*be'er heitev*) [and write all the words of this teaching on stones so that they may be adequately understood].[114] In his commentary on the words *be'er heitev*, Hirsch cites the Talmud (*BT*, Sotah, 32a), which interprets these words to mean that Moses added a *translation of the Torah* so that all the other nations would be able to understand it. Hirsch comments on the universal message implicit in this idea, writing, "Far from the particularism ascribed to it

111 See p. 341 of this volume.

112 Hirsch, *GS*, 2:434–435; *CW*, 7:65–66. See pp. 25–31 of this volume. Also see Gottlieb, "Mendelssohn's Metaphysical Defense of Religious Pluralism."

113 Hirsch, GS, 2: 434–435; CW, 7:65–66.

114 Hirsch, *Der Pentateuch*, 5:469; *The Hirsch Chumash*, 5:646.

by outsiders, Israel was to understand from the very outset that its mission was to help bring about the spiritual and moral redemption (*Erlösung*) of all humanity. With the entry of the divine law (*göttlichen Gesetzes*) into the land, the future salvation of all peoples could begin."[115] While many Christians (and some Jews) regarded Judaism as parochial and clannish, for Hirsch the Hebrew Bible imagined its own translation as a means of benefitting not just the Jewish community, but humanity, by spreading the Torah's universal moral message to the world.

Translation trouble

While Hirsch sees translation as having great value, like Mendelssohn he is keenly aware of the obstacles to translation in general and particularly to translating the Bible. For Hirsch, a problem that can affect any translation is when the source language has words that distinguish between different types of objects *within a class*, while the target language has only one word for *the entire class*. In his preface to the Psalms, Hirsch notes that Hebrew has many more words for describing joy than German, which makes it hard to translate these Hebrew terms. Hirsch observes that Hebrew has five words that indicate joy: *alatz*, *alaz*, *gil*, *sos*, and *same'ah*, each with different nuances, and there are no adequate German equivalents for these words. Similarly, he notes that Hebrew has words that describe forms of musical expression that have no German equivalent. Thus the Hebrew word *zemer* means singing a wordless melody while the word *shir* indicates singing a melody with words. But German has only a single word, *singen*. In this way Hirsch indicates that Hebrew is an aesthetically rich and sophisticated language.[116]

Hirsch explains that when encountering translation problems, he generally takes one of two approaches. If he feels that precision is absolutely essential to understanding the Hebrew original, he will paraphrase the Hebrew word by using several German words to translate it. But if he decides that precision is not essential for understanding the Hebrew text, he

115 Hirsch, *Der Pentateuch*, 5:470; *The Hirsch Chumash*, 5:647 (Commentary to Deuteronomy 27:8).

116 Hirsch, *Die Psalmen*, 1:vi–vii; *The Psalms*, 1:xvii. Hirsch gives several other examples of Hebrew words for which there are no German equivalents. On the differences between *shir* and *zemer*, also see Hirsch, *Der Pentateuch*, 1:496–497; *The Hirsch Chumash*, 1:792–793 (Commentary on Genesis 43:11).

will use a single German word even though it fails to convey the nuances of the original.[117]

These types of problems are not unique to translating Hebrew. But Hirsch thinks that there are specific obstacles to translating Hebrew due to its unique metaphysical status.

Hebrew as a divine language

The roots of Hirsch's conception of Hebrew go back to a medieval Jewish debate. In the eleventh-century dialogue *Kuzari*, Judah Halevi argued that in all languages *except Hebrew* some words designate the essence of the object they refer to while others are arbitrary referents. But, claimed Halevi, Hebrew is a divinely created language whose words most accurately match the essence of the things they designate.[118] Menachem Kellner notes that Halevi's conceiving Hebrew as the only divinely created language leads him to endow it with magical powers.[119] By contrast, Maimonides claims that Hebrew is no different than any other language and designates conventionally.[120] For Maimonides, the only reason that Hebrew is called the "holy tongue" is because it is a refined language that contains no words for genitalia, sex, urination, or excrement.[121]

Hirsch's most important discussion of Hebrew occurs in his commentary on the story of the Tower of Babel (Exodus 11). Hirsch distinguishes between "objective" and "subjective" language formation, writing that a language is "objective" if it designates "things and their relations" in a way that corresponds to the "thing in itself" (*Ding an Sich*) and its relations to the world. By contrast, a language is "subjective" if it merely designates the ways that a certain "nation" (*Volk*) conceives the object and its relation to the world.[122] Hirsch

[117] Hirsch, *Die Psalmen*, 1:vi–vii; *The Psalms*, 1:xvii.

[118] See Halevi, *Kuzari*, 4:25, 229. For discussion of Halevi's view of language, see Kellner, *Maimonides' Confrontation with Mysticism*, 156–158; Bacher, "The Views of Jehuda Halevi Concerning the Hebrew Language"; Septimus, "Maimonides on Language," 48–49.

[119] In particular, Kellner notes that for Halevi Hebrew has a special ability to influence angels. Kellner, *Maimonides' Confrontation*, 158.

[120] See Maimonides, *Guide of Perplexed*, II:30, 357–358.

[121] Maimonides, *Guide of the Perplexed*, III:8, 435–436. Kellner provides other sources that indicate that Maimonides regarded Hebrew as conventional. See Kellner, *Maimonides' Confrontation*, 162–173. Kellner argues that Maimonides emphasized the conventional nature of Hebrew to oppose Jewish thinkers who thought that Hebrew could be used to magically manipulate reality. See ibid., 173–175.

[122] Hirsch, *Der Pentateuch*, 1:201; *The Hirsch Chumash*, 1:274 (Commentary to Genesis 11:7).

explains that the language used by the people of Babel, namely Hebrew, was "objective," as it comprised a single view of "jurisprudence, ethics, physics and metaphysics" that reflected God's will for humanity. This linguistic objectivity existed because the language was not formed by individuals, but inherited from a tradition going back to Adam, whom God had taught this original language. According to Hirsch, the Bible recounts that the division of languages occurred with the fall of the Tower of Babel and the dispersal of humanity.[123] Living in varied territories and climates, peoples developed languages that expressed different human perspectives.[124] Hirsch's view of language here is clearly much closer to Halevi's than to Maimonides's.[125]

[123] According to Hirsch, the cause of this division was communal oppression of the individual. When some individuals began to question the objective view of things expressed by the language of the men of Babel, the community despotically sought to silence them and assert its right over them. For Hirsch, this is implied by the phrase the people of Babel used in constructing the tower, namely, *na'aseh lanu shem/so wollen wir uns einen Name machen* (let us make a name for ourselves). See Hirsch, *Der Pentateuch,* 1:196; *The Hirsch Chumash,* 1:265–269. As a result, individuals' self-respect moved them to rebel and refuse to submit to the community's viewpoint and norms. Even though this represented a rebellion against divine tradition, God punished the people of Babel because they were wrong to seek to crush the individual for the sake of communal conformity. The punishment was dispersion so that the dignity of the individual could be reasserted. As Hirsch puts it, "the organized community misused its power . . . and sought to subject the individual to its rule . . . given such a community, decentralization is the only path to human beings' redemption." Hirsch, *Der Pentateuch,* 203–204; *The Hirsch Chumash,* 277–278 (Commentary to Genesis 11:7). Hirsch thus interprets the moral of the Tower of Babel as being the importance of individuality and liberty of conscience in the face of tyrannical communal oppression, even where the community is upholding a divine tradition. It is no accident that Hirsch wrote these words during his struggle for the right of his Orthodox congregation to secede from the official Jewish community. I will discuss this in the next chapter.

[124] Hirsch, *Der Pentateuch,* 1:204; *The Hirsch Chumash,* 279 (Commentary to Genesis 11:7). Compare Hirsch's commentary on Genesis 10:5 and 11:1. See Hirsch, *Der Pentateuch,* 1:185–186, 192–193; *The Hirsch Chumash,* 1:252–253, 262–263.

[125] See Hirsch, *Der Pentateuch,* 1:202–203; *The Hirsch Chumash,* 1:276–277 (Commentary to Genesis 11:7). In his commentary on Genesis 2:19, Hirsch seems to contradict the view he expresses in his commentary on Genesis 11:7. Genesis 2:19 describes God's bringing Adam the animals to name. Hirsch's translation of the verse is as follows: *Da trieb G o t t alles Thier des Feldes und alles Geflügel des Himmels von der Menschen-Erde zusammen und brachte sie zum Menschen, damit er sehe, was er sich nennen werde, und Alles, was sich's der Mensch als lebendiges Wesen nennt, das ist sein Name* [Then G o d herded together from the human-earth all the animals of the field and all the birds of the sky and brought them to the human being to see what he would name them and everything that the human being himself named as a living being, that is its name]. Hirsch comments that Adam gave names to things as a "living being," that is, as a finite creature. For this reason, these names reflected Adam's "individual standpoint" based on the impressions that the things made on him, whether pleasing or unpleasing. Hirsch writes that this knowledge was "subjective," as no mortal being can know the essence of things. He sees this alluded to by the fact that the text states that the human being "himself" (*sich's/lo*) named things, which indicates that the names Adam gave reflected his finite perspective. Hirsch points out that, nevertheless, the verse states that the names that Adam gave "are its name" (*das ist sein Name/hu shmo*) to indicate that while human beings can never fully know the truth about things, they can still capture a fraction of it. See Hirsch, *Der Pentateuch,* 1:65–66; *The Hirsch Chumash,* 1:86–87. Here Hirsch seems to present a different view of how Hebrew designates (at least as regards the names of the animals and of Eve—see Genesis 2:23) that is closer to Maimonides's view, though unlike Maimonides, he still indicates that Adam's names capture something essential about reality.

For Hirsch, the fact that Hebrew encodes a divine perspective while other languages encode human perspectives creates serious problems for the translator.[126] For example, the Hebrew word *adon* means "lord." Its German equivalent would be *Herr.* The problem is that *Herr* implies domination (from the verb *herrschen*), while according to Hirsch the Hebrew word *adon* is from the root א.ד.נ, which means to bear a burden.[127] So while German conceives the leader as one who dominates his people, Hebrew reflects the divine understanding that the true leader supports his people.[128] Another example is the Hebrew word *yosher*, meaning "simple" or "straightforward." For Hirsch, the Hebrew word denotes an admirable quality, thereby encoding the divine view that being simple and straightforward is good. The German equivalent of *yosher* is *schlicht.* Hirsch tells us that the problem with translating *yosher* as *schlicht* is that *schlicht* is related to *schlecht*, which means bad, thereby encoding the human perspective that being straightforward is bad, while being cunning and wily are good.[129] A third example is *ish* and *ishah.* Genesis 2:23 recounts that Adam called his mate *ishah* since she was taken from man (*ish*). The rabbis already saw in this biblical etymology evidence that Adam spoke Hebrew since in all other ancient languages the words for man and woman share no common root.[130] For Hirsch, it is highly significant that *ish* and *ishah* are nearly identical words, for they indicate the divine view that the sexes are equal. By contrast, Hirsch writes that in other languages the words for "man" and "woman" are very different, which indicates inequality between the sexes. Men are generally understood either to dominate women

[126] Hirsch does, however, note that at times the divine and human worldview coincide. For example, he observes that the Hebrew word *gan* (garden) is connected to the word *ganan* (guard), as a garden is something that must be preserved. Hirsch notes that this connection is also found in German (and English) (*Garten/garten—garden/guard*). See Hirsch, *Der Pentateuch,* 1:56–57; *The Hirsch Chumash,* 1:75 (Commentary to Genesis 2:8).

[127] Hirsch, *Der Pentateuch,* 1:202; *The Hirsch Chumash,* 1:275–276 (Commentary to Genesis 11:7). Hirsch notes that *adon* means the base of a pillar, implying support. Through the principle of "phonetic relation," Hirsch notes that *adon* is related to *eden*, which means comfort and support (as in the Garden of Eden) and to the word *aton*, which means "donkey," since a donkey supports its rider. See *Der Pentateuch,* 1:57, 228; *The Hirsch Chumash,* 1:75, 311 (Commentary to Genesis 2:8, 12:16). This claim that the Bible connects true rulership with a donkey recalls the image of the king arriving in Jerusalem riding on a donkey in Zachariah 9:9, which the Talmud (*BT, Sanhedrin,* 98a, 99a) and New Testament (John 12:14–15) interpret as referring to the Messiah.

[128] See Hirsch, *Der Pentateuch,* 1:202; *The Hirsch Chumash,* 1:276 (Commentary to Genesis 11:7). In support of this Hirsch cites Psalms 144:14 *alufeinu mesubalim* (our leaders bear our burden). In his commentary on Psalms 144:14, Hirsch writes, "Our great men do not feed on the strength of the nation; instead it is they who bear the heavy burdens of the state . . . the highest strata of our nation set a precedent in the performance of duty." Hirsch, *Die Psalmen,* 2:344–345; *The Psalms,* 2:466–467 (Commentary on Psalms 144:14).

[129] Hirsch, *Der Pentateuch,* 1:201; *The Hirsch Chumash,* 1:274 (Commentary to Genesis 11:7).

[130] See *Genesis Rabbah* 18:4.

or to put them on a pedestal. For this reason, translating *ish* and *ishah* with the German equivalent *Mann* and *Weib* is inadequate, as it fails to convey the undertones of the Hebrew.[131] Practically, Hirsch's general approach in his translation is to use a basic German equivalent for the Hebrew word and then explain the concept embedded in the Hebrew in the commentary.

In some cases, Hirsch observes that Hebrew lacks an equivalent for a German word. He notes that every European language contains a word for *religion.* As we noted previously, Hirsch claims that Hebrew has no word for *religion* because *religion* implies that devotion to God occupies one limited sphere of life while in Judaism devotion to God is supposed to permeate all spheres of one's life.[132] In his commentary on Genesis 11:7, Hirsch adds that the word *religion* derives from the Latin *religare,* which mean "to bind." So in Christianity religion is a form of bondage. By contrast, Hirsch cites the talmudic sages' interpretation of the word *harut,* occurring in Exodus 32:16, as connected to the word *herut,* meaning "freedom." The verse refers to the Decalogue as being "engraved (*harut*) on the tablets."[133] The connection between *harut* (engraved) and *herut* (freedom) encodes the divine view that obedience to God's law is freedom.[134]

Hirsch's benign view of Yiddish

While for Hirsch every language encodes a particular worldview, aside from Hebrew no language is superior to another. This is reflected in Hirsch's attitude to Yiddish, which is very different than that expressed by Mendelssohn and Zunz. As we have seen, both Mendelssohn and Zunz disparage Yiddish for being a hybrid, corrupt language. By contrast, Hirsch writes relatively little about Yiddish and expresses no negative attitude toward it. In one of the few passages discussing Yiddish, Hirsch notes that the large number of Bible translations into Yiddish for females reflects the recognition of the importance of teaching females Torah.[135] Of course, Hirsch's benign view of Yiddish may also be due to the fact that in his time few German Jews

[131] Hirsch, *Der Pentateuch,* 1:203, 67; *The Hirsch Chumash,* 1:277, 90 (Commentary to Genesis 11:7, 2:23).

[132] See p. 322 of this volume.

[133] See *BT,* Eruvin, 54a.

[134] Hirsch, *Der Pentateuch,* 1:201–202; *The Hirsch Chumash,* 1:275 (Commentary to Genesis 11:7). There is an obvious connection here between Hirsch's view of Torah law and Kant's view of moral autonomy.

[135] See Hirsch, *Der Pentateuch,* 5:164; *The Hirsch Chumash,* 5:225 (Commentary to Deuteronomy 11:19). See pp. 285–286 of this volume.

still used Yiddish, which meant that it posed little threat to Jews becoming middle-class Germans.[136]

Hirsch's rejection of comparative Semitics

Hirsch's view of Hebrew as a divine language also explains one of the most controversial elements of his Pentateuch, namely, his idiosyncratic etymologies that eschew comparative Semitics.[137] Hirsch's rejecting comparative Semitics is especially striking given that Hirsch will compare the Hebrew of the Pentateuch not only to the Hebrew of the later books of the Bible, but also to rabbinic Hebrew and even to biblical and rabbinic Aramaic. This despite the fact that Hirsch recognizes that the meaning of Hebrew often changed over time and that Aramaic is a distinct language.[138]

Hirsch's not engaging in comparative Semitics is a direct consequence of his considering Hebrew the only divine language and all other languages as derivative from it. Nevertheless, Hirsch's approach raises several questions. Since other languages are derivative from Hebrew, could there not be value in comparing Hebrew to them? Why is Hirsch willing to compare Hebrew to biblical and rabbinic Aramaic, but not, for example, to Syriac?

136 Lowenstein notes that by 1800 no new Yiddish literary works were being published in Germany and that by the late 1830s literary Yiddish ceased to be published at all. The last edition of the *Tsenerene* was published in Sulzbach in 1836, and traditional Jewish printers in Frankfurt an der Oder, Dyhrenfurt, and Sulzbach went out of business in 1826, 1834, and 1851, respectively. See Lowenstein, "The Yiddish Written Word," 180–182; Lowenstein, "The Pace of Modernization," 45.

137 Max Heller writes that Hirsch was "blissfully ignorant of all Oriental languages outside of Hebrew and Aramaic." See Heller, "Samson Raphael Hirsch," 201. Kaufmann Kohler is much harsher, writing, "But no sooner is the scientific method of philological, historical, and psychological investigations applied to it [Hirsch's biblical etymology] than the whole structure proves a fabric of cobwebs." See Kohler, "Response to Heller," 212. Hirsch's failure to employ comparative Semitics stands in marked contrast to the approach taken by his teacher Isaac Bernays in *The Biblical Orient*. For example, Bernays claimed that the biblical name *Abram* derived from the Indian word *Brahma*, which referred to the creator god. See *Der Bibelsche Orient*, 1:20, 22. Scholars dispute the authorship of *The Biblical Orient*. Hans Bach and Isaac Heinemann argue that Bernays was the author or at least coauthor. See Bach, "Der Bibel'sche Orient und sein Verfasser"; Heinemann, "The Relationship between S.R. Hirsch and His Teacher Isaac Bernays," esp. 69–77. Rivka Horwitz argues that a Christian scholar H.A. Kalb authored the work, but that Bernays assisted him. See Horwitz, "On Kabbala and Myth in 19th Century Germany," esp. 139–156. Whether or not Bernays authored *The Biblical Orient*, Hirsch was clearly familiar with the work and knew that Bernays was widely assumed to be its author. See Hirsch, "Die Distellese des Herrn Kirchheim," 133.

138 On Hirsch's recognizing changes in Hebrew, see Hirsch, *Der Pentateuch* 1:344; *The Hirsch Chumash*, 1:478 (Commentary to Genesis 21:33); Hirsch, *Die Psalmen*, 2:91–92; *The Psalms*, 2:123 (Commentary to Psalm 89:3). Hirsch writes that Aramaic "should only be consulted if the vocabulary of the source language [Hebrew] does not provide the solution to the problem." See Hirsch, *Der Pentateuch*, 1:179; *The Hirsch Chumash*, 1:245 (Commentary to Genesis 9:27). See Breuer, "Preface," 10.

The answer lies in Hirsch's view that *language encodes worldview.* Hirsch regards the worldview of the Sages and the Bible as unified because of the inseparable connection between the Oral Torah and the Written Torah. But this worldview is radically distinct from that found in works written in other Semitic languages such as Syriac.[139]

When Hirsch speaks of Hebrew as a divine language that designates essentially, he does so for a very different purpose than Halevi. While for Halevi Hebrew designating essentially explains its magical powers, this view is anathema to Hirsch for reasons we have seen.[140] For Hirsch the significance of Hebrew designating essentially is that Hebrew reveals the *moral purpose of things.* Again we find Hirsch *prioritizing the moral over the metaphysical.*

Hirsch's translation method in his Pentateuch and Psalms

Hirsch's translation method in his Pentateuch and Psalms is guided by his response to *four factors* he sees as alienating readers from the Torah: (1) historicist approaches of the Bible that situate it in an ancient Near Eastern context far removed than the present; (2) the inability of most German Jews to appreciate the nuances of the Biblical texts; (3) Jews' acceptance of pessimistic, otherworldly *Christian* interpretations of the Bible and, in the case of the Pentateuch (4) *Wissenschaft*/Reform approaches that question the divinity of the Oral Torah and whether it constitutes the definitive interpretation of the Written Torah.

I will show that Hirsch seeks to address these problems through his translations in four ways: *first*, by presenting the Bible as a compelling living text through a vivid translation into proper, elegant German; *second*, by communicating the etymological nuances of the original Hebrew text in translation; *third*, by excluding pessimistic, otherworldly Christian interpretations of the Bible, and *fourth,* by accomodating midrashic interpretations in his translation.

139 See Breuer, "Preface," 10.
140 See p. 319 of this volume.

Balancing elegance and accuracy

Hirsch's preference for proper, elegant German over hyper-literalism can be seen by comparing translations from his Pentateuch (1867–1878) with Mendelssohn's *Be'ur*, Zunz's Pentateuch, and his own early Bible translations in *Horeb* (1837). I will again use the example of the law of chasing away the mother bird (Deuteronomy 22:6–7):[141]

Mendelssohn: *Wen dir auf dem Wege ein Vogelnest mit Küchlein oder Eiern aufstößt, am Baume oder auf der Erde, wo die Mutter auf den Küchlein oder Eiern sitzt. So sollst du nicht beide, die Mutter samt den Jungen ausheben. Die Mutter must du fligen lassen, und die Jungen kanst du dir nehmen. Damit es dir wohlgehe und du lange lebest.*[142]

Hirsch (*Horev*): *Wenn geführt wird Nest reinen Vogels in deine Richtung im Wege auf irgend Baum oder auf der Erde, aufblühende Junge oder Eier, und die Mutter ruhend auf den aufblühenden Jungen oder auf den Eiern, sollst du nicht nehmen die Mutter auf den Jungen. Vielmehr freyschicken sollst du die Mutter, und die Jungen magst du dir nehmen, drob wird dir Gutes werden, und du wirst Zeiten durchdauern.*[143]

Zunz: *Wenn ein Vogelnest sich vor dir findet auf dem Wege, auf irgend einem Baume oder auf der Erde, Küchlein oder Eier, und die Mutter liegt auf den Küchlein oder auf den Eiern; so sollst du nicht nehmen die Mütter über den Jungen. Fliegen lasse die Mutter und die Jungen nimm dir, auf daß es dir wohlgehe und du lange lebest.*[144]

Hirsch (*Der Pentateuch*) *Wenn ein Vogelnest vor dir auf dem Wege betroffen wird, auf irgend einem Baum oder auf der Erde, Junge oder Eier, und die Mutter ruht auf den Jungen oder auf den Eiern, sollst du nicht die Mutter auf den Jungen nehmen. Freischicken sollst du die Mutter, die Jungen aber darfst du dir nehmen; darob wird es dir gut ergehen, und du wirst lange leben.*[145]

Of all the translations, Mendelssohn's most forsakes the Hebrew form for the German. He follows German style by placing verbs at the end of clauses

[141] Because the texts are lengthy, I will not include English translations of the German.
[142] Mendelssohn, *JubA*, 9.2:216–217.
[143] Hirsch, *Horev*, Kap. 58, #411, 379; *Horeb*, Ch. 58, #411, 289.
[144] Zunz, *Die vier und zwanzig Bücher*, 188.
[145] Hirsch, *Der Pentateuch*, 5:369–371; *The Hirsch Chumash*, 5:509–511.

rather than putting them in the middle like Hebrew. Mendelssohn alone omits the Hebrew article ***b'khol*** in the phrase ***b'khol** eitz* (**in every** tree), and he alone omits the repetition of the article ***al*** in the phrase ***al** haefrohim **v'al** habeitzim* (**on** the chicks and **on** the eggs). Mendelssohn adds explanatory words not found in the original, such as the word ***beide*** (both), when translating the phrase that one should not take the mother and the chicks. Finally, Mendelssohn alone moves the verb beginning verse seven ***shale'ah teshalah*** *et ha'em* (**send away** the mother) to the end of the first clause, adding the interpretive word ***must*** (must) in his translation.

But with the exception of Mendelssohn's translation, Hirsch's translation in his Pentateuch is the one that most favors German style over Hebrew. Both Zunz and Hirsch in *Horeb* replicate the Hebrew form by placing verbs in the middle of clauses, while in his Pentateuch, Hirsch, like Mendelssohn, places verbs at the end of clauses. Similarly, in *Horeb*, Hirsch seeks to capture the precise meaning of the Hebrew by translating *efrohim* (chicks) as *aufblühende Junge* (blossoming young), while in his Pentateuch Hirsch uses the less precise but simpler and more elegant *Junge* (young).[146]

Perhaps surprisingly, Hirsch's translation in *Horeb* is often closer to the Hebrew even than Zunz's. For example, in *Horeb* Hirsch translates the reward promised for observing the law of *veha'arakhta yamim* highly literally as *und du wirst Zeiten durchdauern* (and you will prolong your days), while in his Pentateuch he translates it more colloquially as *und du wirst lange leben* (and you will live long), which is similar to Zunz, who follows Mendelssohn's translation of *und du lange lebest* (and you will live long). Hirsch alone in *Horeb* translates the Hebrew word *lefanekha* in the phrase ***lefanekha*** *baderekh*, which he renders as *in deine Richtung* (in your direction).[147]

Another example of Hirsch's attentiveness to German literary style involves his translation of names. Like Mendelssohn and Zunz, Hirsch seeks to preserve Hebrew names by transliterating them as *Mosche*, *Jaakob*, etc. But in the case of plurals, while Mendelssohn and Zunz transliterate the entire Hebrew name, Hirsch combines a transliteration of the Hebrew name with a German ending. For example, in translating the reference to the Ishmaelites

146 Zunz follows Mendelssohn in seeking a German equivalent for the Hebrew by using *Küchlein*.

147 I am not certain why Hirsch stays closer to the Hebrew in *Horeb* than in his Pentateuch, but one possibility is that in *Horeb* he is addressing alienated Jewish youth who lack familiarity with Hebrew, which Hirsch seeks to convey through his translations, while his Pentateuch is for members of his Orthodox community who generally have a greater familiarity with Hebrew. I will discuss the sectarian nature of Hirsch's Pentateuch in greater detail in the next chapter.

in Genesis 37:28, Mendelssohn follows the Hebrew by rendering the name as *Jischmeelim*, and Zunz follows the Hebrew even more closely by translating it as *Jischmaëlim*. But Hirsch translates it as *Jischmaeliten*, thereby Germanizing the Hebrew.

Making room for Midrash

While Hirsch seeks to produce an elegant German translation, in cases where the Oral Torah derives interpretations from the *form of the Hebrew*, Hirsch, like Mendelssohn, will often preserve this form in his Pentateuch even if it sounds odd in German. For example, we saw that Mendelssohn preserved the Hebrew form of Genesis 23:1, which he translated as *Es war das Lebensalter der Sarah, **hundert Jahr, und zwangzig Jahr und siben Jahr**; dises waren die Lebens Jahre der Sarah* (The lifespan of Sarah was **one hundred years, and twenty years and seven years**. These were Sarah's years of life). Mendelssohn's intent was to make room for the verse's midrashic interpretation. By contrast, Zunz adopted a translation that was not as close to Hebrew as Mendelssohn's: *Und es war die Lebenszeit Sarah's **hundert und sieben und zwanzig Jahre**; dies die Jahre der Lebenszeit Sarah's* (And the lifespan of Sarah was **one hundred and seven and twenty years**; These were the years of Sarah's lifetime). Guided by a historicist sensibility, Zunz was not concerned with making room for the midrashic interpretation.[148] Hirsch's translation is much closer to Mendelssohn's: *Es war das Leben Sara's **hundert Jahre und zwanzig Jahre und sieben Jahre**: Jahre des Lebens Sara's* (The life of Sara was **one hundred years, and twenty years, and seven years**; years of the life of Sara). In his commentary, Hirsch cites the famous Midrash on the verse.[149]

Hirsch especially seeks to preserve the form of the Hebrew in legal sections when it is midrashically interpreted. For example, Hirsch translates the phrase in Deuteronomy 16:20, *tzedek tzedek*, as *Recht, Recht verfolge* (Justice, justice pursue).[150] In his commentary, Hirsch cites the Talmud (*BT*, Sanhedrin, 32b), which interprets the repetition in the verse as meaning that justice must be pursued impartially whether one is issuing a judgment

[148] See 186–187 of this volume.

[149] See Hirsch, *Der Pentateuch*, 1:358–359; *The Hirsch Chumash*, 1:499–500 (Commentary to Genesis 23:1). See *Genesis Rabbah*, 58:1.

[150] In *Horev* he translates it similarly as *Gerechtigkeit, Gerechtigkeit, erstrebe!* See Hirsch, *Horev*, Kap. 44, #321, 285; *Horeb*, ch. 44, #321, 217.

or seeking a compromise.[151] Mendelssohn similarly translates the repetition as *Gerechtigkeit, Gerechtigkeit sollstu nachtrachten* (Justice, justice you shall pursue).[152] By contrast, Zunz does not translate the repetition, instead rendering the verse as *Der Gerechtigkeit sollst du nachjagen* (Justice you shall pursue).[153] In this case, Hirsch's translation is closest to the form of the Hebrew. While both Mendelssohn and Zunz use three words to translate the Hebrew word *tirdof* (Mendelssohn: *sollst du nachtrachten* and Zunz: *sollst du nachjagen*), Hirsch only use only one word (*verfolge*).

Like Mendelssohn and unlike Zunz, Hirsch translates according to the rabbinic interpretation in cases where the rabbinic interpretation of law contradicts the *peshat*. But unlike Mendelssohn, Hirsch makes no attempt to distinguish *peshat* from the rabbinic legal interpretation by adding parentheses. So while Mendelssohn translates Exodus 21:24–25 as (*Rechtswegen sollte*) *Auge für Auge* (*seyn*) . . . (*daher muß der Tädter Geld dafür geben*), ([according to justice it should be] eye for an eye . . . [therefore the offender must give money instead]), Hirsch translates it as *Auge Ersatz für Auge* (compensation of an eye for an eye).[154] Hirsch sees no reason to add parentheses since he considers the Pentateuch as the notes of the Oral Torah, which is the true meaning of the text.

Conveying nuance: Hirsch's etymological translations

Hirsch often translates in ways that seek to convey the Hebrew etymology. For example, Leviticus 1:2 states *adam ki* ***yakriv*** *mikem* ***korban*** *l'YHWH*. Mendelssohn translates the phrase as: *wen jemand von euch dem Ewigen zu Ehren ein* ***Opfer darbringen*** *wil* (if anyone among you wishes to **offer a sacrifice** to honor the Eternal).[155] Zunz translates it in a similar fashion as *So jemand von euch dem Ewigen* ***ein Opfer darbringen*** *will* (anyone among you who wishes to **offer a sacrifice** to the Eternal).[156] Hirsch, however, seeks to convey the etymological sense of the Hebrew by translating it as *ein Mensch, wenn er von euch ein* ***Opfer*** *G o t t* ***nahebringen*** *will* (If any human being

[151] Hirsch, *Der Pentateuch*, 5:270–271; *The Hirsch Chumash*, 5:373 (Commentary to Deuteronomy 16:20).
[152] Mendelssohn, *JubA*, 9.2:207.
[153] Zunz, *Die vier und zwanzig Bücher*, 183.
[154] Hirsch, *Der Pentateuch*, 2:273; *The Hirsch Chumash*, 2:397.
[155] Mendelssohn, *JubA*, 9.2:3.
[156] Zunz, *Die vier und zwanzig Bücher*, 94.

among you wishes to **bring near a sacrifice** to *God*).[157] While Hirsch follows Mendelssohn and Zunz in using the standard German word for sacrifice, *Opfer*, to translate *korban*, he translates the word *yakriv*, which designates the act of bringing the sacrifice, as *nahebringen* (bring near) rather than the more standard *darbringen* (offer).

In his commentary, Hirsch explains that Western languages have no word that can adequately express the concept expressed by the term *korban*. The German word *Opfer* (sacrifice) connotes "destruction, annihilation, and loss," while the Hebrew word *korban* has no such connotation. Even the Latin word *offero*, which does not imply loss, fails to adequately capture the sense of *korban*, for it implies that one is offering something to a recipient who needs to be satisfied. By contrast, the Hebrew word *korban* derives from the root ק.ר.ב, which means "to draw near," and refers solely to the needs of the one presenting it, not to the needs of the recipient. Hirsch explains that *korban* implies "positive attainment, the realization of a more noble existence," which comes from drawing near to God. Not only does *Opfer* fail to convey this, but it also conveys the opposite since it implies that worshipping God requires self-annihilation. While Hirsch retains the standard translation of *korban* as *Opfer for* the sake of elegance, he conveys the sense of *korban* as "drawing near" by translating *yakriv as nahebringen*.[158]

Another example of Hirsch seeking to preserve the Hebrew etymology in his translation occurs in Genesis 1:26. The first part of the verse reads *vayomer elohim na'aseh adam*. Mendelssohn translates it as *Got sprach, nun wollen wir einen Mensch machen* (God said, now we wish a human being to make). Zunz similarly translates: *Und Gott sprach: Laßt uns machen einen Menschen* (And God said: let us make a human being). Hirsch, however, translates: *Gott sprach: Wir wollen einen Adam (Stellvertreter) machen* (God said: we wish an Adam [representative] to make).

Hirsch understands the word *adam* (אדם) as connected to *hadom* (הדום), meaning "footstool," since human beings are God's "footstools," that is, the "agents and bearers" of God's glory on earth. In his Pentateuch commentary Hirsch similarly notes that *adam* (אדם) is related to *hatam* (חתם), meaning "seal," explaining that human beings are the seal through which God can be seen on earth.[159]

157 Hirsch, *Der Pentateuch*, 3:4; *The Hirsch Chumash*, 3:3.

158 Hirsch, *Der Pentateuch*, 3:3; *The Hirsch Chumash*, 3:5–6. Buber and Rosenzweig follow Hirsch on this point, taking him even further by translating *yakriv korban* as *Nahung darnaht* (near a nearing).

159 See Hirsch, *Der Pentateuch*, 1:30–31; *The Hirsch Chumash*, 1:39–40 (Commentary to Genesis 1:26). Hirsch could have also cited Ezekiel 28:12: "O mortal (*ben adam*), intone a dirge over the king of Tyre and say to him: Thus said God YHWH you were the seal (*hotam*) of perfection: full of wisdom and flawless in beauty."

Hirsch conveys this etymological meaning by transliterating the Hebrew word *adam* and adding in parentheses that it means "representative" in his translation.

Countering Christianity

We have seen that in Mendelssohn's time respectable Protestant Bible scholars still interpreted the Old Testament Christologically and that Mendelssohn worried about young Jews using Christian Bible translations. By contrast, Zunz was animated by a *Wissenschaft* ethos and took for granted that no serious Protestant Bible scholar would interpret the Old Testament Christologically. As such, Zunz was not particularly concerned with excluding such interpretations.[160]

Like Mendelssohn, Hirsch is concerned with Christian interpretations of the Bible, but for different reasons. Hirsch is not particularly worried that such interpretations will tempt Jews to convert. His much greater concern is that such interpretations *alienate young Jews from Judaism*.

Hirsch's greatest concern is with Christian interpretations of the Bible that treat human beings as irredeemably sinful, demand irrational faith as the condition for salvation, and assert that peace will only come to the world through apocalyptic destruction. He worries that such understandings of the Bible lead young Jews committed to moral freedom, reason, and the value of this worldly existence to reject *all biblically based religion, including Judaism*.[161] Hirsch sees an important task of his Pentateuch and Psalms as showing that these interpretations of the Torah are wrong. As he puts it in an 1866 essay, "Should we not consider . . . that we are performing an act of rescue if we guide our young directly to the original source of this spirit? They will then see that the ideas actually expressed in that source are completely different from what is being taught."[162]

Original Sin

In his Pentateuch, Hirsch rejects the doctrine of original sin, writing that Christians "concocted [this] lie (*Lüge*) that undermines the moral future of humanity (*sittliche Zukunft des Menschen*)," through interpretations of the

[160] See pp. 185–186 of this volume.
[161] See Hirsch's 1866 essay "Some Suggestions Regarding the Role of Hebrew in General Education," in Hirsch, *GS*, 2:445; *CW*, 7:76.
[162] Ibid.

Garden of Eden. Hirsch claims that a Jew must protest "with his entire being" against this "regrettable error."[163]

For Hirsch, the problem with original sin is that it assumes that human beings have "lost the ability to do good." This naturally leads to the idea that the only way to achieve salvation is through faith in a divine "intermediary who has died and been resurrected." In fact, Hirsch asserts, not only are these teachings not found in the Torah, they are also diametrically opposed to it. Hirsch acknowledges that the Torah teaches that Adam and Eve defied God, were expelled from the Garden of Eden, punished for their sin, and that life has been more difficult for humanity ever since. But Hirsch explains that the reason that the "world no longer smiles" on humanity is not because human beings have inherited sinfulness, but because they continue to follow Adam and Eve in disobeying God. For Hirsch, the Torah teaches that the way to escape sin is not through irrational faith in a divine redeemer but, rather, by "ascending the highest levels of morality and spirituality" by obeying God's commandments.[164] Rather than see the world as an irredeemable vale of tears, Hirsch writes that the *"sum-total of God's Torah"* is the teaching that humanity's task is to *"transfigure and elevate earthly life to God and the divine by exercising the inalienable moral power given to each human being"* (emphasis in original).[165]

The dignity of the body: Eve and the Serpent (Genesis 3:15)

We have seen that Genesis 3:15, which describes the enmity between Eve and the serpent, is an important test case for Christology. Consider Luther's, Mendelssohn's, and Hirsch's translation of the last part of the verse:

Luther: *Der selbe soll dir den Kopf zertreten, und du wirst ihn in die Ferse stechen* [he will crush your head and you will bite his heel]

[163] Hirsch, *Der Pentateuch,* 1:84–85; *The Hirsch Chumash,* 1:113–114 (Commentary to Genesis 3:19). See Hirsch, *GS,* 2:445; *CW,* 7:76.

[164] Hirsch also emphasizes that in contrast to Christianity, Judaism stresses the humanity of its redeemer (Moses). See Hirsch, *Der Pentateuch,* 2:64; *The Hirsch Chumash,* 2:92–93 (Commentary to Exodus 6:14).

[165] Hirsch, *Der Pentateuch,* 1:84–85; *The Hirsch Chumash,* 1:113–114 (Commentary to Genesis 3:19). Elsewhere Hirsch writes that the fundamental problem with Christian interpretations of the Bible is that Christians view it primarily as a work of theology, teaching "transcendental dogmas" (*transcendentalen Dogmas*) about God that one needs to believe to be saved; while in reality the Torah is a work of "divine anthropology" (*göttliche Anthropologie*), teaching one how to orient oneself in world and live according to God's will. See Hirsch, *GS,* 2:433–434, 445; *CW,* 7:63–64, 76–77.

Mendelssohn: *Diser soll dir den Kopf verwunden, und du ihm die Ferse verwunden* [**this one** will wound your head and you will wound his heel]
Hirsch: *Er wird dich auf das Haupt treffen und du wirst ihn auf die Ferse treffen* [**it** will strike at your head and you will strike at his heel][166]

Luther translates the verse as referring to Jesus's battle with the devil, interpreting it to mean that only Jesus "can overcome sin, death, and hell and deliver us from the violence of the snake." By contrast, Mendelssohn translates the verse to mean that Eve's "seed" will crush the head of the snake while the seed of the snake will bite their heels.[167] Citing Ibn Ezra, Mendelssohn interprets the story as referring to a real snake. Originally, the snake walked and talked, but as a punishment for tempting Eve its descendants slither on their bellies and do not talk. Genesis 3:15 refers to the subsequent enmity between human beings and snakes.[168]

Like Luther, Hirsch does not understand Genesis 3:15 as referring to actual snakes. But while for Luther the Bible is speaking about a real being, namely, the devil, Hirsch interprets the snake as a metaphor for sensual desire. Hirsch makes clear that sensual desire is not intrinsically bad. Animals only know and fulfill God's will by following their sensual desires. But for human beings who are granted moral freedom, God's will is known through the revealed commandments and is fulfilled by obeying them. Hirsch interprets God telling Eve that her seed will experience enmity with the seed of the snake as referring to human beings' moral struggle between following God's commandments or following sensual desire.

Hirsch translates ***hu** yeshufkha rosh **ve'atah** teshufenu akev* as **Er** *wird dich auf das Haupt treffen und du wirst ihn auf die Ferse treffen* (**it** will strike at your head and you will strike at his heel). Hirsch explains that in stating that the human being will strike the head of the serpent but the serpent will only strike the human being's heel, the Torah is teaching that "human beings have greater power over desire (*Begierde*) than it has over them." While Christianity teaches that human beings have no power over desire and that sin can be only be overcome by giving up the struggle and having faith in

166 Hirsch, *Der Pentateuch*, 1:79–80.
167 See p. 61 note 181, pp. 184–185 of this volume.
168 See Mendelssohn, *JubA*, 15.1, 30 (Commentary to Genesis 3:1); 34–35 (Commentary to Genesis 3:15).

Jesus, for Hirsch the Torah teaches that human beings are capable of obeying God's commandments.[169]

Hirsch stresses that in speaking of the importance of mastering desire, the Bible contradicts the Christian teaching that the body is bad. Genesis 1:26 states that humans were created in God's *tzelem*, which is generally translated as "image." As we have seen, Mendelssohn translates the word as *Ebenbilde* (likeness) and interprets it to refer to human beings' capacity to know truth and rule the earth through intellect.[170] Hirsch, however, translates *tzelem* as *würdigen Hülle* (worthy covering), referring to the human body. For Hirsch, the Torah is teaching one "to recognize the divine dignity of the human *body* . . . [and] that the purpose of the entire law (*ganze Gesetz*) is not only to sanctify the spirit but also to sanctify the body . . . [which] is the basis of all human morality" (emphasis in original).[171]

The perfectibility of the world: against apocalypticism (Psalm 110)
Hirsch's approach to eschatology and apocalypticism can be understood by comparing his translation of Psalm 110:1, 6, to Luther's and Mendelssohn's translations.

> **Luther**: (1) *Ein Psalm Davids: Der HERR sprach zu meinem Herrn: Setze dich zu meiner Rechten, bis ich deine Feinde zum Schemel deiner Füße lege . . .* (6) *er wird richten unter den Heiden, er wird ein großes Schlagen unter ihnen tun, er wird zerschmettern das Haupt über große Lande.*
>
> **Mendelssohn**: (1) *An David: ein Psalm. Der Ewge spricht zu meinem Herrn Verweile hier zu meiner Rechten! Ich werde deine Feinde dir, zum Schemel deiner Füsse legen . . .* (6) *Er wird Nationen richten Auf hochgethürmten Leichen, Der itzt das Haupt von Rabba schlug.*
>
> **Hirsch:** (1) *An David. Ein Psalm. Es sprach G o t t zu meinem Herrn: warte nur mir zur Rechten, bis Ich deine Feinde zum Schemel deiner Füß gebe . . .* (6) *Er wird einst unter Völkern das Leichenvolle richten, nachdem er das über mächtiges Land gebietende Haupt gespalten.* [To David. A Psalm. The Lord

[169] See Hirsch, *Der Pentateuch,* 1:71–72; 78–80; *The Hirsch Chumash,* 1:94–96, (Commentary to Genesis 3:1); 106–107 (Commentary to Genesis 3:15).

[170] Mendelssohn, *JubA,* 15.2:13 (Commentary on Genesis 1:26). See pp. 98–99 of this volume.

[171] Hirsch, *Der Pentateuch,* 1:32–33; *The Hirsch Chumash,* 1:42–43 (Commentary to Genesis 1:27). Also see Hirsch, *GS,* 5:188–189; *CW,* 8:54. For Hirsch, the Bible refers to human beings' *spiritual likeness* to God through the world *demut,* which he translates as *Ebenbilde* (likeness). See Hirsch, *Der Pentateuch,* 1:30–31; *The Hirsch Chumash,* 1:40; Hirsch, *GS,* 188–189; *CW,* 8:54. Hirsch's approach to the term *tzelem* in his Pentateuch differs from his approach in the *Nineteen Letters.* See p. 268 of this volume.

said to my master: wait at My right hand, until I make your enemies your footstool... He shall one day judge the cadaverous among the nations, after He will have cleft the head that commands over the mighty land.]

Like Mendelssohn, Hirsch translates the first verse of the Psalm as being addressed *to* David with God instructing David to sit as God's right hand as God vanquishes David's enemies. In his commentary, Hirsch notes that David had two missions: an earthly one to subdue nations militarily and a "spiritual" (*geistigen*) mission "to win the hearts of men for God, by the power of his word and the influence of his actions." Hirsch makes clear that this latter task was the more important one. He interprets verse 1 as God telling David that he has done enough militarily and that God will do the rest. David's task henceforth is to dedicate himself solely to his spiritual mission.[172]

The key element of Hirsch's translation is his translation of verse 6. Luther had interpreted it eschatologically as referring to Jesus's apocalyptic judging the pagans and wreaking destruction on them during his Second Coming. Mendelssohn interpreted the verse non-eschatologically as referring to the historical event of King David's victory over the King of Rabba.

Like Luther, Hirsch interprets verse 6 eschatologically. But he rejects the apocalyptic elements of Luther's translation. The key phrase is *yadin bagoyim malei geviyot.* While Luther interprets this as referring to Jesus judging the pagans by striking a heavy blow resulting in many corpses, Hirsch interprets *malei geviyot* as referring not to the *result* of the judgment, but to its *cause.* The reason that God judges the nations is because they are "cadaverous" (*Leichenvolle*), having amassed their wealth through murder. For Hirsch, the Christian apocalyptic interpretation of the Psalm that the world must be destroyed for righteousness to prevail contradicts the Torah's true teaching that the world is morally perfectible.[173]

Against the Trinity: God's breath (Genesis 1:2)

Hirsch's approach to the *ru'ah elohim* of Genesis 1:2 provides another good example of how he rejects Christian theology. We have seen that Luther translates *ru'ah elohim* as *Geist Gottes* (spirit of God) and understands this as a reference to the Holy Ghost, the third person of the

172 Hirsch, *Die Psalmen,* 2:206; *The Psalms,* 2:281–282.
173 Hirsch, *Die Psalmen,* 2:208; *The Psalms,* 2:284.

Godhead. Mendelssohn translates it as *götliche Geist* (divine spirit) to avoid this Christological interpretation but understands *ru'ah elohim* as referring to spirit separate from matter.

Hirsch translates the phrase entirely differently, as *ein Gottes-Odem* (a breath of God). In his commentary, Hirsch explains that this phrase conveys the fact that while today "the breath of God is interwoven into the earthly matter and produces life from it," at the time of creation it was "hovering over the waters."[174] In other words, the *ru'ah elohim* is a divine generative principle infusing earthly existence. Rather than conceive God's spirit as a person of the Godhead or as God being radically separate from the world, Hirsch stresses that God's spirit permeates the physical world while not being identical or reducible to it. Hirsch regards the emphasis on God's spirit dwelling in the earthly world as a central teaching of the Torah, which is expressed by the rabbinic phrase *ikkar shekhinah batahtonim* (God's primary presence is below), a phrase that Hirsch cites multiple times in his commentary.[175]

In addition to the aims that I have mentioned here, there was an immediate, cause for Hirsch publishing his Pentateuch, which is central to understanding its purpose: the stunning success of a new Jewish Bible translation and commentary, to which I now turn.

[174] Hirsch, *Der Pentateuch*, 1:8–9; *The Hirsch Chumash*, 1:9–10 (Commentary to Genesis 1:2).

[175] See *Genesis Rabbah* 19:7. Hirsch quotes this phrase in at least three separate places. See Hirsch, *Der Pentateuch*, 1:75, 183, 426–427; *The Hirsch Chumash*, 1:100–101, 250, 598 (Genesis 3:8, 9:27, 28:10). There is an obvious affinity between Hirsch's embodied translation of *ru'ah elohim* as *Gottes-Odem* and Buber-Rosenzweig's translation of it as *Braus Gottes* (God's surging).

8

The Fracturing of German Judaism

Ludwig Philippson's Inclusive *Israelite Bible* and Hirsch's Sectarian Neo-Orthodox Pentateuch

Ludwig Philippson (1811–1889) was one of the most effective nineteenth-century Reform leaders. Rabbi of a congregation in Magdeburg, he edited the most important nineteenth-century German Jewish newspaper, was an activist for Jewish emancipation, and wrote historical novels aimed at Jewish communal edification.

Philippson convened the first Reform rabbinical assembly in Brunswick and is typically described as a "moderate Reformer."[1] He did not, however, primarily define himself denominationally. In an imaginary dialogue in which he was asked whether he was Orthodox or Reform, Philippson responded, "Neither! I am an Historical Jew."[2]

In January 1834 at age 23, Philippson published the first volume of a new magazine titled *Israelite Sermon and Synagogue Magazine* (*Israelitisches Predigt und Schul Magazin*). In his opening editorial Philippson surveyed the history of the "spiritual and religious life" of German Jews over the past century. Philippson was particularly concerned by widening fissures within German Jewry.

Philippson began his history conventionally. A hundred years earlier the condition of German Jews was no different than it had been for the previous centuries. Despised by Christians and occupying the lowliest position in civil society, German Jews suffered from the greatest "ignorance" (*Unbildung*), their only learning being in traditional Jewish texts. Philippson noted that from this "cinder heap" (*Zunderhaufen*) a "spark" (*Funken*) shot forth—Mendelssohn.[3] Through his German and Hebrew writings, especially his

[1] See Meyer, *Response to Modernity*, 108. On his convening the Brunswick assembly, see pp 308–309 of this volume.

[2] See Philippson, "Ein Glaubensbekenntniss," in *AZJ* 19 (1855): 1, cited in Shargel, "Ludwig Philippson," 32–33.

[3] Philippson, "Einleitung: Über das Leben des Judenthums," 5–6.

The Jewish Reformation. Michah Gottlieb, Oxford University Press (2021). © Oxford University Press.
DOI: 10.1093/oso/9780199336388.003.0009

Bible translation and commentary, Mendelssohn and his associates effected an "enormous change" in the outlook of German Jews. By elevating Bible study over Talmud study, Mendelssohn laid the groundwork for a "revolution in Jewish religious life."[4]

According to Philippson, Mendelssohn's efforts led Jews to renewed study of the Bible and greater participation in European cultural life, resulting in closer connections between Jews and Christians. But Philippson noted that Mendelssohn's reformatory efforts soon led to an impasse. Mendelssohn had constructed a philosophical concept of Judaism out of the Bible while remaining committed to the ceremonial law and rabbinic Judaism. But his approach did not satisfy many of his students and followers who came to regard the ceremonial law as unnecessary and oppressive. Some embraced Deism, which Philippson described as a "superficial" French philosophy that Kant had already "destroyed."[5]

While these Jewish Deists had little use for Judaism, another group soon emerged that sought to reform Judaism's "ancient constitution" to meet the demands of "contemporary *Bildung*." Consisting primarily of "educated youths" and successful businessmen, this group of Reformers "withdrew themselves from rabbinism" and sought to create a new house of worship that would hold "improved" religious services. "German Israelite Temples" (*deutsch-Israelitscher Tempel*) were rapidly established in Hamburg, Berlin, and Leipzig.[6]

As the Reform faction grew, it was met by an energetic, rigidly "Orthodox" (*Orthodoxen*) party that sought to preserve the older forms of German Judaism. The majority of German Jews were not willing to surrender the "laws and regulations of their fathers" for the sake of *Bildung* and aligned with the Orthodox party. Hatred and persecution raged, at times even dividing families. Philippson noted that in the midst of this struggle an increasing number of Jews turned away from both Reform and Orthodoxy and instead inclined to "shallow indifferentism" (*schalen Indifferentismus*) or "*Hyperbildung*," which equated culture with materialism and sensual pleasure. For Philippson, this "indifferentism" was much more dangerous than old German Judaism, as it undermined all striving for the good and the beautiful.[7]

4 Ibid., 6.
5 Ibid., 7.
6 Ibid., 11.
7 Ibid., 11–13.

For Philippson, a new vision for German Jewry was needed that would unite Reform and Orthodoxy while renewing Jewish commitment among the indifferent. He writes: "What is the most important need of Judaism? *Unity* and *Oneness.* This involves respect for the old [forms of Jewish] existence in which Judaism moved for a thousand years and was handed down, continual striving for *Bildung*, and relevance. *History and Reason* together form the foundation of the human race. When separated they are destructive, but when united they preserve truth, justice, and religion" (emphasis in original).[8] For Philippson, scholarly historical study would save Judaism by uniting Jews. It would do so by promoting respect for Jewish texts and traditions alongside the striving for *Bildung.*

Three years after launching the *Israelite Sermon and Synagogue Magazine*, Philippson replaced it with a new newspaper, the *General Newspaper of Judaism: A Nonpartisan Voice for All Jewish Interests* (*Allgemeine Zeitung des Judenthums: Ein unpartheiisches Organ für alles jüdische Interesse*). The newspaper's name expressed Philippson's desire to create a unified, nonsectarian platform for German Jewry.[9]

Philippson's efforts to unify German Jewry were not limited to his journalistic projects. In 1836, he decided to produce the first German Jewish translation and commentary on all twenty-four books of the Bible.[10]

Publishing an Israelite Bible

Philippson published his Bible, with the Hebrew title *Mikra Torah Nevi'im Ketuvim* (*Scripture: Torah, Prophets Writings*) and the German title *Die Israelitische Bibel* (*The Israelite Bible*), from 1839 to 1854.[11] In 1858, he published a second edition in three large volumes.

On March 21, 1859, Philippson issued a call in his newspaper to create an Israelite Bible Institute (*Israelitischen Bibelanstalt*) to finance a new edition of his Bible. To generate support, Philippson warned his readers that a new edition of his Bible was desperately needed because missionaries were "infiltrating the Jewish masses" by supplying them with cheap Lutheran Bible

[8] Ibid., 14. See Gillman, *A History of German Jewish Bible Translation,* 162.

[9] See Shargel, "Ludwig Philippson," 33–34.

[10] See Philippson's 1877 "Overview of Biblical Works," translated in Shargel, "Ludwig Philippson," 271.

[11] Philippson authored the entire translation and commentary with the exception of the Former Prophets, which his brother Phoebius produced.

translations that "frequently contradict the Jewish viewpoint."[12] Philippson's call was a resounding success. By 1862 there were over 100,000 Philippson Bibles in circulation, and within four years that number had tripled.[13] The Bible that Freud's father gifted him for his thirty-fifth birthday was a Philippson Bible.[14]

That Philippson regarded his Bible as a way to unify German Jewry is clear both from his description of it and from the title he gave it. He described his Bible as "an estimable gift *for all confessions*." Its title *The Israelite Bible* expressed his aspiration that it become *the* Bible for all German Jews.[15]

Philippson's desire to create a Bible that would be adopted by all German Jews can be discerned in the introduction to the Pentateuch that he included in the first edition of the work in 1844. Philippson repeatedly uses the word "unity" (*Einheit*) to describe his exegetical approach. He distinguishes between the "inner unity" (*innere Einheit*) and "external unity" (*äussern Einheit*) of the Pentateuch. For Philippson, the Pentateuch's "inner unity" refers to the consistency of its basic "ideas" (*Ideen*), "direction" (*Tendenz*), and "teachings" (*Lehre*), as he claims that the Pentateuch presents a consistent, compelling vision for life.[16] The Pentateuch's central teachings are: (1) a single, eternal, immutable, incorporeal, holy God created the world; (2) God created human beings in God's image by giving them a free spiritual essence (*freies, geistiges Wesen*) through which knowledge of God and the path to holiness is revealed; (3) holiness is attained by loving God, loving one's neighbor by practicing justice and compassion, and purifying the body by not eating blood (see Genesis 9:4); (4) God provided a special revelation to the Israelites, which includes: (i) religious rituals that remind them of the existence of the unique God; (ii) the strictest laws of justice and specific injunctions about helping the needy that promote love of one's neighbor; (iii) laws of marriage and chastity, restrictions on food, and prohibitions on contacting dead bodies that promote "purity" (*Reinigkeit*); (5) the Israelites received this special revelation to bear "witness" (*bezeugen*) to God and show humanity the path to holiness.[17]

12 See Philippson, "Overview of Biblical Works," in Shargel, "Ludwig Philippson," 273; Hermann, "Translating Cultures and Texts in Reform Judaism," 173–175. Hermann quotes part of the appeal.

13 See Kayserling, *Ludwig Philippson: Eine Biographie*, 268; Kornfeld, "Ludwig Philippson," 175.

14 Hermann, "Translating Cultures and Texts," 171.

15 See Hermann, "Translating Cultures and Texts in Reform Judaism," 174.

16 Philippson, *Die Israelitische Bibel*, "Einleitung in die fünf Bücher Moscheh," 1:viii.

17 Ibid., 1: vii.

For Philippson, the Bible portrays vivid characters to promote its central teachings. Biblical heroes were "*never idealized, but rather [depicted] in their natural simplicity . . . painted with the aura of pure truth.* Virtue and vice, praiseworthy and blameworthy actions are represented with the same detail and shades without praise or reproach except when coming from the actors themselves" (emphasis in original).[18] The fact that the Bible depicts both the virtues and vices of its characters makes them relatable. It also shows that the Bible is a realistic work that should be classified as "pure *history* (*Geschichte*), never as *poetry* (*Dichtung*)" (emphasis in original).[19]

In addition to the Pentateuch's "inner unity," Philippson stresses its "external unity." This refers to the accuracy of Pentateuchal history, geography, and chronology; the integrity of the Masoretic Text; and its being composed by a single author.[20] To ground the Pentateuch's "external unity," Philippson uses *Wissenschaft* methods favored by Reformers, but for conservative ends favored by Orthodox Jews.

To show the accuracy of biblical history and geography, Philippson cites travel literature and scholarship to show that the Pentateuch's description of various localities and peoples conforms to knowledge gleaned from extra-biblical sources.[21] For example, Philippson writes that "the dishes that the Israelites craved in the wilderness [upon leaving Egypt] were the same foods as eaten by the local Arab *fallahin* who live there today."[22] To bring the Bible's historicity to life, Philippson includes hundreds of woodcuts that depict ancient "topography, antiquities, and natural history."[23] For example, in his commentary on Genesis 8:4, Philippson supplies a woodcut of Mount Ararat, telling us that it is 17,260 feet high, lies at latitude 39.30 north and longitude 44.30 east in the Taurus mountain chain, and is today called *Kuhi Nuch*.[24] He further notes that the Armenian city of Nakshivan, which is near

[18] Ibid., 1: viii.

[19] Ibid. Philippson probably has Herder in mind.

[20] Philippson, *Die Israelitische Bibel*, "Einleitung in die fünf Bücher Moscheh," 1:xii–xxxvii.

[21] See Kayserling, *Ludwig Philippson*, 70.

[22] Philippson, *Die Israelitische Bibel*, "Einleitung in die fünf Bücher Moscheh," 1:xii. Like many nineteenth-century Bible scholars, Philippson believed that "oriental" culture remained largely frozen in time. While precipitous changes such as the adoption of Islam occasionally occurred, "oriental" culture was immune to gradual change. See Philippson, *The Development of the Religious Idea*, 168, 224. On other German Bible scholars who held similar views, see Hess, *Germans, Jews and the Claims of Modernity*, pp. 51–52, 58–79.

[23] See Philippson, "Overview of Biblical Works," cited in Shargel, "Ludwig Philippson," 271–272. For a recent study of the source of Philippson's woodcuts, see Wittler, "Towards a Bookish History of German Jewish Culture."

[24] Philippson, *Die Israelitische Bibel*, 1:36 (Commentary to Genesis 8:4).

Ararat, draws its name from Nak, which is a reference to Noah, and Shivan, which means "fixed," and alludes to the fact that Noah's ark grounded on Mount Ararat.[25]

Philippson also argues at length for the unity of the Pentateuch by citing dozens of places where later biblical books reference the Pentateuch. For Philippson this shows that the Pentateuch is a single book that was completed before the later books of the Bible were written.[26] On the basis of this and other considerations, Philippson concludes that the Bible originated "from *one* author" (*von einem Verfasser*), that the books were "*a product of the Mosaic period*," and finally that "*the author could only be Moses himself*" (emphasis in original).[27] In these ways, Philippson casts himself as an ardent opponent of biblical criticism, which he calls "hypothesis-hunting" (*Hypothesenjagd*) leading to "bottomless confusion" (*bodenlose Verwirrung*).[28]

To get a sense of Philippson's exegetical method, it is worth exploring an example from his commentary.

How long were the Israelites in Egypt?

Philippson defends Pentateuchal chronologies that nineteenth-century Bible critics had analyzed to question the Pentateuch's historicity.[29] A famous problem concerns the length of time that the Israelites sojourned in Egypt. Exodus 12:40 states that the Israelites dwelt there for 430 years. But the Bible's genealogies of the Israelites who dwelt in Egypt up to the Exodus do not add up to 430 years. The medieval Jewish commentators were already aware of this problem and contended that when Exodus 12:40 states that the Israelites dwelled in Egypt for 430 years, these years begin with events in Abraham's life.[30] In the *Be'ur*,

[25] Ibid., 1: 42–43 (Commentary to Genesis 9:20). See Figure 22.

[26] Philippson, *Die Israelitische Bibel*, "Einleitung in die fünf Bücher Moscheh," 1:xvi–xxii.

[27] Ibid., 1: xxiv–xxvi.

[28] See the passages cited in Kayserling, *Ludwig Philippson*, 70. Philippson's assertions and methods are very similar to those used by the conservative Protestant Bible critic Ernst Wilhelm Hengstenberg, especially in his 1839 *Beiträge zur Einleitung ins Alte Testament* (*Contributions to an Introduction to the Old Testament*), Volume 3, which is subtitled "Die Authentie des Pentateuches" ("The Authenticity of the Pentateuch"). Philippson cites Hengstenberg frequently in his biblical commentary, and a comparison of their work is a scholarly desiderata.

[29] See Philippson, *Die Israelitische Bibel*, "Einleitung in die fünf Bücher Moscheh," 1:xiv, note 1. Philippson's general approach is similar to Hengstenberg's who devotes a section of his *Beiträge* to resolving "chronological contradictions" (*Chronologische Widersprüche*) in the Pentateuch raised by Bible critics such as Peter von Bohlen, Ferdinand Hitzig, De Wette, and others. See Hengstenberg, *Beiträge zur Einleitung ins Alte Testament*, 2:347–359.

[30] For example, Rashi enumerates the 430 years from the time of the "Covenant of the Pieces" (Genesis: 15:13) when God promised Abraham that his descendants would be slaves in Egypt before

Mendelssohn addresses the problem of the 430 years by engaging with the medieval Jewish exegetes, ultimately siding with Nahmanides.[31]

In a long comment on Exodus 12:40, Philippson outlines the problem and the answers given to it by the medieval Jewish exegetes.[32] But while the medieval exegetes and Mendelssohn seek to resolve the problem solely on the basis of *biblical texts* to solve it. Philippson also adduces *extra-biblical texts.* He cites the Septuagint version (in the original Greek) which states that the Israelites dwelt in Egypt *and Canaan* for 430 years, and the Samaritan Bible which states that the Israelites *and their ancestors* dwelt in Egypt *and Canaan* for 430 years, as well as Targum Jonathan, Paul's Letter to the Galatians, and Josephus's *Antiquities of the Jews*, to show that the "conjectures" (*Annahme*) raised by the medieval Jewish exegetes that the 430 years begin in Abraham's life are ancient traditions.[33] But Philippson defends the Masoretic Text by employing the principle of *lectio difficilior potior* (the more difficult reading is the stronger) to argue that the textual variants found in the Septuagint and Samaritan Bible are interpolations.[34]

Philippson then presents his own approach. His begins by noting another problem, namely, that according to the book of Numbers, approximately two and half million Israelites left Egypt.[35] As Genesis states that only sixty-six Israelites went down to Egypt (see Genesis 46:26) and records only three or four generations from Jacob to the Exodus, Philippson notes that many Bible scholars have regarded the Bible's accounting of the number of Israelites who left Egypt as absurd. He seeks to resolve the problem by linking it with the problem of the 430 years.[36]

Philippson observes that according to Genesis, Levi had three sons whom he brought down to Egypt, one of whom was named Kehat (see Genesis 46:8, 11). Moses was Levi's grandson through his mother and great-grandson

being freed. Ibn Ezra enumerates the 430 years from the time Abraham left his home in Ur of the Chaldees. Nahmanides enumerates the 430 years from the birth of Isaac.

31 See the previous note. Mendelsohn, *JubA*, 16:102–103 (Commentary on Exodus 12:40).

32 See Philippson, *Die Israelitsche Bibel*, 1:365 (Commentary to Exodus 12:40).

33 Philippson cites Targum Jonathan to Exodus 12:40, Galatians 3:17, and Josephus, *Antiquities of the Jews*, Part II, ch. 15.2. The references to Targum Jonathan and Josephus make sense, but it is unclear why Philippson cites Galatians, which simply states that the Israelites were in Egypt for 430 years without discussing how those years are enumerated.

34 Philippson, *Die Israelitsche Bibel*, 1:365 (Commentary to Exodus 12:40).

35 Philippson notes that Numbers 1:46 states that 603,550 adult males over age twenty left Egypt, which does not include an additional 22,000 Levites. Philippson reckons that when one adds women and children one gets about two and half million Israelites who left Egypt.

36 Philippson, *Die Israelitsche Bibel*, 1:365 (Commentary to Exodus 12:40).

through his father through the line of Kehat (see Exodus 6:16–20). Exodus 6:18 states that Kehat had four sons, the oldest of whom was Amram. Amram had two sons, Aaron and Moses, and Aaron and Moses had six children combined (see Exodus 6:18–20, 23; 18:3–4). So Amram's family had nine blood members (including himself) before the Exodus. Of the other three sons of Kehat (Yizhar, Hevron, and Uziel), Exodus tells us that two of them (Yizhar and Uziel) each had three children (see Exodus 6:21–22). But Philippson notes that according to Numbers 3:27–28, there were 8,600 members of the Kehat family serving in the tabernacle in the desert with Moses and Aaron, which is "utter nonsense" (*barrer Unsinn*) if there were only three generation from Kehat to the Exodus. Philippson further notes that even if the Israelites were in Egypt for only 215 years, it is hard to believe that there were only three generations born from Kehat, as this would mean that one generation was born about every seventy years.[37] He therefore concludes that when the Bible provides genealogies, it purposefully leaves out many generations, only mentioning key ancestors.[38]

Returning to the question of how long the Israelites dwelled in Egypt, Philippson notes that if one assumes that (1) a new generation was born at least every thirty years, (2) due to polygamy and early marriage, each male had on average six children (three boys and three girls), (3) people lived long lives, as the Bible indicates, and (4) the Israelites were in Egypt for 430 years, then an increase from 67 to 600,000 males (or 2.5 million Israelites in total) is very reasonable.[39]

Philippson concludes by rejecting the medieval commentators' assumption that the 430 years begin from the time of Abraham and instead concludes that the Israelites dwelled for the full 430 years in Egypt. The reason that the genealogies in the Bible suggest that the Israelites dwelt in Egypt for far fewer years is because the Pentateuch does not provide a complete genealogy of the Israelites born during this period. Philippson therefore dates the Exodus to year 2668 from creation rather than the traditional accounting of it as year 2453 from creation.[40]

In sum, Philippson uses a scholarly historical approach to defend the textual integrity and accuracy of the Masoretic text, but he does not feel bound

[37] Rashi contends that the Israelites were in Egypt for 210 years (see Rashi's comment on Genesis 15:13), but Philippson asserts that they were there for 215 years based on his own calculations.
[38] Philippson, *Die Israelitsche Bibel,* 1:365–366 (Commentary to Exodus 12:40).
[39] Ibid.
[40] Philippson, *Die Israelitsche Bibel,* 1:xiv, 366.

to accept the methods of the medieval commentators like Mendelssohn. By using a historical scholarly method that engages with non-biblical and non-Jewish sources as favored by Reformers to defend the integrity and accuracy of the Masoretic Bible as believed by Orthodox Jews, Philippson seeks to create a Bible that will be acceptable to *all* German Jews.

Orthodoxy attacks

Philippson's Bible project was enormously successful. In addition to prodigious sales, 170 rabbis from Germany, Bohemia, Moravia, Hungary, Galicia, Russia, and America endorsed it, including many of a "strictly conservative bent."[41] But Philippson's Bible also provoked a strong Orthodox reaction.

In 1860, an anonymous pamphlet titled *Torch of Truth* (*Fackel der Wahrheit*) appeared. Subtitled "A critical examination of Philippson's Bible by an Orthodox friend of the Bible," its author was the Rabbi of Würzburg, Seligmann Bamberger. Bamberger begins by recording a question he was posed: "Can an Orthodox man . . . read the Philippson Bible?"[42] Bamberger's answer is unequivocally negative, and he details four ways that the Philippson Bible contradicts Orthodoxy.[43] First, Bamberger objects to Philippson's "attributing weaknesses and faults (*Schwächen und Fehler*) to the [Bible's] sacred heroes (*Heroen der Heiligkeit*), the pious patriarchs and matriarchs." For Bamberger, this is "objectionable beyond comment," as it clearly contradicts the Talmud.[44] Second, Bamberger objects that Philippson sometimes interprets the Bible in ways that oppose accepted rabbinic legal interpretations. For example, Philippson interprets Exodus 21:6 to mean that even a female Hebrew slave can choose to extend her slavery past the seventh year.[45] But, notes Bamberger, the rabbinic legal work *Sifre* interprets the verse as stipulating that only a male slave may extend his slavery, and Maimonides codifies this as law.[46] Third, Bamberger notes places where Philippson simply

[41] See Kayserling, *Ludwig Philippson*, 264.

[42] Bamberger, *Fackel der Wahrheit*, 3.

[43] Ibid., 4.

[44] Ibid., 8. Bamberger cites Talmud (*BT*, Shabbat, 55b), which, commenting on the biblical account of Reuben sleeping with his father's concubine Bilhah (Genesis 35:22), states that "whoever claims that Reuben sinned is mistaken." The Talmud instead interprets the verse to mean that Reuben moved his father's bed out of Bilhah's tent into his mother Leah's.

[45] Philippson draws on Deuteronomy 15:12–17 to support his interpretation. See Philippson, *Die Israelitische Bibel*, 1: 424 (Commentary to Exodus 21:6).

[46] Bamberger, *Fackel der Wahrheit*, 9–10. Bamberger cites *Sifrei* on Deuteronomy 15:17, and Maimonides, *Mishneh Torah* "Laws of Slaves," 3:13.

misunderstands rabbinic teachings. For example, in his commentary on Leviticus 11, Philippson asserts that the talmudic rabbis interpreted the thrice-repeated commandment not to boil a kid in its mother's milk (Exodus 23:18, 34:26; Deuteronomy 14:21) as including the prohibition of boiling poultry in milk.[47] Bamberger criticizes Philippson's commentary as ignorant noting that the Talmud (*BT,* Hullin, 113a) as well as the later legal codifiers "without exception" (*ohne Ausnahme*) make clear that the prohibition of mixing chicken with milk is rabbinic, not biblical.[48] Finally, Bamberger notes that while Philippson had affirmed Moses as the author of the Pentateuch, he conceded that the Pentateuch contains a few post-Mosaic glosses.[49] For example, commenting on the genealogy of Edom found in Genesis 36:31–43, Philippson writes that it must be post-Mosaic since it enumerates the kings who ruled in Edom "before a king ruled over Israel" (verse 31) and there was no king in Israel until long after Moses's death.[50] Bamberger stresses that this contravenes the talmudic view (*BT,* Sanhedrin, 99a) codified by Maimonides, which states that "whoever says that a single verse in the Bible is not from God, but rather from Moses, has denied the entire teaching of God and belongs to those who despise the divine law."[51]

In the wake of Bamberger's pamphlet as well as other Orthodox objections, Rabbi Wolf Feilchenfeld, with the strong backing of Rabbi Esriel Hildesheimer, sought to produce a new Bible with a German translation and commentary that would be fully faithful to rabbinic tradition, and thus acceptable to Orthodox Jews.[52] To this end, an *Orthodox Israelite Bible Institute* (*Orthodoxe Israelitische Bibelanstalt*) headed by rabbis Jacob Ettlinger, Seligmann Bamberger, Esriel Hildesheimer, and Marcus Lehmann was created to rival Philippson's *Israelite Bible Institute.*[53] The aim was to publish "a new translation that would morally recommend our side in the circles of

47 See Philippson, *Die Israelitische Bibel,* 1:594–595 (Commentary to Leviticus 11:34).

48 Bamberger, *Fackel der Wahrheit,* 10.

49 Philippson *Die Israelitische Bibel,* "Einleitung in die fünf Bücher Moscheh," 1:xxiv–xxv, note. Philippson mentions as late glosses Genesis 36:31–43; Genesis 4:8–27; Exodus 6:10–17:7; Numbers 21:14–20, 27–30.

50 Philippson, *Die Israelitische Bibel,* 1: 190–191 (Commentary to Genesis 36:31).

51 Bamberger, *Fackel der Wahrheit,* 13–14. I follow Bamberger's translation.

52 A leaflet titled "To the Faithful Believers of Israel" ("An die treuen Gläubigen Israels") argued against the use of Philippson's Bible in Orthodox synagogues and schools. Forty Orthodox rabbis signed it. I have been unable to locate a copy of this leaflet. See Kayserling, *Ludwig Philippson,* 266.

53 Breuer, *Modernity within Tradition,* 184–185. The Pentateuch they eventually produced was Bamberger, Adler, Lehmann, *Uebersetzung der fünf Bücher Moses.* It was published in 1873.

Wissenschaft."[54] In other words, these rabbis sought to create a new Bible that would defend Orthodoxy using academic methods.

Hirsch was, no doubt, opposed to Philippson's Bible and concerned about its penetrating Orthodox communities. But he pointedly did not support the *Orthodox Israelite Bible Institute*. This was because Hirsch opposed using academic, historical methods to study biblical and rabbinic writings, even if these methods were deployed to defend Orthodoxy. In 1873 while Hirsch was in the midst of publishing his Pentateuch, he warned the scholar and staunch defender of Orthodoxy, David Zvi Hoffmann, not to publish his dissertation *Mar Samuel: Head of the Jewish Academy of Nehardea in Babylonia: The Life of a Talmudic Sage* (*Mar Samuel: Rector der jüdischen Akademie zu Nehardea in Babylonien: Lebensbild eines talmudischen Weisen*). Hirsch objected that Hoffmann's use of academic methods had led him to positions irreconcilable with Orthodoxy, such as that the Mishnah and Talmud introduced new laws in response to changing historical circumstances and that certain halakhic decisions derived from Mar Samuel's personality traits. But Hirsch was especially concerned that by citing the works of *Wissenschaft* scholars who denied the divine origin of the Oral Law, Hoffmann was granting their research legitimacy.[55] Hoffmann was a leading figure in the Berlin branch of German Orthodoxy led by Hildesheimer, and Hirsch's dispute with Hoffmann over whether Orthodoxy should engage with the academic, historical study of Judaism led to a break between Frankfurt and Berlin, which split German Neo-Orthodoxy.[56]

Hirsch's Pentateuch as sectarian Orthodox alternative to Philippson's

We have seen that Hirsch adopted the moniker "Orthodox" soon after arriving in Frankfurt and his sectarianism is reflected in the name of the monthly he established there. While Philippson called his newspaper *General Newspaper of Judaism: A Nonpartisan Voice for All Jewish Interests* to signal his desire to appeal to all Jewish factions, Hirsch titled his journal

[54] See Breuer, *Modernity within Tradition*, 185–186.

[55] See ibid. David Ellenson notes that Hoffmann's approach to rabbinic literature "was clearly distinct from his efforts in the discipline of Bible." See Ellenson, *Rabbi Esriel Hildesheimer*, 150–156. On the dispute between Hirsch and Hildesheimer more generally, see ibid., 135–165; Breuer, "Three Orthodox Approaches to *Wissenschaft*," 856–865.

[56] See Breuer, *Modernity within Tradition*, 186.

Jeschurun: A Monthly for the Promotion of Jewish Spirit and Jewish Life in the Home, Community, and School (*Jeschurun: Ein Monatsblatt zur Förderung jüdischen Geistes und jüdischen Lebens in Haus, Gemeinde und Schule*). In the prospectus to the first issue, Hirsch explained that he deliberately used the expressions "Jewish spirit and Jewish life" (*jüdischen Geistes und jüdischen Lebens*) in the journal's subtitle to signal its guiding principle that the writings and institutions of *rabbinic Judaism* are the only legitimate sources for *Jewish* existence.[57] Hirsch made clear that central to the monthly would be defending the convictions of that group "which is usually designated with the name 'Orthodox Judaism'" and that vigorous polemics would be used to this end.[58] That Hirsch chose the name *Jeschurun* for his journal reflected his seeing himself as speaking for the views of his Orthodox congregation, whose Hebrew name was *Kahal Adath Jeschurun*, and which he saw as embodying authentic Judaism.

In 1867 thirteen years after he began publishing *Jeschurun*, Hirsch published the first volume of his Pentateuch. Hirsch was deeply concerned that Philippson's Bible was contributing to the popularization of a historical-critical understanding of the Bible and he presented his Pentateuch as an Orthodox alternative to it. That Hirsch envisioned his Pentateuch as an alternative to Philippson's is evident by comparing their formal features. Hirsch gave his Pentateuch the same title as Philippson's, both in German (*Der Pentateuch*) and in Hebrew (*Hamishah Humshei Torah*), while all other existing German Jewish Pentateuchs had different titles.[59] The format of Hirsch's Pentateuch also directly mirrored Philippson's. While Mendelssohn's *Be'ur* replicated the format of the traditional *Mikra'ot Gedolot*,[60] and the next generation of Pentateuchs by Joseph Johlson, Gotthold Salomon, and Leopold Zunz only contained a German translation,[61] Philippson's

[57] Hirsch, "Prospectus", n.p., *Jeschurun*, vol. 1, October 1854, 1–2. As we have seen for many Christians, the term *jüdische* implied rabbinic.

[58] Ibid., 2–3.

[59] Philippson gave a German and Hebrew title to his entire Bible as well as to its major sections. The entire Bible was called *Mikra Torah Nevi'im Ketuvim/Die Israelitische Bible*, and each of the sections *Torah* (Pentateuch), *Nevi'im* (Prophets), and *Ketuvim* (Writings) also had individual German and Hebrew titles. In German Philippson's Pentateuch was called *Der Pentateuch: Die fünf Bücher Moscheh*, Mendelssohn's 1780–1783 Pentateuch had no German title, Joseph Johlson's 1831 and Gotthold Salomon's 1837 Pentateuchs were called *Die fünf Bücher Mose*, Zunz's 1837 Pentateuch was called *Die Lehre* on one page and *Der Pentateuch das ist die fünf Bücher Moses* on another, and Herxheimer's 1840 Pentateuch was called *Der Pentateuch oder die fünf Bücher Mose's*. In Hebrew, Philippson's and Johlson's Pentateuchs were titled *Hamishah Humshei Torah*, Mendelssohn's was called *Sefer Netivot Hashalom*, Salomon's was called *Torah Tziva Lanu Mosheh*, and Zunz's and Herxheimer's were simply called *Torah*. See Appendix, Table A.1.

[60] See Figures 3 and 4.

[61] See Figures 7, 8, and 5.

Pentateuch contained a German translation in Gothic characters facing the Hebrew original with an extensive German commentary below, interspersed with Hebrew script.[62] Hirsch's Pentateuch used the exact same format as Philippson's.[63] The only other German Jewish Bible at the time that had this format was Salomon Herxheimer's, but there are good reasons for thinking that Hirsch was much more concerned about Philippson's Bible than about Herxheimer's.[64]

In addition to modeling the *formal features* of his Pentateuch on Philippson's, Hirsch follows Philippson in several *substantive respects*. Like Philippson, Hirsch presents the Pentateuch as teaching a unified religious message that should guide contemporary German Jews, and Hirsch's account of this message is quite similar to Philippson's. Both see the Pentateuch as teaching that the world was created by a single, eternal God who gave human beings intellect and free will and commanded worship of God though acts of justice. Both see the Pentateuch as teaching that God revealed special commandments to the Israelites whose purpose was to remind them of God's existence, specify how to practice justice and charity, and help them master sensual desire with the aim that Jews model moral obedience to God to improve humanity.[65]

Hirsch also follows Philippson against Bamberger on the question of the fallibility of biblical heroes. For Hirsch, the idea that all biblical heroes were faultless creates the danger that they will be deified, which is Christianity's error.[66] Like Philippson, Hirsch claims that the Torah's recounting the flaws of its heroes *increases* its credibility because it shows that the Torah "does not hide from us the faults, errors, and weaknesses of our great men" and narrates events simply "because they took place."[67] Hirsch also agrees with Philippson that recounting heroes' failings furthers the Torah's pedagogic goals by making biblical characters more relatable.[68]

[62] See Figure 9.

[63] See Figures 9 and 10.

[64] See Figure 11. Unlike Philippson, Herxheimer aimed at creating a Bible that would be used by Jews and Christians and he enjoyed some success in this. On Herxheimer's Bible, see Gillman, *A History of German Jewish Bible Translation*, 133–141.

[65] See pp. 267–276, 387 of this volume.

[66] Hirsch, *Der Pentateuch*, 1:194; *The Hirsch Chumash*, 1:304 (Commentary to Genesis 12:10–13).

[67] Ibid.

[68] Hirsch, *Der Pentateuch*, 1:195; *The Hirsch Chumash*, 1:305–306 (Commentary to Genesis 12:10–13). In making this claim, Hirsch cites the authority of the medieval Jewish commentator Nahmanides writing, "From our great Torah teachers, and Nahmanides (Ramban) truly ranks among them, we learn that it is never our duty to be apologists (*Apologeten*) for the spiritual and moral heroes of our past. They don't need or suffer our apologies. *Emet*, truth is the seal of our Torah and truthfulness is the essential feature of all [the Torah's] greatest and truest commentators and

Hirsch was also sympathetic to Philippson's commitment to the Bible's "external unity" that is to the accuracy of Pentateuchal history, geography, and chronology; the integrity of the Masoretic Text; and its being composed by a single author.[69] But for Hirsch, Philippson's use of academic historical methods ultimately compromised the Bible's unity.

Philippson wrote that he aimed "to explain the Bible through the Bible itself" (*die Bibel durch die Bibel selbst zu erklären*), and Hirsch used very similar language, writing that he sought to "explain the biblical text from itself" (*Den biblischen Text aus sich selber zu erklären*).[70] But the two had very different conceptions of what this meant. For Philippson explaining the Bible through itself, meant using extra-biblical sources and historical context to elucidate its original meaning, which he distinguished from later biblical interpretation, including rabbinic exegesis.[71] By contrast, Hirsch regarded the Pentateuch as notes of the Oral Torah, both of which God dictated to Moses, so explaining the Pentateuch through itself meant interpreting it through rabbinic lenses and ignoring its Ancient Near Eastern context.[72]

These different approaches are reflected in Hirsch's and Philippson's translations. We have seen that Hirsch alludes to rabbinic law by translating Exodus 21:24 as *Auge Ersatz für Auge* (compensation of an eye for an eye), and in his commentary Hirsch defends the rabbinic interpretation as the plain meaning of the text.[73] By contrast, Philippson translates the verse literally as *Auge um Auge* (eye for eye) and in his commentary explains the biblical law historically, noting that this "strict law of vengeance" was commonly practiced in the ancient world and was codified in the "ancient Attic laws" (*alt-attischen Gesetzen*) and in the Twelve Tables of ancient Rome. But

teachers." See Hirsch, *Der Pentateuch*, 1:224 (Commentary on Genesis 12:10–13). For discussion of the views of several medieval and modern Jewish commentators, including Nahmanides and Hirsch, on whether biblical heroes sinned, see Frisch, "The Sins of the Patriarchs as Viewed by Traditional Jewish Exegesis."

[69] See pp. 388–389 of this volume.

[70] See Philippson, "Overview of Biblical Works", 385, translated in Shargel, "Ludwig Philippson," 271–272; Hirsch, Der Pentateuch, 1:v; The Hirsch Chumash, 1:i.

[71] Philippson gave a clear exposition of his historical conception of rabbinic literature in a series of lectures that he delivered in 1847 and subsequently published. See Philippson, *Die Entwickelung der Religiösen Idee im Judenthume, Christenthume und Islam*. The work was translated into English in 1855 under the title *The Development of the Religious Idea in Judaism, Christianity and Mahomedanism*. On his understanding of the relationship between rabbinic exegesis and the Bible, see Philippson, *The Development of the Religious Idea*, 132–137, 205–217.

[72] See Gottlieb, "Orthodoxy and the Orient." As we have seen, with the Psalms explaining the biblical "through itself" meant empathizing with the frame of mind of the biblical author for Hirsch. See p. 354 of this volume.

[73] See Hirsch, *Der Pentateuch*, 2:273–273 (Commentary on Exodus 21:25).

Philippson notes that the Talmud later ruled that monetary compensation is necessary, a view that Maimonides codified.[74]

Hirsch's opposition to Philippson's approach was connected to a broader polemic against biblical scholarship in his Pentateuch. In the short preface to the work, Hirsch hinted that one of his aims was to oppose academic approaches to the Torah. But his commentary never mentioned academic Bible scholars by name or engaged with their claims. Hirsch's desire to oppose academic biblical scholarship through his Pentateuch was noted almost immediately. The year that Hirsch's Genesis volume appeared, his son-in-law Joseph Gugenheimer published a series of essays on it in Hirsch's journal *Jeschurun*, which were clearly approved of by Hirsch. Gugenheimer argued that an important aim of Hirsch's Pentateuch was to respond to Bible critics without engaging them directly by showing how interpreting the Pentateuch in light of the Oral Torah successfully resolved textual problems that motivated Bible criticism.[75]

Gugenheimer noted Hirsch's claim that Bible critics did not study the biblical text independently of any prior assumptions but, rather, assumed naturalism, namely, that the Pentateuch was a humanly composed work with a complex textual history. As such, when Bible critics discerned problems such as contradictions, repetitions, and inconsistencies in the Pentateuch, they took this as evidence of multiple authors and sources and that the Pentateuch was redacted over an extended period of time. By contrast, Orthodoxy began with the supernaturalist assumption that God revealed the entire Torah, both Oral and Written, to Moses and that it was preserved perfectly. For Gugenheimer, a central aim of Hirsch's Pentateuch was to show that on the basis of Orthodoxy's assumption that God revealed both the Oral and Written Torah, the textual difficulties that motivated Bible critics to conclude that the Pentateuch was a composite, maculate text could be successfully resolved. Gugenheimer further claimed that for Hirsch

[74] See *BT*, Baba Kamma, 83b and Maimonides, *Mishneh Torah*, "Laws of Injuring a Person or Property," 1:3–6. For Philippson, the Talmud replacing taking a literal eye with monetary compensation reflected changes in the broader society. He cites the report of the traveler and orientalist Johann Ludwig Burckhardt who observed that the "Arabs" pay compensation in livestock for damaging another person's body. Philippson is referring to Burckhardt's *Observations concerning the Bedouin and Wahabi* (*Bemerkungen über die Beduinen und Wahaby*) that appeared in 1831. As we have seen, Philippson regarded oriental culture largely as frozen in time. See p. 388 note 22 of this volume.

[75] Gugenheimer's essays appeared in seven installments in *Jeschurun*. See Joseph Gugenheimer, "Die Hypothesen der Bibelkritik und der Commentar zur Genesis von Herrn Rabbiner S.R. Hirsch," *Jeschurun* 13 (1866–1867): 293–313, 397–409; *Jeschurun* 14 (1867–1868): 1–17, 173–190, 312–324; *Jeschurun* 15 (1868–1869): 81–100; 179–192.

Wissenschaft's naturalism and Orthodoxy's supernaturalism were both unprovable assumptions that were utterly irreconcilable. As such, dialogue between these approaches was impossible.[76] As we have seen, Hirsch had expressed this point of view over a quarter century earlier in his reply to Geiger.[77]

While Hirsch knew that Philippson defended a relatively conservative stance on the unity and authorship of the Pentateuch, this did not make his use of academic historical methods any more acceptable to Hirsch. For Hirsch, the *premises* underlying academic biblical scholarship, no matter how conservative, inevitably weakened the authority of halakhah. The assumption that the Pentateuch was composed in a specific historical context to address the needs of a particular time, and that the rabbis later reinterpreted it to meet the needs of a new era, naturally led to the conclusion that halakhah did not bind absolutely and should be adapted to the needs of the present.[78] By contrast, for Hirsch the Torah, both Oral and Written, reflects the eternal, unmediated will of God, and its obligations are categorical and immutable. Changing halakhah means obeying human beings instead of God. While Reformers claimed that their religious position was based on objective, value-free scholarship in contrast to their Orthodox opponents, whose religious position relied on imposing subjective interpretations on the Torah to defend their religious beliefs, Hirsch contended that the approach of Reformers who employed academic methods to study the Torah was no more objective or value-free than that of Orthodox Jews who studied the Torah as the product of divine revelation. Each depended on an unprovable assumption that was motivated by a specific goal.[79]

[76] As Gugenheimer put it: "The present work [Hirsch's Bible] can also prove to Bible critics that the basic premise of biblical criticism depends on rejecting revelation and [thereby] withdraws itself from scientific discourse. For the truthfulness of revelation, like the truthfulness of any historical fact, is neither provable nor falsifiable through reason . . . Rabbi Hirsch's commentary circumvents biblical criticism . . . [but] is able to clear away the objections that biblical criticism raises . . . by means of a rational and strictly *Wissenschaftliche* interpretation." Gugenheimer, "Die Hypothesen," 13:294.

[77] See pp. 296–297 of this volume.

[78] See Hirsch, *GS*, 4:65–66; Hirsch, *CW*, 2:348.

[79] See Hirsch, *Jeschurun* 2 (1861): 89; *CW*, 7:43–44; Hirsch, *GS*, 6: 415; *CW*, 5:311–312; *GS*, 6:520; *CW*, 8:321. Isaac Heinemann agrees with Hirsch's critique of *Wissenschaft des Judentums*, concluding that Hirsch's claim that study of Torah must serve life was more intellectually honest than the language of scholarly disinterest used by many Reform and Positive-Historical scholars to explain their approach to the study of Jewish texts. See Heinemann, "Rabbi Samson Raphael Hirsch and His Teacher Rabbi Isaac Bernays," 85. Heinemann was no Orthodox apologist, but rather a premier *Wissenschaft* scholar who was a professor at the Jewish Theological Seminary in Breslau and the penultimate editor of the flagship journal of the Positive-Historical school, the *Monatsschrift für Geschichte und Wissenschaft des Judentums*.

Philippson clearly rejected Hirsch's sharp dichotomy between academic biblical scholarship and Orthodoxy. In seeking to appeal to both Reform and Orthodox Jews, Philippson would have likely claimed that he was taking no position on whether or not the Torah was divinely revealed but simply using objective scholarly methods to uncover Pentateuchal authorship and determine whether or not the text had been preserved intact. His conclusion was that unbiased scholarly investigation confirmed Orthodox views of the Pentateuch's authorship and integrity. For Hirsch, however, Philippson's use of academic methods *necessarily* compromised Orthodoxy no matter how conservative his conclusions. An example will illustrate Hirsch's point.

The humility of Moses

One of the most famous verses cited by early Bible critics to show that Moses could not have authored the entire Pentateuch was Numbers 12:3, which states that "Moses was exceedingly humble (*anav*) beyond all people on earth." Since a truly humble person would never boast of his humility, the fact that Moses is so described in the third person is clear evidence that this verse must have been written by someone else.[80]

Philippson observes that many readers have suspected that this verse was a later gloss. But he seeks to refute this claim. Philippson translates Numbers 12:3 as follows: *Der Mann Moscheh aber war sehr* ***ergeben*** (***anav***), *mehr irgend ein Mensch auf dem ganzen Erdboden* (But the man Mosheh was very **resigned** more than any other person on the entire earth). In his commentary, Philippson considers the meaning of the Hebrew word *anav*. He cites Rashi, who interprets it as "humble" (*demütig*) and others who interpret it as "patient" (*geduldig*), "afflicted" (*geplagt*), or "oppressed" (*niedergedrückt*). Philippson explains that whenever the word *anav* appears, it designates someone in low spirits who is resigned to God's will, which Philippson tells us is really "ambiguous praise" (*zweideutig Lob*). Moses calling himself *anav* must be understood in the context of other passages where he concedes his failings and in relation to the immediately preceding verses, which describe Miriam and Aaron criticizing him for marrying a Cushite woman and questioning Moses's special status as a prophet of God. Understood in

[80] Spinoza had already cited this phrase as post-Mosaic. See Spinoza, *Opera,* 3:121; *Collected Works,* 2:196 (*Theological-Political Treatise,* ch. 8).

this context, Philippson interprets Moses describing himself as "the most *anav* person on earth" as a hyperbolic description of his low feelings.[81] Since Philippson rejects the interpretation of *anav* as humble, he deems it "unnecessary" to consider it a post-Mosaic gloss.

Hirsch, however, translates the verse quite simply as *Und der Mann Mosche war äußerst* **demüthig**, *mehr als alle Menschen, welche auf der Erbenfläche leben* (And the man Moses was exceedingly **humble**, more than all human beings living on the face of the earth). In his commentary, Hirsch explains that the word *anav* denotes "the trait of extreme selflessness," and he interprets the verse in relation to those immediately preceding it. Aaron and Miriam had spoken maliciously about Moses, but because of his extremely humility Moses would not answer them, so "God took up his [Moses'] cause." For Hirsch, in Numbers 12:3 *God* is testifying that Moses was extremely humble for three reasons: *first*, to show that had Aaron and Miriam considered Moses's humility, they would not have questioned his separating from his wife, which they assumed was the result of spiritual arrogance (see Hirsch's interpretation of Numbers 12:1–2); *second*, to explain why God had to defend Moses who would not respond to his siblings (see Numbers 12:4–9); and *third*, to explain why Aaron and Miriam had thought it appropriate to criticize Moses in the first place. Because Moses was so humble and never spoke of his special relationship with God, Aaron and Miriam were unaware of it and thought that their prophecies were on par with his, which is why they questioned Moses's separating from his wife. Hirsch suggests that because of his great humility Moses himself may have been unaware that his prophecy was superior to that of his siblings and always presented himself as their equal.[82]

For Hirsch, the fact that Moses is called the most humble person in the world poses absolutely no challenge to the Orthodox view of Pentateuchal authorship. For the Orthodox assumption is not that Moses wrote the Torah on his own accord but, rather, that God dictated it to him.[83] While it would be

[81] See Philippson, *Die Israelitiche Bible*, "Einleitung in die fünf Bücher Moscheh," 1:xxvii, note; 1: 738 (Commentary to Numbers 12:3).

[82] Hirsch, *Der Pentateuch* 4:170; *The Hirsch Chumash*, 4:232 (Commentary on Numbers 12:3).

[83] This view is supported by the Talmud (*BT*, Sanhedrin, 99a), which states: "Another [Baraita] taught: 'Because he has despised the word of the Lord' (Numbers 15:31) this refers to one who maintains that the Torah is not from heaven. *And even if he asserts that the whole Torah is from heaven excepting a particular verse which he maintains was not uttered by God but by Moses himself*, he is included in the statement 'Because he has despised the word of the Lord,'" (emphasis mine). The talmudic view affirmed by Hirsch is that God authored the entire Pentateuch, with Moses serving as God's copyist and that asserting that Moses authored even a single verse on his own initiative constitutes heresy.

problematic to assume that Moses would call *himself* the humblest person on earth, it is surely no problem for God to testify to this *about him*. For Hirsch, while Philippson ostensibly defends the Orthodox view of Pentateuchal authorship, in reality he undermines Orthodoxy by assuming that Moses is the Pentateuch's author. Given Hirsch's view that human, not divine authorship of the Pentateuch is the unspoken assumption of Philippson's Bible, one can understood why he deems it a completely unacceptable translation for Orthodox Jews.

But just as Hirsch does not think that a Bible grounded in academic methods is acceptable for Orthodox Jews, so he does not imagine that his Pentateuch, which relies on Orthodox assumptions about divine authorship, would be acceptable to Reform Jews. Hirsch therefore conceived his Pentateuch as a sectarian Orthodox work aimed solely at educating and inspiring members of his own community. For Hirsch, the problem with Philippson's Bible was not that it relied on assumptions inimical to Orthodoxy, but that it did so while presenting itself as an inclusive *Israelite Bible*.

The translator and the politician: Hirsch's Pentateuch and the Secession Controversy

The conception of community underlying Hirsch's and Philippson's Bibles found political expression during the famous "Secession Controversy" (*Austrittsstreit*) that roiled German Jewry during the second half of the nineteenth century. In 1847, Prussia passed regulations making membership in the local Jewish community mandatory. The only way that a Jew could leave the community was to convert to Christianity.[84] But following the 1848 socialist revolutions, the complete separation of church and state was publicly debated. Almost immediately, Philippson worried that such a separation would have deleterious effects on the Jewish community, opining that the Jewish community could only avoid falling into "chaos and complete dissolution" if the state preserved the requirement that Jews be members of their local Jewish communities.[85]

[84] See Baron, "Freedom and Constraint," 11–12; Katz, *A House Divided*, 9.

[85] See Philippson, *AZJ*, 1848, 337–338, cited in Liberles, *Religious Conflict in Social Context*, 266, note 20. Also see Philippson, *AZJ*, 1848, 437–438, cited in Liberles, *Religious Conflict in Social Context*, 171.

Following the establishment of the North German Confederation (*Norddeutscher Bund*) in 1867, several Jews, including Philippson, worked to form a national German Jewish organization, and in 1872 the Union of German Jewish Congregations (*Deutsch-Israelitischer Gemeindebund*) was formally established.[86] But with the founding of the German empire and Bismarck's attempt to consolidate German unity by waging a *Kulturkampf* against Catholicism, new impetuses for Jewish communal fracture emerged.

In May 1873, the German Parliament passed a Secession Law (*Austrittsgesetz*), according to which a Catholic or Protestant could resign from their National Church without forfeiting the right to be considered Catholic or Protestant by the state.[87] This law did not, however, extend to Jews. A Jew could now leave the Jewish community without becoming a Christian but would still have to renounce her affiliation with Judaism.[88]

In a memorandum written to the Prussian parliament in response to the law's proposal, Hirsch pleaded that Jews be accorded the same freedom as Protestants and Catholics. He understood that one reason Jews were not granted the right to secede was because the government believed that the religious differences between Orthodoxy and Reform were minimal. In his memorandum Hirsch asserted that the gap between Orthodoxy and Reform was greater than that between "any of the existing Christian confessions."[89] The division between Orthodoxy and Reform resulted from their opposing views of the origin and authority of the Torah. As Hirsch put it, ". . . there can be no greater confessional difference than that existing between Jews who accept the divinity and hence the eternal inviolability of Jewish religious law based on the Bible and Tradition and Jews who deny the divinity and inviolability of this law."[90] For Hirsch, either the entire Torah, Written and Oral, is divine and eternal, or it is human and subject to change. In a later article, Hirsch expressed the dichotomy between Orthodoxy and Reform in the starkest terms, using the term *Neology* to include Reform: "If Orthodoxy is truth, then Neology is a lie. If Neology is truth, then Orthodoxy is a lie . . . it is not possible to confess both at the same time without playing games with both."[91]

[86] See Liberles, *Religious Conflict,* 196; Schorsch, *Jewish Reactions to German Anti-Semitism,* 24–30.
[87] See Katz, *A House Divided,* 239–247.
[88] See Katz, *A House Divided,* 247.
[89] Hirsch, *GS,* 4:243; *CW,* 6:158. In an 1863 essay Hirsch explicitly wrote that gap between Orthodoxy and Reform was greater than that between Protestants and Catholics. See Hirsch, *GS,* 5:274–275; *CW,* 6:88.
[90] Hirsch, *GS,* 4:243; *CW,* 6:159.
[91] Hirsch, *GS,* 4:298; *CW,* 6:174. See Gottlieb, "Does Judaism have Dogma? Moses Mendelssohn and a Pivotal Nineteenth-Century Debate."

Hirsch argued that denying an Orthodox Jew to right secede from the Jewish community was an intolerable infringement of liberty of conscience. But Philippson also invoked liberty of conscience in arguing against the right to secede. Isaiah Berlin's essay "Two Concepts of Liberty" helps clarify the assumptions underlying each's position.

Berlin famously distinguished between "negative liberty" and "positive liberty." He defined negative liberty as the ability to act "unobstructed by others." On this view, a person is unfree if she is "prevented from attaining a goal by [other] human beings."[92] By contrast, Berlin defined "positive freedom" as the freedom to "be one's own master," that is, to "take control of one's life and realize one's fundamental purposes."[93]

In opposing a Jew's right to secede, Philippson appealed to positive liberty. For Philippson, the ability to participate in the Jewish community and its institutions was essential for a Jew to fully actualize herself. Unlike Christians, Jews did not form separate sects. The confessional differences between Jews were relatively minor, focusing mainly on differences in the synagogue service and could be accommodated within a unified community. As such, Philippson argued that individuals who withdrew from the Jewish community should be regarded as leaving Judaism altogether.[94] Philippson further argued that the Jewish community could only sustain its institutions through its compulsory tax system. Granting a Jew the right to secede would cause many Jewish communities to collapse, which would effectively strip the vast majority of Jews of the freedom to actualize themselves religiously. As such, allowing a right to secede undermined the positive liberty of the majority of Jews.[95]

At first glance, Hirsch's counterargument seems to depend on an appeal to negative liberty. He argued that forcing an Orthodox Jew to remain a member of a community whose institutions he deemed heretical and pay taxes to it constituted an "outrageous coercion of conscience (*Gewissensdruck*)."[96] On closer consideration, however, it is clear that for Hirsch secession was also a matter of positive liberty. Hirsch argued that there were two main types of communal organizations, political and religious. Prior to Jewish emancipation in the early nineteenth century, Jewish communities were both political

92 Berlin, *Four Essays on Liberty*, 122.
93 Ibid., 131; see Carter, "Positive and Negative Liberty."
94 Philippson, "Offenes Sendchreiben an Herrn Dr. Lasker," 782–783.
95 Ibid., 782.
96 Hirsch, *GS*, 5:275; *CW*, 4:89.

and religious. But with political equality, the Jew became "integrated into the larger civil and civic community of his place of residence and his country," and Jewish communities lost their political function, remaining religious organizations alone.[97] In an 1863 essay Hirsch wrote that the Orthodox Jew fulfilled her life's purpose by being the "bearer of a moral ideal" upheld by the Jewish community and working to "actualize the collective's ideals into an ever-growing reality."[98] And in the *Nineteen Letters*, he made clear that this involved modeling submission to God's ethical law by obeying all the commandments of the Torah.[99] Given that Reformers denied the divinity of the Torah and deemed most of its laws no longer binding, forcing an Orthodox Jew to remain a member of a Reform-controlled community impeded her liberty to fulfill her mission as a Jew since this type of Jewish community could not credibly model submission to God's commandments.[100]

Hirsch further argued that forcing an Orthodox Jew to remain a member of a Reformed-controlled Jewish community violated liberty of conscience *even if* the community supported both Reform and Orthodox congregations. In such a community Orthodoxy and Reform would naturally both be regarded as valid expressions of Judaism. This would impede the Orthodox Jew's ability to impart his religious convictions to his children, since the child would be faced with the dilemma of whether to follow the practices of her parents or the practices of the majority of Jews represented by the community, and it was much easier to be Reform Jew than an Orthodox one.[101] Hirsch thus saw denying Orthodox Jews the right to secede from the official Jewish community as undermining their positive liberty.

A final argument that Hirsch used in favor secession is worth noting. On July 28, 1876, the German Secession Law was officially extended to include Jews. At this point, Hirsch and a few members of his congregation seceded. But most members of Hirsch's congregation demurred, fearing a complete break with the Jewish community. Many of those hesitating to secede were from old Frankfurt families who worried that seceding would mean losing

[97] Hirsch, *GS*, 4:299; *CW*, 6:175.
[98] Hirsch, *GS*, 2:33; *CW*, 6:3.
[99] See Hirsch, *Neunzehn Briefe*, Brief 9, 44–45; *Nineteen Letters*, Letter 9, 128.
[100] In his 1877 Open Letter to Rabbi Bamberger, which will be discussed shortly, Hirsch described remaining in a community with Reformers as a *hillul hashem*, a desecration of the divine name given that Reformers were heretics. See Hirsch, *GS*, 4:321–322; *CW*, 6:204. In his earlier *Horeb* Hirsch wrote that the Jewish task was to sanctify God's name by "upholding the Torah's teachings about God and humanity (*Menschthum*)" for all "humanity" (*Menschheit*). See Hirsch, *Horev*, Kap. 97, #613, 622; *Horeb*, ch. 97, #613, 465.
[101] Hirsch, *GS*, 5:288–289; *CW*, 6:103.

the right to be buried next to their relatives in the Frankfurt community cemetery. These "Community Orthodox" (*Gemeinde Orthodoxen*), as they came to be called, entered into negotiations with the Reform-controlled community and extracted significant concessions, including the assurance that none of their tax money would be used to support Reform institutions, that the community would fund a ritual bath (*mikvah*), and that all community matters bearing on halakhah would be under the supervision of an Orthodox rabbi hired and paid for by the community. A highly respected local scholar from an old Frankfurt family named Rabbi Mosheh Mainz affirmed that under these conditions secession was unnecessary.[102]

For the reasons we have seen, Hirsch was unmoved, and his followers wrote to the Würzburg Rav, Seligmann Bamberger, widely acknowledged as the foremost living Orthodox legal decisor (*posek*) in Germany, for support. Knowing that four years earlier in 1872 Bamberger had ruled that secession from a community that introduced religious reforms was necessary, Hirsch's supporters implored Bamberger to come to Frankfurt to convince Mainz that it was halakhically obligatory to secede.[103] Bamberger initially did not want to get involved but when pressed he acceded and met with Mainz. Learning of the concessions that the Orthodox had won, Bamberger ruled that while seceding from the Jewish community in Frankfurt was halakhically permissible, it was not obligatory. For Bamberger, there was value to remaining part of a unified Jewish community even when the majority no longer observed halakhah, as long as one could observe halakhah undisturbed.[104]

Hirsch was livid. In his 1877 Open Letter to Bamberger, Hirsch explained why he rejected Bamberger's ruling:

> Jewish Orthodoxy and Jewish Reform are irreconcilable opposites . . . Only a person to whom religious truth has become altogether meaningless, who pays attention to religious matters only out of extraneous considerations could support the proposition that such opposing religious trends should remain together in one union. Only such a person could deplore the secession of those loyal to the law (*Gesetzestreuen*) from a union with law-denying (*Gesetz verwerfenden*) Reform as if truth could be an object of haggling (*feilschen*). [Only such a person] could cast about for artful

102 See Japhet, "The Secession from the Frankfurt Jewish Community," 115.
103 See Ellenson, *After Emanicipation*, 273.
104 See Liberles, *Religious Conflict in Social Context*, 219–220; Japhet, "The Secession from the Frankfurt Jewish Community," 113–115; Katz, *A House Divided*, 260–261.

compromise formulas capable of duping insight and conscience (*Gewissen*) and suited to jeopardizing religious truth and integrity on both sides.[105]

For Hirsch, given the opposite principles of Orthodoxy and Reform, one could only advocate that Orthodox Jews remain in the same community as Reform Jews if one did not care about religious truth. Reformers were heretics. For an Orthodox Jew to remain a member of a united community with Reformers obscured this fact. For Hirsch, papering over substantial religious differences violated freedom of conscience. While Hirsch was addressing the Orthodox Bamberger, he probably also had in mind Reformers like Philippson.

Not surprisingly, Bamberger took umbrage at Hirsch's accusation. In his letter, Hirsch had also argued that by contradicting his ruling Bamberger had violated the talmudic principle that one rabbi cannot permit what another has forbidden (see *BT*, Berekhot, 63b). But Bamberger responded that this principle only applied when the two rabbis were equal. When, however, one was a much greater Talmud scholar, the principle did not apply. Hirsch replied by conceding Bamberger's superior talmudic knowledge. But he denied that it entitled him to greater halakhic authority since Bamberger's knowledge was based on "vain pilpul" (*harifut shel hevel*). For Hirsch, the authority to issue a halakhic ruling depended on clear reasoning and knowledge of the local facts, both of which Bamberger lacked in this case. By prioritizing independent, individual judgment in religious matters over blind obedience to contemporary rabbinic authority, Hirsch presented a Neo-Orthodox position that sharply contrasted with Bamberger's Ultra-Orthodox position.[106]

Hirsch's argument that it violates freedom of conscience to force Orthodox Jews to remain in the same community as Reformers should sound familiar. It is an application of an argument that Mendelssohn used at the end of *Jerusalem* to oppose religious union between Jews and Christians. Speaking of those seeking such a union, Mendelssohn wrote, "The gentle souls who make this proposal are ready to go to work. They wish to meet as negotiators and make the humanitarian effort to bring about a compromise

105 Hirsch, *GS*, 4:325–326; *CW*, 6:207–208.

106 See Bamberger's letter to Hirsch in Hirsch, *GS*, 4:518–520; *CW*, 6:228–230, and Hirsch's response in Hirsch, *GS*, 4:352–354; *CW*, 6:261–263. In the nineteenth-century the doctrine of blind obedience to contemporary rabbinic authority known as "Daat Torah" became a central pillar of Ultra-Orthodoxy. For a critical discussion of this doctrine, see Kaplan, "Daas Torah: A Modern Conception of Rabbinic Authority"; Katz, "Daat Torah: The Unqualified Authority Claimed for Halakhists"; Brown, "The Daat Torah Doctrine- Three Stages."

between the faiths, to bargain for truth as if they were rights, like haggling for merchandise (*wie feiles Kaufmannsgut*) . . . At bottom, a union of faiths, should it ever come about, could have but the most unfortunate consequences for reason and liberty of conscience (*Gewissensfreiheit*)."[107]

Writing in 1783, Mendelssohn assumed a unitary conception of Judaism and argued that freedom of conscience required respecting religious differences *between* Jews and Christians. Nearly a century later, German Judaism had fractured. While Philippson fought to preserve a unified Judaism, Hirsch deployed Mendelssohn's reasoning to argue that freedom of conscience required respecting religious differences *within* Judaism. For Hirsch, preserving the integrity of Orthodoxy was impossible if Orthodox Jews were forced to remain members of a Reform-controlled community, even if concessions were granted.[108] Confronting a new reality, we once again find Hirsch turning to Mendelssohn for support.

Conclusion

The careers of Hirsch and Philippson began in parallel. In the mid-1830s both worried about divisions that had formed within German Jewry and sought to articulate a new middle-class vision of German Judaism that would unite opposing factions by inspiring renewed religious commitment. But Hirsch and Philippson did so in different ways. In his 1836 *Nineteen Letters*, Hirsch presented a unifying account of Judaism founded on the Bible that weaved together the partial truths within the four major German Jewish ideologies of the time. In his 1844 Pentateuch translation and commentary, Philippson also presented a unifying conception of middle-class German Judaism that he discerned in the Bible. But rather than synthesize the partial truths of Orthodoxy and Reform, Philippson sought a compromise between the two by using academic methods favored by Reform to defend conservative positions on Pentateuchal authorship and accuracy that would be acceptable to the Orthodox. Philippson expressed his goal of producing a Bible for all German Jews by titling his work *The Israelite Bible*.

While Hirsch's and Philippson's careers began with similar goals, their aims ended up diverging. As Reform grew and radicalized and Positive-Historical

[107] Mendelssohn, *JubA*, 8:202–203; *Jerusalem*, 136–137.
[108] See pp. 314–317 of this volume.

Judaism emerged, Hirsch understood that his views were held by an ever-dwindling minority. As early as 1837 Hirsch had recognized that Reform and Orthodoxy depended on radically different premises, neither of which was provable, with Reform seeing the Torah as a historical work composed by human beings and Orthodoxy regarding it as a timeless, divinely revealed work that was perfectly preserved. Throughout the 1840s Hirsch still clung to the hope that a unified German Judaism could be salvaged, but when appointed head of the Separatist Orthodox community in Frankfurt in 1851, he understood that this was no longer feasible. Instead, Hirsch sought to create a model middle-class Neo-Orthodox German Jewish community grounded in strict adherence to the Torah, understood as a timeless, divinely revealed text. Recognizing that Positive-Historical Judaism was based on historicizing the Oral Torah, and seeking to reply to increasingly influential Bible criticism, Hirsch developed a new account of the relationship between the Oral Torah and the Written Torah by adapting an idea from his opponent Zacharias Frankel. Hirsch came to conceive the Oral Torah as the true text of the Torah, and the Written Torah as its written trace, which was incomprehensible without it.

Unlike Philippson, who sought to have his Bible accepted in all German Jewish communities, Hirsch conceived his Pentateuch translation and commentary as a sectarian project aimed only at Orthodox Jews. An important motivation for Hirsch's publishing his Pentateuch was to prevent Orthodox communities from accepting Philippson's Bible.

Hirsch's and Philippson's opposing attitudes toward Jewish communal fracture were expressed in their opposing positions during the Secession Controversy. Hirsch's campaign to grant Orthodox Jews the right to secede was successful, and it became clear that German Judaism was destined to remain fragmented for the foreseeable future.

Conclusion

The Jewish Counter-Reformation

I have argued that Mendelssohn, Zunz, and Hirsch can all be considered exponents of a Jewish Reformation that aimed to create middle-class, bourgeois German Judaism and that Bible translation was central to their project. They all criticized the traditional Ashkenazic educational system, which centered on near-exclusive study of the Talmud from a young age for boys, and instead advocated a balanced curriculum that included general studies along with Torah study, placing the Bible and grammatical knowledge of Hebrew at the center of the curriculum. They stressed the value of rabbinic teachings, which they deemed crucial for preserving Judaism as a living force and thought deeply about the relation between the Oral Torah and Written Torah. The translators were highly suspicious of mysticism and saw Judaism's goal as promoting *Bildung*. Their translations were educational tools whose aim was to balance conveying the form of the Hebrew original with an elegant, comprehensible German text, thereby expressing their desire to combine Judaism with the best of German culture. Their middle-class German Judaism was never parochial—they regarded Judaism's purpose as not only benefitting Jews, but also as benefitting German Christians, and ultimately all humanity.

When Buber and Rosenzweig first began publishing their Bible translation in 1925, they took aim at the bourgeois German Judaism defended by Jewish Reformation translators.[1] Their disillusionment with Jewish Reformation translators is epitomized by Buber's recollection that reading

[1] For a vivid expression of Rosenzweig's opposition to middle-class German Judaism, see the opening words of Nahum Glatzer's biography of Rosenzweig: "When, after the end of the First World War, Franz Rosenzweig took residence in Frankfurt on Main and assumed the leadership of the *Freies Jüdische Lehrhaus* he said in one of his first lectures, '. . . I intend to shatter ideas that have become very dear to you.' Thus did he make his appearance in bourgeois, well-to-do, traditionalist, and rather stolid Frankfurt." See Glatzer, *Franz Rosenzweig*, ix.

The Jewish Reformation. Michah Gottlieb, Oxford University Press (2021). © Oxford University Press.
DOI: 10.1093/oso/9780199336388.003.0010

Zunz's Bible as a youth destroyed the Bible's living character for him, making it an "unbearable" book.[2]

Part of the reason that Buber and Rosenzweig did not find the Jewish Reformation translators appealing is that their concerns were very different due to the enormous changes that German Judaism had undergone in the intervening years. Traditional Talmud-centered Ashkenazic education had long ceased to be a significant factor among German Jews, and knowledge of rabbinic texts and a sense of their authority had deeply declined among the non-Orthodox. As such, while engagement with rabbinic literature was not entirely absent from the Buber-Rosenzweig translation, it did not play a major role.[3] Buber's and Rosenzweig's main audience was young German Jews who had been raised in bourgeois, middle-class German Jewish homes but who had become alienated from this vision of Judaism. Mendelssohn, Zunz, and the early Hirsch had also addressed alienated young Jews, but there was an important difference. The "pseudo-enlightened" Jews addressed by Mendelssohn, Zunz, and Hirsch were often hostile toward Judaism because they had received a traditional talmudic Jewish education, which they rejected.[4] By contrast, the young Jews addressed by Buber and Rosenzweig

[2] See Buber's essay "The How and Why of Our Bible Translation" in Buber and Rosenzweig, *Scripture and Translation,* 207–208. Glatzer notes that Rosenzweig also used the Zunz Bible as a youth. See Glatzer, *Franz Rosenzweig,* xxxvii.

[3] Mara Benjamin notes that Rosenzweig did not have much knowledge of rabbinic texts or medieval Jewish commentators. See Benjamin, *Rosenzweig's Bible,* 125, note 53. Buber was probably more familiar with rabbinic writings, having been raised by his grandfather, the critical Midrash scholar Salomon Buber. But Buber was much less familiar with these texts than Mendelssohn, Zunz, or Hirsch and, more importantly, was not especially interested in them. Rosenzweig occasionally mentions the influence of rabbinic tradition on his Bible translation. In a 1927 letter to Jacob Rosenheim he writes that his Bible translation was guided by a sense of the unity of the Written Torah and Oral Torah, which he glosses as "the unity of the book as written through the unity of the book as read" or as "the unity of teaching" with the "unity of learning . . . of centuries." Rosenzweig aligns his view of the Oral Torah with Hirsch's. But in stressing rabbinic tradition's quality as communal interpretation, his position is closest to Zunz's. Rosenzweig further remarks that rabbinic Midrash, both halakhic and aggadic, plays a role in his and Buber's Bible translation, as they regarded Midrash as a "complement" to *peshat* and so crafted translations that left room for midrashic interpretations. In this respect, Buber's and Rosenzweig's approach seems closest to Mendelssohn's. Rosenzweig provides a couple of examples where he and Buber left open the midrashic interpretation in their translation (e.g., Deuteronomy 23:20, Exodus 17:16), and Rosenzweig occasionally writes approvingly of a rabbinic interpretation. See Buber and Rosenzweig, *Die Schrift und ihre Verdeutschung,* 48–49, 252; *Scripture and Translation,* 23–24, 137. But through a careful analysis of the working papers Buber and Rosenzweig exchanged as they worked on their translation, Maren Niehoff has shown that Midrash and medieval Jewish commentary actually play a very minor role in their translation choices. See Niehoff, "The Buber-Rosenzweig Translation," 261–263.

[4] While Jewish youth in Mendelssohn's, Zunz's or Hirsch's time often felt little enthusiasm for *Judaism*, Hirsch recognized that they often felt enthusiasm for the *Jewish people.* In an 1835 letter to Z.H. May describing his plan for *Horeb,* Hirsch writes, "I see a younger generation aglow with noble enthusiasm for Judaism-or rather for Jews. These young men do not know authentic Judaism, and what they believe they know of it they consider empty forms without meaning." See Hirsch, *Horeb,* cxliii. I thank my student Kylie Unell for this point.

had often received minimal or no Jewish education, and while alienated from Judaism, they were often open to or even longed to return to it.[5] Buber's and Rosenzweig's distance from the Jewish Reformation project is reflected in their using the word *Erziehung* to describe their educational efforts rather than the bourgeois term *Bildung*. As Gillman has shown, while *Bildung* implies intellectual and character formation, *Erziehung* connotes "the forging of social identity often with an emancipatory aspect." Buber and Rosenzweig were seeking to inculcate a new Jewish identity for German Jews as *ba'alei teshuvah* (returnees to Judaism).[6]

For Rosenzweig, the key to returning to Judaism was a "naked encounter" with the biblical text uncovered by its "traditional garments," that is, "the Jewish millennia" of biblical interpretation. Buber echoed a similar sentiment.[7] While Mendelssohn, Zunz, and Hirsch presented the Oral Torah as the spirit that animated the biblical letter, for Buber and Rosenzweig the letter alone provided access to the spirit.[8] For this reason they sought to reproduce the form, cadences, and word roots of the Hebrew in their translation with almost fanatical consistency to the point that their translation sounded foreign and was often incomprehensible to the typical German reader.[9] Mendelssohn's and Hirsch's Pentateuchs reflected their view that revelation belonged to the past and contemporary Jews could access it by engaging with the tradition of Jewish Bible interpretation.[10] By contrast, through their Bible

[5] As Rosenzweig put it, "This [modern] person is no believer, but no unbeliever either. He believes and doubts . . . Everything can become credible for him, even the incredible." See Rosenzweig's essay "Scripture and Luther" in Buber and Rosenzweig, *Scripture and Translation*, 58–59; *Die Schrift und ihre Verdeutschung*, 108–109.

[6] See Gillman, *A History of German Jewish Bible Translation*, 207.

[7] Buber explains that Rosenzweig came to this understanding by taking Eduard Strauss's class on the Bible at the *Lehrhaus*. See Buber's essay "The How and Why of Our Bible Translation" in Buber and Rosenzweig, *Scripture and Translation*, 207. In his essay "The Contemporary Person and the Jewish Bible," Buber writes of the need to free oneself from familiar interpretations of the Bible, arguing that people of his time "must take up Scripture as if they had never seen it . . . they must place themselves anew before the renewed book, hold back nothing of themselves, let everything happen between themselves and it, whatever may happen." See Buber and Rosenzweig, *Scripture and Translation*, 7; *Die Schrift und ihre Verdeutschung*, 19.

[8] As Rosenzweig put it, "We do not know from what words teaching and comfort may come; we believe that the hidden springs of teaching and comfort may some day break through to us from every word of this book." See Buber and Rosenzweig, *Scripture and Translation*, 59; *Die Schrift und ihre Verdeutschung*, 110.

[9] Weintraub explains that in reproducing the form of the Hebrew in German, Buber and Rosenzweig adopted a three-step process. If they found a German word that rendered the original Hebrew word in its multiple meanings and nuances, they would use it. If they could not find such a word they would seek an archaic German word. Their extensive use of Grimm's nineteenth-century dictionary led Buber to playfully refer to him as "Reb Grimm." Finally, if they could not find any appropriate German word, they would coin a neologism. See Weintraub, *The German Translations*, 38; Niehoff, "The Buber-Rosenzweig Translation," 273–274.

[10] Zunz's view of revelation is less clear.

translation Buber and Rosenzweig signaled that an emotionally charged revelatory experience of God was possible in the present through an encounter with the "naked" biblical text. This was expressed in the layout of their Bible whose page was almost entirely empty aside from their translation and in the fact that their Bible translation contained no explanatory information, not even an introduction. By intimating their erasure, Buber and Rosenzweig suggested that through their translation the reader could access the unmediated original biblical text which would enable a living revelatory encounter with God.[11]

It is common to contrast meek, insecure, religiously empty bourgeois German Judaism with Buber's and Rosenzweig's defiant, proud, spiritually rich return to Judaism. Seidman gives vivid expression to this view when she describes the Buber-Rosenzweig Bible as a "moment of colonial resistance", which contrasts with "Mendelssohn's colonial deference."[12]

In important respects this contrast reflects Rosenzweig's narrative. Raised in a bourgeois German Jewish home, he came to harshly criticize Mendelssohn, whom he saw as originating bourgeois German Judaism.[13] In a 1920 lecture Rosenzweig condemned Mendelssohn's synthesis of Judaism and German culture as a sleight of hand. He characterized Mendelssohn's philosophy of Judaism as primarily apologetic, arising from the need to justify his Judaism to Christians, and charged that Mendelssohn's defense of Judaism rested on compartmentalizing it from German culture by leaving truth, including religious truth, in the realm of universal philosophy while Judaism focused on obedience to the ritual laws revealed to Moses, which were binding to Jews alone. As Rosenzweig put it, Mendelssohn "was no unified person"; the Jew and human being resided "next to one another" within him.[14]

[11] See Figure 12. Mendelssohn's, Zunz's, and Hirsch's Pentateuchs included the standard chapter and verse numbers, the name of the biblical book in Hebrew, and the name of the weekly portion in Hebrew on each page. The Buber-Rosenzweig Bible lacked all these features, with only the standard chapter and verse numbers appearing in a small innocuous space at the bottom of the page. In the second edition, Buber and Rosenzweig included the name of the biblical book in German and moved the chapter numbers to the top of the page. See Gillman, "Between Religion and Culture," 109–110. Mendelssohn's spare edition of the Psalms was closest to the layout of the Buber-Rosenzweig Bible.

[12] Seidman, *Faithful Renderings*, 177.

[13] At an event celebrating the bicentenary of Mendelssohn's birth in 1929, Rosenzweig called Mendelssohn "the first German Jew." See Rosenzweig, *Zweistromland*, 457. Glatzer and Niehoff note that in the Rosenzweig household Zunz was regarded as a "family saint." See Glatzer, *Franz Rosenzweig*, xxxv–xxxviii; Niehoff, "The Buber-Rosenzweig Translation of the Bible," 267.

[14] See Rosenzweig, *Zweistromland*, 566–567; Mendes-Flohr, "Mendelssohn and Rosenzweig," 206. Rosenzweig's criticism of Mendelssohn recalls Hirsch's criticism nearly a century earlier in the *Nineteen Letters*. See pp. 251–252 of this volume. While I have characterized Rosenzweig as opposing the Jewish Reformation translators, of the translators I have explored he is closest to Hirsch.

Rosenzweig aimed to merge his Jewishness and Germanness much more deeply than had Mendelssohn and the other Jewish Reformation translators I have explored. As scholars have shown, initially Rosenzweig considered German a Christian language and therefore concluded that the only possible German Jewish translation would be a revision of Luther's Bible. But after Buber and Rosenzweig unsuccessfully attempted to revise the first chapter of Luther's translation of Genesis, they came to realize that *as Jews* they could produce a translation that would more faithfully convey the Hebrew than had Luther. Given the role of Luther's translation in the formation of German language and culture, Buber and Rosenzweig saw their translation as a means of more deeply fusing Jewishness and Germanness. This resulted in the paradox that while the Buber-Rosenzweig translation was closer to the Hebrew and sounded more foreign than the Jewish Reformation translations, unlike these translations its intended audience included Christians as well as Jews.[15]

The Buber-Rosenzweig Bible was informed by deep anxiety about the place of Jews in German society. Buber mentioned this when he recalled that opposing Neo-Marcion trends in Germany that aimed to "Germanize Christianity" by decoupling Christianity from its connection to the Old Testament was a factor motivating his and Rosenzweig's translation.[16] Klaus

Rosenzweig acknowledged his connection to Hirsch in a famous 1927 letter to Jacob Rosenheim, then leader of the Hirschian Neo-Orthodox community in Frankfurt, writing that his Bible translation was "consciously more closely related to Hirsch's than to any of its other predecessors." Rosenzweig explained that he shared Hirsch's conviction that Bible was the work of "a single mind," a view rejected by Bible critics. For Rosenzweig, the difference was that Hirsch regarded this single mind as Moses, while for himself and Buber this single mind was the Pentateuch's anonymous redactor. Of course, this was a misreading of Hirsch since for Hirsch the single mind behind the Pentateuch was God, not Moses. Rosenzweig found a further affinity with Hirsch in that both stressed the unity of the Oral Torah and Written Torah. But again Rosenzweig misread Hirsch, to whom he attributed the view that the Oral Torah "is a stream parallel to the written rising from the same spring." In fact, Hirsch's view was that the Written Torah is notes of the Oral Torah, which is the true text of revelation. See Rosenzweig's letter to Rosenheim in Buber and Rosenzweig, *Scripture and Translation,* 22–24. Niehoff observes that in his working notes to Buber, the translation that Rosenzweig most often recommends aside from Luther's is Hirsch's. See Niehoff, "The Buber-Rosenzweig Translation," 264. On other affinities between Buber and Rosenzweig and Hirsch, see p. 256 note 130, p. 321 note 149, p. 322 note 154, p. 341 note 14, p. 361, p. 377 note 158, p. 383 note 175 of this volume. In 1931 Raphael Breuer upbraided Buber for not acknowledging his and Rosenzweig's debt to Hirsch's Pentateuch translation. See Breuer, "Eine Offene Anfrage an Martin Buber." See Gillman, *A History of German Jewish Bible Translation,* 236–237.

15 See Benjamin, *Rosenzweig's Bible,* 103–134, and the various sources she cites. Also see Fox, "Franz Rosenzweig as Translator," 372; Levenson, *The Making of the Modern Jewish Bible,* 82–84; Weintraub, *The German Translations,* 37. The one exception is Mendelssohn's translation of the Psalms, which, as we have seen, was intended for both Jews and Christians. See pp. 19 and 37 of this volume.

16 See Buber's essay "The How and Why of Our Bible Translation" in Buber and Rosenzweig, *Scripture and Translation,* 209–211. For discussion of the role opposing Marcionism plays in the Buber-Rosenzweig Bible translation, see Mendes-Flohr, *Divided Passions,* 224–230. For a more general discussion of the role of anti-Marcionism in Rosenzweig's thought, see Pollock, *Rosenzweig's Conversions.*

Reichert has similarly argued that Buber's and Rosenzweig's work was animated by a desire to counter German nationalists who sought to "purify" Germany of foreign influences by returning German language and culture to its medieval Teutonic roots.[17] Scholem clearly intuited this subterranean angst, remarking that "Rosenzweig's translations live in the demonic glamor of a hybrid existence. His activity as a translator was determined by his magic wish for a deeper and deeper marriage with the *German*." Scholem was unsparing in his assessment of this endeavor: "A *disaster* for the Jewish perspective."[18]

But Buber and Rosenzweig were animated not only by unease about their Germanness, but also by deep unease about their Jewishness. That they aimed for a return to Judaism based on direct encounter with the Bible largely independent of rabbinic literature reflects an alienation from historical Judaism that for millennia had been defined and sustained by rabbinic exegesis. Scholem once again put his finger on the point when he detected what he called "fanaticism" in Rosenzweig's return to Judaism.[19] This fanaticism was expressed in Rosenzweig's striving to return his fellow Jews to authentic Judaism through emotionally charged revelatory religious experience accessed through an almost fundamentalist return to the biblical letter.[20] Peter Gordon interprets the Buber-Rosenzweig translation project as an example of an early twentieth-century phenomenon he calls "archaic modernism." The "archaic modernist" is an angst-filled, alienated, rootless modern who longs for a lost religious past, seeing "modern culture and modern thought" and having "gone astray from some original truth," but regarding modernity as inevitable. To heal moribund modernity, she seeks to return to cultural urtexts, which she reads in modernist fashion while asserting that she is, in fact, recovering the texts' original meaning that has been forgotten.[21]

[17] See Reichert, "It Is Time," 184–185.

[18] See Reichert, "It Is Time," 182.

[19] See Fox, "Franz Rosenzweig as Translator," 383.

[20] Fox writes, "A final biographical observation concerns Rosenzweig's character . . . that of a *Ba'al Teshuvah*, the 'returner' to Judaism . . . The person who 'discovers' his or her religious faith often becomes a proselytizer, or at least one who urgently needs to share his discovery with the world." See Fox, "Franz Rosenzweig as Translator," 383.

[21] See Gordon, *Rosenzweig and Heidegger*, 307–308. Rosenzweig's "archaic modernism" is also evident in his articulating a racial concept of Jewish nationhood rooted in what he called "the naturalness of *blood*." See Rosenzweig, *Der Mensch und sein Werke: Briefe und Tägebucher*, 1: 158; *Star of Redemption*, 285, 298–299. See Dagan, "The Motif of Blood and Procreation in Franz Rosenzweig." For Rosenzweig, the racial elements of Judaism had been obscured by apologetic, bourgeois Jewish writers such as Mendelssohn, Zunz, Hirsch, and Hermann Cohen. Rosenzweig may have conceived the importance of Jewish blood symbolically. See Batnitzky, *Idolatry and Representation*, 73–76; Gordon, *Rosenzweig and Heidegger*, 212–214. Yet one cannot imagine Mendelssohn, Zunz, or Hirsch speaking of blood as central to Jewish nationhood, even metaphorically. On the modernist context of Rosenzweig's turn to a racial/ethnic conception of Judaism, see Schwarzschild, "Franz Rosenzweig and Martin Heidegger: The German and Jewish Turn to Ethnicism." Also see Mosse, *German Jews Beyond Judaism*, 47–48.

Rosenzweig's and Buber's anxiety-ridden endeavor to leap over millennia of rabbinic exegesis and return to an imagined biblical urtext by an almost fanatical attempt to recreate the Hebrew in their German translation with the aim of triggering a dramatic revelatory experience contrasts with the approach to the Bible taken by the Jewish Reformation translators. More organically connected to Jewish tradition through their deep knowledge of rabbinic literature and more secure in their Judaism, they deeply probe the relation between Midrash and the Bible, seek to balance German elegance with the form of the Hebrew, and promote a harmonious religious vision grounded in obedience to God's moral will, while being suspicious of dramatic revelatory experience.

Rather than contrast Buber's and Rosenzweig's bold Jewish Counter-Reformation with the timid Jewish Reformation, one can suggest a different narrative. Buber's and Rosenzweig's assertiveness is compensatory bluster masking deep insecurity about both their Jewishness and Germanness, while the Jewish Reformation writers present a learned, quietly confident, yet deeply spiritual Judaism harmoniously blended with the noblest elements of middle-class German values.

APPENDIX

Mendelssohn on the Decalogue

The different versions of the Decalogue found in Exodus and Deuteronomy provided fodder for Bible critics. Beginning with Spinoza, Bible critics cited differences between the Decalogues as evidence of the Pentateuch's historical development. As we have seen, Mendelssohn was committed to the unity and reliability of the Masoretic Bible and deployed his concept of multiple levels of meaning to undercut Bible criticism. Spinoza's and Mendelssohn's treatments of the two versions of the Decalogue provide a good example of how Mendelssohn uses literary analysis to respond to biblical criticism.

The most significant differences between the two Decalogues occur in the fourth commandment. I begin by citing both versions, placing additions in the second version in italics and marking variations between the two texts by underlining them:[1]

> *Version 1*: Exodus 20: 8–11
> [8]<u>Remember</u> (*zakhor*) the Sabbath day and keep it holy (*l'kadsho*). [9]Six days you shall labor and do all your work, [10]but the seventh day is a Sabbath of the Lord your God; you shall not do any work—you, your son or daughter, your male or female slave, or your cattle, or the stranger who is within your settlements. [11]<u>For in six days the Lord made heaven and earth and sea, and all that is in them, and He rested on the seventh day; therefore the Lord blessed the Sabbath day and hallowed it.</u>
>
> *Version 2*: Deuteronomy: 5: 12–15
> [12]<u>Guard</u> (*shamor*) the Sabbath day and keep it holy (*l'kadsho*), *as the Lord your God has commanded you.* [13]Six days you shall labor and do all your work, [14]but the seventh day is a Sabbath of the Lord your God; you shall not do any work—you, your son or daughter, your male or female slave, *your ox or your ass, or any* of your cattle, or the stranger who is within your settlements, *so that your male and female slave may rest as you do.* [15]<u>Remember (*v'zakharta*) that you were a slave in the land of Egypt and the Lord your God freed you from there with a mighty hand and an outstretched arm; therefore the Lord your God has commanded you to keep (*la'asot*) the Sabbath day.</u>

In the *TTP* Spinoza notes that in the fortieth year after the departure of the Israelites from Egypt, Moses explained to the people all the laws and bound them to observe them.[2] Moses then wrote a book containing this legal covenant, which he titled *The Book of the Law of God* (*Sefer Torat Elohim*). This book included the version of the Decalogue found in Exodus. Moses gave *The Book of the Law of God* to the priests to guard and read to the people, and Joshua later added to this book.[3]

Spinoza surmises that when the Jews were exiled, Ezra retrieved the *Book of the Law of God,* which had been lost or fallen into neglect. He presented the book to the people but expanded it. Ezra's revised *Book of the Law of God* became the book of Deuteronomy.[4]

[1] I use the 1985 Jewish Publication Society translation, which I have amended where I have seen fit.
[2] See Deuteronomy 1:5, 9–14.
[3] See Deuteronomy 31:9–13; Joshua 24:25–26. See Spinoza, *Opera,* 3:122–123; *Collected Works,* 2:198 (*Theological-Political Treatise,* ch. 8).
[4] See Spinoza, *Opera,* 3:126–127; *Collected Works,* 2: 204 (*Theological-Political Treatise,* ch. 8).

In Ezra's view the Jews were exiled because they had forsaken Moses's law. To bolster the authority of this law, Ezra claimed that the Israelites had only received the land of Israel because of divine promises made to Abraham and the commandments given to Moses. Using documents that he found and redacted, Ezra appended what came to be the first four books of the Pentateuch to the book of Deuteronomy. He then redacted what became the books of Joshua, Judges, Ruth, Samuel, and Kings as a way of showing by historical example that as long as the Israelites observed the law, they prospered, but when they abandoned it, they suffered.[5]

For Spinoza, the Decalogue in Deuteronomy reveals Ezra's editorial hand quite perspicuously. That is why it is fuller and contains more explanations than the original version recorded by Moses, which is preserved in its original form in Exodus. Ezra's zeal for the observance of the law is made manifest by the fact that he changes the emphasis and rationale of the original Decalogue. Whereas the original the Decalogue focused on "remembering" (*zakhor*) the Sabbath as a way of affirming God's creation of the world in six days, Ezra emphasizes "observing" (*shamor*) the laws of the Sabbath. Furthermore, Ezra justifies this law by appealing to God's taking the Jews out of Egypt. The implication is that if the Jews return to observing the Law of Moses God will liberate them from their current exile just as God freed them from the exile of Egypt.[6]

While Spinoza sees the discrepancies between the two versions of the Fourth Commandment as containing clues to their historical origins, Mendelssohn draws on four Midrashim to establish the perfect harmony between these two versions:

1. "Remember" (*zakhor*) and "guard" (*shamor*) were said in one utterance— something that the mouth cannot utter and the ear cannot hear (*BT*, Shevu'ot, 20b).
2. R. Abin citing R. Ila'i laid down: Wherever the expressions "guard yourself" (*hishamer*), "lest" (*pen*), or "do not" (*al*) are used, a negative commandment is invariably intended (*BT*, Eruvin, 96a).
3. "Remember"—you might think with your heart, when it says "guard" it means with your heart, so what does "remember" refer to? That you should study with your mouth (*shone befikha*) (Sifra, Behukotai, Parshata).
4. "Remember (*zakhor*) the Sabbath to keep it holy" (Exodus: 20:8)—mention it (zokhreihu) over wine (*BT*, Pesachim, 106a).

Mendelssohn's approach to the Fourth Commandment is informed by his classification of truth. In *Jerusalem*, he distinguishes between eternal-necessary and historical truths.[7] Eternal-necessary truths are logically necessary. Historical truths are contingent truths that become actual at a certain time because God wills them into existence though it is logically possible for God never to have done so.

Mendelssohn maps Judaism onto this division. Judaism includes eternal-necessary truths such as God's existence and divine providence. These are universal truths knowable to all people through reason or common sense. What distinguishes Judaism from other

[5] See Spinoza, *Opera*, 3:125–128; *Collected Works*, 2:202–205 (*Theological-Political Treatise*, ch. 8).
[6] Ibid.
[7] See Mendelssohn, *JubA*, 8:157–158; *Jerusalem*, 90–91. Mendelssohn also refers to "eternal contingent truths," that is, truths that are true at all times in this world but not in every possible world. These truths become actual because God wills them into existence since they are for the best.

religions is that it also includes historical truths such as the biblical narratives and the ceremonial laws given to the Jews alone following their exodus from Egypt.[8]

According to a rabbinic adage, the Sabbath is equivalent to the entire Torah.[9] Mendelssohn adapts this idea, claiming that in the Sabbath one finds all of the major components of Judaism. Following the first Midrash, Mendelssohn explains that the Fourth Commandment has a particular character. Through one utterance God communicated multiple things in a miraculous way that is impossible to replicate in writing.[10] To convey a sense of what God had commanded, God recorded two versions of the Decalogue in the Pentateuch, encoded with multiple layers of meaning.

For Mendelssohn, the *peshat* of *zakhor* and *shamor* mean the same thing. In the *kal* form, which is the form used in Exodus 20:8, the root ז.כ.ר means "to remember."[11] Similarly, the *kal* form of the root ש.מ.ר used at Deuteronomy 5:12 refers to guarding an idea in one's mind.[12] So on the level of *peshat* both verses address *thought* enjoining a person to remember the Sabbath.[13] Mendelssohn further observes that according to *peshat* the word *l'kadsho* ("to sanctify it") used in both verses means that one should mentally distinguish the Sabbath from the other days of the week by marking it as a special time for clearing the mind of temporal matters.[14] So the "it" of *l'kadsho* ("to sanctify it") refers to the Sabbath.[15]

But for Mendelssohn *zakhor* and *shamor* also have secondary meanings. These secondary meanings enjoin *actions* one should take to remember the Sabbath. Drawing on the third and fourth Midrashim, Mendelssohn notes that in the *hif'il* form, the root ז.כ.ר means "to mention," for mentioning is a means of recalling something through speech.[16] The third Midrash, which interprets *zakhor* to mean that one should "study with one mouth," indicates that the choice of the term *zakhor* in Exodus hints to a secondary meaning of the term according to its *hif'il* form. This secondary meaning is that the Sabbath should be a time for gathering with friends and family to sanctify and bless God's name by discussing God's majesty as evidenced by the wonders of creation.[17] This is similarly indicated by the fourth Midrash, which states that one should mention the Sabbath over wine, since wine is something that often accompanies a social meal that centers on important discussions such as the Greek symposium.[18] Further evidence

[8] See Mendelssohn, *JubA,* 8:192–193; *Jerusalem,* 126–127; *JubA,* 18:340 (Commentary to Deuteronomy 5:15).

[9] See *Exodus Rabbah* 25:12.

[10] See Mendelssohn, *JubA,* 16:195. See Rashi, Exodus 20:8 s.v. *zakhor*; Rashi, Deuteronomy 5:12: s.v. *shamor.*

[11] See Mendelssohn, *JubA,* 16:191 (Commentary to Exodus 20:8). See Rashbam, Exodus: 20:8 s.v. *zakhor.*

[12] Mendelssohn, *JubA,* 14:148; 16:325 (Commentary on Exodus 31:16); 17:263 (Commentary to Leviticus 19:3).

[13] Ibid.

[14] Compare Nahmanides, Exodus: 20:8 s.v. *l'kadsho.*

[15] See Mendelssohn, *JubA,* 14;148. In Ibn Ezra's commentary to Exodus 20:1, he likewise notes that *zakhor* and *shamor* both mean "to remember," though Ibn Ezra claims that this "remembering" refers to the fact that one should always recall what day of the week it is so that one does not come to violate the Sabbath by doing labor. But unlike Mendelssohn, for Ibn Ezra *shamor* and *zakhor* are completely interchangeable; they have no secondary meanings.

[16] See Mendelssohn, *JubA,* 16:191 (Commentary to Exodus 20:8).

[17] See Mendelssohn, *JubA,* 18:339, 340 (Commentary to Deuteronomy 5:12, 15)

[18] See Mendelssohn, *JubA,* 18:339, 340 (Commentary to Deuteronomy, 5:12, 15); Nahmanides, Commentary on Exodus 20:8 s.v. *l'kadsho.*

for this secondary meaning is found in the fact that in Exodus the rationale for the Sabbath derives from the universal event of God's creation of the world.[19] So according to the secondary meaning of Exodus 20:8, *zakhor* instructs one how to cultivate an appreciation for eternal religious truths, and the "it" in *l'kadsho* ("to sanctify it") refers to God.[20]

Turning to the Deuteronomic Decalogue, Mendelssohn claims that the extra phrase "as the Lord your God commanded" (Deuteronomy 5:12) indicates that though employing different words the Deuteronomic version refers to the same utterance recorded in Exodus.[21] But as the second Midrash notes, the root ש.מ.ר also has a secondary meaning—"guard yourself," that is, to refrain.[22] So unlike Exodus 20:8, Deuteronomy 5:12 alludes to refraining from work on the Sabbath. And as the Midrash makes clear, this refraining from work is of a technical sort involving specific prohibitions, the so-called "negative commandments" (*mitzvot lo ta'aseh*). That the Deuteronomic version is referring to legal prohibitions is also indicated by the fact that, unlike the Exodus version, it ends with the words "therefore the Lord your God has commanded you to keep (*la'asot*) the Sabbath day"[23] for the word *la'asot* can mean "to perform."[24] A further indication that the Deuteronomic version refers to legal prohibitions is the rationale given for resting. While in Exodus this rationale is based on God's having rested following six days of creation, in Deuteronomy it involves commemorating God's having freed the Israelites from slavery. For in so doing God became the Israelites' sovereign, which was a prelude to God's binding the Israelites to God's law.[25] So for Mendelssohn, *shamor* points to the major historical truths that define Judaism, namely, God's providential governance of the Israelites and the laws God revealed to them. Unlike the eternal truths, these historical truths are particular to the Jews and distinguish them from Gentiles.[26] Hence, the secondary meaning of *l'kadsho* is that one should refrain from work on the Sabbath, as this sanctifies the Jews among the nations. Here the "it" of *l'kadsho* refers to the Jewish people.[27]

In sum, Mendelssohn's literary-philosophical interpretation of the Pentateuch undercuts biblical criticism. Mendelssohn explains that the repetitions and contradictions found in the Fourth Commandment of the Decalogue are not evidence of the historical development of the Pentateuch and multiple authorship, but rather reflect multiples levels of meaning that point to the major elements of Judaism.

[19] See Mendelssohn, *JubA*, 16:188.

[20] See Mendelssohn, *JubA*, 18:339 (Commentary to Deuteronomy, 5:12). In Hebrew, the suffix *vav* in *l'kadsho* refers to the third person singular, which can be an object ("it") or a person ("him").

[21] See ibid. Compare Ibn Ezra's comments to Exodus 20:1.

[22] See Mendelssohn, *JubA*, 18:339–340 (Commentary to Deuteronomy, 5:12).

[23] Deuteronomy, 5:15. See Mendelssohn, *JubA*, 18:340 (Commentary to Deuteronomy 5:15).

[24] Ibid.

[25] Ibid. See Harvey, "Mendelssohn's Heavenly Politics," 403–412.

[26] See Mendelssohn, *JubA*, 16:188; 18:340 (Commentary to Deuteronomy, 5:15); 8:165; *Jerusalem*, 98; Rashi, Commentary to Deuteronomy 5:15 s.v. *vezakharta*.

[27] See Mendelssohn, *JubA*, 16:324 (Commentary to Exodus 31:11); 18:340 (Commentary to Deuteronomy 5:15).

Table A.1. Titles of German Jewish Pentateuch Translations until Hirsch

Author	Year of Publication	Hebrew Title	German Title
Moses Mendelssohn	1780–1783	*Sefer Netivot Hashalom*	
Joseph Johlson	1831	***Hamishah Humshei Torah***	*Die fünf Bücher Mose*
Gotthold Salomon	1837	*Torah Tziva Lanu Mosheh*	*Die fünf Bücher Mose*
Leopold Zunz	1837	*Torah*	*Die Lehre/**Der Pentateuch** das ist die fünf Bücher Moses*
Salomon Herxheimer	1840	*Torah*	***Der Pentateuch** oder die fünf Bücher Mose's*
Ludwig Philippson	1844	***Hamishah Humshei Torah***	***Der Pentateuch.** Die fünf Bücher Moscheh*
Samson Raphael Hirsch	1867–1876	***Hamishah Humshei Torah***	***Der Pentateuch***

Bibliography

Allison, Henry. *Lessing and the Enlightenment; His Philosophy of Religion and Its Relation to Eighteenth-Century Thought*. Ann Arbor: University of Michigan Press, 1966.

Alter, Robert. *The Art of Biblical Poetry*. New York: Basic Books, 1985.

Altmann, Alexander. *Die Trostvolle Aufklärung: Studien zur Metaphysik und Politischen Theorie Moses Mendelssohns*. Stuttgart-Bad Cannstatt: Frommann-Holzboog, 1982.

Altmann, Alexander. *Essays in Jewish Intellectual History*. Hanover, NH: Brandeis University Press, 1981.

Altmann, Alexander. "Introduction." In *Jerusalem, or on Religious Power and Judaism*, edited by Allan Arkush, 3–29. Hanover, NH: Brandeis University Press, 1983.

Altmann, Alexander. "Mendelssohn on Education and the Image of Man." In *Studies in Jewish Thought: An Anthology of German Jewish Scholarship*, edited by Alfred Jospe, 387–403. Detroit, MI: Wayne State University Press, 1981.

Altmann, Alexander. "Moses Mendelssohn as the Archetypal German Jew." In *The Jewish Response to German Culture: From the Enlightenment to the Second World War*, edited by Walter Schatzberg and Jehuda Reinharz, 17–31. Hanover, MA: University Press of New England, 1985.

Altmann, Alexander. *Moses Mendelssohn: A Biographical Study*. Philadelphia, PA: Jewish Publication Society of America, 1973.

Altmann, Alexander. *Moses Mendelssohns Frühschriften zur Metaphysik*. Tübingen: Mohr Siebeck, 1969.

Altmann, Alexander. "Moses Mendelssohns Kindheit in Dessau." *Bulletin des Leo Baeck Instituts* 40 (1967): 237–275.

Altmann, Alexander. "Zur frühgeschichte der jüdischen Predigt in Deutschland: Leopold Zunz als Prediger." *The Leo Baeck Institute Year Book Annual* 6 (1961): 3–59.

Aptroot, Marion. "Bible Translation as Cultural Reform: The Amsterdam Yiddish Bibles (1678–1679)." Thesis (Ph.D.), Oxford University, 1989.

Aptroot, Marion. "'In Galkes They Do Not Say So, but the Taitsh Is as It Stands Here': Notes on the Amsterdam Yiddish Bible Translations by Blitz and Witzenhausen." *Studia Rosenthalia* 27 (1993): 136–158.

Aptroot, Marion. "Yiddish Bibles in Amsterdam." In *The Bible in/and Yiddish*, edited by Shlomo Berger. Amsterdam: Menasseh ben Israel Institute, 2007.

Arendt, Hannah. *The Human Condition*. Chicago: University of Chicago Press, 1958.

Arendt, Hannah. *Rahel Varnhagen: The Life of a Jewess.* Translated by Richard and Clara Winston. Baltimore, MD: Johns Hopkins University Press, 2000.

Arkush, Allan. *Moses Mendelssohn and the Enlightenment*. Albany: State University of New York Press, 1994.

Asad, Talal. *Genealogies of Religion: Discipline and Reasons of Power in Christianity and Islam*. Baltimore, MD: Johns Hopkins University Press, 1993.

Ascher, Saul. *Leviathan, oder über Religion in Rücksicht des Judenthums*. Berlin: Franckeschen Büchhandlung, 1792.

Assaf, Simcha. *A Source-Book for the History of Jewish Education from the Beginning of the Middle Ages to the Period of the Haskalah* [in Hebrew]. Edited by Shmuel Glick. 5 vols. New York: The Jewish Theological Seminary of America, 2002.

Augusti, Johann Christian Wilhelm. "Vorrede." In *Die Schriften des Alten Testaments*, edited by Johann Christian Wilhelm Augusti and Wilhelm Martin Leberecht De Wette, i–xi. Heidleberg: Mohr und Zimmer, 1809.

Augusti, Johann Christian Wilhelm, and Wilhelm Martin Leberecht De Wette. *Die Schriften des Alten Testaments*. 5 vols. Heidelberg: Mohr und Zimmer, 1809.

Baader, Benjamin Maria. *Gender, Judaism, and Bourgeois Culture in Germany, 1800–1870*. Bloomington: Indiana University Press, 2006.

Baader, Benjamin Maria. "Jewish Difference and and the Feminine Spirit of Judaism in Mid-Nineteenth-Century Germany." In *Jewish Masculinities*, edited by Benjamin Maria Baader, Sharon Gillerman, and Paul Lerner, 50–71. Bloomington: Indiana University Press, 2012.

Bach, Hans. "Der Bibel'sche Orient und sein Verfasser." *Zeitschrift für die Geschichte der Juden in Deutschland* 7 (1937): 14–45.

Bach, Hans. "Isaac Bernays." *Monatsschrift für Geschichte und Wissenschaft des Judentums* 83, no. 1 (1939): 533–547.

Bacher, Wilhelm. "The Views of Jehuda Halevi Concerning the Hebrew Language." *Hebraica* 8, no. 3/4 (1892): 136–149.

Baeck, Leo. *Mendelssohn Gedenkfeier der Jüdischen Gemeinde zu Berlin am 8. September 1929: Gedenkrede*. Berlin: n.p., 1929.

Baer, Yitzhak, *A History of the Jewish in Christian Spain*. Translated by Louis Schoffman, 2 vols. Philadelphia, PA: Jewish Publication Society, 1971.

Bamberger, Seligmann. "Fackel der Wahrheit: Eine kritische Beleuchtung des Philippson'chen Bibelwerkes von einem Orthodoxen Bibelfreunde." Würzburg: J.M. Richter, 1860.

Bamberger, Seligmann, Abraham Adler, and Marcus Lehmann, Eds. *Uebersetzung der fünf Bücher Moses*. Frankfurt: J. Kauffmann, 1873.

Baron, Salo. "Freedom and Constraint in the Jewish Community: An Historic Episode." In *Essays and Studies in Memory of Linda R. Miller*, edited by Israel Davidson, 9–24. New York: Jewish Theological Seminary, 1938.

Barzilay, Isaac. "Smolenskin's Polemic against Mendelssohn in Historical Perspective." *Proceedings of the American Academy of Jewish Research* 53 (1986): 11–48.

Batnitzky, Leora. *How Judaism Became a Religion: An Introduction to Modern Jewish Thought*. Princeton, NJ: Princeton University Press, 2011.

Batnitzky, Leora. *Idolatry and Representation: The Philosophy of Franz Rosenzweig Reconsidered*. Princeton, NJ: Princeton University Press, 2000.

Bauer, Bruno. "The Jewish Problem." In *The Jew in the Modern World*, edited by Paul Mendes-Flohr and Jehuda Reinharz, 297–300. New York: Oxford University Press, 1843.

Baumgarten, Jean, and Jerold C. Frakes. *Introduction to Old Yiddish Literature*. Oxford; New York: Oxford University Press, 2005.

Bechtoldt, Hans-Joachim. *Jüdische deutsche Bibelübersetzungen vom ausgehenden 18. bis zum Beginn des 20. Jahrhunderts*. Stuttgart: W. Kohlhammer, 2005.

Beck, Lewis White. *Early German Philosophy; Kant and His Predecessors*. Cambridge, MA: Harvard University Press, 1969.

Behm, Britta. "Moses Mendelssohns Beziehungen zur Berliner Jüdischen Freischule zwischen 1778 und 1786." In *Jüdische Erziehung und Aufklärerische Schulreform*, edited by Uta Lohmann Britta Behm and Ingrid Lohmann, 107–136. Munster: Waxmann, 2002.

Behm, Britta *Moses Mendelssohn und die Transformation der jüdischen Erziehung in Berlin* Münster: Waxmann, 2002.

Behrens, Katja. *Der Kleine Mausche aus Dessau: Moses Mendelssohns Reise nach Berlin im Jahre 1743*. München: Hanser, 2009.

Beiser, Frederick. *Diotima's Children: German Aesthetic Rationalism from Leibniz to Lessing*. Oxford: Oxford University Press, 2009.

Benjamin, Mara H. *Rosenzweig's Bible: Reinventing Scripture for Jewish Modernity*. Cambridge; New York: Cambridge University Press, 2009.

Benjamin, Walter. *Illuminations*. Translated by Harry Zohn. New York: Schocken Books, 1986.

Berlin, Isaiah. *Four Essays on Liberty*. New York: Oxford University Press, 1969.

Berman, Antoine. "Translation and the Trials of the Foreign." In *The Translation Studies Reader*, edited by Lawrence Venuti, 276–289. New York: Routledge, 2004.

Biale, David. *Not in the Heavens: The Tradition of Jewish Secular Thought*. Princeton, NJ: Princeton University Press, 2010.

Bilik, Dorothy. "Tsene-Rene: A Yiddish Literary Success." *Jewish Book Annual* 51 (1993): 96–111.

Bitzan, Amos. "Leopold Zunz and the Meanings of Wissenschaft." *Journal of the History of Ideas* 78, no. 2 (2017): 233–254.

Bleich, Judith. "Jacob Ettlinger, His Life and Works: The Emergence of Modern Orthodoxy in Germany." Thesis (Ph.D.), New York University, 1974.

Blitz, Yekutiel. *Torah, Nevi'im, Veketuvim* [in Yiddish]. Amsterdam: Uri Phoebius ben Aharon Halevi, 1679.

Bloch, Philipp. *Heinrich Graetz: A Memoir*. London: Jewish Publication Society of America, 1898.

Blum, Jean. *J.A. Starck et la Querelle du Crypto-Catholicisme en Allemagne, 1785–1789*. Paris: Alcan, 1912.

Blutinger, Jeffrey. "'So-Called Orthodoxy': The History of an Unwanted Label." *Modern Judaism* 27, no. 3 (2007): 310–328.

The Book of Concord: The Confessions of the Evangelical Lutheran Church. Edited by Robert Kolb and Timothy J. Wengert, Minneapolis, MN: Fortress Press, 2000.

Boyarin, Daniel. *Dying for God: Martyrdom and the Making of Christianity and Judaism*. Stanford: Stanford University Press, 1999.

Boyarin, Daniel. "Pilpul: The Logic of Commentary." In *The Talmud: A Personal Take-Selected Essays*, edited by Tal Hever-Chybowski, 47–65. Tübingen: Mohr-Siebeck, 2017.

Brämer, Andreas. *Rabbiner Zacharias Frankel: Wissenschaft des Judentums und Konservative Reform im 19. Jahrhundert*. Hildesheim Olms, 2000.

Brämer, Andreas. "Revelation and Tradition: Zachariah Frankel on the Controversy Concerning the 'Hodegetica in Mischnam'; from His Letters to Bernhard Beer." *Jewish Studies Quarterly* 5, no. 2 (1998): 171–186.

Brann, Marcus. "Aus H. Graetz Lehr-und Wanderjahren (1. Artikel)." *Monatsschrift für Geschichte und Wissenschaft des Judentums* 62, no. 3 (1918): 231–265.

Brann, Marcus. "Aus H. Graetz Lehr-und Wanderjahren (2. Artikel)." *Monatsschrift für Geschichte und Wissenschaft des Judentums* 63, no. 1 (1919): 34–47.

Brann, Marcus. "Aus H. Graetz Lehr-und Wanderjahren (3. Artikel)." *Monatsschrift für Geschichte und Wissenschaft des Judentums* 63, no. 3 (1919): 343–363.

Brann, Marcus. "Mittheilungen aus dem Briefwechsel zwischen Zunz und Kaufmann." *Jahrbuch für jüdische Geschichte und Literatur* 30 (1937): 131–172.

Brenner, Michael. *Prophets of the Past: Interpreters of Jewish History*. Princeton, NJ: Princeton University Press, 2010.

Breuer, Edward. *The Limits of Enlightenment: Jews, Germans, and the Eighteenth-Century Study of Scripture*. Cambridge, MA: Harvard University Press, 1996.

Breuer, Edward, and David Sorkin. "Moses Mendelssohn's First Hebrew Publication: An Annotated Translation of the Kohelet Mussar." *Leo Baeck Institute Year Book Annual* 48 (2003): 3–23.

Breuer, Joseph. "Aus den Vorarbeiten zum Horeb." *Nahalath Zwi* 5 (1935): 142–145.

Breuer, Mordechai. *Asif: From the Fruits of the Time and the Pen* [in Hebrew]. Jerusalem: Rimonim, 1999.

Breuer, Mordechai. "Chapters in the Life of Rabbi Samson Raphael Hirsch: Geiger a Friend Who Became an Enemy." [In Hebrew]. *Hama'ayan* 3, no. 1–2 (1956): 39–50.

Breuer, Mordechai. "Chapters in the Life of Rabbi Samson Raphael Hirsch: Graetz a Wayward Student." [In Hebrew]. *Hama'ayan* 3 (1956): 42–47.

Breuer, Mordechai. "Chapters in the Life of Rabbi Samson Raphael Hirsch: In Rabbi Jacob Ettlinger's Yeshiva in Mannheim." [In Hebrew]. *Hama'ayan* 12, no. 2 (1972): 55–62.

Breuer, Mordechai. "Chapters in the Life of Rabbi Samson Raphael Hirsch: On the Elimination of Kol Nidre in Oldenburg." [In Hebrew]. *Hama'ayan* 4, no. 2 (1963): 7–12.

Breuer, Mordechai. "Index of Word Roots." [In Hebrew]. In *Pentateuch with the Commentary of Rabbi Samson Raphael Hirsch*, edited by Mordechai Breuer, 17–39. Jerusalem: Mosad Yitzhak Breuer, 2002.

Breuer, Mordechai. "Modernism and Traditionalism in Sixteenth-Century Jewish Historiography: A Study of David Gans' Tzemah David." In *Jewish Thought in the Sixteenth Century*, edited by Bernard Cooperman, 49–88. Cambridge, MA: Harvard University Press, 1983.

Breuer, Mordechai. *Modernity within Tradition: The Social History of Orthodox Jewry in Imperial Germany*. New York: Columbia University Press, 1992.

Breuer, Mordechai. "Preface to the Hebrew Edition." [In Hebrew]. In *Pentateuch with the Commentary of Rabbi Samson Raphael Hirsch*, edited by Mordechai Breuer, 7–11. Jerusalem: Mosad Yitzhak Breuer, 2002.

Breuer, Mordechai. "Rabbi Samson Raphael Hirsch's Commentary on the Torah." [In Hebrew]. *Mahanayim* 4 (1999): 348–359.

Breuer, Mordechai. "Review of *Tradition in an Age of Reform: The Religious Philosophy of Samson Raphael Hirsch* by Noah Rosenbloom." *Tradition: A Journal of Orthodox Jewish Thought* 16, no. 4 (1977): 140–149.

Breuer, Mordechai. "Samson Raphael Hirsch (1808–1888)." In *Guardians of Our Heritage*, edited by Leo Jung, 265–299. New York: Bloch Publishing Company, 1958.

Breuer, Mordechai. *The Tents of Torah* [in Hebrew]. Jerusalem: Zalman Shazar, 2003.

Breuer, Mordechai. "Three Orthodox Approaches to Wissenschaft." [In Hebrew]. In *Jubilee Volume in Honor of Moreinu Ha-Gaon Rabbi Joseph Soloveitchik*, edited by S. Israeli et al., 856–865. Jerusalem: Mosad Harav Kook, 1984.

Breuer, Mordechai. *The Torah Im Derekh Eretz of Samson Raphael Hirsch*. New York: Feldheim, 1970.

Breuer, Raphael. "Eine Offene Anfrage an Martin Buber." *Nahalath Zwi* 1, nos. 9–10 (1931): 308–318.

Breuer, Raphael. *Unter seinem Banner: Ein Beitrag zur Würdigung Rabbiner Samson Raphael Hirsch*. Frankfurt am Main: Gebrüder Knauer, 1908.

Brown, Benjamin, "The Daat Torah Doctrine: Three Stages." [In Hebrew]. In *The Path of the Spirit: The Eliezer Schweid Jubilee Volume: Volume Two*, edited by Yehoyada Amir, 537–600. Jerusalem: Magnes Press, 2004.

Bruford, Walter Horace. *Germany in the Eighteenth Century: The Social Background of the Literary Revival*. Cambridge: The University Press, 1971.

Brüll, Joel. *Sefer Zemirot Israel* [in Hebrew]. 5th ed. Pest: M.E. Löwy Sohn, 1864.

Buber, Martin, and Franz Rosenzweig. *Die Schrift*. Heidelberg: Schneider, 1976.

Buber, Martin, and Franz Rosenzweig. *Die Schrift und ihre Verdeutschung*. Berlin: Schocken, 1936.

Buber, Martin, and Franz Rosenzweig. *Scripture and Translation*. Translated by Lawrence Rosenwald and Everett Fox. Edited by Lawrence Rosenwald and Everett Fox. Bloomington: Indiana University Press, 1994.

Carlebach, Elisheva. *Divided Souls: Converts from Judaism in Germany, 1500–1750*. New Haven: Yale University Press, 2001.

Carlebach, Elisheva. "La communauté juive et ses institutions au début de L'époque moderne." In *Aux Origines du Judaïsme*, edited by Julien Darmon and Jean Baumgarten, 358–389. Paris: Actes Sud, 2012.

Carter, Ian. "Positive and Negative Liberty." *Stanford Encylopedia of Philosophy* (2016).

Chiarini, Luigi. *Théorie du Judaïsme appliquée à la Réforme des Israelites de Tous les Pays de L'Europe et servant en Même Temps D'ouvrage Préparatoire à la Version du Talmud de Babylone*. 2 vols. Paris: J. Barbezat, 1830.

Clark, Matityahu. *Etymological Dictionary of Biblical Hebrew: Based on the Commentaries of Rabbi Samson Raphael Hirsch*. Jerusalem: Feldheim Publishers, 1999.

Cohen, Hermann. *Jüdische Schriften*. Edited by Franz Rosenzweig and Bruno Strauss. 3 vols. Berlin: C.A. Schwetschke & Sohn, 1924.

Cohen, Jeremy. *Living Letters of the Law: Ideas of the Jew in Medieval Christianity*. Berkeley, CA: University of California Press, 1999.

Cohen, Richard. "Urban Visibility and Biblical Visions: Jewish Culture in Western and Central Europe in the Modern Age." In *Cultures of the Jews*, edited by David Biale, 731–798. New York: Schocken, 2003.

Cohon, Samuel. "Zunz and Reform Judaism." *Hebrew Union College Annual* 21 (1960): 251–276.

Dagan, Haggai. "The Motif of Blood and Procreation in Franz Rosenzweig." *AJS Review*, 26, no. 2 (2002): 241–249.

Dauber, Jeremy. "New Thoughts on 'Night Thoughts': Mendelssohn and Translation." *Journal of Modern Jewish Studies* 2, no. 2 (2003): 132–147.

"Der Bibelsche Orient." München: E.A. Fleischmann, 1821.

De Wette, Wilhelm Martin Leberecht. *Beiträge zur Einleitung in das Alte Testament*. 2 vols. Halle: Schimmelpfenning und Compagnie, 1806.

De Wette, William Martin Leberecht. *Die Heilige Schrift des Alten und Neuen Testaments*. 2nd ed., 3 vols. Heidelberg: J.C.B. Mohr, 1831.

De Wette, Wilhelm Martin Leberecht. *Theodore; or the Skeptic's Conversion*. Translated by James Clarke. 2 vols. Boston: Hillard, Gray and Company, 1841.

De Wette, Wilhelm Martin Leberecht. "Vorrede." In *Die Heilige Schrift des Alten und Neuen Testaments*, iii–vii. Heidelberg: J.C.B. Mohr, 1831.

"Die Religiösen Wirren in der Israelitischen Gemeinde zu Frankfurt am Main." Frankfurt am Main: F.B. Auffahrt, 1854.

Di Giovanni, George. "Hegel, Jacobi, and Crypto-Catholicism, or, Hegel in Dialogue with the Enlightenment." In *Hegel on the Modern World*, edited by A. Collins, 53–72. Albany: State University of New York, 1995.

Dimitrovsky, Haim. "On the Method of Pilpul." [in Hebrew]. In *Jubilee Volume for Salo Baron*, edited by Saul Lieberman, 111–182. Jerusalem: JAAR, 1975.

Dohm, Christian Wilhelm von. *Concerning the Amelioration of the Civil Status of the Jews*. Translated by Helen Lederer. Cincinnati, OH: Hebrew Union College-Jewish Institute of Religion, 1957.

Dohm, Christian Wilhelm von. *Ueber die bürgerliche Verbesserung der Juden*. Berlin and Stettin: Friedrich Nicolai, 1783.

Dole, Andrew. *Schleiermacher on Religion and the Natural Order*. New York: Oxford University Press, 2010.

Ducat, Jean. *Spartan Education: Youth and Society in the Classical Period*. Swansea: Classical Press of Wales, 2006.

Duckesz, Eduard. *Chachme AHW* [in Hebrew]. Hamburg: Goldschmidt Verlag, 1908.

Duckesz, Eduard. "Zur Biographie des Chacham Isaak Bernays." *Jahrbuch der jüdisch-literarichsen Gesellschaft* 5 (1907): 297–320.

Duckesz, Eduard. "Zur Genealogie Samson Raphael Hirsch's." *Jahrbuch der Jüdisch-Literarichsen Gesellschaft* 17 (1926): 103–132.

Eastwood, C. Cyril. *The Priesthood of All Believers; an Examination of the Doctrine from the Reformation to the Present Day*. Minneapolis, MN: Augsburg Pub. House, 1962.

Efron, John M. *German Jewry and the Allure of the Sephardic*. Princeton, NJ: Princeton University Press, 2016.

Ehrenberg, Philipp. "Die Samson'sche Freischule zu Wolfenbüttel." *Der Orient* 5, no. 5 (1844): 65–77.

Eisen, Arnold. "Divine Legislation as 'Ceremonial Script': Mendelssohn on the Commandments." *AJS Review* 15, no. 2 (1990): 239–267.

Eisenmenger, Johann Andreas. *Entdecktes Judentum*. 2 vols. Königsberg: n.p., 1711.

Elias, Joseph. "Editor's Notes to *Nineteen Letters*." In *The Nineteen Letters about Judaism*. New York: Feldheim Publishers, 1996.

Eliav, Mordechai. *Jewish Education in Germany in the Period of Enlightenment and Emancipation* [in Hebrew]. Tel Aviv: Hakibbutz Hame'uhad, 1960.

Ellenson, David. *After Emancipation: Jewish Religious Responses to Modernity*. Cincinnati, OH: Hebrew Union College Press, 2004.

Ellenson, David. "Antinomianism and Its Responses in the Nineteenth Century." In *The Cambridge Companion to Judaism and Law*, edited by Christine Hayes, 260–286. New York: Cambridge University Press, 2017.

Ellenson, David. *Rabbi Esriel Hildesheimer and the Creation of a Modern Jewish Orthodoxy*. Tuscaloosa: University of Alabama Press, 1990.

Ellenson, David. "Samuel Holdheim and Zacharias Frankel: On the Legal Character of Jewish Marriage." In *Redefining Judaism in an Age of Emancipation: Comparative Perspectives on Samuel Holdheim*, edited by Christian Wiese, 191–205. Leiden: Brill, 2006.

Emanuel, Yonah. *Modern Commentators and Decisors in Rabbi Samson Raphael Hirsch's Commentary on the Torah* [in Hebrew]. Jerusalem: n.p., 1962.

Epstein, Klaus. *The Genesis of German Conservatism*. Princeton, NJ: Princeton University Press, 1966.

Euben, Roxanne Leslie, and Muhammad Qasim Zaman. "Introduction." In *Princeton Readings in Islamist Thought: Texts and Contexts from Al-Banna to Bin Laden*, edited by Roxanne Leslie Euben and Muhammad Qasim Zaman, 1–48. Princeton, NJ: Princeton University Press, 2009.

Euben, Roxanne Leslie, and Muhammad Qasim Zaman, Eds. *Princeton Readings in Islamist Thought: Texts and Contexts from Al-Banna to Bin Laden*. Princeton Studies in Muslim Politics. Princeton, NJ: Princeton University Press, 2009.

Euchel, Isaac Abraham. *Toldot Rabbenu Hakhaham Mosheh Mendelssohn*. Berlin: Hinukh Ne'arim, 1788.

Ewald, Heinrich. "Recension der *Kritische Untersuchungen über die Genesis* von J. Stähelin." *Theologische Studien und Kritiken* 3 (1831): 595–606.

Feiner, Shmuel. "Educational Agendas and Social Ideals: 'Jüdische Freischule' in Berlin, 1778—1825." [In Hebrew]. *Zion* 60, no. 4 (1995): 393–424.

Feiner, Shmuel. *The Jewish Enlightenment*. Translated by Chaya Naor. Philadelphia: University of Pennyslvania Press, 2002.

Feuchtwang, David. "Samson Raphael Hirsch als Oberlandesrabbiner von Mähren." In *Samson Raphael Hirsch Jubiläums-Nummer*, 19–26. Frankfurt am Main: Israelit, 1909.

Fishbane, Michael. *Biblical Interpretation in Ancient Israel*. Oxford: Oxford University Press, 1985.

Fishman, Isidore. *The History of Jewish Education in Central Europe, from the End of the Sixteenth to the End of the Eighteenth Century*. London: E. Goldston, 1944.

Fokkelman, J.P. *Reading Biblical Poetry: An Introductory Guide*. Louisville, KY: Westminster John Knox Press, 2001.

Fox, Everett. "Franz Rosenzweig as Translator." *Leo Baeck Institute Year Book Annual* 34 (1989): 371–384.

Frankel, Zacharias. *Darkhei Hamishnah; Hodgetica in Mischnam*. Leipzig: H. Hunger, 1859.

Frankel, Zacharias. "Erklärung, Die Schrift 'Hodegetik in die Mishna' betreffend." *Monatsschrift für Geschichte und Wissenschaft des Judentums* 10, no. 4 (1861): 159–160.

Frankel, Zacharias. *Über den Einfluss der Palästinischen Exegese auf die Alexandrinische Hermeneutik*. Leipzig: J.A. Barth, 1851.

Frankel, Zacharias. "Über Reformen im Judenthume." *Zeitschrift für die religiösen Interessen des Judenthums* 1, no. 1 (1844): 3–27.

Frankel, Zacharias. *Vorstudien zu der Septuaginta*. Leipzig: F.C.W. Vogel, 1841.

Fredrikson, Paula. *Augustine and the Jews: A Christian Defense of Jews and Judaism*. New Haven: Yale University Press, 2010.

Freimark, Peter. "Language Behaviour and Assimilation: The Situation of the Jews in Northern Germany in the First Half of the Nineteenth Century." *The Leo Baeck Institute Year Book Annual* 24 (1979): 157–178.

Freudenthal, Gad. "Rabbi David Fränckel, Moses Mendelssohn, and the Beginning of the Berlin Haskalah: Reattributing a Patriotic Sermon." *European Journal of Jewish Studies* 4, no. 2 (2007): 3–33.

Freudenthal, Gideon. *No Religion without Idolatry: Mendelssohn's Jewish Enlightenment*. Notre Dame, IN: University of Notre Dame Press, 2012.

Frevert, Ute. *Women in German History: From Bourgeois Emancipation to Sexual Liberation*. Oxford; New York: Berg, 1989.

Friedländer, David. "Etwas über die Mendelssohnische Psalmenübersetzung." *Berlinische Monatschrift* 8 (1786): 523–550.

Friedländer, David. *Lesebuch für jüdische Kinder*. Berlin: Christian Freidrich Voß und Sohn, 1779.

Friedländer, David, Friedrich Schleiermacher, and Wilhelm Abraham Teller. *A Debate on Jewish Emancipation and Christian Theology in Old Berlin*. Edited by Richard Crouter and Julie A. Klassen. Indianapolis, IN: Hackett Pub., 2004.

Friedlander, Yehuda. *Studies in Hebrew Satire. Volume 1: Hebrew Satire in Germany (1790–1797)* [in Hebrew]. Tel Aviv: Papyrus Publishing House, 1979.

Fries, Jakob Friedrich. *Über die Gefährdung des Wohlstandes und Charakters der Deutschen durch die Juden*. Heidelberg: Mohr und Winter, 1816.

Frisch, Amos. "The Sins of the Patriarchs as Viewed by Traditional Jewish Exegesis." *Jewish Studies Quarterly* 10, no. 3 (2003): 258–273.

Gafni, Chanan. "'Rulebook for Students in the Wolfenbüttel Study House' (from the Zunz Archive): On a Pedagogic Revolution in Its Making." [In Hebrew]. *Dor leDor* 49 (2015): 28–44.

Gans, David. *Zemah David*. Warsaw: n.p., 1878.

Gay, Ruth. *The Jews of Germany: A Historical Portrait*. New Haven, CT: Yale University Press, 1992.

Geiger, Abraham. *Abraham Geiger and Liberal Judaism: The Challenge of the Nineteenth Century*. Translated by Ernst Schlochauer. Edited by Max Wiener. New York: Hebrew Union College Press, 1981.

Geiger, Abraham. *Abraham Geiger's Nachgelassene Schriften*. Edited by Ludwig Geiger. 5 vols. Berlin: Louis Gerschel Verlagsbuchhandlung, 1875.

Geiger, Abraham. "Die Rabbinerzusammenkunft: Sendschreiben an einen befreundeten jüdischen Geistlichen." *WZJT (Wissenschaftliche Zeitschrift für jüdische Theologie)* 3, no. 3 (1837): 313–332.

Geiger, Abraham. "Nachrichten." *WZJT* 3, no. 3 (1837): 450–453.

Geiger, Abraham. "Recension der *Briefe über Judenthum* (1)." *WZJT* 2, no. 2 (1836): 351–359.

Geiger, Abraham. "Recension der *Briefe über Judenthum* (3)." *WZJT* 3, no. 1 (1837): 74–91.

Geiger, Abraham. "Recension der Hirsch's *Versuche*." *WZJT* 4, no. 3 (1839): 355–381.

Geiger, Abraham. *Urschrift und Uebersetzungen der Bibel in ihrer Abhängigkeit von der innern Entwickelung des Judenthums*. Breslau: J. Hainauer, 1857.

Geiger, Ludwig. "Zunz im Verkehr mit Behörden und Hochgestellten." *MGWJ (Monatsschrift für Geschichte und Wissenschaft des Judentums)* 60 (1916): 245–262; 321–347.

Geiger, Ludwig. "Zunz' Tätigkeit für die Reform (1817–1823)." *Liberales Judentum* 11–12 (1917): 113–120.

Gillman, Abigail. "Between Religion and Culture: Mendelssohn, Buber, Rosenzweig and the Enterprise of Biblical Translation." In *Biblical Translation in Context*, edited by Frederick Knobloch, 93–114. Baltimore: University of Maryland Press, 2002.

Gillman, Abigail. *A History of German Jewish Bible Translation*. Chicago: The University of Chicago Press, 2018.

Gillman, Abigail. "The Jewish Quest for a German Bible: The Nineteenth-Century Translations of Joseph Johlson and Leopold Zunz." *SBL Forum* 7, no. 5 (2009).

Gillman, Abigail. "Not Like Cherries, but Like Peaches: Mendelssohn and Rosenzweig Translate Yehuda Halevi's 'Ode to Zion.'" In *The German Hebrew Dialogue*, edited by Rachel Seelig, 19–39: Walter de Gruyer, 2017.

Gilman, Sander L. *Jewish Self-Hatred: Anti-Semitism and the Hidden Language of the Jews*. Baltimore, MD: Johns Hopkins University Press, 1986.

Gilon, Meir. *Mendelssohn's Kohelet Mussar in Its Historical Context* [in Hebrew]. Jerusalem: Israel Academy of Sciences and Humanities, 1979.

Glatzer, Nahum. *Franz Rosenzweig: His Life and Thought*. New York: Schocken Books, 1961.

Glatzer, Nahum. *Leopold and Adelheid Zunz: An Account in Letters*. London: East West Library, 1958.

Glatzer, Nahum. *Leopold Zunz: Jude, Deutscher, Europeaer: Ein Jüdisches Gelehrtenschicksal des 19. Jahrhunderts in Briefen an Freunde*. Tübingen: J.C.B. Mohr, 1964.

Glikl. *Glikl: Memoirs 1691–1719*. Edited by Chava Turniansky. Translated by Sara Friedman. Waltham, MA: Brandeis University Press, 2019.

Goldenbaum, Ursula, and Frank Grunert. *Appell an Das Publikum: Die Öffentliche Debatte in der Deutschen Aufklärung 1687–1796*. 2 vols. Berlin: Akademie Verlag, 2004.

Goldschmidt, Hermann Levin. *The Legacy of German Jewry*. Translated by David Suchoff. New York: Fordham University Press, 2007.

Gordon, Peter Eli. *Rosenzweig and Heidegger: Between Judaism and German Philosophy*. Berkeley: University of California Press, 2003.

Goto, Masahide. "Modern Judaism and Religious Tolerance: On the Paradoxical Phenomenon of 'Exclusivism in Enlightenment.'" *Journal of Interdisciplinary Study of Monotheistic Religions* 3 (2007): 78–97.

Gottlieb, Michah. *Faith and Freedom: Moses Mendelssohn's Theological-Political Thought*. New York: Oxford University Press, 2011.

Gottlieb, Michah. *Faith, Reason, Politics: Essays on the History of Jewish Thought*. Brighton, MA: Academic Studies Press, 2013.

Gottlieb, Michah. "From Tolerance to Acceptance: Moses Mendelssohn's Solution to the Jewish Problem." In *Moses Mendelssohns Rechtsphilosophie im Kontext*, edited by Ursula Goldenbaum, Stephan Meder and Matthias Armgardt, 265–290. Hannover: Wehrhahn Verlag, 2020.

Gottlieb, Michah. "Does Judaism have Dogma? Moses Mendelssohn and a Pivotal Nineteenth-Century Debate." *Yearbook of the Maimonides Centre for Advanced Study* 4 (2019): 219–242.

Gottlieb, Michah. "Mendelssohn's Metaphysical Defense of Religious Pluralism." *The Journal of Religion* 86, no. 2 (2006): 205–225.

Gottlieb, Michah. "Oral Letter and Written Trace: Samson Raphael Hirsch's Defense of the Bible and Talmud." *Jewish Quarterly Review* 106, no. 3 (2016): 316–351.

Gottlieb, Michah. "Orthodoxy and the Orient: Samson Raphael Hirsch on the Location of Judaism." In *Wissenschaft des Judentums beyond Tradition: Jewish Scholarship on the Sacred Texts of Judaism, Christianity and Islam*, edited by D. Saltzer, C. Gafni, and H. Harif, 53–72. Berlin: De Gruyter, 2019.

Gottlieb, Michah. "Spinoza's Method(s) of Biblical Interpretation Reconsidered." *Jewish Studies Quarterly* 14, no. 3 (2007): 286–317.

Gottlieb, Michah. "The Study of Scripture and the Study of Nature: Spinoza and Modern Jewish Thought." In *Spinoza and Modern Jewish Philosophy*, edited by Michael Rosenthal, New York: Palgrave Macmillan, forthcoming.

Graetz, Heinrich. *Geschichte der Juden vom Untergang des jüdischen Staates bis zum Abschluß des Talmud.* Berlin: Veit und Comp., 1853.

Graetz, Heinrich. *Gnosticismus und Judenthum.* Krotochin: B.L. Monasch, 1846.

Graetz, Heinrich. *History of the Jews.* Translated by Bella Lowy. vol. 5, Philadelphia, PA: Jewish Publication Society of America, 1895.

Graetz, Heinrich. *History of the Jews from the Downfall of the Jewish State to the Conclusion of the Talmud.* Translated by James Gutheim. New York: American Jewish Publication Society, 1873.

Grunfeld, Isidor. "Introduction." In *Horeb: A Philosophy of Jewish Laws and Observances,* edited by Isidor Grunfeld, xix–cxl. London: Soncino, 1962.

Grunfeld, Isidor. "Samson Raphael Hirsch: The Man and His Mission." In *Judaism Eternal: Selected Essays from the Writings of Samson Raphael Hirsch,* edited by Isidor Grunfeld, xiii–xlvii. London: Soncino, 1951.

Gugenheimer, Joseph. "Die Hypothesen der Bibelkritik und der Commentar zur Genesis von Herrn Rabbiner S.R. Hirsch." *Jeschurun* 13 (1867): 293–313, 397–409; *Jeschurun* 14 (1867–1868): 1–17, 173–190, 312–324; *Jeschurun* 15 (1868–1869): 81–100; 179–192.

Guttmann, Julius. *The Philosophy of Judaism: the History of Jewish Philosophy from Biblical Times to Franz Rosenzweig.* Translated by D. Silverman. Northvale, NJ: J. Aronson. 1988.

Haberman, Jacob. "Kaufmann Kohler and His Teacher Samson Raphael Hirsch." *The Leo Baeck Institute Year Book Annual* 43 (1998): 73–103.

HaCohen, Ran. *Reclaiming the Hebrew Bible: German-Jewish Reception of Biblical Criticism.* New York: De Gruyter, 2010.

Halbertal, Moshe. *Maimonides: Life and Thought.* Translated by Joel Linsider. Princeton, NJ: Princeton University Press, 2014.

Halevi, Judah. *The Kuzari (Kitab Al Khazari): An Argument for the Faith of Israel.* Translated by Hartwig Hirschfeld. New York: Schocken Books, 1964.

Hamburger, Moses Mendelssohn. *Pnei Tevel.* Amsterdam: Levisohn Brothers, 1872.

Harris, Jay Michael. *How Do We Know This?: Midrash and the Fragmentation of Modern Judaism.* Albany: State University of New York Press, 1995.

Harvey, Warren Zev. "Mendelssohn and Maimon on the Tree of Knowledge." In *Sepharad in Ashkenaz: Medieval Knowledge and Eighteenth Century Enlightened Jewish Discourse,* edited by Andrea Schatz, Resianne Fontaine, and Irene Zwiep, 185–192. Amsterdam: Koninklijke Nederlandse Akademie van Wetenschappen, 2007.

Harvey, Warren Zev. "Mendelssohn's Heavenly Politics." In *Perspectives on Jewish Thought and Mysticism,* edited by Alexander Altmann, Alfred Ivry, Elliot Wolfson, and Allan Arkush, 403–412. Amsterdam: Harwood Academic Publishers, 1998.

Harvey, Warren Zev. "Moses Mendelssohn on the Land of Israel." [In Hebrew]. In *The Land of Israel in Modern Jewish Thought,* edited by Aviezer Ravitzky, 301–312. Jerusalem: Yad Yitzhak ben Zvi, 1998.

Harvey, Warren Zev. "Spinoza on Ibn Ezra's 'Secret of the Twelve.'" In *Spinoza's Theological-Political Treatise: A Critical Guide,* edited by Yitzhak Melamed and Michael Rosenthal, 41–55. New York: Oxford University Press, 2010.

Harvey, Warren Zev. "Why Philosophers Quote Kabbalah: The Cases of Mendelssohn and Rosenzweig." *Studia Judaica* 2008 (2008): 120–125.

Hausen, Karin. "Family and Role Division: The Polarisation of Sexual Stereotypes in the Nineteenth Century—an Aspect of the Dissociation of Work and Family." In *The German Family: Essays on the Social History of the Family in Nineteenth and Twentieth*

Century Germany, edited by Richard Evans and W. R. Lee, 51–83. Totowa, NJ: Barnes & Noble Books, 1981.

Hegel, Georg Wilhelm Friedrich. *Lectures on the History of Philosophy*. Translated by Elizabeth Sanderson Haldane. 3 vols. London: K. Paul, Trench, Trübner, & Co., 1892.

Heine, Heinrich. *Gesammelte Werke*. Edited by Gustav Karpeles and C. Buschheim. 9 vols. Berlin: G. Grote, 1887.

Heine, Heinrich. *On the History of Religion and Philosophy in Germany and Other Writings*. Translated by Howard Pollack-Milgate. Edited by Terry P. Pinkard. New York: Cambridge University Press, 2007.

Heinemann, Isaac. "The Formative Years of the Leader of Modern Orthodox Judaism." *Historia Judaica* 10 (1951): 29–54.

Heinemann, Isaac. "The Relationship between S.R. Hirsch and His Teacher Isaac Bernays." [In Hebrew]. *Zion* 16, no. 1-2 (1951): 44–90.

Heller, Max. "Samson Raphael Hirsch: In Honor of the Centenary of His Birth." *Yearbook of the Central Conference of American Rabbis* 18 (1908): 179–210.

Hengstenberg, Ernst Wilhelm. *Beiträge zur Einleitung ins Alte Testament*. 3 vols. Berlin: Ludwig Oehmigke, 1831–1839.

Herder, Johann Gottfried. *Against Pure Reason: Writings on Religion, Language, and History*. Edited by Marcia J. Bunge. Minneapolis, MN: Fortress Press, 1993.

Herder, Johann Gottfried. *Johann Gottfried Herder: Selected Early Works, 1764–1767: Addresses, Essays, and Drafts; Fragments on Recent German Literature*. Translated by Ernest A. Menze and Michael Palma. Edited by Ernest A. Menze and Karl Menges. University Park, PA: Pennsylvania State University Press, 1992.

Herder, Johann Gottfried, *The Spirit of Hebrew Poetry*. Translated by James Marsh. Burlington, VT: E. Smith, 1833.

Herder, Johann Gottfried. *Vom Geist der ebräischen Poesie*. 2 vols. Dessau: Buchhandlung der Gelehrten, 1782–1783.

Hermann, Klaus. "Translating Cultures and Texts in Reform Judaism: The Philippson Bible." *Jewish Studies Quarterly* 14, no. 2 (2007): 164–197.

Hertz, Deborah Sadie. *How Jews Became Germans: The History of Conversion and Assimilation in Berlin*. New Haven, CT: Yale University Press, 2007.

Herzberg, Isaak. *Moses Mendelssohn: Ein Lebensbild für die Israelitische Jugend*. 2nd ed. Leipzig: Kaufmann, 1929.

Heschel, Abraham Joshua. *God in Search of Man: A Philosophy of Judaism*. Philadelphia, PA: Jewish Publication Society, 1955.

Heschel, Susannah. *Abraham Geiger and the Jewish Jesus*. Chicago: University of Chicago Press, 1998.

Hess, Jonathan M. *Germans, Jews and the Claims of Modernity*. New Haven, CT: London: Yale University Press, 2002.

Hess, Moses. *Ausgewählte Schriften*. Edited by Horst Lademacher. Köln: J. Melzer, 1962.

Hess, Peter. "The Two Books." In *Encyclopedia of Religion*, edited by Lindsay Jones, 9421–9424. Detroit, MI: Macmillan Reference, 2005.

Hildesheimer, Meir. "Rabbi Zvi Hirsch Kalischer and Rabbi Samson Raphael Hirsch." [In Hebrew]. In *Sefer Aviad*, edited by Isaac Raphael, 195–214. Jerusalem: Mosad Harav Kook, 1985.

Hilfrich, Carola. *"Lebendige Schrift": Repräsentation und Idolatrie in Moses Mendelssohns Philosophie und Exegese des Judentums*. München: Fink, 2000.

Hirsch, Emil. "Zunz, Leopold." In *The Jewish Encyclopedia: A Descriptive Record of the History, Religion, Literature, and Customs of the Jewish People from the Earliest Times to the Present Day*, edited by Isidore Singer, vol. 12, 699–704. New York: Funk and Wagnalls, 1906.

Hirsch, Samson Raphael. "Beiträge zum Verständnis der ersten Blätter des Pentateuch." *Jeschurun* 11, no. 4 (1865): 141–154.

Hirsch, Samson Raphael. *Chapters of the Fathers*. Translated by Gertrude Hirschler. Jerusalem: P. Feldheim, 1967.

Hirsch, Samson Raphael. *The Collected Writings*. Edited and Translated by Marc Breuer, Jacob Breuer, Meta Bechhofer, and Elliott Bondi. 9 vols. New York: Feldheim, 1984–2012.

Hirsch, Samson Raphael. Jüdische Anmerkungen zu den Bemerkungen eines Protestanten über die Confession der 22 Bremlischen Pastoren. Oldenburg: Gerhard Stalling, 1841.

Hirsch, Samson Raphael. "Das Mainzer Journal und die Ideen der Nationalität und Humanität, der Civilisation und Freiheit." *Jeschurun* 11, no. 3 (1864): 89–94.

Hirsch, Samson Raphael. *Der Pentateuch, übersetzt und erläutert*. 5 vols. Frankfurt am Main: J. Kauffmann, 1867–1878.

Hirsch, Samson Raphael. "Die Distellese des Herrn Kirchheim." *Jeschurun* 15, no. 4–5 (1868): 113–133.

Hirsch, Samson Raphael. "Die Ehe." *Jeschurun* 18, no. 4 (1885), 51–52.

Hirsch, Samson Raphael. *Die Psalmen, übersetzt und erläutert*. 2 vols. in 1. Frankfurt am Main: J. Kauffmann, 1882.

Hirsch, Samson Raphael. *Erste und Zweite Mitteilung aus einem Briefwechsel*. Frankfurt am Main: Sänger & Friedberg, 1920.

Hirsch, Samson Raphael. *Gesammelte Schriften*. 6 vols. Edited by Mendel Hirsch. Frankfurt am Main: J. Kauffmann, 1902.

Hirsch, Samson Raphael. *From the Wisdom of Mishlé*. Edited by Raphael Moller. Translated by Karin Paritzky. New York: Feldheim, 1976.

Hirsch, Samson Raphael. *The Hirsch Chumash*. Translated by Daniel Haberman. 5 vols. New York: Feldheim, 2010.

Hirsch, Samson Raphael. *Horeb; a Philosophy of Jewish Laws and Observations*. Translated by Isidor Grunfeld. Edited by Isidor Grunfeld. London: Soncino Press, 1962.

Hirsch, Samson Raphael. *Horev: Versuche über Jissroels Pflichten in der Zerstreuung*. Altona: Johann Friedrich Hammerich, 1837.

Hirsch, Samson Raphael. *Israels Gebete*. Frankfurt am Main: J. Kauffmann, 1895.

Hirsch, Samson Raphael. *Judaism Eternal; Selected Essays from the Writings of Samson Raphael Hirsch*. Translated by Isidor Grunfeld. London: Soncino Press, 1956.

Hirsch, Samson Raphael. *Neunzehn Briefe über Judenthum*. Altona: J.F. Hammerich, 1836.

Hirsch, Samson Raphael. *Neunzehn Briefe über Judentum Zweite Auflage*. Frankfurt: J. Kauffmann, 1889.

Hirsch, Samson Raphael. *The Nineteen Letters about Judaism*. Translated by Karin Paritzky. Edited by Joseph Elias. New York: Feldheim Publishers, 1995.

Hirsch, Samson Raphael. *Pentateuch with the Commentary of Rabbi Samson Raphael Hirsch* [in Hebrew]. Translated by Mordechai Breuer. Edited by Mordechai Breuer. 5 vols. Jerusalem: Mosad Yitzhak Breuer, 2002.

Hirsch, Samson Raphael. *Postscripta zu den unter dem Titel Horev Betzion erschienen Briefen*. Altona: Johann Friedrich Hammerich, 1840.

Hirsch, Samson Raphael. "Prospectus." *Jeschurun* 1 (1854): n.p.

Hirsch, Samson Raphael. *The Psalms*. Translated by Gertrude Hirschler. 2 vols in 1. New York: Feldheim, 1978.

Hirsch, Samson Raphael. *Sefer Shemesh Marpe*. Edited by Eliyahu Meir Klugman. New York: Mesorah, 1992.

Hirsch, Samson Raphael. *Timeless Torah: An Anthology of the Writings of Rabbi Samson Raphael Hirsch*. Translated by Jacob Breuer. New York: P. Feldheim, 1957.

Hirsch, Samson Raphael. "Vom dem pädagogischen Werte des Judentums." *Nahalath Zwi* 7, no. 1 (1937): 1–27.

"Hirsch Testimonial for the British Chief Rabbinate." London: John Wertheimer, 1844.

Horwitz, Rivka. "Mendelssohn's Interpretation of the Tetragrammaton as the Eternal." [In Hebrew]. *Jewish Studies* 37 (1997): 185–214.

Horwitz, Rivka. "On Kabbala and Myth in 19th Century Germany: Isaac Bernays." *Proceedings of the American Academy for Jewish Research* 59 (1993): 137–183.

Huebner, Sabine. "'Brother-Sister' Marriage in Roman Egypt: A Curiosity of Humankind or a Widespread Family Strategy?" *The Journal of Roman Studies* 97 (2007): 21–49.

Isaacs, A.S. *Step by Step: A Story of the Early Days of Moses Mendelssohn*. Philadelphia, PA: Jewish Publication Society of America, 1910.

Jacobs, Jonathan. "Rabbi Samson Raphael Hirsch as a Peshat Commentator: Literary Aspects of His Commentary on the Pentateuch." *Review of Rabbinic Judaism* 15, no. 2 (2012): 190–200.

Japhet, Saemy. "The Secession of the Frankfurt Jewish Community under Samson Raphael Hirsch." *Historia Judaica* 10, no. 2 (1948): 99–122.

Joskowicz, Ari. *The Modernity of Others: Jewish Anti-Catholicism in Germany and France*. Palo Alto, CA: Stanford University Press, 2014.

Jospe, Raphael. "The Superiority of Oral over Written Communication: Judah Halevi's Kuzari and Modern Jewish Thought." In *Essays in Honor of Marvin Fox*, edited by E. Freirichs, J. Neusner, and N. Sarna, 127–156. Atlanta, GA: Scholars Press, 1989.

Kant, Immanuel. *Critique of Pure Reason*. Translated and Edited by Paul Guyer and Allan Wood. New York: Cambridge University Press, 2016.

Kaplan, Lawrence. "Daas Torah: A Modern Conception of Rabbinic Authority." In *Rabbinic Authority and Personal Autonomy*, edited by Moshe Sokol, 1–60. Northvale, NJ: Jason Aronson, 1992.

Kaplan, Lawrence. "On the Boundary between Old and New: The Correspondence between Moses Mendelssohn and R. Jacob Emden." Unpublished manuscript, 1984.

Kaplan, Marion. *The Making of the Jewish Middle Class: Women, Family, and Identity in Imperial Germany*. New York: Oxford University Press, 1991.

Katz, Jacob. "Daat Torah: The Unqualified Authority Claimed for Halakhists." *Jewish History* 11, no. 1 (1997): 41–50.

Katz, Jacob. *Divine Law in Human Hands: Case Studies in Halakhic Flexibility*. Jerusalem: Magnes Press, 1998.

Katz, Jacob. *Emancipation and Assimilation: Studies in Modern Jewish History*. Farnborough, UK: Gregg, 1972.

Katz, Jacob. *From Prejudice to Destruction: Anti-Semitism, 1700–1933*. Cambridge, MA: Harvard University Press, 1980.

Katz, Jacob. *A House Divided: Orthodoxy and Schism in Nineteenth-Century Central European Jewry*. Translated by Ziporah Brody. Hanover, NH: University Press, 1998.

Katz, Jacob. "Marriage and Sexual Life among the Jews at the Close of the Middle Ages." [In Hebrew]. *Zion* 10 (1944): 21–54.

Katz, Jacob. "Orthodoxy in Historical Perspective." In *Studies in Contemporary Jewry*, edited by Peter Medding, 3–17. Bloomington: Indiana University Press, 1986.

Katz, Jacob. *Out of the Ghetto: The Social Background of Jewish Emancipation, 1770–1870*. Cambridge, MA: Harvard University Press, 1973.

Katz, Jacob. "Rabbi Samson Raphael Hirsch: To the Right and to the Left." [in Hebrew]. In *Torah Im Derekh Eretz*, edited by Mordechai Breuer, 13–31. Ramat Gan: Bar-Ilan University Press, 1987.

Katz, Jacob. *Tradition and Crisis; Jewish Society at the End of the Middle Ages*. Translated by Bernard Cooperman. Syracuse: Syracuse University Press, 2000.

Kaufmann, David. *Gesammelte Schriften*. Edited by M. Brann. 3 vols. Frankfurt: J. Kauffmann, 1908.

Kayserling, Meyer. *Ludwig Philippson: Eine Biographie*. Leipzig: Hermann Mendelssohn, 1898.

Kayserling, Meyer. *Moses Mendelssohn; sein Leben und seine Werke*. Leipzig: H. Mendelssohn, 1862.

Kellner, Menachem Marc. *Maimonides' Confrontation with Mysticism*. Oxford: Littmann, 2006.

Klugman, Eliyahu Meir. *Rabbi Samson Raphael Hirsch: Architect of Torah Judaism for the Modern World*. Brooklyn, NY: Mesorah, 1996.

Knapp, Georg Christian. *Die Psalmen: Uebersetz und mit Anmerkungen*. Halle: Johann Jakob Curt, 1782.

Kocka, Jürgen. "Bürgertum und Bürgerlichkeit als Probleme der deutschen Geschichte vom späten 18. zum frühen 20. Jahrhundert." In *Bürger und Bürgerlichkeit im 19. Jahrhundert*, edited by Jürgen Kocka, 21–63. Göttingen: Vandenhoeck & Ruprecht, 1987.

Kocka, Jürgen. "The European Pattern and the German Case." In *Bourgeois Society in Ninteenth-Century Europe*, edited by Jürgen Kocka and Allen Mitchell, 3–39. Oxford: Berg, 1993.

Kocka, Jürgen. "The Middle Classes in Europe." *The Journal of Modern History* 67, no. 4 (1995): 783–806.

Kohler, Kaufmann. "Response to Rabbi Max Heller." *Yearbook of the Central Conference of American Rabbis* 18 (1908): 210–214.

Köhler, Johann Bernhard. "Rezension *Probe einer jüdische-deutschen Uebersetzung der fünf Bucher Moses des Herrn Moses Mendelssohn*." *Allgemeine Deutsche Bibliothek* 40 (1780): 44–52.

Koller, Aaron. *The Flower of Human Perfection: Moses Mendelssohn's Defense of Rationalist Aesthetics*. Thesis (Ph.D.), Syracuse University, 2011.

Koltun-Fromm, Ken. *Abraham Geiger's Liberal Judaism: Personal Meaning and Religious Authority*. Bloomington: Indiana University Press, 2006.

Kornfeld, Joseph. "Ludwig Philippson." *Central Conference of American Rabbis Year book* 21 (1911): 149–190.

Koselleck, Reinhart. *The Practice of Conceptual History: Timing History, Spacing Concepts*. Translated by Todd Samuel Presner. Stanford, CA: Stanford University Press, 2002.

Krochmalnik, Daniel. "Scheintod und Emanzipation. Der Beerdigungsstreit in seinem historischen Kontext." *Trumah. Zeitschrift der Hochschule für jüdische Studien, Heidelberg* 6 (1997): 107–149.

Kugel, James L. *The Idea of Biblical Poetry: Parallelism and Its History*. New Haven, CT: Yale University Press, 1981.

Lässig, Simone. "The Emergence of Middle-Class Religiosity: Social and Cultural Aspects of the German-Jewish Reform Movement during the First Half of the Nineteenth Century." In *Towards Normality? Acculturation and Modern German Jewry*, edited by Rainer Liedtke and David Rechter, 127–158. Tübingen: Mohr-Siebeck, 2003.

Lässig, Simone. *Jüdische Wege ins Bürgertum: Kulturelles Kapital und sozialer Aufstieg im 19. Jahrhundert*. Göttingen: Vandenhoeck & Ruprecht, 2004.

Leibniz, Gottfried Wilhelm. *Die Philosophischen Schriften von Gottfried Wilhelm Leibniz*. Edited by C. I. Gerhardt. Hildesheim: Olms Verlagsbuchhandlung, 1960.

Leibniz, Gottfried Wilhelm. *Philosophical Essays*. Edited by Roger Ariew and Daniel Garber. Indianapolis, IN: Hackett Pub. Co., 1989.

Leibniz, Gottfried Wilhelm. *Philosophical Papers and Letters*. Edited by Leroy Loemker. Dordrecht: D. Reidel, 1976.

Lessing, Gotthold Ephraim. *Philosophical and Theological Writings*. Translated by H. Nisbet. Edited by H. Nisbet. Cambridge: Cambridge University Press, 2005.

Lessing, Gotthold Ephraim. *Werke und Briefe*. Edited by Wilfried Barner et al. 14 vols. Frankfurt: Deutscher Klassiker Verlag, 1985.

"Letter from a Native of Hamburg." [In Hebrew]. *Hame'asef* October (1809): 22–28.

Levenson, Alan T. *The Making of the Modern Jewish Bible: How Scholars in Germany, Israel, and America Transformed an Ancient Text*. Lanham, MD: Rowman & Littlefield, 2011.

Levenson, Edward Richard. "Moses Mendelssohn's Understanding of Logico-Grammatical and Literary Construction in the Pentateuch." Thesis (Ph.D.), Brandeis University, 1972.

Liberles, Robert. "Dohm's Treatise on the Jews: A Defence of the Enlightenment." *Leo Baeck Institute Year Book Annual* 33 (1988): 29–42.

Liberles, Robert. "From Toleration to Verbesserung: German and English Debates on the Jews in the Eighteenth Century." *Central European History* 22, no. 1 (1989): 3–32.

Liberles, Robert. *Religious Conflict in Social Context: The Resurgence of Orthodox Judaism in Frankfurt Am Main, 1838–1877*. Westport, CT: Greenwood Press, 1985.

Litvak, Olga. *Haskalah: The Romantic Movement in Judaism*. New Brunswick, NJ: Rutgers University Press, 2012.

Lohmann, Ingrid. *Chevrat Chinuch Nearim—Die jüdische Freischule in Berlin (1778–1825)*. Münster; New York: Waxmann, 2001.

Losch, Andreas. "What Is behind God's Name? Martin Buber's and Franz Rosenzweig's Reflections on the Name of God." *Leo Baeck Institute Year Book Annual* 60 (2015): 91–106.

Lowenstein, Steven. "The 1840s and the Creation of the German-Jewish Religious Reform Movement." In *Revolution and Evolution, 1848 in German-Jewish History*, edited by Arnold Paucker, Werner Mosse, and Reinhard Rürup, 255–298. Tübingen: J.C.B. Mohr, 1981.

Lowenstein, Steven. *The Berlin Jewish Community Enlightenment, Family, and Crisis, 1770–1830*. New York: Oxford University Press, 1994.

Lowenstein, Steven. "The Complicated Language Situation of German Jewry, 1760–1914." *Studia Rosenthalia* 36 (2003): 3–31.

Lowenstein, Steven. "The Readership of Mendelssohn's Bible Translation." *Hebrew Union College Annual* 53 (1982): 179–213.

Lowenstein, Steven. "The Yiddish Written Word in Nineteenth-Century Germany." *The Leo Baeck Institute Year Book Annual* 24 (1979): 179–192.

Lowth, Robert. *Lectures on the Sacred Poetry of the Hebrews*. 2 vols. London, 1816.

Luther, Martin. *Biblia: Das ist die Gantze Heilige Schrift: Deutsch*. Wittemburg: Hans Lufft, 1545.

Luther, Martin. *Luther's Works*. Edited by Helmut T. Lehmann. 55 vols. Saint Louis, MO: Concordia, 1955.

Mahmood, Saba. *Religious Difference in a Secular Age: A Minority Report*. Princeton: Princeton University Press, 2015.

Mahmood, Saba. "Religious Reason and Secular Affect: An Incommenserable Divide?." In *Is Critique Secular? Blasphemy, Injury, and Free Speech*, edited by Wendy Brown Talal Asad, Judith Butler, and Saba Mahmood, 64–100. Berkeley: University of California Press, 2009.

Maimon, Salomon. *The Autobiography of Solomon Maimon: The Complete Translation*. Translated by Paul Reitter. Edited by Yitzhak Melamed and Abraham Socher. Princeton, NJ: Princeton University Press, 2018.

Maimon, Salomon. *Salomon Maimons Lebensgeschichte*. Edited by Zwi Batscha. Frankfurt am Main: Insel, 1984.

Maimonides, Moses. *Commentary on the Mishnah: Tractate Sanhedrin*. Translated by Fred Rosner. Edited by Fred Rosner. New York: Sepher-Hermon Press, 1981.

Maimonides, Moses. *The Guide of the Perplexed*. Translated by Shlomo Pines. Edited by Shlomo Pines. 2 vols. Chicago: University of Chicago Press, 1963.

Maimonides, Moses. *Mishneh Torah: The Book of Knowledge*, Translated by Moses Hyamson. Edited by Moses Hyamson. Jerusalem: Feldheim, 1962.

Manuel, Frank. *The Broken Staff: Judaism through Christian Eyes*. Cambridge, MA: Harvard University Press, 1992.

Marchand, Suzanne L. *German Orientalism in the Age of Empire: Religion, Race, and Scholarship*. New York: Cambridge University Press, 2009.

Marcinkowski, Roman. "Luigi Chiarini (1789–1832), an Anti-Judaistic Reformer of Judaism." *Studia Judaica* 7, no. 2 (2004): 237–248.

Marcus, Ivan. "Beyond the Sephardic Mystique." *Orim* 1 (1985): 35–53.

Melamed, Yitzhak. "Mendelssohn, Maimon, and Spinoza on Excommunication and Toleration." In *Moses Mendelssohn: Enlightenment, Religion, Politics, Nationalism*, edited by Michah Gottlieb and Charles Manekin, 49–60. Bethesda: University Press of Maryland, 2015.

Mendelssohn, Joseph. *Aufsätze und Arbeiten von Joseph Mendelssohn angefangen im Jahre 1783 am 15. October*. Leo Baeck Institute, AR10327.

Mendelssohn, Moses. *Brautbriefe*. Edited by Ismar Elbogen. Berlin: Schocken Verlag, 1936.

Mendelssohn, Moses. *Jerusalem, or on Religious Power and Judaism*. Translated by Allan Arkush. Edited by Alexander Altmann. Hanover, NH: University Press of New England, 1983.

Mendelssohn, Moses. *Morning Hours: Lectures on God's Existence*. Translated by Daniel Dahlstrom and Corey Dyck. Dordrecht: Springer, 2011.

Mendelssohn, Moses. *Moses Mendelssohn Gesammelte Schriften, Jubiläumsausgabe*. Edited by Alexander Altmann et al. 25 vols. Stuttgart-Bad Cannstatt: F, Frommann, 1971–.

Mendelssohn, Moses. *Moses Mendelssohns Gesammelte Schriften*. Edited by G.B. Mendelssohn. 7 vols. Leipzig: F.A. Brockhaus, 1843–1845.

Mendelssohn, Moses. *Moses Mendelssohn's Hebrew Writings*. Translated by Edward Breuer. Edited by Edward Breuer and David Sorkin. New Haven, CT: Yale University Press, 2018.

Mendelssohn, Moses. *Moses Mendelssohn: Writings on Judaism, Christianity, and the Bible.* Translated by Curtis Bowman, Elias Sacks, and Allan Arkush. Edited by Michah Gottlieb. Hanover, NH: University Press of New England, 2011.

Mendelssohn, Moses. *Phaedon: or on the Immortality of the Soul.* Translated by Patricia Noble. New York: Peter Lang, 2007.

Mendelssohn, Moses. *Philosophical Writings.* Translated by Daniel O. Dahlstrom. Edited by Daniel Dahlstrom. New York: Cambridge University Press, 1997.

Mendelssohn, Moses. *Verzeichniß der Auserlesenen Büchersammlung des seeligen Herrn Moses Mendelssohn.* Leipzig: F.A. Brockhaus, 1926.

Mendes-Flohr, Paul. *Divided Passions: Jewish Intellectuals and the Experience of Modernity.* Detroit, MI: Wayne State University Press, 1991.

Mendes-Flohr, Paul. "Mendelssohn and Rosenzweig." *Journal of Jewish Studies* 38, no. 1 (1987): 203–211.

Mendes-Flohr, Paul R., and Jehuda Reinharz, Eds. *The Jew in the Modern World: A Documentary History.* 3rd ed. New York: Oxford University Press, 2011.

Meyer, Herrmann. *Moses Mendelssohn Bibliographie.* Berlin: de Gruyter, 1967.

Meyer, Michael. "From Combat to Convergence: The Relationship between Heinrich Graetz and Abraham Geiger." In *Reappraisals and New Studies of the Modern Jewish Experience Essays in Honor of Robert M. Seltzer*, edited by Brian Smollett and Christian Wiese, 145–161. Leiden: Brill, 2015.

Meyer, Michael, Ed. *German-Jewish History in Modern Times.* 4 vols. New York: Columbia University Press, 1996.

Meyer, Michael. "'Most of My Brethren Find Me Unaccepatable': The Controversial Career of Rabbi Samuel Holdheim." In *Redefining Judaism in an Age of Emancipation*, edited by Christian Wiese, 3–22. Leiden: Brill, 2005.

Meyer, Michael. *The Origins of the Modern Jew: Jewish Identity and European Culture in Germany, 1749–1824.* Detroit, MI: Wayne State University Press, 1967.

Meyer, Michael. "The Religious Reform Controversy in the Berlin Jewish Community, 1814–1823." *The Leo Baeck Institute Year Book Annual* 24 (1979): 139–155.

Meyer, Michael. *Response to Modernity: A History of the Reform Movement in Judaism.* Studies in Jewish History. New York: Oxford University Press, 1988.

Meyer, Michael. "Two Persistent Tensions within Wissenschaft des Judentums." *Modern Judaism* 24, no. 2 (2004): 105–119.

Meyer, Michael. "Women in the Thought and Practice of the European Jewish Reform Movement." In *Gender and Jewish History*, edited by Marion Kaplan and Deborah Dash More, 139–157. Bloomington: Indiana University Press, 2011.

Michaelis, Johann David. *Commentaries on the Laws of Moses.* Translated by Alexander Smith. 4 vols. London: F.C. and J. Rivington; and Longman, Hurst, Rees, Orme, and Brown; and A. Brown, 1814.

Michaelis, Johann David. *Critisches Collegium über die drey wichtigsten Psalmen von Christ.* Frankfurt: Johann Gottlieb Garbens, 1759.

Michaelis, Johann David. *Deutsche Uebersetzung des Alten Testaments, mit Anmerkungen für Ungelehrte.* 13 vols. Göttingen: Bey J.C. Dieterich, 1769–1785.

Miller, Michael Laurence. *Rabbis and Revolution: The Jews of Moravia in the Age of Emancipation.* Palto Alto, CA: Stanford University Press, 2011.

Mintz, Adam. "Translating the Talmud." In *Printing the Talmud: From Bomberg to Schottenstein*, edited by Gabriel M. Goldstein and Sharon Liberman Mintz, 121–141. New York: Yeshiva University Museum, 2006.

Morgan, Michael. "History and Modern Jewish Thought: Spinoza and Mendelssohn on the Ritual Law." *Judaism* 30, no. 4 (1981): 467–478.

Mosse, Werner. "From "*Schutzjuden*" to "Deutsche Staatsbürger Jüdischen Glaubens": The Long and Bumpy Road of Jewish Emancipation in Germany." In *Paths of Emancipation: Jews, States, and Citizenship*, edited by Pierre Birnbaum and Ira Katznelson, 59–93. Princeton, NJ: Princeton University Press, 1995.

Mosse, Werner. *German Jews Beyond Judaism*. New York: Hebrew Union College Press, 1997.

Mosse, Werner. "Jewish Emancipation between *Bildung* and Respectability." In *The Jewish Response to German Culture: From the Enlightenment to the Second World War*, edited by Jehuda Reinharz and Walter Schatzberg, 1–16. Hanover, NH: University Press of New England, 1985.

Moynahan, Gregory B. *Ernst Cassirer and the Critical Science of Germany, 1899–1919*. London: Anthem Press, 2013.

Muller, Richard *Dictionary of Latin and Greek Theological Terms, Drawn Principally from Protestant Scholastic Theology*. Grand Rapids, MI: Baker Book House, 1985.

Muncker, Franz. "Mendelssohn und die deutsche Literatur." *Zeittschrift für die Geschichte der Juden in Deutschland* 1 (1887): 45–64.

Myers, David. "Hermann Cohen and the Quest for Protestant Judaism." *Leo Baeck Institute Year Book Annual* 46 (2001): 195–214.

Niebuhr, Barthold Georg. *Lectures on Ancient History*. Translated by Leonhard Schmitz. 3 vols. Philadelphia, PA: Blanchard and Lea, 1852.

Niehoff, Maren Ruth. "The Buber-Rosenzweig Translation of the Bible within Jewish-German Tradition." *Journal of Jewish Studies* 44, no. 2 (1993): 258–279.

Niehoff, Maren Ruth. "Moses Mendelssohn's Translation of Judah Halevi's 'Ode to Zion.'" [In Hebrew]. In *The Land of Israel in Modern Jewish Thought*, edited by Aviezer Ravitzky, 313–325. Jerusalem: Yad Yitzhak ben Zvi, 1998.

Niehoff, Maren Ruth. "Zunz's Concept of Haggadah as an Expression of Jewish Spirituality." *The Leo Baeck Institute Year Book Annual* 43 (1998): 3–24.

Niewöhner, Friedrich. "Mendelssohn als Philosoph-Aufklärer-Jude Oder: Aufklärung mit dem Talmud." *Zeitschrift für Religions- und Geistesgeschichte* 41, no. 2 (1989): 119–133.

"Offene Anfrage an die Leiter der zu Folge des Programms vom Februar dieses Jahres in Breslau zu eröffnen den Seminars für Rabbiner und Lehrer." *Allgemeine Zeitung des Judentums* 18, no. 20 (1854): 244–246.

Pasto, James. "W.M.L. De Wette and the Invention of Post-Exilic Judaism." In *Jews, Antiquity and the Nineteenth-Century Imagination*, edited by Hayim Lapin and Dale Martin, 33–52: Bethesda: University of Maryland Press, 2003.

Petuchowski, Jacob. "Abraham Geiger and Samuel Holdheim: Their Differences in Germany and Repercussions in America." *Leo Baeck Institute Year Book Annual* 22 (1977): 139–159.

Petuchowski, Jacob. "Manuals and Catechisms of the Jewish Religion in the Early Period of Emancipation." In *Studies in Nineteen Century Jewish Intellectual History*, edited by Alexander Altmann, 47–64: Cambridge, MA: Harvard University Press, 1964.

Philippson, Ludwig. *Der Pentateuch, Die fünf Bücher Moscheh*. 2 vols. Leipzig: Baumgärtner's Buchhandlung, 1844.

Philippson, Ludwig. *The Development of the Religious Idea in Judaism, Christianity and Mahomedanism*. Translated by Anna Maria Goldsmid. London: Longman, Brown, Green, and Longmans, 1855.

Philippson, Ludwig. *Die Entwickelung der Religiösen Idee im Judenthume, Christenthume und Islam*. Leipzig: Baumgärtner, 1847.

Philippson, Ludwig. *Die Israelitische Bibel*. 2nd ed. 3 vols. Leipzig: Baumgärtner, 1858.

Philippson, Ludwig. "Einleitung: Über das Leben des Judenthums seit der Mitte des vorigen Jahrhunderts." *Israelitisches Predigt und Schul Magazin* 1, no. 1 (1834): 5–14.

Philippson, Ludwig. "Offenes Sendchreiben an Herrn Dr. Lasker." *Allgemeine Zeitung des Judentums* 37, no. 48 (1873): 782–783.

Philippson, Ludwig. "Uebersicht über biblische Arbeiten." *Allgemeine Zeitung des Judentums* 39, no. 24 (1875): 384–386.

Philipson, David. *The Reform Movement in Judaism*. New York: The Macmillan Company, 1907.

Philipson, David. "Samuel Holdheim, Jewish Reformer." *Yearbook of the Central Conference of American Rabbis* 16 (1906): 305–333.

Pinto, Jacqueline. *The Story of Moses Mendelssohn*. London: Vallentine Mitchell, 1960.

Plaut, Gunther. *German-Jewish Bible Translations: Linguistic Theology as Political Phenomenon*, New York: Leo Baeck Institute, 1992.

Plaut, Gunther. *The Rise of Reform Judaism: A Source Book of Its European Origins*. Lincoln, NE: *Jewish Publication Society*, 2015.

Pollock, Benjamin. *Franz Rosenzweig's Conversions: World Denial and World Redemption*. Bloomington: Indiana University Press, 2014.

Prell, Riv Ellen, "The Vision of Woman in Classical Reform Judaism." *Journal of the American Academy of Religion* 50, no. 4 (1982): 575–589.

"Protocolle der ersten Rabbiner-Versammlung Abgehalten Zu Braunschweig." Brunswick, 1844.

"Protokolle und Aktenstücke der zweiten Rabbiner-Versammlung." Frankfurt, 1845.

Rahden, Till Van. "Jews and the Ambivalences of Civil Society in Germany, 1800–1933: Assessment and Reassessment." *The Journal of Modern History* 77, no. 4 (2005): 1024–1047.

Reichert, Klaus. "'It Is Time': The Buber-Rosenzweig Bible Translation in Context." In *The Translatability of Cultures: Figurations of the Space Between*, edited by Sanford Budick and Wolfgang Iser, 169–185. Stanford, CA: Stanford University Press, 1996.

Reiner, Elchanan. "Changes in the Polish and German Yeshivot in the 16th and 17th Centuries and the Dispute over Pilpul." [In Hebrew]. In *Ke-Minhag Ashkenaz U-Polin: Sefer Yovel Le-Ḥonah Shmeruk*, edited by Israel Bartal et al., 9–80. Jerusalem: Zalman Shazar, 1993.

Ritter, Immanuel. "Samuel Holdheim: The Jewish Reformer." *The Jewish Quarterly Review* 1, no. 3 (1889): 202–215.

Rogerson, J.W. *Old Testament Criticism in the Nineteenth Century: England and Germany*. Philadelphia, PA: Fortress Press, 1985.

Rogerson, J.W. *W.M.L. De Wette, Founder of Modern Biblical Criticism: An Intellectual Biography*. Sheffield, UK: JSOT Press, 1992.

Rosenbloom, Noah. *Tradition in an Age of Reform: The Religious Philosophy of Samson Raphael Hirsch*. Philadelphia, PA: Jewish Publication Society of America, 1976.

Rosenstock, Bruce. *Philosophy and the Jewish Question: Mendelssohn, Rosenzweig, and Beyond*. New York: Fordham University Press, 2010.

Rosenstock, Moritz. *Festschrift zur hunderjährigen Jubelfeier der Samsonschule zu Wolfenbüttel*. Wolfenbüttel: Julius Zwißler, 1886.

Rosenzweig, Franz. *On Jewish Learning*. Translated and edited by Nahum Glatzer. New York: Schocken Books, 1965.

Rosenzweig, Franz. Der Mensch und sein Werke Gesammelte Schriften: Briefe und Tagebücher. 2 vols. Edited by Rachel Rosenzweig, Edith Rosenzweig-Scheimann, Bernhard Casper. The Hague: Springer, 1979.

Rosenzweig, Franz, The Star of Redemption. Translated by William Hallo. Notre Dame, IN: Notre Dame University Press, 1985.

Rosenzweig, Franz. *Zweistromland; Kleinere Schriften zur Religion und Philosophie*. Berlin: Philo Verlag, 1926.

Rosin, David. "Die Zunz'sche Bibel." *Monatschrift für die Geschichte und Wissenschaft des Judenthums* 11 (1894): 504–514.

Rühs, Friedrich. *Ueber die Ansprüche der Juden an das deutsche Bürgerrecht*. Berlin: Realschulbuchhandlung, 1816.

Sachs, Michael, and Moritz Veit. *Michael Sachs und Moritz Veit: Briefwechsel*. Frankfurt am Main: J. Kauffmann, 1897.

Sacks, Elias. *Moses Mendelssohn's Living Script: Philosophy, Practice, History, Judaism*. Bloomington: Indiana University Press, 2017.

Samet, Moshe. "The Beginnings of Orthodoxy." *Modern Judaism* 8, no. 3 (1988): 249–269.

Samet, Moshe. *The New Is Forbidden by the Torah: Chapters in the History of Orthodoxy* [in Hebrew]. Jerusalem: Merkaz Dinur, 2005.

"Samson Raphael Hirsch—ein Lebensbild." In *Samson Raphael Hirsch—Jubiläums—Nummer*, 5–17. Frankfurt am Main: Verlag des '"Israelit," 1908.

Sandler, Perez. *Mendelssohn's Edition of the Pentateuch* [in Hebrew]. Jerusalem: R. Mass, 1940.

Saperstein, Marc. *Jewish Preaching, 1200–1800: An Anthology*. New Haven, CT: Yale University Press, 1989.

Sarna, Nahum. *Studies in Biblical Interpretation*. Philadelphia, PA: JPS, 2000.

Schacter, Jacob Joseph. "Rabbi Jacob Emden: Life and Major Works." Thesis (Ph.D.), Harvard University, 1988.

Schelling, Friedrich. *On University Studies*. Translated by E.S. Morgan. Edited by Norbert Guterman. Athens: Ohio University Press, 1966.

Schleiermacher, Friedrich. *On Religion: Speeches to Its Cultured Despisers*. Translated by Richard Crouter. New York: Cambridge University Press, 1996.

Schleiermacher, Friedrich. "On the Different Methods of Translation." In *The Translation Studies Reader*, edited by Lawrence Venuti, 43–63. London: Routledge, 2012.

Schmelzer, Menahem. "Hebrew Printing and Publishing in Germany, 1650–1750: On Jewish Book Culture and the Emergence of Modern Jewry." *The Leo Baeck Institute Year Book Annual* 33 (1988): 369–383.

Schmidt, Ferdinand. *Moses Mendelssohn: Ein Lebensbild*. Kreuznach: Voigtländer, 1886.

Schmidt, Johann Lorenz. *Die göttlichen Schriften vor den Zeiten des Messie Jesus* Wertheim: Johann Georg Nehr, 1735.

Scholem, Gershom. *On Jews and Judaism in Crisis: Selected Essays*. New York: Schocken Books, 1976.

Scholem, Gershom. *On the Kabbalah and Its Symbolism*. New York: Schocken, 1969.

Schorsch, Ismar. *From Text to Context: The Turn to History in Modern Judaism*. Hanover, NH: University Press of New England, 1994.

Schorsch, Ismar. "In the Shadow of Wellhausen: Heinrich Graetz as Biblical Critic." *Jewish Quarterly Review* 109, no. 3 (2019): 384–405.

Schorsch, Ismar. *Jewish Reactions to German Anti-Semitism, 1870–1914.* New York: Columbia University Press, 1972.

Schorsch, Ismar. *Leopold Zunz: Creativity in Adversity*. Philadelphia, PA: University of Pennsylvania Press, 2016.

Schorsch, Ismar. "Leopold Zunz on the Hebrew Bible." *Jewish Quarterly Review* 100, no. 3 (2012): 431–454.

Schorsch, Ismar. "Missing in Translation: The Fate of the Talmud in the Struggle for Equality and Integration in Germany." In *Wissenschaft des Judentums beyond Tradition: Jewish Scholarship on the Sacred Texts of Judaism, Christianity and Islam*, edited by D. Saltzer, C. Gafni, and H. Harif, 167–184. Berlin: De Gruyter, 2019.

Schreiber, Emanuel. *Reformed Judaism and Its Pioneers. A Contribution to Its History*. Spokane, WA: Spokane Printing Company, 1892.

Schwarzschild, Steven. "Franz Rosenzweig and Martin Heidegger: The German and Jewish Turn to Ethnicism." In *Der Philosoph Franz Rosenzweig (1886–1929)*, edited by Wolfdietrich Schmied Kowarzik, vol. 2., 887–889. Munich: Verlag Alber Freiburg, 1988.

Seidman, Naomi. *Faithful Renderings: Jewish-Christian Difference and the Politics of Translation*. Chicago: University of Chicago Press, 2006.

Seidman, Naomi. *Sarah Schenirer and the Bais Ya'akov Movement: A Revolution in the Name of Tradition*. London: Littmann Library, 2019.

Sela, Yael. "The Voice of the Psalmist: On the Performative Role of Psalms in Mendelssohn's *Jerusalem*." In *Psalms In/On Jerusalem*, edited by Ilana Pardes and Ophir Münz-Manor, 109–134. Berlin: De Gruyter, 2019.

Septimus, Bernard. "Maimonides on Language." In *The Heritage of the Jews of Spain*, edited by Aviva Doron, 35–54. Tel Aviv: Levinsky College, 1994.

Shargel, Norton David. "Ludwig Philippson, the Rabbi as Journalist: An Anthology of His Writings with an Introductory Essay." Thesis (Ph.D.), Jewish Theological Seminary of America, 1990.

Shavit, Jacob, and Mordechai Eran. *The Hebrew Bible Reborn: From Holy Scripture to the Book of Books: A History of Biblical Culture and the Battles over the Bible in Modern Judaism*. Translated by Chaya Naor. Berlin: Walter de Gruyter, 2007.

Shavit, Zohar. "David Friedländer and Moses Mendelssohn Publish the Lesebuch für Jüdische Kinder—A Turning Point in the History of Books for Jewish Children." In *Yale Companion to Jewish Writing and Thought in German Culture, 1096–1996*, edited by Sander L. Gilman and Jack Zipes, 68–74. New Haven, CT: Yale University Press, 1997.

Shavit, Zohar. "From Friedländer's Lesebuch to the Jewish Campe: The Beginning of Hebrew Children's Literature in Germany." *Leo Baeck Institute Year Book Annual* 33 (1988): 385–415.

Sheehan, Jonathan. *The Enlightenment Bible: Translation, Scholarship, Culture*. Princeton, NJ: Princeton University Press, 2005.

Silber, Michael. "Orthodoxy." In *The Yivo Encyclopedia of Jews in Eastern Europe*, edited by Gershon Hundert. New Haven, CT: Yale University Press, 2008.

Simon, Ernst. "Are We Israelis Still Jews?: The Search of Judaism in the New Society." *Commentary*, 1953, 357–364.

Simon, Ernst. *Are We Still Jews? Essays* [in Hebrew]. Tel Aviv: Sifri'at Po'alim, 1982.

Sommer, Benjamin *Revelation and Authority: Sinai in Jewish Scripture and Tradition*. New Haven: Yale University Press, 2015.

Sorkin, David. "The Genesis of the Ideology of Emancipation: 1806–1840." *Leo Baeck Institute Year Book Annual* 32 (1987): 11–40.

Sorkin, David. *Moses Mendelssohn and the Religious Enlightenment*. Berkeley: University of California Press, 1996.

Sorkin, David. *The Religious Enlightenment: Protestants, Jews, and Catholics from London to Vienna*. Princeton, NJ: Princeton University Press, 2008.

Sorkin, David. *The Transformation of German Jewry, 1780–1840*. New York: Oxford University Press, 1987.

Spalding, Paul. *Seize the Book, Jail the Author: Johann Lorenz Schmidt and Censorship in Eighteenth-Century Germany*. West Lafayette, IN: Purdue University Press, 1998.

Spalding, Paul. "Toward a Modern Torah: Moses Mendelssohn's Use of a Banned Bible." *Modern Judaism* 19, no. 1 (1999): 67–82.

Spinoza, Benedict. *The Collected Works of Spinoza*. Edited and Translated by Edwin Curley. 2 vols. Princeton, NJ: Princeton University Press, 2016.

Spinoza, Benedict. *Complete Works*. Translated by Samuel Shirley. Edited by Michael L. Morgan. Indianapolis, IN: Hackett Pub., 2002.

Spinoza, Benedict. *Opera*. Edited by Carl Gebhardt. 4 vols. Heidelberg: C. Winter, 1925.

Spinoza, Benedict. *Theological-Political Treatise*. Translated and edited by Samuel Shirley. 2nd ed. Indianapolis, IN: Hackett Pub. Co., 2001.

Stanislawski, Michael. *A Murder in Lemberg: Politics, Religion, and Violence in Modern Jewish History*. Princeton, NJ: Princeton University Press, 2007.

Stoeffler, F. Ernest. *German Pietism during the Eighteenth Century*. Leiden: Brill, 1973.

Sulzbach, A. "Zur Geschichte der Schulanstalten." In *Festschrift zur Jubiläums-Feier Des 50 jährigen Bestehens der Israelitischen Religionsgesellschaft zu Frankfurt A.M.*, 1–45. Frankfurt am Main: Louis Golde, 1903.

Tal, Uriel. *Christians and Jews in Germany: Religion, Politics, and Ideology in the Second Reich, 1870–1914*. Ithaca, NY: Cornell University Press, 1975.

Talmage, Frank. *Apples of Gold in Settings of Silver: Studies in Medieval Jewish Exegesis and Polemics*. Toronto: Pontifical Institute of Mediaeval Studies, 1999.

Tänzer, Aron. "Samuel Holdheim als Rabbinatskandidat." *Allgemeine Zeitung des Judentums* 62, no. 2 (1898): 19–20.

Tasch, Roland. *Samson Raphael Hirsch: Jüdische Erfahrungswelten im historischen Kontext*. Berlin: De Gruyter, 2011.

Trautmann-Waller, Céline. *Philologie Allemande et Tradition Juive: Le Parcours Intellectuel de Leopold Zunz*. Paris: Cerf, 1998.

Turner, R. Steven. "The Prussian Universities and the Research Imperative, 1806–1848." Thesis (Ph.D.), Princeton University, 1972.

Turniansky, Chava. "Heder Education in the Early Modern Period." [In Hebrew.] In *The Heder: Studies, Documents, Literature, and Memoirs*, edited by David Assaf and Immanuel Etkes, 3–36. Tel-Aviv: Institute for the History of Polish Jewry, 2010.

Veltri, Giuseppe. *Alienated Wisdom: Enquiry into Jewish Philosophy and Scepticism*. Berlin: De Gruyter, 2018.

Veltri, Giuseppe. "Altertumswissenschaft und Wissenschaft des Judentums: Leopold Zunz und seine Lehrer F.A. Wolf und A. Böckh." In *Friedrich August Wolf: Studien, Dokumente, Bibliographie*, edited by Reinhard Markner and Giuseppe Veltri, 32–47. Stuttgart: Franz Steiner Verlag, 1999.

Veltri, Giuseppe. "A Jewish Luther? The Academic Dreams of Leopold Zunz." *Jewish Studies Quarterly* 7, no. 4 (2000): 338–351.

Wallach, Luitpold. *Liberty and Letters; the Thoughts of Leopold Zunz*. London: East and West Library, 1959.

Weinberg, Werner. "Einleitungen." In *Moses Mendelssohn Jubilaümsausgabe*, edited by Alexander Altmann et al, vol. 10.1, ix–xciii. Stuttgart-Bad Canstatt: Friedrich Fromann Verlag.

Weinberg, Werner. "Einleitung: Die Orthographie von Mendelssohns deutscher Pentateuchübersetzung in hebräischer Schrift." In *Moses Mendelssohn Jubilaümsausgabe*, edited by Alexander Altmann et al, vol. 9.1: vii–xlii. Stuttgart-Bad Canstatt: Friedrich Fromann Verlag, 1985.

Weinberg, Werner. "Language Questions Relating to Moses Mendelssohn's Pentateuch Translation." *Hebrew Union College Annual* 55 (1984): 197–242.

Weinberg, Werner. "A Word List for Teaching 18th Century Jews Some Fine Points of High German." *Leo Baeck Institute Year Book Annual* 39 (1984): 277–293.

Weinreich, Max. *History of the Yiddish Language*. Chicago: University of Chicago Press, 1980.

Weintraub, William. *The German Translations of the Pentateuch* [in Hebrew]. Chicago: Judaica Press, 1967.

Welch, Claude. *Protestant Thought in the Nineteenth Century*. New Haven, CT: Yale University Press, 1972.

Wessely, Naphtali Herz. *Divrei Shalom Ve'emet*. Berlin: Hinukh Ne'arim, 1782.

Wessely, Naphtali Herz. "Mehalel Re'a.". In *Moses Mendelssohn Jubilaümsausgabe*, edited by Alexander Altmann et al. Stuttgart-Bad Canstatt: Friedrich Fromann Verlag, 1985, vol. 15.1: 8–10.

Wessely, Naphtali Herz. *Rav Tuv Leveit Israel*. Berlin: Hinukh Ne'arim, 1782.

Wiese, Christian. *Challenging Colonial Discourse: Jewish Studies and Protestant Theology in Wilhelmine Germany*. Leiden; Boston: Brill, 2005.

Wiese, Christian. "'Let His Memory Be Holy to Us!': Jewish Interpretation of Luther from the Enlightenment to the Holocaust." *Leo Baeck Institute Year Book Annual* 54 (2009): 93–126.

Wiesemann, Falk. "Jewish Burials in Germany—between Tradition, the Enlightenment, and the Authorities." *The Leo Baeck Institute Year Book Annual* 37 (1992): 17–31.

Wilke, Carsten. "Holdheim's Seven Years in Schwerin: The Rabbi as an Ecclesiastical Councillor." In *Redefining Judaism in an Age of Emancipation: Comparative Perspectives on Samuel Holdheim*, edited by Christian Wiese, 81–110. Leiden: Brill, 2006.

Wittler, Kathrin. "Towards a Bookish History of German Jewish Culture Travelling Images and Orientalist Knowledge in Philippson's Israelitische Bibel (1839–1854)." *Leo Baeck Institute Year Book Annual* 62 (2017): 151–177.

Witzenhausen, Yosel. *Torah, Nevi'im, Veketuvim*. Translated by Yosel Witzenhausen. Amsterdam: Joseph Attias, 1678.

Wolf, F.A. *Ueber Erziehung, Schule, Universität*. Quedlinburg: n.p., 1835.

Wolf, Immanuel. "On the Concept of a Science of Judaism." *The Leo Baeck Institute Year Book Annual* 2 (1957): 194–204.

Zimmerman, Erich. "Erinnerungen des Hamburger Bibliothekars Meyer Isler (1807–1888)." *Zeitschrift des Vereins für Hamburgische Geschichte* 47 (1961): 45–86.

Zirkle, Alexandra. "Heinrich Graetz and the Exegetical Contours of Modern Jewish History." *Jewish Quarterly Review* 109, no. 3 (2019): 360–383.

Zunz, Leopold. "Beleuchtung der Théorie du Judaisme Chiarini's." Berlin: Haude und Spenersche Buchandlung, 1830.

Zunz, Leopold. *Das Buch Zunz*. Edited by Fritz Bamberger. Berlin: Soncino, 1931.

Zunz, Leopold. *Deutsche Briefe*. Berlin: F.A. Brockhaus, 1872.

Zunz, Leopold. *Die gottesdienstlichen Vorträge der Juden, historisch entwickelt. Ein Beitrag zur Alterthumskunde und biblischen Kritik, zur Literatur- und Religionsgeschichte.* Frankfurt am Main: J. Kaufmann, 1892.

Zunz, Leopold. Ed. *Die Heilige Schrift: Hebräische-Deutsch.* Basel: Victor Goldschmidt Verlag, 1997.

Zunz, Leopold. *Die Monatstage des Kalenderjahres; ein Andenken an Hingeschiedene.* Berlin: M. Poppelauer, 1872.

Zunz, Leopold. *Die Ritus des synagogalen Gottesdienstes, geschichtlich entwickelt.* Berlin: J. Springer, 1859.

Zunz, Leopold. *Die Synagogale Poesie des Mittelalters.* Hildesheim: Georg Olms, 1967.

Zunz, Leopold, Ed. *Die vier und zwanzig Bücher der Heiligen Schrift nach dem Masoretischen Texte.* Berlin: Veit, 1838.

Zunz, Leopold. "Geist der Rabbiner." *Allgemeine Zeitung des Judentums* 80, no. 35 (1916): 413–414.

Zunz, Leopold. *Gesammelte Schriften.* 4 vols. Berlin: L. Gerschel, 1875.

Zunz, Leopold. "Leopold Zunz' Plan." In *Chevrat Chinuch Nearim: Die Jüdische Freischule in Berlin (1778–1825),* edited by Ingrid Lohmann, 1061–1082. Berlin: Waxman Münster, 2001.

Zunz, Leopold. *Literaturgeschichte der Synagogalen Poesie.* Hildesheim: Georg Olms, 1966.

Zunz, Leopold. "Mein erster Unterricht in Wolfenbüttel." *Jahrbuch für jüdische Geschichte und Literatur* 30 (1937): 131–140.

Zunz, Leopold. *Predigten.* Berlin: Schlesingerschen Buch und Musikhandlung, 1823.

Zunz, Leopold. "Solomon ben Isaac genannt Rashi." *Zeitschrift für die Wissenschaft des Judenthums* 1 (1823): 277–384.

Zunz, Leopold. "Thefillin, Eine Betrachtungen." *Jahrbuch für Israeliten* 2 (1843): 133–139.

Zunz, Leopold. *Toldot Rashi.* Warsaw, n.p., 1862.

Zunz, Leopold. *Zur Geschichte und Literatur.* Berlin: Veit und Comp., 1845.

Zweig, Arnulf. "Biographical Sketches." In *Immanuel Kant. Correspondence*, edited by Arnulf Zweig, 563–616. Cambridge: Cambridge University Press, 1999.

Index

Note: A page number followed by "n." indicates a footnote, and "nn." indicates a set of consecutive footnotes.

Biblical and Rabbinic Sources

New Testament

Mishnah